The Workers' Movement and the National Question in Ukraine

Historical Materialism Book Series

Editorial Board

Loren Balhorn (*Berlin*)
David Broder (*Rome*)
Sebastian Budgen (*Paris*)
Steve Edwards (*London*)
Juan Grigera (*London*)
Marcel van der Linden (*Amsterdam*)
Peter Thomas (*London*)

VOLUME 229

The titles published in this series are listed at *brill.com/hm*

The Workers' Movement and the National Question in Ukraine

1897–1918

By

Marko Bojcun

BRILL

LEIDEN | BOSTON

Library of Congress Cataloging-in-Publication Data

Names: Bojcun, Marko, 1951- author.
Title: The workers' movement and the national question in Ukraine : 1897-1918 / by Marko Bojcun.
Description: Leiden ; Boston : Brill, [2021] | Series: Historical materialism book series, 1570-1522 ; volume 229 | Includes bibliographical references and index.
Identifiers: LCCN 2021017589 (print) | LCCN 2021017590 (ebook) |
  ISBN 9789004223707 (hardback ; alk. paper) | ISBN 9789004466302 (ebook)
Subjects: LCSH: Communism–Ukraine–History. | Working class–Political activity–Ukraine–History. | Ukraine–History–Revolution, 1917-1921. | Ukraine–Politics and government–1917-
Classification: LCC HX315.45.A6 B65 2021 (print) | LCC HX315.45.A6 (ebook) |
  DDC 335.4309477–dc23
LC record available at https://lccn.loc.gov/2021017589
LC ebook record available at https://lccn.loc.gov/2021017590

Typeface for the Latin, Greek, and Cyrillic scripts: "Brill". See and download: brill.com/brill-typeface.

ISSN 1570-1522
ISBN 978-90-04-22370-7 (hardback)
ISBN 978-90-04-46630-2 (e-book)

Copyright 2021 by Koninklijke Brill NV, Leiden, The Netherlands.
Koninklijke Brill NV incorporates the imprints Brill, Brill Nijhoff, Brill Hotei, Brill Schöningh, Brill Fink, Brill mentis, Vandenhoeck & Ruprecht, Böhlau Verlag and V&R Unipress.
All rights reserved. No part of this publication may be reproduced, translated, stored in a retrieval system, or transmitted in any form or by any means, electronic, mechanical, photocopying, recording or otherwise, without prior written permission from the publisher. Requests for re-use and/or translations must be addressed to Koninklijke Brill NV via brill.com or copyright.com.

This book is printed on acid-free paper and produced in a sustainable manner.

Contents

Acknowledgements VII
List of Maps and Tables VIII
Transliteration and Dates IX
Abbreviations X

Introduction 1

1 State Power and the Development of Capitalism 9

2 The Working Class 36

3 Social Democracy and the National Question 62

4 February to October 1917 112

5 November 1917: Attempts at Reconciliation 168

6 December: The Failure of Reconciliation 212

7 The First Treaty of Brest Litovsk 262

8 Battles for Kyiv 279

9 Kyiv under Bolshevik Rule 309

10 The Pogroms in March and April 1918 331

11 Resistance to the Austro-German Occupation 344

12 Last Days of the Rada 364

Epilogue 393

References 395
Index 404

Acknowledgements

Ivan Maistrenko, Panas Fedenko and Vsevolod Holubnychy introduced me to the 1917 Revolution in Ukraine. I had the good fortune to meet Maistrenko and Fedenko in Munich in 1974. In their youth they took part in the Revolution and wrote extensively about it. Around the same time I came across Vsevolod Holubnychy's writings and met him in 1976 in Toronto. A Marxist economist and historian, he was a rarity in the Ukrainian diaspora. I first glimpsed the significance of the Ukrainian national question for the working class and peasantry through the lives and works of these three people.

Edward Palmer Thompson deeply influenced me with his great historical study, *The Making of the English Working Class* (1963). His work showed me the value of approaching the workers' movement through its origins in different social strata, nationalities and political traditions. This was a necessary foundation for understanding its further evolution, the difficult quest for unity in its own ranks and with the peasantry during the Revolution and Civil War. I gained the confidence to investigate a relationship that Stalinist historians dismissed as largely irrelevant and nationalist historians denied even existed: namely that between the workers' movement and the Ukrainian national question as a problem of the radical destruction and reconstruction of state power.

I would like to acknowledge and thank the people who supported me when completing my PhD dissertation in 1986, which was the first draft of the present work: my parents, Anna and Roman Bojcun, my sister Alexandra, and my previous partner, the late Marta Danylewycz. Bohdan Krawchenko and Roman Senkus at the Canadian Institute of Ukrainian Studies supported me in those years as academics and political allies.

I thank Christopher Ford in London for sharing with me his wide knowledge of Ukrainian, English, Scottish and Irish labour history, and for repeatedly urging me to publish my work. Zakhar Popovych in Kyiv assured me that I have something new to offer to readers in Ukraine as well as other countries. Maksym Kazakov and Lesia Bidochko, who translated this work into Ukrainian, offered valuable critical observations and factual corrections which I have incorporated into my finished work.

My thanks go to Halya Kowalsky for her personal support and her hard work proofreading both the English and Ukrainian versions.

Finally, I thank Jane Greenwood, my partner in life who has given me her unfailing support over many years, which has helped me to bring this work to completion.

Maps and Tables

Maps

1 Hetmanate, the Ukrainian Cossack state, 1648   17
2 Ukrainian provinces of the Russian Empire   20

Tables

1   Branches of production in Ukraine, 1904   26
2   Imports and exports of Ukraine for 1909–1911   30
3   State taxes and expenditures in Ukraine, 1898–1910 (in millions of roubles)   32
4   Industrial plant workers in Ukraine, 1861–1917   44
5   Wage earners in Ukraine, 1897–1917   45
6   Industrial workers in Ukraine, 1910–1917 (in thousands)   48
7   Wage earners in Ukraine, January 1917 (in thousands)   51
8   Structure of the working class in Ukraine by national group, 1897   53
9   Distribution of Ukrainian workers, 1897 (in thousands)   54
10 Population of major cities by native language speakers, 1897   56

Transliteration and Dates

Transliteration is based on the Modified Library of Congress system. Ukrainian names of towns, cities and provinces used before the Revolution have been retained.

All dates are designated by the Julian calendar up to 31 January 1918; thereafter they follow the Gregorian calendar, when 1 February by the Julian calendar became 14 February by the Gregorian.

Abbreviations

Black Hundreds	Union of Russian Peoples
Bund	Jewish General Workers' Union
CEC	Central Executive Committee of the Councils of Ukraine
CP(B)U	Communist Party (Bolsheviks) of Ukraine
CPC	Council of People's Commissars
Fareinigte	United Jewish Workers' Party
Folkspartei	Jewish People's Party
Kadets	Russian Constitutional Democratic Party
MRC	Military Revolutionary Committee
Poale Zion	Jewish Social Democratic Party (Workers of Zion)
PPS	Polish Socialist Party
RCP	Russian Communist Party
RSDWP	Russian Social Democratic Workers' Party
RUP	Revolutionary Ukrainian Party
Spilka	Ukrainian Social Democratic Union
SUP	Socialist Ukrainian Party
TUP	Society of Ukrainian Progressives
UDFP	Ukrainian Democratic Farmers Party
UJF	Union of Jewish Fighters
UMRC	Ukrainian Military Revolutionary Committee of the Petrograd Soviet
UPR	Ukrainian People's Republic
UPSF	Ukrainian Party of Socialist Federalists
UPSI	Ukrainian Party of Socialist Independentists
UPSR	Ukrainian Party of Socialist Revolutionaries
URDP	Ukrainian Revolutionary Democratic Party
USDWP	Ukrainian Social Democratic Workers' Party
UTP	Ukrainian Labour Party

Introduction

> The Great Revolution is a historical fact of exceptional importance for the Ukrainian people. Above all, the people discovered their identity in it ... every peasant and worker knows now that he or she is a Ukrainian ... The national identity of the urban workers has grown enormously. In 1917 they came forward as Russians and today more than half identify themselves as Ukrainians. This is an important conquest of the revolution and of our difficult struggle.[1]

The exiled Socialist Revolutionary leader Mykyta Shapoval[2] drew this conclusion during one of his speeches to Ukrainian workers living in Canada in 1927. Although Ukrainians had failed to secure their independence in the recent upheaval, Shapoval remained optimistic about the future. Tsarism had been swept away. Among workers as well as peasants there was a new sense of national awareness which the Soviet government could not ignore. Like many other socialists and communists living in Ukraine and abroad, Shapoval believed in 1927 that the Revolution had not yet run its full course.

Such optimism was dispelled soon afterwards by Stalin's collectivisation of agriculture, the 1932–33 Famine and the purges. Yet Shapoval's claim about the adoption of a Ukrainian national identity by the lower classes became all the more credible in the following decades. Before the Revolution, the price that peasants paid for their social mobilisation, their transition from agricultural to industrial occupations, was assimilation into the Russian and Polish culture of the towns and cities. Not all were assimilated nor did they submit to it without resistance. But before 1917 they were fighting a losing battle. After the Revolution, however, the peasantry came into the cities and the working class more and more on their own terms. In 1897 44 percent of the working class identified themselves as Ukrainians, by 1926 it was 55 percent, by 1939 66 percent, and by

---

1 Mykyta Shapoval, *Velyka Revoliutsiia i Ukrains'ka Vyzvol'na Prohrama* (Prague: Vilna Spilka i Ukrainskyi Robitnychyi Instytut, 1927), p. 251.
2 Mykyta Shapoval (1882–1931): poet, literary critic, agronomist and political activist; founding member of the Ukrainian Party of Socialist Revolutionaries (UPSR) and an organiser of the November 1918 uprising against Hetman Pavlo Skoropadsky's regime. Exiled in Czechoslovakia after the Civil War, he helped establish several organisations, including the Ukrainian Workers' Institute in Prague. Shapoval also co-edited the journal *Nova Ukraina* with the Ukrainian Social Democratic leader Volodymyr Vynnychenko.

1959 69 percent. By 1970 three-quarters of the working class in the Ukrainian Soviet Socialist Republic identified as Ukrainians.[3]

Rapid industrialisation in the twentieth century drew the rural population to urban centres at an unprecedented rate and profoundly changed the ethnolinguistic composition of urban society. Yet the adoption of a national identity by members of the working class was a result not only of the peasant sources of the class, but also of conscious political choice. The assertion of Ukrainian national identity arose from the historic clash between classes of a stateless people mobilised by industrialisation and classes with the levers of industrialisation and state power already in their hands. A decisive turning point in this process when the choice of national identity began to be made by the majority of peasants and workers in Ukraine was 1917.

1   The Scope of the Work

This is a study of the formation of the working class in Ukraine and its relationship to the national question. It examines the working class as a force in the labour process and in politics from 1897 to 1918. It endeavours to explain how the formation of the working class was shaped by the national question, what interests workers had in its resolution and the kinds of solutions they pursued through their mass organisations and political parties.

The study focuses on eight provinces (*gubernia*) of the Russian Empire in which Ukrainians were a majority at the turn of the century.[4] It excludes from consideration the territories of Western Ukraine under Austro-Hungarian rule until the end of 1918 and after that under Poland until 1939. It maps out a broad view of the historical process: the succession of state powers on Ukrainian territories, the emergence of the capitalist mode of production and the formation of the working class as a labour force and as a political force. It examines the debates about the national question among internationally prominent Marxists of the era and analyses the positions taken by the Ukrainian, Rus-

---

[3] Bohdan Krawchenko, *Social Change and National Consciousness in Twentieth Century Ukraine* (Basingstoke: Macmillan, 1985), p. 206.

[4] They are the Right Bank provinces (of the Dnipro River) of Kyiv, Podillia and Volyn, the Left Bank provinces of Chernihiv, Poltava and Kharkiv; and the southern provinces of Katerynoslav, Kherson and Tavria. In this study, the Right and Left Bank provinces are also referred to as the northern tier provinces. At the eastern edge of the tier, Kharkiv shared characteristics of economic development both with the other five, largely agrarian, northern provinces and the industrialising south. Strictly speaking, the industrialising provinces were in the southeastern part of Ukraine but are referred to simply as the southern provinces or 'the south'.

sian and Jewish social democratic parties active in the Ukrainian provinces. These themes provide a context for examining in detail the first 'long year' of the Revolution from February 1917 to April 1918.

2   A Theory of the National Question

Throughout the study I use the terms 'national question', 'national movement', 'nation' and 'nation state'. They refer respectively to the genesis, politicisation, mobilisation and unification of nations. Used in such a way, they are merely signposts, heuristic indicators of historical stages of national development. A viable *theory* of national development, however, should explain how and why the national question arises in the first place.

I have adopted and extended Karl Marx's use of the concept of the division of labour in order to explain the origins of the national question. Marx observed in the development of capitalism an increasing separation and specialisation of human labour: agricultural and industrial, menial and intellectual, and male and female labour. These separations in social labour were not peculiar to capitalism, but were the product of a much longer evolution of human society. However, as the capitalist mode of production emerged it incorporated the city-country, menial-intellectual and gender divisions of earlier modes of production and accentuated them in an even sharper way.

For Marx the division of labour was the infrastructure of class society, while private property was but a juridical expression and defence of the division of labour peculiar to capitalism.[5] The European social democratic movement which inherited his ideas had a tendency to reduce Marx's concept of class society to its juridical expression, as the relationship between the owners of labour and the owners of the means of production. This notion of ownership served as a general indicator or the 'last word' on class under capitalism, but it was not of much use for understanding class struggles other than economic ones. Nor could it provide insight into the contradictions within the working class itself, divided as it was by occupational privileges based on location, education and gender.

How does all this apply to the national question? The division of labour did not stop evolving with the advent of capitalism. Since the end of the nineteenth century, capitalism as a global economic system has built an *international* divi-

---

5   Karl Marx and Friedrich Engels, *The German Ideology*, Parts I and III, edited and with an introduction by R. Pascal (New York: International Publishers, 1947), pp. 8–16, 21–7, 43–4.

sion of labour. It is now characterised by the imposition of specific economic tasks by the economically powerful metropoles upon the ever more distant peripheral societies it draws onto the world market.[6] Regions of the world and their inhabitants have taken different paths of social and economic evolution depending on the time they were linked to the world market, the resources most readily exploitable in them and the relative strength of the state power already in control of their territories.

For different historical reasons, the boundaries of states in peripheral societies seldom conform to the boundaries of compact ethno-linguistic groups. As a rule they encompass several of them. Such groups within single states are drawn into the process of industrialisation and urbanisation at varying rates. These rates depend on the readily exploitable natural resources and human labour in their vicinity, the influence of these groups' leaders in the central state institutions, the groups' knowledge of the language of modern industry and government, their possession of industrial skills and work habits and their willingness to assimilate into a new urban-industrial culture. Because the resources available for industrialisation are limited, they are applied only in selected parts of the country. Invariably industrialisation will benefit the ethno-linguistic group or groups that control the state power. Even if new industries are not located on their own group's traditional territory, they are in control of the state mechanisms for centralising and redistributing a major portion of the surplus product produced over the whole territory of the state.

Thus, the division of labour that has emerged on a global scale between the industrialised and industrialising regions is reproduced once again within the confines of the latter, the industrialising region. Here the division of labour incorporates the potential attributes of a national identity (language, culture, attachment to territory, etc.) that affect an ethno-linguistic group's capacity for social mobility through the class structure of the industrialising region – that is, the capacity to secure urban, intellectual and 'male' designated occupations in the modernising economy. Thus it is the crystallisation of a division of labour between established and incipient nations within an existing state, a process that holds back the social mobility of the incipient nation and redistributes the surplus product of the whole society inequitably in favour of the estab-

---

6 Marx studied the beginning of this process. In *Capital*, Vol. 1 (Moscow: Progress Publishers, 1977), p. 425, he writes: 'A new and international division of labour, a division suited to the requirements of the chief centres of modern industry springs up, and converts one part of the globe into a chiefly agricultural field of production for supplying the other part which remains a chiefly industrial field'.

lished nation, which politicises these well known attributes of national identity (language, culture, attachment to territory) and provokes national movements among the incipient nations.[7]

One can therefore argue that labour in contemporary world society is divided not only along gender, menial-intellectual and city-country lines, but also along national lines. If one accepts such a view of the division of labour, it follows that national movements, that is movements which contest this division, are one of the expressions of class struggle. For class struggle is in the first instance nothing more than a struggle over the division of labour and the distribution of wealth stemming from that labour.

I have proposed above in a most general way a concept of the historical development of a division of labour between state-established and incipient nations at three distinct levels: in the globalising capitalist economy, in the industrialising region of the peripheral state and within the working class itself. In the chapters below I have applied this concept to the case of Ukraine and examined how the workers' movement and its social democratic parties dealt with the national question from their inception in the late nineteenth century up to and including the first year of the Revolution.

3 The Historical Debate

The historical literature on the Revolution and Civil War presents three distinct assessments of the efforts of the mass organisations and political parties of the working class in relation to the national question and the movement for independence. The first of these originated in the Ukrainian Social Democratic Workers' Party (USDWP), one of the parties vanquished in the Revolution. Volodymyr Vynnychenko, a prominent USDWP leader has argued that

> in its great majority, our proletariat was denationalised and Russified by force of historical circumstances. Because of this we did not have a broad proletarian base ... to support us ... to demand resoluteness from us ... We rested on the peasantry, not on the poor strata but for the most part on the well-to-do peasants who were more politically mature and conscious.
>
> Instead of going to our proletariat even though it had not awakened nationally, instead of awakening it and drawing social resoluteness and

---

7 Michael Hechter, *Internal Colonialism: The Celtic Fringe in British National Development* (Berkeley: University of California Press, 1975), pp. 33–9.

confidence from it ... approaching it with a social programme and giving it national leadership, we turned away from it. We became scared of it and even of the peasants who went after the proletariat. That was our main mistake and shortcoming.[8]

Vynnychenko attributed the failure of the national independence movement to attract working-class support mainly to the USDWP's own limitations. On the other hand, Isaak Mazepa, another USDWP leader, stressed more the subjective and organisational immaturity of the Ukrainian speaking proletariat:

> ... the Ukrainian nation began to awaken and muster its forces only a few decades before the outbreak of the revolution. It is not surprising that the trade union and political organisation of the Ukrainian proletariat began considerably later than among the Russians and that the Ukrainian intelligentsia approached its proletarian masses very late in the day .... The Ukrainian proletariat proved young and disorganised. The revolution came too soon for it.[9]

The leaders of the vanquished Social Democrats and others, such as the Ukrainian Party of Socialist Revolutionaries (UPSR), continued in exile to debate their defeat in the Civil War at the hands of the Bolsheviks. Their thinking about 1917 evolved from regarding it as a social revolution, as they had called it in 1917, to remembering it also, and even more so, as a national liberation struggle. They attributed the defeat of their state building efforts to an immature Ukrainian proletariat, which denied them an adequate social base in the cities, and to a Russian proletariat hostile towards any kind of Ukrainian state.

The second interpretation of working-class practice on the national question, which became dominant among Soviet Ukrainian historians, originated in a debate among the victors of the Civil War at the end of the 1920s. After the Civil War the Bolsheviks embarked upon a programme of 'indigenisation' or 'Ukrainisation', in order to broaden the social base of their regime from its narrow, mainly Russian and Jewish urban base. The ranks of the Communist Party (Bolsheviks) of Ukraine (CP(B)U) were swelled by large numbers of Ukrainians for the first time, among them former members of the USDWP and UPSR, their rivals in the Civil War. This second interpretation was advanced by the Stalinist faction that fought 'nationalist deviations' appearing in CP(B)U as a result of the

---

8 Volodymyr Vynnychenko, *Vidrodzhennia Natsii*, 3 vols (Kyiv-Vienna: Dzvin, 1920), Vol. 2, p. 97.
9 Isaak Mazepa, *Bol'shevyzm i Okupatsiia Ukrainy. Sotsiial'no-ekonomichni prychyny nedozrilosty syl ukrains'koi revoliutsii* (Lviv-Kyiv: Znattia to Syla, 1922), pp. 17–18.

Ukrainian influx. It guided party thinking and historical scholarship thereafter, until the collapse of the Soviet Union. It was made up of several interlocking propositions: that the working class was the leading force in the Revolution; that its Russian section led the other nations in the working class; that the Communist Party led the working class as a whole; and that the national question was of insignificant concern in the order of problems faced by the working class. This set of propositions provided a clear framework in which Soviet scholars from the 1930s onwards explained how the working class came to power in the Revolution and Civil War, established a multinational state of its own and resolved the national question in the process.[10]

One of its most serious consequences was the committal of all other parties of the working class to historical oblivion. The Mensheviks, USDWP and Bund were seldom mentioned. When they were, it was to the tune of accompanying epithets as to their 'opportunist', 'bourgeois nationalist' or 'counterrevolutionary' activities. Another consequence was the studious denial of the peasantry, the class that had a greater social weight than the working class and that deeply affected the fortunes of all urban based state building projects.

The so-called state school of the history of the Revolution and Civil War provides a third interpretation of the role of the working class with regard to the national question. Ukrainian historians after 1991 were freed from the restrictions of Stalinist historiography to approach the revolutionary period 1917–21 from a wide variety of perspectives, to focus on the full spectrum of its participants. However, almost without exception they adopted the term and concept of the 'Ukrainian revolution' and the explanatory framework of national liberation struggle or movement. They rejected the concept and the study of the social revolution of this period and considered the parties and movements that addressed it as such as carriers of a foreign ideology. So, too, they downplayed, if not denied, the links of the Ukrainian revolution to the

---

10 P. Hrytsenko, *Robitnychi Fortetsi Sotsialistychnoi Revoliutsii* (Kyiv: Naukova Dumka, 1965); P.P. Hudzenko, *Sotsialistychna Natsionalizatsiia Promyslovosti v Ukrains'kii RSR* (Kyiv: Naukova Dumka, 1965); I.O. Hurzhii, *Zarodzhennia Robitnychoho Klasu Ukrainy* (kinets' XVIII–persha polovyna XIX st.) (Kyiv: Derzhavne Vydavnytstvo Politychnoi Literatury URSR, 1958); Yu. Y. Kirianov, *Rabochie Iuga Rossii 1914–fevral 1917 g.* (Moscow: Izdatelstvo Nauka, 1971); F. Ie. Los (gen. ed.), I.O. Hurzhii, I.T. Shcherbyna, O.I. Luhova (eds), *Istoriia Robitnychoho Klasu URSR*, 2 vols (Kyiv: Naukova Dumka, 1967); O.O. Nesterenko, *Rozvytok Promyslovosti na Ukraini. Chastyna II* (Kyiv: Vydavnytstvo Akademii Nauk URSR, 1962); Ye. M. Skliarenko, *Robitnychyi Klas Ukrainy v Roky Hromadians'koi Viiny* (Kyiv: Naukova Dumka, 1966); and *Narys Istorii Profspilkovoho Rukhu na Ukraini 1917–20* (Kyiv: Naukova Dumka, 1974).

Russian, and of the turbulent growth of the national movement to the democratic gains made by the February 1917 overthrow of Tsarism.[11]

This school, which has dominated the field of enquiry into this period since 1991, identifies with the conclusions reached by moderate and conservative participants in the Revolution and Civil War, with individuals like Dmytro Doroshenko[12] and organisations like the Ukrainian Party of Socialist Federalists (UPSF). In addition to its basic proposition that a national liberal struggle, rather than a social revolution, lay at the heart of the upheavals of 1917–21, this school also contends that the behaviour and choices of elite forces, rather than of the masses of workers and peasants, determined the outcome of this struggle. It concludes that Ukrainian elites of the time made the wrong choices by favouring radical social policies and downplaying the task of independent nation state building; and, ultimately, that the Ukrainian masses succumbed to the demagogy of foreign, Bolshevik forces and so abandoned their leaders and the struggle for their own nation state.

The state school's propositions provoke several important questions that this study seeks to answer. Were indeed the social revolution and the national liberation struggle counterposed as mutually exclusive alternatives in the reasoning and the actions of participants in the Revolution and Civil War? If not, then just how did they understand the relationship between them in a broader, unifying historical process? Finally, can we speak of a social class as a subject, a maker of history? In other words, did the working class demonstrate any capacity for independent reasoning and action, or should we accept the proposition of the primacy of elites in the revolutionary process of those times? In the following chapters I consider these three interpretations of a turbulent period of Ukraine's history as I attempt to disclose the relationship of the working class to the national question of that time on the basis of my own study of the original sources.

---

11   A comprehensive review of Ukrainian historical writing about this period is provided by Valerii Soldatenko, 'Novi pidkhody v osmyslenniu istorychnoho dosvidu i urokiv revoliutsiinoi doby 1917–20 rr. v Ukraini', *Naukovi pratsi istorychnoho fakul'tetu Zaporiz'koho Derzhavnoho Universytetu*, 24 (2008), pp. 93–203.

12   Dmytro Doroshenko, *Moi Spomyny pro Nedavnie Mynule, 1914–20* (Munich: Ukrainske Vydavnytstvo, 1969); *Istoriia Ukrainy*, 2nd edn (Augsburg: P. Pohasyi, 1947).

CHAPTER 1

State Power and the Development of Capitalism

Capitalism had a long, uncertain and fitful history in Ukraine until the end of the nineteenth century. One of the reasons for its slow and uneven gestation was an extended struggle between regional state powers for control of Ukrainian territories and their eventual absorption by Russia, whose feudal system survived until the mid-nineteenth century. This chapter examines the succession of Lithuanian, Polish, Cossack and Russian state powers, their influence on the growth of the market and bourgeoisie in Ukraine and the particular relationship established between the Russian state and European finance capital at the end of the nineteenth century in the division of the country's social product. The historic evolution of these economic and political forces is the basis upon which conclusions are offered about Ukraine's colonial predicament on the eve of the Revolution. They are examined summarily in three stages: from the fall of Rus to the 1648 Revolution; from the Treaty of Pereiaslav in 1654 to the abolition of serfdom in 1861; and the period of rapid industrialisation before the First World War.

1   The 1648 Revolution

Between the ninth and the mid-thirteenth centuries a large section of present-day Ukraine was ruled by the tributary state of Kyivan Rus. With its capital anchored in the upper Dnipro Basin on the border between the northern forests and the southern steppes, Kyivan Rus controlled the trade between Scandinavia and Byzantium. Its power crumbled in the thirteenth century as Crimean Tatars living on the Black Sea coast moved northwards, conquering Rus principalities, sacking Kyiv and cutting off the old trade route along the Dnipro River. The southern reaches of the Dnipro and all lands east of the Rivers Buh and Dnipro remained under their sway until the end of the sixteenth century.[1]

---

[1] Dmytro Doroshenko, *Istoriia Ukrainy*, 4th edn (Augsburg: P. Pohasyi, 1947), p. 20; Matvii Yavorsky, *Revoliutsiia na Vkraini v ii Holovnishykh Etapakh* (Kharkiv: Derzhavne Vydavnytstvo Ukrainy, 1923), p. 5; Isaak Mazepa, *Pidstavy Nashoho Vidrodzhennia* (n.p.: Prometei, 1946), Vol. 1, pp. 30–2, 50.

From the north, the Lithuanian nobility began occupying Rus in the fourteenth century, settling in Podillia, Kyiv and Eastern Volyn. In the fifteenth century, the Polish kingdom expanded south eastward into Galicia and Western Volyn. The boyars and princes of Rus who remained on their land joined the ranks of the colonising nobilities. Lithuanian and Polish systems of tributary obligation were imposed on the rural commoners.[2]

Stimulated by mercantile opportunities with European cities in the sixteenth century, the Polish nobility in Western Ukraine stepped up its exploitation of serf labour.[3] The profits to be gained from long distance trade in agricultural and forestry products through the Baltic Sea ports encouraged noblemen to restrict peasants' mobility and to exact more working hours on their land. At the same time they extended their fields at the expense of traditional peasant holdings. Although rent in money and kind were in widespread use elsewhere by the sixteenth century, the Polish nobility preferred an original, more oppressive and labour exacting system called *panshchyna* – corvée or labour days.[4]

Social evolution in the Dnipro Basin below Kyiv followed a different path after the fall of Rus. Here the indigenous people who withstood the Crimean Tatar invasions, and even supported them to get rid of their own princes and retainers,[5] continued to live as armed communities of hunters, foragers, beekeepers and fishermen. Because the old Rus nobility was all but destroyed in these parts the surviving communities governed themselves by the principles of an earlier epoch. Households chose representatives to an assembly (*viche*) which periodically re-allocated the use of the habitat, ruled on disputes and elected the community's leaders in war. The people of the Dnipro Basin resisted all feudal obligations and upheld a conception of independence they remembered collectively as their 'ancient rights and privileges'.

From the end of the fifteenth century the communities in the forest-steppe were joined each summer by expeditions of young men from the Lithuanian realm who came down the rivers to hunt, fish and take horses. As these expeditions became more frequent the nobility began applying taxes to the sale of goods brought back each autumn to the northern towns and fortress outposts.

---

2   Mazepa, *Pidstavy*, Vol. 1, pp. 36–40, 47; M. Antonovych, *Istoriia Ukrainy*, 2nd edn (Winnipeg: UVAN, 1966), Vol. 2, p. 61; Yavorsky, *Revoliutsiia na Vkraini*, p. 5; Perry Anderson, *Lineages of the Absolutist State* (London: New Left Books, 1974), p. 280.
3   Michael (Mykhailo) Hrushevsky, *A History of Ukraine* (New Haven: n.p. 1944), p. 174.
4   K.K. Dubyna (gen. ed.), *Istoriia Ukrains'koi RSR* (Kyiv: Naukova Dumka, 1967), Vol. 1, p. 126; Antonovych, *Istoriia Ukrainy*, Vol. 2, pp. 62–3.
5   Doroshenko, *Istoriia Ukrainy*, pp. 62–3.

Over time participants in these expeditions spent the winter in the south to avoid taxes and other feudal obligations. Eventually they settled there and turned to farming.[6]

The burdens of *panshchyna* grew in Volyn and Galicia, and many serfs escaped to settle frontier land in Central Ukraine. Some arriving at the fortress outposts of the Polish crown on their way east were readily recruited by resident nobles to military service and maintenance of their properties and fortifications. Like the emigrants from Lithuanian controlled territories, some of the fugitives from serfdom continued moving further east and south into the realm of the cossack host.[7]

Emerging at the end of the fifteenth century on the frontier between the Lithuanian-Polish and Turkish realms, cossack society was the product of a fusion between economically motivated migrants and fugitives from serfdom and the earlier, pre-feudal order of Central Ukraine which had survived the demise of Rus. A nomadic warrior class that turned increasingly to farming and trade, the cossacks led the reoccupation of lands depopulated by the Crimean Tatar invasions. In 1552 they founded an army state on the lower rapids of the Dnipro River (*Zaporiz'ka Sich*) and managed to push the Crimean Tatars back to the Black Sea coast by the end of the sixteenth century. The *Sich* was a rallying point for communities in the Dnipro Basin, guardian of the river traffic and a staging ground for maritime wars against Turkey and military expeditions to Muscovy and Moldova. The *nyzovi* cossacks (those of the lower reaches of the river) conducted trade and diplomatic relations with all of these states and became an important factor in the balance of power between Turkey, Poland and Russia. The *Sich* stood until 1775 when Catherine II destroyed it and the *nyzovi* migrated into the Kuban and Danubian Basin.[8]

Poland and Lithuania united into a Commonwealth in 1569. Poland formally annexed Eastern Volyn, Kyiv and lands east of the Dnipro. The Polish nobility set its sights on new land and followed in the footsteps of its fugitive serfs into Central Ukraine. The most powerful nobles organised large transfers of supplies and serfs to stake out new latifundia. They occupied uninhabited land and, where necessary, threw cossack farmers off land they wanted. Compared to their estates in Western Ukraine, the aristocracy's new holdings were enormous. The Wisnowiecki family was granted title to 'almost half of Poltava' by the

---

[6] Mazepa, *Pidstavy*, Vol. 1, p. 49; Antonovych, *Istoriia Ukrainy*, Vol. 2, pp. 4–6; Hrushevsky, *History of Ukraine*, p. 152.
[7] Hrushevsky, *History of Ukraine*, p. 174; Antonovych, *Istoriia Ukrainy*, Vol. 3, p. 6.
[8] Hrushevsky, *History of Ukraine*, p. 157; Anderson, *Lineages*, p. 209.

king and had 230,000 people working on its properties. The Potocki family took over three million acres. Title to new land was granted also in Podillia, Kyiv and Chernihiv.[9]

In order to secure sufficient labour for their frontier estates nobles offered serfs exemptions from customary obligations for up to 20 years if they consented to move east. They also accepted fugitive serfs already in Central Ukraine and defended them from their former masters. The nobility imposed limits on the outlets of ale, applied taxes, mill rates, road and bridge tolls and took one-tenth of all beehives and livestock, yet the system of taxes and obligations between lord and commoner in Central Ukraine was still less onerous than in Western Ukraine. Here rent in money and produce prevailed; 'real serfdom' did not exist.[10]

Faced with a new wave of colonisers, many people living on the frontier migrated further east and south. Others stayed on their land and tried to adapt. They were the *horodovi* Cossacks (town Cossacks) who farmed land near the fortress outposts and were valued by the Polish crown as an important military reserve on the frontier. In 1555, three years after the foundation of the *Sich*, the crown began to register *horodovi* as paid soldiers and exempted them from all obligations to the nobility. The registered cossacks also retained the right to elect officers and govern themselves. Many frontier townspeople, who in their majority were fugitives from Western Ukraine, were eager to join their ranks and benefit from the same rights and exemptions.[11]

The migration of the Polish nobility now joined Central Ukraine to the mercantile trade with Europe through the Baltic Sea ports. In contrast to the situation in Western Ukraine, however, where the mercantile connection served to accentuate serfdom, in Central Ukraine it stimulated production that employed a much larger proportion of free labour. Here the natural resources for industry were more abundant. Unable to impose obligations to the same degree as elsewhere, the nobility left serfs with a greater margin in time and labour to apply to wage earning occupations. Moreover, almost 40 percent of the peasants in Central Ukraine owned no land at all and a high proportion of the population, by one estimate over 46 percent,[12] enjoyed the status of town

---

9   Doroshenko, *Istoriia Ukrainy*, p. 93; Anderson, *Lineages*, p. 285.
10 Hrushevsky, *History of Ukraine*, p. 175; Antonovych, *Istoriia Ukrainy*, Vol. 1, pp. 16–17; Konstantyn Kononenko, *Ukraine and Russia: A History of Economic Relations between Ukraine and Russia (1654–1917)* (Milwaukee: Marquette University Press, 1958), p. 9.
11 Hrushevsky, *History of Ukraine*, pp. 162–4; Antonovych, *Istoriia Ukrainy*, Vol. 1, p. 28; Mazepa, *Pidstavy*, Vol. 1, p. 52.
12 Mykhailo Braichevsky, 'Pryiednannia chy Voziednannia?', in *Shyroke More Ukrainy: Dok-*

dweller. That is to say, many people with the rights of town dwellers actually lived beyond the town walls. Thus the mobility of labour and its products was greater than in Western Ukraine.

Still another factor contributing to the spread of commodity production and wage labour was the de facto ownership of means of production in land by the earlier cossack settlers. Not only did industries in Central Ukraine employ less serf labour than in the west, but they also sprang up as home industries on the properties of cossack farmers. This contributed to a vital industrial environment with a growing domestic market and good opportunities for long distance trade. The greatest number of wage earners were employed by enterprises that produced mainly for export: iron foundries and glass works, lumber mills, breweries, distilleries, potash and saltpetre mines.[13]

While the Polish nobility grew rich from the grain trade, it did not consolidate political power. The presence of the *horodovi*, close proximity of the *nyzovi* and the fact that for every 'obedient' town dweller, there were a dozen 'disobedients', the fugitives of serfdom in Western Ukraine, all contributed to keeping the nobility in check as 'a small potentate caste superimposed over an ethnically alien peasantry'.[14]

But the compromise of the crown with the *horodovi* way of life and their employment as frontier soldiers conflicted with the ambitions of the landed nobles, who wanted as much land and labour as possible under their control. They conspired with the town nobles to have the registered Cossack ranks decreased and their privileges denied. The register was reduced to several thousand. Nobles assumed leading positions in cossack regiments and sold lower ranks to the highest bidders. They taxed the soldiers' pay, forced them to perform supplementary labour on their land and enserfed their widows and children. Cossacks were taxed for fishing and hunting, using roads and bridges, and were prohibited from making beer and vodka.[15]

In addition to losing their land to the most powerful nobles, violation of the original terms upon which the *horodovi* accepted membership in the crown's armed forces made them all the more violently disposed to the new ruling classes. There were frequent armed rebellions, occupations of estates and

---

umenty Samvydavu z Ukrainy (Paris-Baltimore: PIUF-Smoloskyp, 1972), p. 285. This group included farmers who were not enserfed and fulfilled minor obligations to the town nobility as well as merchants and artisans.

13 Braichevsky, 'Pryiednannia chy Voziednannia?', pp. 287–8.
14 Anderson, *Lineages*, p. 284.
15 Mykhailo Hrushevsky, *Istoriia Ukrainy-Rusy*, 2nd edn, 10 vols (New York: Knyhospilka, 1954–58), Vol. 6, pp. 285–6.

seizures of munitions and supplies. The most serious rebellions occurred in 1590, 1596, 1624, 1630, 1637 and 1638.[16] It was not only the growing scope and intensity of feudalism in Central Ukraine that provoked opposition but its very existence. Many settlers who had escaped *panshchyna* were not happy to see the nobles follow them east 'like swarms of mosquitoes'.[17] Another segment of the population had not known tribute for over two hundred years. For the *nyzovi* cossacks especially, the nobiliary colonisation was not to be compromised with, but simply resisted.

Towns in the Polish-Lithuanian Commonwealth had no influence on state legislation because they were not represented in the *Sejm*. The gentry controlled the *Sejm*, 'systematically exploited the urban centres for their own advantage'[18] and discouraged members of their class from settling in them. According to the Magdeburg Charter, only Roman Catholics could serve on municipal councils or join artisan guilds. Thus the autonomous political and economic institutions of the towns were reserved for Poles and Germans. Belonging to other faiths, Armenians, Jews and Ukrainians had no access to them.[19]

As the only autonomous institution of the Ukrainians, the Orthodox Church was subjected to official persecution and persistent attempts to assimilate its clergy, laity and property into the Roman Catholic Church. Ukrainian townspeople mounted campaigns to defend Orthodoxy, recruiting the *horodovi* and later *nyzovi* Cossacks to them as well.[20]

Mounting antagonisms between the two main colonising groups in Central Ukraine over land, religious and political rights, and the introduction of serfdom lie at the roots of the 1648 Revolution, 'the most formidable peasant war of the epoch in the East'.[21] Sparked by a nobleman seizing land from Bohdan Khmelnytsky, a registered cossack in Chyhyryn, a revolt of 500 men quickly turned into an outright challenge to the entire structure of Polish rule in Central Ukraine. In May 1648 an army of 70,000 peasants and cossacks defeated the Polish army and took control of a large area on both sides of the Dnipro River. Subsequent negotiations with Jan Kasimir, the newly elected king, res-

---

16 Doroshenko, *Istoriia Ukrainy*, pp. 98–119.
17 Hrushevsky, *History of Ukraine*, p. 175.
18 Hrushevsky, *History of Ukraine*, p. 171.
19 Mazepa, *Idstavy*, Vol. 1, p. 44; Dubyna, *Istoriia Ukrains'koi RSR*, Vol. 1, p. 126; Antonovych, *Istoriia Ukrainy*, Vol. 1, p. 68.
20 Doroshenko, *Istoriia Ukrainy*, pp. 105–8, 111–12.
21 Anderson, *Lineages*, p. 210.

ulted in the Treaty of Zboriv, which recognised part of this area (see Map 1) as an autonomous Ukrainian cossack state, or Hetmanate, within the Commonwealth.[22]

The leaders of the 1648 Revolution secured important political gains for the Ukrainian population. According to the Treaty of Zboriv, all political offices in the Hetmanate were reserved for persons of the Orthodox faith. The *het'man* himself and all judicial and administrative positions were to be elected by the ranks of registered cossacks whose numbers were raised to 40,000. The Polish army was to be withdrawn from the Hetmanate. But the Treaty also represented a compromise between the Revolution's leaders and the Polish ruling classes on the burning social questions facing the peasants and rank and file cossacks. The Crown administration was permitted to return to its offices and the nobility to its land. Those not included in the new register, together with the peasantry as a whole, were ordered to report to their masters and submit to previous obligations. Khmelnytsky thus parted ways with the anti-feudal aspirations of the bulk of his army in exchange for privileges for the cossack leadership which aspired to become an independent, progressive, yet nobiliary class.[23]

Subsequent edicts of Hetman Khmelnytsky ordering peasants and unregistered cossacks to return to their masters had a demoralising and fragmenting effect on the popular mobilisation. When the *Sejm* rejected the terms of the Zboriv Treaty and war broke out again, Khmelnytsky did not have the kind of support he had previously enjoyed. In September 1651 he was defeated at Bila Tserkva after losing thirty thousand men and was forced to sign a new and less generous treaty with the Poles. He then turned to other neighbouring rulers to bolster his strength – the Crimean Tatar Khan, the Turkish Sultan, the Swedish King and eventually to Oleksii, the Russian Tsar. In January 1654 representatives of the Hetman and Tsar met at Pereiaslav and signed a treaty making all territories under Khmelnytsky's army's control an autonomous Russian protectorate.[24]

The Revolution of 1648 was a struggle between two historic waves of settlers in Central Ukraine. An anti-feudal revolution against the Polish crown and landed nobility, it was waged under the ideological banners of Rus identity and Orthodoxy. After Khmelnytsky triumphed over the Polish army he declared to the emissaries of the Polish crown:

---

22   George Gajecky, *The Cossack Administration of the Hetmanate*, 2 vols (Cambridge, MA: Harvard University Research Institute, 1978), Vol. 1, p. 1.
23   Mazepa, *Idstavy*, Vol. 1, pp. 73–4.
24   Doroshenko, *Istoriia Ukrainy*, pp. 129–31.

> I shall free the entire people of Rus from the Poles [liakhy] ... all of the commoners will help me in this task ... I have become the independent and supreme ruler of Rus! And I will maintain two or three hundred thousand soldiers.[25]

Yet the ideological unity of Khmelnytsky's forces concealed divergent social interests of peasants, smallholders and their political-military leaders. When the leaders sought a compromise with the Polish ruling class over the social order, they lost the support of their peasant and cossack base. The compromise itself began to be made not when Khmelnytsky suffered his first defeats but at the height of his power. During the election of Jan Kasimir to the Polish throne, which coincided with the 1648 uprising, cossack leaders sent emissaries to the *Sejm* to argue for Orthodox rights, cossack 'rights and privileges' and for a division in society where 'a cossack is a cossack and a peasant remains a peasant'.[26] Kasimir responded by promising many favours in exchange for the cossacks' support and begged them to postpone further military operations against his army. The peasantry and the cossack ranks had turned Khmelnytsky's revolt into a revolution. Thus, as 'the independent and supreme ruler of Rus' Khmelnytsky secured the national and religious aspirations of the Ukrainian masses, but he would not uphold their social struggle to free themselves from feudal bondage.[27]

2 After Pereiaslav

The 1654 Treaty of Pereiaslav showed in another way that the anti-feudal aspirations of the lower classes were being abandoned by the cossack leaders in favour of their own nobiliary ambitions. Although the feudal order in Russia was more developed and entrenched than in Central Ukraine, the leaders of the 1648 Revolution were drawn into an alliance with Russia against Poland in order to defend these ambitions.[28]

---

25   Mykhailo Hrushevsky, *Istoriia Ukrainy-Rusy*, Vol. VIII, Chapter XII.
26   Mazepa, *Idstavy*, Vol. 1, pp. 73–4.
27   Hrushevsky, *History of Ukraine*, p. 283.
28   Discussions about the relative importance of national, religious and social motives in the 1648 Revolution are to be found in Hrushevsky, *Istoriia Ukrainy-Rusy*, Vol. 8, p. 118; Mazepa, *Idstavy*, Vol. 1, pp. 73–82; and Mykyta Shapoval, *Sotsiolohiia Ukrains'koho Vidrodzhennia* (Prague: Ukrainskyi Sotsiolohichnyi Instytut v Prazi, 1936), p. 26.

STATE POWER AND THE DEVELOPMENT OF CAPITALISM 17

MAP 1   Hetmanate, the Ukrainian Cossack state, 1654
© DMYTRO VORTMAN, 2019

As a protectorate of Russia, the Hetmanate encompassed Poltava, Chernihiv, Kyiv and the eastern edge of Podillia. Poland held onto almost the entire Right Bank despite a continuous war with peasants and cossacks from both sides of the border that lasted into the eighteenth century. Many peasants fled the Right Bank and settled in the Hetmanate and further east in what became Kharkiv, Kursk and Voronezh provinces.

The nobility and gentry split into three camps: the supporters of Khmelnytsky who were for the most part descendants of the indigenous nobles of Rus; the Polish nobles who fled Ukraine during the Revolution; and those who fled, but returned later to claim their property under the terms of the Zboriv Treaty. As early as 1654, leading cossack officers petitioned the Tsar for official title to lands vacated by the nobility. The Tsar looked favourably on their petitions as he was eager to build a landed aristocracy capable of dealing with anti-feudal opposition, which was mounting in Russia at the time and would peak in 1670 in Stenka Razin's revolt. The cossack elite appropriated large tracts of land and parcelled out portions to its lower officers in return for army service. It granted permission to peasants from the Right Bank to occupy plots in the regimental districts of the Hetmanate.[29]

Yet the 1648 Revolution left a strong imprint on the peasants' consciousness. Believing that all feudal ranks and obligations had been abolished 'by the cossack sword', peasants considered occupied land as their own. Except for an annual tax to the state treasury to maintain the army and diplomatic corps, they honoured no other obligations in the early years after 1648. As long as land remained plentiful and the Revolution stuck in the memory of the peasants, the old and the new nobility could do little to bring rural labour under their control. It was only after all available land was occupied and the cossack nobility began seeking title to land already settled by the peasantry that dues and obligations made an appearance again. Free settlers became known as sharecroppers and started to pay rent. Over time other obligations were added, including road repair, sentry duty on estates, hay making on the noble's fields and work on his dams and millponds. From 1701, a tax in oats and two days labour per week for the noble were demanded.[30]

Serfdom in the Hetmanate at the end of the seventeenth century was considerably less exacting on the peasants than it was in Poland or Russia, but it was already reasserting itself. In 1648, the *Zemskyi Sobor* in Moscow had codified and universalised serfdom throughout Russia in an agreement with the Tsar

---

29   Braichevsky, 'Pryiednannia chy Voziednannia?', p. 305; Doroshenko, *Istoriia Ukrainy*, p. 151.
30   Kononenko, *Ukraine and Russia*, p. 5.

that made him an absolute monarch. Laws were passed in 1658 making peasant flight a felony.[31] These political decisions paved the way to complete serfdom in Russia. The peasantry in the Hetmanate withstood their implementation until the end of the seventeenth century and only after Hetman Mazepa's defeat at Poltava in 1709 were they applied there in force. Serfdom was extended to the lands of the Zaporozhian host in the lower Dnipro Basin in the latter half of the eighteenth century when the Russian nobiliary colonisation of the steppes took place.[32]

The reintroduction of serfdom and accession of the cossack elite to the ranks of the landed nobility ruptured the social alliance which upheld the political autonomy of the Hetmanate. During the latter half of the seventeenth century, Khmelnytsky's successors retained a good deal of political autonomy from their protector state, but it declined slowly and steadily as the pendulum of power in the region swung to the east and Russia boldly annexed Polish controlled territories to the west of the Hetmanate in three great Partitions of pre-1772 Poland. The leaders of the Hetmanate tried to extricate themselves from the protectorate status by launching wars against Poland, making alliances with the enemies of Poland and Russia and attempting to unite Central with Western Ukraine. The Tsars intervened decisively against these attempts, whittling away at their domestic authority, introducing their own garrisons to the towns and cities, changing laws and diverting taxes to the imperial treasury. Russia's victory over Mazepa and the Swedes in 1709 was the occasion for a radical diminution of the Hetmanate's autonomy. After Hetman Skoropadsky died in 1722, the Tsar prohibited the election of a successor. Attempts were made to revive the authority of the hetman's office, but it was abolished finally in 1764 by Catherine II and the entire administrative structure of the Hetmanate was dismantled by 1783.[33]

The Russian Empire annexed sections of Western Ukraine in the course of the Partitions of Poland in 1772, 1793 and 1795. The nobiliary colonisation of the south, 'the largest single geographic clearance in the history of European feudal agriculture'[34] sealed Russian control of the lower Dnipro Basin, the steppes and the Black Sea coast. In this way, the greater part of Ukrainian ethnographic territories came under the control of the Russian Empire by the end of the eighteenth century. The remainder was taken by Austro-Hungary from the ruins of the Polish state (see Map 2).

---

31   Anderson, *Lineages*, pp. 203–4, 339–41.
32   Mazepa, *Idstavy*, Vol. 1, pp. 95–6.
33   Ibid, Vol. 1, pp. 93–102; O.I. Luhova, 'Pro stanovyshche Ukrainy v period kapitalizmu', *Ukrains'kyi Istorychnyi Zhurnal*, March 1967, p. 16.
34   Anderson, *Lineages*, p. 345.

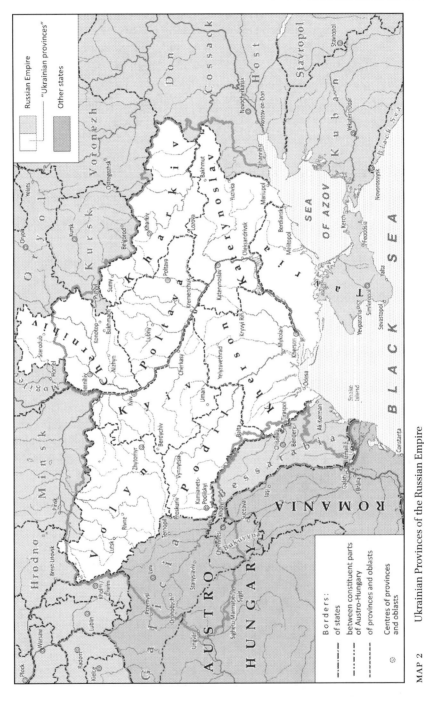

MAP 2   Ukrainian Provinces of the Russian Empire
© DMYTRO VORTMAN, 2019

Alongside the loss of its national autonomy and the resurgence of serfdom, the third long-term consequence for Ukraine of annexation by Russia was registered in the pace of industrial development and formation of the bourgeoisie. After 1654 Poland controlled the economically developed sections of Right Bank Ukraine which continued to serve as her richest agricultural possessions. In the more recently colonised lands of the Hetmanate, home industries had appeared during the latter half of the seventeenth century. A regional market in agricultural produce and artisan wares took shape. Trading links between the Hetmanate and mercantile centres on the Baltic Sea coast were secured. During Khmelnytsky's term in office, the state treasury began imposing export and import duties at its borders. However, these early signs of a national market faded as the Hetmanate lost its political autonomy. In 1714 the Tsar decreed that all exports should pass through Russian borders on their way abroad. In 1720 all foreign trade conducted in the Hetmanate was reserved for Russian merchants and Russian currency became the sole medium of domestic exchange. Laws passed in 1752 freed imports to the Hetmanate from duties. In 1754 all duties on imports and exports collected at the Hetmanate's borders were abolished.[35]

At the end of the eighteenth century when sections of Western Ukraine were annexed by Russia from Poland, German merchants had already established a strong presence in the region. They sold manufactured goods there, bought up raw materials and arranged transit for their wares onto the Left Bank. The younger and economically weaker class of Russian merchants could not compete effectively in the newly annexed region without a measure of state intervention on its behalf. In 1822 a protectionist tariff helped the nascent Russian bourgeoisie gain a better grip on the situation. Large duties were imposed on foreign goods and some were barred from entering the country altogether. Export, on the other hand, became easier. These duties and tariffs undermined the trade between German manufactured goods and Ukrainian potash, tar, saltpetre, glass and other semi-finished products. This in turn reduced the volume of production of the latter products, placing Ukrainian industries in an unfavourable competitive position domestically with similar products made in other parts of the Empire that had free access onto the Ukrainian market.[36]

---

[35] Doroshenko, *Istoriia Ukrainy*, p. 153; Vsevolod Holubnychy, *Try Liektsii pro Ekonomiku Ukrainy* (Munich: Vydavnytstvo Ukraina i Diiaspora, 1969), p. 3; Luhova, 'Pro stanovyshche Ukrainy', p. 17.

[36] O.P. Ohloblyn, 'Problema ukrains'koi ekonomiky v naukovyi i hromads'kyi dumtsi XIX–XX v.', *Chervonyi Shliakh*, October–November 1928, pp. 166–7; I. Redkina, 'Do pytannia proletars'koi revoliutsii na Ukraini', *Litopys Revoliutsii*, June 1926, p. 336; M. Volobuiev, 'Do

In the case of the glass industry, the rising unit cost of production after 1822 opened domestic markets to cheaper Russian products. A similar predicament befell the Ukrainian textile industry which had made a promising start using locally grown raw materials, including merino wool. Heavy cloth was being produced in Chernihiv and Volyn, finer weaves in Kyiv, Podillia and Poltava, rugs in Kharkiv and silks in the vicinity of Okhtyrka. A series of customs ordinances that reduced import duties on English wool during the early 1840s brought the Ukrainian industry into serious decline. Between 1842 and 1847, production of woollens in Kyiv province dropped by 44 percent. As a result Russian textile merchants all but controlled the wholesale markets in Ukraine by the mid-1850s.[37] State intervention on behalf of Russian trading capital also contributed to the decline of alcohol production in the 1860s and of coal mining in the Donbas in the late 1870s.

In the larger towns and cities, the first position in the economy occupied by Russian capital was trade.

> During the mid-eighteenth century, most trade in Kyiv was in the hands of local merchants. But in 1782 foreigners were permitted to settle in Kyiv … A struggle ensued between local and Russian entrepreneurs that ended with the defeat of the former in the mid-nineteenth century. Local merchants retained control of less lucrative sectors – the fish trade, bakeries, market gardening and leatherwork – and were forced to reside in the worse sections of the city.[38]

By the time manufacturing fever gripped the Empire in the 1830s Russian capitalists had assumed leading positions in the trade and manufacturing sectors. According to Mykhailo Volobuiev, 44.6 percent of industrialists in Ukraine in 1832 were Russians, followed by Ukrainians (28.7 percent) and Jews (17.4 percent). Among merchant capitalists, 52.6 percent were Russians, 22.2 percent Ukrainians and 20.9 percent Jews.[39] By the mid-nineteenth century Ukrainians and Jews, who made up the original layer of the capitalist class in Ukraine, remained only in branches of production closely associated with agriculture:

---

problemy ukrains'koi ekonomiky', in I. Maistrenko (ed.), *Dokumenty Ukrains'koho Komunizmu* (New York: Prolog, 1962), p. 142.
37   Kononenko, *Ukraine and Russia*, p. 118; Volobuiev, 'Do problemy ukrains'koi ekonomiky', p. 170.
38   Luhova, 'Pro stanovyshche Ukrainy', pp. 17–18.
39   Volobuiev, 'Do problemy ukrains'koi ekonomiky', p. 154.

soap, tobacco, sugar refining, lumber, milling and distilling. In the manufacturing sectors of iron, steel and machine building there were practically none.[40]

3 Industrialisation

The greatest single obstacle to industrialisation was serfdom. It limited the productivity and mobility of labour as well as the disposable cash income of the peasantry. The lower productivity of serf labour in industry became apparent in the first half of the nineteenth century when firms employing free wage labourers grew more rapidly than the semi-feudal factories of the nobility and made inroads into branches of production they once dominated. Whereas serf labour predominated in the production of sugar, alcohol, textiles, lumber, paper, glass and saltpetre, wage labour was employed primarily in paraffin, soap, leather goods, canvas and tobacco industries. Between 1828 and 1861 the share of enterprises owned by the nobility declined dramatically from 53.8 percent of their total number to 5.8 percent, mainly as a result of 'more capitalist' firms taking over glass, paper, metals and textile production. Serfs remained in widespread use only in sugar refining. On the eve of the Reform, there were approximately 85,000 industrial workers in Ukraine.[41]

The abolition of serfdom was intended, above all, to free labour for industry and open up the market in manufactured goods to the peasantry.[42] However, the 1861 Reform did not provide a sufficient stimulus for the development of industry or the market because the Tsarist regime made too many compromises with the landed nobility when it was drafted. According to one of its provisions, peasants were obliged to remain on the properties of their former masters as paid workers for up to seven years if the masters so desired. The landed nobility in Ukraine who built up agricultural businesses in grain and sugar and needed large reserves of cheap seasonal labour took advantage of this provision more than did the large landowners in Russia where commercial agriculture was less profitable. The Reform also assured a high price for land offered to the emancipated peasants. Extended payments limited their disposable income for many years after 1861, preventing them from buying manufactured consumer goods

---

40 Luhova, 'Pro stanovyshche Ukrainy', p. 21.
41 I.O. Hurzhii, *Zarodzhennia Robitnychoho Klasu Ukrainy* (*kinets XVIII–persha polovyna XIX st.*) (Kyiv: Derzhavne Vydavnytstvo Ukrainy, 1958), pp. 13–15; Matvii Yavorsky, *Istoriia Ukrainy v Styslomu Narysi* (Kharkiv: Derzhavne Vydavnytstvo Ukrainy, 1928), pp. 190–1.
42 Kononenko, *Ukraine and Russia*, pp. 12–13; Anderson, *Lineages*, p. 348.

in appreciable quantities and holding back both industrial production and the penetration of the market into the countryside. Between 1861 and the late 1870s, industrialisation faltered in Ukraine.[43]

The Russian Empire stood in last place among the European powers in terms of its level of industrial development. It did not possess the domestic capital necessary for rapid industrialisation and was falling behind the British, French, Belgian and German economies in the scramble for foreign markets and raw materials on its own eastern and southern borders. The relative weakness of the Russian bourgeoisie in the European constellation and its lack of an economic strategy made state intervention imperative. In order to secure investments for railroads, mining and manufacturing industries, the government turned to agriculture, the Empire's most developed economic sector. Imposing a state monopoly on foreign grain sales in 1870, it collected and exported up to five million tons a year to European markets, underwriting long-term investments from European banks with its profits. In this way the world market was used to channel the domestic capital flow from agriculture to industry, exchanging the country's grain for European machinery and technique.

The Ukrainian region played a part on both sides of the equation. It supplied most of the grain for export and attracted a good deal of foreign capital to the anthracite coal, iron ore and manganese fields in the south. On the basis of southern mining, foreign capital began building Ukraine's heavy industrial complex during the 1880s and 1890s.

The post-Reform slump ended when French, German, Belgian and British capital began flowing into the Empire. In 1870, foreign corporations had 26.5 million roubles invested in the Empire. The figure climbed to 97.7 million in 1880, 214 million in 1890, 911 million in 1900 and to 1,832 million roubles in 1917. On the eve of the Revolution, foreign companies controlled over half of all capital in industrial corporations and just under half in the banking and credit system.[44]

Approximately 450 million roubles were invested in the Ukrainian provinces before the War, an amount exceeding foreign investments in the Central Industrial Region of Russia and the Urals combined. French and Belgian companies accounted for 50 percent and 33 percent of this amount respectively, followed by German firms (10 percent), British (5 percent) and American (1 percent). These companies controlled 98 percent of all mining concerns, 90 percent of all metallurgical production, 88 percent of the machine building industry and

---

43   Kononenko, *Ukraine and Russia*, p. 100.
44   Ibid, p. 159.

81 percent of chemical plants. By 1913, they had also taken over sugar refining and tobacco curing.[45]

Foreign investors also played a major role in transportation. Back in the 1860s two thirds of all cargo loaded at Azov and Black Sea ports was being delivered from the interior by *chumaky*, teamsters on oxen drawn carts. By 1876, when 17,652 versts of railway line had been laid down in the Empire, the Ukrainian provinces had a mere 587 versts.[46] It was not until 1872 that Odesa and Moscow were connected by rail. Kyiv and Odesa were connected in 1876.[47] Intensive railroad construction started in Ukraine in the 1880s under pressure from French capitalists who financed the building of railways throughout the Empire and had invested heavily in the exploitation of southern Ukraine's mineral resources. Their priorities in Ukraine were to connect Donbas coal and Kryvyi Rih iron ore with the smelters, rolling mills and machine building plants in Katerynoslav and Kharkiv. The Black Sea ports were more important to foreign capitalists in Ukraine than were those on the Baltic Sea. Although the Russian government was mindful of the particular interests of its own bourgeoisie, it had no choice but to accede to the demands of French and other foreign investors and approve railroad construction in Ukraine.[48]

Industrialisation in the south began in earnest after these railways were built. The demand for coal by railways and by iron and steel industries soon made the Donbas the major producer in the Empire. Its share of imperial output in 1913 was 70.2 percent, followed by the Dombrova Basin in Poland (19.2 percent), Siberia (6.2 percent) and the Urals (3.1 percent). Similar developments occurred in the mining of iron ore and manganese. Ukraine produced one half of the manganese exported from the Empire before the War. By 1913, 72 percent of the iron ore mined in the Empire came from Ukraine as did 73.4 percent of all pig iron, 63.7 percent of the steel, 52.9 percent of the agricultural machinery and 35 percent of all locomotives.[49]

---

45   Yu. Kulyk, 'Do rozvytku kapitalizmu na Ukraini', *Chervonyi Shliakh*, June–July 1923, p. 115. Kulyk estimates foreign investment before the War at around 414 million roubles. See also Volobuiev, 'Do problemy ukrains'koi ekomoniky', p. 180; Holubnychy, *Try Liektsii*, p. 6.
46   One verst equalled 1.067 kilometres.
47   Patricia Herlihy, 'Ukrainian Cities in the 19th Century', in *Rethinking Ukrainian History*, edited by Ivan Rudnycky and J.P. Himka (Edmonton: Canadian Institute of Ukrainian Studies, 1981), p. 147.
48   F. Ie. Los (gen. ed.), *Istoriia Robitnychoho Klasu Ukrains'koi RSR*, 2 vols (Kyiv: Naukova Dumka, 1967), Vol. 1, pp. 102–3; Ohloblyn, 'Problema ukrains'koi ekonomyky', p. 172; Mykola Porsh, *Pro Avtonomiiu* (Kyiv: Prosvita, 1907), p. 76.
49   Basil Dmytryshyn, *Moscow and the Ukraine 1918–1953: A Study of Russian Bolshevik Nationality Policy* (New York: Bookman Associates, 1956), pp. 184–5; N.N. Popov, *Narys Istorii*

TABLE 1   Branches of production in Ukraine, 1904

	Production value in 000s of roubles	Percentage of total value of production in all branches
Food processing	505,482.2	66.1
Mineral processing	84,483.7	11.1
Metallurgy and machine building	60,442.6	7.9
Shipbuilding	541.6	0.05
Other metal manufacturing	5,010.8	0.7
Railroad workshops	22,543.4	3.0
Machine repair	1,388.5	0.2
Chemical industry	18,514.6	2.4
Other mineral processing	15,600.6	2.0
Paper	11,389.4	1.5
Mechanised woodworking	10,604.3	1.4
Processing of animal products	11,035.6	1.4
Woollens	9,461.3	1.2
Hemp and linen	6,567.7	0.9
Cotton goods	475.0	0.05
Other textiles	733.6	0.1
TOTALS	764,274.9	100.0

SOURCE: K. KONONENKO, *UKRAINE AND RUSSIA: A HISTORY OF ECONOMIC RELATIONS BETWEEN UKRAINE AND RUSSIA (1654–1917)* (MILWAUKEE: MARQUETTE UNIVERSITY PRESS, 1958), P. 122.

As Table 1 indicates, the leading branches of industry in Ukraine in 1904 were food processing (accounting for 66.1 percent of the total rouble value of industrial production), mining (11.1 percent) and metallurgy and machine building (7.9 percent). Manufacturing of consumer goods such as paper, textiles, and wood products was not developed at all. In 1913 the leading industrial branches remained the same as in 1904. However, there had been important changes in their proportional weight: mining had expanded its share of production to 43.9 percent, machine building rose marginally to 10.4 percent and food pro-

Komunistychnoi Partii (bil'shovykiv) Ukrainy (Kharkiv: Vydavnytstvo Proletaryi, 1930), pp. 4–5; A.I. Epshtein, *Robitnyky Ukrainy v Borot'bi za Stvorennia Material'no-tekhnichnoi Bazy Sotsializmu 1928–32* (Kharkiv: Vydavnytstvo Ordena Trudovoho Chervonoho Prapora Derzhavnoho Universytetu im. O.M. Horskoho, 1968), p. 10.

cessing declined to 36.2 percent. These branches accounted for 90.5 percent of all industrial production and employed 86.7 percent of the industrial working class.[50]

The late arrival of industrialisation was not without its benefits. Initial stages of industrialisation in Western Europe could be 'skipped'. Foreign corporations introduced the latest European technique and organisation, building the largest and most modern plants in the world. The high concentration of the industrial workforce was one of the consequences of the tardiness of industrialisation in Ukraine. According to 1902 government statistics, there were 252,222 workers employed in 4,776 of the largest factories; in 91 of these (or 1.9 percent of all factories covered), 110,319 or 44 percent of all workers were employed. Katerynoslav province had the highest concentration of all with 76.3 percent of its workers in 4.5 percent of its factories.[51]

Foreign investors enhanced their control over industrial production in Ukraine by establishing territorial syndicates and cartels. Prodamet controlled almost all metallurgical plants. Eighty percent of all coal mines were organised into the Produgol syndicate. The Urozhai syndicate united 72 percent of all agricultural machinery production while Prodarud controlled 80 percent of Kryvyi Rih ore mining. These syndicates were formed between 1902 and 1908 at the congresses of Mining Industrialists of Southern Russia which took place annually in Kharkiv. Much earlier in 1887, a sugar refiners' syndicate was organised. Thus by the early years of the twentieth century practically every important branch of industry in Ukraine was controlled by a syndicate or cartel. Most of them were directed from Paris, Brussels and other European capitals by the head offices of the investing companies. Their main purpose was to compete with European controlled syndicates based in other industrialising centres of the Empire.[52]

Vsevolod Holubnychy[53] has argued that selective investment by European capitalists in different parts of the Empire and the subsequent territorial organisation of industrial production through syndicates and cartels prevented the economic integration of the Empire into an 'All-Russian' market during the period of rapid industrialisation. Rather, such investment and organisation by

---

50 O.O. Nesterenko, *Pozvytok Promyslovosti na Ukraini. Chastyna II* (Kyiv: Vydavnytstvo Akademii Nauk URSR, 1962), p. 380.
51 S. Ostapenko, 'Kapitalizm na Ukraini', *Chervonyi Shliakh*, January–February 1924, p. 127.
52 Holubnychy, *Try Liektsii*, p. 7.
53 Born in Bohodukhiv, Ukraine in 1928, died in New York City, USA in 1977, foremost Marxist economist and historian of the Ukrainian diaspora, founding member of the Ukrainian Revolutionary Democratic Party, editor of *Vpered*, a Ukrainian workers' paper.

European capitalists unleashed strong tendencies of regional economic differentiation and competition between distinct territorial economies that were marked off from one another by the interdependence of their constituent branches and the geographic radius of price competitiveness of their commodities. These tendencies contributed to the formation of six industrial regions in the Empire: Petrograd-Baltic (machine building, textiles and chemicals); Moscow (textiles and metallurgy); Urals (mining and metallurgy); Baku-Grozny (petroleum); Poland (textiles and metallurgy); and Ukraine (mining, metallurgy, machine building, chemicals and food processing). While the Moscow and Petrograd regions were long connected through trade, the newly industrialising regions became tied to the old centres and with one another only later, in the process of competition in certain commodities. The Urals and Ukrainian regions competed fiercely for control of metal sales on Moscow and Petrograd markets. Polish coal producers fought English imports and later Ukrainian producers for a share of these same markets.[54]

The extent of market integration between Ukraine and the rest of the Empire was not far advanced before the industrial revolution. Trade between Ukrainian and Russian provinces, for example, did not exceed 1–2 percent of production and consumption on both sides. Banks played an insignificant role in the economy as organisers and mediators of investment. The only common integrative force was currency – the Russian rouble.[55] Although integration did accelerate in the early period of industrialisation, as the foregoing discussion about the inroads of the Russian bourgeoisie into the sectors held by their Ukrainian and Jewish competitors suggests, it was confronted by even stronger centrifugal tendencies when foreign capital moved into the Empire and began organising itself territorially.[56]

The only countervailing force to these centrifugal tendencies was the Russian state whose economic policies attempted to consolidate an All-Russian market dominated by the northern bourgeoisie. Mykhailo Volobuiev writes that

> the pre-revolutionary Russian economy ... was united on an antagonistic and imperialist basis. But in view of the centrifugal forces in the colonies that it oppressed, it was a complex of *national* economies.[57]

---

54 Holubnychy, *Try liektsii*, pp. 3–6.
55 Ibid, p. 4.
56 Ibid.
57 Volobuiev, 'Do problemy ukrains'koi ekonomiky', p. 185.

The representatives of Banque de Paris et des Pays Bas, Credit Lyonnais, Société Generale pour L'Industrie en Russe, Société Generale de Belgique, Nadelmackers et Fils and Deutsche Bank and Co. formed the most powerful contingent of the bourgeoisie in Ukraine. Russian merchants and industrialists who had moved into the region in the late eighteenth and early nineteenth centuries and displaced the original layers of the bourgeoisie were themselves relegated by foreign firms to a secondary role in the new constellation of capital.[58]

4 Trade, Taxation and Capital Repatriation

Ukraine's level of industrial development before the War is revealed also in the content and balance of its trade on the foreign market and with other parts of the Empire. Karlo Kobersky, an economist of the interwar years, prepared a composite table of imports and exports for the years 1909–11 which is reproduced here as Table 2. It shows that exports from the nine provinces were divided almost equally in rouble value between those destined for the foreign market (46.4 percent) and for other parts of the Empire (53.6 percent).

Processed food (mainly sugar), metals and semi-finished metal products accounted for over two thirds (67.7 percent) of exports to other parts of the Empire. Grain accounted for one fifth (20.5 percent), much of which was already milled or processed as pasta. Ukraine did not export much grain to other parts of the Empire. The Russian provinces, for example, grew most of the wheat and rye their populations consumed.[59]

The Ukrainian region participated in the world market chiefly as an exporter of grain, processed food, cattle and animal by-products. These goods made up 97.7 percent of the rouble value of all exports abroad. Britain was the main purchaser of Ukrainian grain until 1908 when cheaper Argentinean, American and Canadian grain came onto European markets.

The bulk of Ukraine's exported grain was sold to Germany, Holland and countries of the Near East.[60] Imports to Ukraine were less evenly divided than exports as far as their sources were concerned. The foreign market supplied

---

[58] Holubnychy, *Try Liektsii*, p. 4; see also V.I. Lenin, 'The Socialist Revolution and the Right of Nations to Self-Determination', in *Collected Works*, Vol. XIX (New York: International Publishers, 1942), p. 126.

[59] Karlo Kobersky, *Ukraina v Svitovomu Hospodarstvi* (Prague: Ukrainska Strilets'ka Hromada v S. Sh.A., 1933), pp. 16–17; Mykola Porsh, *Pro Avtonomiiu Ukrainy* (Kyiv: Prosvita, 1908), p. 23.

[60] Porsh, *Pro Avtonomiiu Ukrainy*, pp. 19–22.

TABLE 2   Average annual imports and exports of Ukraine, 1909–1911

EXPORTS

Product	Percentage of total export	Percentage of export abroad	Percentage of export to other parts of Empire
Agricultural	50.1	84.4	20.5
Cattle and animal by-products	7.1	7.3	6.9
Wood products	0.6	1.3	0
Processed food (including sugar)	27.8	6.0	44.6
Mining products	1.6	1.0	2.1
Raw and semi-finished metal	1.3	0	1.1
Other	1.5	0	2.6
TOTAL	100.0	100.0	100.0
PERCENTAGE OF TOTAL EXPORT	100.0	46.4	53.6

IMPORTS

Product	Percentage of total import	Percentage of imports from abroad	Percentage of imports from other parts of Empire
Timber and wood products	3.6	0.01	4.6
Manufactured goods	39.0	0.7	51.4
Petroleum and mining products	7.2	2.4	8.3
Machines and metal goods	7.5	28.0	1.5
Fish	6.0	5.3	6.5
Hides and leather goods	6.7	3.2	7.4
Alcoholic beverages	5.5	2.7	6.3
Textiles	5.9	4.0	6.6
Chemical products	1.6	7.1	0
Colonial products	7.2	25.6	1.6
Other	9.7	21.0	5.6
TOTAL	100.0	100.0	100.0
PERCENTAGE OF TOTAL IMPORT	100.0	22.5	77.5

SOURCE: KARLO KOBERSKY, *UKRAINA V SVITOVOMU HOSPODARSTVI* (PRAGUE: UKRAINS'KA STRILETS'KA HROMADA V S.SH.A., 1933), P. 14.

22.5 percent and other parts of the Empire 77.5 percent. Manufactured goods made up 51.4 percent of the total rouble value of imports from other regions of the Empire, with petroleum, textiles, hides, alcoholic beverages and fish accounting for another 35.1 percent. The high proportion of imperial products in the total value of imports did not signify, however, more integration of the Ukrainian region with the Russian region proper because many of these products came from Poland, Baku and the Urals.[61]

Ukraine enjoyed a positive balance of trade in the period 1909–11 with average annual surpluses of 323.1 million roubles. Vis-à-vis other parts of the Empire, the surplus stood at 60.7 million roubles; on the foreign market it totalled 262.4 million roubles. According to the estimates of the economist A. Koporsky, the trade surplus in 1913 stood at 413.2 million roubles. M.I. Halytsky's calculation for 1913 is even higher – 528.1 million roubles. Whoever is closer to the actual figure, it seems clear that Ukraine not only had a healthy trade surplus before the War, but that it was growing from year to year.[62]

This trade surplus provides some indication of the Ukrainian region's potential to accumulate capital. The question to be asked is how much of it was re-invested and how much left the region? The principal routes for capital outflow were state taxes and repatriation of profits by foreign investors.

The balance of state taxes and expenditures in Ukraine between 1898 and 1910 presented in Table 3 shows that the central government consistently collected more taxes than it spent there. The annual deficits grew from 168.7 million roubles in 1898 to 284.8 million in 1910. Northern Tavria was the only province where more taxes were spent than collected; this was due mainly to government contracts to build the Black Sea fleet. In all other provinces, the opposite tendency prevailed. The industrialising provinces of Katerynoslav and Kherson stood in the next best position with 57.9 percent of all taxes collected being spent there, followed by the Left Bank provinces (56.2 percent) and the underdeveloped Right Bank (53.6 percent).[63]

Expenditures by central state institutions and the armed forces as well as payments on the state debt should be taken into account as costs assumed by the entire imperial tax base. Yet even when these costs are calculated for Ukraine in proportion to its share of the population and then added to taxes already spent there, they fail to make up for the deficit. Mykòla Porsh calculates that a shortfall of 115 million roubles remained in 1903 after these additional

---

61 Kobersky, *Ukraina v Svitovomu Hospodarstvi*, pp. 25–6; Holubnychy, *Try Lektsii*, p. 5.
62 Holubnychy, *Try Liektsii*, pp. 14–15.
63 Mykola Porsh, *Ukraina v Derzhavnomu Biudzheti Rosii* (Katerynoslav: Kameniar, 1918), p. 22.

TABLE 3   State taxes and expenditures in Ukraine, 1898–1910 (in millions of roubles)

Year	Taxes collected	Taxes spent	Balance
1898	352.1	183.4	168.7
1899	369.1	198.4	170.7
1900	361.3	213.8	141.5
1901	375.1	218.9	156.1
1902	424.4	227.9	197.5
1903	449.8	242.9	206.9
1904	443.0	253.1	189.9
1905	443.2	250.6	192.6
1906	518.5	260.8	257.7
1907	512.5	294.3	218.2
1908	449.3	304.9	194.8
1909	538.3	320.3	218.4
1910	607.1	321.3	284.8
TOTAL	5,894.8	3,289.6	2,605.2

SOURCE: MYKOLA PORSH, *UKRAINA V DERZHAVNOMU BIUDZHETI ROSII* (KATERYNOSLAV: KAMENIAR, 1918), P. 16.

expenditures (20 percent of the cost of maintaining central state institutions, the army and servicing the debt) were added to expenditures already made in the nine provinces. That is to say, these 115 million roubles in 1903 were invested or consumed in other parts of the Empire.[64]

Petrograd, on the other hand, spent four times as much as the taxes it collected in its province during the period from 1879 to 1897. At the same time, the central industrial and agricultural provinces of Russia claimed 118 percent of their tax base, Poland 98 percent, the Baltic region 76 percent and Ukraine only 48 percent.[65] In the first decade of the twentieth century, Ukraine's share of state expenditures climbed to 55.7 percent of taxes collected on its territory, but this was far from a qualitative improvement over the previous period. Between 1868 and 1891, 17 percent of all state taxes were collected in Ukraine and 9.5 percent of them spent there. For the period from 1906 to 1910, the respective

64   Porsh, *Pro Avtonomiiu Ukrainy*, pp. 27–8.
65   Ibid, p. 4.

percentages were 22.1 percent and 13.2 percent.[66] Thus it may be argued that the central government recovered through taxation as much as, and probably more than, the Ukrainian provinces gained through their positive balance of domestic trade with other parts of the Empire.

Little is known about repatriation of profits by foreign companies, the second main route of capital outflow. In the two decades before 1917, approximately 7 billion roubles left the Empire in this way, more than three times the total foreign capital invested in banks, municipalities and industry.[67] If these proportions are applied to foreign capital invested only in Ukraine, which totalled 450 million roubles before the War, the outflow of capital may have been as high as 1.35 billion roubles.

Porsh's calculations of the 1903 gross domestic product provide some clues about the actual extent of capital outflow. He estimates that 1.18 billion roubles out of a total of 1.6 billion were used up in consumption and replacement of fixed capital. This left a surplus of 420 million roubles, of which approximately 200 million left Ukraine as tax deficits and 100 million as mortgage and interest payments on loans made in Russian and foreign controlled banks, income of absentee landlords and dividends paid out to foreign investors. Porsh estimates these dividends at between 20 and 25 million roubles. Thus 120 million roubles in surplus value remained in the nine provinces for reinvestment there, approximately one quarter of the total surplus generated in 1903.[68]

5   Conclusion

Several important facets of the national question emerge from this historical overview. The leaders of the 1648 Revolution failed to establish an independent nation state and ruling class. Ukraine was subsequently annexed by Russia and experienced a resurgence of feudal relations. After the abolition of feudalism in 1861 the Russian state collaborated with European capitalists to industrialise Ukraine and share in its surplus product. As a result of these developments, industrialisation in Ukraine at the end of the nineteenth and in the early twentieth centuries was directed by foreign bourgeoisies to its east and west. The European bourgeoisie's strength lay in its capital resources. The Russian bour-

---

[66] Porsh, *Ukraina v Derzhavnomu Biudzheti*, pp. 16–18; Ohloblyn, 'Problema ukrains'koi ekonomyky', p. 173.
[67] M.I. Suprunenko (gen. ed.), *Istoriia Ukrains'koi RSR*, 7 vols (Kyiv: Naukova Dumka, 1977), Vol. 5, p. 10.
[68] Porsh, *Pro Avtonomiiu Ukrainy*, p. 8.

geoisie in Ukraine had comparatively less investment capital, but it enjoyed political and fiscal support from the Russian state. The indigenous bourgeoisie that originated in the period of mercantilism before Russian state annexation did not play much of a role in industrialisation at all. Clearly, Ukraine was not a colonial dependency typical of late nineteenth-century European imperialism that simply supplied raw materials to industrialised metropoles and imported their manufactured goods. Though such trade was important, Ukraine's gross domestic product also grew on the strength of its own heavy industry and capitalist agriculture, and semi-processed goods constituted a large portion of its exports to other parts of the Empire. Moreover, its domestic production was beginning to diversify and its branches of industry were being organised into an increasingly self-sufficient and interdependent territorial economy.

The principal brakes upon Ukraine's economic development, however, were the disproportionate growth of heavy industry over the manufacturing sector, the continual extraction of its annual surpluses and the underdevelopment of its domestic market for consumer goods. Ukraine was producing 70 percent of the Empire's raw materials before the War, but only 15 percent of its manufactured goods.[69] Had not so much surplus left the country via taxation deficits and the repatriation of profits on invested foreign capital, a manufacturing sector would have had ample capital resources to expand. Yet the underdevelopment of the manufacturing sector should not be exaggerated. After all, the Ukrainian region was one of six industrialising centres of the Empire with a 15 percent share in the Empire's manufacturing output. Ukraine's ample natural resources and its formidable mining and heavy industries merely lead one to conclude that the manufacturing sector had enormous potential to grow far more than it did and that this potential was being stifled by the flight of capital.

Karl Kautsky summed up Ukraine's predicament before the War in the following way:

> Capitalism develops in only one dimension for the Ukrainian people – it turns them into proletarians, while the other dimension – the flowering of the productive forces, the accumulation of surplus and wealth – is mainly for the benefit of other countries. Because of this, capitalism reveals to Ukrainians only its negative, revolutionising dimension ... It does not lead to an increase in their wealth.[70]

---

69   Epshtein, *Robitnyky Ukrainy*, p. 10.
70   Cited in Porsh, *Pro Avtonomiiu Ukrainy*, p. 11.

In view of the weakness of the indigenous layer of the bourgeoisie in Ukraine at the turn of the century, it is difficult to imagine how the idea of an independent Ukrainian bourgeois state could have gained much currency among the upper classes and native petit bourgeoisie. However, the absence of an independent state power on Ukrainian territory meant that much of the surplus created by the labour of workers and peasants would not be reinvested there, but abroad and in other parts of the Empire. Thus the national question as a problem of unequal development and of state power remained on the agenda of the Ukrainian nation. If it could not be solved by an indigenous bourgeoisie, the national question would fall sooner or later to the working class, the peasantry and their own leaders in the political process.

CHAPTER 2

The Working Class

The working class is a child of the industrial revolution. Although its origins in Ukraine can be traced to the sixteenth century, the working class assumed a significant role in economic production only after the abolition of serfdom and the priming of industrialisation by European finance capital. It reached a high point in its development on the eve of the First World War. While the number of workers continued to grow during the War, their cohesion, stability of membership and level of skill were seriously undermined by militarisation of the economy and conscription to the Russian army. Internal fragmentation continued during the Revolution and Civil War. In numerical terms the working class declined dramatically. It did not regain its pre-War stature until the years of the First Five Year Plan (1928–32).

This chapter presents an overview of the formation of the working class and investigates several of its salient characteristics, namely its numerical size, distribution throughout the economy, level of urbanisation, literacy and national composition.

By the term 'working class' I mean people who have departed or are in the process of departing from subsistence farming or the artisanal and commercial occupations prevalent in feudal society, and who have secured seasonal or full-time wage earning jobs. This definition is fairly broad because I am not so much concerned with the end point as with the process, with the numerous passages to wage labour and the combinations of incentive and constraint that different groups encountered on their way into the working class.

At the end of the eighteenth century, the overwhelming majority of the 10,000 people working in industry were serfs, pressed into service by their noblemen who had become entrepreneurs and established small industries on their estates. By 1828, when their numbers had grown to 14,000, 74 percent of industrial workers were serfs.[1] As the previous chapter points out, wage labour proved more productive than serf labour and the industries of merchant capitalists employing wage earners grew more rapidly than the semi-feudal factories of the nobility. By 1861, approximately three quarters of the industrial workforce in Ukraine were freely hired workers, while the majority of serfs working

---

1 F. Ie. Los (gen. ed.), *Istoriia Robitnychoho Klasu URSR* (Kyiv: Naukova Dumka, 1967), Vol. 1, pp. 59, 68.

in sugar refineries were earning some wages as well. Estimates of the total number of industrial workers in 1861 range from between 82,000 and 85,000.[2]

The three major sources of working-class recruits after 1861 were peasants, migrants from neighbouring Russian, Polish and Belarusian provinces, and the artisans of small industries and craft shops being ruined by competition from mass commodity producers. The dominant peoples in these sources were Ukrainians, Russians and Jews.

1   Peasant Sources

The high price for land demanded by the nobility after 1861 and a rapid rate of natural increase of the rural population meant that the Ukrainian peasantry had less arable land per capita at its disposal by the end of the nineteenth century than it did before the Reform.[3] Between 1868 and 1902, the price of land rose each year by over five percent on average. Peasant holdings decreased by 30 percent in acreage per unit, while in Eastern Europe as a whole they declined by 10 percent. Although land hunger in Ukraine was generally not as bad as in Russia, on the Right Bank 'the degree of rural overpopulation and poverty was the most acute in the Empire'.[4] Harvest yields were increasing by two percent per annum, less than the rate of rural population growth. At the same time one quarter of the grain harvest was being exported to finance industrialisation.[5] Although per capita production of grain in the nine provinces was higher than in Germany, Russia and Denmark, and almost as high as in Hungary and Bulgaria, per capita consumption was the lowest in all Europe.[6]

Peasants who could no longer subsist on the land had two alternatives: to seek wage earning jobs or emigrate. Between 1896 and 1914, over 1.6 million

---

2   I.O. Hurzhii, *Zarodzhennia Robitnychoho Klasu Ukrainy (kinets XVIII–persha polovyna XIX st.)* (Kyiv: Derzhavne Vydavnytstvo Politychnoi Literatury URSR, 1958), pp. 13–15; Mykhailo Yavorsky, *Istoriia Ukrainy v Styslomu Narysi* (Kharkiv: Derzhavne Vydavnytstvo Ukrainy, 1928), pp. 190–1.
3   Mykyta Shapoval, *Velyka Revoliutsiia i Ukrains'ka Vyzvol'na Prohrama* (Prague: Vil'na Spilka i Ukrains'kyi Robitnychyi Instytut, 1927), p. 66.
4   Vsevolod Holubnychy, 'The Agrarian Revolution in Ukraine', in *Selected Works of Vsevolod Holubnychy: Soviet Regional Economics*, edited by Iwan S. Koropeckyj (Edmonton: Canadian Institute of Ukrainian Studies, 1982), p. 4.
5   Ibid, p. 5.
6   Konstantyn Kononenko, *Ukraine and Russia: A History of Economic Relations between Ukraine and Russia (1654–1917)* (Milwaukee: Marquette University Press, 1958), p. 51.

people left for Siberia and Kazakhstan to settle new land.[7] But their departure did little to relieve land hunger or pressure on the labour market because up to 70 percent of the emigrants failed to settle abroad and soon returned.[8]

Wage earning occupations first accessible to the peasants were on the large capitalist farms. Such jobs were close to home and peasants already possessed the required skills. Sugar beet plantations and refineries in Kyiv, Kharkiv and Podillia provinces provided an important source of employment for 70 to 100 days a year, depending on the harvest. In 1911, for example, when the harvest and refining took 98 days to complete, one hundred thousand temporary workers were taken on. Distilleries offered seasonal employment for up to 180 days a year for about 9,000 people. Another seventy thousand were taken on at flour mills for 30 to 40 days. Seasonal workers were employed also on tobacco and hop farms, in woolsheds, brick kilns and construction.[9]

However, these industries hardly satisfied the demand for wage earning jobs as land hunger in the northern provinces became more acute. The big grain farms on the steppes, in the neighbouring Russian provinces of Don, Samara, Saratov and Orenburg as well as Bessarabia in the south west, attracted growing numbers of poor peasants each year from Poltava, Chernihiv, Kyiv and Podillia provinces. Men and single women prepared for the annual migration right after Easter, travelling to the hiring towns in the south where they waited for farm foremen to come and select them for the summer's work. They did not know if they would find work and, if they did, what their wages would be. Often they waited for weeks, selling their clothes and stealing in order to eat, sleeping in the fields or under stores in the towns. By the turn of the century they had achieved some measure of self-organisation; prospective migrants elected a representative who went south ahead of time to negotiate with a foreman on numbers of workers and wages. The representative then telegraphed home and told his people to come. In the best of circumstances such practices worked well. On many occasions, however, the migrant workers were cheated out of their wages or told to leave if they would not accept wage cuts on the spot. Given the large numbers of hands available for work it was easy for employers and their foremen to treat migrants as they wished.

Another group of poor peasants headed for towns and cities to work as day labourers in construction, stable hands in trade and servants in the homes of

---

7 Shapoval, *Velyka Revoliutsiia*, p. 65.
8 Holubnychy, 'The 1917 Agrarian Revolution', p. 5.
9 Yavorsky, *Istoriia Ukrainy*, p. 190; N.N. Popov, *Narys Istorii Komunistychnoi Partii (bil'shovykiv) Ukrainy* (Kharkiv: Proletaryi, 1931), p. 28; Ostapenko, 'Kapitalizm na Ukraini', *Chervonyi Shliakh*, January–February 1924, p. 196; Los, *Istoriia Robitnychoho Klasu*, Vol. 1, p. 76.

the middle and upper classes. Little is known about this large group of urbanising peasants, but it may well be assumed that their working conditions and wages, as well as a lingering desire to return home and buy land with their savings, discouraged many at first from settling permanently in the towns.

The second rung on the ladder of wage earning occupations for peasants was mining, an industry that paid relatively well but had terrible working conditions. Only a third of the people who took jobs in southern coal and iron ore mining during the 1870s and 1880s stayed on during the summer months when additional hands were needed on the family farm. By the end of the 1890s the proportion of Donbas coal miners who still had ties to the land dropped to 40 percent. However, in the iron ore mines of Kryvyi Rih, it remained considerably higher. As late as 1906 mine operators continued to cut back production in the summer months, unable to keep those who had some land from staying on.[10]

Peasants resisted a decisive leap into full time wage labour for several reasons. At first, many peasants considered wage labour as a temporary need, a means to earn money, buy land and become successful farmers.[11] The oppressive climate in modern industries, with labour supervision more calculated and administrations who 'dealt with the workers like animals'[12] gave them little incentive to stay. Although there was a general labour surplus in Ukraine, coal mine operators complained endlessly about labour shortages and resorted occasionally to the use of convict labour.[13] But peasants who had been accustomed for generations to working in the daylight and varying the types of labour with the seasons resisted initiation into the modern habits of industrial production. 'They run from the underground kingdom and barracks of the mining barons because it is their only salvation. The residents of hell would flee too, if only they could'.[14]

Most peasants got low paying and arduous work. The pay for unskilled work in mines and factories was about the same as the average wage in agriculture.[15] On a farm an adult male worker earned on average 183 roubles a year in 1913. The average in industry was 229 roubles, but variations in pay were high. An unskilled helper in a trade earned about 100 roubles annually, less than a minor

---

10 Valentyn Sadovsky, *Pratsia v USSR* (Warsaw: Ukrainskyi Naukovyi Instytut, 1932), pp. 20–1; O.O. Nesterenko, *Rozvytok Promyslovosti na Ukraini. Chastyna II* (Kyiv: Vydavnytstvo Akademii Nauk URSR, 1962), p. 432; Los, *Istoriia Robitnychoho Klasu*, pp. 189, 226.
11 Mykhailo Ye. Slabchenko, 'Do metodolohii istorii robitnychoho klasu', *Chervonyi Shliakh*, April 1927, p. 82.
12 Panas Fedenko, 'Isaak Mazepa v Zhytti i v Politytsi', *Nashe Slovo*, no. 3 (1973), p. 9.
13 Sadovsky, *Pratsia*, pp. 8–9.
14 Cited in Nesterenko, *Rozvytok Promyslovosti*, p. 433.
15 Holubnychy, 'Robitnytstvo'.

received for farm work (125 roubles in 1913). In tanneries the average wage was 216 roubles, in the garment industry 210. A miner working the coal face could make up to 400 roubles, but a sled pusher or water pump attendant working above ground earned between 197 and 211 roubles. And these unskilled, relatively low-paying jobs were all that many peasants could get at first.[16]

Farm workers who lived in their ancestral home did not have to pay rent or build a new house. Those who took work in the new industries on the steppe often squatted a patch of land nearby, built a crude earthen dug-out home and planted a vegetable garden. It was the most urbanised, full time section of the working class living in company barracks and row housing and buying food in company stores who spent a lot of their relatively high income on such necessities. Industrial workers were also subject to an array of fines for poor workmanship, breakage of tools, absenteeism and down time that cut into their wages. Taking these facts into account it is difficult to argue that wages alone could make industrial work a desirable alternative to staying on the land. Rather it was the peasants' inability to survive on the land that drove them to search for wages.

2 Migrant Sources from Central Russia

One of the greatest obstacles peasants faced when seeking well-paid jobs was their lack of industrial skills. Factory employment, a third rung on the ladder of wage earning occupations, required skills, experience and a rudimentary knowledge at least of Russian, the language of supervision on the shop floor. Although industries sprouted like mushrooms at the end of the nineteenth century they did not meet the local demands for wage labour provoked by rural overpopulation and growing land hunger in the Ukrainian provinces. The available full time jobs in industry that required skill were at first taken mainly by migrant Russian workers, and to a lesser extent by Poles and Belarusians, who competed for them with greater advantages than the local peasants.

Well before the abolition of serfdom, industrial development in Russia prompted the nobility to release their serfs from labour duty and allow them instead to honour obligations by paying rent. Russian serfs acquired industrial skills sooner than Ukrainians who continued to do *panshchyna*, labour duty on the big commercial farms of the landed nobility. More nobles in Ukraine than

---

16   V. Sukhyno-Khomenko, 'Z pryvodu osoblyvostei proletars'koi revoliutsii na Ukraini', *Litopys Revoliutsii*, April 1928, p. 83; Nesterenko, *Rozvytok Promyslovosti*, p. 245.

in Russia took advantage of the clause in the Reform act allowing them to hold onto former serfs for seven more years as wage labourers. Thus the Ukrainian peasant entered the market less prepared to compete for industrial jobs than his fellow Russian.[17]

During the 1870s and 1880s new industries demanded an immediate supply of skilled labour and they offered high wages to attract it. Migrants from the overpopulated agricultural region of Central Russia, close to the industrialising Donbas, initially provided the lion's share of this labour. By the 1890s, however, the situation began to change as Ukrainians competed more successfully for industrial jobs than before. In mining, for example, 82 percent of the workforce in 1871 were migrants from the Central Russian provinces; in 1884 they made up 60 percent and in 1900 just over 55 percent.[18]

3 Jewish Sources

Artisans did not contribute to the formation of the working class in Ukraine to the same extent as they did in Western Europe because Ukrainian towns had declined in cultural and economic importance and lost their political autonomy under the rule of the Tsars. Rather than serving as locations for economic development, the towns were mainly administrative, military and long distance trading centres in which at least half of the population was composed of soldiers, civil servants, merchants and clergy.[19] Most new industries in Ukraine at the end of the nineteenth century, moreover, were established on the southern steppe, far from traditional urban centres.

The Jewish community in Ukraine contained a sizeable stratum of craftsmen and artisans, a potentially large source of working class recruits. However, their passage into the working class was hampered by state policies and popular prejudice. In Western Europe the democratic revolutions of the eighteenth and nineteenth centuries abolished the feudal hierarchy of estates and, over time, began breaking down the caste status of Jews as an estate permitted to practice

---

17 Bohdan Krawchenko, *Social Change and National Consciousness in Twentieth Century Ukraine* (Oxford: Macmillan, 1985), pp. 16–17; Sadovsky, *Pratsia*, p. 8.
18 Holubnychy, 'Robitnytstvo'; Popov, *Narys Istorii*, p. 27.
19 I.K. Rybalka and F.H. Turchenko, 'Sotsiial'no klasova struktura naselennia Ukrainy naperedodni Zhovtnevoi Revoliutsii', *Ukrains'kyi Istorychnyi Zhurnal*, November 1981, p. 30; Isaak Mazepa, *Pidstavy Nashoho Vidrodzhennia*, 2 vols (n.p.: Prometei, 1946), Vol. 1, pp. 110–11; Patricia Herlihy, 'Ukrainian Cities in the Nineteenth Century', in *Rethinking Ukrainian History*, edited by Ivan L. Rudnycky and J. Himka (Edmonton: Canadian Institute of Ukrainian Studies, 1981), pp. 137–9.

only certain occupations for a living. In the Russian Empire, their caste status survived intact until the 1905 Revolution. Jews remained excluded from the political process and restricted in their economic and educational endeavours as well as in their places of permanent residence. A combination of juridical, political and repressive measures together with popular prejudice that took its extreme form in waves of pogroms enforced Jews' 'savage exclusion' from the societal mainstream.[20] During the last four decades of Tsarist rule, their predicament grew steadily worse.[21]

Jews were confined to the Pale of Settlement, a territory which encompassed around 20 percent of the European part of the Empire and which included most of Right Bank Ukraine. After the abolition of serfdom in 1861 those living in small towns where they had worked as agents for the nobility were forced to seek new occupations.[22] However, the Temporary Rules promulgated by Tsar Alexander II in 1882, and reinforced in 1885, forbad Jews to undertake new settlements in rural areas, to purchase land or fixed capital there or to conduct business on Sundays and Christian holidays. They crowded into the towns and cities of Right Bank Ukraine, where work was scarce. Further legal restrictions on their admission to higher education, professions and political office in 1887, 1890 and 1891 all contributed to their subsequent impoverishment as a community.[23]

According to 1818 statistics of the Finance Ministry, 12 percent of the Jewish population in the Empire were craftsmen and their employees.[24] In Lithuania, Poland and Belarus, where Jews constituted a majority of the population in many urban centres and were the largest ethnic group in the remainder, their stratum of craftsmen and wage earners was very large. By 1897 there were 1.9 million Jews living in the Ukrainian provinces of whom 268,000 (or about 14 percent) were wage earners. Here they made up 17 percent of the working class (see below).

It was not a lack of industrial skills that prevented Jews from entering wage earning occupations. As industrialisation took off in the late nineteenth cen-

---

20   Jonathan Frankel, *Prophesy and Politics: Socialism, Nationalism and Russian Jews, 1862–1917* (Cambridge: Cambridge University Press, 1981), p. i.
21   Frankel, *Prophecy and Politics*, pp. 52–3, 135, 143–5; Henry J. Tobias, *The Jewish Bund in Russia from its Origins to 1905* (Stanford: Stanford University Press, 1972), pp. 221, 223, 227, 229, 251–2; S.M. Dubnow, *History of the Jews in Russia and Poland*, 2 vols, translated by I. Friedlaender (n.p.: n.p., 1975), pp. 2, 348, 354, 386, 400; Matvii Yavorsky, *Istoriia Ukrainy v Styslomu Narysi* (Kharkiv: Derzhavne Vydavnytstvo Ukrainy, 1925), p. 235.
22   Tobias, *Jewish Bund*, p. 7.
23   Dubnow, *History of the Jews*, Vol. 2, p. 312.
24   Salo Baron, *The Russian Jew under Tsars and Soviets* (New York: Macmillan, 1964), p. 97.

tury Jewish small industries and trades were hard pressed to compete with mass commodity production. Their owners, therefore, could not hire as many co-religionists as before. If at the beginning of the nineteenth century a young apprentice in a trade could reasonably expect to open a shop of his own later in life, it was far more likely at the close of the century that he would earn wages all his life. And if there were insufficient opportunities for wage labour in the community itself, young Jews had to look for work beyond it.

But the legal restrictions on Jews as well as the antisemitism of industrialists and industrial workers made the transition to wage earning occupations outside the community quite difficult for them. Hundreds of thousands chose emigration instead.[25] Those who remained were trapped inside an occupationally circumscribed, increasingly urbanised and impoverished community whose members' passage into wage earning occupations was blocked despite their possession of the requisite skills. Jews did contribute to the formation of the working class in Ukraine as 1897 statistics show. But the artisan contingent of the Jewish community would certainly have contributed more had not official and popular antisemitism restrained their social mobility and forced so many to emigrate abroad.

4   Numerical Growth

Between 1861 and 1897 the number of industrial workers in the nine Ukrainian provinces climbed from approximately 85,000 to 327,000. The growth rate was not uniform. An absolute decline in the number of industrial workers was registered in the 1870s when a paucity of domestic capital combined with the depressed purchasing power of the rural population held back industrialisation (see Table 4). The influx of West European capital in the 1880s restarted the process and drove the growth rate of industrial production and labour up again until the outbreak of the First World War.

The lack of accurate annual data makes a precise estimation of the size of the working class in the years leading up to 1917 a difficult task. The 1897 census, the first and only census to be conducted in the Russian Empire (the following one was the 1926 Soviet census), was both incomplete and inaccurate. Like other statistics prepared by the government, it divided the population by occupational and status-oriented categories that are not easily adapted to the definition of the working class advanced at the beginning of this chapter.

---

25   Frankel, *Prophesy and Politics*, p. 135.

TABLE 4   Industrial plant workers in Ukraine, 1861–1917

Annual averages for decades

1861–70	1871–80	1881–90	1890–1900
142,604	130,391	170,442	259,131

Annual totals in thousands from 1901 to 1917

1901	360.2	1907	431.3	1913	631.6
1902	354.7	1908	449.5	1914	631.4
1903	370.7	1909	441.7	1915	635.3
1904	372.4	1910	481.0	1916	812.5
1905	371.0	1911	513.4	1917	893.0
1906	418.0	1912	549.4		

SOURCE: V. SADOVSKY, *PRATSIA V SSSR* (WARSAW, 1932), P. 11.

This analysis relies on the findings of scholars working with the 1897 census, reports of the Tsarist factory inspectorate (which covered only large industrial enterprises), studies of the labour force conducted by industrial syndicates and the All-Russian agricultural censuses of 1916 and 1917.

The 1897 All-Russian census reported 5,719,499 self-supporting individuals (4,679,310 men and 1,040,189 women) living in the nine provinces out of a total population of 23,430,437. Wage earners made up approximately 1,480,000 of that number, of whom 425,000 were employed in factories, industrial plants, trade and transport. An equal number of people, 425,000, worked in agriculture, forestry, fishing, hunting and small rural trades. A further 582,000 were journeymen, servants and unskilled labourers.[26] Of those in the first category of industrial, trade and transport workers, approximately half lived in Southern Ukraine and the remaining half were evenly divided between the Right and Left Bank provinces.[27]

Table 5 presents the general trend from 1897 to 1917 in the growth of the full-time and seasonal wage earning population. If the 1897 census is taken at face value, it would appear that the number of wage earners grew from 1.5 to 3.6 million by 1917. However, the census was conducted in January, the middle

---

26   Ibid, Vol. 1, p. 125.
27   Sadovsky, *Pratsia*, pp. 11–12.

TABLE 5   Wage earners in Ukraine, 1897–1917

	1897	1913	1917
Total population	23,430,437	33,000,000	31,214,500
Wage earners	1,480,000	3,000,000	3,612,000
of which:			
industrial	327,400	631,600	893,000
Agricultural	425,413	1,500,000	1,200,000

SOURCES: I.K. RYBALKA AND F.H. TURCHENKO, 'SOTSIIAL'NO KLASOVA STRUKTURA NASELENNIA UKRAINY NAPEREDODNI ZHOVTNEVOI REVOLIUTSII', *UKRAINS'KYI ISTORYCHNYI ZHURNAL*, NOVEMBER 1981, P. 30; M.A. RUBACH, 'PROLETARIAT UKRAINY NAPEREDODNI SOTSIALISTYCHNOI REVOLIUTSII', *UKRAINS'KYI ISTORYCHNYI ZHURNAL*, APRIL 1963, P. 31; F. YE. LOS (ED.), *ISTORIIA ROBITNYCHOHO KLASU URSR*, 2 VOLS (KIEV: NAUKOVA DUMKA, 1967), P. 1:348; S. GOLDELMAN, 'PRO UMOVY HOSPODARS'KOI VIDBUDOVY UKRAINY', *NOVA UKRAINA*, 30 MAY 1922, P. 21; K.K. DUBYNA (ED.), *ISTORIIA UKRAINS'KOI RSR*, 2 VOLS (KIEV: NAUKOVA DUMKA, 1967), P. 1: 602.

of winter, and therefore it failed to include all workers employed seasonally in agriculture. M.A. Rubach and other Soviet-era scholars have suggested that by the end of the nineteenth century the agricultural proletariat numbered approximately 2 million at the height of harvest each year.[28] This estimate can be supported indirectly by working backwards from the 1917 calculation of the agricultural proletariat's size and the ratio between full time and seasonal workers in its ranks.

Two contemporary demographers estimate that in 1917 there were 394,000 full-time workers out of 1.2 million earning wages in agriculture (a ratio of full-time to seasonal workers of approximately 1:2).[29] Given that in the two decades before the Revolution mechanisation was invested almost continually into large-scale agriculture, the ratio between full-time and seasonal workers in 1897 was probably somewhere in the range of 1:3 to 1:4. Now the 425,413 proletarians in agriculture reported in the 1897 census were undoubtedly full-timers in their great majority because the census was conducted in January when little seasonal labour was required. The total number of workers in the agricultural

---

28   Los, *Istoriia Robitnychoho Klasu*, Vol. 1, p. 359; M.I. Suprunenko (gen. ed.), *Istoriia Ukrains'koi RSR*, 7 vols (Kyiv: Naukova Dumka, 1977), Vol. 4, p. 25; M.A. Rubach, 'Proletariat Ukrainy naperedodni sotsialistychnoi revoliutsii', *Ukrains'kyi Istorychnyi Zhurnal*, April 1963, p. 31.
29   Rybalka and Turchenko, 'Sotsialno klasova struktura', p. 24.

sector in the summer and fall of 1897 could have been four to five times that number (if 1897 ratios were 1:3 or 1:4), in the vicinity of 1.7 to 2.2 million. Therefore, if this figure were to replace the official 1897 estimate, the first salient trend in the evolution of the working class observed is the decline in the size of its agricultural contingent from approximately 2 million in 1897 to 1.5 million in 1913, and to 1.2 million in 1917. At the same time, the proportion of full-time workers to seasonal help in agriculture changed possibly from as much as 1:4 or 1:3 to 1:2 by 1917.

Over the same period, the industrial workforce (defined as those who work in plants hiring at least 15 workers and having mechanical power or 30 workers without mechanical power) rose from 327,000 to 893,000 in an almost steady upward climb that rose sharply between 1915 and 1917. The most important branches of Ukrainian industry were food processing, mining, metallurgy and machine building. In 1913, they accounted for 90.5 percent of the gross domestic product (mining: 43.9 percent; food industry: 36.2 percent; metallurgy and machine building: 10.4 percent) and employed 86.7 percent of the industrial workforce (48.7 percent in mining, 27.9 percent in food and 10.1 percent in metallurgy and machine building).[30]

These industrial sectors were heavily dependent on the international market for their trade. Production levels in mining, steel, machine building and the food industry fluctuated in response to international cycles of recession and boom, which at the time were recurring every ten years on average. The sharp drop in prices for coal, steel and sugar during the European recession of 1900–03 forced producers in Ukraine to cut back output and lay off workers. The economic recession in the Empire was ameliorated partially by military orders from the government during the Russo-Japanese War, but the country failed to recover until 1907 because of economic disruptions caused by the 1905 Revolution and the uneasiness of European investors afterwards.[31]

Barely had the economy emerged from the recession of 1900 when a new economic decline began in the United States and Western Europe. It bottomed out in Europe at the beginning of 1909, but continued to deepen in the Russian Empire until the end of that year suppressing coal, iron and steel production, the foundations of Ukraine's industrial sector.[32]

The uneven rate of economic growth before the War is reflected in the annual growth rate of the industrial workforce presented in Table 4. Due to

---

30 Los, *Istoriia Robitnychoho Klasu*, Vol. 1, p. 334.
31 Nesterenko, *Rozvytok Promyslovosti*, pp. 314, 338.
32 Ibid, p. 380.

the heavy industrial economy's reliance on the world market, cycles of international recession and recovery had a longer lasting impact upon it than they did upon countries with strong internal demand.

Generally speaking, industrial workers enjoyed growing security of employment in the years leading up to the War. One of the main reasons for this trend was the systematic replacement of unskilled manual labour by mechanical power throughout industry. Employers had to offer higher wages to skilled workers, but they benefitted from less labour turnover. This in turn promoted a more efficient and evenly paced tempo of production.[33]

In addition, the Stolypin land reform of November 1906 created large reserves of labour in the countryside. The reform abolished communal obligations of peasants to their villages, giving them the options to consolidate their land allotments or sell them off to richer farmers and move away permanently to wage earning occupations. Because many peasants had insufficient land, draught power and farm implements to survive as individual producers, the 1906 reform stimulated social differentiation in the countryside, strengthening the layers of middle and rich peasants on the one hand and driving the poor from their small plots on the other. In this way, the Stolypin reform enlarged the pool of reserve labour by increasing the number of rural dwellers who had no land of their own and had to start looking for full-time jobs.[34]

At the end of the nineteenth century, wages offered for industrial work in Ukraine were approximately 40 percent higher than in neighbouring Russian provinces. This had attracted migrant workers to the south in the 1880s and 1890s. After 1900, however, industrial wages in Russia rose to 12 percent above their average in Ukraine.[35] The reversal suppressed the flow of migrant labour into the Ukrainian provinces and opened up the job market to more of the indigenous population.

Only 5.8 percent of the workforce in metalwork and machine building industries was seasonal by 1914. Foundries and smelters, the suppliers of these industries, employed more seasonal labour, about 21.7 percent of their workforce in 1914.[36] In the mining industry, conditions of work discouraged workers from staying on the job and so the number of part-timers continued to be high even in times when the demand for coal and iron ore was strong.[37] The seasonal nature of agricultural production made it impossible for the food industry to

---

33   Ibid, p. 431.
34   Los, *Istoriia Robitnychoho Klasu*, Vol. 1, pp. 348, 357.
35   Holubnychy, 'Robitnytstvo'.
36   Los, *Istoriia Robitnychoho Klasu*, Vol. 1, p. 354.
37   Nesterenko, *Rozvytok Promyslovosti*, p. 432.

TABLE 6   Industrial workers in Ukraine, 1910–1917 (in thousands)

	1910	1913	1917
HEAVY INDUSTRY	288.2	440.1	636.2
of which:			
Coal	110.2	168.4	280.3
Ferrous metallurgy	44.5	71.7	114.1
Iron ore and salt	14.6	27.5	23.2
Metalwork and machine building	47.7	67.1	98.4
Chemicals	9.1	10.1	16.0
Silicates	27.8	39.4	28.2
Locomotives and wagons	34.3	55.9	76.0
LIGHT INDUSTRY	187.0	215.3	256.9
of which:			
Sugar	110.7	126.3	142.7
Flour	10.2	11.0	10.6
Textiles	13.5	14.1	13.8
Printing	5.8	6.8	4.7
Woodwork	18.7	24.1	21.8
TOTALS	474.2	655.4	893.1

SOURCE: M.A. RUBACH, 'PROLETARIAT NA UKRAINI NAPEREDODNI SOTSIALISTYCHNOI REVOLIUTSII', *UKRAINS'KYI ISTORYCHNYI ZHURNAL*, APRIL 1963, P. 29.

retain more than a fraction of its workers year round. But even in the agricultural sector, mechanisation must have contributed to some increase in the proportion of full-time workers before the War.

Table 6 presents a breakdown of workers employed in different branches of heavy and light industry in 1910, 1913 and 1917. From 1910 to 1913, a period of rapid economic expansion, the workforce in heavy and light industry registered impressive rates of growth. Coal miners were the largest section of the heavy industry workforce, growing from 110,200 in 1910 to 168,400 in 1913. They were followed by iron and steel foundry workers, metalworkers and machine builders. Of the 215,300 workers in light industry on the eve of the War, those in sugar refineries made up more than half of the total, dwarfing all other sections in this category.

During the War years, the working class grew numerically from 655,400 in 1913 to 893,100 in 1917. But while heavy industry registered strong gains in all branches except iron ore, salt mining and silicates, only the sugar workers grew significantly in number among those in light industry. Wood workers advanced marginally, while the number of workers in textiles, flour mills and printing declined. Construction also slowed during the War years, with the number of builders declining from about 400,000 in 1913 to 300,000 in 1917.[38] It has been estimated that before the War there were 132,000 full-time wage earners and salaried employees on the railways in Ukraine, with an additional 70,000 day labourers building new lines. During the War the full time workforce appears to have remained rather stable in number. Rubach estimates that in 1917 there were 121,000 wage earners on the railways.[39]

Russia's entry into the War was accompanied by increased state intervention into the industrial sector. Private capital was squeezed out of domestic trade. Capital investments and all available labour reserves were put into military production. While such measures enhanced the Russian state's capacity to wage war, they had long-term destructive consequences for the whole economy. Large numbers of able bodied men died on the fronts. Production was geared principally to serve military needs, so its impressive quantitative output did little, if anything, to regenerate the twin foundations of the economy – living labour and fixed capital. Under the strain of mounting military orders, whole industries used up their fixed capital without replacing it in the hope that industries of the enemy would collapse sooner than their own. Sectors of the economy not vital to the war effort stagnated for lack of raw materials, fuel and labour. The total acreage under cultivation declined by 20 percent during the War years.

A real struggle between the belligerent powers took place behind the front lines of warfare to exhaust one another's economic reserves. Russia was the weakest among the imperialist powers in terms of its industrial capacity. It failed to keep up with the frantic pace of military production set by Germany, exhausted its fixed capital sooner and resorted finally in 1916 and 1917 to mass offensives on the front against a better equipped, better clothed and better fed opponent. A combination of huge human losses in the fighting and the crumbling of production at home led to its eventual defeat and the outbreak of revolution.[40]

---

38 Los, *Istoriia Robitnychoho Klasu*, Vol. 2, pp. 13–14.
39 Rubach, 'Proletariat Ukrainy', p. 35. Estimates vary; see also Nesterenko, *Rozvytok Promyslovosti*, p. 426, and Ostapenko, 'Kapitalizm', p. 201.
40 J.V. Koshiw, 'The Number of People, Proletarians and Industrial Workers in the Russian Empire on the Eve of the February Revolution', April 1983 (mimeographed), p. 9.

Over 15 million men were conscripted into the Russian army. Four million came from Ukraine, accounting for one half of its adult male population. The mobilisation undermined the farms of poor peasants. Their productivity depended almost exclusively on the number of hands available in the family. Richer peasants with horses, mechanical implements and larger families than the rural poor were not as seriously affected by conscription. The best off farmers could hire labour from farms that failed or apply to the government for prisoners of war to work their land.[41]

Large numbers of industrial workers were conscripted before the government began granting deferments to those employed in war production industries. The first mobilisation in 1914, for example, took 40 percent of Donbas miners, 30 percent of workers in big foundries and 17 percent of metalworkers in Ukraine.[42] The conscripted workers were replaced by less skilled recruits from the villages, greater numbers of women and adolescents, refugees from other states, prisoners of war and migrant workers from Central Asia.[43] Conscription served as a means to tighten labour discipline. After receiving basic military training, many workers were sent back to work in the crucial war industries. Out of 104,000 workers employed in Ukraine's metallurgical industries in 1916, for example, 31,000 were conscripts and 16,000 were prisoners of war (45 percent of the total). More than two thirds of the 291,000 coal, iron ore, manganese and salt miners in January 1917 were conscripts and prisoners of war.[44]

Women workers were concentrated in agricultural, textile and chemical industries before the War. They made up practically half of the workforce in the tobacco industry and one fifth of all textile workers. The proportion of women workers throughout the economy grew in the years leading up to the War. In the industries monitored by the Tsarist factory inspectorate, women and girls made up 13 percent of the workforce in 1901, 16 percent in 1907 and 18 percent in 1914 when their numbers reached 58,000.[45] By 1916 there were approximately 103,000 female workers throughout Ukrainian industries. They were beginning to take jobs in coal and iron ore mining, sectors where few had worked before 1914. Between 1913 and 1916, the female workforce in coal mining grew from 2,400 to 12,400 (or from 1.6 percent to 4.5 percent of the total workforce). By 1916 4.5 percent of iron ore miners were women.[46] The proportion of

---

41 Sukhyno-Khomenko, 'Z pryvodu osoblyvostei', p. 89.
42 Los, *Istoriia Robitnychoho Klasu*, Vol. 2, p. 12.
43 Sadovsky, *Pratsia*, pp. 35–6; Sukhyno-Khomenko, 'Z pryvody osoblyvostei', pp. 88–9.
44 Nesterenko, *Rozvytok Promyslovosti*, p. 558.
45 Los, *Istoriia Robitnychoho Klasu*, Vol. 1, pp. 347–8.
46 Ibid, Vol. 1, p. 432.

TABLE 7 Wage earners in Ukraine, January 1917 (in thousands)

Agricultural proletariat	1,200
Industrial	893
Railways	121
Urban small industries	230
Rural small industries	444
Construction	300
Domestics and servants	365
Trade and urban transport	59
Total	3,612

SOURCE: M.A. RUBACH, 'PROLETARIAT UKRAINY NAPEREDODNI SOTSIALISTYCHNOI REVOLIUTSII', *UKRAINS'KYI ISTORYCHNYI ZHURNAL*, APRIL 1963, P. 35.

adult women workers throughout industry grew from 7.2 percent to 16.2 percent between 1914 and 1917.[47]

Per capita productivity declined during the War years because the industrial labour force became progressively less skilled and more coerced. The phenomenon bears a resemblance to the lower productivity of serfs in industry before 1861 compared to that of free wage earners. The main factors behind the rapid growth in the size of the working class were this decline in labour productivity and the using up of fixed capital.[48] Thus the number of workers in heavy industry grew by 57 percent between 1913 and 1917 with the industries under state control accounting for the lion's share of the growth. Manufacturing that remained under private control experienced an absolute decline in its workforce.[49]

M.A. Rubach has constructed a composite table of wage earners in the nine provinces in January 1917, reproduced here as Table 7. It includes full-time and seasonally employed people in agriculture, industry, small urban and rural trades, transport, trade, construction and services. It shows, among other things, that there were almost 700,000 wage earners scattered throughout the

---

47   Ibid, Vol. 2, p. 13.
48   Koshiw, 'Number of people', p. 9.
49   Ibid, p. 8.

country in small trades, and 365,000 domestics and servants. Of all the sections of the working class, the least is known about these two.[50]

The 3.6 million wage earners in 1917 made up 12 percent of the population of the nine provinces. Counted together with their dependents for a total of 6,501,000, the working class defined in the broader sense constituted 21 percent of the population. Less than a quarter of these 6.5 million workers and their families lived in officially designated towns and cities.[51] The estimated number of wage earners in the Russian Empire in January 1917 was 18,631,000. Ukraine, therefore, accounted for approximately 19 percent of the All-Empire total.[52]

5 National Composition

In 1897 Ukrainians made up 72.6 percent of the population, slightly more than 17 million people out of 23.4 million living in the nine provinces. There were 2.8 million Russians (11.8 percent), 1.9 million Jews (8.1 percent), and 1.75 million people belonging to other nationalities (7.5 percent).[53]

Estimates of the national composition of the working class vary according to the way occupational categories in the 1897 census are grouped and interpreted. Bohdan Krawchenko estimates that Ukrainians made up 44 percent of all wage earners, Russians 28 percent, Jews 17 percent and other nationalities 11 percent. The major national groups were concentrated in different sectors of the economy (see Table 8). Among day labourers and servants who made up 43 percent of the wage earning population, Ukrainians were in a majority (52.1 percent), followed by Russians (26.3 percent) and Jews (9.6 percent). In mining, heavy industry, mineral processing and manufacturing, which together employed 19 percent of the workforce, 38 percent were Ukrainians, followed by Russians (32.5 percent) and Jews (18.4). In the garment industry, which employed 14.7 percent of wage earners, Jewish and Ukrainian workers were practically equal in size (39.2 percent and 39.3 percent respectively). In the

---

50 See Ostapenko, 'Z pryvodu osoblyvostei', for a breakdown of workers in small industries and trades.
51 Rybalka and Turchenko, 'Sotsial'no klasova struktura', p. 30.
52 L.S. Gaponenko, *Rabochyi Klas Rossii v 1917 godu* (Moscow: Nauka, 1970), p. 72.
53 Bohdan Krawchenko, 'Aspects of the Social Structure of Ukraine before the Revolution', Paper presented to the Canadian Association of Slavists Annual Conference, Fredericton, 13–17 June 1977, p. 2.

TABLE 8   Structure of the working class in Ukraine by national group, 1897

Occupation	Total number	Percent Ukrainians	Percent Russians	Percent Jews
Mining	31,115	30.0	61.8	2.0
Metallurgy	102,314	38.8	35.0	16.0
Chemicals	27,448	48.3	27.7	15.8
Textiles	43,154	57.2	18.6	17.6
Woodworking	78,117	37.9	27.7	22.6
Printing	11,388	12.9	29.6	51.9
Diverse manufacturing	5,344	10.9	28.3	48.0
Sub-total	298,910	38.0	32.5	18.4
Garment	229,045	39.3	17.0	39.2
Forestry	11,605	30.7	44.6	9.5
Processing of animal products	20,646	35.6	26.0	31.5
Food processing	60,011	28.5	29.5	26.5
Distilling and tobacco	32,341	16.8	11.1	18.6
Sub-total	124,603	31.7	25.5	23.8
Construction	110,603	38.0	42.0	11.9
Transport and communications	120,476	36.5	41.1	13.1
Day labourers and servants	676,026	52.1	26.3	9.6
TOTAL	1,559,663	43.7	28.3	17.2

SOURCE: BOHDAN KRAWCHENKO, 'ASPECTS OF THE SOCIAL STRUCTURE UKRAINE BEFORE THE REVOLUTION', PAPER PRESENTED TO THE CANADIAN ASSOCIATION OF SLAVISTS ANNUAL CONFERENCE, FREDRICTON, CANADA, 13 JUNE 1977, P. 39, TABLE XV.

construction industry, Russians were the largest national group (42 percent), followed by Ukrainians (38 percent) and Jews (11.9 percent). The proportions of these national groups in transport and communications was practically the same as in construction.

Isaak Mazepa, whose count of the wage earning population differs from Krawchenko's calculates that Ukrainians made up 73 percent of all wage earners, 50 percent of the working class in industry, trade and transport, 80 percent of all day labourers and servants and 88 percent of the agricultural proletariat. Similarly, Mykola Porsh identifies proportions of Ukrainians in various

TABLE 9   Distribution of Ukrainian workers, 1897 (in thousands)

| | All workers in Ukraine || Ukrainian workers ||
	Total numbers	Percent of all workers	Percent of all workers in sector	Percent of All-Ukrainian workers
Industry, trade and transport	425.4	28.8	50.0	19.6
Agriculture, fishing and hunting	424.6	28.6	88.2	34.4
Servants	430.7	29.1	80.0	46.0
Journeymen and unskilled workers	199.5	13.5		
Total	1480.2	100.0	73.0	100.0

SOURCE: ISAAK MAZEPA, *BOL'SHEVYZM I OKUPATSIIA UKRAINY* (LVIV-KYIV: ZNATTIA TO SYLA, 1922), P. 13.

occupations ranging from 32.4 percent in large factories, 33.8 percent in mining, 37.8 percent in construction, to 41.5 percent on the railways.[54]

All of the estimates reveal a similar pattern. In comparison to their proportional representation in the working class as a whole, Ukrainians were underrepresented in heavy industry and mining in 1897 (except in the Kryvyi Rih ore mines). They were overrepresented in service occupations and agricultural industries. Russian workers, on the other hand, were concentrated in the heavy industry of the south, while Jewish workers (of whom two thirds were living in the Right Bank provinces) made up a large proportion of the craft proletariat in small industries and trades. Day labourers and servants were the bottom layer of the working class in terms of pay, job security and prestige. According to Krawchenko's figures in Table 8, more than half of All-Ukrainian wage earners were day labourers and servants. Among Russian and Jewish workers, the respective percentages in these occupations were 40 percent and 24 percent.[55]

Ukrainians accounted for 83.4 percent of the peasantry in 1897. Peasants made up 93.1 percent of the Ukrainian nationality. The elite classes, on the

[54]   Holubnychy, 'Robitnytstvo'.
[55]   Nesterenko, *Rozvytok Promyslovosti*, p. 436; Krawchenko, 'Aspects of the Social Structure'; Pavlo Khrystiuk, *Ukrains'ka Revoliutsiia. Zamitky i Materiialy do Istorii Ukrains'koi Revoliutsii 1917–20rr*, 4 vols (Vienna: Ukrains'kyi Sotsiolohichnyi Instytut, 1921), Vol. 4, p. 4; Popov, *Narys Istorii*, p. 21.

other hand, were comprised mainly of the members of national minorities. Just over half of the nobility in 1897 was Russian (50.2 percent), one fifth was Polish (20.2 percent) and one quarter Ukrainian (26.2 percent). Among civil servants, members of free professions and persons living from inheritance and invested capital, 37.5 percent were Russians, 30.9 percent were Ukrainians, 15.8 percent were Jews and another 15.8 percent belonged to other national minorities. Jews made up the majority of people engaged in trade and commerce (62.2 percent), followed by Russians (17.4 percent), Ukrainians (13.1 percent) and other national groups (7.3 percent).[56]

> The national minorities in Ukraine were 'minorities' only in the pure mathematical sense of the word. In terms of their social weight, they dominated society. In the social division of labour, industry, trade, culture, political administration, the military – all were by and large in the hands of non-Ukrainians … Taking the Ukrainian nobility, those drawing their income from capital or an inheritance, the merchants and tradesmen, the clergy as well as those involved in state administration, the liberal professions and other intellectual work – all together, the entire 'elite' of the Ukrainian nation totalled 1.3 percent of the Ukrainian population. On the other hand, over 12 percent of the Russian population of Ukraine could be included in the elite as defined (rather loosely) above.[57]

6   Urbanisation

The level of urbanisation in the Ukrainian provinces in 1897 stood at 13 percent, higher than in European Russia, where it stood at 10 percent.[58] Overall, Russians made up 34 percent of the urban population, Ukrainians 30 percent and Jews 27 percent. In Odesa, the largest Ukrainian city at the time with a population of 404,000, only 9 percent of the inhabitants were Ukrainians. In Kyiv, with a population of 248,000, 22 percent were Ukrainians; in Kharkiv (174,000) 25 percent and Dnipropetrovsk (113,000) 16 percent. Poltava was the only city with a population of more than 50,000 in which Ukrainians constituted a majority

---

[56] Krawchenko, 'Aspects of the Social Structure', Tables VII, X, XI, XIX.
[57] Ibid, pp. 16, 22. See also O.I. Luhova, 'Pro stanovyshche Ukrainy v Period Kapitalizmu', *Ukrains'kyi Istorychnyi Zhurnal*, April 1967, p. 21.
[58] George Y. Boshyk, 'The Rise of Ukrainian Political Parties in Russia 1900–1907. With Special Reference to Social Democracy', PhD thesis, Oxford University, 1981, pp. 12–13.

TABLE 10   Population of major cities by native language, 1897

City	Population	Ukrainian	Russian	Jewish
Odesa	403,815	9.4	49.0	30.8
Kyiv	247,723	22.2	54.2	12.1
Kharkiv	173,989	25.9	63.2	5.7
Katerynoslav	112,839	15.8	41.8	35.4
Mykolaiv	92,012	8.5	66.3	19.5
Zhytomyr	65,895	13.9	25.7	46.4
Kremenchuk	63,007	30.1	19.3	46.9
Yelyzavethrad	61,488	23.6	34.6	37.8
Kherson	59,076	19.6	47.2	29.1
Poltava	53,703	56.0	20.6	19.9
Berdychiv	53,351	8.2	8.6	77.1

SOURCE: STEVEN GUTHIER, 'UKRAINIAN CITIES DURING THE REVOLUTION AND INTERWAR ERA', UNIVERSITY OF MICHIGAN, N.D. (MIMEOGRAPHED), P. 2.

(56 percent). The number of Ukrainians in a town tended to be inversely proportional to the town's total population.[59]

Between 1897 and 1917 the population of major urban centres grew rapidly and many villages in the industrialising south became towns. The situation in Kyiv, where a census of the population was conducted in September 1917, seems to indicate that 'the acceleration of urban growth before the revolution was not paralleled by any significant improvement in the position of the Ukrainian nationality in cities'.[60] In the two decades leading up to the Revolution, the proportion of Ukrainians in Kyiv actually declined from 22 percent to 16 percent. The number of Russians doubled while the Jewish population tripled in size. Steven Guthier attributes these changes to the weak influx from the surrounding countryside and 'the inroads of Russianisation among the Ukrainian minority in the cities'. It was also the result of the increasingly untenable position of small trades in the face of mass commodity production. These pressures forced Jews out of the villages and hamlets at the end of the nineteenth century and into Kyiv and other big urban centres.

---

59   Krawchenko, 'Aspects of the Social Structure', p. 4; Steven Guthier, 'Ukrainian Cities during the Revolution and Interwar Era', University of Michigan (mimeographed), p. 2; Shapoval, *Velyka Revoliutsiia*, p. 74.
60   Guthier, 'Ukrainian Cities', p. 4.

M. Vasylenko, an enumerator of voters in Kharkiv in 1917, argues that national self identification in censuses did not reflect the real state of affairs in the cities. He claims that there was no basis to accept the dominant view before the Revolution that the urban population in Ukraine was being Russified in an irreversible sense.

> Russification set down its strongest roots in the cities, but it actually affected language, customs and other national characteristics in a limited way. It did not manage to eradicate national differences in any final sense.[61]

While the level of urbanisation was higher in Ukraine than Russia, the situation was reversed as far as the working class was concerned. According to 1902 statistics, less than one third (29.5 percent) of the industrial workforce in the Ukrainian provinces lived in urban centres. In the southern Ukrainian provinces the proportion was 49.3 percent. In northern Russia, on the other hand, 69.3 percent of the industrial workforce was urbanised, in the Central Industrial Region 53.3 percent.[62] Official figures are misleading, however, because the official reclassification of villages into towns lagged behind their de facto growth in population. Around the new industries in the south, localities officially classified as villages soon acquired populations greater than those of officially designated towns. The mining villages of Donbas had a population of 374,000 by 1913. The village of Yuzivka, for example, had 55,000 residents in that year and was served by several banks, schools and trading companies.[63]

An overall lower level of urbanisation of workers in Ukraine compared to their fellow workers in Russia had to do with the entire history of industrial development under serfdom: its rural location, the importance of agricultural industries in Ukraine, the retention of peasants on the land after 1861 when modern heavy industries were starting to be located on the steppe close to the sources of raw materials but far from the traditional urban centres. Provincial capitals like Kyiv, Kharkiv and Kherson had a smaller share of the working-class population of their provinces than did Moscow, Petrograd and Warsaw.[64]

---

61   *Robitnycha Hazeta*, 20 June 1917, p. 2.
62   Mazepa, *Bol'shevyzm*, p. 9; Krawchenko, 'Aspects of the Social Structure', p. 18.
63   Nesterenko, *Rozvytok Promyslovosti*, p. 432.
64   Ibid, p. 438. See also Sadovsky, *Pratsia*, p. 12; Sukhyno-Khomenko, 'Z pryvodu osoblyvostei', p. 87; and M. Larin, 'Yak ne treba pysaty istoriiu', *Litopys Revoliutsii*, June 1928, p. 322. Larin disputes Sukhyno Khomenko's views, arguing that 'Odesa, Mykolaiv, Kherson and Yelyzavethrad had 91.9 percent of all workers in their provinces'.

7 Literacy

Around the time of the Revolution of 1648, the majority of the population in Ukraine, 'almost all members of households, and not only the men but women and their daughters' could read.[65] Censuses conducted in seven regimental districts of Chernihiv and Poltava in 1740 and 1748 showed there was one school for every 740 souls, a total of 866 schools serving 1,034 villages. City censuses conducted a century later between 1866 and 1874 recorded levels of literacy among men of between 33 and 50 percent and among women between 27 and 40 percent.[66] In 1875 a mere 3.7 percent of all recruits to the Russian army from Ukraine were literate, compared to 20 percent of conscripts from Russia.[67] By 1897, 18.8 percent of the population in Ukraine remained literate, compared to a level of 23.2 percent for all of European Russia. Among Ukrainians themselves, the level stood at 13 percent, the lowest of any nation in the Empire recorded in the census.[68]

Among Ukrainian men literacy stood at 22.2 percent, for Ukrainian women it was a mere 3.5 percent. Among Russians living in Ukraine, literacy stood at 26.8 percent (among men 35.5 percent and women 17.3 percent). Slightly higher levels of literacy among Ukrainians were to be found in Katerynoslav and Kharkiv provinces (14 percent), Kherson (15 percent) and former territories of the Hetmanate – Poltava (14 percent) and Chernihiv (16 percent). In Podillia and Volyn provinces on the Right Bank it fell to 11 percent and 9 percent respectively.[69]

Just over half of the industrial working class in Ukraine was literate in 1897, a higher proportion than that for officially classified urban dwellers as a whole. Literacy levels among industrial workers was highest in the biggest cities like Kyiv (62.3 percent), Kharkiv (62.6 percent) and Odesa (59 percent).[70]

The level of literacy in specific occupations naturally increased with the intellectual requirements of labour, improvements in working conditions and

---

65   This according to the Archdeacon Alepsky in 1652. Cited in Mykhailo Braichevsky, 'Pryiednannia chy Voziednannia?', in *Shyroke More Ukrainy: Dokumenty Samvydavu z Ukrainy* (Paris-Baltimore: PIUF-Smoloskyp, 1972), pp. 274–5.
66   Holubnychy, 'Robitnytstvo'.
67   Mykhailo Drahomanov, *Vybrani Tvory*, edited by Bohatsky (Prague-New York: Ukrainski Postupovi Tovarystva v Amerytsi, 1937), p. 22.
68   Mykola Porsh, *Pro Avtonomiiu* (Kyiv: Prosvita, 1907), pp. 71–3.
69   Krawchenko, 'Aspects of the Social Structure', p. 13; Porsh, *Pro Avtonomiiu*, pp. 71–3.
70   Mykola Porsh, 'Robitnytstvo Ukrainy: Vysnovky z Pratsi pro Ukrains'ku Ekonomiku i Robitnytstvo', *Zapysky N.T. Sh.*, Book XII, 1913, p. 142.

shortening of the working day: 87.4 percent of printers were literate, as were 66.7 percent of metalworkers, 53.9 percent of construction workers and 33.5 percent of miners. Concentrated in agricultural industries, small trades, domestic service and the lower strata of workers in heavy industry, Ukrainians were the least literate nation of the working class. In Kyiv province, for example, literacy among Russian workers was twice as high as among Ukrainian workers – 45 percent to 23 percent. In Podillia, it was the same – 40 percent to 18 percent, and in Volyn Russian workers were four times as literate as their fellow Ukrainians (37 percent to 9 percent). The levels of literacy between these two groups were more evenly matched in the industrialising south.[71]

Industrialisation abetted the reacquisition of literacy, but the state's long-standing policy of Russification continued to hold it back for the Ukrainian nationality. As early as 1720, the Tsar had prohibited the publication of all books in the Hetmanate except reprints of existing Church literature and ordered the correction of these texts to conform with the Church Slavonic used in Russia.[72] Alexander I declared Ukrainian a backward dialect of Russian in 1804 and forbad its use in schools as a language of instruction or separate subject.[73] Alexander II added the infamous Ems *ukaz* in 1876 which prohibited all publications in the language, except belles lettres, or singing of any folksongs except in French translation.[74] In October 1881, the Ministry of the Interior added 'the organisation of Little Russian theatres and troupes' to the prohibition clauses of the *ukaz*. Employees of the Petrograd central censor bureau received instructions in 1892 to take special note of original Ukrainian manuscripts submitted for clearance and to reject as many as possible 'strictly on grounds of national security'.[75] It was not until 1905 that the bans on the Ukrainian language were lifted; by 1906 many of them were being re-introduced unofficially as part of the regime's clawing back of the democratic gains of the 1905 Revolution.

The laws were designed to prevent revolutionary ideas reaching the peasants and to suppress separatist currents in the western periphery of the Empire. The prohibition on education kept the peasantry ignorant; bans on publications,

---

71   Los, *Istoriia Robitnychoho Klasu*, Vol. 2, p. 146; Mykola Porsh, *Pro Avtonomiiu Ukrainy* (Kyiv: Prosvita, 1908), p. 19; Mykyta Shapoval, *Sotsiolohiia Ukrains'koho Vidrodzhennia* (Prague: Ukrainskyi Sotsiolohichnyi Instytut v Prazi, 1936), p. 18.
72   Luhova, 'Pro stanovyshche Ukrainy', p. 22.
73   Porsh, *Pro Avtonomiiu*, p. 71.
74   Los, *Istoriia Robitnychoho Klasu*, Vol. 2, p. 161.
75   Luhova, 'Pro stanovyshche Ukrainy', p. 22.

theatre and other cultural endeavours in the native language kept the radicals away from them. Combined with the dominance of the Russian language and culture in the urban and industrial centres, they promoted the assimilation of socially mobile Ukrainians into the ruling nation.

In the course of becoming socially mobile, educated and urbanised, Ukrainians parted with their peasant nation. Their original culture remained synonymous with rural life. Many city dwellers associated it with backwardness and isolation. The development of capitalism deepened the division between the city and countryside in linguistic and cultural as well as social and economic terms. In Ukraine, Russian (and Polish on the Right Bank) were the languages of social mobility, while Ukrainian remained the language of most illiterates. Although the process of industrialisation was accompanied by an increase in the literacy of those drawn into wage earning occupations, the rate at which it spread among proletarians depended upon their national origins, facility in Russian, the requirements of their jobs, incentives to improve one's position at work, free time after working hours and the institutions available for education. In this process Ukrainian sections of the working class had few incentives and considerable barriers in the economy and civil society to become more literate.

8 Conclusion

The previous chapter showed how the Ukrainian provinces became an economically advanced 'internal' colony of the Russian state and its European financiers. This chapter has examined the working class which arose from the same historical process. It has analysed some of the salient characteristics of the working class: its numerical growth, its distribution throughout the economy, urbanisation, its national sources and its levels of literacy. These characteristics taken together reveal a class that was internally stratified along the lines of geographic location, gender, skill and nationality. Such stratification was not merely the outcome of the functional needs of capitalists for wage labour. It was also shaped by history and by the policies of the Russian state. The Ukrainian peasant, the Jewish artisan and the Russian migrant variously enjoyed advantages and encountered obstacles in their social mobilisation into the working class that were peculiar to their national status – as a member either of the historically oppressed or ostracised or oppressing nation of that society. It therefore seemed inevitable that social antagonisms internal to the working class would appear to its members also as national antagonisms. In other words the working class had its own internal national question to deal with, which in the final analysis concerned its unity. The 1917 revolution brought to the surface such antagonisms. How the workers' movement prepared to deal with them is the subject of the next chapter.

CHAPTER 3

Social Democracy and the National Question

One of the main features of capitalism in the late nineteenth century was its rapid spread into peripheral societies, the creation of a globally connected economy, and the economic division of the world by a handful of imperialist powers. By the turn of the century, Britain, France and Germany had seized colonies encompassing almost 28 million square miles inhabited by over 380 million people. Together with Russia, Japan and the United States, they carved up among themselves 90 percent of the African continent, 57 percent of Asia, all of Polynesia and over a quarter of the Americas, gaining access to huge reserves of raw materials, cheap labour and new markets for goods manufactured in the metropolitan centres.[1] Without this new economic territory, the astronomical growth of capitalism in its heartlands at the turn of the century is inconceivable.

The national movements maturing in peripheral societies at the end of the nineteenth century were a political response to their penetration and subordination by the metropolitan states. Although these movements demanded state independence as a solution to this predicament, they were historically different kinds of national movements from those which created nation states in Western Europe beforehand. Philosophically they were indebted to European revolutionary thinking, but ultimately they were a reaction to European imperialism.

National movements posed a challenge to the coherence of Marx's revolutionary vision. It was predicated on the victory of capitalism over feudalism, capitalism's spread throughout the world and the organisation of an international proletarian movement to lead world society beyond capitalism. Marx and his political descendants therefore supported capitalism's maturation, its suppression of feudal relations and its creation of the wage earning class. They were confident that both the spread of capitalism and the working class movement itself would erase not only the hostilities between nations, but national differences between them, leading to a culturally and linguistically more homogenous world society. However, imperialism complicated their vision because it united nations into a world economy that bestowed its wealth

---

1 V.I. Lenin, 'Imperialism. The Highest Stage of Capitalism', in *Collected Works*, Vol. XIX (New York: International Publishers, 1942), pp. 149–50.

unequally among them. It fostered national identities among the peripheral peoples, including their nascent working classes. It presented new problems to the international workers' movement and its political parties because imperialist policies benefited the English, French and German working classes, the new aristocracy of world labour whose living standards were underwritten by the workers and peasants of peripheral societies being drawn into the world economy. Imperialism demanded from Marxists another attempt to separate the revolutionary and retrogressive tendencies of capitalist development, the tendencies they should support or oppose. It challenged them to take up the national question as a concern of the international workers' movement.

1 Marx and Engels

The social democratic workers' movement in Ukraine inherited two fairly distinct assessments of the national question from the Marxist tradition. They are both rooted in the works of Marx and Engels, representing the two poles between which their ideas developed from the 1840s to the 1880s. In the Communist Manifesto of 1848, Marx and Engels stated that

> The bourgeoisie ... draws all nations, even the most barbarian into civilisation ... Just as it has made the country dependent on the towns, so it has made barbarian and semi-barbarian countries dependent on the civilised ones, nations of peasants on nations of bourgeois, the East on the West.[2]

Not all nations were destined to create their own state. Only those nations with an indigenous capacity for capitalist development, as opposed to an external stimulus, could take this road. As capitalist relations matured in the core European states, the politically weak and economically backward nations would be assimilated by modern nations, the 'standard bearer[s] of historical development'.[3]

Considering the Scots, Gaels and Basques as peoples historically unprepared for nationhood, Marx predicted

---

[2] Karl Marx and Frederick Engels, *The Communist Manifesto* (New York: International Publishers, 1948), p. 13.

[3] Cited by Rosa Luxemburg, *The National Question: Selected Writings by Rosa Luxemburg*, edited and with an introduction by Horace B. Davis (New York: Monthly Review Press, 1976), p. 124.

such national left overs will become and will remain until their final extermination or denationalisation fanatical partisans of counterrevolution, since their entire existence is in general a protest against the great historical revolution.[4]

'The Moravians and Slovaks', he wrote, 'have long since lost every vestige of national feeling and vitality ... Bohemia could exist henceforth only as a portion of Germany'.[5]

The 1848 Manifesto says that 'workingmen have no country' only to add that they can have one if they 'rise to the leading class of the nation' and constitute themselves as 'the nation'; the proletariat is 'itself national' when it attains political power 'though not in the bourgeois sense of the word'.

> Though not in substance, yet in form, the struggle of the proletariat with the bourgeoisie is at first a national struggle. The proletariat of each country must, of course, first of all settle matters with its own bourgeoisie.[6]

For the young Marx and Engels, the national movements of their day were neither 'in the way of' nor 'on the way' to revolutionary change. Each national movement had to be assessed by its contribution to the suppression of autocracy, the promotion of capitalism and the political freedom of the proletariat. The 'right' to national self-determination had to be weighed in such terms for every claimant.[7]

Marx subordinated national movements in Central and Eastern Europe to such criteria of progress. Tsarist Russia, 'the policeman of Europe' represented for him the greatest threat to capitalism and democracy in the region. Movements he perceived as under its influence were dismissed as reactionary. Because they rebelled against Tsarist rule, the Poles were admired and supported by Marx as a bulwark for Europe against the Russian autocratic menace. He opposed Pan-Slavism, believing that it strengthened Russia's influence in Europe.[8] He supported Turkey against Russia in the Crimean War for the same

---

4   Ibid.
5   Ibid, p. 117.
6   Marx and Engels, *The Communist Manifesto*, p. 20.
7   Solomon F. Bloom, *The World of Nations: A Study of the National Implications in the Work of Karl Marx* (New York: AMS Press, 1967), p. 20.
8   Ibid, pp. 40–4.

reasons and judged the movements for national independence among Slavs in the Balkan Peninsula as 'only the machinations of Russian Tsardom trying to irritate the Turks'.[9]

Marx and Engels's early views about the fate of stateless nations in Europe and on its periphery were based more on their original projections about capitalist development than on empirical studies of their national movements. They expected capitalism to spread outward into peripheral societies, reproducing itself and creating favourable conditions for the birth of the proletariat. However, the potential for the revolutionary transformation of capitalist society remained concentrated in the original centres of industrial production where the proletariat was strongest. The metropoli of Europe were destined to show the way forward for other parts of the world, and the more they extended their influence into peripheral societies the more capitalism would displace feudalism and create the agent for capitalism's own transformation there. The capitalist mode of production on a world scale would break down national differences and antagonisms between peoples as would the growing international unity of the proletarian struggle against it.[10]

This vision underwent considerable revision in later years. The Irish question with which Marx and Engels became closely acquainted in the 1850s and 1860s presented perhaps the first real challenge to its basic assumptions. Marx and Engels learned that the real threat to English landlordism in Ireland came from the impoverished Irish peasantry and not the mainland bourgeoisie and that the radicalism of English workers was blunted and continually undermined by their prejudice against fellow Irish immigrant workers. So they began to reconsider the revolutionary potential in peripheral society and its relationship to political change in the metropolitan country that dominated it. Marx went so far as to say that the national liberation of Ireland and its political separation from the British Empire was 'the first condition' for the emancipation of the English working class. The Irish question provided Marx with an opportunity to draw the connection between national and social emancipation in the peripheral society:

> The destruction of the English landed aristocracy in Ireland is an infinitely easier operation than in England itself because the land question has hitherto been the exclusive form of the social question in Ireland, and because it is a question of existence, of life and death for the immense

---

9 Luxemburg, *The National Question*, p. 114.
10 Marx and Engels, *The Communist Manifesto*, p. 28.

majority of the Irish people and because it is at the same time inseparable from the national question.[11]

During the 1870s, Marx came to the conclusion that the capitalist penetration of India was not contributing much to its industrial development. Capital appeared mainly in the commercial form, as trade in readily available commodities, which resulted in an enormous drain of India's wealth to Britain without an equivalent replacement. Rather than being merely the phase of Europe's 'primitive accumulation' of capital, the plundering of colonies now assumed a permanent place in the overall, long-term process and was in fact a key contributing factor to European capitalism's astronomical growth. Marx then set out to revise the final section of Capital to accord with this development in his thought. He stressed that Capital described just one phase of the European experience and other countries need not follow its example.[12]

In 1882, Engels wrote to Karl Kautsky about the significance of the national question for the workers' movement. Focusing mainly on the Polish situation, Engels's letter in February of that year made several proposals of a general, principled nature:

> Until there is national independence, a great historical people cannot even approach half seriously any internal problems ... An international proletarian movement is possible only among independent nations ... International co-operation is possible only between different entities ... As long as Poland is partitioned and subjugated, neither a strong socialist party inside the country nor a truly international union of proletarian parties of Germany and other countries can emerge or flourish ... The removal of national oppression is the fundamental condition of all healthy and free development.[13]

In another letter to Kautsky in September 1882, Engels urged that 'India, Algeria, the Dutch, Portuguese and Spanish possessions ... be taken over for the time being by the proletariat and led as rapidly as possible towards independence'.[14]

---

11   Cited in Bloom, *The World of Nations*, p. 113.
12   Raya Dunayevskaya, 'A 1980s View of the Two Way Road between the US and Africa', *News and Letters*, January–February 1984, pp. 8–9.
13   Cited in Hryhorii Kostiuk, *Teoriia i Diisnist'* (Munich: Suchasnist', 1971), pp. 18–19.
14   Cited in V.I. Lenin, *Collected Works*, Vol. XIX (New York: International Publishers, 1942), p. 298.

Marx and Engels did not live to see the phase of finance capital at its height, but the implications in their last writings seemed rather clear: it was not only that peripheral societies overseas or territorially adjacent to the European metropoles should not follow the European example; they *could not* precisely because they were being locked into the metropolitan economies' division of labour which sapped their wealth and prevented them from developing as rounded, self sufficient entities. The forces of revolutionary change, therefore, were as likely to gather in the peripheral societies as in the metropolitan. Far from being 'fanatical partisans of counterrevolution', national movements in peripheral societies were likely to be more on the way to revolution than in its way. These peripheral societies, moreover, would not necessarily have to pass through the way station of capitalism.

2   Two Views on the National Question

Marx and Engels's ideas about nations under capitalism dispersed along two main paths. The first, which emphasised the assimilationist, big power and 'internationalising' tendency of capitalism, has a lineage from the early Marx and Engels to Karl Kautsky, Vladimir Lenin and Rosa Luxemburg. In Ukraine, it found a home in the Russian Social Democratic Workers' Party (RSDWP). The second path, which emphasised growing national differentiation under capitalism, can be traced from Marx and Engels's later writings to Austro-Marxism, the Jewish General Workers' Union (Bund), the Ukrainian Social Democratic Workers' Party (USDWP) and at least seven other social democratic parties in the Russian Empire.

Rudolf Hilferding, the Austro-Marxist upon whose work Lenin based many of his own ideas about imperialism, foresaw growing and increasingly violent opposition to the European powers' scramble for economic territory:

> In the newly opened up countries themselves, the capitalism imported into them intensifies contradictions and excites the constantly growing resistance against intruders on the peoples who are awakening to national consciousness. This resistance can easily become transformed into dangerous measures directed against foreign capital. The old social relations become completely revolutionised. The age-long agrarian incrustation of 'nations without a history' is blasted away and they are drawn into the capitalist whirlpool.
>
> Capitalism itself gradually procures for the vanquished the means and resources for their emancipation and they set out to achieve the same

goal which once seemed highest to the European nations: the creation of a united national state as a means to economic and cultural freedom.

This movement for national independence threatens European capital just in its most valuable and promising fields of exploitation, and European capital can maintain its domination only by continually increasing its means of exerting violence.[15]

Otto Bauer, another member of the Austro-Marxist school, argued that the development of capitalism sharpened national distinctions because it brought education to the lower classes and heightened their self identity. If socialism promised democracy and popular education, then national identity would only continue to deepen after capitalism was overthrown. Bauer supported the national movements appearing in Central and Eastern Europe in the late nineteenth century and called for a federal system of government in the Austro-Hungarian state based on a particular form of national autonomy. Because nations in the Austro-Hungary lived in widely ranging degrees of territorial compactness, he proposed that members of each nation be registered on a country-wide list as a separate public corporation. Such corporations should have control of their registered members' educational and cultural affairs and the right to represent them in parliament and courts of law. Concessions to national aspirations of this kind would alleviate tensions in the multinational state which Bauer feared were leading to its breakup.[16]

Delegates to the 1899 Brunn Congress of the Austro Hungarian Social Democrats devoted much time to the national question. A group of South Slav delegates introduced Bauer's proposals for federalism and the 'personality principle' in the organisation of national cultural autonomy. It reads:

> Every nation inhabiting Austria, irrespective of the territory on which its members reside, shall constitute an autonomous group which shall quite independently administer its national affairs.[17]

The motion was defeated in favour of another one put forward by Austrian delegates who also supported national autonomy, but only for territorially compact nations. The five main clauses of the adopted motion read as follows:

---

15 Rudolf Hilferding, *Finance Capital*, p. 406, cited by Lenin, 'Imperialism', p. 190.
16 Horace B. Davis, *Marxist and Labour Theories of Nationalism to 1917* (New York: Monthly Review Press, 1967), pp. 151–7.
17 Cited by V.I. Lenin in 'Critical Remarks on the National Question', in Hyman Lumer (ed.), *Lenin and the Jewish Question* (New York: International Publishers, 1974), pp. 95–6.

Austria is to be transformed into a democratic federation of nationalities.

The historic Crown lands are to be divided by nationally homogenous self ruling bodies whose legislation and administration shall be in the hands of national chambers elected on the basis of universal, equal and direct franchise.

All self-governing regions of one and the same nation are to form together a nationally distinct union which shall take care of this union's affairs autonomously.

We do not recognise any national privilege, therefore we reject the demand for a state language. Whether a common language is needed, a federal parliament can decide.[18]

Both the adopted and defeated resolutions gained a wide hearing among socialists outside Austro-Hungary. They were well received in the Russian Empire. Across the border in the Ukrainian provinces, they lent support to Ukrainian and Jewish social democrats who wanted to make the national question a central issue of the workers' movement.

A leading theoretician of the German social democratic movement, Karl Kautsky feared that his comrades in Austro-Hungary made too many concessions to the stateless nations. A programme of federalism and national autonomy went against the grain of economic and political centralisation that Kautsky evidently discerned in the maturation of capitalism. Moreover, such a programme divided unnecessarily the workers' movement in existing multinational states. Kautsky leaned towards the belief that the assimilation of economically backward and stateless nations into the more 'advanced' ones was inevitable under capitalism. And the transition from capitalism to socialism, he believed, would only advance the centralisation of economic, political and cultural life even further.[19]

But Kautsky did not seem to share the optimism of the 1848 Communist Manifesto in which Marx and Engels foresaw the spread of capitalism breaking down national differences and the international unification of the proletariat 'caus[ing] them to vanish still faster'.[20] In the Erfurt Programme of 1891, which Kautsky drafted for the German social democrats and was meant to update the Manifesto, he had characterised the national question as a 'remarkable contradiction in the historical process':

---

18   Cited by Luxemburg, *The National Question*, pp. 104–5.
19   Davis, *Marxist and Labour Theories*, p. 159.
20   Marx and Engels, *The Communist Manifesto*, p. 28.

> The more complex becomes international commerce ... the fiercer grows the competitive struggle and the greater becomes the danger of conflicts between nations. The closer the international relations which are developed, the louder swells the demand for attention to separate national interests ... Hand in hand with the movement toward international brotherhood goes the tendency to emphasise national differences.[21]

Kautsky traced the conflict between nations to established and aspiring territorial groups of the bourgeoisie within them. He counselled the workers' movement to stay clear because their interests would not be served by lining up with one or another side of the bourgeoisie.[22] In his study *Nationality and Internationalism*, he predicted the 'gradual withdrawal and, ultimately, the complete disappearance of the languages of smaller nations' and the unification of all civilised countries by 'one language and one nationality'. Kautsky extrapolated this future from the existing links between the bourgeoisie and petit bourgeoisie of different nations through commerce, communications, education and culture. He believed that the workers' movement should support such links because they prefigured the future international socialist order. Rather than foreseeing the further development of separate national cultures, an idea Kautsky considered 'very strange' at first, he predicted their gradual coalescence into an international culture united by just a few universal languages. The stateless nations would gravitate towards such universal languages as they entered the world of capitalist production.[23]

In his later years, Kautsky studied more the other side of the coin. He acknowledged that national movements in Austro-Hungary and Russia were intimately connected to movements for democracy. They were 'children of the same mother', the eastward spread of capitalism.[24] Though not prepared to concede to their demands for political independence, Kautsky nevertheless agreed that some measure of cultural and linguistic autonomy for territorially compact peoples was necessary.[25] Now Kautsky advised the proletariat not to be indifferent or opposed to national movements, but 'very much interested

---

21 Karl Kautsky, *The Class Struggle (Erfurt Programme)*, translated by William E. Bohn (Chicago: Charles H. Kerr and Co., 1910), p. 203.
22 Ibid, p. 205.
23 Cited in Luxemburg, *The National Question*, p. 127.
24 Karl Kautsky, *The National Question in Russia*, cited by Lev Yurkevych, *Kliasy i Suspilstvo* (Kyiv: Dzvin, 1913), p. 34.
25 Henry J. Tobias, *The Jewish Bund in Russia from its Origins to 1905* (Stanford: Stanford University Press, 1972), p. 109.

in having such movements continue to develop ... Although the proletarian stands on the principle of internationalism, this does not mean he rejects national identity; it means he seeks the freedom and equality of all nations'.[26]

In the years leading up to the First World War, the epicentre of revolutionary upheavals shifted eastward through Europe and into Asia. Kautsky was obliged to think about the consequences of this shift for the anticipated transition from capitalism to socialism on the continent. He stuck to the idea that national struggles were part and parcel of the movement towards bourgeois democracy. They had to be supported insofar as the bourgeois democratic revolutions had only reached Austro-Hungary; they still had to overthrow Russian autocracy and to open the political process to the rapidly growing proletariat in the east. The proletariat in the west still retained the leading role in the drama, as Marx had written. Only now it faced the question of revolution in the semi-capitalist east where national movements had as important a role to play in the struggle against autocracy as did its fledgling workers' movements.

V.I. Lenin, chief theorist of the Bolshevik faction in the RSDWP, would have nothing to do with Austro-Marxism on the national question, whose programme he called 'a plan of capitalists and opportunist philistine intelligentsia'.[27] His views were based on Kautsky, the early Marx and Engels and his own assessment of national movements in the Russian Empire. Lenin attributed the importance of the national question in the Empire to four facts: the non-Russian peoples formed a majority of its population (57 percent); the borderlands of the Empire inhabited by these nations frequently had a higher level of capitalist development than central Russia; their national oppression was worse than in Austro-Hungary; and several oppressed nations in the southern and western regions of the Empire had compatriots across the border in Austro-Hungary.[28]

Lenin located the origin of national movements in the transition from feudalism to capitalism; they were motivated by the needs of the bourgeoisie for a unified market, a common language of commerce and protection of its home territory. The nation state was 'the rule and 'norm' of capitalism'. But once capitalism expanded beyond its original national bases, it tended to subordinate the less developed nations in its path, denying their bourgeoisies the same kind of state organisation. Lenin approved of this big power, assimilationist tendency of capitalist expansion, characterising it as 'one of the greatest driving forces

---

26 Ibid.
27 Lumer (ed.), *Lenin on the Jewish Question*, p. 90.
28 V.I. Lenin, 'On the Right of Nations to Self-determination', in *Collected Works* (Moscow: Progress Publishers, 1977), pp. 20–1.

transforming capitalism into socialism'. He argued that 'the requirements of economic exchange will themselves decide which language of the given country it is to the advantage of the majority to know in the interests of commercial relations. This decision will be all the firmer because it is adopted voluntarily by a population of various nationalities'.[29]

Observing this process unfold in Ukraine at the end of the nineteenth and early twentieth centuries, he remarked:

> For several decades a well-defined process of accelerated economic development has been going on in the South, that is Ukraine, attracting hundreds of thousands of peasants and workers from Great Russia to the capitalist farms, mines, and cities. The 'assimilation' – within these limits – of the Great-Russian and Ukrainian proletariat is an indisputable fact. And this fact is undoubtedly progressive. Capitalism is replacing the ignorant, conservative, settled muzhik of the Great-Russian or Ukrainian backwoods with a mobile proletarian whose conditions of life break down specifically national narrow mindedness, both Great-Russian and Ukrainian. Even if we assume that, in time, there will be a state frontier between Great Russia and Ukraine, the historically progressive nature of the 'assimilation' of the Great-Russian and Ukrainian workers will be as undoubted as the progressive nature of the grinding down of nations in America. The freer Ukraine and Great Russia become, the more extensive and more rapid will be the development of capitalism, which will still more powerfully attract the workers, the working masses of all nations from all regions of the state and from all the neighbouring states (should Russia become a neighbouring state in relation to Ukraine) to the cities, the mines, and the factories.[30]

Yet the assimilation of the Ukrainian workers into the Russian urban and industrial culture was neither voluntary nor progressive. It was a historical consequence of conquest by the Russian state and its nationality policies, of industrialisation and land hunger. That is to say, the 'choice' of national affiliation was as much a product of political and economic coercion as it was a response to political and economic opportunity.

Lenin emphasised the economic superiority of big states over small ones and argued that they prefigured the socialist future. It flowed from this posi-

---

29   Ibid.
30   V.I. Lenin, 'On the Right of Nations to Self-determination', in *Collected Works* (Moscow: Progress Publishers, 1977), pp. 20, 31.

tion that the fragmentation of existing big states, including his own, was a step backwards from the point of view of the proletariat. The proletariat had to contend with the big state in its struggle against autocracy in the east. It had to be united on an all-state level in order to be effective, and the assimilation of workers into a single language and culture objectively promoted this unity.

This argument can be contested even with the facts Lenin himself introduced into the debate. The level of capitalist development in the hinterlands of the Russian Empire was higher than at its centre; if political movements in the hinterlands aimed for the breakup of the semi-feudal, autocratic state and the organisation of independent nation states, was this not to the advantage of capitalist development on a big terrain of the Eurasian continent? Was not the Russian state the policeman of Europe because the bourgeois democratic revolutions had stopped at its borders and were long overdue there? Yet Lenin also believed another historical path was possible – in place of the bourgeoisie, the workers' movement could lead the next revolutionary wave in Tsarist Russia. Its solution to the national question would be different from that of the bourgeoisie.

Lenin did not deny the existence of national oppression. He simply believed that the workers' movement was the best possible historical force to resolve it. National movements complicated the tasks of the workers' movement because they led to the breakup of big states and, as Lenin claimed, they were invariably led by bourgeois or pro-bourgeois classes. If the working class could seize power on its own (the Russian bourgeoisie distinguished little political independence from the autocracy) the proletarian state could resolve national oppression in its own way: by guaranteeing the right of national self-determination while seeking the maximum political unity between proletarians of different nations.

While he continually stressed that national movements advanced the interests of the bourgeoisie, Lenin acknowledged their contribution to the struggle for democracy. It was not easy to distinguish the revolutionary tendencies of national movements that were compatible with the aims of Social Democracy from the reactionary ones:

> It is impossible to estimate beforehand all the possible correlations between the bourgeois emancipation movements of the oppressed nations and the proletarian emancipation movement of the oppressing nation, the very problem which makes the national question so difficult in Russia.[31]

---

31   Lenin, 'On the Right of Nations to Self-determination', p. 278.

Lenin's scheme for a democratic centralist Russian social democratic party was motivated by more than the needs of conspiracy and unity in action. He wanted to create a party that also prepared the assumption of power by mass movements of the working class. As one means to that end, the social democratic party would prefigure socialism. Lenin believed the proletarian state would inherit from the capitalist epoch the advantages of big states, macroscopic economies and international cultures based on the languages of the dominant nations. Like its long-term goal, the social democratic party had to be state-wide, centralised to the maximum degree and not federated, promoting the merger of nations, not their differentiation.

Lenin was the author of a resolution on the national question passed at the 1903 Second RSDWP Congress that 'emphatically refute[d] federation as the organisational principle of a Russian party'. From the floor of the Congress he denounced federalist proposals advanced by Jewish, Polish and Latvian delegates as 'harmful, running counter to the principles of Social Democracy as applied to existing Russian conditions ... Federalism can be justified theoretically only on the basis of nationalist ideas'.[32] He maintained this position on party structure to the end of 1917, conceding a right of autonomy in organisational matters only at a local level.[33]

Against the Austro-Marxist programme of national autonomy and federalism, Lenin advanced the slogan of 'the right of nations to self-determination'. After the 1905 Revolution, he called upon the RSDWP

> to fight against all nationalism and above all against Great Russian nationalism; to recognise not only the complete equality of rights for all nations in general, but also ... the right of nations to self-determination ... [while] preserving the unity of the proletarian struggle and of proletarian organisations.[34]

In his *Theses on the National Question* written in June 1913, Lenin emphasised that the self-determination slogan 'cannot be interpreted to mean anything but political self-determination, that is the right to secede and form a separate state'.[35] At the same time, support for this slogan was not to be confused 'with the expediency of a given nation's secession'. In a resolution prepared for the Bolsheviks' 1913 conference of Central Committee members, Lenin argued

---

32   Lumer (ed.), *Lenin on the Jewish Question*, pp. 26–8.
33   Ibid, p. 70.
34   Lenin, 'On the Right of Nations to Self-determination', p. 292.
35   Lumer (ed.), *Lenin on the Jewish Question*, p. 87.

that support for national self-determination 'most certainly does not mean that Social Democrats reject an independent appraisal of the advisability of the state secession of any nation'. Rather, the Bolsheviks should be prepared to support 'wide regional autonomy and fully democratic local self government' in the Russian Empire and even the secession of Poland and Finland, 'more civilised and more isolated' countries that 'could most easily and most 'naturally' put into effect their right to secession'.[36] That was the limit of concessions as far as he was concerned:

> the proletariat ... far from undertaking to uphold the national development of every nation, on the contrary warns against such illusions, stands for the fullest freedom of capitalist intercourse and welcomes every kind of assimilation of nations except that which is founded on force or privilege.[37]

Lenin's self-determination slogan was more like a promise to the oppressed nations in the Russian Empire that, should the attainment of a democratic republic not also remove national oppression and inequality, they would have full freedom to secede. However, he believed they would not take up that option because

> the more closely the democratic system of state approximates to complete freedom of secession, the rarer and weaker will the strivings for complete freedom of secession be in practice. For the advantages of large states, both from the point of view of economic progress and ... of the interests of the masses, are beyond doubt, and these advantages increase with the growth of capitalism.[38]

Until the social democrats were given a chance to prove their point, workers of all nations should remain in a single revolutionary party and not seek independent roads to national freedom. Democracy would satisfy their demands once autocracy was overthrown, and to achieve this end a united front against Tsarism was needed.

Rosa Luxemburg's position on the national question won many adherents in the Bolshevik party, probably more than Lenin's. Her conclusions seemed

---

36   Ibid, p. 76.
37   Ibid, p. 112.
38   Lenin, *Collected Works*, Vol. XIX, p. 50.

clearer and more consistent with Bolshevik conceptions of democratic centralism than Lenin's self-determination slogan. She charged that the Bolsheviks' official support for national self-determination, notwithstanding the conditions and reservations Lenin voiced about this slogan, stood 'in sharp contradiction to their otherwise outspoken centralism in politics' and could be explained only as 'the result of some opportunistic kind of policy'.[39]

Luxemburg had more reasons to fight the self-determination slogan than to steer the Bolsheviks away from adaptation to national movements. Her party, the Social Democrats of Poland and Lithuania were fighting the nationalist Polish Socialist Party for a base in the working class. Luxemburg strongly opposed Polish nationalism, charging that it blunted workers' attention to the broader struggle, its socio-economic dimension and international context in particular. However, she was confronted by a European socialist tradition that since the days of Marx and Engels had supported Poland's national aspirations. Luxemburg wanted to bury this tradition. She believed that conditions in the Russian Empire had changed so much since the mid-nineteenth century when the Polish rebellions were 'the few rays of light in the dark days of Tsarism'[40] that Marx and Engels's support for Poland's independence was no longer defensible. Because she viewed their support merely as a 'foreign policy' of European socialists against Russian feudalism on behalf of capitalism,[41] Luxemburg set out to devise a new foreign policy. European socialists, she contended, should abandon their traditional homage to Poland and concentrate instead on the new workers' movement emerging throughout the Russian Empire.

Luxemburg echoed the early Marx and Engels by making her support for national movements conditional upon their harmony with capitalist development. Scientific socialism bestowed no eternal rights, national or otherwise, she said. Rather, all rights were determined 'only by the material social conditions of the environment in a given historical epoch'. Her analysis of the capitalist epoch singled out the same dominant tendencies of development to be found in Lenin's work: 'as comprehensive a centralisation as possible in all areas of social life ... the development of world powers' and the ruin of small nations as 'both a necessity and a condition of development for capitalist world powers'.[42] Like Lenin, she identified some of the preconditions of socialism in these dominant tendencies: the point of departure of the world revolution was big state development; centralisation of economic and political power under

---

39 Luxemburg, *The National Question*, p. 292.
40 Ibid, p. 161.
41 Ibid, p. 62.
42 Ibid, pp. 111, 129–30, 189.

capitalism was 'one of the main bases of the future socialist system'; the socialist movement itself possessed 'the same eminently centralist characteristic as the bourgeois society and state'.[43]

Here end the similarities between Luxemburg and Lenin. Luxemburg focused her attention almost exclusively on the centralising, big power tendencies of capitalism and relegated national oppression to last place among the concerns of the proletariat. It was 'only a drop in the ocean of the entire social privation, political abuse and intellectual disinheritance that the wage labourer suffers'.[44] Lenin, on the other hand, detected contradictory tendencies of national assimilation and differentiation in capitalist development. He restrained himself from speculating about an 'inevitable' course for capitalism and, however much he may have disagreed with national movements' separatist trajectory, he acknowledged their revolutionary potential and responded with his self-determination slogan.

Luxemburg's approach boiled down to the position that the independence of weaker nations was no longer possible under capitalism and would be unnecessary under socialism.[45] Then Luxemburg wavered. Acknowledging the Polish proletariat's strong attachment to its language and national culture, she offered a transitional, compensatory slogan. Against Lenin's slogan she put forward the demand for Polish national autonomy. She conceded that 'local autonomy also grows simultaneously out of the objective development and ... needs of bourgeois society' and that it was a requirement of the proletariat as much as of the bourgeoisie. It expressed a general desire 'to overthrow absolutism and ... achieve political freedom in the country at large'.

> The Polish proletariat needs for its class struggle all the components of which a national culture is made ... the elimination of national oppression ... a normal, broad and unrestricted cultural life. ... Our proletariat can and must fight for the defence of national identity as a cultural legacy that has its own right to exist and flourish.[46]

Luxemburg made clear she meant autonomy in cultural and linguistic matters only. She opposed national liberation becoming 'a political goal of the international proletariat' because it was 'a utopian objective'.[47] National liber-

---

43   Ibid, p. 190.
44   Ibid, pp. 46–7.
45   Ibid, p. 140.
46   Ibid, pp. 97, 214, 259.
47   Ibid, p. 57.

ation should be sought not through political independence but by 'overthrowing despotism and solidly implanting the advantages of culture and bourgeois life throughout the entire country, as has long since been done in Western Europe'.[48]

Having distanced herself from the self-determination slogan and relegated the national question to linguistic and cultural demands realisable in a bourgeois democracy, Luxemburg began imposing her own conditions. Whereas Lenin acknowledged the right of self-determination for all nations only to mount strong arguments against its practical implementation for most cases in the Russian Empire, Luxemburg delineated from the outset which nations could aspire to national autonomy and which could not. National autonomy was realisable where the urban classes were 'promoters of the national movement ... where the respective nationality possess[ed] its own bourgeois development, urban life, intelligentsia, its own literary and scholarly life' and a compact territory on which it was the majority.[49]

Of course, the Poles were ready for national autonomy, even in Lithuanian and 'Ruthenian', that is Ukrainian, lands where they were in a minority. 'The only nationality culturally fit to manage national autonomy is the Polish with its urban population, intelligentsia ... the Polish language, the Polish school, Poles in public offices would be the natural expression of the autonomous institutions of the country'.[50]

Like the Ukrainians and Lithuanians, Jews did not qualify for autonomy, 'an entirely utopian idea'. Neither did the Belarusians ('simply impractical'), nor Georgians (the nation was too small), nor any of the peoples of the Caucasus ('no intellectual creativity in their native language').[51] The situation for Ukrainians was not promising at all, Luxemburg noted again in 1918:

> Ukrainian nationalism was something quite different from ... Czech, Polish or Finnish nationalism in that the former was a mere whim, a folly of a few dozen petty bourgeois intellectuals without the slightest roots in the economic, political or psychological relationships of the country; it was without any historical tradition, since Ukraine never formed a nation or government, was without any national culture, except for the reactionary romantic poems of Shevchenko.[52]

---

48   Ibid, p. 97.
49   Ibid, p. 265.
50   Ibid, p. 272.
51   Ibid, pp. 278–9.
52   Ibid, p. 298.

Thus Rosa Luxemburg came full circle by a strange route, departing with the idea that the national question was but 'a drop in the ocean' of the proletariat's misery, passing on to national autonomy as a concession to the proletariat's cultural and linguistic inheritance, and arriving at the conclusion that national autonomy in the Russian Empire was justified only for the Poles! All the other oppressed nations were too small, too mixed up with one another, lacking in creative potential, too reactionary or simply not bourgeois enough to muster the resources necessary for self rule.

Neither Lenin nor Luxemburg studied national movements. Lenin relied almost exclusively on his knowledge of Switzerland, Finland and Norway to back up his arguments. Luxemburg's characterisation of the Ukrainian movement and her list of nations unfit for self-determination speak for themselves. Vsevolod Holubnychy has written that

> As far as the theory of the national question was concerned, scientific socialism ended with Kautsky. Everything after that was pure politics and voluntarism. Marx's prognosis of the assimilation of nations was turned into a programmatic objective by the Bolsheviks, into one of their political goals. While Marx said that under socialism nations will merge, Lenin said that the merger of nations was necessary for socialism and that they should already begin to merge.[53]

3   Social Democracy in Ukraine

A Jewish socialist tradition in the empire dates back to the 1870s when study circles, fraternal insurance societies and strike funds were first organised in the community. Jewish socialist circles multiplied across the Pale of Settlement after the pogroms of 1881–82 and Alexander II's Temporary Rules drove many Jews out of the rural areas into the bigger towns and cities. There they set to work among a new generation of urbanised and increasingly proletarianised Jews. As the growth of mass commodity production destroyed small enterprises and trades, young Jews faced ever diminishing prospects of becoming self employed artisans or traders as their parents had been. At the same time they faced the daunting predicament of competing for wage labour with other nationalities in urban centres of the Pale which traditionally had had

---

[53] Vsevolod Holubnychy, 'Sotsiialistychni Teorii Natsional'noi Problemy', *Suchasnist'* August 1961, p. 75.

little industry to speak of. The first shoots of a militant workers' movement in the Jewish community appeared in such circumstances during the 1890s. This movement, while forwarding economic and generally democratic demands, could not ignore the national question. The rapid social changes combined with the intensification of official and popular antisemitism were politicising Jewish perceptions of their language, customs, history and religion, their community, transforming them into objects of collective self-defence.

Many Jews chose emigration as their best chance for survival. Those who stayed behind chose to organise and fight for equal rights with the rest of society. Formed in 1897, the Jewish General Workers Union (Bund) was a leading exponent of this second alternative for Jews, which it called 'auto-emancipation'.[54] At a Mayday rally outside Vilnius in 1897 organised by the Bund, Julius Martov declared that

> the aim of Jewish social democrats who are active among the Jews is to build a special Jewish workers' organisation that will educate the Jewish proletariat and lead it in the struggle for economic, civil and political rights ... the pressing task is to win for every nation if not political autonomy then at least full equal rights.[55]

The first major discussion on national rights among Bund members that went beyond considerations of civil rights took place at their Third Congress in 1899. No resolution was forthcoming because the Bund feared a public declaration of national rights might be misinterpreted as splitting the working class movement.[56] However, at the party's Fourth Congress in May 1901 delegates adopted a resolution asserting that

> Each nationality, apart from its aspirations for economic, civil and political freedom and full rights, also has national aspirations based on ... language, customs, way of life, culture in general – which ought to have full freedom of development.[57]

---

[54] Jonathan Frankel, *Prophecy and Politics: Socialism, Nationalism and Russian Jews 1862–1917* (Cambridge: Cambridge University Press, 1981), p. 49.

[55] Martov later became a prominent Menshevik. See Henry J. Tobias, *The Jewish Bund in Russia from its Origins to 1905* (Stanford: Stanford University Press, 1972), p. 55. Gozhansky, another Bundist, wrote that 'the working class which can reconcile itself to the ill fate of a particular nation will never rise up against the ill fate of a particular class'. Cited by Frankel, *Prophecy and Politics*, p. 192.

[56] Tobias, *The Jewish Bund*, pp. 105–6.

[57] Ibid, p. 160.

They proposed that each nation in the Russian Empire have the right to 'full national autonomy regardless of the territory it occupies',[58] echoing the defeated resolution of the South Slav delegation at the 1899 Brunn Congress. In line with this programmatic objective, the Bund called for a federated social democratic party in the Russian Empire in which it would be recognised as 'a representative of the Jewish proletariat'.[59] The Sixth Bund Congress in October 1905 repeated the call for national autonomy and demanded that state and local authorities relinquish control of all matters dealing with culture and education to elected assemblies of each nation.[60]

In 1902 the Bund created armed self-defence committees to fight pogroms. Its members agitated for the abolition of legal restrictions and urged the community not to wait for government reforms but to organise and press for change. It conducted strikes, often against Jewish employers, smuggled revolutionary literature into the Empire and published clandestine Yiddish language literature of its own.[61]

The Bund was also in the forefront of efforts to convene an Empire-wide social democratic party. The Russian Social Democratic Workers Party envisaged by Bund leaders was quite different from the one envisaged by Lenin. The Bund wanted the national question addressed differently in the RSDWP's principles, programme and organisational structure. While it sought unity with social democratic organisations throughout the Empire, it also guarded its political and organisational independence and insisted upon special attention to the needs of the Jewish working class.

The Bund's approach to the national question in the workers' movement did not sit well with the luminaries of European socialism. Marx, Kautsky, Lenin and Luxemburg all denied that Jews were a nation. They characterised them as a caste that would disappear with the advent of democracy in European society.[62] Lenin referred to 'the Zionist idea of a Jewish nation' as being 'absolutely untenable scientifically and reactionary politically'.[63] Kautsky claimed that 'Jews have ceased to be a nation' and that hostility toward them would disappear only when they had assimilated completely into the dominant nations.[64]

---

58   Frankel, *Prophecy and Politics*, p. 220.
59   Tobias, *The Jewish Bund*, p. 165.
60   Salo Baron, *The Russian Jew under Tsars and Soviets* (New York: Macmillan, 1964), pp. 171–2; Frankel, *Prophecy and Politics*, p. 246.
61   Tobias, *The Jewish Bund*, pp. 226–7.
62   Lumer (ed.), *Lenin on the Jewish Question*, pp. 23, 39, 48–9, 71; Tobias, *The Jewish Bund*, p. 172; Frankel, *Prophecy and Politics*, p. 198.
63   Lumer (ed.), *Lenin on the Jewish Question*, pp. 48–9.
64   Cited in Lumer (ed.), *Lenin on the Jewish Question*, p. 47.

But the authority of ideas in the social democratic movement found a strong opponent in the reality of numbers. When the RSDWP was being formed, the Jewish workers' movement was its most experienced and numerically strongest section. The Bund simply could not be excluded from the RSDWP nor expected to join on terms contrary to its basic positions. At the RSDWP's founding congress in 1898, it was accorded 'full autonomy ... both in organisation and in coping with problems related specifically to Jewish workers'.[65]

In the period leading up to the 1903 Second RSDWP Congress, Lenin led the Iskra group in the party in the fight for a democratic centralist organisation. He secured a narrow majority in support of his ideas which forced Jewish, Latvian and Polish social democrats to quit the RSDWP after the 1903 Congress rejected all proposals for a federated structure.[66] The Bund made repeated attempts to rejoin the RSDWP, but found a fierce opponent in Lenin until 1906. The Stockholm 'Reunification' Congress of 1906 readmitted the Bund and recognised it as 'the sole representative of the Jewish proletariat'. Although the Stockholm Congress explicitly rejected federative schemes of party building, it adopted no general resolution on the national question. Bund members were free to pursue their own programme although they were not supposed to have a separate leadership.[67] Of the 58 votes cast in favour of their readmission, 41 came from Bolshevik delegates and 17 from Mensheviks. Thirty-eight Mensheviks were opposed.

During the entire debate on the Bund's application, Lenin remained uncharacteristically silent.[68] How is one to interpret his silence and the fact that the Stockholm Congress passed no resolution on the national question? Lenin was acutely aware that the balance of forces in the social democratic camp before and during the 1905 Revolution increasingly leaned in favour of national autonomy in principle and party organisation. National branches of Social Democracy were organised before 1905 by Jews, Ukrainians, Belarusians, Armenians, Georgians and Latvians, all of whom wanted to join a federated RSDWP as autonomous members.[69] At the Stockholm Congress, the Bund reported a membership of 33,000, the Social Democrats of Poland and Lith-

---

65   Tobias, *The Jewish Bund*, p. 79.
66   Matvii Yavorsky, *Istoriia Ukrainy v Styslomy Narysi*, 2nd edn (Kharkiv: Derzhavne Vydavnytstvo Ukrainy, 1928), p. 249.
67   Frankel, *Prophecy and Politics*, pp. 248–9.
68   Ibid.
69   Tobias, *The Jewish Bund*, pp. 172, 284; Lumer (ed.), *Lenin on the Jewish Question*, pp. 152–3.

uania 26,000, the Latvians 14,000, the USDWP, whose application was rejected at Stockholm, 6,000. The RSDWP's membership stood at 31,000.[70]

The Bund's readmission to the RSDWP in 1906 without opposition from Lenin or binding resolutions on the national question as such was an indication of the RSDWP's leaders' respect for the Bund's influence in the workers' movement and of the RSDWP's rank and file members' desire to forego programmatic unity in favour of unity in action. Even the Bolsheviks and Mensheviks were making amends in 1906 under pressure from their rank and file. Most of the national social democratic parties stood closer to the Bolsheviks than the Mensheviks on practically all issues except the national question during the 1905 Revolution. Lenin apparently did not want the national question to be a source of damaging divisions at the time, for there was much to be gained by the Bolshevik faction from admitting people to the party who stood close to it in most other respects. So he clenched his teeth, hoping to soften antagonisms with the Bund for the moment and return to the national question at a future date.

The Bund distinguished itself among Jewish political parties by its resolute opposition to Zionism, a movement that was rapidly gaining adherents across the Diaspora at the turn of the century. Zionists advocated the establishment of an entirely separate state for Jews as the only lasting solution to their historic predicament as a discriminated, excluded and stateless people. As Zionism gained currency right across the ideological spectrum of organised politics in Jewish communities, it was embraced by some social democrats who sought to cross fertilise it with Marxism.

Foremost among such synthesisers was Ber Borochov, an early exponent of Labour Zionism. Borochov was born and raised in Poltava province and cut his teeth in the RSDWP in Katerynoslav before being expelled for his Zionist views. He subsequently organised, in 1900, a 150-strong Labour Zionist Socialist Alliance in Katerynoslav which deployed a self-defence group during the Pesach pogrom in 1901 and organised a tailors' strike, the first strike of Jewish workers in the city, in the same year.

Whereas the Bund's branches were concentrated in Poland and Lithuania, Labour Zionist groups emerged further south, first in Minsk in 1897, then Katerynoslav in 1900, and Odesa in 1902. From such groups the Jewish Social Democratic Party Poale Zion (Workers of Zion) was constituted in July 1905 at a conference in Kyiv, which in February of the following year adopted its programme and organisational structure at a conspiratorial congress in Poltava.

---

70   Lumer (ed.), *Lenin on the Jewish Question*, p. 63.

Once established Poale Zion's work in the Russian Empire was concentrated in the Ukrainian and Belarusian provinces.[71]

The party's ultimate goal was a global socialist society, and its immediate aim was Zionism: preparing the Jewish people to establish their own homeland. In it they would develop a complete social structure, with a proletariat and a bourgeoisie rooted directly into the means of production in land, rather than being excluded from the land and other means of production, restricted in their occupations and their area of settlement. This homeland would be Palestine, where Jews would enjoy political territorial autonomy alongside Arabs already settled there, and where the class struggle between the proletariat and bourgeoisie would unfold and lead to socialism. To ensure socialism was achieved, however, Poale Zion advocated building a Jewish proletarian movement to consciously prepare Palestine for settlement and to lead the Jewish exodus there from out of the Diaspora. To those ends, Poale Zion systematically sent activists from its own ranks to establish and maintain branches in Palestine, Europe and North America. Borochov recalled that 'Russia was for a long period the foundry in which Poale Zionist thought was molten and cast for the whole world'.[72]

Labour Zionists assumed also that a large part of the Jewish people would remain behind in their Diaspora, and so national political autonomy for minorities, the second strand of Austro-Marxists' solution to the national question, was demanded for Jewish communities living in every separate state. However, Borochov believed this was an unsatisfactory resolution of the problem for Jews living in the Russian state because national autonomy did not address the abnormal conditions in which they were forced to live, which he feared would only worsen with the further development of capitalism in the autocratic state.[73] In the long run, Poale Zion found itself under tension between three objectives: seeking unity in action with other social democratic and workers' parties to advance general working class goals; national political autonomy for Jews in the empire; and national territorial autonomy for Jews in a new state in Palestine.

The origins of the Russian Social Democratic Workers Party (RSDWP) can be traced to social democratic circles of the intelligentsia established in the late

---

71　Ber Borochov, 'Reminiscences. On the Occasion of the Tenth Anniversary of the Poale Zion in Russia, 1906–1916', http://www.marxistsfr.org/archive/borochov/1916/reminiscences.htm [accessed 5 July 2017].

72　Ibid.

73　Ber Borochov, *Class Struggle and the Jewish Nation: Selected Essays in Marxist Zionism*, edited with an introduction by Mitchell Cohen (New Brunswick: Transaction Books, 1984), p. 91.

1880s and 1890s which made contact with radical workers during the strikes of 1896–99. In Ukraine, such circles appeared first in Kharkiv, Odesa, Kyiv, Kherson, Mykolaiv, Poltava and Katerynoslav. They spread into the Donbas in 1900–02 with the active assistance of social democratic committees based in Katerynoslav and Rostov-on-Don. RSDWP militants gained initial experience working with proletarians on a day-to-day basis in the South Russian Workers' Unions, which were active in Odesa, Kyiv, Kharkiv and Mykolaiv between 1875 and 1897, in the Unions of Struggle for the Emancipation of the Working Class in Kyiv, Odesa, Katerynoslav, Mykolaiv and Kharkiv between 1892 and 1903, and in the unemployment insurance and strike fund societies (*kasy*) which had a long history in the labour movement and became widespread at the end of the nineteenth century. The first Russian language periodicals in Ukraine to popularise social democratic ideas and to report extensively on working class unrest were *Vpered* and *Rabochaia Gazeta* in Kyiv, *Nashe Delo* in Mykolaiv and *Yuzhnii Rabochii* in Katerynoslav.[74]

The initiative to form the RSDWP came from the Bund and the Kyiv Union of Struggle for the Emancipation of the Working Class. Six of the nine delegates to its founding Congress in Minsk in 1898 were from these organisations. The Kyiv Union's newspaper *Rabochaia Gazeta* became the RSDWP's first official publication.[75]

At its Second Congress in 1903, the RSDWP adopted a resolution on the national question prepared by Lenin. It called for the right of all nations to self-determination, broad local self government, use of native languages in educational and administrative institutions and full equality of nations before the law. These demands served as the party's basic programme throughout the period leading up to the 1917 Revolution.[76]

Twelve of the 43 delegates attending the Second Congress were from Ukraine. Although they did not constitute an identifiable bloc in programmatic debates, the delegates from *Yuzhnii Rabochii* in Katerynoslav formed a bloc to oppose Lenin's scheme for the subordination of Russian operations to emigre

---

74 F. Ie. Los (gen. ed.), *Istoriia Robitnychoho Klasu Ukrains'koi RSR*, 2 vols (Kyiv: Naukova Dumka, 1967), Vol. 1, pp. 194–5; Isaak Mazepa, *Bol'shevyzm i Okupatsiia Ukrainy: Sotsiial'no-ekonomichni prychyny nedozrilosty syl Ukrains'koi Revoliutsii* (Lviv-Kyiv: Znattia to Syla, 1922), pp. 15–16; N.N. Popov, *Narys Istorii Komunistychnoi Partii (Bil'shovykiv) Ukrainy* (Kharkiv: Proletaryi, 1930), pp. 37–9; Yavorsky, *Istoriia Ukrainy*, p. 244; M. Ravich Cherkassky, 'Robitnychi Orhanizatsii na Ukraini v 70-kh, 80-kh i 90-kh rokakh', *Chervonyi Shliakh*, November 1923.

75 R. Carter Elwood, *Russian Social Democracy in the Underground* (Assen: Van Gorcun and Co., 1974), pp. 11–12.

76 Ibid, p. 256.

control and were instrumental in splitting the party into its Menshevik and Bolshevik wings.[77]

By 1905, the RSDWP had branches in Tahanrih, Yuzivka, Sloviansk, Mariupol, Katerynoslav, Luhansk, Kyiv, Kremenchuk, Poltava, Yelyzavethrad, Mykolaiv and Odesa. Party cells existed in Zhytomyr, Oleksandrivsk, Berdychiv, Kherson, Chernihiv and Konotop. The Mensheviks had a bigger following in the Ukrainian branches of the RSDWP than the Bolsheviks. Of the 12 delegates from Ukraine to the 1903 Congress, 7 were Mensheviks. At the 1907 RSDWP Congress, 78 percent of all Bolshevik delegates were Russians, 11 percent were Jews and 3 percent Georgians. Russians made up only 34 percent of the Menshevik delegation, followed in size by Georgians at 28 percent, Jews 22 percent and Ukrainians 6.5 percent.[78]

Except in periods of great social crisis, the Mensheviks had more supporters in the labour movement in Ukraine than the Bolsheviks. They had more experienced leaders in big industries and a broad following among workers of different nationalities employed in small industries and trades. N.N. Popov argues that Menshevism owed its strength in Ukraine mainly to the weight of the Jewish craft proletariat, whose political representative the Bund went mainly into the Menshevik faction in 1906 when it was readmited to the RSDWP.[79]

The Bolsheviks had strongholds in the south among miners and metalworkers. Relatively young, unskilled but inclined to radical labour action, the heavy industry and assembly line proletariat remained loyal to the Bolsheviks when the years of reaction rolled in after the defeat of the 1905 Revolution. Bolshevik committees of the RSDWP survived only in Katerynoslav, Mykolaiv, Odesa and throughout the Donbas.[80] Elsewhere they fell apart and were practically non-existent in the Right Bank provinces. One of the main reasons for their poor showing outside the Donbas was the 'completely unclear slogan' of self-determination put forward by Lenin and their reputation as an RSDWP faction accessible only to Russian workers.[81] Another important reason was that the Bolsheviks lacked a stable leadership based permanently in Ukraine. Mykola Skrypnyk, a prominent Ukrainian Bolshevik, recalls that professional organisers were sent periodically into Ukrainian branches with specific assign-

---

77 Ibid, p. 14.
78 Popov, *Narys Istorii*, pp. 39, 63; Los, *Istoriia Robitnychoho Klasu*, Vol. 2, p. 257.
79 Popov, *Narys Istorii*, p. 63.
80 Isaak Mazepa, *Ukraina v Ohni i Buri Revoliutsii 1917–21*, 3 vols, 2nd edn (n.p.: Prometei, 1950) Vol. 1, p. 10; A.S. Pidhainy, 'The Formation of the Communist Party (Bolsheviks) of Ukraine', PhD thesis, McGill University, 1977, p. 35; Popov, *Narys Istorii*, p. 77.
81 Volodymyr Levynsky, *Yedyna Nedilyma Sovits'ka Rosiia* (Kyiv-Vienna: n.p., 1920), p. 11.

ments but did not remain for long. During periods of political decline, including downturns in the Civil War, the most capable Bolshevik cadres headed for Russia.[82]

The Ukrainian Social Democratic Workers Party (USDWP) was a latecomer to the social democratic camp, emerging as the major faction in its predecessor organisation, the Revolutionary Ukrainian Party (RUP) between 1902 and 1905. Like the Bund, the USDWP drew some of its theoretical heritage from the late Marx and Engels and the Austro-Hungarian social democrats. It built a national following in the working class and sought membership in the RSDWP on terms of autonomy and federation. It saw its first task as the mobilisation of agricultural workers and their political unification with industrial workers.

It would be misleading, however, to define the USDWP's ideological profile solely as the net result of affinities and differences with different strands of the Marxist tradition and other social democratic parties in its vicinity. Such a definition gives some idea of the USDWP's place in the social democratic camp, but it says nothing of the formidable influence exerted on the USDWP by earlier generations who attempted to wed national liberation to particular revolutionary ideologies of their time. The Ukrainian national movement was a hundred years old by 1900. As a social democratic expression of this movement, the USDWP was following on from earlier generations of populists and anarcho-socialist revolutionaries. Populism dominated Ukrainian history writing in the 1830s and 1840s, focusing attention on movements of the lower classes and on the cossack tradition in particular.[83] Demands for Ukrainian self-determination were voiced already in the 1820s by members of the Decembrist movement and in 1830 by supporters of the Polish insurrection.[84]

The first explicit programme of the Ukrainian national movement, however, was the 1847 Manifesto of the Brotherhood of Saints Cyril and Methodius, formed in 1846 in Kyiv. The Manifesto called for political freedom and equality, the abolition of serfdom and all social rank, a federation of independent Slavic republics to replace the Russian Empire and the direct, universal election of government deputies and all state functionaries. One of its members was the poet Taras Shevchenko, whom Rosa Luxemburg was to denounce in

---

[82] M.O. Skrypnyk, 'Nacherk istorii proletars'koi revoliutsii na Ukraini', *Chervonyi Shliakh*, April 1923, p. 99.

[83] Isaak Mazepa, *Pidstavy Nashoho Vidrodzhennia*, 2 vols (n.p.: Prometei, 1946), Vol. 1, pp. 108, 113; Hans Kohn, *The Idea of Nationalism: A Study in its Origins and Background* (New York: Macmillan, 1944), pp. 715–16.

[84] M. Yavorsky, *Revoliutsiia na Vkraini v ii holovnishykh etapakh* (Kharkiv: Derzhavne Vydavnytstvo Ukrainy, 1923), pp. 8–10.

her ignorance as a 'romantic reactionary'. Shevchenko was the most outspoken Ukrainian critic of Tsarism of his generation. He spent ten years in Siberian exile for his membership in the Brotherhood of Sts Cyril and Methodius.[85]

A formidable influence on Ukrainian Social Democracy in its youth was Mykhailo Drahomanov. Originally a member of the 1860s student generation which upheld the political traditions of the Brotherhood, Drahomanov was deeply involved in the 'turn to the people' advocated by the populists.[86] This generation in Ukraine contributed many leaders to the militarist organisation *Narodnaia Volia*, to populist propaganda cells in the cities and to the South Russian Workers' Unions.[87] Drahomanov was the link between the generation of the 1860s and 1870s and the radical circles of the 1890s from which the Ukrainian social democratic movement emerged.[88]

A publicist and scholar, Drahomanov was well known abroad in Europe as a representative of Russian anarcho-socialism. He corresponded with Herzen, Lavrov, Marx and Bakunin at different times in his life. He associated with Andrii Zheliabov, leader of *Narodnaia Volia*, who asked him to represent the organisation in Western Europe.[89] He was a student of Jewish history and politics and tried to promote a working relationship between Ukrainian and Jewish socialists in the 1870s.[90]

As an anarcho-socialist, Drahomanov opposed the centralised state as a goal for revolutionaries. He advocated the self organisation of labouring communities and their spontaneous federation on a local, regional, national and international level. His conception of national self-determination grew out of this federalist conviction rather than from latter day socialist ideas about the seizure, destruction and wholesale replacement of state powers.

> People require equality and communal economy above all. These are the roots of freedom for people whether they already have a state or not … Such a large number of people as those inhabiting Ukraine cannot belong to one association. Otherwise it will cease to be a free association. They

---

85 D.I. Bahalii, *Taras Shevchenko i Kyrylo-Metodiivtsi* (Kharkiv: Derzhavne Vydavnytstvo Ukrainy, 1925), pp. 27, 36; Yavorsky, *Revoliutsiia na Vkraini*, pp. 12–13.
86 Yavorsky, *Istoriia Ukrainy*, p. 200.
87 Mykhailo Drahomanov, *Vybrani Tvory*, edited by P. Bohatsky (Prague/New York: Ukrainski Postupovi Tovarystva v Amerytsi, 1937), p. 16; Ivan Maistrenko, *Borot'bism: A Chapter in the History of Ukrainian Communism* (New York: Research Programme on the USSR, 1954), p. 51.
88 Mazepa, *Pidstavy*, Vol. 1, p. 150.
89 Maistrenko, *Borot'bism*, p. 6.
90 Frankel, *Prophecy and Politics*, pp. 101–3.

> must become an association of associations, a union of communities, each free in its own matters ... only small states, or better put, communities and associations can be truly free ... [those] which deal with one another directly or through elected representatives in each separate matter .... It is more worthwhile for Ukrainian communities to seek the greatest possible freedom for themselves than to strive for a more or less centralised state power in Ukraine.[91]

Drahomanov concluded from his fieldwork that, although Ukrainians had not been united previously in a single state and were poorly educated, they identified with one another across their common national territory. Peasants invariably travelled to areas already settled by their co-nationals in search of work, disregarding existing state boundaries. 'Times of the most powerful peasant rebellions against the nobility revealed the greatest efforts of communities from all over Ukraine to associate with one another'. A collective memory of the *Zaporiz'ka Sich*, which Drahomanov found resided among peasants in all parts of the country, was his clearest evidence of their attachment to a national territory.

> Only among the literate people have such memories faded ... the literate people respect state borders and partitions because they have little to do with the commoners [*muzhyky*] and more with the ruling class. They have been educated in foreign schools in preparation for service in the kingdom and the state between which our Ukraine is partitioned.[92]

Drahomanov saw as one of his most important tasks the unification of radicals in the populist and national movements. When he became politically active in the 1860s, the Ukrainian national movement had lost much of its political edge and was immersed in cultural pursuits. Its most promising activists turned to Russian populist organisations as soon as they embraced radical politics. Turning to Ukrainians in Russian populist organisations, Drahomanov urged them to begin to think of their own organisations and different methods of work applicable to the real conditions of life in their country.[93] Without rejecting the cultural work undertaken by the Ukrainophile milieu, he urged the younger generation in it to turn to politics and broaden the national movement's social base.

---

91 Drahomanov, *Vybrani Tvory*, pp. 114–15, 141.
92 Ibid, p. 93.
93 Ibid, p. 122.

Drahomanov was convinced that whatever their national affiliation, revolutionaries who worked among the peasants in Ukraine would be drawn to the Ukrainophile persuasion of Shevchenko and other leaders of the 1840s generation.

> We believe that all community work in Ukraine should be clothed in Ukrainian garb. Of course, 'Ukrainianism' is not part of the aims of this work. The goals of human labour are the same throughout the world – they are the product of the same scientific thinking. However, the applied science is not the same everywhere, and so it is with community work. For every country, every community and even each individual, there have to be separate approaches to the attainment of the same solutions. These are the lessons drawn from the efforts of the International Workingmen's Association.[94]

Drahomanov was forced by the authorities into exile in 1875. He settled in Geneva and together with a small group of co-thinkers began issuing the first Ukrainian language socialist periodical, *Hromada*, and a series of pamphlets aimed at a peasant audience. The *Hromada* circle exerted a strong influence on the socialist movement in Galicia as well as in Russian Ukraine. It persuaded radicals on both sides of the border between Russia and Austro-Hungary to establish contact and co-operate in smuggling literature into the east.[95]

Serhii Podolynsky was one of its most active members. A physician by training, Podolynsky cultivated a range of interests including the relationship of solar energy to the labour theory of value (taking coal and sugar as his case studies), the health standards of the peasantry and the history of industry and trade in Ukraine. During the ten years of his life in which he was able to study and write, Podolynsky produced about twenty journal articles, several major studies and four propagandistic brochures. He authored the first three pamphlets put out by the Geneva circle: *Parova Mashyna* (The Steam Engine) which appeared in several other European languages as well, *Pro Bidnist'* (On Poverty), a popular exposition of Marx's labour theory of value, and *Pravda* (Truth), an adaptation of the Russian brochure *Khytraia Mekhanika* (The Cunning Trick), which dealt with the injustices of taxation. In 1880, his *Remesla i Fabryky na*

---

94   Ibid.
95   Yavorsky, *Istoriia Ukrainy*, p. 209; Mazepa, *Pidstavy*, Vol. 1, pp. 140–1; Drahomanov, *Vybrani Tvory*, p. 155.

Ukraini (Crafts and Industry in Ukraine) appeared in print. Like Drahomanov, Podolynsky spent much of his adult life in exile.[96]

Mykola Ziber, another close associate of Drahomanov, was the first university professor in the Russian Empire to lecture on Marx's *Capital*. In 1870, Ziber and Podolynsky organised a workers' study group in Kyiv that looked into Marx's economic thought. Ziber was also a member of the South Russian Geographical Society whose activities in the early 1870s had prompted the authorities to exile Drahomanov and bring in the infamous Ems *ukaz*.[97]

The relatively small number of people involved in the first Ukrainian socialist initiative had much to do with harassment by the authorities, a lack of legal channels for work in the Ukrainian language and the exile of its most promising leaders. Added to this, the indifference and sometimes outright hostility of Russian populist organisations to national demands discouraged Ukrainian radicals from raising them themselves. Drahomanov corresponded with Zheliabov, a member of *Narodnaia Volia*, on this issue. Asked about his organisation's silence on the national question, Zheliabov replied:

> How can we place in a programme of immediate demands those which have no real support or defence, just a lot of fierce enemies? Where are our Fenians, where's our Parnell?[98]

Personal misfortunes also removed prematurely from the scene both Podolynsky and Ziber. Podolynsky became mentally ill and was confined in French psychiatric institutions. His mother brought him back to Kyiv in 1885 where he died six years later without recovering. Mykola Ziber also suffered a mental breakdown and died in 1885.[99]

Drahomanov became a solitary figure in the 1880s in his various places of exile. He died in Sofia, Bulgaria in 1895. His archives are there at the university. Shunned by moderate Ukrainophiles for his socialist views and by Russian socialists for his stress on the national question, Drahomanov reserved his energy for the younger generation becoming politically active in Russian Ukraine. During the 1880s and 1890s clandestine student groups that read and discussed Shevchenko, Drahomanov, the economist Mykola Yasnopolsky, also

---

96 Roman Serbyn, 'In Defence of an independent Ukrainian socialist movement: Three letters from Serhii Podolynsky to Valeriian Smirnov', *Journal of Ukrainian Studies*, 13 (Fall 1982), pp. 3–33.
97 Ibid.
98 Cited in Mazepa, *Pidstavy*, Vol. 1, pp. 120–1.
99 Serbyn, 'In Defence of an Independent Ukrainian Socialist Movement', p. 8.

a member of the South Russian Geographical Society, and a range of Galician radical thinkers appeared in Kyiv, Chernihiv, Kherson, Katerynoslav, Kharkiv and in many towns of Poltava province.[100] These circles were indebted mainly to Drahomanov for their initial conversion to political action and their attention to the national question. They were the organisers of the Socialist Ukrainian Party in 1897, the Revolutionary Ukrainian Party in 1900 and the Ukrainian Social Democratic Party in 1905.[101]

The first group to attempt a critique of Drahomanov's orientation to the peasantry was a social democratic circle organised in 1893 by Ivan Steshenko, poet and philosophy student at Kyiv University. The circle included people like Lesia Ukrainka, *nom de plume* of Liarysa Kosach, the poet and niece of Drahomanov, the writer Mykhailo Kotsiubynsky and Pavlo Tuchapsky, a founding member of the Kyiv Union of Struggle for the Emancipation of the Working Class. Their main criticism of Drahomanov was that he failed to recognise the social differentiation of the peasantry in the late nineteenth century into wage earning, small holding and wealthy (*kurkul'*) strata. While a part of the peasantry thrown off the land was going into the industrial working class, much of it remained in the countryside as a seasonal wage labour force employed by big agricultural industries. The Steshenko group decided to concentrate their efforts on this rural contingent of the working class and to prepare it for collaboration with urban workers.[102]

In 1897 its members established the Socialist Ukrainian Party (SUP). The long-term goal facing the party was to unite rural and urban workers in Ukraine into a single political movement. This objective required a differentiated approach: raising the national consciousness of urban workers 'so that they would not become strangers to their original identity and to their brothers, the village workers', whereas the priority in the rural areas was to spread socialist propaganda among the village workers and small holding peasantry.[103]

---

[100] George Boshyk, 'The Rise of Ukrainian Political Parties in Russia 1900–1907. With Special Reference to Social Democracy', PhD Thesis, Oxford University, 1981, p. 30. See also O. Ohloblyn, 'Problema ukrains'koi ekonomyky v naukovyi i hromads'kyi dumtsi XIX–XXV', *Chervonyi Shliakh*, 9–10 (1928), p. 178; Drahomanov, *Vybrani Tvory*, p. 27; Yurij Borys, *The Russian Communist Party and the Sovietisation of Ukraine: A Study in the Communist Doctrine of the Self-determination of Nations* (Stockholm: n.p., 1960), p. 75; O. Hermaize, *Narysy z Istorii Revoliutsiinoho Rukhu na Ukraini. Tom 1: RUP* (Kyiv: Knyhospilka, 1926), pp. 52, 54–5; Yuliian Bachynsky, *Ukraina Irredenta*, 3rd edn (Berlin: Vydavnytstvo Ukrains'koi Molodi, 1924), pp. vi–vii.

[101] O. Hermaize, '25 Littia RUP', *Zhyttia i Revoliutsiia*, no. 3 (1925), p. 20.

[102] Yavorsky, *Istoriia Ukrainy*, p. 251; Hermaize, *Narysy z Istorii*, p. 43; Boshyk, 'The Rise of Ukrainian Political Parties', pp. 41–2.

[103] Boshyk, 'The Rise of Ukrainian Political Parties', p. 100; O.M. Fed'kov, V.A. Dubins'kyi,

Except for a modest network of contacts with communities of rural workers around Kyiv, the SUP failed to sink roots into a broad social base. However, it survived until 1903 when it fused with the Revolutionary Ukrainian Party and endowed it with the general strategy its members had worked out in the 1890s.[104]

A numerically larger and more heterogenous alliance of Drahomanovists, Marxists and nationalists, the Revolutionary Ukrainian Party (RUP) was founded in Kharkiv in February 1900 by a group of students led by D. Antonovych and M. Rusov.[105] Initially RUP was based among high school, university and theological seminary students, the sons and daughters of peasants, Ukrainian gentry and clergy. RUP branches were established across the northern tier province towns and cities of Kyiv, Poltava, Chernihiv, Nizhyn, Pryluky and Romny as well as Petrograd, Lviv and Chernivtsi. The Party's Foreign Committee worked out of the last two centres in the Austro-Hungarian state editing, publishing and smuggling literature across the border.[106]

RUP was deeply involved in the student movement and played a major part in the university strikes of 1900 and 1901. During the widespread peasant disturbances in the summer of 1902 and workers' strikes in 1903, RUP had an opportunity to broaden its social base. Its members moved first into the countryside and organised successful strikes of agricultural workers in the Left and Right Bank provinces. RUP's rural work boosted its prestige in the towns and attracted some urban Ukrainian workers to the party. The secret police also pricked up their ears and began infiltrating the organisation.[107]

Most of its new urban recruits were transient workers from the villages, including porters, servants, stable hands, laundry and bakery workers. The Kyiv branch organised a circle at the end of 1902 in which painters, goldsmiths and wood carvers who produced icons mainly for village churches and who travelled regularly to outlying districts assumed an active role. These *ikonostas* workers previously belonged to Russian socialist committees in the city and were experienced agitators. The branch also made contact with workers in small factories in nearby towns that produced lace and wood products. Although most Ukrainians employed there were seasonal workers and thus

---

'Ahrarne pytannia v programnykh dokumentakh natsional'nykh politychnykh partii nadniprians'koi Ukrainy u 90-kh pokakh XIX st.', *Politolohichni Studii*, 3 (2013).

104 Yavorsky, *Istoriia Ukrainy*, p. 251.
105 Borys, *The Russian Communist Party*, p. 72; Popov, *Narys Istorii*, p. 40; Mazepa, *Bols'hevyzm*, p. 16.
106 Boshyk, 'The Rise of Ukrainian Political Parties', pp. 106–9; Hermaize, '25 Littia RUP', p. 21.
107 Boshyk, 'The Rise of Ukrainian Political Parties', pp. 106–9, 144–5; Hermaize, *Narysy z Istorii*, pp. 84–5, 98; Yavorsky, *Istoriia Ukrainy*, p. 232.

limited in their ability to organise on the job, they were valued by RUP as agitators and couriers of political literature into the countryside. During the summer of 1903, these migrant workers acted as foot soldiers for another strike movement in the northern provinces which at its height involved over two hundred thousand estate workers.[108]

The Kharkiv RUP branch made contact with railway workers living in nearby Liutotyn and Nova Bavaria in the autumn of 1902. Andrii Zhuk, one of RUP's Kharkiv leaders, managed to set up a study circle that read and distributed party literature in villages along the railway lines its members worked. After the July 1903 strike wave

> a group calling itself the Organising Committee of the Railway Lines of South Russia joined the RUP. Its members, who worked on several lines ... were mostly machinists, stokers, conductors, telegraphists, clerks and switchmen ... The Committee's general intentions were to spread socialist and revolutionary ideas among the railway employees and to organise the more politically conscious workers into one organisation ... The Committee accepted the RUP programme.[109]

In 1904, the Galician socialist publication *Volia* reported that RUP had 'good workers' organisations' in Kharkiv, Poltava, Nizhyn, Katerynodar, Lubny, Romny, Pryluky, Hlukhiv, Kremenets and Bila Tserkva. The Lubny RUP branch was credited with three workers' committees totalling 150 men and women.[110]

While RUP was based in urban centres and made attempts to reach workers living there, it kept in the forefront an imperative to recruit workers who travelled periodically through the countryside and could act as radical agents among rural workers. The villager who spent time in the town and knew something about the workers' movement there was the ideal RUP activist. He was the link between the urban and rural workers, a link the RUP wanted to build into a strategic alliance over the long term.[111]

RUP literature focused on the concerns of the poor peasant and the seasonal worker. While its urban branches produced their own May Day proclamations, leaflets and brochures that took up urban workers' concerns, RUP's main literary arsenal that issued from across the border articulated the desires of rural

---

108   S. Shupak, 'RUP v periodi 1905 roku na Kyivshchyni', *Zhyttia i Revoliutsiia*, 11 (1925), p. 80; Hermaize, *Narysy z Istorii*, p. 87; Boshyk, 'The Rise of Ukrainian Political Parties', pp. 153–4.
109   Boshyk, 'The Rise of Ukrainian Political Parties', p. 157.
110   Ibid, pp. 235, 306.
111   Shupak, 'RUP v periodi 1905', p. 45.

workers. It also addressed issues of general concern such as the Russo-Japanese War and the struggle for democratic rights. However, the social questions it posed were of concern mainly to rural people. The strike weapon was explained in terms of its successful previous application in the countryside.[112]

Urban workers in small industries, most of them still transient and unorganised, were a precarious stepping stone for the RUP's anticipated entry into the industrial proletariat. The party needed a period of patient organising and rethinking of its programme in order to take that step. It grappled with this problem throughout 1904 and it assumed a central place in its internal debates just before and during the 1905 Revolution.

RUP's turn to Social Democracy began in 1901 when a majority of its members rejected the nationalist platform put forward by Mykhailo Mikhnovsky, a founding member, because it lacked a social programme. In 1902, the party's offical organ *Haslo* defined RUP's main objective as

> an independent Ukrainian republic of the working masses, socialisation of the means of production, nationalisation of land and the dictatorship of the proletariat – in short a socialist state ... Without rejecting work among the industrial proletariat where agitation is being conducted by Russian, Polish and Jewish socialists, RUP in the main turns to the village.[113]

Between 1902 and 1903, RUP's leadership moved away from the independence position in favour of national autonomy in a federated Russian republic. The change seems to have been an accommodation to the RSDWP which it wanted to join. Dmytro Antonovych, a prominent Foreign Committee member justified it by arguing there was little evidence Ukraine was a colony of Russia or Austro-Hungary or that its productive forces were unduly stifled by the burden of state taxes. If proof of colonial status could be furnished, Antonovych was prepared to change his mind.[114] A tendency opposed to the Foreign Committee sprang up in RUP branches in Ukraine. Mykola Porsh, then a twenty-six year old activist in the Poltava branch, was its main exponent. Porsh was not as eager as the Foreign Committee to abandon the goal of independence. Even if the party opted for national autonomy as a transitional slogan, he felt it should not forsake organisational independence and fuse with the RSDWP on the terms

---

112   Hermaize, *Narysy z Istorii*, pp. 174–6; Shupak, 'Rup v periodi 1905', pp. 50, 79.
113   Hermaize, '25 Littia RUP', p. 22.
114   Boshyk, 'The Rise of Ukrainian Political Parties', pp. 185–6, 262; Yavorsky, *Istoriia Ukrainy*, p. 253.

of democratic centralism outlined in the latter's 1903 programme. The Foreign Committee believed that fusion with the RSDWP would facilitate RUP's entry into the industrial working class. Porsh, on the other hand, saw in the Bund's approach, the nationality principle in self organisation and federation with the RSDWP, a better alternative.[115]

The Revolutionary Ukrainian Party was strongly influenced by the Bund in its early years. Contacts between the organisations first began on an individual basis as early as secondary school, mostly on the Left Bank and especially in Poltava province.[116] They co-operated in smuggling literature across the border. A number of militants, like M. Hechter and M. Hutnyk in Kyiv belonged simultaneously to the RUP and Bund. After 1903, the RSDWP's influence on RUP's evolution grew stronger, manifesting itself strongly in the party's first major split in 1905.

Marian Melenevsky, a Foreign Committee member, set about organising a faction in the Ukrainian branches to wage war on Porsh's 'new course'. Without questioning RUP's priority to organise Ukrainian speaking proletarians, first in the countryside and then in the urban centres, Melenevsky believed that fusion with the RSDWP on its terms would facilitate RUP's entry into the industrial sector. He accused Porsh of accommodating to the moderate Ukrainophile middle class, preferring good relations with it over a broader proletarian base for the party. Melenevsky laid stress on social, economic and political issues comprehensible to industrial workers rather than the national question in programme and organisation. He urged the party to join with other nationalities in the RSDWP even at the risk of disbanding the RUP.[117]

The debate raged throughout 1904. At the second RUP Congress in January 1905, on the eve of the Revolution, the party split down the middle. Porsh's tendency had a slight majority. Melenevsky's group quit the Congress and immediately issued a manifesto under the name 'Ukrainian Social Democracy'. The manifesto called on 'proletarian elements' to leave the party 'and begin organising the Ukrainian proletariat, turning its forces into the powerful stream of the all-Russian proletarian movement ... to build a centralised party for all Russia and not allow the Ukrainian proletariat to be dragged down in the direction of a bourgeois radical "independent" Ukraine'.[118]

A few days later, the Ukrainian Social Democratic Union, later known as the Spilka, joined the RSDWP. Meanwhile the RUP Congress went on. The remain-

---

115   Yavorsky, *Istoriia Ukrainy*, p. 234.
116   Ibid, p. 199.
117   Hermaize, *Narysy z Istorii*, pp. 255, 275.
118   Ibid, pp. 257–8.

ing delegates adopted Porsh's draft programme which called for national autonomy as a minimum and independence as a maximum goal, a separate Ukrainian social democratic party and unification with Russian and Jewish parties on a federative basis.[119]

In December 1905, RUP convened another Congress and renamed itself the Ukrainian Social Democratic Workers Party. It was decided to seek membership in the RSDWP at its next gathering as a self governing group and 'the sole representative of the Ukrainian proletariat'. But the RSDWP's Stockholm Congress was under no pressure to accept the USDWP's application because it had won over the Spilka on less demanding terms. The attempt at union ended in failure and the USDWP's application rejected.[120]

It was not until after the 1905 Revolution that Mykola Porsh prepared a more systematic analysis of the national question in Ukraine, the central issue raised by Dmytro Antonovych in 1904 that led to the split in RUP. In 1907 and 1908, Porsh published two lengthy pamphlets in Kyiv[121] that dealt with the relationship of the national question to capitalist development, the role of the state in this relationship and the possible political forms of national self-determination. His main concern was to demonstrate the socio-economic basis of national oppression and the complicity of the Russian state in the unequal development of its subject peoples. The pamphlets addressed proportionality of growth of industrial sectors in Ukraine, tariffs, the balance of trade, state taxes and expenditures. Porsh concluded from his analysis that the underdevelopment of the manufacturing sector was the Ukrainian economy's principal flaw and attributed it to state fiscal policies and short term interests of investing capitalists. Industries in Ukraine contended with 'higher taxes … a lack of productive investments from the state budget, hostile tariff policies and a lower productivity of the working class, a consequence of national and cultural oppression'. Long-term economic growth and industrial diversification were stifled by the flight of surplus capital, the absence of an indigenous bourgeoisie, increases in land rent and declines in agricultural workers' incomes.

> The only way to improve Ukraine's current situation is through autonomy. One of the principal aims of autonomy must be to halt the outflow of capital which is ruining Ukraine's productive forces. Everything that can possibly be taken out of the hands of the central state administration should be placed under the control of an autonomous government, including

---

119 Popov, *Narys Istorii*, p. 96; Hermaize, *Narysy z Istorii*, p. 251.
120 Popov, *Narys Istorii*, pp. 68–9; Boshyk, 'The Rise of Ukrainian Political Parties', p. 363.
121 *Pro Avtonomiiu* (Kyiv: Prosvita, 1907) and *Pro Avtonomiiu Ukrainy* (Kyiv: Prosvita, 1908).

all taxation. As far as the expenditures on institutions remaining under central government control are concerned, the Ukrainian treasury's contribution should be proportional to its share of the population. The same principle should apply to paying the interest on state debts.[122]

Porsh envisaged an autonomous Ukrainian government with broad executive and legislative powers over agriculture, labour, education, culture, roads and railways, credit and banking, vital statistics and medicine. The central state would have control of state-wide transport and communications, legislation on human rights and citizenship, insurance and banking laws, tariffs and duties, patents, weights and measures.[123]

There were all kinds of overlapping responsibilities between autonomous and central state institutions in Porsh's scheme. One can only imagine the numerous ways in which human rights legislation could affect labour, tariffs the railways, citizenship culture and so forth. So he proposed four rules to preserve the balance of power in a federation of autonomous states: an autonomous government had the right to block efforts of the central power to suppress its region's productive forces; the central power could block an autonomous government if it promoted policies detrimental to the entire state's productive forces; the central power should set standard democratic rights and could not restrict them for any member of the federation. The autonomous government could broaden these rights but not restrict them for any part of its population.

Porsh was writing under the eye of the censor. His pamphlets were to be published legally in Kyiv by the Prosvita Society. Like other publicists of the day, he resorted to the Aesopian way, substituting Ireland and India for Ukraine in numerous passages describing imperialism and national oppression. Although he discussed autonomy as something realisable through reform in both pamphlets, Porsh asserted in one part of *Pro Avtonomiiu Ukrainy* (About the Autonomy of Ukraine) that

> the Great Russian bourgeoisie will never agree voluntarily to give up tens of millions of roubles coming from the Ukrainians and accept a progressive tax system that throws the burden onto its own back ... Autonomy or independence? Which is easier? The struggle for independence is impossible without long wars ...[124]

---

122   Porsh, *Pro Avtonomiiu Ukrainy*, pp. 26–7.
123   Porsh, *Pro Avtonomiiu*, pp. 99–100; and *Pro Avtonomiiu Ukrainy*, p. 27.
124   Porsh, *Pro Avtonomiiu Ukrainy*, pp. 29–30.

Porsh also took issue with the Austro-Marxist conception of national cultural autonomy. He said that unless an oppressed nation took control of its economy, 'the foundation from which every people's culture springs', efforts to gain literacy, education and cultural enrichment in one's own language would always be inadequate. The supporters of national cultural autonomy believed that resources for education and culture could be gained by taxing the registered members of each nation's 'public corporation'. Porsh suggested the scheme was faulty. Regardless of their national origin, most members of the bourgeoisie would sign into the corporation of the already dominant nation because it had the best educational and cultural facilities in place. Their wealth would not be taxed for the benefit of the nations into which they were born.[125]

As for the Ukrainians, 'non-territorial autonomy is not only useless, but even harmful', wrote Porsh. Unless there was a territorial government, Ukrainians could not take control of their economy, community and culture to their fullest potential. The needs of national minorities in Ukraine would be served best by direct apportionment of taxes proportionate to their numerical size. He agreed that a workers' party must support some form of national cultural autonomy to satisfy the needs of minorities for self government, but the national majority should seek an autonomous territorial government.[126]

Citing Kautsky, Porsh noted that both workers and capitalists of an oppressed nation were interested in autonomy. However, workers wanted autonomy in the spirit of equality for all nations, whereas the bourgeoisie was interested solely in its own future and the possibility to dominate more nations than just its own. In Ukraine there was not much of an indigenous bourgeoisie with a political project of its own, while the peasantry and petit bourgeoisie were not prepared to lead.

> Thus only the proletariat can assume leadership in the struggle for autonomy ... the Ukrainian national movement will not be a bourgeois movement of triumphant capitalism as in the case of the Czechs. It will be more like the Irish case, a proletarian and semi-proletarianised peasant movement.[127]

Lev Yurkevych, a leader of the USDWP's left wing before the 1917 Revolution, expressed similar ideas in a book titled *Kliasy i Suspils'tvo* (Classes and Society),

---

125   Ibid, pp. 30, 53.
126   Porsh, *Pro Avtonomiiu*, pp. 57–8.
127   Porsh, *Pro Avtonomiiu Ukrainy*, p. 31.

published in Kyiv in 1913. Yurkevych added something to Porsh's views about the national movement's evolution. After the defeat of the 1905 Revolution, a wave of politically moderate middle class Ukrainians joined the struggle for democratic rights and Ukrainisation of the educational system. Many rural radicals and moderates became active in the co-operative movement. Their entry into the national movement in a period of political decline and reaction and the simultaneous creation of a strong economic base for the movement created fertile conditions for a pro-capitalist current within it. Yurkevych suggested that the national movement now also contained a stratum of the Ukrainian petit bourgeoisie that took part only to improve its competitive economic position vis-à-vis the Jewish and Russian petit bourgeoisie. He warned the USDWP to stay clear of the moderate Ukrainophile camp and build an alternative to it by linking the national struggle with the movement against capitalism as well as autocracy. The USDWP was living through hard times, with a few working class branches still active and many of its former leaders inactive or in exile. To drive his point home that the working class was a necessary base for the national movement, he quoted with approval a resolution submitted by Katerynoslav workers to Hryhorii Petrovsky, their Bolshevik deputy in the State Duma:

> We believe that national oppression, which is one aspect of the capitalist domination in our society, leads to the cultural, economic and political ruin of oppressed nations. It is therefore an obstacle to the development of these nations' proletariat and its class struggle ... We value our national language. It is a powerful means of cultural development, something without which our political class consciousness cannot mature.[128]

During the First World War, Lev Yurkevych moved to Geneva to publish the newspaper *Borot'ba* (Struggle) which reflected the views of the USDWP's left wing. There he released a pamphlet that attacked Lenin's views on the national question and defended the independence of the Ukrainian social democratic movement.[129] Relations between Yurkevych and Lenin, who also was living in Geneva at the time, were far from cordial. Lenin referred to Yurkevych as 'that disgusting, foul, nationalistic petit bourgeois who, under the flag of Marx-

---

[128] Lev Yurkevych, *Kliasy i Suspil'stvo* (Kyiv: Dzvin, 1913), p. 49.
[129] Rybalka (Lev Yurkevych), *Rosiis'ki sotsiial-demokraty i natsional'ne pytannia*, 2nd edn (New York: Suchasnist', 1969).

ism, preaches the division of workers by nationality and especially the national organisation of Ukrainian workers'.[130]

In a letter to Inessa Armand Lenin described another leading Ukrainian social democrat, the novelist and playwright Volodymyr Vynnychenko, as 'pretentious, completely idiotic', describing one of his novels as 'what filth, what nonsense'.[131] Such epithets led the historian Ralph Carter Elwood to sense in Lenin's letters and articles 'a contempt for things Ukrainian ... and a condescension towards backward minorities in general. One suspects that many of the Great Russian and educated Jewish members of the RSDWP shared his opinion'.[132]

Yurkevych's pamphlet took up Lenin's 1916 theses entitled 'The Socialist Revolution and the Right of Nations to Self-determination' in which Lenin coupled support for the principle of self-determination with advice against its practical implementation and spoke in favour of 'the undoubtable advantages of big states both from the point of view of economic progress ... and the interests of the masses'.[133]

Yurkevych argued that Lenin's positions cancelled each other out.

> The preference Russian social democrats have for 'big states' and for centralism within them destroys their capacity to look upon the national question from a genuinely internationalist point of view ... The 'merger of nations' is not internationalism speaking. It is the voice of the contemporary system of centralised big states and their continued assimilation of oppressed nations.[134]

Even if a democratic republic were achieved, Yurkevych countered, the Russian bourgeoisie would follow the example of its counterparts in Western Europe and centralise the Russian state even more. Little could be expected in the way of national liberation simply by gaining a bourgeois democracy. On the contrary, it would exacerbate national conflicts. Lenin's belief that the more democratic a multinational state such as Russia, 'the rarer and weaker will the strivings for complete freedom of secession be in practice' was pure speculation.

---

[130] Carter Elwood, *Russian Social Democracy*, p. 262, citing V.I. Lenin, *Polnoe Sobranie sochinenii*, 55 vols, 5th edn (Moscow, 1958–65), Vol. XLVIII, p. 277.
[131] Ibid, citing Lenin, *Polnoe Sobranie sochinenii*, Vol. XLVII, p. 295.
[132] Ibid, p. 263.
[133] Lenin, *Collected Works*, Vol. XIX, p. 50.
[134] Yurkevych, *Rosiis'ki sotsiial-demokraty*, pp. 21, 24.

Yurkevych noticed a definite similarity between the views of Lenin and Alexander Herzen on the national question. In 1859 Herzen declared in the journal *Kolokol* (The Bell) that Poland had a 'full and inalienable right to state independence from Russia' only to add that 'we do not want it to separate'. Both he and Lenin were for self-determination in theory and against it in practice. Lenin's programme was 'nothing more than a return to the Great Russian liberal patriotic programme formulated in the era of the peasantry's emancipation from serfdom'.[135] It contrasted with the spirit of the Zimmerwald camp of anti-war socialists to which both Yurkevych and Lenin belonged. The second Zimmerwald conference came out in favour of national autonomy, opposed all annexations of the big powers in the past and during the War and called upon the European working class to make 'an energetic rebuttal through class struggle of all oppression of the weaker nations and the defence of national minorities and their autonomy on the basis of full democracy'.[136]

Lenin's 1916 theses were less generous. Russian social democrats had never raised national oppression in Ukraine in a systematic way although they benefited objectively from it by having access to a large territory and population which gave their movement considerable support. Lenin recognised national movements in the Russian Empire as a potent threat to the autocracy but regarded them as an unreliable ally of the proletariat. He welcomed their opposition to autocracy but opposed their desire to break up its state completely. Yurkevych's view of the national movement and the working class was different, as were the programmatic and organisational conclusions flowing from it:

> National liberation movements of the oppressed nations ... and especially those in which the proletariat takes an active and revolutionary role, tying its national emancipation to its class emancipation in general, serve the cause of social progress without any doubt ... We support the federalist principle both in the reconstruction of the Russian Empire and in the organisation of Russian Social Democracy.[137]

---

135 Ibid, pp. 12–13.
136 Ibid, pp. 24–5.
137 Ibid, pp. 27, 29.

4   1905 and After

On 5 January 1905 over 100,000 Petrograd workers and their families gathered in front of the Winter Palace to present a petition to the Tsar. They were demanding political freedom and improved working conditions. Army units guarding the Palace were ordered to fire into the crowds. A thousand people died and another 5,000 were wounded. News of the massacre spread quickly across the country, eliciting protest strikes and demonstrations by over 400,000 workers and setting off the year long chain of events that came to be known as the 1905 Revolution.[138] The immediate demands raised by workers across the Empire were the same: an eight-hour working day, basic democratic rights, abdication of the Tsar, a constituent assembly and an end to the war with Japan.

The January strikes continued into the spring. A lull in the summer was followed by an even stronger wave of strikes in October and November that culminated in armed insurrections in December. In the Ukrainian provinces they took place in Katerynoslav, Kyiv, Odesa, Mykolaiv, Kharkiv, Oleksandrivsk and many Donbas towns. The insurrections were put down by the army and the revolutionary upsurge subsided. There followed a year of intensive trade union organising, brought to a halt in 1907 by new measures of repression. During the first quarter of 1905, 170,000 workers in Ukraine went on strike; in the second quarter 83,000; the third 13,000 and the fourth 203,000. The first wave precipitated the formation of factory committees in the largest industrial enterprises. In October, these committees began uniting on a city-wide basis into soviets or councils. They appeared first in Odesa, Katerynoslav, Mykolaiv and Kyiv in October, Luhansk, Kamians'k and the Donbas in November and December. The December insurrections were organised by the soviets.[139]

The soviets took the initiative to organise trade unions. The period of intensive organising began in September. On 4 March 1906 trade unions were legalised. By the end of that year they had approximately 246,000 members throughout the Empire, 38,000 of whom were in Ukraine. Practically all of the unions limited their membership to workers in a single enterprise or a particular trade. They averaged in size from 150 to 200 members.[140]

---

138   M.I. Suprunenko (gen. ed.), *Istoriia Ukrains'koi RSR*, 7 vols (Kyiv: Naukova Dumka, 1977), Vol. 4, p. 83.
139   Los, *Istoriia Robitnychoho Klasu*, Vol. 1, p. 305.
140   *Entsyklopediia Ukrainoznavstva*, 9 vols (Paris-New York: Vydavnytstvo Molode Zhyttia, 1973), s.v. Vsevolod Holubnychy, 'Robitnytstvo'; V. Grinevich, *Professionalnoe dvizhenie rabochikh v Rosii* (Moscow: Izdatel'stvo Krasnaia Nov, 1923), p. 210; V. Sadovsky, *Pratsiia v USSR* (Warsaw: Ukrains'kyi Naukovyi Instytut, 1932), p. 33.

The authorities made a concerted attempt in 1906 to smash the largest and best organised unions, leaving smaller associations alone until the following year. They concentrated on unions in Katerynoslav, Luhansk, Mariupol and other southern industrial centres. In October 1906 leaders of a metalworkers' union in Katerynoslav with over three thousand members were arrested.[141] The union's ranks shrank to fewer than 200 by 1908. Authorities in Kyiv tolerated the activities of over 30 unions but forbad the election of a central council. Harassment drove down both membership and activism of the unions. Only 70 of the 600 registered members of a Kyiv garment workers' union were paying dues by 1908, as were an insignificant number of the 250 organised bakery workers. By the beginning of 1908 only three unions were operating legally while 13 maintained a conspiratorial illegal existence.[142] In Volyn province, where the authorities were particularly harsh, only the printers' union was still tolerated at the end of 1907 and its activities had been all but completely stifled. A union of retail workers legally registered there in March 1906 was closed down for attempts to discuss political matters at meetings, a common charge invoked against many unions across the country.[143]

Efforts to unify unions on an industry wide basis were in evidence among railways workers in 1905, postal and telegraph employees, tailors and retail workers in 1906, and mechanics, metalworkers and printers in 1907. These were initiatives on an all-Empire scale. No attempts were made to bring together workers from the same industry or occupation in Ukraine alone.[144] Early in 1905, a Kharkiv mechanics' union began organising a state-wide central council of trade unions. Three conferences with this aim in mind were held in Moscow and Petrograd. There were no attempts to organise an all-Ukrainian trade union central council in this period. In December 1906 a regional conference of various trade unions active in the Donbas elected a leadership body but its aspirations to lead were restricted to the Donbas.[145]

All of the social democratic parties profited from the working-class mobilisation in 1905 and 1906. The RSDWP gained the most because it was implanted in large industries where factory committees, soviets and trade unions were first organised and in which both Bolshevik and Menshevik factions were heavily involved – the Mensheviks more in the unions, the Bolsheviks in factory com-

---

141 *Rada*, 24 October 1906, p. 3.
142 D. Shlosberg, 'Profesiinyi Rukh 1905–07 r.r. na Ukraini', *Litopys Revoliutsii*, 6 (1930), p. 38.
143 Sadovsky, *Pratsiia*, pp. 32–5.
144 Shlosberg, 'Profesiinyi Rukh', p. 53.
145 Ibid.

mittees and soviets.[146] The RSDWP's ranks in Ukraine were strengthened also by the entry of the Spilka and the Bund as well as many novices to the workers' movement. They grew from several hundred members on the eve of the Revolution to 20,000 in 1906. Of this number, 7,000 belonged to the Spilka and an equal, if not larger number to the Bund. Total Bund membership in the Empire grew to 40,000 by the end of 1906. In Ukraine it had large branches in several cities, with 2,000 members in Kyiv, 300 in Odesa and 150 in Katerynoslav. The USDWP, which remained outside the RSDWP after the Stockholm Congress, claimed 6,000 members in December 1905.[147]

All of these gains were short lived as party membership declined as rapidly as it had grown. RSDWP ranks in Ukraine were halved by 1907, dropping to about one thousand in 1907 and 220 in 1910. By 1911 its network had been all but destroyed by repressions, emigration of leading members and the closure of legal organisations brought temporarily to life by the upsurge in 1905 and 1906. After 1907 there was no mandated RSDWP Congress until 1917.[148]

The Bund's membership dropped to 25,000 throughout the Empire in 1907 and to a few thousand in 1908.[149] While the party faced the same conditions that drove down the membership of the RSDWP as a whole, Bund militants were further demoralised by the wave of anti-Jewish pogroms that broke out in October 1905 and in 1906.[150]

Between December 1905 and March 1907, USDWP membership was halved to 3,000. Of this number about 1,000 were based in the cities and 500 belonged to trade unions.[151] The Party's Third Congress in March 1907 was the last to be convened until 1917. In the interim, a few hundred still active members were grouped around two solid working-class branches, Katerynoslav and Kharkiv, and four publications: *Dzvin* (The Bell) in Kyiv, *Ukrains'kaia Zhizn* (Ukrainian Life) in Moscow, *Nash Holos* (Our Voice) in Lviv, and *Borot'ba* (Struggle) in Geneva. The USDWP's decline stemmed from its poor showing in 1905 when its agitation among urbanised workers ended in failure,[152] the loss of the Spilka faction to the RSDWP, the general climate of reaction and the defection of many disillusioned socialists to the moderate Ukrainophile camp.[153]

---

146 Suprunenko, *Istoriia Ukrains'koi RSR*, Vol. 4, pp. 90, 122–4.
147 Popov, *Narys Istorii*, p. 72; Elwood, *Russian Social Democracy*, p. 23.
148 Elwood, *Russian Social Democracy*, pp. 35, 38, 115.
149 Ibid, p. 37.
150 Frankel, *Prophecy and Politics*, pp. 146–9.
151 Popov, *Narys Istorii*, p. 72.
152 Shupak, 'RUP v periodi 1905', p. 77.
153 *Robitnchyi Prapor* (Sofia), 2 (June 1915), p. 4; *Borot'ba*, 1 (February 1915), p. 4.

The government banned All-Ukrainian language publications again except the Kyiv daily *Rada* and closed down Prosvita societies and other popular educational and cultural institutions. Yet the intellectuals who had quit the USDWP and gone into these projects did not return to the party after the repressions closed off avenues to legal work. On the eve of the War, when the RSDWP was able to launch at least some initiatives, the USDWP remained a fairly isolated group without much of a working-class base. Its leading members withdrew from political activity. Mykola Porsh practiced law in Kyiv. Dmytro Antonovych left for Italy to study art. Volodymyr Vynnychenko spent much of his time writing books and plays which provided him with a modest income. Andrii Zhuk, Oksen Lola, Mykhailo Rusov and others emigrated to Western Europe. Lev Yurkevych bemoaned the party's fate in a *Dzvin* article in 1913:

> The Ukrainian Marxist intelligentsia has almost no interest in a workers' press although such work is much needed and would bring invaluable benefit to the Ukrainian workers' cause. Our generation, carelessly and without perspectives of its own, got involved in Ukrainian bourgeois affairs. Its path and that of the Ukrainian workers' movement have parted ways, apparently forever.[154]

The kind of workers' organisations that emerged in 1905 seemed to vindicate the strategy of the Spilka. Factory committees, soviets and trade unions brought together workers of different nationalities. As part of the RSDWP, the Spilka had access to thousands of radicalising Ukrainian workers. But the opportunities for concerted intervention quickly faded. And while Spilka was closer to the mark in 1905 and 1906, it fared even worse than the USDWP in the long run. After reaching a high point of 7,000 members in 1906, its ranks declined to 4,500 in 1907 and 200 in 1908.[155] Spilka members became disillusioned with their strategy because they were unable to unite Ukrainian speaking workers in the RSDWP branches once they joined. The RSDWP's leaders viewed the Spilka contingent as ideal peasant organisers because they were the only ones in the party who spoke Ukrainian and pressured them to expand their work into neighbouring Russian provinces. Scattered throughout the RSDWP and without an ongoing leadership of their own, Spilka members lost sight of their original perspectives.[156] By 1909 they had disbanded altogether. Some of them rejoined

---

154 Lev Yurkevych, 'V spravi Ukrains'koi robitnychoi hazety', *Dzvin*, 14 (1913), p. 277.
155 Elwood, *Russian Social Democracy*, p. 38.
156 Popov, *Narys Istorii*, pp. 64–6; Boshyk, 'The Rise of Ukrainian Political Parties', p. 334.

the USDWP; others joined the Bolsheviks.[157] Some of the Spilka leaders resurfaced during the War as members of the Union for the Liberation of Ukraine (*Soiuz Vyzvolennia Ukrainy*), an organisation that took Austro-Hungary's side in the War against Russia, worked among Ukrainian soldiers in Austrian prisoner of war camps and agitated for Ukraine's state independence in the capitals of Europe.

As a dress rehearsal for 1917, the 1905 Revolution gave some indication of the working class's capacity for united action. The soviets and trade unions were good examples of this capacity. At the local level, RSDWP, Bund and USDWP branches worked out common programmes of action.[158] Representatives of these and other social democratic parties in the Empire made an agreement in Riga in January 1905 to pursue a common minimum programme which included demands to abolish all exceptional laws against nations and to allow education in one's native language.[159]

Neither the workers' movement nor the social democratic parties paid much attention to the national question because they did not confront the problem of state power in any practical or constructive way except for a series of aborted insurrections. They did not develop any strong relations with the peasant movement in 1905, which put forward more far reaching national demands, including the demand for the territorial autonomy of Ukraine. There was little pressure on the RSDWP to advance a positive programme for national self-determination because its Ukrainian and Jewish sections had subordinated the national question to other political and social demands for the moment. The USDWP was simply too weak to raise the issue forcefully on its own in the workers' movement. As the first major opportunity for the social democratic parties to test the regime, the 1905 Revolution demanded from them a maximum of unity in action. The cost of such unity was temporary subordination of political differences between them. This feeling was strongest among rank and file workers who came into the struggle to win first their basic, universally agreed upon minimum demands.

After the defeat of the Revolution and the regime's retrenchment, every party paid the price for failure. Recent recruits to the revolutionary movement deserted *en masse*, some joining legal organisations while others dropped out of politics altogether. A revealing sign of the times was the growth of nationalist currents in the Ukrainian, Jewish and Russian intelligentsia. Rus-

---

157   Yavorsky, *Revoliutsiia na Vkraini*, p. 29.
158   Stepaniuk, 'Z spohadiv robitnyka', p. 337.
159   Tobias, *The Jewish Bund*, p. 303.

sian nationalism grew in response to the impending threat of imperial fragmentation. Ukrainian and Jewish nationalism was defensive, a response to the post-revolutionary reaction and a judgment on the apparent failure of the internationalist strategy to win national rights and freedoms.

5   The First World War

The War presented the workers' movement and its parties with their second major test of unity. Judging from the positions taken by European socialists on the question of war before 1914, a common stand seemed likely in the event it broke out. Congresses of the Second International in Paris (1889), Brussels (1891), Zurich (1893), Stuttgart (1907), Copenhagen (1910) and Basel (1912) had all passed resolutions opposed to war.[160] The Zurich Congress called upon all social democratic parties 'to protest against the maintenance of standing armies and demand disarmament'. A vote against war credits by socialist deputies in every European parliament was deemed obligatory. The Stuttgart Congress resolved that all working class organisations had a duty to prevent the outbreak of war. In case their efforts failed, they should utilise the crisis to hasten the downfall of capitalism. The 1912 Basel Congress, whose resolutions were accepted 'by all the socialist parties in the world' characterised war as a product of rivalries between imperialist powers seeking new territories and a redivision of the world's markets.

> War cannot be justified by the slightest pretext of being in the interests of the people ... [but is waged] in the interests of the profits of capitalists and the ambitions of dynasties.[161]

When the World War finally broke out in July 1914, socialist deputies in the parliaments of France, Belgium, Britain and Germany voted for war credits to their respective governments. The Mensheviks declared their support for the Russian war effort. Socialists opposed to the war were in a minority in their parties practically everywhere in Europe with the exception of Bulgaria and Serbia. Defence of the fatherland became an acceptable slogan for social democrats

---

[160]   V.I. Lenin, 'Militant Militarism and the Anti-Militarist Tactics of Social Democracy', in *The Years of Reaction and the New Revival* (New York: International Publishers, n.d.), p. 325; and Lenin, *Collected Works*, Vol. XIX, p. 329.

[161]   V.I. Lenin, 'Opportunism and the Collapse of the Second International', in *Collected Works*, Vol. XIX, p. 15.

and bourgeois parties alike. Workers of different nations were pressed into uniform to fight one another, for Germany's claims on British and French colonies, for Austro-Hungary's claims on the Balkans, for Britain's claims on Mesopotamia and Palestine, for France's claims on Alsace Lorraine, and for Russia's claims on the Dardanelles, Armenia and Galicia. The Great Powers justified their claims by alleging to defend the oppressed nations under the yoke of their opponents. They tried to exploit all national movements in their enemy's camp. Germany 'championed' the Irish cause, France the Czech movement, Austro-Hungary Ukrainian aspirations in the Russian Empire.[162]

A wave of patriotic fervour swept the Russian Empire in 1914 when its government declared war. Workers in Petrograd took to the streets in thousands and paraded with Russian flags.[163] Deputies in the State Duma rose to declare the loyalty of the nationalities they represented to the Tsar. Only the Ukrainians failed to muster a speaker. Five deputies, all of them Bolsheviks (Petrovsky, Badaiev, Muranov, Shagov and Samoilov) dared to protest Russia's declaration of war. They were duly arrested, put on trial and exiled to Siberia.[164]

The mood in Kyiv was like that in Petrograd. Kyivan Bolsheviks put up a fight in the surviving trade unions but Menshevik defensists (*oborontsi*) outnumbered them with their strong base among railway workers, the older generation of printers and employees at the Greter steel mills. They controlled the executive committees of trade unions, workers' co-operatives and clubs in the city, from which they sent representatives to sit on the government sponsored War Productions Committee. The Mensheviks were rewarded for their efforts by being allowed to work without official harassment for the duration of the War.

> Russia's invasion of Galicia [Halychyna, the western Ukrainian region of the Austro-Hungarian Empire] in August 1914 charged the patriotic sentiment even of the Mensheviks. Under the influence of their patriotic loyalty, they silently condoned the policies of [military governor] Bobrynsky in Galicia, notwithstanding the fact that these policies amounted to pogroms against Jews and deportations of Galician independentists.[165]

---

162 Lenin, *Collected Works*, Vol. XIX, pp. 303, 329.
163 Dmytro Doroshenko, *Moi Spomyny pro Nedavnie Mynule 1914–1920* (Munich: Ukrains'ke Vydavnytstvo, 1969), p. 18.
164 Lenin, *Collected Works*, Vol. XIX, p. 29.
165 Yavorsky, *Revoliutsiia na Vkraini*, p. 30.

A majority of active USDWP members were opposed to the War.[166] Among their leaders, Symon Petliura was one of the notable exceptions. Taking up residence in Moscow in 1912, Petliura began publishing the Russian language *Ukrains'kaia Zhizn*, a newspaper designed for Ukrainians living in Russia. Dmytro Doroshenko claims that after Petliura learned that no deputies in the State Duma had declared Ukrainians' loyalty to the regime, he prepared a special issue of the newspaper to set the record straight. The editorial stated that Ukrainians in the Empire had no choice but to support the Russian war effort.[167]

Members of the USDWP branch in Katerynoslav concentrated on anti-war propaganda and suffered repeated police raids on their homes. Together with Bolshevik, Socialist Revolutionary and anarchist committees, the USDWP planned a general strike at the end of 1916 to protest the War. It failed to materialise. By February 1917, however, its members had collected a small arsenal 'for the coming battle' with the regime.[168]

Lev Yurkevych's Geneva newspaper *Borot'ba* devoted itself mainly to anti-war propaganda and polemicised equally with the pro-Russian orientation of Petliura's newspaper in Moscow and the pro-Austrian sympathies of the Vienna based Union for the Liberation of Ukraine.[169] Yurkevych wrote:

> We Ukrainian social democrats must come out with redoubled energy against the arrangements that provoked this war and against our classes and their parties who pursue a policy of 'reconciliation' with those arrangements. The struggle today for Ukrainian liberation is the same as the struggle against the war, for a revolutionary overthrow in Russia ... We place no hope in the generosity of Tsarist Russia, but only in its *death*.[170]

Increasing numbers of people began changing their stand on the War as fatalities mounted and the domestic economy cracked and strained under the pressure of militarisation. Nationalist sentiments among Ukrainians also grew. The coincidence of nationalist and defeatist sentiments in their case is not difficult to understand. When War was declared, the government banned Ukrain-

---

166 V. Sukhyno-Khomenko, 'Z pryvodu osoblyvostei proletars'koi revoliutsii na Ukraini', *Litopys Revoliutsii*, 4 (1928), p. 91.
167 Doroshenko, *Moi Spomyny*, p. 19.
168 Yu. Y. Kirianov, *Rabochie Iuga Rossii 1914–fevral 1917 g.* (Moscow: Izdatel'stvo Nauka, 1971), pp. 133–6.
169 *Borot'ba*, 1 (February 1915), p. 5; Popov, *Narys Istorii*, p. 99.
170 *Borot'ba*, 5 (November 1915), p. 4.

ian language publications even before German ones. The moderate Kyiv daily *Rada* was closed down two weeks after it published a statement of loyalty to the government. When the Russian army occupied Galicia, All-Ukrainian language schools, newspapers, bookstores, cultural and educational institutions were closed down and their employees deported to the Russian interior. In Lviv, Chernivtsi and Stanislav, occupation authorities burned all the Ukrainian language literature they could find. Post offices in Galicia refused to accept letters written in Ukrainian, although Polish, German, French and English language correspondence was permitted.[171]

The territory of Ukraine was a major theatre of the War. Large garrisons were stationed in Ukrainian cities close to the South Western and Romanian fronts. Forty-five out of a total of 76 divisions of the Russian army were committed to these fronts. Galicia suffered extensive losses in human life and material wealth from the conflict; 60 percent of all standing structures there were razed to the ground. Once it became clearer in whose interests and at whose cost the War was being prosecuted, appeals to Ukrainians on both sides of the front by their respective governments increasingly rang hollow. Loyalty to either belligerent faded, giving way to demands for an end to the War, the defence of human life from the carnage and the withdrawal of the warring parties altogether from their national territory.

---

171   *Borot'ba*, 2 (April 1915), p. 2; Doroshenko, *Moi Spomyny*, p. 24.

CHAPTER 4

February to October 1917

In the winter of 1916–17 the privations of war became intolerable for soldiers on the front and poor people behind the lines. Bread queues in Petrograd grew longer by the day. Heating fuel ran out. Women and children protested in the streets, demanding bread and herring. The army was failing to get its bread rations, not to mention other basic provisions. After the commemoration on 9 January[1] of the Bloody Sunday massacre in 1905, workers' strikes began to spread across the empire. Official estimates put the number of strikers at a quarter of a million in January and double that in February. In the Russian capital itself work stoppages swelled on International Women's Day, celebrated in Russia by the Julian calendar on 23 February, coinciding with the hunger protests on the streets. And then four days later the Volyn regiment, made up of Ukrainian peasant conscripts, mutinied and took the side of the hungry workers. Other regiments joined them. By the evening of 27 February several strategic locations in the capital were in the hands of insurgents, including police stations, law courts, the Interior Ministry and the Fortress of Saints Peter and Paul.

The authorities sent punitive army battalions to put down the revolt. However, they failed to quell it even after five days of shooting left 13 people dead and more than 1,500 injured.[2] The situation came to a breaking point for the Tsar's loyal opposition in the State Duma, who formed a Provisional Government on 2 March in an attempt to restore law and order. Tsar Nicholas II, having lost the support of his ministers and the loyalty of his troops, was forced to abdicate.

Workers' leaders being held since early January in the Fortress of Saints Peter and Paul were freed by soldiers on 27 February. On that same day they convened the first meeting of the Petrograd Soviet of Workers' Deputies. USDWP activists at the meeting proposed the Soviet should work jointly and on the basis of equal representation with a Soviet of Soldiers' Deputies. Their proposal was approved and the first meeting of the Petrograd Soviet of Workers' and Soldiers' Deputies convened on 1 March.[3]

---

1 All dates are by the Julian calendar up to 31 January 1918. Thereafter they follow the Gregorian calendar, when 1 February by the Julian calendar became 14 February by the Gregorian.
2 V.F. Soldatenko, *Ukraina v revoliutsiinu dobu: Istorychne ese-khroniky*, 4 vols (Kyiv: Svitohliad, 2010), Vol. 1, pp. 25–33.
3 More than 60 deputies of this first meeting belonged to the USDWP. M. Avdienko, 'Liutneva Revoliutsiia v Petrohradi i USDRP', *Litopys Revoliutsii*, 1 (January–February 1928).

There were now two foci of political power in the Russian capital: the Petrograd Soviet of Workers' and Soldiers' Deputies and the Provisional Government. Each institution enjoyed a distinct kind of popular support based on the demands and promises it espoused at its inception. The Petrograd Soviet was dominated by an alliance of Mensheviks, Socialist Revolutionaries, Bundists and members of other small socialist parties. They gathered under the banner of 'revolutionary defencism', calling for military defence of the Empire, an end to the War by way of a negotiated peace, radical social and economic policies and co-operation with the Provisional Government. The alliance held majority control in the Petrograd and Moscow Soviets and most provincial soviets throughout the country until September 1917.

In the Provisional Government the Constitutional Democrats (Kadets), a liberal bourgeois party, co-operated with the Mensheviks, Socialist Revolutionaries, and smaller moderate socialist parties like the Labourists (*Trudovaia gruppa*) and the Popular Socialists (*Narodni sotsiialisty*) in a series of coalition cabinets formed between February and October 1917.

The Government enjoyed widespread support at first because it held out the hope for democratic elections to a constituent assembly that could deal resolutely with the War, land reform, the collapse of industry and demands of the non-Russian peoples for national self-determination. It steadily lost this support when it did not call elections or deal with the domestic situation and continued to take part in the War on the side of the former Tsar's allies. Under pressure from radical movements of soldiers, workers and peasants, the Provisional Government began to falter, its cabinets resigning and reforming in an attempt to appease and head off the radicalisation.

The Petrograd Soviet was the Provisional Government's watchdog, its conscience so to speak, because it expressed the desires of deputies elected by hundreds of thousands of people and of millions when it called All-Russian congresses of soviets. As it became clear to these millions that the Government was not committed to the goals of the February Revolution, and above all did not try to end the War, the initiative passed to the Petrograd Soviet and a power struggle took shape between them. The bloc of revolutionary defencists in the Soviet was challenged by increasingly popular Bolsheviks, Left Socialist Revolutionaries and Menshevik Internationalists. They were opposed to coalitions between socialist and bourgeois parties in the Provisional Government and called for an immediate halt to the War. Instead of general elections to a constituent assembly, they proposed an altogether new form of state based solely on soviets, that is councils of elected workers', soldiers' and peasants' deputies. In October, the Second All-Russian Congress of Soviets overthrew the Provisional Government in Petrograd after a concentrated military assault on its institutions and elected a Council of Peoples' Commissars (CPC) to take its place. The Bolsheviks held the majority in the CPC.

The dynamic of the dual power struggle that took shape in the summer of 1917 was complicated in two ways. First, by the participation of Mensheviks and Socialist Revolutionaries simultaneously in the Provisional Government alongside the Kadets and other bourgeois parties, and in the Soviets alongside the Bolsheviks and other radical socialist parties. Second, by the presence in the non-Russian regions of the emancipation movements of imperial Russia's oppressed nations. Thus in Ukraine, the period from February to October is better described as a treble power struggle between the Provisional Government, the urban councils of workers' deputies that looked to the Petrograd Soviet for leadership, and the Ukrainian national movement, whose institutional focus became the Tsentral'na Rada (Central Council in Ukrainian).

Formed in Kyiv on 3 March the Rada set as its minimum programme 'the attainment of territorial autonomy, making Ukrainian a language of government and protecting the rights of national minorities – Russians and others'.[4] In the following months the overwhelming majority of soldiers' and peasants' councils in Ukraine rallied to its side. Together with a modest delegation of workers' deputies, they made up the greater part of the Tsentral'na Rada's general assembly in Kyiv. The Rada gained sufficient popular support to force the Provisional Government to recognise Ukraine's right to territorial autonomy in July and then to overthrow the Government itself in October. It took power in Kyiv at the behest and with the military backing of the Third All-Ukrainian Soldiers' Congress at the same time as power changed hands in Petrograd.

It is well known that peasants and semi-proletarians on the land and in the army were the spine of the Tsentral'na Rada, its most committed supporters from the beginning. The working class, on the other hand, was divided at the outset and for the longest time it looked to Petrograd for a political solution to the crisis. In its majority, the working-class movement in Ukraine was unprepared for the Rada's seizure of power. Only after the seizure did the urban councils of the working class begin to deal with the national question and the national movement as a problem of state power.

The remaining chapters of this book examine the working class coming to terms with this particular problem of state power from February 1917 to April 1918, the first 'long year' of the Revolution. They focus on developments in the urban centres where two big movements held the keys to power: the working-class movement organised into factory committees, soviets and trade unions

---

4 *Visty Ukrains'koi Tsentral'noi Rady*, 1 (19 March 1917), p. 1; 4 (April 1917), p. 3.

and the soldiers' movement in the garrisons and on the front. Of primary importance to this study is how these mass movements influenced the outcome of the struggle for state power. While much has been written about political leaders, parties and governments, a great deal remains to be learned about the mass mobilisations on whose crests they rode into power and in whose wake they lost it. It is necessary to learn more about their tempos and cycles, the numbers of people who took part in them and the patterns of interaction between distinct movements of workers, soldiers and peasants. In the last analysis, these movements were the adjudicators in the revolutionary crisis, the source of its possibilities and its objective limitations.

Not a calendar year, the first year of the Revolution spans the period from the collapse of Tsarism in February 1917 to the Austro-German occupation and fall of the Tsentral'na Rada in April 1918. It has four periods: mobilisation and self organisation of the lower classes from February to July; contestation and seizure of state power between August and October; attempts in November and December to reconcile the interests of the mass movements in the new state power; the failure of these attempts and the outbreak of civil war and foreign interventions between January and April 1918.

1   First Days of the Rada

After the fall of the autocracy practically all enterprises and public institutions stopped working for several days. Crowds of people gathered in the streets to share the news and consider the future. Demonstrations and attacks on state institutions occurred in many towns and cities. In Kyiv crowds gathered on 1 March outside the city council building, moved on to the city garrison, destroyed its headquarters and then freed the political prisoners in the Lukianivka prison. Workers' councils formed in the first week of March in Kyiv, Kharkiv, Katerynoslav, Odesa, Poltava, Mariupol and in towns of the Donbas. In some places they disarmed the police, dismissed reactionary officials of the old regime and assumed control of city councils (*dumy*) and district councils (*zemstva*).[5]

The city council of Odesa was driven out of its premises, its Black Hundreds chairman, Pelikan, and his assistants were arrested. Monarchist officers were driven out of their units as soldiers and sailors took up the call from the Petrograd Soviet of Workers' and Soldiers' Deputies to elect their own committees

---

5   M.A. Rubach, 'Treba diisno vypravyty', *Litopys Revoliutsii*, 3–4 (May–June 1930), p. 265.

and councils and to obey only their orders. Across the front passive resistance to the war became the norm under the slogan: 'Hold the front but don't advance'. Soldiers returning home from the front called public meetings in towns and villages along the way, often at the railway station, to deliver news from the cities and the front. The correspondent of the Petrograd Telegraph Agency visiting Zhytomyr, Lutsk and Novhorod-Volynsk on Right Bank Ukraine reported:

> Everywhere, without tears or regret the village parted with the past political order. It took the news of the overthrow as something that was needed, in fact was inevitable ... everyone breathed a sigh of relief. The village awoke. Hope that better times had finally arrived shone in everyone's eyes. There would now be land, pasture, freedom.[6]

Political exiles made their way home from Siberia and abroad. Proscribed political parties were revived, the opposition presses restarted. A period of intense organising by students, soldiers, workers, the intelligentsia and professional classes began, creating cultural associations, neighbourhood committees, trade unions and councils. The active restoration of democracy from below quickly brought into popular usage new expressions to denote what was now taking place. Among them three terms in particular gained widespread currency. 'The social revolution' was the process in its broadest scope by which the lower classes were now taking control of workplaces, schools and public institutions from the old regime. 'The democracy' identified the community positively involved in this revolution, as opposed to the temporarily silenced supporters of the old regime. And 'national autonomy' summed up the oppressed nations' and national minorities' goal of self-government in a future federated republic.

In Ukraine the Tsentral'na Rada took up the goal of national autonomy. The moderate Society of Ukrainian Progressives (*Tovarystvo Ukrains'kykh Postupovtsiv* – TUP) in Kyiv took the initiative on 1 March to establish the Rada as a national co-ordinating body for its own members. However, its founding meeting was interrupted by members of other Ukrainian organisations in the city who demanded the Rada include them. So on 3 March over one hundred people attended another meeting in the Rodina club at which the Tsentral'na Rada was redefined as a central council empowered to co-ordinate the activity of its Ukraine-wide member organisations, to work as a coalition of the Ukrainian national movement. Its initial members included co-operatives, cultural and educational societies, students', teachers', soldiers' and workers' organisa-

---

6 Soldatenko, *Ukraina v revoliutsiinu dobu*, Vol. 1, p. 79.

tions. Ukrainian social democrats and socialist revolutionaries were active in all these bodies.

On 7 March the Rada elected its head, a presidium and eight commissioners overseeing different policy areas. Mykhailo Hrushevsky, the renowned historian, was elected head. He was at the time still in Moscow, the last place of internal exile imposed on him by the Tsarist authorities in 1916. He assumed the post on 13 March after returning to Kyiv. Most of the other positions went to members of TUP, the Ukrainian Social Democratic Workers' Party (USDWP) and the Ukrainian Labour Party (*Ukrains'ka Trudova Partiia* – UTP), the latter based in the co-operative movement. At the end of March the USDWP and the Ukrainian Party of Socialist Revolutionaries (UPSR) formally announced their endorsement and support of the Rada. These two parties now came alongside the TUP, soon to be renamed as the Ukrainian Party of Socialist Federalists (*Ukrains'ka Partiia Sotsialistiv Federalistiv* – UPSF) to form the core of the executive bodies. Over time the moderate UPSF would yield the leadership to the USDWP. Its programme declared the party on the side of the working class and peasantry, although in reality the UPSF was fearful of mass movements and tried to dampen their radicalism. It was similar in political outlook to the Russian Kadets but had included socialism in its name under the pressure of rising revolutionary sentiments among the populace.

The Rada was launched as a civic organisation, consciously modelled on the committees of civic organisations that were being formed to support the provincial, city and district executives of the Provisional Government. But unlike them it aimed to become a national organisation and to unite a set of provinces that were not yet recognised in Russian law or public administration as a distinct national entity. The Rada was about to seek such recognition from the Provisional Government on the way to securing Ukraine's national territorial autonomy, and in the process transforming the Rada itself from a civic organisation into an autonomous government.

The Provisional Government in Petrograd started asserting its authority by removing the Tsarist provincial governors and vice-governors and replacing them with their own Commissariats at provincial and district levels of administration. It appointed its commissars to Kyiv on 1 March, Kharkiv on 3 March and then across the other Ukrainian provinces. Typically they were representatives of the urban bourgeoisie and big landowners. The Commissariats relied on the support of the committees of civic organisations, formed under their patronage. It was common for the commissar to be made the head of the civic committee as well. Moderate and right wing Mensheviks and Russian Socialist Revolutionaries were active in the civic committees, alongside a wide cross section of merchants, lawyers, teachers, civil servants and workers' organisations.

Where they were well established, Ukrainian political parties, co-operatives and cultural organisations also secured representatives in such committees and sometimes even a commanding position. For example, the Kyiv provincial executive committee of civic organisations, elected in mid-March, 'fell almost completely into Ukrainian hands'.[7]

Despite these changes in government personnel and civic participation the old order still survived in the administration of government. Senior administrators maintained their well established ties to the big landowners, entrepreneurs and industrialists. The Provisional Government remained committed to the War on the side of its allies, the Entente, for which it had to marshal the needed resources and secure the active co-operation of the upper classes, the press and the military. By 1917 the economic situation was critical, while mass expectations of positive change soared with the collapse of the autocracy. There was evident concern that, despite the replacement of Tsarist authority by a Provisional Government at the pinnacle of power, the situation could get out of hand. Lurking in the background were those who could not accept the passing of the old order, nor the dismemberment of Russia, 'united and indivisible'. They included the notorious Black Hundreds, the Union of Russian People, who numbered around 190,000 in the Ukrainian provinces, half their total membership in the empire.[8]

Supporters of the old regime had good reason to be worried. In the first two weeks of March there were four mass demonstrations by soldiers in Kyiv calling for constituent assembly elections and Ukraine's territorial autonomy in a federated, democratic republic, Ukrainisation of schools and public services, and separate Ukrainian regiments in the army commanded by elected officers.[9] Twenty-five thousand workers and soldiers in a March 12 Petrograd demonstration raised the same demands.[10] And on 19 March 100,000 people marched in Kyiv, a third of them soldiers, to demand national autonomy and to declare their support for the Tsentral'na Rada as the political representative of the Ukrainian people.[11]

Hrushevsky in his memoirs recalled the 19 March demonstration 'left a mighty impression that Ukrainian identity was not a fiction in the heads of a

---

[7] Soldatenko, *Ukraina v revoliutsiinu dobu*, Vol. 1, p. 108.
[8] Oleksandr Reient, *Robitnytstvo Ukrainy i Tsentral'na Rada* (Kyiv: Akademiia Nauk, Instytut Istorii Ukrainy, 1993), pp. 20–6.
[9] *Visty Ukrains'koi Tsentralnoi Rady*, 1 (19 March 1917), pp. 1–2.
[10] M. Avdiienko, 'Liutneva Revoliutsiia v Petrohradi i USDRP', *Litopys Revoliutsii*, 1 (January–February 1928), p. 230.
[11] V. Skorovstansky (Vasyl Shakhrai), *Revoliutsiia na Ukraine* (Saratov: n.p., 1919), p. 22.

little band of romantics or maniacal intellectuals. It was a living force which had power over the masses, which moved them and lifted them up'.[12] It was widely regarded as the beginning of a national democratic revolution, echoing powerfully the developments in Petrograd and setting down a bulwark against the threat of a restoration of the old order. However, it also introduced a quite unexpected current into the stream of the all-Russia revolution, one which posed an even wider set of possible outcomes than those envisaged by the Russian democratic camp.

The Rada called a National Congress in Kyiv in early April. According to Hrushevsky the organisers wanted to impress upon the Provisional Government the gravity of the situation with regard to Ukrainian national demands, that they could no longer be ignored:

> The Provisional Government had a tendency to put everything off until after Constituent Assembly elections and that's where it filed away the Ukrainian situation, in a general folder on the national question. However, it considered Finland, Poland and the South Caucasus sufficiently self-evident issues that it could decree them political rights on the basis of its own existing authority, not waiting for the outcome of Constituent Assembly elections. That meant we had to demonstrate forcefully and unambiguously that Ukrainian demands were very widely supported and of an urgent nature if we wanted to achieve a resolution of the Ukrainian question.[13]

Judging by the turnout the National Congress was a great success – 900 delegates, a majority of them soldiers, workers and peasants.[14] The congress heard greetings from Russian, Jewish, Polish and Estonian organisations. At the end of deliberations the delegates adopted motions supporting national territorial autonomy for Ukraine within a democratic, federated Russian republic, protection of the rights of national minorities living in Ukraine and the rights of Ukrainians living outside its borders; that borders be decided henceforth

---

12   Mykhailo Hrushevsky, 'Spomyny: Chastyna 11', *Kyiv*, 8 (1989), p. 143.
13   Hrushevsky, 'Spomyny: Chastyna 11', p. 144.
14   *Robitnycha hazeta*, 9 April 1917, p. 2. Estimates of the number of delegates vary from 700 to 1,500 in the following literature: Pavlo Khrystiuk, *Ukrains'ka Revoliutsiia: Zamitky i Materiialy do Istorii Ukrains'koi Revoliutsii 1917–20 rr*, 4 vols (Vienna: Ukrains'kyi Sotsiolohichnyi Instytut, 1921), Vol. 1, pp. 38–41; Mykyta Shapoval, *Velyka Revoliutsiia i Ukrains'ka Vyzvol'na Prohrama* (Prague: Vilna Spilka i Ukrains'kyi Robitnychyi Instytut, 1927), p. 78; Volodymyr Vynnychenko, *Vidrodzhennia Natsii*, 3 vols (Kyiv-Vienna: Dzvin, 1920), Vol. 1, pp. 92–3.

by plebiscites of border populations; that national territorial autonomy be implemented before elections to an All-Russian constituent assembly, with the immediate establishment of a regional Ukrainian council (*Kraieva Rada*); and finally, that stateless peoples, not only states, be represented at international peace talks to bring the War to an end.

Hrushevsky was elected head of the Rada almost unanimously in a secret ballot. The author and playright Volodymyr Vynnychenko from the USDWP and Serhii Yefremov, a journalist and historian from the UPSF, were elected in an open ballot as his deputies. They headed the *mala rada*, a standing body which adopted decisions of policy between general assemblies of Rada deputies. Numbering 20 in all, it was drawn overwhelmingly from the intelligentsia and in its majority from the moderate UPSF. Only one member of the *mala rada*, Pavlo Khrystiuk, was a socialist revolutionary from the UPSR.

The congress elected deputies to the Rada's general assembly: 13 from Kyiv civic associations, eight from soldiers' organisations, five each from co-operatives, the Peasant Union, students and teachers, one from the Ukrainian Women's Union; from the UPSF five, USDWP four, UPSR and Ukrainian Revolutionary Democratic Party (URDP) three each; and one from a small group of nationalist independentists. Each provincial capital got three deputies and the province's population outside its capital four. Ukrainian communities living in the Kuban, Bessarabia, Petrograd, Moscow, Rostov and Saratov also sent deputies into the Rada.[15]

Thus the Rada's first elected leadership was moderate and even conservative in outlook compared with the more radical bent of its assembly deputies.

2   Peasants in the City

The first year of the Revolution was distinguished from the ones that followed by the strength of the soldiers' movement in the cities and the link it provided between urban workers and peasants on the land. Right from the beginning this new, momentarily urban force tipped the balance of social forces in favour of the working class against the upper classes. The peasant conscripts who joined the bread protests in Petrograd precipitated the fall of the autocracy. They were the pride of the revolutionary movement in 1917. 'The soldier was a *persona grata*. He made the Revolution. Everywhere he was accorded first place'.[16]

---

15   Soldatenko, *Ukraina v revoliutsiinu dobu*, Vol. 1, pp. 193–213.
16   Dmytro Doroshenko, *Moi Spomyny pro Nedavnie Mynule, 1914–20* (Munich: Ukrains'ke Vydavnytstvo, 1969), p. 156.

By 1917 there were 4.5 million Ukrainian soldiers in the Russian army. They had come to hate the War, in which they were fighting on behalf of a state that denied them land and rights and that sent them into battle against men like themselves, including Ukrainian soldiers on the Austro-Hungarian side. Militant village teachers in their ranks taught them to fashion their hatred into demands for an end to the War, for land, national equality and self-determination. The Ukrainian soldiers' movement was like others in the Russian army in 1916 and 1917 which demanded its reorganisation into national armies, solely for the defence of each nation's homeland against all the belligerent powers in the War.[17] Soldiers formed clubs and associations, read newspapers to one another to share news and discussed ways to defend their interests. They agitated for the election of officers and the establishment of separate regiments and demanded to be stationed on Ukrainian soil or as close as possible to it on the front.

In the early days of the soldiers' movement a struggle broke out between Ukrainian nationalist officers in the army, who wanted solely to organise and lead national regiments from the ranks already under their own command, and Ukrainian socialist revolutionaries and social democrats who supported the demands of the ranks to elect their own officers and make them accountable to councils of elected soldiers' deputies.[18] This internal struggle was resolved in favour of the latter soon afterwards, when the soldiers' movement swelled to massive proportions and dispelled any notions of officers' authority without soldiers' consent.

An early example of the soldiers' movement in formation was a spontaneous gathering of three thousand unassigned recruits in April in the centre of Kyiv. They wanted to leave together for the front as the First Ukrainian Regiment of Bohdan Khmelnytsky. Electing their own officers, the recruits dispatched them to headquarters of the Kyiv Military District to seek its approval. When they were refused the soldiers turned to the Rada to request its intercession with the military authorities. The Rada supported them, while the Kyiv Council of Workers' Deputies and the Executive Committee of the Provisional Government stood strongly opposed. The Khmelnytsky regiment was eventually accepted into the army on its own terms. However, as it left Kyiv for the front in the wake

---

17   Mark von Hagen, 'A Socialist Army Officer Confronts War and Nationalist Politics: Konstantin Oberuchev in Revolutionary Kyiv', *Journal of Ukrainian Studies*, 33–34 (2008–09); Mikhail Frenkin, *Russkaia armiia i revoliutsiia 1917–1918* (Munich: Logos, 1978); Alan Wildman, *The End of the Russian Imperial Army*, 2 vols (Princeton: Princeton University Press, 1980, 1987).
18   N.N. Popov, 'Moskovs'ka hrupa "livykh" u USDRP', *Litopys Revoliutsii*, 6 (1928).

in July, nationalist Russian officers raked its train with machine gun fire and killed 16 soldiers on board.[19]

Other regiments were formed, including the Shevchenko heavy artillery regiment in Berdychiv, the Ivan Honta regiment in Uman, the Polubotok regiment in Chernihiv, regiments named after Taras Shevchenko, Pylyp Orlyk, Chyhyryn and Nalyvaiko in Petrograd, until there were 30 of them in the city garrisons and another 27 on the front, a combined force of a million and a half soldiers. In Kyiv alone, there were 50,000 soldiers in the Ukrainian regiments by the end of June.[20] In the councils of soldiers' deputies, they worked mainly with the UPSR.

On 5 May, 700 elected deputies representing 993,400 soldiers met in Kyiv for the First All-Ukrainian Soldiers' Congress. They adopted resolutions calling on the Provisional Government to recognise Ukraine's national autonomy in principle and to begin negotiating with the Tsentral'na Rada on its practical implementation. The deputies called for an end to the War, reorganisation of the entire Russian army into national regiments, the training of a Ukrainian officer corps and for regular provision of Ukrainian language newspapers to the front. The Congress chose the Rada as its political representative and identified itself as 'the foundation of the organised military might of the Ukrainian democracy'. It elected a General Military Committee headed by the social democrat Symon Petliura to advise the Rada on all matters pertaining to the army and the War.[21]

The Tsentral'na Rada's rural base of support came from the *selians'ki spilky*, village unions of poor and middle peasants organised by the UPSR in April and May. They adopted a common programme at the First All-Ukrainian Peasants' Congress, held in Kyiv on 28 May–4 June and attended by 2,500 deputies from approximately 1,500 *spilky*.[22] It called for the expropriation of all landed estates without compensation, its division and redistribution by local peasant councils, and a ban on the sale of land or the hiring of labour. The Congress also demanded an end to the War without indemnities or annexations, recognition

---

19   Khrystiuk, *Ukrains'ka Revoliutsiia*, Vol. 1, p. 48.
20   I.F. Kuras, 'Borot'ba bils'hovykiv za zmitsnennia soiuzu syl sotsialistychnoi revoliutsii i natsional'no-vyzvol'noho rukhu (ber.-zhovt. 1917 r.)', *Ukrains'kyi Istorychnyi Zhurnal*, 12 (December 1976), p. 40; Isaak Mazepa, *Ukraina v Ohni i Buri Revoliutsii 1917–1921*, 3 vols (n.p.: Prometei, 1950), Vol. 1, p. 29.
21   Khrystiuk, *Ukrains'ka Revoliutsiia*, Vol. 1, pp. 53–4; Andrii Zdorov, *Ukrains'kyi Zhovten'* (Odesa: Astroprint, 2007), pp. 66–9.
22   Khrystiuk, *Ukrains'ka Revoliutsiia*, Vol. 1, p. 65; *Encyclopedia of Ukraine*, 1984 edn, s.v. 'All-Ukrainian Peasant Congresses'.

of the Tsentral'na Rada by the Provisional Government and the establishment of an autonomous Ukrainian government.[23]

The Congress elected a Council of Peasants' Deputies which delivered to the Rada a proposal that it adopt immediately a plan for the autonomy of Ukraine in a federal democratic Russian republic. It called upon the Rada to convene a congress of peoples of the empire who supported the federal principle as a basis for rebuilding the existing state and urged it to use all its resources to bring forward general elections in Ukraine, to democratise all civic institutions and local governments to ensure they represented their resident populations.

There was not a single congress in 1917 at which the peasants' representatives did not demand the confiscation of land without compensation nor an immediate end to the War. They made these demands with impatience, insisting that the Rada act expeditiously to secure them. Kovalevsky, a delegate from Uman, put it to the first peasants' congress that if the Provisional Government refused to satisfy their demand for national autonomy

> then we should take it ourselves, relying on the revolutionary self-organisation of the entire Ukrainian people and on the peasantry in particular. Our children will not forgive us if we don't win at least national territorial autonomy. If words don't help then swords will! The time has come to take what's ours! We won't plead or bow anymore because this is ours![24]

The Rada's leaders responded to the resolutions of the First All-Ukrainian Soldiers' Congress by composing a declaration to the Provisional Government and the Petrograd Soviet of Workers' and Soldiers' Deputies. They sent it to Petrograd on 13 May with a delegation headed by Volodymyr Vynnychenko. Now the Rada spoke to those it regarded as its counterparts in Russia, as a mandated representative of the Ukrainian people and as their equal:

> The growth of the Ukrainian movement, which has revealed itself with such intensity in these days of revolution, demands new methods for its assessment, new political approaches, not to mention just getting to know what it is saying ... in this regard, however, everything remains as it was in the past and the Russian citizenry by and large rests on its old, undefined position.

---

23 *Robitnycha hazeta*, 3 May 1917, p. 1; Shapoval, *Velyka Revoliutsiia*, p. 80.
24 Soldatenko, *Ukraina v revoliutsiinu dobu*, Vol. 1, pp. 360–1.

This is already impacting negatively on the mutual relations between our two fraternal peoples, while for the future it threatens us with very undesirable complications. To avoid them and to overcome these difficulties both sides should take action on a state and civic level ...

But how does the Russian community living in Ukraine treat this truly fabulous reawakening of a 35 million strong people? We have to say right away that its relationship is a superficial one and not in the interests of revolutionary Russia. On the contrary, it is what threatens the entire cause of freedom with so many problems. There are a lot of reasons for this, but the main one is class interest. The ruling classes in Ukraine are not Ukrainian. Industry is in the hands of a Russian, Jewish and French bourgeoisie; a big part of the commercial and agricultural bourgeoisie is made up of Poles, Russians, and Ukrainians who have long since called themselves *russki*. Similarly all administrative posts are in the hands of non-Ukrainians.

It is also necessary to consider in the round the national dimension. Having been suckled on the milk of autocracy and centralism, being accustomed to looking at Ukraine as merely the southwestern region of the Russian Empire and at Ukrainians as *khakhly*[25] who differ from Russians only in some minor aspects of everyday life, never having bothered to acquaint themselves with the life of these *khakhly* and what their ideals are, ideals which never died even under the oppression of Tsarism, the bourgeois intelligentsia cannot find in itself the strength to rise to a clear understanding of what has been going on here all the time. And by succumbing to these two forces of class and national egoism, it has taken the path of strongly resisting the formation of the Ukrainian democracy, resorting to every available means.

Twisting the facts in the press and at public meetings, they are spreading rumours that the *khakhly* want to separate from Russia, that they are preparing to expel all non-Ukrainians from Ukraine because, allegedly their slogan is 'Ukraine only for the Ukrainians', that in its entirety the Ukrainian movement is, without regard for its internal social or political differences, a counterrevolutionary movement that must be stopped immediately. They have become so frightened by the massive growth of this movement that they have infected with their fears even the democratic non-Ukrainian milieux. The Russian democracy has been so infected with the attitudes of the Russian bourgeoisie, with the idea that the

---

25   A pejorative term in Russian for a Ukrainian.

Russians rule over Ukraine ... that an unusually high level of hostility now persists. Such hostility has, for example, led the head of the Kyiv Council of Workers' and Soldiers' Deputies to appear before a conference of socialist organisations of all nationalities and to threaten to use bayonets to break up a Ukrainian congress.[26]

Believing they were ill informed by their representatives in Ukraine the Rada wanted to impress upon the Provisional Government and the Petrograd Soviet the mass character of the Ukrainian national movement and the alarm and hostility it was provoking among the Russian minority. The Rada's delegation was instructed to seek a way out of the looming conflict by proposing to the Provisional Government 'the adoption of an act of agreement in principle of Ukraine's right to national autonomy, appointment of a commissar of Ukrainian affairs in the Provisional Government and a governing commissar for all Ukraine with a Regional Council attached to him, and the assignation of funds for the national cultural needs of the Ukrainian people and for other matters'.[27]

The Rada's delegation met with Prince Lvov, head of the Council of Ministers, but could not persuade him to bring its demands for consideration before the government as a whole. Instead the delegation was granted a meeting with a commission, which informed them after some discussion that it could not respond to any of their proposals. The delegation then informed the commission that the Rada henceforth could not be held responsible for maintaining order in Ukraine. Delegation members also met for talks with Nikoloz Chkheidze, head of the Petrograd Soviet. The Soviet offered no formal response to the Rada's proposals. After waiting for three weeks in the capital for an official statement from the Provisional Government the delegation returned empty-handed to Kyiv.

The Rada then recalled the soldiers' deputies to Kyiv. Defying a ban imposed by Aleksandr Kerensky, then Minister of Defence, 2,308 deputies mandated by over 1.6 million soldiers travelled to Kyiv to take part in the Second All-Ukrainian Soldiers' Congress. Convened on 5 June, the Congress charged the Provisional Government with

> misunderstanding completely the national relations prevalent in Ukraine and not estimating properly the degree of self-organisation and elemental power of the awakening Ukrainian democracy ... If it wants to uphold the

---

26 Oleksandr Reient, *Robitnytstvo Ukrainy i Tsentral'na Rada* (Kyiv: Akademiia Nauk, Instytut Istorii, 1993).
27 *Visty z Ukrains'koi Tsentral'noi Rady*, 8 (May 1917).

gains of the Revolution … then its first task must be to change its attitude to the demands forwarded by the Tsentral'na Rada and to accept them without delay.[28]

Promising its full support, the Congress demanded the Rada halt further negotiations with the Provisional Government, unilaterally declare Ukraine's autonomy and begin putting it into practice. It also demanded the Government recognise the authority of its General Military Committee to command organised Ukrainian ranks in the Russian army. Volodymyr Vynnychenko came from the Rada on the last day of the Congress with the text of the First Universal, a unilateral declaration of autonomy. He read it to the assembled deputies:

> Let Ukraine be free. Without separating from all-Russia, without breaking with the Russian state, let the Ukrainian people have the right to govern their own lives in their own land. Let universal, equal, direct and secret elections to a Ukrainian National Assembly (Parliament) bring order and harmony to Ukraine. Only our own Ukrainian Assembly should have the right to make laws that provide such order here in Ukraine. And the laws which should provide order across the whole Russian state should be issued by an All-Russian Parliament.[29]

The soldiers' deputies then adopted the First Universal and sang Taras Shevchenko's revolutionary poem *Zapovit* (*Testament*) on their knees. The Universal was read out a few days later to the citizens of Kyiv on the square around Khmelnytsky's monument.[30]

3   Ukrainian Workers

The daily newspaper of the USDWP, *Robitnycha hazeta*, published many reports in the first months of the Revolution describing the turbulent growth of national consciousness among Ukrainian workers. While the party already had a modest cadre of working class militants from before 1917 to lend it some direction, it now witnessed a largely spontaneous process of politicisation released by the collapse of the autocracy and driven by the promise of fundamental change. There were thousands of factory and railway workers, teachers, postal

---

28   Vynnychenko, *Vidrodzhennia Natsii*, Vol. 1, p. 201.
29   Ibid, Vol. 1, pp. 219–20.
30   Ibid, Vol. 1, pp. 202, 225.

and telegraph employees at the first mass demonstration in Kyiv that backed the Tsentral'na Rada on 19 March.[31] Similar meetings and demonstrations were taking place in towns and cities across Ukraine.

Teachers and sugar refinery workers in Kalnyk, Kyiv province, organised a demonstration bearing red flags and national blue and gold flags on the second day of Easter to back demands for Ukrainian national autonomy.[32] On 3 April, 300 garment workers and peasants in the town of Myropillia, Kursk province, composed a resolution calling for 'the right of self-determination ... every nation must decide for itself with which state it wants to associate or if it wants to live independently'. The resolution expressed a desire of Myropillia residents, who lived in the far north eastern tip of Ukrainian ethnographic territories, to associate with Kyiv. It also expressed their concern for Galicia, over the western border with Austro-Hungary and then under military occupation, 'where our countrymen, the Ukrainians live'.[33]

Ukrainian workers marched in their own contingents in the May Day parade in Kharkiv. Most of them were employed at the Helferich Sade and Shymansky factories. They were joined by railways workers on the southern lines and soldiers carrying national flags inscribed in the slogans 'Long live socialism' and 'Down with militarism'. After the May Day ceremony in the Kharkiv Hippodrome, they marched again through the city led by a soldiers' orchestra.[34]

The first organised manifestation of Kateryslov Ukrainians was also on May Day when their contingents received huge ovations from the crowds lining the march.[35] In Poltava, the USDWP attracted many May Day marchers to its section in the parade.[36] In Petrograd, over forty thousand workers and soldiers marched under USDWP banners on that day.[37] The town of Lubny, Poltava province, was adorned for the May Day holiday with red and blue and gold flags. Among the eighty-seven groups taking part in the march there were numerous contingents carrying banners with the slogans 'Long live the International', 'Long live socialism', 'Long live a free Ukraine' and 'Long live an autonomous Ukraine'. When the first speaker to address the participants in the Ukrainian language began, a roar of approval went up. 'It was hard to tell' wrote *Robit-*

---

31   Clarence Manning, *Twentieth Century Ukraine* (New York: Bookman Associates, 1951), p. 37; Khrystiuk, *Ukrains'ka Revoliutsiia*, Vol. 1, p. 29.
32   *Robitnycha hazeta*, 6 April 1917, p. 4.
33   *Robitnycha hazeta*, 22 April 1917, p. 3.
34   *Robitnycha hazeta*, 2 May 1917, p. 3.
35   Mazepa, *Ukraina v Ohni*, Vol. 1, p. 18.
36   *Robitnycha hazeta*, 4 May 1917, p. 4.
37   Avdiienko, *'Liutneva Revoliutsiia v Petrohradi'*, p. 231.

nycha hazeta's correspondent in Lubny 'just where the workers' holiday ended and the national one began'.[38]

The first mass demonstration by Ukrainians in Luhansk took place on 11 May. It was held in honour of Shevchenko. Of the ten flags carried in the demonstration, four were red ones bearing socialist slogans and demands for national autonomy. The participants were addressed by speakers from the USDWP, UPSR and the Luhansk Council of Workers' and Soldiers' Deputies.[39] Such demonstrations were an overt sign of a significant growth in national awareness among Ukrainian workers during the War, which then affected the way they looked upon the prospects opened up by the collapse of Tsarism. It brought the national question squarely into the realm of concerns of the labour movement and stimulated a debate on the issue between workers in numerous places of employment.

A thousand railway workers and soldiers assembled on 13 April at the No. 2 passenger station in Kyiv to discuss disagreements between Russian and Ukrainian workers over the national question and the future of Ukraine. Vynnychenko spoke to the gathering on 'the spontaneous rebirth of national consciousness among the Ukrainian people'. Hortynsky, a member of the Kyiv Council of Workers' Deputies (most likely from the USDWP) spoke of 'the necessity for a successful struggle by the working class with the capitalist order, for the free development of workers' spiritual strength and, as a first condition, that teaching in the schools be conducted in their native language'. He was joined by a Menshevik speaker who supported the principle of national autonomy and Ukrainisation of schools. According to the report in *Robitnycha hazeta* 'the friendly and comradely tone of the comrades from both parties made a good and uplifting impression on the Ukrainian and Russian workers alike'.[40]

Workers at the Kyiv Arsenal gathered in the first week of April to hear speeches from Ukrainian deputies of the Petrograd Soviet and the Odesa and Katerynoslav Councils. They adopted a resolution supporting the Petrograd Soviet and calling for 'the reconstruction of the Russian state into a democratic, federated republic'.[41] On 15 April, the Poltava USDWP branch sponsored a meeting attended by a thousand railway workers at which a spirited debate on the national question was joined by representatives of all socialist parties in the city.[42] At the Shymansky factory in Kharkiv, where over half of the work-

---

38   *Robitnycha hazeta*, 30 April 1917, p. 4.
39   *Robitnycha hazeta*, 25 May 1917, p. 4.
40   *Robitnycha hazeta*, 2 May 1917, p. 4.
41   *Robitnycha hazeta*, 12 April 1917, p. 3.
42   *Robitnycha hazeta*, 27 April 1917, p. 3.

force was Ukrainian, fierce debates were taking place throughout April over the type of literature that they should collect and send to army units on the front. Ukrainian workers demanded that at least 30 percent of the literature be in their own language 'because whole regiments of the army are composed of Ukrainians and they need newspapers and books written in our language'. Bolsheviks among Shymansky's workers opposed this demand and accused the Ukrainians of chauvinism, of wanting to divide the workers. Eventually, two literature collections were held, one for Russian and another for Ukrainian material.[43]

The Tsentral'na Rada's First Universal drew resolutions of support from workers on the railway lines between Moscow, Voronezh and Kyiv, at Katerynoslav foundries and rolling mills, the Kyiv railway depots, Odesa water works, sugar refineries in Chernihiv and elsewhere.[44] The Myrhorod (Poltava province) Council of Workers', Soldiers' and Peasants' Deputies resolved on 13 June 'to implement all of the directives of the Tsentral'na Rada in regards to establishing the autonomy of Ukraine'.[45] The executive committee of the Zinkov Council of Workers' and Soldiers' Deputies recognised the Rada 'as its own national government' and promised 'to use all means to implement immediately and comprehensively the First Universal in town and country'.[46] An executive member of the Poltava Council of Workers' and Peasants' Deputies and a member of the UPSR, Leonard Bochkovsky appeared before the Rada's general assembly in June to declare its support for the Universal. Significantly, Bochkovsky called for the expansion of the assembly to include delegates from all workers', soldiers' and peasants' councils in Ukraine.[47]

4 First All-Ukrainian Workers' Congress

Support for the Tsentral'na Rada came initially from those workers' councils in which Ukrainians constituted a significant bloc of the deputies. By mid-1917 it was a sufficiently strong current to warrant bringing together its leaders and co-ordinating their local work at a national level. USDWP and UPSR deputies

---

43 *Robitnycha hazeta*, 25 April 1917, p. 4.
44 *Robitnycha hazeta*, 20 May 1917, p. 4; 24 May 1917, p. 3; 29 May 1917, p. 4.
45 Yu. M. Hamretsky, 'Stavlennia Rad Robitnychykh i Soldats'kykh Deputativ Ukrainy u Periodi Dvovladdia do Pytan' Natsional'no-Vyzvol'noho Rukhu', *Ukrains'kyi Istorychnyi Zhurnal*, 7 (July 1966), p. 13.
46 Ibid.
47 *Visty Ukrains'koi Tsentral'noi Rady*, 10 (June 1917), p. 3.

in the Kyiv Council of Workers' Deputies took the initiative in June to organise a national congress of Ukrainians active in the workers' movement. Held in Kyiv from 11–14 July, the First All-Ukrainian Workers' Congress attracted 400 participants delegated to represent forty thousand workers. The USDWP commanded the largest fraction of 175 delegates, followed by the UPSR fraction of 75 delegates. The Congress received greetings from the Bund, Poale Zion and the Polish Socialist Party (PPS). It was a gathering of militants active mainly among the Ukrainian agricultural proletariat and the workers of industries closely associated with agriculture. Although it was significantly smaller than the peasants' and soldiers' congresses that preceded it, this congress nevertheless was an important first attempt in 1917 to build a bridge between the Ukrainian national movement and the multinational workers' movement.

In line with a longstanding tradition the congress adopted at the outset a resolution of solidarity with the struggle of Irish workers against the British bourgeoisie.[48] Delegates then heard speeches and deliberated on eight subjects, adopting resolutions on all of them: the political situation in Russia; the War; Ukraine's autonomy in a federated Russian republic and Constituent Assembly elections; the land question; the supply of basic provisions to the population; employment and industrial relations policy; on workers' organisations; and state education policy. Their resolutions called for an immediate end to the War, the confiscation of landed estates without compensation and a ban on the sale of all land. The congress addressed essentially the same big issues as the first soldiers' and peasants' congresses and adopted broadly similar resolutions.

The devil, however, hid in the details of the debates taking place on the congress floor. The delegates disagreed with one another and with the Rada's leaders whom they had invited to address them over three closely intertwined issues: first, the nature of the revolutionary process then underway; second, the class nature of the Tsentral'na Rada, its willingness and capacity to undertake all the tasks on the agenda of the revolution; and third, the tasks facing Ukrainian workers and their relationship to the multinational working class of Ukraine.

The USDWP's centrist leaders dominated the congress debates, pushing aside their own left wing members and the even more radical socialist revolutionaries. The centrists in the USDWP expected the revolutionary process to culminate in democratic elections to constituent assemblies for a federated

---

48   A.P. Hrytsenko, *Ukrains'ki Robitnyky na shliakhu tvorennia natsional'noi derzhavy: pershii vseukrains'kii robitnychii z'iizd 11–14/24–27 lypnia 1917r* (Kyiv: Instytut Istorii Ukrainy, National'na Akademiia Nauk Ukrainy, 1992), pp. 5, 18.

Russian republic and for an autonomous Ukrainian republic within it. Only in these assemblies would the main tasks of the revolution be definitively resolved. They also acknowledged that bourgeois interests, as well as those of workers and peasants, were represented, and indeed should be represented, in the Rada. They believed the resolution of the national question and overcoming the economic crisis both required a combined effort of all the social classes. Vynnychenko in his address to the congress spoke out against turning the Rada into a council representing workers, soldiers and peasants alone, cautioning the revolutionary democracy not to take on all government responsibility. If the industrial and landowning bourgeoisie was excluded from the Rada, he argued, there would be chaos in the event of the Rada's failure to create a functioning national government. Likewise, constituent assembly elections for a federated Russian republic should lead to a government of all classes. Socialism, he said, was still some way off in the future:

> No-one will cope with this ruin that now envelops us. Because the socialists themselves and the Councils of Workers' Deputies don't build the trains, they can't give us bread, and they won't deliver the goods. So that responsibility is shared out between all the classes they first must have their representatives in our parliament.[49]

The USDWP's leaders did not see beyond this horizon, which was dominated for them by the revolution's national tasks. Of course, an autonomous national government should become an important site for the resolution of other struggles over social, economic and political inequalities. Thus the social democrats envisaged co-operation with the bourgeoisie simultaneously with a struggle against it. Their vision clashed with the expectations of more radical participants in the congress who wanted the Rada to start implementing the social and economic demands of the workers and peasants immediately. Like the Bolsheviks they were advocating these demands with a sense of urgency. But unlike the Bolsheviks they were looking to Kyiv rather than Petrograd as the capital in which to assemble the organised power to resolve them.

'The Rada must win power', argued the delegate Dubovy, 'and get involved in a new struggle, a social and economic one'. To which Mykola Porsh replied: 'We can be at ease once power is in the hands of the Tsentral'na Rada here and when in Russia it is in the hands of the revolutionary democracy's representatives'. To which the USDWP delegate from Moscow Andrii Richytsky countered:

---

49 Hrytsenko, *Ukrains'ki Robitnyky na shliakhu tvorennia natsional'noi derzhavy*, pp. 22–3.

'Only when the Rada has been completely rebuilt on the model of the Council of Workers' and Soldiers' Deputies will we have a strong government'.[50]

The Declaration adopted at the end of proceedings reflected the dilemma facing those who adhered to the centrist USDWP faction's vision and strategy:

> The Ukrainian Tsentral'na Rada holds not only workers but also bourgeois classes of the Ukrainian and non-Ukrainian population. Bound to fight in concert with them for its national, cultural and political liberation the Ukrainian proletariat must fight simultaneously against all kinds of bourgeoisie, which includes the Ukrainian bourgeoisie. Once again this path is slippery and dangerous because conscious Ukrainian workers do not have the right in any way to back down from their own class interests and needs. But they should also not push the Ukrainian bourgeoisie away from themselves in the common struggle for national freedom and Ukraine's autonomy.[51]

What, then, did the Ukrainian workers' representatives at this congress see as their immediate tasks? By mid-1917 a majority of Ukrainian workers belonged to unions and worked in enterprises that elected and sent delegates to the local workers' council. The Ukrainian fraction of the Kyiv Council of Workers' Deputies which initiated the workers' congress had called upon similar fractions in other workers' councils, as well as organisations such as the sugar workers' union where Ukrainian workers were concentrated, to send their delegates. One of its objectives was simply to find out just how many organised and unorganised Ukrainian workers there were in every locality.

The congress resolution on workers' organisation called upon Ukrainian workers to build and take part in industrial and trade unions, which should be open to all without regard for political or religious conviction, nationality or race. These unions should eventually coalesce into a single Industrial Workers' Union of Ukraine. The role of the unions was threefold: to improve workers' economic standing, to reduce their hours of work, and to equip them through training and education 'to bring to life the socialisation of the means of production', that is to say, workers' control, ownership and management of the economy.

Within this broad objective the congress resolution also set out specific tasks for the unions with regard to their Ukrainian members: 'In view of the need to

---

50   Ibid, p. 17.
51   Ibid, Appendix.

improve the cultural level of Ukrainian workers which has sunk very low after many years of national oppression, the congress calls upon workers to create their own cultural and educational societies ... to form an All-Ukrainian central bureau of workers' educational societies which should provide general direction to the societies and shed light on the class position of the proletariat in our existing social order'.[52]

Finally, the congress elected 100 deputies, 70 USDWP members and 30 from the UPSR, to represent it in the Rada's general assembly. The deputies, who were seated in the Rada on 5 August, were instructed to retain their independence as a voting bloc and to seek a united course of action with the workers of other nationalities.[53] In his speech Vynnychenko assured them that

> in the Rada they will meet the workers of other nations of Ukraine and together they will represent all the working people of Ukraine. We can't have any discord, so that the working class can indeed join battle in the Tsentral'na Rada with the Ukrainian and non-Ukrainian bourgeoisie ... in this parliament the working people will fight for their freedom without regard for nationality. They will be actively creating our national political life in the name of our bright future – socialism.[54]

Vynnychenko's optimism could not dispel the doubts about the USDWP strategy that many must have felt at the end of the congress. There were no other nationalities yet formally represented in the Rada, let alone delegations of workers of other nationalities. Was this the way to proceed, given that the focus of workers' self organisation and representation in 1917 was the burgeoning movement of councils of workers' deputies? The First All-Ukrainian Workers' Congress had not even discussed, let alone adopted, a policy on the workers' councils nor the role that Ukrainian workers' fractions should play within them.

5   A National Autonomy of Sorts

It was quite understandable why the Ukrainian social democrats and their milieu felt wary, if not pessimistic, about staking their claim in the wider working class movement. It was not just a question of their relatively small numbers, but of the hostility to their national demands from the wider democratic camp.

---

52   Ibid.
53   Khrystiuk, *Ukrains'ka Revoliutsiia*, Vol. 1, p. 104.
54   Hrytsenko, *Ukrains'ki Robitnyky na shliakhu tvorennia natsional'noi derzhavy*, p. 11.

Liberal and conservative Russians were protesting to the Petrograd government that their own national rights were being threatened by the Ukrainian national movement, while Russian social democrats protested that it was threatening the unity of the working class. 'There was frequent clamour of the kind that "Ukrainians have stabbed the revolution and democracy in the back"'.[55] The First Universal was denounced as a German intrigue in Kyiv's Russian newspapers of the right and as 'bourgeois nationalism' in papers of the left.[56] The Katerynoslav city *duma* mounted a campaign against 'Ukrainian separatism'.[57] Upon learning of the First Universal the All-Russian Council of Peasants' Deputies under the leadership of the Russian SRs supported national autonomy and federalism *in principle* but called upon the Rada to *withdraw* the Universal.

> Issuing this Universal is dangerous because its immediate implementation introduces new and massive complication to state life, threatens to cause national hostility, contributes to national conflicts, weakens the capacity of the state to resist its external enemy, undermines the authority of the Provisional Government, encourages similar demands by other nationalities and altogether weakens and tears the revolution apart.[58]

Yet there were dissenters from this viewpoint in the left flank of the democracy. The First All-Russian Congress of Soviets in Petrograd, meeting eleven days after the Rada issued the First Universal, resolved to support the attainment of national autonomy for Ukraine, but noted also that it could only be confirmed after All-Russian constituent assembly elections. The Congress' support for the Rada's efforts was largely the result of the Bolsheviks' work among its delegates, while the condition attached to the resolution was the insurance demanded by the Mensheviks and Russian SRs against any further unilateral moves by the Ukrainian movement.

Lenin attacked Aleksandr Kerensky, who as Minister of Defence tried to ban the Ukrainian soldiers' congress, and the Provisional Government as a whole for its refusal to recognise the legitimacy of the Rada's demands:

> No democrat, to say nothing about a socialist, will dare to deny the completely lawful nature of Ukrainian demands. Nor can any democrat deny Ukraine's right to freely separate from Russia: it is precisely the uncon-

---

55 Soldatenko, *Ukraina v revoliutsiinu dobu*, Vol. 1, p. 360.
56 Khrystiuk, *Ukrains'ka Revoliutsiia*, Vol. 1, pp. 82–3.
57 Mazepa, *Ukraina v Ohni*, Vol. 1, p. 18.
58 Vynnychenko, *Vidrodzhennia Natsii*, Vol. 1, p. 237.

ditional recognition of this right that alone makes it possible to agitate for a free union of Ukrainians with Great Russians, for the voluntary unification of both peoples into one state. It is precisely the unconditional recognition of this right that is capable of breaking in practice, irreversibly and finally, with that accursed Tsarist past which did everything to alienate these peoples from one another, who are so close in language, place of settlement, in character and history. Accursed Tsarism made the Great Russians into the oppressors of the Ukrainian people, who in turn came to hate those who even prohibited Ukrainian children to speak and learn their own native language.[59]

Lenin, however, was in a minority among the Bolsheviks. The leading Kyivan Bolshevik Hryhorii Piatakov opposed the Ukrainian movement, saying 'this movement is not convenient for the proletariat':

We can see in this movement the national bourgeoisie in struggle against elements of the social revolution. It is trying to use national means to tie the hands of the revolutionary movement and turn back the wheel of history. This movement is against the social revolution ... We stand before two tasks: to protest against the government's actions, including Kerensky's, and to fight against the chauvinistic efforts of the Ukrainians.[60]

Piatakov went on to argue that only a plebiscite of the entire population could empower a body like the Rada to speak in the name of the Ukrainian people. Without such empowerment the Bolsheviks would oppose these demands, if necessary by force.

The divisions in the democratic camp over the Ukrainian question were most evident among the intelligentsia and petit bourgeoisie, who readily became involved in the political process after the February Revolution and took seats in all the new institutions vying for political power, including the urban workers' and soldiers' councils. Their presence made it very unlikely that these councils would be guided in their actions solely by the economic and social interests of the proletariat and peasantry without regard for their national interests and sensibilities or, indeed, prejudices. Serhii Mazlakh, a Ukrainian Bolshevik, pointed out that the councils were no more purely class organs

---

[59] Lenin, *Collected Works*, Vol. 32, pp. 333–4; cited in Soldatenko, *Ukraina v revoliutsiinu dobu*, Vol. 1, pp. 450–1.
[60] Soldatenko, *Ukraina v revoliutsiinu dobu*, Vol. 1, p. 443.

than the Tsentral'na Rada was a purely national organ. From the outset of the Revolution, leadership in the workers' councils was assumed by the Russian petit-bourgeois intelligentsia, most of whom belonged to or sympathised with the Mensheviks.[61] Andrii Richytsky noted that

> in the first few months of this unstable period, the councils of workers' deputies became props and places of refuge for the Great Power, nationalist, urban petit bourgeoisie (Mensheviks, Socialist Revolutionaries, Bundists). In its struggle to retain national privileges in Ukraine, the petit bourgeoisie covered itself with a fig leaf of democracy, revolution and even internationalism. While in Russia even the most conciliatory workers' councils had strained relations with the Provisional Government and opened up a dual power contest with it that was so hated by the bourgeoisie, in Ukraine until the Kornilov offensive ... they were propagators of the 'All-Russian' [*obshcherusskoe*] point of view and of the Provisional Government's policies. Instead, they had strained relations with the Tsentral'na Rada ... they fed off the struggle of the urban petit bourgeoisie and were a conservative force that blocked with the big bourgeoisie against the Ukrainian national and peasant petit bourgeoisie.[62]

Leon Trotsky writes in his *History of the Russian Revolution*:

> The difference in nationality between the cities and the villages was painfully felt also in the soviets, they being predominantly city organisations. Under the leadership of the compromise parties the soviets would frequently ignore the national interests of the basic population. This was one cause of the weakness of the soviets in Ukraine ... Under a false banner of internationalism, the soviets would frequently wage a struggle against the defensive nationalism of the Ukrainians or Mussulmans [Muslims], supplying a screen for the oppressive Russifying movement of the cities.[63]

---

61   Skorovstiansky, *Revoliutsiia na Ukraine*, pp. 121–2; Yavorsky, *Revoliutsiia na Vkraini*, p. 39; M.A. Rubach, 'Proty revizii bil'shovytskoi skhemy rushiinykh syl ta kharakteru Revoliutsii 1917 roku na Ukraini', *Litopys Revoliutsii*, 5 (September–October 1930), p. 42; Hamretsky, Tymchenko and Shchus, *Rady Ukrainy*, pp. 19, 83.
62   Cited by Rubach, 'Treba diisno vypravyty', pp. 263–4.
63   Leon Trotsky, *History of the Russian Revolution*, 3 vols (London: Sphere Books, 1967), Vol. 3, pp. 47–8.

Vynnychenko believed already in the spring of 1917 that the democratic, pro-Government wing of the Russian petit bourgeoisie had made a tacit alliance with the bourgeoisie to derail the Ukrainian national movement. The most active promoter of the alliance was the Black Hundreds daily newspaper *Kyivlianin* whose insinuations that the Rada was a German intrigue were believed and repeated by democrats. 'The Russian intelligentsia needed some justification for their conservatism and chauvinism'.[64]

The Provisional Government's reading of the situation changed substantially after the Rada declared Ukraine's autonomy. Its initial shock at the defiance shown by the second soldiers' congress and the Rada's unilateral declaration of autonomy gave way to pragmatism. The Russian army's June offensive on the western front had collapsed, demoralisation and insubordination grew in the soldiers' ranks. The Rada could be useful to the Government in helping to maintain order in the army divisions stationed on its territory given that the Ukrainian soldiers' movement already recognised the Rada's authority. However, the growth of the Ukrainian national movement alarmed the Russian minority. The Government could reconcile the Russian parties to the devolution of some limited power to the Rada by including them in Rada's decision-making bodies, by ensuring they had a hefty share of its power. If that could be done, the Government could also rely on them to hold the Ukrainian majority in the Rada in check. For their part, the Rada's existing leaders were ready to co-operate with the Government, wanting its recognition and approval. They had been rebuffed once, they had since acquired even more popular support, but they were still looking for formal legitimacy from Petrograd.

The Bund played an important role in bringing the Government around to this point of view. Its members in Ukraine were concerned about the growth of opposing nationalisms as the Mensheviks and the Russian SRs more vigorously put forward their all-Russian unity position in the face of Ukrainian demands for autonomy. To prevent an escalation to open war between them the Bund proposed an autonomous administration on terms that would likely be acceptable to both the Provisional Government and most parts of the revolutionary democracy in Ukraine. A resolution of the Bureau of the Bund's Southern Oblast Committee argued that the growing division in the camp of the revolutionary democracy between the Tsentral'na Rada and the councillist movement threatened to become a catalyst to national conflict. In order to avoid it and at the same time 'to satisfy the lawful demands of the Ukrainian nation and all other nations living in Ukraine' the Provisional Government should set

---

64   Vynnychenko, *Vidrodzhennia Natsii*, Vol. 1, p. 106.

up a 'general territorial organ ... in the form of a representative body of the All-Russian Provisional Government'

> to realise the consistent democratisation of all aspects of life ... to combine the territorial autonomy of Ukraine with the autonomy of its national minorities, which in turn will guarantee for each one of them the right to national cultural autonomy and equality with other nations in all questions of national and state life ... A draft statute of territorial autonomy drafted by a territorial assembly, including the guarantee of national rights for minorities, should be presented for ratification by an All-Russian Constituent Assembly.[65]

The Bureau's resolution was adopted with a few minor changes by the Southern Conference of the Bund and was ratified by the Bund's Central Committee July meeting in Kyiv, which declared an autonomous Ukrainian government administration 'unconditionally necessary' and once established should become the only local authority. The Central Committee added that the participation of social democrats in the Rada was conditional on it having the competence and an action programme to secure the rights of all national minorities.

The Bund then carried this resolution to the nationalities commission of the First All-Russian Congress of Soviets on 21 June, where it was adopted and forwarded to the Provisional Government 'in the context of strengthening the revolution's gains and uniting the labour democracy of all nations'. Moshe Rafes, a leading Bund member, claimed it was this intervention that finally persuaded the Provisional Government 'to make peace with Ukraine'.[66]

At the end of June, four ministers of the Government, A. Kerensky, I. Tsereteli, M. Tereshchenko and M. Nekrasov, came to Kyiv to seek a compromise with the Rada. The negotiations produced a Government position paper on 3 July and a parallel text of the Tsentral'na Rada. This was its Second Universal, which called for an autonomous government responsible for finances, food supply, land reform, justice, education, nationalities, trade and industry, transport and postal and telegraph services. In return for such authority the Rada pledged to halt 'the unauthorised realisation of autonomy' until after All-Russian constituent assembly elections were held and to relinquish all matters to do with the military to the Provisional Government so as to ensure that the Ukrainian movement did not compromise the army's combat capacity.[67]

---

65   Rafes, *Dva goda*, footnote on p. 38.
66   Ibid, p. 39.
67   Soldatenko, *Ukraina v revoliutsiinu dobu*, Vol. 1, p. 481.

A key issue in the negotiations was the proportion of seats in the Tsentral'na Rada's *mala rada* and General Secretariat which should be given to representatives of the Russian, Jewish and Polish minorities. Proposals discussed with the Government's envoys ranged from between one third to a half of the seats in the Rada's executive organs being given over to them.[68] No firm agreement on this issue seems to have been reached.

The Government delegation returned to Petrograd, where the agreement it had reached with the Rada deepened an already mounting crisis in the Provisional Government. Economic chaos and dislocation were driving up unemployment, yet the Government failed to heed the call of the factory committees to increase its regulation of production and halt factory closures and workplace lockouts. The army's June offensive had collapsed within days. Attempts made by the military command to use the offensive to rein in the powers of soldiers' committees over their officers further alienated the troops. In Petrograd army units were refusing to leave for the front. One of these, the First Machine Gunners Regiment, set up outposts in strategic positions in the capital. On 3 July demonstrations of armed soldiers and workers descended on the Soviet's executive committee headquarters demanding it take power from the Provisional Government. The Bolsheviks and the anarchists now commanded much wider influence among workers and soldiers, with the Bolsheviks holding a majority in the workers' section of the Petrograd Soviet. The Bolsheviks supported the demonstrators but resisted their demand for a seizure of power from the Provisional Government, judging rightly that they still lacked sufficient support across the country.

The crisis unfolding in Petrograd echoed strongly in Kyiv. Here both the Government's authority and the Rada's capacity to assume control of the situation on the ground were tested on 4 and 5 July by the actions of five thousand conscripts of the self-styled Polubotok Regiment. The conscripts were refusing to be sent to the front and demanded to be recognised by the military authorities as a self governed regiment. They placed their own guard posts over government buildings, arrested Kyiv's chief of police, seized several police stations and destroyed the private residence of the commander of the Kyiv Military District. The Rada managed to deploy other troops to disarm the Polubotok insurgents and restore order in the centre of Kyiv. The incident heightened fear and mistrust of the Ukrainian national movement in several quarters. Both the military command in Kyiv and Kerensky in Petrograd insisted that Ukrainian soldiers obey orders and leave for the front. They did not want to see the

---

68   Ibid, Vol. 1, p. 96.

Rada surrounded by army units sympathetic to its assumption of even greater authority. More ominous still, the revolt of the Polubotok Regiment evoked vengeance from Russian nationalist officers who ordered troops under their command to fire upon two trains carrying another Ukrainised unit, the Bohdan Khmelnytsky regiment, as it left Kyiv for the front. Sixteen soldiers were shot dead and 30 were injured. Their attackers suffered no casualties. The Khmelnytsky regiment's commanders were disarmed, the trains looted and the Ukrainian soldiers duly humiliated.[69]

The entire incident exposed the deep ambivalence, if not outright opposition, of the USDWP leaders of the Rada towards the Ukrainisation movement in the army. As anti-militarists the Ukrainian social democrats were in principle opposed to standing armies. Rather, they stood for local popular militias, but they could not see how existing units of the Russian army, albeit with a large measure of rank and file control over officers and orders, could be reconciled with their conception of armed force. Moreover, as federalists, they believed the armed forces and foreign policy were prerogatives of a future Russian federal government, not an autonomous Ukrainian one. The Social Democratic leaders in the Rada actually opposed the formation of the Polubotok regiment as well as other attempts, before and after the Polubotok revolt, to Ukrainise the armed forces. Only under great pressure and with reluctance did they intervene on behalf of such regiments with the Provisional Government and its military general staff. The pressure to support them came from soldiers and officers, the UPSR, the moderate UPSF and the small contingent of nationalist independentists in the Rada itself.[70] The Polubotok revolt thus left the strong impression that the Rada would struggle to contain the mass mobilisations rising up around it, especially if it did not want to command an armed force of its own or would not be entrusted with such a command by the Provisional Government.

It was precisely in the midst of the so called July days that the Government's delegation returned from Kyiv to Petrograd with the negotiated agreement on autonomy. Charging that it had offered the Rada far too much power, all the Kadets in the Cabinet except Nekrasov resigned in protest. The Cabinet was in the midst of trying to replace the Kadets and the Prime Minister, Prince Lvov, who resigned over the Government's handling of the land reform issue, when a delegation from the Rada, composed of Moshe Rafes, Volodymyr Vynnychenko and Khrystian Baranovsky arrived in the capital to resume the negotiations.

---

69 Soldatenko, *Ukraina v revoliutsiinu dobu*, Vol. 1, pp. 499–618.
70 Ibid, Vol. 1, pp. 336–9.

They brought with them a draft Statute of a Higher Administration of Ukraine. However, the Government's attention was elsewhere: demonstrations of armed soldiers and workers had broken out, demanding the Petrograd Soviet assume power from the Government and deal with the deteriorating situation in the economy and on the front. All this made it unlikely the Rada delegation would even be seen. As with the Rada's attempt to negotiate with Petrograd in May, this delegation was rebuffed by senior government officials and lectured by lower officials on its lack of legal expertise. Following three weeks of fruitless effort, Rafes and Vynnychenko returned to Kyiv, leaving Baranovsky behind to wait for a formal response to its draft statute on autonomy.

On 4 August the Provisional Government made its final offer in the form of a 'Temporary Instruction to the General Secretariat of the Provisional Government in Ukraine'. The Instruction did not recognise the Tsentral'na Rada, but only its General Secretariat which it defined as an institution representing the Provisional Government itself. Four of the nine posts in the General Secretariat were reserved for representatives of minority nationalities. Its jurisdiction was to extend over five, rather than nine gubernia – Kyiv, Volyn, Podillia, Poltava and Chernihiv. The General Secretariat was accorded nine ministerial portfolios: interior, agriculture, finances, education, trade and industry, labour, nationalities, recording secretary and the post of general controller. The army, railways, post and telegraph, and food supply remained under the control of the Provisional Government. The General Secretariat had no authority in the provinces of Kharkiv, Katerynoslav, Kherson and Northern Tavria. All of its decisions would require Petrograd's approval. The Tsentral'na Rada was not even mentioned in the Temporary Instruction, neither as a representative body nor as an interlocutor with the Provisional Government.

The Temporary Instruction was denounced roundly in the Rada's plenary session that opened on 5 August. Had it not been for repeated interventions by Vynnychenko it would have been rejected. On 9 August the Rada accepted it by a vote of 247 to 16. A resolution appended to the motion to accept declared the Instruction, 'dictated by mistrust towards the aspirations of the entire democracy of Ukraine, is steeped in the imperialistic tendencies of the Russian bourgeoisie ... and completely fails to meet the needs not only of the Ukrainian people but also of the national minorities that live in Ukraine'.[71]

The soldiers', peasants' and workers' congresses described above had all sent permanent delegations to take seats in the Rada. One hundred and fifty-eight

---

71   Vynnychenko, *Vidrodzhennia Natsii*, Vol. 1, pp. 339–40.

seats were taken by soldiers' deputies, 212 by peasants and 100 by workers.[72] The assembly included representatives of the main Ukrainian political parties – the UPSR, USDWP and UPSF – in separate delegations in addition to their presence in the soldiers' peasants' and workers' delegations. The first meeting of the Rada in which representatives of national minorities took part occurred on 25 July. After the Rada adopted the terms outlined in the Temporary Instruction, the assembly was increased to 822 and apportioned among the following blocs of delegations:[73]

All-Ukrainian Council of Peasants' Deputies:	212
All-Ukrainian Council of Soldiers' Deputies:	158
All-Ukrainian Council of Workers' Deputies:	100
City Councils of Workers' and Soldiers' Deputies:	50
Russian parties:	40
Jewish parties:	35
Ukrainian parties:	20
Polish parties:	15
Representatives of cities and provinces:	84
Trade union, educational, co-operative and community organisations:	108
Total	822

Alongside the USDWP, UPSR and UPSF the Rada now seated the following parties: the Russian SRs, Mensheviks and the Russian Popular Socialist Party (*Trudoviki*); the Polish Democratic Centre; the Jewish General Workers' Union (Bund), Jewish Social Democratic Party (Poale Zion), the United Jewish Socialist Party (Fareinigte), the Zionists and Folkspartei.[74] The Bolsheviks refused to take the seats they were offered because they disagreed with any allocation on the basis of nationality.[75]

The UPSR remained numerically the strongest party by virtue of its commanding influence in the soldiers' and peasants' councils. A youthful organisation whose leaders averaged 25 years in age, the UPSR was less skilled in parliamentary tactics than the USDWP, whose members' average age was ten years greater. As a result, the UPSR was unable to translate its numerical weight

---

72   Shapoval, *Velyka Revoliutsiia*, p. 94.
73   Ibid.
74   Shapoval, *Velyka Revoliutsiia*, p. 83.
75   Soldatenko, *Ukraina v revoliutsiinu dobu*, Vol. 1, p. 628.

in the assembly into effective leadership. The USDWP took up the leading role instead and maintained it to the end of 1917.[76] It resorted frequently to blocking with the moderate UPSF in order to keep control of the Rada's 40-strong day-to-day decision-making chamber, the *mala rada*, and the General Secretariat, its executive cabinet. Rather than building an alliance with the more powerful, mass based peasant party, it appeared as a left flank for the UPSF and occasionally its critic.[77] The UPSR's lack of influence in the Rada's leadership and the social democrats' seemingly unprincipled alliance with the older generation of moderates and conservatives caused the young socialist revolutionaries endless frustration and provoked them on several occasions to walk out for a day or two. Their demonstrative protests did little to move, let alone dislodge the USDWP.

6   The Workers' Movement

Industrial workers in Ukraine organised themselves along three principal lines in 1917: at the point of production they established factory committees; on a town or city-wide basis they convened councils of workers' deputies; and on an industry-wide basis or within specific occupations they formed industrial and trade unions. These institutions of the workers' movement involved themselves in the struggle for power mainly through the economy and at the level of city politics. Leading members of the workers' movement who were interested in the larger picture, the struggle for state power, looked to the contest in Petrograd between the Government and the Soviet for guidance and signs of its ultimate resolution. The Tsentral'na Rada did not figure in their calculations until it demonstrated its appeal to soldiers and peasants, challenged the Provisional Government's authority in Ukraine and began drawing support from the lower, Ukrainian speaking strata of the working class. The fact that the struggle for power would involve three contenders in Ukraine dawned slowly, but it was evident to all by the summer of 1917. It obliged the urban and industrial working class to come to terms with the aspirations of the peasantry and soldiers being voiced in the Rada's assembly, as well as in its own multinational ranks.

---

76   M. Yavorsky, *Revoliutsiia na Vkraini v ii holovnishykh etapakh* (Kharkiv: Derzhavne Vydavnytstvo Ukrainy, 1923), p. 45; N.N. Popov, *Narys Istorii Komunistychnoi Partii (Bil'shovykiv) Ukrainy* (Kharkiv: Proletaryi, 1931), pp. 109–10.
77   Khrystiuk, *Ukrains'ka Revoliutsiia*, Vol. 3, p. 117.

The factory committee was a fundamental base organisation of the workers' movement. Its origins can be traced to the War when state controlled military industries set up factory committees made up of employers' and employees' representatives. Fashioned on West European models of the time, the committees were charged with strengthening labour discipline and boosting war production. Fitters, turners, mechanics and electricians were invariably placed on the factory committees because they were also the foremen of unskilled workers on the shop floor. When opposition to the War grew stronger among the industrial workforce in 1916 and workers' representatives began voicing this opposition as well, the committees were dissolved and many Mensheviks and anarchists serving on them, as well as some Bolsheviks, were thrown into prison.[78]

Factory committees were revived after the fall of the autocracy, but without management participation. Strengthened by the release of thousands of political prisoners returning to their jobs, the committees set out to win basic rights for workers at the point of production: modern practices of collective bargaining, an eight hour day and elementary conditions of safety and hygiene on the job.[79] They tried to develop a common policy towards the owners of industry and the Provisional Government. An exploratory conference of factory committees in Petrograd decided in April that the committees should assume responsibility for the organisation of production in each factory, firing and firing workers, deciding the length of the working day and vacations, 'the factory manager to be kept notified'.[80] On 23 April the Provisional Government recognised the factory committees in all private and state run enterprises. Its decree stipulated that committees be elected by the entire workforce and have the power to negotiate wages, hours and working conditions on its behalf. The decree did not recognise any managerial role or control over production by the factory committees.[81]

Industrialists were afraid of the factory committee movement and combated it with lockouts and transfer of assets out of the country. This only drove the committees onto a more radical path in an effort to save jobs. Having secured most of their original demands, they aspired to take greater control of produc-

---

[78] Chris Goodey, 'Factory Committees and the Dictatorship of the Proletariat', *Critique*, 3 (Autumn 1974), pp. 31–40.
[79] Ibid.
[80] Maurice Brinton, *The Bolsheviks and Workers' Control 1917–21* (Montreal: Black Rose Books, 1972), p. 2.
[81] F.I. Kaplan, *Bolshevik Ideology and the Ethics of Soviet Labour 1917–20. The Formative Years* (New York: Philosophical Library, 1968), pp. 47–8.

tion. At first this meant coercing capitalists to co-operate with them. Later it took the form of outright takeovers and the removal of factory managers.[82]

The First Conference of Factory Committees in Petrograd and Environs from 30 May to 3 June opposed by an overwhelming majority all co-operation with either the Provisional Government or the bourgeoisie.[83] The 568 delegates who took part represented over one third of a million workers in 236 factories. They passed resolutions in which control of production assumed a comprehensive scope. Organs of the Provisional Government were to be composed of a majority or two thirds' representation from factory committees, councils and trade unions. Participation of factory owners and technical specialists in worker-controlled production was to be made 'compulsory'. Employees' committees were expected to take over the banks as well. The financial records of companies were to be made public.[84]

Factory committees were established in Ukraine in a majority of enterprises during March and April.[85] A regional conference of factory committees held in Kharkiv on 29 May defined their tasks in terms similar to those being adopted at the time in Petrograd: 'The factory committees must take over production, protect it and develop it ... look after hygiene, fix wages, control the technical quality of products, decree all internal factory regulations and determine solutions to all conflicts'.[86]

Whereas workers' councils had first appeared only towards the end of the 1905 Revolution, they were organised anew at the very beginning of 1917. In Ukraine, councils appeared in 11 major cities in the first week of March: Kyiv, Kharkiv, Katerynoslav, Kremenchuk, Luhansk, Poltava, Odesa, Mykolaiv, Vynnytsia, Kherson and Zhytomyr. In the following weeks they spread throughout the Donbas, appearing there first in Makiivka, Kramatorsk, Horlivka, Shcherbynivtsi, Lysychansk and Shosta.[87]

The councils were composed of delegates from factory committees, trade unions and socialist parties. As city-wide organisations they competed with the local Executive Committees of the Provisional Government for municipal authority and the allegiance of garrison soldiers. In Kharkiv, Katerynoslav,

---

82   B. Kolos, 'Profesiinyi Rukh na Ukraini', *Vpered. Kaliendar dlia Ukrains'koho Robitnytstva na Rik 1925* (New York: Soiuz Ukrains'kykh Robitnychykh Orhanizatsiiakh v Zluchenykh Derzhavakh, 1925), p. 194; Brinton, *Bolsheviks and Workers' Control*, p. 12.
83   Kaplan, *Bolshevik Ideology*, pp. 57–8.
84   Dewar, *Labour Policy in the USSR 1917–28* (London: Oxford University Press, 1956), p. 8.
85   M.I. Suprunenko (gen. ed.), *Istoriia Ukrains'koi RSR*, 8 vols (Kyiv: Naukova Dumka, 1977), Vol. 5, pp. 57–8.
86   Brinton, *Bolsheviks and Workers' Control*, p. 4.
87   Suprunenko, *Istoriia Ukrains'koi RSR*, Vol. 5, p. 25.

Odesa, Poltava, Mariupol and in towns of the Donbas, the workers' councils disarmed the police, dismissed reactionary officials of the former regime and assumed control of the city councils (*dumy*) and district councils (*zemstva*).[88]

Workers' and soldiers' councils began meeting in joint session in Kharkiv, Poltava, Chernihiv, Vynnytsia and Kherson during the first weeks of the Revolution. They joined forces in Mykolaiv in April, Katerynoslav in May, Kremenchuk in August and Zhytomyr, Uman and other northern towns in September. The Kyiv and Odesa Councils of Workers' and Soldiers' Deputies did not begin working together until the eve of the October crisis.[89] By that time there were approximately 320 urban councils in Ukraine, the majority of them composed of both workers' and soldiers' deputies.[90] They were grouped into three regional organisations, each with their own executive committee: the Southwestern organisation's committee was in Kyiv, Donets-Kryvyi Rih in Kharkiv and the Romanian Military Front, Black Sea Fleet and Odesa Military District (*Rumcherod*) in Odesa. Their territories corresponded to the old Tsarist administrations of gubernia-general of Kyiv, Kharkiv and Novorosiia. These regional organisations of workers' councils did not co-ordinate their work with each other, but liaised directly with Petrograd.[91]

It is difficult to make precise estimations of the changing balance of party influences in the workers' movement. Delegates to the urban councils, moreover, did not always vote along party lines, especially in the first months of the Revolution when political differences were submerged by a general enthusiasm to unite the class and to stand firmly behind the Provisional Government. Even the Bolsheviks and Mensheviks 'dreamed of unity' and displayed little of the sharp antagonisms that characterised their pre-1917 history.[92] Decisions in the councils were made by reconciling and amalgamating a broad range of views from independent deputies and the members of established parties. This remained the case until the Kadets resigned from the Provisional Government over the question of Ukraine's autonomy and the Petrograd Soviet began to split on the issue of collaboration with bourgeois parties.

The Bolsheviks in Ukraine concentrated their efforts on building the factory committees. They were their most consistent organisers and leaders. In the south, their influence in the factory committees was matched only by the

---

88 M.A. Rubach, 'Treba diisno vypravyty', *Litopys Revoliutsii*, 3–4 (May–June 1930), p. 265.
89 Suprunenko, *Istoriia Ukrains'koi RSR*, Vol. 5, p. 25.
90 Hamretsky, Tymchenko and Shchus, *Rady Ukrainy*, pp. 13, 282.
91 Zdorov, *Ukrains'kyi Zhovten'*, p. 138.
92 H. Lapchynsky, 'Zarodzhennia radians'koi vlady ta pershi ii kroky v odnomu z mist ukrains'kykh', *Chervonyi Shliakh*, 1–2 (January–February 1925), p. 121.

anarchists.[93] Since the anarchists were suspicious of state building projects, the Bolsheviks were the only party to offer leadership to the factory committees as a whole and to co-ordinate their development with the councillist and union movements. By April, they had majorities in the factory committees of Kharkiv, Kyiv, Luhansk, Katerynoslav and many Donbas towns. They were especially strong in the coal and steel industries and on the railways. By August they controlled 70 percent of all factory committees in Ukraine.[94]

The Mensheviks dominated the workers' councils by virtue of their strength in the unions. Their experienced cadres played an important role in the city *dumy* as well as in the urban workers' councils, and their unqualified support for the Provisional Government was very popular among the urban petit bourgeoisie and working class in the first months of 1917. They faced a sustained challenge from the Bolsheviks in the summer when new elections of deputies to the councils were called, but the Mensheviks managed to keep control of most of them, including those in the Donbas.[95]

The USDWP fared poorly in the councils and did not record gains of the same order as the Bolsheviks when the political situation became critical over the summer months. Between September and November, the Ukrainian social democrats acquired sufficient numbers of delegates to workers' councils in Katerynoslav, Kharkiv and Kyiv (about 10 percent) to elect members to their executive committees. In Odesa, USDWP members made up only 6 percent of the workers' council at the end of 1917.[96]

The organisation of industrial and trade unions began in the first weeks of the Revolution.[97] By May most cities in Ukraine had a Central Bureau of Trade Unions composed of delegates from the locals.[98] Union membership in Ukraine rose to 275,000 by the summer and to 617,000 in January 1918. At that time there were approximately three million workers in unions across the Russian state.[99] Many unions, especially in Ukraine's northern provinces, were organised along craft or occupational lines. In the south, where the concen-

---

[93] K.K. Dubyna (gen. ed.), *Istoriia Ukrains'koi RSR*, 2 vols (Kyiv: Naukova Dumka, 1967), Vol. 2, p. 14.

[94] Suprunenko, *Istoriia Ukrains'koi RSR*, Vol. 5, pp. 57–8.

[95] Ibid, Vol. 5, pp. 19, 83; Yavorsky, *Revoliutsiia na Vkraini*, p. 39.

[96] Iu. Hamretsky, 'Kryza dribnoburzhuaznykh partii na Ukraini v 1917 r.', *Ukrains'kyi Istorychnyi Zhurnal*, 12 (December 1976), p. 79.

[97] B. Kolesnikov, *Professional'noe dvizhenie i Kontrrevoliutsiia: Ocherki iz istorii professional'nogo dvizheniia na Ukraine* (n.p.: Gosudarstvennoe Izdatel'stvo Ukraine, 1923), p. 17.

[98] Ie. M. Skliarenko, *Narysy Istorii Profspilkovoho Rukhu na Ukraini 1917–20* (Kyiv: Naukova Dumka, 1974), p. 13.

[99] Ibid, pp. 13, 18.

tration of workers in plants was much higher and assembly line production prevailed over the bay system, the craft mentality was superseded by industrial unionism. Miners, metalworkers and machine builders had the largest and best organised industrial unions.[100]

The Mensheviks were the most influential political party in the unions in Ukraine, as they were in Russia. They had a strong following not only in the numerous single shop unions spread out in small industries and trades but also in the big industrial unions where they competed with the Bolsheviks for their leadership.[101] The union movement in Ukraine swung behind the Bolsheviks in times of acute social crisis, but invariably handed leadership back to the Mensheviks when crises passed.

Ukrainians were the least organised of the three major nationalities in the working class at all levels of economic and political struggle. Few belonged to craft unions because they were mainly unskilled. In the south where industrial unionism took root there were more Ukrainians in unions, but on the whole they were in a minority of their class. Those who did not speak Russian well could not easily seek leadership positions or take active part in union meetings, educational and cultural programmes. Such factors, combined with the Mensheviks' and Bolsheviks' negative attitude to national demands contributed to the formation of breakaway unions in Ukraine and to agitation within the unions organised on an All-Russian scale for their reconstruction along territorial and federalist lines. National tensions of this kind were evident among railway workers, teachers, paramedics and midwives, postal and telegraph employees and sugar refinery workers. Their attempts to build All-Ukrainian unions in 1917 presaged a much bigger effort along such lines in 1918.

An official history of the Soviet Ukrainian republic published in 1977 decried the breakaway unions as attempts to divide the union movement into separate organisations based on the nationality principle.[102] The original sources convincingly show that was not the case. Rather, these were attempts to establish territorial union organisations that could participate as autonomous members in the All-Russian union movement. The resolutions of the First All-Ukrainian Workers' Congress in July spelled out this strategy; they merely restated resolutions on the national question adopted by the Third All-Russian Congress of Trade Unions held in Petrograd in the previous month, adding the demand for

---

100 Ibid, pp. 15–16; Kolesnikov, *Professional'noe dvizhenie*, p. 17.
101 A. Shlosberg, 'Professional'ny Soiuzy v Borb'e za Oktiabr', *Litopys Revoliutsii*, 1 (January–February 1928), pp. 9–10; Suprunenko, *Istoriia Ukrains'koi RSR*, Vol. 5, p. 143.
102 Suprunenko, *Istoriia Ukrains'koi RSR*, Vol. 5, p. 56.

territorial autonomy to them.[103] The USDWP fought against the idea of an ethnic union movement and denounced a feeble campaign to set up a union of Ukrainian workers in Kyiv as 'feudal nationalism'.[104]

At the same time it cannot be denied that many Ukrainian workers in 1917 first organised themselves on a nationality principle, that is as Ukrainian language speakers, into educational societies and clubs. Ukrainian socialists among them were the first to raise the call for territorially based unions and an All-Ukrainian union central council. A majority of the existing unions did not support this call until May 1918, so the attempt to reform the union movement first took the form of breakaway unions that were open to workers of all nationalities, but were being joined overwhelmingly by Ukrainians.[105] The All-Ukrainian Railway Workers Union, which began organising in April, competed with the five All-Russian railway unions on all the lines.[106] Its leaders claimed the need for a new union because the existing ones did not adequately represent Ukrainian workers nor take heed of their needs. For example, Ukrainians made up over 50 percent of the workforce on the South Western Lines, but not one of them was elected to the union's regional executive committee.[107] They also wanted to bring railways and other means of long distance transport under the control of a single organisation 'to advance the goal of autonomy for Ukraine in union with other free states of the Russian republic'.[108]

Three hundred delegates took part in the First All-Ukrainian Railway Workers' Congress held in Kharkiv from 29 June to 1 July. They adopted resolutions recognising the Tsentral'na Rada as their government, calling for national territorial autonomy in a federated, democratic republic, and the Ukrainisation of railway services and training of railway workers.[109] The union's second congress, which convened in Kyiv in September right after Kornilov's coup was quashed, demanded the removal of all railway officials 'who have exposed themselves as enemies of the new political order and of the Ukrainian movement' and their replacement by candidates approved by the unions. Its resolutions called for an immediate end to the War on the basis of the self-

---

103 Yu. Mykolov (ed.), *Putevoditel' po Rezoliutsiiam Vserossiis'kykh Siezdov i Konferentsii Professional'nikh Soiuzov* (Moscow: V.Ts.S.P.S. 1924), p. 59.
104 *Robitnycha hazeta*, 2 May 1917, p. 1; 17 May 1917, p. 3; 23 December 1917, p. 7.
105 'The Non-Ukrainian Democracy Forced Workers to Organise in This Way', *Robitnycha hazeta*, 24 December 1917, p. 1.
106 *Robitnycha hazeta*, 22 April 1917, p. 3; Khrystiuk, *Ukrains'ka Revoliutsiia*, Vol. 1, p. 185.
107 M. Redin, 'Do Istorii Vsekrains'koho Zaliznychnoho Straiku 1918 roku', *Litopys Revoliutsii*, 6 (October–December 1928), p. 26.
108 *Robitnycha hazeta*, 30 April 1917, p. 4.
109 *Robitnycha hazeta*, 10 July 1917, p. 3; 15 July 1917, p. 2.

determination of nations, extension of the Tsentral'na Rada's jurisdiction into Kharkiv, Katerynoslav and Kherson provinces, and the formation of a workers' militia to guard the railways from sabotage.[110] There are widely ranging estimates of the numerical size of the All-Ukrainian Railways Workers' Union. The First Congress of the union in Kharkiv claimed to represent two hundred thousand workers on twelve railway lines in the Russian state. The *Encyclopedia of Ukraine* gives the same figure, unusually high and possibly a misprint.[111] *Robitnycha hazeta* reported on 25 April 1917 that 15,000 workers on the Moscow Lines out of a total of 50,000 Ukrainian employees had signed up with the new union. The union's membership on the South Western Lines was set at five thousand in December 1917.[112]

A committee of Kyiv workers began organising an All-Ukrainian Postal and Telegraph Workers' Union soon after the February Revolution. Despite opposition from the All-Russian union, a Congress attended by one hundred delegates took place in Kyiv on 22 August. The new union supported the Tsentral'na Rada and wanted to remain in the All-Russian union as a federated, autonomous section.[113]

An article in the 23 July issue of *Vistnyk* describes the founding congress of a telegraphists' union on the Kherson railway network which took place at the Katerynoslav *Prosvita* popular education society hall on 9 July:

> During the preparation of the union's statutes Russian members started to voice a lot of protest over the issue of Ukrainising the telegraph services. Without paying too much attention to the outbursts of their brothers, the Great Russian workers, a majority of those present supported Zubkovsky's advice that 'one shouldn't crawl into a monastery and expect others to obey one's own Rule' and nominated him and comrade Chernomaz to formulate the union's statutes .... Russians, Poles and other nations belong to the union ... it is a political and economic organisation. All comrades are bound by the statutes to defend actively the national and territorial autonomy of Ukraine and to recognise the Tsentral'na Rada as the highest authority in the land.[114]

---

110   *Robitnycha hazeta*, 22 September 1917, p. 2; Khrystiuk, *Ukrains'ka Revoliutsiia*, Vol. 2, p. 8.
111   *Litopys Revoliutsii*, 3 (May–June 1928), p. 327; *Encyclopedia of Ukraine*, 1984 edn, s.v. 'All-Ukrainian Railway Workers' Congresses'.
112   F. Soldatenko and V.I. Polokhalo, 'Borot'ba Bil'shovykiv Ukrainy za Seredni Verstvy Mis'koho Naselennia iak Reserv Sotsialistychnoi Revoliutsii', *Ukrains'kyi Istorychnyi Zhurnal*, 2 February 1977, p. 21; *Robitnycha hazeta*, 25 April 1917, p. 4.
113   Khrystiuk, *Ukrains'ka Revoliutsiia*, Vol. 1, p. 186; *Robitnycha hazeta*, 27 August 1917, p. 2.
114   *Vistnyk Tovarystva Prosvity v Katerynoslavi*, 23 July 1917, p. 3.

An All-Ukrainian Union of Paramedics and Midwives based on the same principles as these was founded in Kyiv in August 1917. Its membership was multinational and spread out in eight provinces (excluding Northern Tavria).[115]

The All-Ukrainian Teachers' Union was not a breakaway organisation like the railway or telegraph workers' unions, but it shared their objective of a national territorial union movement. The union was composed mainly of village teachers who had a long history of self-organisation in Ukraine and were a majority of their profession. It would be fair to say that the urban based teachers broke away from these rural teachers rather than the other way around, and that the reasons for the split were mainly political in nature. Ukrainian village teachers were among the first to organise insurance co-operatives (*kasy dopomohy*) that often served additional purposes in the early days of the workers' movement. Under their cover they conducted populist agitation in the countryside and held regional teachers' conferences. The All-Ukrainian Teachers' Union followed in this tradition when it was organised in the spring of 1905. During the post-1905 reaction and the First World War, the union agitated for universal access to public education and the use of the native language in schools. Many village teachers went into the army where they contributed to the formation of the soldiers' movement.[116] Whereas village teachers tended to side with radical peasant parties, urban teachers were mostly liberals and often members of the Kadet party. University professors were conservative in the main and among the last to turn against the old regime.[117]

When the regime collapsed in February 1917 village teachers took the initiative to organise district and provincial conferences of their profession. These gatherings sided overwhelmingly with the Tsentral'na Rada.[118] The All-Ukrainian Teachers' Congress held in Kyiv in April seated 600 delegates from all parts of Ukraine as well as the Don and Kuban where sizeable Ukrainian minorities lived. The Congress called for the introduction of Ukrainian language instruction to the schools and minority language instruction where numbers warranted it, the establishment of teacher training institutes at public cost and the revival of the *Prosvita* popular education movement.[119] By the end of

---

115 *Robitnycha hazeta*, 3 August 1917, p. 3.
116 *Visti Vseukrains'koho Tsentral'noho Vykonavchoho Komitetu*, 13 January 1925, p. 3. *Encyclopedia of Ukraine*, 1984 edn, s.v. 'All-Ukrainian Teachers' Association' by Polishchuk.
117 Ibid.
118 *Visty Ukrains'koi Tsentral'noi Rady*, 5 (May 1917), p. 3; *Litopys Revoliutsii*, 4 (1928), p. 9.
119 *Robitnycha hazeta*, 6 April 1917, p. 4; Khrystiuk, *Ukrains'ka Revoliutsiia*, Vol. 1, p. 21.

1918, the union had 78 local branches with 20,000 members. Its first president in 1917 was S. Rusova.[120]

Sugar workers were the largest single contingent of wage earners in the countryside. Practically all sugar beet plantations in the Empire were located in Ukraine due to the narrow range of climatic and soil conditions conducive to its profitable cultivation. Sugar refineries were located both in Ukraine and Russia along the freight lines to the Baltic Coast and close to domestic urban markets. The seasonal workforce on plantations and in refineries was composed mainly of semi-proletarianised Ukrainian peasants while the skilled workers and administrative personnel in refineries were mainly Russians, Poles, Jews and Belarusians.

After the February Revolution Ukrainian sugar workers began organising cultural societies, reading rooms and libraries. They turned to the USDWP for help in these efforts and in the resolution of conflicts with employers.[121] However, the party seemed unable to advance their interests.

The first All-Russian Congress of Sugar Industry Workers was held in Kyiv in May with the objective of creating a new union. Two hundred delegates representing approximately 100,000 workers in 140 refineries took part in its deliberations.[122] During the debate on the union's statutes Slonymsky, a USDWP member, argued that the most suitable form of organisation was not a centralised union, but a federation of territorial unions. Another USDWP member, Dovzhenko, reasoned that the union's structure should conform to the political and economic reorganisation of the Russian state which he anticipated would lead to a federal republic with a broad measure of national autonomy. Sugar workers in Ukraine, therefore, needed a territorial union to defend their economic and cultural interests. The USDWP's intervention did not have the desired effect. As Dovzhenko wrote afterwards in *Robitnycha hazeta*, a majority of the delegates were Ukrainians while the working commissions were dominated by Russian Mensheviks who remained resolutely opposed to a federal organisation of autonomous sections.[123]

Over 500 delegates from 220 refineries came to the Second Congress of the union two months later. Ukrainians made up 47 percent of those present, Russians 26 percent, Poles 16 percent and Jews 7 percent. Two delegates gave their national affiliation as 'internationalists' in the registration forms. Salar-

---

120   *Encyclopedia of Ukraine*, 1984 edn, s.v. 'All-Ukrainian Teachers' Association', by Polishchuk.
121   *Robitnycha hazeta*, 27 June 1917, p. 3; 9 October 1917, p. 3.
122   Suprunenko, *Istoriia Ukrains'koi RSR*, Vol. 5, p. 56; *Robitnycha hazeta*, 17 May 1917, p. 4; *Visti Vseukrains'koho Tsentral'noho Vykonavchoho Komitetu*, 16 June 1925, p. 1.
123   *Robitnycha hazeta*, 21 May 1917, pp. 3–4.

ied employees, as opposed to wage earners in production, made up 43 percent of those in attendance. For reasons unexplained in *Robitnycha hazeta*, which reported extensively on both Congresses, there was no discussion at all on the national question during the second conference.[124]

7 The Seizure of Power

The first period of the Revolution came to an end in July when the equilibrium struck between the Provisional Government, Tsentral'na Rada and the workers' movement in the first phase of peaceful self-organisation was dissolved by new mass mobilisations from below. The simultaneous soldiers' mutinies in Petrograd and Kyiv signalled the beginning of a major tilt in the balance of power. The soldiers and workers now understood that the Provisional Government was not committed to the same goals as they were. Allegiances began shifting more firmly to the other two poles in the power triad.

The collapse of the Russian army's offensive on the Southwestern front shattered all hopes for a speedy end to the War. The Provisional Government needed stability in the Ukrainian provinces in order to hold the front against Austro-Hungary and Germany. But the Tsentral'na Rada's demand for territorial autonomy challenged the Government for a share of control over resources and infrastructure that were vital to the war effort, while the Ukrainisation movement in the army further weakened the authority of the military command. Growing numbers of soldiers' councils on the front began issuing threats to lead their regiments back into Ukraine, partly in protest against the Government's failure to sue for peace and partly out of fear that the Tsentral'na Rada might be dispersed by troops loyal to the Government.[125]

In their great majority these soldiers were peasants; their demobilisation by whatever means could only strengthen the movement for land reform, which was led by peasant unions. As this movement gained momentum it adopted new forms of struggle at each turn in the agricultural cycle. During the sowing season peasants fought big landowners for the use of more land and restrictions in rent increases. In July and August they fought for a greater share of the harvest picked on landowners' estates. Between August and October, they began to confiscate and redistribute the land. In many places peasants formed into armed brigades to guard their locality against bandits and to resist army

---

124 *Robitnycha hazeta*, 7 July 1917, p. 1; 10 July 1917, p. 2.
125 Khrystiuk, *Ukrains'ka Revoliutsiia*, Vol. 1, p. 59.

units sent in to protect estates from confiscation.[126] In districts of Podillia and Volyn which were directly adjacent to the front between 50 and 60 percent of all estates were seized and partitioned by October. In the interior of these gubernia as well as in Kyiv further east 20 to 25 percent of big landholdings were seized. On the Left Bank the biggest number of confiscations and the greatest amount of destruction of landowners' capital occurred in Chernihiv province, crammed with landless agricultural workers. Here the landowners lost between 15 and 20 percent of their land. Further to the east and south on the steppe and in the most industrialised provinces peasants took over only 5 to 10 percent of all big estates by October. Altogether, about 25 to 30 percent of the landed estates in Ukraine was confiscated and redistributed by the peasant unions before the fall of the Provisional Government.[127]

The peasant unions did not restrict their demands to land. The War, national autonomy and public education were other major subjects of discussion at their provincial and national congresses. The demands they put forward to the Tsentral'na Rada were always more radical than anything the USDWP, the Rada's leading party, was prepared to pursue. We have already noted the demands issued by the First All-Ukrainian Peasants' Congress on 28 May to 2 June. The Second Plenum of the All-Ukrainian Council of Peasants' Deputies on 2 September continued in the same vein, calling for an immediate end to the War and conclusion of peace among the belligerent states. The plenum spoke out in favour of workers' control of industry as the best guarantee of continued production and distribution of consumer goods, stable prices and the re-opening of factories locked or closed down by their owners.[128]

The peasant unions continued to look to the Tsentral'na Rada as the representative body through which to advance and resolve the political, social and economic problems they faced. Vynnychenko wrote that 'the realistic and monistic mind of the peasant fused these two categories, the national and social, into a single, indivisible and organic whole. Whoever wanted land also wanted Autonomy; if you were against Autonomy you were also against the seizure of land'.[129]

---

126 Khrystiuk, *Ukrains'ka Revoliutsiia*, Vol. 2, p. 14; V. Sukhyno-Khomenko, 'Z pryvodu osoblyvostei proletars'koi revoliutsii na Ukraini', *Litopys Revoliutsii*, 4 (1928), pp. 92–5.
127 Vsevolod Holubnychy, 'The 1917 Agrarian Revolution in Ukraine', in *Selected Works of Vsevolod Holubnychy: Soviet Regional Economics*, edited by Iwan S. Koropeckyj (Edmonton: Canadian Institute of Ukrainian Studies, 1982), p. 56.
128 Iwan Maistrenko, *Borot'bism: A Chapter in the History of Ukrainian Communism* (New York: Research Programme on the USSR, 1954), p. 45; Khrystiuk, *Ukrains'ka Revoliutsiia*, Vol. 2, pp. 24–5.
129 Vynnychenko, *Vidrodzhennia Natsii*, Vol. 1, p. 178.

Relations between the Tsentral'na Rada and the Provisional Government continued to deteriorate after the Rada accepted the humiliating terms of the Temporary Instruction. It boycotted the 12 August Moscow Conference called by the Government to cement a coalition cabinet of bourgeois and socialist parties under Alexandr Kerensky, the new prime minister. The Ukrainians' lack of confidence in it came through clearly during the debate in the *mala rada* on the Government's invitation to Moscow. USDWP member Tkachenko was one of the first there to openly call for the complete replacement of the Provisional Government: 'The Russian bourgeoisie has proven itself completely incapable of organising the country. That is why it must be deposed and power passed into the hands of the workers and peasants ... Ukraine's autonomy should be secured de facto and in its fullest possible scope'.[130]

Others, however, were already plotting its overthrow. On 25 August Lavr Kornilov, Commander in Chief of the Russian armed forces, mounted a coup against the Provisional Government. Kornilov publicly declared his intention was to restore order to Petrograd and the army. He called for the return of capital punishment, courts martial and the ruthless suppression of the Bolsheviks. However, Kerensky saw in his march on the capital an attempt to overthrow the Government itself and install a military dictatorship. Lacking the authority or popularity to mobilise opposition to the coup attempt, Kerensky was forced to appeal to the Petrograd Soviet for support. He agreed to release imprisoned Bolsheviks and to arm workers so that they could guard the approaches to the capital. The coup was crushed in a matter of days. The entire episode served to undermine further the authority of the Provisional Government and to strengthen that of the Petrograd Soviet, which had called for resistance to the coup conspirators right across the country.

Kornilov was relying on the support of the general staff, including A.I. Obeleshev, chief of staff of the Kyiv Military District, General Kaledin in Eastern Ukraine and General Denikin on the Southwestern front. Here, as in Petrograd, Kornilov's move was seen widely as an attack on the democratic gains of the Revolution. Workers' and soldiers' councils on the Left Bank started taking control of postal and telegraph services, placing guards at mines and factories. In the Donbas they sent agitators into the ranks of Kaledin's Cossack troops to explain what Kornilov and his allies aimed to achieve. Soldiers' committees on the Southwestern front demanded their officers be arrested and prosecuted as supporters of the coup. In Berdychiv, the second most important location

---

130 Ibid, Vol. 2, p. 31.

of Kornilov's allies in the Russian army after the *Stavka* headquarters of the general staff in Mohilev, soldiers actually arrested General Denikin and other commanders and held them for a time. In Kharkiv a Committee in Defence of the Revolution took control of the city commissariat of the Provisional Government, while its armed guards held the railway lines.

A Committee in Defence of the Revolution was established in Kyiv, composed of the general secretaries of the Rada, commissars of the Provisional Government for Kyiv city and the Kyiv Military District, the mayor, chief of police, representatives of the Kyiv Council of Workers' and Soldiers' Deputies, the trade unions and practically all the political parties of the revolutionary democracy: the Bolsheviks, Mensheviks, Russian SRs, Ukrainian Social Democrats and SRs, the Bund and the United Jewish Social Democratic Party. The Committee arrested Kornilov's key supporters, General Obeleshev and S. Stradomsky, Government commissar for Kyiv and a Kadet.

From the beginning of September the successful resistance to the attempted coup handed the initiative over to the councils in the Donbas, which retained the control they had taken away from Kornilov's sympathisers and collaborators and themselves assumed the responsibilities of local government.[131]

Whereas it had boycotted the Provisional Government's Moscow conference in August the Rada did accept the invitation of the All-Russian Central Executive Committee of the Councils of Workers', Soldiers' and Peasants' Deputies to its Democratic Conference on 18 September. Called to support the Provisional Government against the restorers of the old regime who had flocked around Kornilov, the conference actually revealed the great diversity of political currents in the camp of the democracy. The Tsentral'na Rada handed its twelve delegates to the conference an 'imperative mandate' to defend the following demands:

> Formation of an exclusively revolutionary socialist government answerable to the democracies of all the peoples of Russia … until a constituent assembly is formed the transfer to the management by land committees of all landowners', monastic and church land holdings … the establishment of state and regional [*krai*] government control over economic production and distribution … handing over to regional governments the management of the most important branches of industry … convocation in every *krai* that demands it a national sovereign constituent assembly … [and] the transfer of power in Ukraine to the Ukrainian Tsentral'na Rada

---

131   Soldatenko, *Ukraina v revoliutsiinu dobu*, Vol. 1, pp. 710–18.

and its General Secretariat, formed on the basis of the statute adopted by the Tsentral'na Rada on 16 July.[132]

This last demand referred to the statute the Rada negotiated with the representatives of the Provisional Government in Kyiv, which was rejected afterwards in Petrograd and replaced with the Temporary Instruction.

The Rada's delegation presented its demands to the 2,000 people in attendance and won support for them only from the Bolsheviks and Russian left SRs. The majority refused to consider them while the more right-wing delegates accused the Rada of separatism in the service of Germany's war aims against Russia. When the vote was cast whether to support a coalition government of bourgeois and socialist parties, the Rada's representatives joined the Bolsheviks, left SRs and delegations from other nations seeking autonomy to defeat it.[133] Lenin noted afterwards that

> the national delegations ensured a considerable majority for the opponents of a coalition government ... Their radicalism stands higher than that of the workers' and soldiers' councils ... the conflicts Ukrainians are having with the Government, and especially those of Ukrainian soldiers, grow fiercer all the time.[134]

The demise of the Provisional Government in the autumn of 1917 polarised the political forces within the democracy between three camps: those who still believed a government of bourgeois and socialist parties could work; those who advocated a government made up exclusively of socialist parties 'from the *trudoviki* to the Bolsheviks'; and those who no longer believed the Provisional Government could be reformed sufficiently to serve the goals of the Revolution and that a new state power had to be built from the ground up. The main advocates of the third path were of course the Bolsheviks and the left Socialist Revolutionaries, for whom the ground was already prepared by the councils. And while the Bolsheviks appeared to represent a minority position within the broad camp of the democracy, they were receiving a groundswell of support within the workers' movement, particularly from the industrial proletariat. During re-elections of deputies to the workers' councils in September

---

132 Ibid, p. 767.
133 Shapoval, *Velyka Revoliutsiia*, pp. 87–8; Vynnychenko, *Vidrodzhennia Natsii*, Vol. 2, p. 34; Sukhyno-Khomenko, 'Z prydovu osoblyvostei', p. 101.
134 Hamretsky, Tymchenko and Shchus, *Rady Ukrainy*, p. 166; Dubyna, *Istoriia Ukrains'koi RSR*, Vol. 2, pp. 39–40.

the Bolsheviks in Ukraine made their biggest gains in the Donbas, capturing 79 percent of the seats in Horlivka-Scherbynivtsi, 70 percent in Luhansk, 60 percent in Bokovo-Khrystalskyi, 58 percent in Lozova-Pavlivsk and Makiivka and 44 percent in Mariupol. In Kyiv, Kharkiv, Katerynoslav, Odesa, Mykolaiv and Kryvyi Rih, they increased their proportion of delegates to the councils, but failed to unseat the Mensheviks and moderate Russian SRs. Bolsheviks were already pressing the councils in the Donbas from early September to take on the responsibilities of government, which they did, well before the convocation of the Second All-Russian Congress of Soviets.[135]

One hundred and twenty-eight delegates from Ukraine attended the Second All-Russian Congress of Soviets which opened in Petrograd on 25 October. They represented 12 workers' councils, 12 workers' and soldiers' councils, nine councils of workers', soldiers' and peasants' deputies, three soldiers' councils and one council of peasants' deputies. By political affiliation the delegates from Ukraine were divided into 60 Bolsheviks, 30 Russian SRs, 30 Mensheviks, six USDWP members, four UPSR members and seven independents.[136] Fifty six percent of delegates from Ukraine supported the Bolshevik position to overthrow the Provisional Government and replace it with a new one based on the councils. This compared with 70 percent of all 600 delegates attending the Second Congress going with the Bolsheviks.[137]

The Congress was not representative of all the councils in the Russian state. Had it been representative the alternative of a restructured Cabinet of the Provisional Government composed of all socialist parties would almost certainly have prevailed. Revolutions, however, are not made democratically. They are driven forward by initiatives on a mass scale whose organisers seek approval and reconciliation only after they secure new positions of strength. In Petrograd the Bolsheviks took the initiative to overthrow the Provisional Government. They did so through the Revolutionary Military Committee of the Petrograd Soviet which led soldiers and sailors in an assault on the key institutions, civil and military, of the Government. Among them were Ukrainian soldiers in the Leibgarde (Life Guard) of the First, Second and Third Divisions and sailors of the Baltic Sea Fleet acting under the leadership of the Petrograd USDWP.[138]

---

135 Hamretsky, Tymchenko and Shchus, *Rady Ukrainy*, pp. 107–8; Suprunenko, *Istoriia Ukrains'koi RSR*, Vol. 5, p. 141.
136 Hamretsky, Tymchenko and Shchus, *Rady Ukrainy*, p. 189.
137 Ibid, p. 188.
138 M. Avdienko, 'Liutneva Revoliutsiia v Petrohradi i USDRP', *Litopys Revoliutsii*, 1 no. 28 (January–February 1928).

Developments in Kyiv in the last week of October 1917 culminated like those in Petrograd in the overthrow of the Provisional Government. However, the fundamental difference was that in Kyiv and all the major cities of Ukraine it brought the Tsentral'na Rada to power.

The Third All-Ukrainian Soldiers' Congress convened in Kyiv on 20 October and sat in continuous session until 29 October. More than 3,000 delegates representing 1.5 million soldiers took part, two thirds of them members and supporters of the UPSR. The Congress provided the Rada with the political backing and essential military force needed to take power, adjourning to form into military detachments to defeat the forces loyal to the Provisional Government in Kyiv.[139]

When news of the Bolshevik-led seizure of power in Petrograd reached Kyiv the Soldiers' Congress expressed support for it by a large majority and took the position that the Tsentral'na Rada and the Council of Peoples' Commissars should work together. Asked by a speaker from the floor with whom they were prepared to go, with Lenin or Kerensky, delegates shouted back 'With Lenin! With Lenin!'[140] and adopted a motion declaring that

> This Congress cannot consider the actions of the Bolsheviks to have been antidemocratic, and it will take all measures to ensure that armies from Ukraine as well as separate Ukrainian army units on the front and in the rear are not sent to fight against the representatives of the working people's interests.[141]

The Tsentral'na Rada responded to the news from Petrograd by convening a Committee in Defence of the Revolution and establishing a staff headquarters charged with organising an armed force. The Committee's members were from every party except the Mensheviks, who insisted that the Kyiv Duma was the only authority legitimately empowered to defend the gains of the Revolution and public order in Kyiv.[142]

---

139   Skorovstansky, *Revoliutsiia na Ukraine*, pp. 66–7.
140   Ibid.
141   Khrystiuk, *Ukrains'ka Revoliutsiia*, Vol. II, p. 47.
142   The members of the Kyiv Committee in Defence of the Revolution were: from the Rada, M. Tkachenko and M. Porsh (USDWP), O. Sevriuk, M. Shapoval and M. Kovalevsky (UPSR), A. Nikovsky, M. Matushevsky (UPSF), H. Piatakov (Bolsheviks), and S. Goldelman (Jewish Social Democratic Labour Party – Poale Zion). Political parties sent the following members to the Committee: M. Zilberfarb (Jewish Socialist Workers Party), S. Saradzhev (Russian SRs), M. Rafes (Bund), M. Zatonsky (Bolsheviks) and A. Pisotsky (pseud. Richytsky) – USDWP. From other organisations came I. Kreisberg (Bolshevik), representing the

On the following day the Committee issued a statement to the population of Ukraine in which it spoke in the name of 'all the bodies of the revolutionary democracy, all revolutionary and socialist parties of our country, both Ukrainian and non-Ukrainian' demanding that 'all civic and military authorities in the rear, all organisations of the revolutionary democracy firmly and without wavering implement all its orders and instructions'. It would not tolerate any actions hostile to the interests of the revolution, it would suppress them ruthlessly and, if necessary, by force of arms.[143]

The Committee and the Rada suffered a serious setback within days when the Bolsheviks quit their ranks. The Bolsheviks had insisted that two of their members, M. Zatonsky and Yurii Piatakov, the latter Hryhorii Piatakov's brother, be made members of the *mala rada* as their condition for joining the Committee.[144] It was the body where the strategic objectives of the Committee were being discussed and decided on a daily basis. On 26 October M. Rafes introduced a resolution to the *mala rada* on behalf of the Bund that 'resolutely condemned the Bolshevik seizure of power' in Petrograd and promised to oppose any attempts by the councils to take power in Ukraine.[145] The resolution sparked a major debate. USDWP leaders spelled out their party's position:

> There can be no coalition with the bourgeoisie. Power should pass into the hands of the revolutionary democracy, which does not at all mean it should be handed to the councils of workers' and soldiers' deputies. We are against the uprising of the Petrograd proletariat if that means it will apply such a formula. But at the same time we resolutely oppose putting it down by military force. In the current situation that would mean in reality to hand all power to the actual counterrevolution. The Petrograd conflict must be resolved solely by peaceful means.[146]

      Kyiv Council of Workers' Deputies, M. Shumytsky from the Central Committee of the All-Ukrainian Railway Workers' Union, S. Petliura (USDWP) representing the Ukrainian General Military Committee, M. Telezhynsky and Ye. Kasianenko from the All-Ukrainian Council of Soldiers' Deputies. Finally, there were representatives on the Committee from the Kyiv Council of Soldiers' Deputies, and the Odesa, Kharkiv and Katerynoslav Councils of Workers', Soldiers' and Peasants' Deputies. See Soldatenko, *Ukraina v revoliutsiinu dobu*, Vol. 1, pp. 790–2; S. Volin, *Mensheviki na Ukraine 1917–21* (New York: Inter-University Project on the History of the Menshevik Movement, paper no. 11, September 1962), p. 20.

143   Soldatenko, *Ukraina v revoliutsiinu dobu*, Vol. 1, p. 793.
144   Rafes, *Dva goda*, pp. 46–8.
145   *Robitnycha hazeta*, 28 October 1917, p. 1.
146   Ibid.

This position, which was supported also by the UPSR, differed from the Bund's. The Bund held the Bolsheviks solely responsible for the Petrograd uprising without acknowledging the broader motives and involvement of the Petrograd workers, soldiers and sailors and the backing of the Second All-Russian Congress of Soviets. The *mala rada* refused to condemn the uprising, adopting a resolution that opposed it for the reasons spelled out by the USDWP.

The Kyivan Bolsheviks nevertheless felt compelled to quit the Committee in Defence of the Revolution as well as the Rada. Their main reason for joining in the first place had been to shield the Petrograd seizure of power from a possible counterrevolutionary riposte. Volodymyr Zatonsky recalled in his memoirs, written in 1920:

> Our basic demand to the Rada was the following: not to allow any military formations out of Ukraine or the Southwestern or Romanian fronts that could suppress the revolution in Moscow and Petrograd. These fronts were the most problematic because we knew that the forces around Kerensky were uniting with the Kornilovists in struggle against the revolution and would try to rely on military units standing in Ukraine. We could take care of this task of, so to speak, giving passive support to the revolutionary centre most easily in union with the Rada, as long as it honourably met its obligations.[147]

The Kyivan Bolsheviks' most important task at that moment was to provide support, *passive support* as Zatonsky put it, to the revolution in 'the centre', in Russia proper. This was a fundamentally different motive for participating in the Committee in Defence of the Revolution from that of the USDWP and the UPSR, who were using it to build another institution of state power in Ukraine. The Ukrainian parties either opposed outright the Bolshevik-led seizure of power or were at least deeply troubled by it. Bolshevik norms of representation in a government based on the councils discriminated against the peasantry, the Rada's main base of support. Moreover, the Bolsheviks had given no indication just what they meant in practice by the right of nations to self-determination.

On quitting the Committee in Defence of the Revolution and the Rada Yurii Piatakov declared in the *mala rada*:

---

147 *U dni Zhovtnia. Spohady uchasnykiv borot'by za vladu Rad na Ukraini* (Kyiv, 1967), p. 3, cited by Soldatenko, *Ukraina v revoliutsiinu dobu*, Vol. 1, p. 795.

> The battle on the streets of Petrograd has been going on for three days. That testifies to the fact that it is not a Bolshevik uprising, but an uprising of the revolutionary proletariat and the army ... By speaking out against the uprising of the Petrograd proletariat and army you have by the same token struck a blow against our party. That is why we are walking out of the *mala rada* with our hands untied. But know that regardless of all this we will be with you in arms the moment you are perishing under the blows of Russian imperialism.[148]

A USDWP deputy responded to Piatakov that the Ukrainian people would not forget the services rendered to them by the Bolsheviks. The hall erupted in applause.[149]

The Bolsheviks then called a meeting on 27 October of the combined Kyiv Council of Workers' and Soldiers' Deputies at which Hryhorii Piatakov accused the Rada of putting a knife in the back of the Petrograd uprising. He considered the battles for control of Petrograd and Moscow to be still unresolved and warned that the Ukrainian people could forget about their national self-determination if the forces of the Provisional Government succeeded in drowning the uprisings there in blood. The meeting adopted the Bolsheviks' resolution of solidarity with the Petrograd workers and soldiers and declared its determination 'to organise a revolutionary committee of the Councils, hand all power in Kyiv over to it, mandate it to implement comprehensively the resolutions of the Second All-Russian Congress of Soviets and to subordinate it (the revolutionary committee) to the Kyiv Councils of Workers' and Soldiers' Deputies which have the right to re-elect its members at any time'.[150]

A revolutionary committee (*revkom*), composed mainly of Bolsheviks and left Russian SRs, set up headquarters in a palatial residence in the centre of the city and brought in some two hundred rifles. However, it failed to take any further action for on the same day a delegation from the Rada, the city Duma, the Russian SRs, Mensheviks and Bund visited the *revkom* and had its headquarters surrounded by an armed detachment. Situated far from the working-class neighbourhoods of the city, the *revkom* could not easily call in reinforcements. It surrendered its arms and its members were arrested. But the Bolsheviks decided to press on and formed a new *revkom* on 29 October. It issued a call

---

148   Soldatenko, *Ukraina v revoliutsiinu dobu*, Vol. 1, pp. 799–800.
149   M. Maiorov, *Z Istorii Revoliutsiinoi Borot'by na Ukraini 1914–1919* (n.p.: Derzhavne Vydavnytstvo Ukrainy, 1928), p. 46; D. Petrovsky, *Revoliutsiia i Kontr-Revoliutsiia na Ukraine* (Moscow: Gosudarstvennoe Izdatel'stvo, 1920), p. 14.
150   Soldatenko, *Ukraina v revoliutsiinu dobu*, Vol. 1, pp. 800–5.

to the workers of Kyiv to rise up against the Provisional Government's forces, but not the Rada. That evening an uprising began in the Pechersk district that was directed against the headquarters of the Kyiv Military District.

The fighting in Kyiv over the following three days and nights was a two-on-one struggle. The Provisional Government had approximately 10,000 troops under its command, including part of the city garrison. Bolshevik forces, which included both Red Guards and regular army detachments loyal to them, numbered 6,600. The Tsentral'na Rada had the support of a detachment formed at the Third All-Ukrainian Soldiers' Congress, the Kyiv Council of Soldiers' Deputies which was vying with officers who supported the Provisional Government for the loyalty of the city garrison, and the 34th Army Corps under General Skoropadsky's command. Together they constituted the largest armed camp in Kyiv, a force of approximately 16,000.[151]

How the ensuing struggle unfolded is the subject of considerable dispute among historians, specifically whether the Bolsheviks and the Rada co-operated or operated autonomously in defeating the forces of the Provisional Government. Hryhorii Piatakov telegrammed the Council of People's Commissars in Petrograd after his release from arrest: 'By the joint efforts of Bolshevik and Ukrainian soldiers and armed Red Guards the headquarters [of the Kyiv Military District] was forced to surrender ... Kerensky's lackeys tried to send different army units against the Ukrainians and Bolsheviks, but none of them would go'.[152]

Piatakov here made the important observation that the outcome of the armed struggle depended not just on the numbers on each side but on the loyalty and strength of conviction of the workers and peasants involved once the fight for power literally became a question of their life or death. In this regard the Provisional Government was least able to retain the loyalty of its troops. Furthermore, Mykhailo Hrushevsky, the Rada president, had persuaded formidable Cossack units in Kyiv to remain neutral, telling them they should not intervene in a conflict taking place in what was for them now a foreign country.[153]

---

151 Hamretsky, Tymchenko and Shchus, *Rady Ukrainy*, p. 192; Rafes, *Dva goda*, p. 46; Soldatenko, *Ukraiina v Revoliutsiinu dobu*, Vol. 1.
152 Soldatenko, *Ukraina v revoliutsiinu dobu*, Vol. 1, pp. 860–1.
153 Soldatenko, *Ukraina v revoliutsiinu dobu*, Vol. 1, pp. 752–6, notes that the Rada convened a Congress of Peoples in Kyiv from 8–15 September that brought together 84 delegates of 12 national movements in the former Empire which, like the Ukrainian movement, were seeking to rebuild the Russian state on the principles of national territorial autonomy and federalism. Among the delegates there were nine representatives of Cossacks from their Tersk, Don, Amur, Kuban, Ural, Transcaspian and Orenburg armies. Some of the units

Historians agree that the Rada emerged the victor from these three days of fighting. Its forces took control of Kyiv, occupying the garrison, the police stations, Lukianivka prison, government buildings, the city's banks, the railways and post office. The Bolsheviks were not strong enough to challenge the Rada and so they withdrew their forces from the streets. Some members of the general staff of the Kyiv Military District were arrested while others evacuated south to join General Kaledin's army on the Don.[154]

On 1 November the General Secretariat of the Rada declared itself the government of Ukraine, asserting that the Rada was chosen by all its people, expressed the will of the entire revolutionary democracy and was, in essence, a national council of peasants', workers' and soldiers' deputies.[155] Holding a decisive military advantage over the Bolsheviks and the Provisional Government largely as a result of the allegiance to it of the soldiers' movement, the Rada was acknowledged as the acting government throughout the Ukrainian provinces. Its assumption of power was peaceful everywhere except in Kyiv and Vynnytsia, where there were armed confrontations between the forces of the Rada, the Bolshevik-led workers' brigades and units of the army still loyal to the Provisional Government. Still, the Rada's forces prevailed in Vynnytsia as they did in Kyiv.[156]

The concluding resolution of the Third Soldiers Congress on 29 October demanded the Tsentral'na Rada's general assembly declare the formation of a Ukrainian People's Republic. Its federative ties with other republics of Russia should be decided, the Congress argued, by an elected, already sovereign Ukrainian constituent assembly.

The Tsentral'na Rada adopted its Third Universal on 7 November, which declared the Ukrainian People's Republic, claimed all ethnographically Ukrainian territories and proposed a settlement of border disputes by plebiscite. The Universal expressed a desire for federation with Russia and other nations of the former Empire, and the hope that a democratically constituted government of the federation would sue immediately for peace. It also outlined the programme to be pursued by the Ukrainian Republic: a combination of state and workers' control of industry, confiscation of all privately owned landed estates without compensation, an eight hour working day, national personal

---

accompanying these delegates stayed behind in Kyiv after the Congress and were a potential, though uncertain, military force on any side in the ensuing struggle for power.

154 Hamretsky, Tymchenko and Shchus, *Rady Ukrainy*, p. 214; Shapoval, *Velyka Revoliutsiia*, p. 91.
155 Soldatenko, *Ukraina v revoliutsiinu dobu*, Vol. 1, p. 809.
156 Andrii Zdorov, *Ukrains'kyi Zhovten'*, pp. 60–4.

autonomy for minorities, defence of basic democratic rights, abolition of the death penalty and a general amnesty of all political prisoners. Elections to a Ukrainian Constituent Assembly were scheduled for 27 December and its convocation for 9 January 1918.[157]

The initial draft of the Third Universal agreed between the Ukrainian social democrats and socialist revolutionaries was subjected to considerable amendment by representatives of the Bund, Mensheviks and Russian SRs before they were prepared to put it to a vote. They insisted that, in declaring a Ukrainian republic, the Universal stresses the desire of its people to remain within the Russian state, for its government to work through the central government and not unilaterally for the conclusion of peace and for the purpose of defending Ukraine's rights at interstate forums. These parties wished to retain all sovereign rights in the Russian state, which should then devolve some of them to Ukraine. They feared that by unilaterally declaring an autonomous republic the Ukrainian national movement was prone to drift towards the maximum goal of a fully sovereign, independent state. Such a move would jeopardise the political influence of the Russian and Jewish minorities in Ukraine. Rafes wrote:

> It was clear to the Bund that this 'Ukrainian democracy' could retain its revolutionary character only in a tight union with all of revolutionary Russia. Declaring its 'independence' would open the sluice gates to the nationalist petit bourgeois reaction and immediately weaken the influence of the 'national minorities' who were strong only by force of their ties with revolutionary Russia, and in whose name they were putting pressure on the Ukrainian Tsentral'na Rada.

The desire to ensure their ongoing influence led these parties to seek stronger representation in the Rada's government. The Third Universal upgraded the vice secretaries for Russian, Jewish and Polish national affairs to the rights and status of full secretaries. The upgrade gave the minorities a third of the votes in the General Secretariat (6 out of 18) and a quarter of the portfolios (6 out of 24).[158]

The Bund's representatives voted for the Third Universal when the amended version was put to the Rada's general assembly. The Mensheviks, Russian SRs and Popular Socialists as well as the Polish Democratic Centre abstained. The Mensheviks justified their abstention by stating they had not wanted to weaken

---

157 *Robitnycha hazeta*, 8 November 1917, pp. 2–3.
158 Rafes, *Dva goda*, p. 58.

'the revolutionary front', and that while they supported national self-determination in principle only an elected All-Russian Constituent Assembly had the power to determine the form such self-determination could take.[159] The Kyivan Bolsheviks dismissed the Third Universal as 'a typical bourgeois democratic melodrama which can be taken to mean one thing or another'. The real issue, they argued, was how and by which classes the objectives contained in it were going to be implemented. Did the Rada stand on the position of a bourgeois democratic revolution or a proletarian-peasant one?[160]

For the Rada's supporters, however, the problem lay elsewhere. Rafes noted that 'the Bund could easily reconcile itself to the declaration of a federal order in Russia, for which the Ukrainian Bundists were long prepared by their previous political work. However, a federated union of Russia and Ukraine in the absence of a central government is a fiction'.[161] That absence, or at least the belief that the Bolsheviks would not succeed in consolidating an alternative central government, left a gaping hole in the Third Universal. It made clear what the Tsentral'na Rada wanted in terms of power in Ukraine, but it failed altogether to take a position on the struggle for power in Petrograd, Moscow and elsewhere. It was silent, neither recognising nor rejecting the new Soviet government. Rather, the Universal described the struggle for power in the Russian metropoli as ongoing and unresolved, the general situation there as one of chaos.

> A grave and difficult hour has befallen the land of the Russian republic. To the north in the capitals a hand-to-hand bloody battle is being waged. The central government is no more and across the state anarchy, disorder and ruin are spreading.

The Universal went on to assure the people that after taking power in Ukraine the Rada 'will use its power and authority to stand guard over their rights and the revolution not only in our own country but in all Russia'. The Rada had made clear on 26 October that it did not recognise the Council of People's Commissars, but wanted the conflict between the socialist parties provoked by the overthrow of the Provisional Government to be resolved by peaceful means. All the party leaders in the Rada disagreed with the Bolsheviks' conception of the revolution and their goal of a proletarian dictatorship. Rather, they espoused the goal of a federal, democratic republic whose central and

---

159 Ibid.
160 Soldatenko, *Ukraina v revoliutsiinu dobu*, Vol. 1, p. 904.
161 Rafes, *Dva goda*, pp. 56–7.

autonomous national governments should be elected by universal suffrage. That was the most they expected of the revolution they saw unfolding before them. The peasantry and working class would be represented amply in such a republic's governing institutions, but they would rule in the long run only in coalition with or opposition to the bourgeoisie. As for this period of exceptional crisis before constituent assembly elections were concluded, the socialist parties should exclude the bourgeois and landowners' parties from government. General elections would then decide the composition of the constituent assemblies of the Ukrainian republic and the federated Russian republic, and who would form the new government in each of them.

The moderate wings of Russian, Jewish and Ukrainian social democracy consoled themselves in their common belief that the nascent Petrograd government of Bolsheviks could not survive for very long. For them there was in fact no viable government in Petrograd on whom the Ukrainian People's Republic could rely as a credible central authority and partner in federation. However, the situation was extremely fluid and the Rada's advantage was momentary, secured by the peasant soldiers who stood for an autonomous Ukrainian People's Republic because they believed it stood ready to satisfy their demands for land, national self-determination and an end to the War. The position of the working class, on the other hand, was far from clear. The workers' councils in the Ukrainian towns and cities of the north, in which the Mensheviks and Bund were strong, were internally divided over such cardinal issues and the kind of government that was needed to resolve them. The Bolsheviks led the workers' councils in the industrial Donbas, supported the seizure of power in Petrograd and sought to bring their region under the authority of the Russian Council of People's Commissars.

The Third All-Ukrainian Soldiers' Congress had also declared its sympathy for the Bolsheviks' course of action in Petrograd. It clearly wanted the Rada to follow the same course in Ukraine without waiting for constituent assembly elections: to sue for peace unilaterally, to distribute land to the peasants immediately, to enforce workers' control of industry, to provide for democratic self government, while securing Ukraine's national independence *as a means to those ends*. The Rada had proven strong enough to overcome the Provisional Government, to reject the Bolsheviks' terms of state power in Ukraine and to declare the Ukrainian People's Republic. But could they consolidate their momentary victory and build a viable state power? And how could they join their republic into a federated Russian republic when they could no longer detect a functioning central government in Russia but only 'anarchy disorder and ruin'?

CHAPTER 5

November 1917: Attempts at Reconciliation

The Tsentral'na Rada overthrew the Provisional Government's forces with the support of the peasantry on the land and in the army. It took control of Ukraine's cities and declared the Ukrainian People's Republic (UPR). It stood at a threshold of state power, but to step over it and to consolidate its momentary victory the Rada had to deal decisively with the demands of the revolutionised masses, namely to end the War, to carry out land reform, to arrest the catastrophic decline of industrial production, and to involve the workers, peasants and soldiers directly in the exercise of that state power. The workers' councils that claimed power at the local level, and in many towns and cities already exercised it, posed a particular challenge. Until October Kyiv was nowhere on their broader horizon; they looked only to Petrograd for a higher state authority that could support them in dealing with the multifaceted crisis their communities faced.

By overthrowing the Provisional Government and declaring the Republic the Rada ended direct rule of Petrograd over Ukraine. It claimed substantial autonomy in a future federated Russian republic to which the Ukrainian Republic would devolve some of its sovereignty, in the first instance in order to negotiate on its behalf an end to the War. In the long run, the respective competences of the central and autonomous governments would be negotiated and then held by new constituent assemblies at both levels of the federal state.

However, this vision of the revolution's trajectory was thrown into disarray at the end of October 1917 when armed forces led by the Petrograd Soviet's Military Revolutionary Committee (MRC) overthrew the Provisional Government in the Russian capital and the Second All-Russian Congress of Soviets elected a government to take its place. We must therefore turn directly to the situation in Petrograd and to the predicament of the Russian state in November 1917 in order to understand the Rada's own predicament and its negative perception of this turn of events. Indeed, how could the Rada incorporate the UPR into a federated Russian republic when it could no longer even detect a functioning central government in Russia, but only 'anarchy disorder and ruin'?

1   The New Power in Petrograd

The Rada's rejection of the Council of People's Commissars as the successor of the Provisional Government mirrored that of a minority of the delegates at the Second All-Russian Congress of Soviets who opposed both the Bolshevik-led overthrow and a government answerable solely to the councils/soviets. Overnight and in the morning hours of 25 October the forces of the Military Revolutionary Committee had seized key points in the capital and surrounded the Winter Palace, seat of the Provisional Government. Fighting around the Winter Palace continued all day and into the evening of 25 October when the Second All-Russian Congress of Soviets opened nearby in the Smolny Institute. The congress was protected by sailors under the command of the MRC.

The uprising and the congress taking place on the same day was no coincidence.

> Trotsky wanted to link the action to the Congress itself, believing that an insurrection conducted on the party's own initiative would have less chance of winning mass support; Lenin believed it 'criminal' to temporize until the Congress, since he feared that the Provisional Government would forestall the insurrection by a vigorous offensive … Lenin wanted the insurrection to precede the Congress, which would have no alternative but to sanction the accomplished deed.[1]

Mensheviks and SRs at the congress denounced the uprising as a Bolshevik conspiracy which rendered the congress illegitimate. They demanded the fighting be stopped and negotiations for a new coalition cabinet take place with the Provisional Government.

The Winter Palace was finally taken, Kerensky fled, ministers of the Provisional Government were arrested and taken to the Fortress of Saints Peter and Paul. Among them were several Menshevik ministers. When Volodymyr Antonov-Ovsiienko, commander of the MRC's assault on the Winter Palace, declared to the Congress that the Provisional Government was finally overthrown, around 60 Mensheviks and SRs, around one tenth of the delegates, walked out in protest. The left SRs and a small group of Menshevik Internationalists remained behind, but continued to protest the Government's overthrow, demanding peaceful negotiations with it instead. They were even supported

---

[1]   Victor Serge, *Year One of the Revolution*, translated and edited by Peter Sedgwick (Holt, Reinhart, and Winston, 1972), p. 66, https://www.marxists.org/archive/serge/1930/year-one/index.htm [accessed 2 October 2017].

by some Bolsheviks led by Zinoviev and Kamenev, who doubted their own party could survive long alone at the helm while the Mensheviks, SRs and the Kadets controlled critical institutions and infrastructure such as the telegraph, the postal services and the railways.

However, the congress sanctioned the overthrow by a majority of around 70 percent and resolved to form a new government answerable to the councils alone. Of the 128 delegates from Ukraine, representing 36 councils of workers', soldiers' and peasants' deputies, 56 percent upheld these positions. The congress elected a Central Executive Committee (CEC) of the Soviets as its legislative assembly, and on 26 October a Council of People's Commissars (CPC) as the governing executive. The composition of the CEC was determined by proportional representation of parties elected to the congress. Vacant seats were retained for the Mensheviks and SRs who had quit the congress should they decide to return. The Council of People's Commissars was made up entirely of Bolsheviks, with Lenin as its chairman. The Bolsheviks invited the left SRs to govern alongside them in the CPC, but they hesitated and remained in opposition within the CEC alone.[2]

The Congress entrusted its government to convene the Constituent Assembly on schedule. It adopted two decrees, on peace and land reform. The first decree called for 'an immediate peace without annexations [without the seizure of foreign territory and the forcible annexation of foreign nationalities] and without indemnities'. The decree on land declared private ownership abolished in perpetuity, that all estates, including those of the crown, church and large landowners, were confiscated without compensation and all their land should be distributed equitably to the peasantry. The decree stated that 'the land question in its full scope can be settled only by the popular Constituent Assembly'.

The Mensheviks and SRs who had quit the Congress joined up with two institutions they held sway in, the powerful All-Russian Executive Committee of the Union of Railway Workers, known in English by its Russian acronym *Vikzhel*, and the Central Executive Committee of the All-Russian Congress of Peasant Deputies. Together they formed a Committee to Save the Fatherland and the Revolution, 'to recreate the Provisional Government' based on the bourgeois as well as the revolutionary parties that should lead the country to the Constituent

---

2 Vladimir Brovkin, *The Mensheviks After October: Socialist Opposition and the Rise of the Bolshevik Dictatorship* (Ithaca: Cornell University Press, 1987), p. 17; 'Session of the Petersburg Committee of the Social Democratic Labour Party of Russia (Bolshevik), November 1(14), 1917', in Lev Trotsky, *The Stalin School of Falsification*, https://www.marxists.org/archive/trotsky/1937/ssf/sfo8.htm#a41 [accessed 1 August 2017].

Assembly elections. They called upon state employees and the population as a whole to obey the Committee, not the new Soviet government, and they desperately sought troops for Kerensky to mount a march on the Russian capital against the Soviet government. Sporadic fighting carried on inside Petrograd, culminating on 29 October in an uprising by officer cadets, which the MRC quickly put down. Thereafter, all publications calling for the overthrow of the Soviet government were ruthlessly suppressed and their publishers arrested.

On 29 October the Bolsheviks agreed to multiparty negotiations mediated by the *Vikzhel* in order to find a way out of the conflict and to forestall the further estrangement of the Mensheviks and SRs from the new government. The threat remained of a march on the capital by troops supporting the ousted government. These talks did not progress, however, as all three parties were themselves split internally over the seizure of power and were now increasingly alienated from one another by their dispute having escalated into an armed conflict. At the heart of the conflict was not whether these parties should govern in coalition, but whether the said government should answer solely to the councils/soviets or to the entire democracy, that is to all the bourgeois and socialist parties represented in the soviets and the Provisional Government.

Kerensky, who fled Petrograd to the camp of General Krasnov, mounted a march of Cossack horsemen on the capital. Thousands of Petrograd workers responded to the new government's call to defend it, dug trenches on the approaches to the city and equipped soldiers, sailors and Red Guards with artillery, munitions and provisions directly from their factories. On the night of 30 October they repelled and completely demoralised a mere one thousand cossacks, who advanced without the reinforcements they had been promised from the front. Thereafter, Kerensky and other members of the Provisional Government departed for the front in a vain attempt to find new forces prepared to march on Petrograd.

The Bolsheviks in Petrograd met for a party conference on 1 November where they continued to disagree among themselves about the composition of their new government, whether it was sufficiently broad to hold and consolidate its power across Russia. Its position remained uncertain as its ability to govern through existing state administrations and to communicate with the rest of the country through the telegraph, postal services and the railways were being blocked by the hostile parties within them. However, the position advocated by Lenin and Trotsky, that it should remain a homogenous Bolshevik government, was gaining ground. They had been elected to this government by the Second Congress while majorities in the other parties had refused to take the seats allocated to them. Lenin argued further that the new government should ruthlessly suppress those who opposed it, to use terror to deny the bourgeoisie any chance to mount a counteroffensive. By 1 November a compromise with the bourgeois parties and those socialist parties that advocated coalition with them appeared less urgent. Kerensky's much feared march on Petrograd had just been repelled and the pro-soviet forces in Moscow, Russia's second city, had prevailed over Provisional Government forces after a week of bloody fighting.[3]

The Mensheviks at their Petrograd conference on 3 November failed to find a common position. Some were calling for armed struggle against the Bolsheviks as usurpers of the revolution while others demanded that civil war be prevented at all costs. The prospects for a united position among themselves and for a peaceful compromise between the three main parties were increasingly remote. Indeed, the seizure of power was testing the unity and coherence of all the parties. On 5 November eleven Bolsheviks on the Central Executive Committee of the Soviets, three of whom also served on the Council of People's Commissars, resigned and demanded an end to the use of terror to maintain the CPC in power as a single party government.[4]

Thus the overthrow of the Provisional Government, the conflict between the parties of the Russian revolutionary democracy over the legitimacy of the new Soviet government and the outbreak of fighting between the supporters of the ousted and the new government was the 'anarchy, disorder and ruin' the Rada referred to in its Third Universal of 7 November. The Rada promised 'to defend the rights and the revolution not only in our country but in all of Russia'. While opposing the Bolshevik-led seizure of power, the Rada also opposed any forcible suppression of the new government, insisting that a compromise be sought through peaceful negotiations. All the parties in the Rada remained in touch with the rapidly evolving situation in Petrograd, the Russian and Jewish parties communicating with their respective Central Committees there, the Ukrainian parties with their comrades in the Petrograd Soviet, the army and the Baltic Sea fleet.

Undoubtedly the Rada's leaders were also wondering what kind of voice and representation the Ukrainian People's Republic could possibly secure in a future coalition government through such negotiations. The Provisional Government had never negotiated with the Rada in good faith, and in its last days turned on it completely, ordering the arrest of Vynnychenko on charges of treason. The Council of People's Commissars addressed the question of national self-determination for the first time on 2 November, a week after

---

3 Ibid.
4 Brovkin, *The Mensheviks After October*, pp. 19–33.

adopting its decrees on peace and land reform. It issued a Declaration of the Rights of Peoples of Russia, signed by Stalin as People's Commissar of Nationalities and Lenin as head of the Council. The Declaration called for 'a voluntary and honest union of the peoples of Russia'. The Provisional Government's lies, provocations and mistrust of peoples 'should be replaced with an open and honest policy leading to complete mutual trust between the peoples of Russia'. A strong union was necessary, the declaration went on, for it 'to be able to withstand all kinds of attacks by the imperialist-annexationist bourgeoisie', a reference to the military advance of the Central Powers on Russia. Proceeding from these motives the Council declared it would place four principles at the heart of its policy in the sphere of nationalities: the equality and sovereignty of the peoples of Russia; their right to self-determination up to separation and establishment of their own independent states; rejection of all national and religious privileges; and the free development of national minorities. However, it proposed no practical steps towards implementing any of these principles other than forming a commission on nationalities within the Soviet government. Ending the War first was its immediate priority, and this required an orderly demobilisation on the military front and remaining united behind the front lines. However, the Bolsheviks saw in 'an honest and voluntary union of the peoples of Russia' more than an immediate requirement to stabilise the Soviet government so it could secure a ceasefire and negotiate a peace. It was their long-term objective to reconcile at least some of Russia's oppressed nations to a new union, to a more equal relationship with their former oppressor nation within the new Soviet state.

Which of these nations were likely to choose to remain with Russia? No less than twelve national movements were seeking a new settlement or outright separation. Ringing the Russian heartland, they were in Finland, Poland, Ukraine, Belarus, Lithuania, Estonia, Latvia, Armenia, Georgia, Azerbaijan, Moldova and the Cossacks in the Kuban, on the Don and other regions across the south. This outer ring of Russia's colonial possessions coincided in many places with the military front with the Central Powers. The latter were seeking to tear these regions away from an enfeebled Russia, while the new Soviet government was committed to halting the war and negotiating a peace. The Bolsheviks surely could not fail to see that the Central Powers wanted to take from Russia by force what imperial Russia had itself once taken by force. The principle of national self-determination denied both of them the right to hold onto these colonies against their nations' will. Yet to release them into the hands of another imperialist power was equally unacceptable. The Bolsheviks had never before had to face the possibility of a break-up of the Russian state. Even though they opposed 'the forcible annexation of foreign nationalities' and advocated the national independence of the colonial possessions of the other European imperialist states, they did not imagine they may themselves one day become responsible for *implementing* the principle of national self-determination up to the separate statehood for any part of their own multinational state. The fact that at this precise point in time their country was being invaded and about to be dismembered by another imperialist state made it practically impossible for the Bolsheviks to see how they could implement this principle in any practical and just way. For them the national question in Russia had to remain a domestic issue to be addressed in practice only after the threat of foreign aggression was repulsed.

2   The Constituent Assembly

Within one week of the Provisional Government's ouster from Petrograd and Kyiv the parties of the revolutionary democracy were deeply and, as it turned out, irrevocably split over the question of the succeeding state power. How should democracy and popular sovereignty be exercised: through the institution of soviet democracy that excluded the bourgeois and landowning classes or through a parliamentary republic that included them? The question was posed immediately and in an entirely practical way, since on 12 November elections finally were held to the Constituent Assembly. More than 44 million people, around 60 percent of the electorate across the country and on the fronts voted, giving a plurality to the Russian SRs of around 45 percent, followed by the Bolsheviks (25 percent), the Ukrainian SRs (9.5 percent), Kadets (5 percent), and the Mensheviks (between 1.8 and 2.5 percent).[5] The Bund's slate won just over 31,000 votes and Poale Zion's around 21,000. Within their own communities these two workers' parties were overshadowed completely by moderate and religious parties which claimed over 80 percent of the half million votes cast for Jewish parties.[6] Like their Russian and Ukrainian counterparts, many Jewish workers cast their votes instead either for Menshevik or Bolshevik candidates.

The Bolsheviks polled strongly in the urban areas and on the military fronts, while the Russian and Ukrainian SRs took majorities in the rural areas.

---

5   The sources give various estimates of the final count. See: http://www.encyclopediaofukraine.com/pagespercent5CApercent5CLpercent5CAll6RussianConstituentAssembly.htm [accessed 9 September 2017], and N.V. Sviatitsky in *A Year of the Russian Revolution: 1917–18* (Moscow: Zemlia i Volia, 1918).

6   Gitelman, *Jewish Nationality*, p. 80.

The returns in the nine Ukrainian provinces taken together gave the Ukrainian SRS 52 percent of the votes, the Russian SRS 25 percent, USDWP 13 percent, Bolsheviks 10 percent and Kadets 3.7 percent. The Bolshevik vote was highest in the more industrialised provinces; in the Donbas it approached 50 percent. The bourgeois and landowning class parties got 12 percent of the votes in Ukraine, which was practically half the votes cast for them across the entire Russian state.[7] The Ukrainian and Russian SRS ran on joint tickets in Kharkiv and Kherson gubernia. The Ukrainian SDS and SRS ran on joint tickets on the military fronts and in some interior districts. Overall, 120 deputies to the Constituent Assembly were elected in Ukraine: 71 Ukrainian SRS, 30 Russian SRS, 11 Bolsheviks, two Ukrainian Social Democrats, one Kadet, one from the Union of Landowners and four from Jewish, Polish and Muslim parties. In addition, another 11 deputies from the bloc of Ukrainian SRS and SDS were elected by soldiers on the fronts. Some of the Ukrainian parties' deputies, around 50 in all, decided at a meeting in Kyiv in December not to take part in the actual Constituent Assembly until elections to the Ukrainian Constituent Assembly were held.[8]

Throughout the period from February to October the Bolsheviks had called for elections to a constituent assembly, but they criticised the election outcome and sought to subordinate the Assembly to the authority of the Soviet government. Trotsky argued that the Constituent Assembly could not truly represent the electorate's wishes because the party lists were drawn up for these elections three months prior to the actual voting, when the right-wing candidates on the Russian SRS' list outnumbered the left by three to one. The balance of forces within the Russian SRS had changed by November, he argued, for the left SRS were in the ascendancy and were splitting away to form a distinct party of their own to champion the poor peasantry.[9] For Trotsky, the Constituent Assembly 'lagged behind the course of political events'. The Russian SRS and the Bolsheviks having taken 70 percent of the votes made this internal correlation of SR forces highly significant, for the fact that the majority of Russian SRS sent to the Constituent Assembly were from its right wing meant that the Bolsheviks could not achieve a working majority with the left SR wing in the Assembly.

---

7   A.P. Hrytsenko, *Politychni Syly u Borot'bi za Vladu v Ukraini* (Kyiv: Akademiia Nauk URSR, 1993), p. 5.
8   http://www.encyclopediaofukraine.com/pagespercent5CApercent5CLpercent5CAll6Russia nConstituentAssembly.htm [accessed 9 September 2017].
9   Trotsky, *From October to Brest-Litovsk*.

Trotsky's criticism of the Assembly was just one illustration of the Bolsheviks' belief that the soviet institution of democracy was more representative and responsive to the lower classes, particularly so in a fast-moving revolutionary situation, than the cumbersome machinery of general elections and parliamentary democracies. Moreover, the institution of soviet power was a reality; it was authorised by the Second All-Russian Congress to govern the country. Thus the Bolsheviks put their efforts into strengthening this government while seeking to subordinate the Constituent Assembly to its will. On 15 November they persuaded the left Russian SRs, who were splitting away from their mother party, to join the Soviet government and give it its first significant peasant representation. From 19 November seats in the Central Executive Committee of the Soviets more than doubled from 119 to 258 and now included 108 deputies from the All-Russian Congress of Peasants' Deputies, 100 soldiers' and sailors' deputies and 50 from the trade unions. There were 108 left Russian SRs and 92 Bolsheviks among them.[10]

The Constituent Assembly's convocation was delayed until 5 January 1918 for various reasons that included the banning of the Kadet party as 'enemies of the people', the domestic disruptions caused by the War and the threat of German forces pressing on Petrograd. The Council of People's Commissars put to the first session of the Assembly the decisions of the Second All-Russian Congress of Soviets and called for their ratification. It was, in effect, a demand that the Assembly recognise the authority and support the programme of the Soviet government. The Assembly refused and so Red Guards were instructed by the government to prevent it from reconvening on the following morning. There were some public protests, but they were not large. That ended what may be considered an extension of the dual power struggle in truncated form which followed the overthrow of the Provisional Government. For the Ukrainian People's Republic a path to autonomy in a federated Russian republic through the Constituent Assembly was irrevocably lost.

3   War and Peace

The new Soviet government, notwithstanding its ongoing struggle to secure its authority at home, now faced the task of extricating Russia from the War. German forces advanced as the Russian army continued to disintegrate on the front. Riga had fallen in September and Petrograd itself was threatened by Ger-

---

[10]   Brovkin, *The Mensheviks After October*, p. 36.

man land and naval forces. Immediately upon the Second Congress's adoption of its decree on peace the government broadcast it internationally in a 'Message to All'. On 7 November Trotsky, as People's Commissar of Foreign Affairs, telegrammed an invitation from his government to the Entente and Central Powers to meet and conclude a general peace. The Entente refused to recognise the Soviet government, rejected its proposal out of hand and threatened grave consequences should it proceed to negotiate separately with the Central Powers.

The Bolsheviks, however, saw an immediate halt to the carnage as their overriding and urgent responsibility. On 11 November they published the secret treaties the Russian state had entered into on the eve of the War and declared they would relinquish all the claims in them that went against the interests of the peoples of the countries concerned. The exposure of these treaties, which detailed how the disputed lands of stateless nations should be carved up between allies as spoils in war, caused consternation in the governments and outrage among the public of all the European imperialist states.

The Russian army was disintegrating on the front, soldiers were deserting in growing numbers to head home where the seizure and division of land was rapidly gaining pace. The Bolsheviks could not and would not try to hold the front, but they wished to demobilise it in as orderly a way as possible. Their government also desperately needed a breathing space to regroup its forces against the threat of a domestic counterrevolution. They understood their bid for power as the opening shot of an international revolution, which needed to break out of Russia and envelop the advanced capitalist countries, especially Germany. So, in seeking peace with the imperialist powers, they remained ready to break the peace with any of these countries as soon as the balance of social forces in them changed and to encourage the spread of social revolution to them.

While the Entente refused to countenance any talk of peace, the Central Powers calculated they stood to gain much from a separate peace with an exhausted Russia. They were pressing on its borders across a wide front stretching from the Black Sea to the Baltic. Peace with Russia would relieve the pressure on their eastern front and enable Germany to turn more of its forces into the western front. By securing peace here Germany could also get much needed food, fuel and other crucial materials for its war effort elsewhere.

Germany's calculations were informed by even bolder ambitions, indeed by a grand strategy for global expansion. Long-term German policy towards Russia aimed to break it up entirely as a state, to destroy its economic and political unity, to link up its dismembered parts directly to Germany to serve its strategic interests. Germany wanted a cordon of client states stretching from the Baltic to the Black Seas, separating it from the Russian core and pushing Russia away into the east. It wanted to evict Russia permanently from the Balkan peninsula and to open a direct land passage for itself from Berlin to Baghdad.[11] Ukraine, it was plain to see, was by far the richest and strategically best placed of all of Russia's colonial possessions that Germany needed to gain in order to destroy Russia, to win the War and implement its grand strategy.[12]

The German Central Command responded positively to Trotsky's invitation, hostilities were suspended on different parts of the front, and on 22 November a truce was signed that halted all fighting. An armistice was concluded on 15 December. The Bolshevik government continued to inform the Entente of its actions and of its intention to conclude a general, democratic peace among all the belligerents. The Entente continued to refuse entering into peace negotiations. So Soviet Russia and the Central Powers initiated separate peace negotiations at Brest Litovsk on 9 December. There the Soviet representatives once again set out the objectives of their 26 October decree, calling for a general, democratic peace without annexations or reparations on the basis of the self-determination of nations.[13]

4   The Political Parties in Ukraine

As in Russia, the parties of the workers' movement in Ukraine were divided over the seizure of power in Petrograd. The Bolsheviks had majorities in the workers' councils across the Donbas. They gained a majority in the Kyiv Council of Workers' Deputies at the very end of October. In other towns and cities the Mensheviks and the Bund remained the dominant parties in the workers' councils, with the USDWP in a distinct minority. These three parties continued to call for a united socialist government for all Russia until general elections and the convocation of the Constituent Assembly. However, a second question was now posed by the Rada's assumption of power in Kyiv and the major cities of Ukraine. All the parties here, the city and district governments and the workers' and soldiers' councils were obliged to take a stand for or against its claim to govern as well.

---

11   Fritz Fischer, *Germany's Aims in the First World War*, with Introductions by Hajo Holdorn and James Joll (New York: Norton and Co., 1967), pp. 479–86.

12   'As much as anything, the First World War turned on the fate of Ukraine'. This is the very first sentence of Dominic Lieven's *Towards the Flame: Empire, War and the End of Tsarist Russia* (London: Penguin, 2016).

13   Trotsky, *From October to Brest Litovsk*.

The Russian Socialist Revolutionaries, Russian Popular Socialists, the Polish Democratic Centre, the Bund and Poale Zion now held portfolios in the General Secretariat alongside the Ukrainian Social Democrats, Socialist Revolutionaries and Socialist Federalists. The Mensheviks insisted they were prepared to join the Secretariat, but they held back after clashing with the USDWP over the portfolio of Labour Secretary, which both wanted to hold. That is to say, all these parties had committed themselves in varying degrees to the Tsentral'na Rada as a Ukrainian autonomous government. However, the Rada's authority remained untested and unsettled despite the evident mass support given to it by the peasantry and the fact that it held military power in Kyiv and other cities. How much did the mass memberships of these workers' parties support their representatives in the Rada? And what did these parties do more widely among the workers to help decide these questions of government? Here we examine the responses of four parties: the USDWP, the Bund, Mensheviks and Bolsheviks.

4.1 The Ukrainian Social Democrats

The USDWP had ten functioning branches in April 1917: Kyiv, Kharkiv, Katerynoslav, Odesa, Cherkasy, Chernihiv, Novhorod-Volynsk, Berdiansk, Moscow and Petrograd. Six more were reported in their newspaper *Robitnycha hazeta* in May: Kremenchuk, Romny, Poltava, Zolotonosh, Dunaiv and Voronezh. New branches were set up in Nyzhnia-Krymka and Luhansk in June, Kherson in July, Bakhmut in August, Mykolaiv in November and Sevastopol on the southern tip of Crimea in December.[14] This still incomplete list of USDWP branches suggests that the party expanded over the year in a broad sweep from north to south. The Fourth Congress of the USDWP in October reported 28 branches. By the end of 1917, the party claimed to have some 40,000 members, an impressive figure that appeared to be based on a very loose definition of membership. The membership of the Kharkiv USDWP branch at its height in 1917, described below, is illustrative of a loose definition.

The USDWP did not have the intellectual or organisational resources needed to take full advantage of the opportunities for growth that presented themselves in 1917, especially in the south. For example, a member of the Mykolaiv branch wrote in November that the deepening political crisis 'had created very

---

14 *Robitnycha hazeta*, 12 April 1917, p. 8; 14 April 1917, p. 3; 15 April 1917, p. 3; 26 April 1917, p. 4; 27 April 1917, p. 3; 2 May 1917, p. 4; 3 May 1917, p. 4; 4 May 1917, p. 4; 5 May 1917, p. 4; 9 May 1917, p. 4; 11 May 1917, p. 4; 16 May 1917, p. 4; 21 May 1917, p. 4; 24 May 1917, p. 4; 26 May 1917, pp. 2–3; 27 May 1917, p. 4; 20 June 1917, p. 4; 22 June 1917, p. 4; 24 June 1917, p. 4; 21 July 1917, p. 3; 27 August 1917, p. 3; 24 October 1917, p. 3; 27 October 1917, p. 3; 5 November 1917, p. 4; 11 November 1917, p. 3; 23 December 1917, p. 4; 29 December 1917, p. 4.

favourable conditions for the work of Ukrainian social democracy in Mykolaiv', but that it was not taking advantage of them for lack of organisers. 'The central organs of our party must pay more attention to the big industrial cities'.[15]

The USDWP had some intellectually powerful orators, publicists and organisers who rose quickly to the leadership of the Tsentral'na Rada. But they lacked experienced organisers and militants on the ground to grow from a vanguard into a mass party. The request made most often to the party headquarters by its branches and by unaffiliated, yet interested, workers was for organisers.[16] Isaak Mazepa noted that in Katerynoslav there were no more experienced organisers in the party's branch at the end of 1917 than there were at the beginning. The overwhelming majority of new recruits were workers, both in the provincial capital and nearby towns of Nizhnedniprovsk, Diivka and Kodaky. At its 28 May meeting in the city railway station, where the USDWP had its headquarters in premises taken from the police, the branch expanded its executive committee to bring in representatives from the Briansk factory, pipe factories 'A' and 'C', the railways workshops and train depot, and from several new cells in the city centre.[17] The party had its own fraction of deputies in the Katerynoslav Council of Workers Deputies, a network of *Prosvita* cultural and educational centres and a choir.[18]

The USDWP in Kharkiv formed branches in the Helferich Sade factory, the Shymansky factory and the locomotive works. It re-opened a defunct branch at the Liubotyn railway depot where it gained 30 new members from the RSDWP. By mid-year the Kharkiv party organisation claimed 700 members. However, only 180 were paying dues and about 80 were actually attending city-wide meetings. The Kharkiv organisation staged public meetings across the city attended by thousands of workers, and it sent its members to outlying villages to address peasant gatherings. In May, it members collected 8,000 pieces of literature for Ukrainian soldiers and sent a delegation to the front to deliver them.[19] They tried to issue their own newspaper *Robitnyk*, but failed to sustain it and

---

15   *Robitnycha hazeta*, 5 November 1917, p. 4.
16   *Robitnycha hazeta*, 29 April 1917, p. 1.
17   *Vistnyk Tovarystva Prosvity u Katerynoslavi*, 31 March 1917, p. 4; 18 June 1917, p. 3; *Robitnycha hazeta*, 27 April 1917, p. 3; 24 May 1917, p. 4.
18   H.F. Kryvoshy, 'Robitnytstvo i Tsentral'na Rada: do pytannia pro sotsial'nu bazu ukrains'koi derzhavnosti', *Naukovi pratsi istorychnoho fakul'tetu Zaporiz'koho Derzhavnoho Universytetu* (Berdiansk: Zaporizhzhia, 1998), Vypusk III: Mizhnarodni Vidnosyny I problemy derzhavnoho budivnytstva v krainakh Yevropy I Ameryky.
19   *Robitnycha hazeta*, 12 April 1917, p. 5; 26 April 1917, p. 4; 3 May 1917, p. 4; 5 May 1917, p. 4; 21 July 1917, p. 3.

decided to concentrate instead on distributing *Robitnycha hazeta*, the party's main paper out of Kyiv.[20]

The Kyiv branch recruited new members at the Arsenal and regularly collected money there for *Robitnycha hazeta*. A second USDWP branch was established in the Podil district. The Luhansk USDWP branch was set up in June by workers from the Hartman factory, a majority of them seasonal workers with ties to the land. Seasonal workers in coal mines and chemical plants predominated also among the USDWP's recruits in Nyzhnia-Krymka and Tahanrih. The Bakhmut organisation had branches at the Sofiiev mine and the grain elevators in the city and in nearby mining towns of Enakiievo, Avdiivka, Nykolovk, Horlivka and Donets. Practically all of these organisations were built from scratch, often taking members from the Prosvita Society and the RSDWP.[21]

> Ukrainian fractions were formed in many councils of workers' deputies, including Kyiv, Katerynoslav, Kharkiv, Poltava, Mykolaiv and Odesa. They confidently put to the leaders of these organisations, which mainly represented Russian and Russian speaking workers, their own Ukrainian requirements. They came out with their own initiatives. The Ukrainian fractions in the councils were either made up of USDWP members or were politically aligned with them. The Ukrainian social democrats ... made up 10 percent of the executive committees of the Katerynoslav council in September, the Kyiv council in October and the Kharkiv council in November. There were somewhat fewer USDWP members in the Odesa council of workers' deputies, between five and seven percent of the total. It was the same picture in other cities of Ukraine, although in the middle sized and smaller urban centres the influence of Ukrainian social democrats on the work of their councils was stronger.[22]

The USDWP attracted a modest, if growing number of workers. Its capacity to grow was limited not only by the small number of its experienced cadres, but also by its inadequate programmatic response to the crisis in 1917. Isaak Mazepa recalled that from the beginning of the Revolution 'the social moment played

---

20 N.O. Bondar, 'Diial'nist' Kharkivs'koi orhanizatsii USDRP v seredovyshchi robitnykiv I selian na pochatku revoliutsiinykh podii 1917 roku' (n.p.: n.d.).
21 *Robitnycha hazeta*, 16 May 1917, p. 4; 26 May 1917, p. 4; 22 June 1917, p. 4; 11 November 1917, p. 3; 23 December 1917, p. 4; M. Ostrohorsky, 'Z Istorii Bil'shovyts'koi Orhanizatsii Horlivs'ko-Shcherbynivs'koho Raionu Donbasa (1901–1918)', *Litopys Revoliutsii*, 5 (September–October 1930), p. 108; Hamretsky, 'Kryza dribnoburzhuaznykh partii', p. 79; *Bor'ba za Oktiabr na Artemovshchine* (Kharkiv: Proletaryi, 1929), p. 95.
22 Kryvoshyi, 'Robitnytstvo I Tsentral'na Rada'.

a great and decisive role ... in the temperament of the Ukrainian masses'.[23] The threat of impending economic collapse spurred workers into action and self organisation. They paid attention to governmental slogans to the extent that they addressed this threat, as much as they did their democratic and national aspirations. Yet the party's leaders and its daily paper *Robitnycha hazeta* continued to focus on the national question with little regard for the socio-economic crisis even as that crisis deepened into the autumn months.

A conference of ten USDWP branches in April had made no decisions at all on ways to combat the economic crisis.[24] An editorial in the 20 May issue of *Robitnycha hazeta* described the dislocation of industry and transport, lack of fuel and raw materials and rising unemployment. It stressed the need to defend the means of production from imminent ruin. But rather than point to the factory committees as instruments for such a defence, the editorial cautioned workers to restrain their economic demands and support the Provisional Government's efforts to keep production going.[25] In October the USDWP Fourth Congress called for 'decisive central and regional government control over production and exchange of industrial goods with the direct participation of the organised proletariat'.[26] Perhaps the party stressed state control of industry because the embryonic levers of state power at its disposal in the Tsentral'na Rada were more tangible to it than those in the workers' movement like the factory committees. Yet more than anything else it was the USDWP leaders' preconceptions about the trajectory of the 1917 Revolution and its objective possibilities and limits that made them think this way. The USDWP's old guard did not believe that the working class could assume state power on its own in 1917, that ultimately it would share power with the bourgeoisie in a democratic republic.[27]

That stance exposed the party's ranks to the appeal of the Bolsheviks' more pro-active response to the economic crisis. At the local level where the USDWP had strong working class branches, its rank and file members were drawn to the Bolshevik view of workers' control and soviet power. USDWP deputies in the Kyiv and Kremenchuk workers' councils described themselves as 'Bolsheviks, only Ukrainian ones'.[28] The Kherson Bolshevik leader Lipshyts recalled 'the Ukrainian social democrats who came along in step with us and saw themselves

---

23   Mazepa, *Ukraina v Ohni*, Vol. 1, p. 13.
24   *Robitnycha hazeta*, 7 April 1917, pp. 2–3; 30 April 1917, p. 3.
25   *Robitnycha hazeta*, 20 May 1917, p. 1.
26   *Robitnycha hazeta*, 6 October 1917, p. 4.
27   Vynnychenko, *Vidrodzhennia Natsii*, Vol. 2, pp. 91–2.
28   Maiorov, *Z Istorii Revoliutsiinoi Borot'by*, p. 37.

as more left wing than the Bolsheviks themselves'.[29] The Kyiv USDWP branch adopted a resolution on 9 September calling for the introduction of workers' control over production and distribution without assigning any role at all to the state.[30] The Bakhmut branch supported workers' control of industry.[31] The Petrograd branch, with a following among the Russian capital's Ukrainian soldiers, sailors and workers, co-operated with the Bolshevik party in conducting anti-war propaganda and voted for their candidates to the city Duma elections.[32] When the Moscow branch split at the end of 1917 the right faction departed for Ukraine while most of the left went over to the Bolsheviks.[33]

The USDWP's Fourth Congress at the beginning of October debated the role of the working class in the exercise of power. From the right wing of the party, Valentyn Sadovsky argued that 1917 had ushered in a bourgeois democratic revolution which would be consummated in the formation of a coalition government of bourgeois and socialist parties. Sadovsky was not even prepared to give a greater share of power inside the Rada to the All-Ukrainian Soldiers', Peasants' and Workers' Congresses. Rather, he contended, it was the parties that should hold onto the reins.[34] From the centre, Mykola Porsh characterised 1917 as a 'social revolution' in which the proletariat and poor peasantry were playing a leading role. Volodymyr Vynnychenko stood between these two positions, characterising the revolution as both socialist and democratic but in the first instance as a national revolution which required cross-class unity to achieve its aims. This view he had consistently enunciated since the Second All-Ukrainian Soldiers Congress in June.[35] From the left wing of the party, Yevhen Neronovych and Mykola Tkachenko argued that working class and peasant parties should break with the bourgeois parties and that the Tsentral'na Rada should co-operate with the workers' councils to transform itself into a national council of workers', peasants' and soldiers' deputies.[36]

Mykola Porsh appeared to side with the left wing:

> When our party entered the Rada, it replaced its class orientation with a national one. Some of our comrades said quite plainly that until we

---

29   Kryvoshyi, 'Robitnytstvo I Tsentral'na Rada'.
30   Popov, *Narys Istorii*, p. 115.
31   *Borot'ba za Oktiabr na Artemovshchine*, p. 95.
32   M. Avdiienko, 'Liutneva Revoliutsiia v Petrohradi I USDRP', *Litopys Revoliutsii*, 1, no. 28 (January–February 1928).
33   N.N. Popov, 'Moskovs'ka hrupa 'livykh' u USDRP', *Litopys Revoliutsii*, 6, no. 33 (1928).
34   *Robitnycha hazeta*, 3 October 1917, p. 3.
35   *Robitnycha hazeta*, 7 June 1917.
36   *Robitnycha hazeta*, 1 October 1917, p. 3; 3 October 1917, pp. 2–3.

achieve the goal of unity there can be no class struggle in the Tsentral'na Rada … As far as I am concerned, Ukrainian social democrats had no right compromising on class interests in deference to general, national ones, about which I have a lot of doubt. That is why the opposition tendency in the Tsentral'na Rada demanded its transformation into a Council of Workers', Peasants' and Soldiers' Deputies, because this tendency stood on a more realistic footing.[37]

Pavlo Khrystiuk in his history of the Ukrainian revolution suggested the USDWP's leaders were more concerned about retaining their own power in the Rada than placing it in the hands of the working class:

During the revolution the party conducted not so much a social class as a national politics among the workers, which even provoked complaints within the party ranks. So too in the Tsentral'na Rada the USDWP fraction was in its majority more a petit bourgeois national democratic party than a socialist proletarian one. For this reason it often more willingly cooperated with the Socialist Federalists than with the Ukrainian Socialist Revolutionaries.[38]

The final resolutions of the Fourth USDWP Congress show the centrist wing forging voting majorities by making compromises with both the left and right. The party recognised that the Revolution was at an impasse. The Provisional Government had not only proved itself incapable of bringing the War to a close or dealing with the urgent questions facing the country, but in fact had prolonged the War and opposed the fundamental demands of the workers, peasants and soldiers.

That is why in the state as a whole as in its separate countries there must immediately be formed a homogenous revolutionary democratic power, a power of the organised proletariat, peasantry and army … bringing the imperialist war to a halt, drawing the proletariat and the entire revolutionary democracy in Russia and the warring states to a democratic peace without annexations or reparations and on the basis of the self-determination of nations … the Ukrainian Tsentral'na Rada should become the supreme revolutionary state authority in Ukraine.[39]

---

37 *Robitnycha hazeta*, 4 October 1917, p. 1.
38 Khrystiuk, *Ukrains'ka Revoliutsiia*, Vol. 2, p. 117.
39 *Robitnycha hazeta*, 6 October 1917, p. 2.

The Congress also pointed out that a majority of deputies in the Rada were still from the intelligentsia, which caused the Rada to waver towards 'petit-bourgeois nationalism'. It therefore resolved that the USDWP strengthen its activity in the All-Ukrainian Councils of Workers', Peasants' and Soldiers' Deputies, build local councils across the country and transform them 'from national organisations into general, territorial ones'. However, the Congress also made clear that 'these organisations by their activity should not obscure the leading role of Social Democracy among workers and suitable, proletarianised groups of peasants and soldiers'.[40]

These objectives appeared both unrealistic and misplaced in view of the weak implantation of the USDWP in the working class and the fact that multi-party, multinational workers' councils were already well established in towns and cities throughout the country. Until now these councils had a tenuous relationship with the Rada, if any at all. The USDWP needed to pursue its goal of expanding direct working-class representation in the Rada by concentrating its work on the councils and among the multinational working class. The UPSR commanded sufficient authority among the peasantry and soldiers to represent their aspirations. The Ukrainian Social Democrats held sway in the Rada but they did not have the same kind of mass support squarely behind their backs as the UPSR did. The Fourth USDWP Congress grasped the significance of the new conjuncture, that the Provisional Government which had so begrudgingly legitimised the Rada in July was all but finished. Authority and legitimacy were now required directly from the mass organisations of workers and peasants. The Congress stood on the brink of a decision to link the Rada's peasant and soldier base with the workers' movement, but the hour was late, the USDWP lacked a viable strategy to do this and the party leadership was afraid to lose its leading role in the Rada. In the end the Fourth Congress resolutions left things much the same way as they were before and set the party's sights on the upcoming Constituent Assembly elections. However, the USDWP now faced a grave and multifaceted social crisis and a struggle for state power in Ukraine, neither of which could be tackled by parliamentary means alone.

4.2 *The Russian Social Democrats*

There were no sharp political differences between Bolsheviks and Mensheviks in Ukraine except on the question of peace until the summer months of 1917. Both factions of the RSDWP were loyal to the Provisional Government. They stayed together in the same branches in Mykolaiv until July, Poltava until

---

40   *Robitnycha hazeta*, 6 October 1917, pp. 2–3.

August, Katerynoslav and Odesa up to October and in Kharkiv for the whole year.[41] Differences between them sharpened in the wake of the disastrous June offensive of the Russian army into Galicia, during Kornilov's attempted coup, and with the mounting popular disaffection over Kerensky's coalition cabinet. It was only then that the arguments Lenin had made upon his return to Russia in his April Theses took hold of a growing number of RSDWP members: that they should give no support to the Provisional Government, but look instead to the soviets/councils as the basis for an alternative government. The catastrophic situation on the front and the war weariness behind the lines gave increasing credence to the Bolsheviks' demand for an immediate peace and their conviction the Provisional Government could not secure it.

Bolshevik ranks throughout Ukraine grew from approximately 1,000 in February to between 7,000 and 8,000 in April. Their Kyiv city organisation had 1,500 members in six branches by May (Pechersk, Podil, Shuliavka, Demiivka, Zaliznodorozhnyi and Horodsky), with a growing base of support at the Arsenal munitions works, the aviation plant and the railway workshops. They were outnumbered in the Kyiv Council of Workers' Deputies by the Mensheviks and the Bund right up to the end of October when they secured a narrow majority. They began working among the soldiers but remained excluded from the Kyiv Council of Soldiers' Deputies by the Octobrists, Kadets and Right Russian SRs who represented units stationed in the Kyiv Military District. At the Sixth RSDWP (Bolsheviks) Congress in August, their branches in Ukraine reported a total membership of 22,303 with 15,818 of them living in the Donbas and Kryvyi Rih. Thereafter, the estimates of their numbers vary, ranging from 45,000 to 60,000 in October 1917. Half of them were based in the industrial region of the south east, with the other half evenly divided between the agricultural provinces and the army.[42] There were several attempts by the Kyiv organisation to create a co-ordinating body for Bolshevik branches across the Ukrainian provinces, but these attempts met with little success until the very end of 1917. Not having a Ukrainian territorial organisation meant not having a strategy towards the Ukrainian social formation, the national question or the Tsentral'na Rada.

The Bolsheviks have been researched far more than the Mensheviks or, indeed, any other party. The late Soviet era historians Yurii Hamretsky and

---

41 Sukhyno-Khomenko, 'Z pryvodu osoblyvostei', pp. 102–10.
42 Yevgeniia Bosh, *God bor'by, Bor'ba za vlast' na Ukraine s aprelia 1917g. do nemektskoi okupatsi* (Moscow: Gosizdat, 1925), pp. 11–15; Volin, 'Pershyi Ziizd', p. 23; Suprunenko, *Istoriia Ukrains'koi RSR*, Vol. 5, pp. 44, 137; Skrypnyk, 'Nacherk istorii proletars'koi revoliutsii', pp. 100–5; Skliarenko, *Narysy Istorii Profspilkovoho Rukhu*, p. 17; Soldatenko, *Ukraina v revoliutsiinu dobu*, Vol. 1, pp. 64, 228, 723.

Yevhen Skliarenko dealt briefly with the Mensheviks in Ukraine. In 1987 Vladimir Brovkin published a study of the Mensheviks that offered some information about their membership here.[43] Hamretsky found that the Mensheviks peaked in their numerical growth by September, while the Bolsheviks continued to grow until at least October or November. Throughout the former Empire, there were about 45,000 Mensheviks in May, expanding to 200,000 by September, but dropping back to 140,000 in October. The Bolsheviks, on the other hand, continued to recruit new members and grew to 350,000 by October.[44] Such a pattern of growth, Hamretsky suggested, reflected a loss of popular confidence in the Mensheviks as they failed to resuscitate the Provisional Government, and the ascent of the Bolshevik faction in the workers' councils between August and October where they were agitating for the Government's complete overthrow.

Hamretsky's estimate of Bolshevik and Menshevik forces in nine Ukrainian towns and cities in October (Katerynoslav, Kharkiv, Luhansk, Enakiievo, Druzhivka, Poltava, Zhytomyr, Yelyzavethrad and Yuzivka) placed them on a par with about twelve thousand members each.[45] But this was just a snapshot and it gave no indication of the total membership of the Mensheviks in Ukraine or the pattern of their growth and decline. Valerii Soldatenko, however, notes that from the beginning of November the Bolsheviks agitated for the re-election of those councils which had refused to support the October seizure of power or recognise the Council of People's Commissars or to seek to establish their own rule locally. Through such re-elections they gained control of councils in at least twenty one cities and towns, as well as in the four armies standing on Ukrainian fronts.[46] Thus the Bolsheviks in Ukraine continued to grow stronger after October both in terms of membership and the exercise of power locally, especially in the south east.

On the other hand, Brovkin found that the Mensheviks did not decline, but rather they grew in number overall between August and December from

---

43 Brovkin, *The Mensheviks After October*.
44 Hamretsky, 'Kryza dribnoburzhuaznykh partii', pp. 74–5.
45 Ibid, pp. 80–1. See also Maiorov, *Z Istorii Revoliutsiinoi Borot'by*, p. 29; Kazymyrchuk, 'Revoliutsionnoe dvizhenie v Horlovo-Shcherbinovs'kom raoine Donbassa', *Litopys Revoliutsii*, 3 (1923), p. 42.
46 Soldatenko, *Ukraina v revoliutsiinu dobu*, Vol. 1, pp. 947–9. These were Kharkiv, Kateryn-oslav (city and province), Yuzivka, Lozova-Pavlivsk, Kadiivsk, Berdychiv, Vynnytsia, Luben', Zhytomyr, Kamianets-Podilsk, Korosten, Lutsk, Mohyliv-Podilsk, Proskuriv, Rivne, Starokostiantynivsk, Tulchynsk, Mykolaiv, Odesa, Kherson 'and many other councils of workers', soldiers' and peasants' deputies'.

139,000 to 246,000. They did not grow everywhere: in Ukraine they declined over these months from 46,000 to 33,000.[47]

We should also recall some other characteristic strengths of these RSDWP factions: the Mensheviks had the support of older, skilled workers, especially in the smaller industries and trades, whereas the Bolsheviks excelled in recruiting the younger generation of assembly line workers in the big factories, mines and steel making plants. The Mensheviks held the leadership of many trade unions, while the Bolsheviks put much of their efforts into the factory committees. Each faction had its own members elected as deputies from the trade unions and factory committees to the workers' councils. In times of mounting crisis and radicalisation workers tended to swing behind the Bolsheviks, but as crises subsided they would hand back leadership, or at least the balance of power, to the Mensheviks.

The Mensheviks held a clear position on the national question: they defended Russia's unity as a state and were prepared to concede only limited autonomy to its nations and national minorities. The Ukrainian Bolshevik Heorhii Lapchynsky described them as 'representatives of the urban petit bourgeoisie and the qualified elite of workers ... who always were determined russifiers and adherents to "a united and indivisible" Russia'.[48] There is considerable evidence to support Lapchynsky's claim. In April 1917 a conference of Mensheviks from the five northern provinces of Kyiv, Volyn, Podillia, Poltava and Chernihiv rejected a federal state system on the grounds that

> it would hinder the development of the workers' movement. To satisfy the demands of separate nationalities, a system of autonomy that simultaneously preserves Russia's unity as a state and economic entity is required. The motion opposes bourgeois nationalist demands that complicate the tasks of the revolution, blur the proletariat's class consciousness and threaten its unity.[49]

In May, another conference of Mensheviks active in Kyiv gubernia adopted a similar resolution that characterised federalism as contradictory to historical progress, the growth of productive forces and unity of the proletariat's class

---

47   Brovkin, *The Mensheviks After October*, p. 42.
48   H. Lapchynsky, 'Z pershykh dniv Vseukrains'koi Radians'koi Vlady', *Litopys Revoliutsii*, 5–6 (1927), p. 49. See also Hamretsky, 'Stavlennia Rad', p. 14; Matvii Yavorsky, *Istoriia Ukrainy v Styslomu Narysi* (Kharkiv: Derzhavne Vydavnytstvo Ukrainy, 1928), p. 325.
49   *Robitnycha hazeta*, 27 April 1917, p. 4.

struggle.[50] The Mensheviks of Katerynoslav campaigned alongside the Russian SRs against the introduction of the Ukrainian language into schools. They were outspoken opponents of the Ukrainian soldiers' movement and they led the opposition to the First Universal in the Petrograd Soviet and in the Kyiv Councils of Workers' and Soldiers' Deputies. They consistently blocked attempts to discuss the national question in the southern urban councils in 1917.[51] They supported national autonomy for Ukraine as long as it was first approved by the Provisional Government. They did not recognise Ukraine's right in principle to separate from Russia. Rather, only Russia as a centralised state had the right to accord any autonomy to its parts. They joined the Tsentral'na Rada in July to participate in the power devolved to the Rada by the Provisional Government and to forestall any alliance developing between the UPSR, USDWP and the Bolsheviks.

Like the Mensheviks, the Bolsheviks were unprepared for the political awakening of the Ukrainian masses. Volodymyr Zatonsky noted that in the Kyiv party organisation

> Unfortunately, practically no-one among us knew the language. Our organisation was almost entirely Russian. Other than myself, only two or three others could speak Ukrainian. For the 'soviets' [Zatonsky uses the Russian term *sovety*] and therefore for the parties of the urban proletariat, for the Bolsheviks as much as for the Mensheviks, Ukraine as such did not exist because it did not exist for the urban worker.[52]

Lapchynsky, who hailed from Kremenchuk, spoke on behalf of the veterans in the party:

> We Bolsheviks of the old generation who emerged from the underground in February ... were very little prepared subjectively to grasp the idea of all-Ukrainian unity, to understand that as a result of this great revolution Ukraine was being reborn as a big independent country – a proletarian country – alongside the other parts of old 'Russia'.[53]

---

50 Volin, *Mensheviki*, pp. 3–4.
51 Ibid, pp. 4, 8–9; Panas Fedenko, 'Isaak Mazepa v Zhytti i v Politytsi', *Nashe Slovo*, 3 (1973), p. 14; Hamretsky, Tymchenko and Shchus, *Rady Ukrainy*, p. 14; Hamretsky, 'Stavlennia Rad', p. 12.
52 Zdorov, *Ukrains'kyi Zhovten'*, p. 115.
53 Heorhii Lapchynsky, 'Z pershykh dniv Vseukrains'koi Radians'koi Vlady (spohady)', *Litopys Revoliutsii*, 5–6, nos. 26–27 (1927), pp. 46–66.

Many Bolsheviks had not considered the issue before 1917. Veteran Bolshevik, Mykola Skrypnyk, pointed out that different sections of the working class and the Bolshevik party were swayed by 'bourgeois, petit bourgeois and Great Power nationalist prejudices'.[54] So the party proved quite unprepared in 1917 when the national question became the focus of an actual mass movement.

> We had ready answers to questions of a general, all-Russian character, answers given to us by our joint congresses and our Central Committee. But we did not have clear, unambiguous answers to questions that applied only to Ukraine. Making agreements with Ukrainian social democrats was decided independently by each local party organisation; there was no common position. Issues concerning mutual relations between Ukraine and Russia were decided on the basis of the abstract formula of 'self-determination of nations', while we, the proletarian vanguard of Ukraine, could not give an answer to what the proletariat of Ukraine was actually demanding with regard to such mutual relations: did it want regional autonomy or federation or independence, or perhaps it didn't want any separate status for Ukraine at all? Perhaps it wanted direct ties of each local soviet with the all-Russian centre. There was no answer, no commitment on this question, nor could there be one because we were not united on an all-Ukrainian basis.[55]

However, rank and file Bolsheviks proved more willing than the Mensheviks to rethink old positions and to respond to the rising national awareness in the working class milieus. C.I. Hopner recalled in his memoirs:

> Not once did we acknowledge we were working in Ukraine. For us Katerynoslav was the biggest city in Southern Russia and that was all. Only later, in June and July when the Ukrainian Social Democrats and Socialist Revolutionaries began to make themselves heard did we feel the need to weigh this question. But even then and later still, closer to October, we were poorly oriented on this question and we made lots of mistakes.[56]

The Katerynoslav Bolshevik newspaper *Zvezda* declared its support on 2 July for the Tsentral'na Rada's demand for territorial autonomy.[57] Hryhorii Pet-

---

54 Cited by Popov, *Narys Istorii*, p. 118.
55 *Komunist*, 5 (1918), cited in Khrystiuk, *Ukrains'ka Revoliutsiia*, Vol. 2, pp. 154–5.
56 Cited by M. Volin, 'Pershyi Ziizd KP(b)U', *Litopys Revoliutsii*, May–June (1928), p. 11.
57 Holubnychy, 'Outline History of the Communist Party of Ukraine', in *Selected Works of Vsevolod Holubnychy*, p. 68.

rovsky addressed a meeting of the Katerynoslav Council of Workers' and Soldiers' Deputies in September to urge its members to support the demand for a federated republic. 'Only then will all people be drawn irresistibly to participate in the task of government. A federated republic will give freedom to all the democratic forces in Russia'.[58]

The USDWP and Bolshevik deputies then steered two key resolutions through the Katerynoslav Council during the October crisis to recognise the Rada at the centre and the Council in Katerynoslav as the legitimate governments.[59]

Similar things were happening in Kremenchuk where Bolshevik sympathies for the Rada grew in proportion to their mutual mistrust for the Provisional Government. One could often hear from Ukrainian workers there

> that they too were 'also Bolsheviks, only Ukrainian ones', who wanted the councils to take power in Ukraine and who regarded the Tsentral'na Rada as a 'soviet' institution because local councils of workers' and peasants' deputies were taking part in elections to it. All this convinced us that the only way to establish soviet power across Ukraine was to call an all-Ukrainian congress of the councils of workers', soldiers' and peasants' deputies and to elect an all-Ukrainian worker and peasant government there, to do the same as was done at the second congress of soviets in Petrograd on 23–25 October.[60]

By October the Bolsheviks in Kharkiv were split. One faction was blocking with the USDWP and UPSR in the Kharkiv Council and wanted the Rada re-elected along soviet lines. A second faction continued to look only to Petrograd, opposed the Rada's jurisdiction over the industrialised Ukrainian provinces and favoured instead an autonomous Donets-Kryvyi Rih Republic which would ally with Soviet Russia. Its capital would be Kharkiv, the main industrial, communications and administrative centre that linked the Donbas with Russia.[61]

---

58 Cited by Kuras, 'Borot'ba bil'shovykiv', p. 36.
59 Yu. Hamretsky, 'Rady Ukrainy v Periodi Nastupu Kontrrevoliutsii (lypen' – serpen' 1917)', *Ukrains'kyi Istorychnyi Zhurnal*, 3 (1970), p. 53; Ye. Kviring, 'Nekotori Popravki k Vospomynaniiam o Ekaterinoslavs'kom Oktiabr', *Litopys Revoliutsii*, 2 (March–April 1928), p. 137; Hamretsky, Tymchenko and Shchus, *Rady Ukrainy*, pp. 200–1.
60 Lapchynsky, 'Z pershykh dniv', p. 55.
61 Sukhyno-Khomenko, 'Z pryvodu osoblyvostei', p. 109; Yu. Hamretsky, 'Do pytannia pro taktyku Bilshovykiv shchodo Tsentralnoi Rady v lystopadi 1917 r.', *Ukrains'kyi Istorychnyi Zhurnal*, 3 (1965), p. 73.

The plan of this second Kharkiv faction was shared by many, if not most Bolsheviks in the Donbas, who considered their region an integral part of Russia and wanted nothing to do with the Rada. Yet there is evidence that even here the Bolsheviks were beginning to recognise and respond to the growth of national awareness among Ukrainian, Jewish, Polish and Latvian workers.[62] A majority of the population of these industrialised provinces was ethnically Ukrainian, even though the Russian language and culture were dominant in the towns. The rise of national awareness among peasants in the countryside and among the garrisoned soldiers inevitably seeped into the Ukrainian migrant communities in the mining and factory towns. The Bolsheviks created Ukrainian speaking sections of the party in the mining towns of Horlivka and Scherbynivtsi in November.[63] Another section was organised in Odesa in December with over one hundred soldiers, sailors and workers.[64]

It was in Kyiv, under the shadow of the Rada and the massive congresses of soldiers' and peasants' deputies, that the Bolsheviks felt most acutely their lack of a programme and strategy on the national question. It eluded them because they were not prepared to engage directly with the Rada and its supporters. In June they protested the Provisional Government's attempt to ban the Second All-Ukrainian Soldiers' Congress as an example of its 'imperialist policy' toward Ukraine. They upheld the principle of national self-determination, supported a wide measure of autonomy for Ukraine, but refused to take a position for or against the Rada itself. The party contented itself with an assertion that carried no apparent practical consequence for them at the time: that national oppression could be abolished only by a government of workers and peasants.[65]

On 2 July, the Kyiv Bolsheviks responded positively to the Tsentral'na Rada's invitation to send their delegates to its expanding assembly. They elected Leonid Piatakov, Mykhailo Maiorov and Isaak Kreisberg.[66] However, the decision provoked a dispute between the majority that insisted their delegates' task in the Rada was information gathering and no more, and the minority who believed the Bolsheviks' mere presence in the Rada would confuse the workers as to its true class character, which it regarded as petit bourgeois. The delegates

---

62   *Borot'ba za Oktiabr na Artemovshchine*, p. 93.
63   Volin, 'Pershyi Ziizd KP(b)U', p. 16.
64   Rezinkin, 'Pro diial'nist hrupy bil'shovykiv-ukraintsiv v m. Odesi', *Litopys Revoliutsii*, 3 (May–June 1931), p. 130.
65   I. Yu Kulyk, 'Kievskaia organizatsiia ot fevralia do oktiabria 1917 goda', *Litopys Revoliutsii*, 1 (1924), pp. 189–99.
66   Popov, *Narys Istorii*, p. 38.

were left with no guidance as to the positions they should advocate in the Rada as their own July conference adopted no resolutions on the national question or the Rada. And even the majority's instruction to their delegates to gather information about the Rada was not implemented because they appeared at meetings of the *mala rada* only to read out their party's proclamations.[67]

The Kyiv organisation tried several times, but with limited success, to create a co-ordinating centre for party branches across the Southwestern region (the provinces of Kyiv, Volyn, Podillia, Chernihiv and Poltava). Bolsheviks in the Donets-Kryvyi Rih region organised a separate co-ordinating centre for their branches in Kharkiv, Katerynoslav and part of Kherson gubernia. The party's branches in the 'free cities' of Odesa, where the Bolsheviks stayed with the Mensheviks in the same organisation until December, Mykolaiv and Katerynoslav operated quite autonomously from either of the two regions.[68]

The Bolsheviks' two regional co-ordinating centres mirrored two of the three regional organisations of the workers' and soldiers' councils. The third was *Rumcherod*, the Central Executive Committee of the Councils of the Romanian Front, Black Sea Fleet and Odesa province. Thus, until October the Bolsheviks in Ukraine were building regional structures for their own co-ordination on the same pattern as the co-ordinating structures of the councillist movement. This made sense because they were concerned primarily with establishing the rule of local councils, consolidating them regionally and then linking them to a central authority in Petrograd. The Rada seizing power disrupted the logic of this political geography and forced them to consider Ukraine as a coherent territory. When the Rada refused to recognise the new Soviet government in Petrograd, it engendered a deep split in the Southwestern regional party organisations between those Bolsheviks who wanted to recognise the Rada as the national government but transform it through peaceful political struggle into a government representing all the councils in Ukraine and those who wanted to overthrow the Rada.

The Bolsheviks' leaders in Donets-Kryvyi Rih region were more united in their estimation of the Rada than their Kyiv comrades. They wanted nothing at all to do with it as they did not consider it had any claim to their region. In many towns the workers' councils had already taken over as their local governments and declared their loyalty to the Council of People's Commissars in Petrograd. Many of them continued to reject the idea that such a thing as Ukraine existed or could come into being. Zatonsky would write in early 1918 that 'many

---

67 I. Yu Kulyk, 'Kievskaia organizatsiia'; Bosh, *God bor'by*, pp. 41–2.
68 Bosh, *God bor'by*, pp. 25–6.

comrades to this day are convinced in the depths of their souls that [historian Mykhailo] Hrushevsky invented Ukraine'.

> And so their search begins for a way out. So, well, go on, they will say, self-determine yourselves all the way to separation. But why the hell must you do it here, in our own party? Let there be a Ukraine, even an independent one if you really can't live without it, wherever, in Australia or, if it must come to it, even in semi-savage Volyn or Podillia. But why must it be in Katerynoslav or over there in Kherson, not to mention Kharkiv?[69]

4.3 The Jewish Social Democrats

The Bund in February 1917 had ten functioning branches in Ukraine – in Kyiv, Odesa, Katerynoslav, Zhytomyr, Berdychiv, Kremenchuk, Bakhmut, Kharkiv, Luhansk and Mariupol. By November, the party had built 75 branches in the nine provinces with a membership of over 16,000, about half of the total Bund membership on the territory of the former Empire. It established a General Ukrainian Committee in Kyiv and regional offices in Odesa and Katerynoslav. It held All-Ukrainian Congresses during the Revolution and Civil War.[70]

The Bund was now only one among several Jewish socialist parties operating in the Russian state. The Jewish Social Democratic Workers Party Poale Zion (Workers of Zion), with a growing proletarian base, was 'particularly effective' in Ukraine.[71] Poale Zion sympathised with the Bolsheviks after the July crises in Petrograd and Kyiv, worked locally with the USDWP and discussed unification with the USDWP's leadership.[72] The Bund, however, retained a distinct and pre-eminent role in the workers' movement as the oldest social democratic party in Russia, one which had given many talented leaders and militants to the RSDWP. So the Bund assumed the role of unifier and mediator between the social democratic parties of different nationalities. It was most sensitive to emergent crises in social and national relations that could and often did turn into pogroms against Jews. Rafes noted with respect to its mediation in June 1917 between the Rada, the Russian parties and the Provisional Government

---

69 *Komunist*, 3–4 (1918); cited in Khrystiuk, *Ukrains'ka Revoliutsiia*, Vol. 2, p. 154.

70 Rafes, *Dva goda*, p. 13; Zvi Gitelman, *Jewish Nationality and Soviet Politics: The Jewish Sections of the CPSU, 1917–1930* (Princeton: Princeton University Press, 1972), pp. 69, 72, 157; Jurij Borys, 'Political Parties in the Ukraine', in *The Ukraine 1917–21: A Study in Revolution*, edited by Taras Hunczak (Cambridge, MA: Harvard Ukrainian Research Institute, 1977), p. 154.

71 Gitelman, *Jewish Nationality*, p. 33.

72 Rafes, *Dva goda*, p. 11.

that 'the Bund at every moment felt responsible for the *entire* revolutionary coalition and strived at every particular moment to do its utmost to ease the coalition's common work'.[73]

Throughout 1917 the Bund remained allied with the Mensheviks. There were both cultural and ideological affinities between them. About half the membership of the Menshevik faction of the RSDWP was Jewish, and both parties took the position that Russia was unprepared for socialism and still awaited its bourgeois democratic revolution. Their common strategy to resolve the question of power was through general elections based on universal suffrage to a constituent assembly. However, as Raphael Abramovich, a prominent Bundist wrote, the party 'always tried to be the left wing of the Mensheviks ... the revolutionary conscience of Menshevism'.[74] This aspiration applied also to the Bund's stand on the national question in Ukraine. Divergence between the Bund and the Mensheviks over Ukrainian autonomy widened even as both parties stood opposed to the Bolshevik government in Petrograd.

The great majority of Jews saw their emancipation being secured through the general gains of the revolution, beginning with the Provisional Government's abolition in March of all restrictions on civil rights that were based on religious or national grounds. This gave impetus to their fuller participation in civic and political life and raised hopes they may have a future as a community in Russia. However, the Zionist movement offered Jews an alternative path to their emancipation: emigration from Russia to build an entirely new state of their own. This alternative became all the more compelling the longer the War dragged on, the deeper grew the domestic crisis, the greater the social tensions and the prospect of renewed pogroms. However, the Revolution broke out and into this novel situation stepped the Rada. The Jewish community was positively impressed by the Rada's advocacy of Ukraine's territorial autonomy and national personal autonomy for its minorities while giving its commitment to the continued unity of the Russian state. There began a process of convergence (in Ukrainian *zblyzhennia*) of interests and efforts between the Jewish and Ukrainian democracies to make the Rada a functioning and authoritative regional government.[75] Having opposed the First Universal in April, the Bund took part in negotiating the Second Universal and published it in Yiddish in

---

73 Rafes, *Dva goda*, p. 35.
74 Cited by Gitelman, *Jewish Nationality*, p. 87.
75 Henry Abramson, *Molytva za vladu. Ukraintsi ta yevrei v revoliutsiinu dobu (1917–1920)*, translation from the English by Anton Kotenko and Oleksandr Nadtoka of *A Prayer for the Government: Ukrainians and Jews in Revolutionary Times (1917–1920)* (Kyiv: Dukh i Litera, 2017), pp. 85–6.

July when it entered the Rada, and then voted for the Third Universal at the beginning of November when the Rada took power in Kyiv.

Three Jewish workers' parties, the Bund, Poale Zion and the United Socialist Workers Party Fareinigte, played an active role building the Rada after they entered it in July together with the Zionists and the Jewish People's Party Folkspartei. Generally speaking, Jews were the most interested of all the minorities in Ukraine to secure their national autonomy through the Tsentral'na Rada as an autonomous government. The Russian and Polish minorities were not so interested because their formal recognition as national minorities downgraded their once privileged status. The slogans of the revolution in Ukraine were directed against the landowning and bourgeois classes that these two minorities dominated. While spokesmen for the Russian minority tried to hold back the Ukrainian movement, Polish leaders took a 'friendly neutral attitude'. They were more concerned about Poland's future in the region, its struggle for independence. They did not want to jeopardise it by spoiling relations with the largest nation separating Poland geographically from Russia, a nation with whom they shared ethnically mixed and potentially contestable borders in Kholm and Podillia.[76]

Solomon Goldelman, a Poale Zion leader, noted that 'the great extent of national autonomy granted the Jewish minority in Ukraine stands alone in the entire history of the Jewish people in diaspora'.[77] Their gains in other parts of the Empire in 1917 could not even be compared to those they made in Ukraine. Moshe Rafes and Oleksandr Zolotariov of the Bund both served as General Controller in the General Secretariat. The Russian, Polish and Jewish parties occupied fifty out of 199 seats, one quarter, in the *mala rada*. In the Rada plenary assembly they had 110 of its 822 seats, or 13 percent of the total. In fact, there were more plenary members from the minorities than those formally allocated to their parties because Russians, Jews and, to a lesser extent, Poles also served as representatives from other bodies seated there, such as workers' and soldiers' councils, trade unions and city governments.

On 16 July the Rada submitted a statute to the Provisional Government that defined the structures and lines of responsibility for implementing autonomy for national minorities. Moshe Zilberfarb of the Fareinigte party became Deputy Secretary of Jewish affairs in the Secretariat of International Affairs. After the Third Universal was adopted in November Zilberfarb's position was upgraded to Secretary, with full voting rights in the General Secretariat. After

---

76   Ibid, pp. 29–30; Vynnychenko, *Vidrodzhennia Natsii*, Vol. 1, p. 297; Dmytro Doroshenko, *Istoriia Ukrainy*, Vol. 1, pp. 272–4.
77   Goldelman, *Jewish National Autonomy*, p. 14.

the adoption of the Fourth Universal, the declaration of Ukraine's independence in January 1918, he served briefly in the post as Minister (as all Secretaries were renamed when the General Secretariat became the Council of People's Ministers). Over this period of time, responsibility for implementing the autonomy policy for the Jewish population was divided between three departments, each headed by a Deputy Secretary: education, headed by Avraam Strashin of the Bund, community self government by Avraam Revutsky of Poale Zion, and general affairs by Isaak Khurgin of Fareignigte. They were nominated by their political parties and approved by a committee of the Rada. The Secretary and his Deputies had a voice in discussions about all policy areas of the General Secretariat. They all had a vote as well as a veto in matters concerning their own minorities policy remit.[78]

The Secretariat of Jewish Affairs had a staff of 125 people and a budget of 604,000 *karbovantsi*, the legal tender of the Ukrainian People's Republic. That was approximately 10 percent of the Rada's overall budget. The Secretariat concerned itself during its relatively short existence with developing the legal basis and institutions of Jewish autonomy and responding to requests for financial support to local governments, for postal, telegraph and other services in Yiddish and providing compensation for losses and injuries caused by military operations on the front and in the rear.[79]

The Secretariat drafted the law on national personal autonomy that was put to the Rada plenary for approval in January 1918, just before the Fourth Universal was adopted (see below). The law recognised the right of any nationality that made a declaration on behalf of at least ten thousand of its members, regardless of their place of residence in Ukraine, to establish a National Union (*Natsional'nyi Soiuz*) on which to build its autonomous community life. There were also significant numbers of Belarusians, Czechs, Bulgarians, Germans, Crimean Tatars, Greeks and Romanians living in the nine Ukrainian provinces. Each Union would have the status of a state organisation financed by public funds, with the right to determine its community's priorities, to tax its own members and to distribute funds to them for their community needs.[80]

The fact that the Jewish socialist parties and not the Zionist or religious parties took the initiative in the Rada to implement its policy of national autonomy for minorities needs some explanation. The outbreak of the revolu-

---

78 Abramson, *Molytva za vladu*, pp. 100–9. A Secretariat for Polish Affairs, headed by Miecheslav Mitskevych, functioned only for a couple of months. The Secretariat for Russian Affairs, headed by Dymtro Odynets, barely got off the ground.
79 Abramson, *Molytva za vladu*, pp. 124–7.
80 Doroshenko, *Istoriia Ukrainy*, Vol. 1, p. 274.

tion called into question the traditional lines of authority within the Jewish community and its relationship to the state. At issue was the separation of religious and secular authority and the elevation in importance of the latter in people's daily lives. This proved a complex undertaking in a community that had lived for centuries in enforced segregation from the rest of society and that dealt with all levels of state authority through its religious and charismatic leaders. Now the question was posed as to the appropriate division of authority and responsibility between the government, the communal institution of self government elected by the religious congregation called *kehilla*, and the newly proposed National Union as the secular body determining the minority's priorities and putting them before the state. Would this new body supplant the traditional role of religious leaders in the community and in its relations with the state? Would Jews now exercise their democratic rights as individual citizens without or with less recourse to community institutions? For example, was one to turn to the Ministry of Jewish Affairs to resolve a complaint regarding provision of postal and telegraphic services in Yiddish or simply to the Ministry of postal and telegraphic services? Should education be provided to children by a state ministry or by the religious school, or by both? While all the political parties agreed that the *kehilla* should remain a cornerstone of local self government, they disagreed over the extent of the competence it should retain. The Bund, for example, wanted to limit it and to transfer control over the institution itself to the community as a whole instead of it remaining under the leadership of religious elders. Such a change would also mean that membership in the *kehilla* should be open to anyone who considered themselves a Jew, rather than only those who professed Judaism. The revolution underway was undermining old mentalities, practices and institutions.[81]

There was also a struggle between the socialist and Zionist parties over which language, Yiddish or Hebrew, should be used. Yiddish was spoken by the vast majority of Jews in the Russian Empire. The Zionist movement, however, wanted to revive Hebrew. The socialists won a victory here when Yiddish was adopted by the Rada as one of its four official languages alongside Ukrainian, Russian and Polish. The Second and Third Universals were published in all four languages. They appeared on *karbovantsi* banknotes. Yiddish appeared on street signs in Kyiv and in government communications. It was intended to become the language of instruction of the first university planned by the Jewish socialist parties. However, four official languages proved unwieldy and expensive for the Rada to implement and practically all laws were subsequently

---

81 Abramson, *Molytva za vladu*, p. 128.

published only in Ukrainian. Nevertheless, the attempt to introduce four official languages signalled the Rada's intent to implement the rights of national minorities to a degree that was historically unprecedented for Ukraine and indeed for the Russian state.

Finally, there was the question of representation of Jews in the Rada government. The legislation being drawn up called for the election of a National Council (*Natsional'na rada*) by the members of their National Union (*Natsional'nyi Soiuz*). Until these institutions were in place, representatives to the *mala rada* and the General Secretariat were selected directly by the political parties. A serious conflict arose over which parties should be permitted to make the selection, in what proportion and which parties should be allowed to stand for election to the National Council. There was also a dispute over the democratic accountability of the Secretary of Jewish Affairs in the Rada. Should the Secretary submit reports of his work to the National Council, which could then approve or reject them, the socialists' position, or should the Council merely advise the Secretary on policy, while he remained independent of the community in determining his policy, the Zionists' position. In the turbulent atmosphere of 1917 who actually belonged to 'the revolutionary democracy' was being disputed: the socialists, to be sure; the Zionists were simply too strong to be ignored or refused a place in the Rada and the National Council; but the religious parties were considered ineligible.

The first Jewish National Council that met on 1 October 1917 was composed of representatives from five parties: the Bund, Poale Zion, Fareinigte, Folkspartei and the Zionists. The Zionists later withdrew, leaving only an observer behind, so the socialist parties became even more dominant. They tried to build the authority and competence of the Secretariat of Jewish Affairs, to make it answerable to the Jewish National Council. The Zionists, on the other hand, wanted to see it reduced in status and authority to a department. They looked upon their community as a diaspora whose members would find national self government ultimately in a state of Israel. For them, this long-term objective stood in the way of Jews' whole-hearted participation in the life of any other state.[82]

Thus, there were several reasons why the Bund and the other socialist parties took the initiative in the Rada. First, the Rada gave them a bigger voice and better representation than they had in Jewish community institutions. Second, it promoted the further secularisation of Jewish society while at the same time respecting its distinct national identity and community. Thirdly, it brought this

---

82 Abramson, *Molytva za vladu*, pp. 106–7, 129.

community into a closer and more co-operative relationship with members of society from whom they had been historically estranged. In short, participation in the Rada was part of their common task of securing a permanent home for Jews in Ukraine.

However, the Bund could not envisage the successful pursuit of Jewish national emancipation occurring solely in the Ukrainian republic, that is in isolation from Jews living in other parts of the Empire. It was an imperative for the Bund that this geographically dispersed community somehow stay united across the extant Russian state. But the War and the Revolution were splitting Russia's peripheries away from the imperial heartland, precisely those peripheries of Ukraine, Poland, Lithuania and Moldova where the overwhelming majority of them lived. If Jews sought national autonomy within the Ukrainian People's Republic, they were obliged to reciprocate and recognise Ukraine's right to territorial autonomy. That was the limit for the Bund: as long as Ukrainians were satisfied with territorial autonomy in a federated Russian state, then the integrity of the wider Jewish community would not be jeopardised. But if Ukraine's territorial autonomy was unrealisable for any reason and the Ukrainian national movement took to separating from Russia, the Bund had to consider the consequences for their community. It was concerned about the possible rise of antisemitism as social conflicts grew, particularly among the urban middle classes and the peasantry. This tension between support for Ukrainian national demands and ensuring such demands did not lead to Ukraine separating from Russia or, even worse, contributing to the outbreak of pogroms, profoundly influenced the evolution of Ukrainian-Jewish relations in 1917 and the subsequent civil war.[83]

5   Reconciliation and the Form of State Power

The downfall of the Provisional Government left two contenders standing: the Tsentral'na Rada, whose power rested on the peasantry, and the urban councils of the working class. There was some complementarity between them as they represented two different classes and different nationalities – Ukrainians on the one hand and Russians and Jews on the other. As members of the revolutionary democracy their political parties shared a good deal in the way of solutions to the burning questions of the day, while still disagreeing among themselves over the class composition and institutional form of the state power

---

83   Goldelman, *Jewish National Autonomy in Ukraine*, pp. 34–5.

needed to resolve them. From this broad complementarity and their search for solutions to the same issues the idea was born that they should reconcile their respective institutions of power. The initiative for reconciliation came from the urban councils and the left-wing factions of the UPSR and USDWP in the Rada.

The Kyivan Bolshevik leader Yevgeniia Bosh recalled that in early November

> A range of workers' and soldiers' organisations, not having representatives in the Tsentral'na Rada, began to elect their delegates and adopt resolutions fully supporting it. Even those working class masses that were fighting actively for Soviet power at that moment hesitated and inclined towards supporting the Tsentral'na Rada, considering it to be the Ukrainian national government.[84]

Mykola Skrypnyk agreed:

> the idea of an All-Ukrainian Congress of Councils and the establishment of a central government based on the councils in Ukraine was received with great enthusiasm by all the workers and broad layers of soldiers.[85]

Transforming the Rada into a central council of this kind was not a new idea. Yulian Bochkovsky, chairman of the Poltava Council of Workers' and Peasants' Deputies, had put it to the Rada in June. It appeared in one of the resolutions of First All-Ukrainian Workers' Congress in July and again at the Third Soldiers' Congress in October. The left wing of the USDWP demanded it at the party's Fourth Congress at the beginning of October. However, the workers' councils began to consider it seriously only after the fall of the Provisional Government when the Rada declared the Ukrainian People's Republic. Now these councils extended their recognition to the Rada, but on condition it recognised them as local governments and agreed to its own re-election by them.

The Kharkiv Council of Workers' and Soldiers' Deputies was the first of the big city councils to recognise the Rada and to demand its reorganisation into a national government elected by local workers', soldiers' and peasants' councils. On 12 September, 81 of its deputies voted in favour of such a resolution, with two opposed and 56 abstentions. The resolution also defended the territorial

---

[84] Yevgeniia Bosh, *Natsionalnoe Pravitel'stvo* (n.p.: n.p., August 1918), p. 110. See also Skrovstiansky, *Revoliutsiia na Ukraine*, p. 74; and Sukhyno-Khomenko, 'Z pryvodu osoblyvostei', p. 111.

[85] M. Skrypnyk, 'Nacherk istorii proletars'koi revoliutsii na Ukraini', *Chervonyi Shliakh*, 2 (May 1923), p. 79.

integrity of Ukraine and protested its effective partition by the Government's Temporary Instruction. The USDWP, UPSR and a majority of Russian SRs in the Council supported the motion, while the Bolsheviks, Mensheviks and a minority of SRs abstained. Other councils in Kharkiv province adopted similar resolutions in the following week.[86]

On 26 October a joint meeting of the executive committee of the Kharkiv city Council, the provincial Council of Soldiers' Deputies and the regional executive committee of workers' councils in the Donets and Kryvyi Rih region recognised the Tsentral'na Rada as Ukraine's government and elected a Military Revolutionary Committee to defend it against forces still loyal to the Provisional Government.[87] The Kharkiv Council declared its support for the Third Universal on 10 November and repeated that 'local and central power must be assumed by a congress of workers', soldiers' and peasants' deputies in the Ukrainian Republic'.[88]

USDWP deputies in the Kharkiv Council supported the Third Universal but opposed the Rada's re-election. As a result of defending this position, the party fared poorly in elections to the Council which were held on 8–12 November, losing all four of its seats on the executive committee.[89] This sequence of resolutions showed that the Council's deputies were not voting along party lines, but were seeking a novel form of state that allowed the peasantry and working class to share political power and to reconcile their particular class and national interests. This process of peasant-worker reconciliation was momentarily facilitated by the fact that the peasant-soldiers garrisoned in Kharkiv were visibly represented by their own council, and it had united with the workers' council for joint deliberation and decision-making.

The Katerynoslav Council of Workers' and Soldiers' Deputies debated the question of state power throughout October and November. At its 12 October plenary session, the USDWP fraction introduced a motion practically identical to the one adopted in Kharkiv a month earlier. It delegated responsibility to the Rada to organise the state power in close co-operation with all institutions of the revolutionary democracy and to include Katerynoslav province in its jurisdiction. The motion was adopted. A Bolshevik sponsored counter motion to resolve the Rada's territorial claims by plebiscite was defeated.[90]

---

86 Hamretsky, Tymchenko and Shchus, *Rady Ukrainy*, p. 162.
87 Ibid, p. 186.
88 Ibid, p. 244; Sukhyno-Khomenko, 'Z pryvodu osoblyvostei', p. 109.
89 Hamretsky, Tymchenko and Shchus, *Rady Ukrainy*, p. 244.
90 *Robitnycha hazeta*, 4 November 1917, p. 3; Hamretsky, Tymchenko and Shchus, *Rady Ukrainy*, p. 103.

A meeting of the Katerynoslav Council, in which the executive committees of local trade unions, factory committees and socialist parties also participated, was called immediately after the October seizures of power. On this occasion, USDWP members and Bolsheviks joined forces and pushed through a resolution supporting the Petrograd uprising, recognising the Rada as the government in Ukraine, and calling on the Katerynoslav Council to take power in the city. The resolution also demanded the Rada's reorganisation 'along the same lines as the councils are based'. When the Third Universal was released, the Katerynoslav Council re-affirmed its recognition and called again for the Rada's reorganisation.[91]

The Kremenchuk Council, elected by 25,000 workers and 15,000 soldiers and in which the Bolsheviks had an absolute majority, recognised the Tsentral'na Rada on 20 November on the condition it be reorganised. Here too, there was an alliance between the Bolsheviks, USDWP and UPSR. The Ukrainian parties supported the assumption of power by the councils at the local level and in a national government. The Bolsheviks reciprocated by recognising Kyiv as the national centre. Similar positions to those developed in Kharkiv, Kyiv, Katerynoslav and Kremenchuk were adopted by many councils in Volyn, Chernihiv and Poltava provinces in which the Bolsheviks had majorities.[92]

On 3 November the Kherson Council of Workers' and Soldiers' Deputies was asked to choose between three resolutions. The one introduced by the USDWP and UPSR called for recognition of the Tsentral'na Rada in Ukraine and the formation of a united socialist government in Petrograd. It received 139 votes. The resolution put forward by the Mensheviks and Russian SRs calling only for a united socialist government in Russia and saying nothing about Ukraine drew 49 votes. The Bolshevik resolution called for local power to the councils and recognition of the Rada on condition it be reorganised by a congress of these councils. It gained 166 votes and was carried.[93]

On the following day, 4 November, a meeting of the Odesa Councils of Workers' and Soldiers' Deputies, attended also by the Kherson provincial Military Revolutionary Committee and *Rumcherod* (Executive Committee of Soldiers' Soviets of the Romanian Front, Black Sea Fleet and Odesa Military Dis-

---

91   Kviring, 'Nekotori Popravki', p. 137; Fedenko, 'Isaak Mazepa', p. 16; Sukhyno-Khomenko, 'Z pryvodu osoblyvostei', p. 109; Hamretsky, Tymchenko and Shchus, *Rady Ukrainy*, p. 200; *Robitnycha hazeta*, 3 November 1917, p. 4; 5 November 1917, p. 3.
92   Lapchynsky, 'Zarodzhennia radians'koi vlady', p. 122; Lapchynsky, 'Z pershykh dniv', p. 56; Steven Guthier, 'The Popular Base of Ukrainian Nationalism in 1917', *Slavic Review* (March 1971), p. 45; Hamretsky, Tymchenko and Shchus, *Rady Ukrainy*, pp. 250–5.
93   Hamretsky, 'Do pytannia pro taktyku Bil'shovykiv', pp. 69–70.

trict), adopted a resolution greeting the Third Universal and recognising the Rada's jurisdiction over the territories it claimed. The resolution called for a united socialist government in Petrograd with representation from autonomous national republics and protection of minority rights on the basis of their national-cultural autonomy.[94] A similar resolution was adopted by a Kherson provincial congress of workers', soldiers' and peasants' deputies early in December.[95]

USDWP members in Konotop took a lesson from meetings they organised in November at the city's railway workshops. On 4 November, 2,000 railway workers voted almost unanimously to recognise the Tsentral'na Rada as the government of Ukraine.[96] The Konotop Council of Workers' Deputies recognised the Rada on 12 November on the condition it was re-elected by a representative congress of councils. The USDWP challenged this condition and called a second meeting which was attended by over 2,500 workers. This meeting re-affirmed their support for the Rada, but when it rejected the 12 November condition by voting to oppose the Rada's re-election, 1,000 workers in attendance quit the meeting.[97] It was a clear sign to the USDWP that its own base in the working class was shifting towards the position of convening an All-Ukrainian Congress of Councils.

The Mykolaiv Council of Workers' and Soldiers' Deputies narrowly passed a resolution, 65 to 60, 'to enter into constructive relations with the Ukrainian Rada on all issues with a general bearing on the state of the country'. Support for the resolution came from the USDWP, UPSR, the Mensheviks and Russian SRs.[98] The Luhansk regional committee of workers' and soldiers' councils representing 11 districts in and around the city resolved to support the Tsentral'na Rada on 20 November on condition it upheld the decisions of the Second All-Russian Congress of Soviets and defended the interests of the lower classes.[99]

A joint meeting of the Kyiv Councils of Workers' and Soldiers' Deputies with the participation of the executives of factory committees and trade unions in the city was called on 4 November. The meeting voted on a set of resolutions introduced by the Bolsheviks. First, it recognised and supported the Council of People's Commissars in Petrograd by a vote of 433 against 119 in favour of

---

94   *Robitnycha hazeta*, 25 November 1917, pp. 3–4.
95   *Robitnycha hazeta*, 15 December 1917, p. 2.
96   *Robitnycha hazeta*, 10 November 1917, p. 4.
97   *Robitnycha hazeta*, 26 November 1917, pp. 3–4.
98   Hamretsky, 'Do pytannia pro taktyku Bilshovykiv', p. 71.
99   Hamretsky, Tymchenko and Shchus, *Rady Ukrainy*, p. 247.

a united socialist government. On the question of local power 438 favoured it passing into the hands of their own councils. Then, 424 deputies supported re-organising the Rada against 271 who wanted to leave it as it was. But when it came to the question concerning what kind of institution the Rada should become, a smaller majority of 389 deputies supported its re-election as an All-Ukrainian Council of Workers' Soldiers and Peasants' Deputies.[100]

Therefore, while a combined majority in the Kyiv workers' and soldiers' councils voted in favour of soviet government for Russia, Ukraine and locally, there was some uncertainty and disagreement over how the Rada should be re-organised and on whose initiative. The Bolsheviks had gathered a majority here, but they remained in a minority in the councils' joint executive committee, which resisted its own re-election. Here the Mensheviks, Bund and Right Russian SRs, together 53, still prevailed over the Bolsheviks' 23 and USDWP's four. On 15 November a majority of this executive committee rejected the 4 November resolutions of their own councils.[101]

However, the executive committee of the Councils of the Southwestern region, which included Kyiv, had already turned to the Rada on 10 November and proposed that they jointly call a congress to resolve the question of state power in Ukraine. The Rada's General Secretariat rejected the proposal. Mykola Porsh, Labour Secretary, said in a meeting with Yosef Stalin and Serhii Bakynsky of the executive committee of Councils of the Southwestern region that such a congress was unnecessary. Undeterred, on 24 November the Southwestern region executive committee resolved to convene an all-Ukrainian congress on 3 December.[102]

It is clear from these resolutions that by mid-November workers' and soldiers' councils in at least seven of the ten most populous cities of Ukraine supported the establishment of a Ukrainian national government. One cannot generalise from these cases and from evidence of similar positions being taken by councils across the northern gubernia to say that an absolute majority of the urban councils in Ukraine favoured this particular solution to the crisis of power. One should bear in mind, however, that the smaller the population of a town, the greater tended to be the proportion of Ukrainians living in it. It is

---

100   Bosh, *God bor'by*, pp. 58–9. The accounts of this meeting vary. See also *Robitnycha hazeta*, 7 November 1917, p. 1; S. Sh. 'Iz istorii Sovlasti na Ukraine', *Litopys Revoliutsii*, 4 (1924), p. 167; Bosh, *Natsional'noe Pravitel'stvo*, p. 19; Hamretsky, Tymchenko and Shchus, *Rady Ukrainy*, p. 242; Zdorov, *Ukrains'kyi Zhovten'*, p. 138.
101   Bosh, *God bor'by*, p. 59.
102   Zdorov, *Ukrains'kyi Zhovten'*, p. 138.

quite likely, therefore, that support for the Tsentral'na Rada in the councils of medium sized and small towns was even stronger than in the cities.[103]

The available evidence calls into question the argument advanced by Yurii Hamretsky that 'all of the conciliatory [Menshevik dominated] councils in November banded together around a common platform of a united socialist government for the whole country and, in Ukraine, recognition of the bourgeois nationalist Tsentral'na Rada as the supreme governing organ'.[104] Hamretsky musters examples to support his contention, but other sources show that Bolsheviks in many councils also backed the Rada. And their call for an All-Ukrainian Congress of Councils to re-elect it was consistent with the soviet platform of direct and recallable representation of the lower classes by their elected deputies in local and central government.[105]

For many urban councils, the real bone of contention in November was not whether there should be a Ukrainian People's Republic, but what should be the class composition of its government. Bolsheviks wanted a government based on the councils; the Mensheviks and the Bund wanted it chosen through elections to a Constituent Assembly on the basis of universal suffrage. The UPSR and USDWP, while defending the Rada as the seat of the UPR's government, were now beginning to splinter over whether its expansion should be achieved by the councils or by elections to a Ukrainian Constituent Assembly, or indeed by a combination of both. However, within the workers' and soldiers' councils as such there grew a powerful tendency cutting across party lines to support the formation of a government of Ukraine as long as it was based on the councils locally and nationally, and on the condition it maintained solidarity with the Russian Soviet government. It was not a question of simply adapting the Russian experience, but of attempting to build with indigenous social forces on the basis of the institutions of popular representation that the revolution in Ukraine had so far created.

The USDWP's leaders rejected calls to hold an All-Ukrainian Congress of Councils. They labelled them as an opportunistic manoeuvre by the Bolsheviks to seize power. 'If the Bolsheviks want to reorganise the Tsentral'na Rada' *Robitnycha hazeta*'s November 7 editorial advised, 'they should take an active part in it, which they have not done yet, and achieve it there'.

---

103 Rubach, 'Treba diisno vypravyty', p. 264; Hamretsky, Tymchenko and Shchus, *Rady Ukrainy*, p. 161; Sukhyno-Khomenko, 'Z pryvodu osoblyvostei', p. 105.
104 Hamretsky, Tymchenko and Shchus, *Rady Ukrainy*, p. 206.
105 XX.

> The Tsentral'na Rada *is* the revolutionary parliament of Ukraine in which all layers of the revolutionary democracy are represented far more fully than they will be at a congress of workers', soldiers' and peasants' deputies ... The Tsentral'na Rada is itself in fact a Council of Workers', Peasants' and Soldiers' [in Ukrainian *Viis'kovykh*] Deputies ... Which is why it cannot be permitted under any circumstances for the Tsentral'na Rada to be elected by a congress of Workers', Soldiers' [in Russian *Saldats'kykh*] and Peasants' Deputies. The Bolsheviks' struggle with the Tsentral'na Rada is motivated by nothing other than their desire to seize power in Ukraine.[106]

Note the difference in the order of deputies in the description of the Rada and of the congress proposed by the Bolsheviks, that is peasants' deputies in second and third place respectively. Note also the use of the Russian *Saldats'kykh* (soldiers') in the latter, as opposed to the Ukrainian *Viis'kovykh* in the former. By these differences the USDWP newspaper's editorial, most likely written by Vynnychenko as editor-in-chief, signalled the party's fear that the Bolsheviks would relegate the Ukrainian peasantry to minority representation, and instead rely on garrisoned Russian soldiers represented in the urban soldiers' councils to offset the Ukrainian soldiers' deputies. Many Ukrainian soldiers and their councils were still stationed on different fronts and Petliura was making every effort to bring them home to the Ukrainian provinces and onto the now single Ukrainian front. There they would replace units of Russian soldiers who would be sent home, which for many was outside the Ukrainian provinces.

Vynnychenko, however, later recalled with some regret that the Rada under his leadership had not agreed to its re-election. But he understood its leaders' reasoning at the time:

> Unfortunately, this way, and the only way out, was rejected by a majority of the Tsentral'na Rada ... on the following grounds. 1. If we agreed to the Rada's re-election by the same token we conceded that our policies were wrong. 2. Such a re-election would have given the majority in the new Rada to Bolshevik elements, to workers in the main, but a russified working class, and so all government power would have gone over into Russian hands.[107]

---

106 *Robitnycha hazeta*, 7 November 1917, p. 2.
107 Vynnychenko, *Vidrodzhennia Natsii*, Vol. 3, pp. 161–4.

Meanwhile, splits were developing in the USDWP's Kyiv, Poltava and Kharkiv branches over the inadequacy of the Rada's social base and its temerity in implementing its programme. In mid-November a majority of the Kyiv branch called on the party to organise a national congress of workers' deputies to broaden the Rada's working-class base.[108] Yevhen Neronovych at a branch meeting on 3 December argued that 'the national postulates of our party have been implemented completely' and that it was time for the USDWP 'to conduct a struggle to transform the Tsentral'na Rada into a genuine All-Ukrainian Council of Workers', Peasants' and Soldiers' Deputies'. He put a resolution before the meeting:

> This period requires us to unfurl fully the flag of proletarian struggle and to break with the bloc containing any of the bourgeois parties, Ukrainian or non-Ukrainian, even if they do call themselves socialist ... the party ... must have in good time a base for the final and complete transition of power to the proletariat and revolutionary peasantry in the Councils of Workers', Soldiers' and Peasants' Deputies locally, with the Tsentral'na Rada at their head, and which they should have the right to recall.

The branch split three ways in the vote on Neronovych's resolution: 31 in favour, 31 opposed and 16 abstentions.[109]

On the eve of the All-Ukrainian Congress of Councils in Kyiv, Yukhym Medvedev, a Kharkiv member of the USDWP's left wing, made a presentation before his party's delegates assembled in Kyiv. Porsh and Vynnychenko were absent from this meeting. Medvedev urged them to seek an alliance with the Bolsheviks to establish a workers' and peasants' government. Only three of the forty USDWP delegates at this pre-Congress meeting voted against Medvedev's resolution. But it was rejected later and without explanation by the USDWP resolutions' commission.[110]

6 The Peasantry and the UPSR

The peasant unions opposed the Bolsheviks' approach to establishing soviet power, but they were not opposed to soviet power as such. Their conception

---

108 *Robitnycha hazeta*, 15 November 1917.
109 *Robitnycha hazeta*, 6 December 1917.
110 Ie. Medvedev, 'Z Kharkova do Kyieva i Nazad', *Litopys Revoliutsii*, 1 (January–February 1928), p. 242.

was different insofar as they already had an institutional base in the Rada on which to build a peasant and worker government. This issue concerning the form and social basis of government, plus the issues of War and land reform, dominated their deliberations at the Third Plenum of the All-Ukrainian Council of Peasant Deputies which met in Kyiv for six days from 18 to 23 November. The Plenum adjourned several times and sent the deputies into the army units stationed in the capital to agitate in favour of its positions on these three issues.

The peasants' deputies were suspicious of the Bolsheviks' demand that the Rada be re-elected. The Rada had declared the Ukrainian People's Republic less than two weeks previously and put forward its programme of action in the Third Universal. They believed it needed a chance to implement that programme. But they also saw the Bolsheviks as foreign interlopers wanting to deny them national self-determination.

> The All-Ukrainian Council of Peasants' Deputies sees in the Russian Bolsheviks' agitation to have the Ukrainian Tsentral'na Rada re-elected their desire to seize power in Ukraine into their own hands. The Council protests this and declares that such re-elections at the present moment will bring nothing but harm to the Ukrainian working people, and that the question itself of the Tsentral'na Rada's re-election is not for the Russian Bolsheviks to decide but for the Ukrainian working people. The All-Ukrainian Council of Peasants' Deputies notes that the labouring peasantry of Ukraine will resolutely oppose any interference in the creative work of the sole, supreme and legitimate body in Ukraine – the Ukrainian Tsentral'na Rada, whose present composition corresponds to the needs of the organised labouring peasantry.[111]

The Plenum resolved that all governing bodies be established on the basis of the formula of four representatives from councils of peasants' deputies to one from councils of workers' and soldiers' deputies, plus minor participation from institutions created by universal suffrage. A provincial government was to be made up of 10 members, eight of them from councils and two from *dumy* and *zemstva*. The provincial commissar was to be chosen by the provincial council of peasant deputies after consulting with the provincial council of workers' and soldiers' deputies.[112]

---

111 Khrystiuk, *Ukrains'ka Revoliutsiia*, Vol. 2, p. 60.
112 Ibid, Vol. 2, pp. 63–4.

The Plenum continued to call for a temporary all-Russian government of socialist parties 'from the Bolsheviks to the popular socialists' to enter immediately into negotiations for peace with the Entente and Central Powers. It also called for the Ukrainian People's Republic to take part in those negotiations through this All-Russian government so as to ensure no part of Ukraine was attached to any state against the wishes of its people. Given the possibility that such talks could fail, the Ukrainian soldiers on the front were instructed to stand firm until the UPR could itself sign a separate peace.

On the question of land reform the Plenum called on the Rada to adopt a law abolishing private ownership in land; the peasantry through the land committees should take control of all land, mines, bodies of water, inventories of landed estates and agricultural research stations. The peasantry was urged to prepare for sowing of cereals and sugar beet. The Plenum pressed on the Rada to act decisively and implement its promise on the land question set out in the Third Universal.

The Ukrainian Party of Socialist Revolutionaries held its Third Congress in Kyiv on 21 to 24 November. Chronologically it was an almost seamless extension of the Plenum of peasants' deputies. However, whereas the Plenum held to the positions of the centre and right wings of the UPSR, it was the left, internationalist wing of the party that held sway over its Congress. Here the party supported the co-existence for a limited time period of two government organs: a parliament elected by universal suffrage and an All-Ukrainian Council of Peasants', Workers' and Soldiers' Deputies. The Tsentral'na Rada should continue until it was replaced by the parliament chosen in the upcoming Ukrainian constituent assembly elections. Therefore, the party opposed the Rada's immediate re-election by the councils. However, this Congress also supported the soviet platform, the rule of councils locally and the establishment of an All-Ukrainian Council of Peasants', Workers' and Soldiers' Deputies that would, in time, supplant the Rada. It backed the call for an All-Ukrainian Congress of Councils to be held in early December, which of course the Executive Committee of Workers' and Soldiers' Councils of the Southwestern Region meeting on 24 November resolved to convene. The UPSR Central Committee elected at the party's Third Congress took the position that it should seek an alliance with the Bolsheviks at the All-Ukrainian congress on the basis of the soviet platform.[113] Khrystiuk contended

---

113 Popov, *Narys Istorii*, p. 126; Skrypnyk, *Statti i Promovy*, Vol. 2, p. 26; Guthier, 'The Popular Base of Ukrainian Nationalism', p. 40.

> This was an original form of state building which grew organically from the development of the Revolution in Ukraine. Its essence lay in the simultaneous existence of two kinds of institutions ... of which the class organs of power clearly had the upper hand – the councils of workers', soldiers' and peasants' deputies locally and in the centre.[114]

It was a daring strategy for the UPSR to pursue, given its lack of previous co-operation with the Bolsheviks. Just as the Bolsheviks had no base in the peasantry, the UPSR had none to speak of in the working class, except on its margins among rural workers, the semi-proletarianised peasants. How were they to unite them in the exercise of power? They disagreed over the proportional weight that the working class and the peasantry should have in decision-making. The Bolsheviks believed the proletariat should lead the peasantry, which the Socialist Revolutionaries could not accept on the grounds of national self-determination and the fact the peasantry was numerically the dominant social class in Ukraine. The second problem for the UPSR was that all the social democratic parties in the Rada opposed the soviet platform; they wanted a multiclass parliamentary institution through which they could govern alone or in coalition with the parties representing other classes. They would give the upper hand to the Rada, not to an All-Ukrainian council of workers', peasants' and soldiers' deputies.

114 Khrystiuk, *Ukrains'ka Revoliutsiia*, Vol. 2, p. 67.

CHAPTER 6

December: The Failure of Reconciliation

1   The Rada Lags behind the Radicalisation

The Rada had declared a good programme in its Third Universal, but the critical issue now was its implementation. It faced considerable obstacles: the destruction of infrastructure and displacement of people; the lack of reliable information, of previous government experience, of a competent and co-operative administration. The old methods and structures of government left behind by the old regime and adapted briefly and superficially by the Provisional Government were not suitable for implementing a radical social programme. The Rada's leaders were naïve to think they could achieve their aims without an even sharper class struggle taking place around them, one moreover in which the councils were necessary institutions for such struggle and its successful resolution. With regard to ending the War, the Rada simply had no experience, information or infrastructure of diplomacy to apply. It was not even recognised as a government by the CPC or the Entente or Central Powers.[1]

On the question of land reform the Third Universal abolished private ownership of all land, declared the confiscation of all landed estates without compensation to their previous owners and the redistribution of land by committees elected by the peasants. However, the Rada's leaders began introducing amendments to their originally clear and simple intent. First, the General Secretariat explained that all land except that held by the peasantry, that is crown, church and big landowner estates, was now national property, and a Ukrainian Constituent Assembly once elected would decide its ultimate redistribution. It left the peasant land committees in limbo, awaiting a future government's directives. Second, a draft land law drawn up by Borys Martov, USDWP Rada secretary for land affairs, and K. Matsievych from the UPSF excluded all holdings of up to forty *desiatyn* from the confiscation and redistribution. Given that poor peasants held on average 2.5 *desiatyn* (approximately 6.7 acres) of land and middle peasants around twenty-five *desiatyn*, there would be insufficient confiscated land in densely populated rural areas to distribute to the poorest peasants and the agricultural proletariat who had no land at all. Peasant depu-

---

1   Khrystiuk, *Ukrains'ka Revoliutsiia*, Vol. 2, pp. 56–7.

ties to the Rada were outraged by the draft law. They rose in the *mala rada* to denounce it.

> The peasants long for the land as much as for their heavenly paradise. And here you are leaving intact up to forty *desiatyn* in separate holdings. Well, these are landlords ... If we go back and report the draft law will leave forty *desiatyn* in one pair of hands, then the people will not recognise the Rada nor anyone for that matter ... That's right, our soldiers will come back from the front and they will remeasure those forty *desiatyn* with their bayonets!

It became evident USDWP leaders were aiming to protect the well off peasants (*kurkuli*) at the expense of the poor. Then the Kyiv press reported Vynnychenko had assured a delegation of wealthy landowners that the new government would compensate them out of public funds for their losses. Meanwhile, peasant seizures of land continued apace. Petliura as Rada secretary for military affairs sent troops into the countryside to quell the 'anarchy' and suppress ongoing land seizures and strikes by workers at sugar refineries.[2]

The Third Congress of the UPSR on 21–24 November saw the retreat on the land question by the USDWP as undermining the Rada's popular base of support:

> We recognise the need to prioritise social reforms and we call attention to the fact that the national revolution at a certain stage of its development begins to threaten the successful pursuit of the socio-economic class struggle ... this Congress is compelled to inform the Tsentral'na Rada that if it continues along this path it will lose from under its feet the support of the working classes of the nation, the peasants and workers of Ukraine. And when it loses its influence and that support it will at a certain point in time provoke a reaction among the masses which will even threaten the national gains of the revolution.[3]

The Congress called on the Rada urgently to implement the Third Universal and abolish private ownership of land in practice, establish state and workers' control of industry, nationalise strategic industrial sectors, restore production and resist the catastrophic rise in unemployment. The deputies were stung

---

2 Zdorov, *Ukrains'kyi Zhovten'*, pp. 134–6; Khrystiuk, *Ukrains'ka revoliutsiia*, Vol. 2, pp. 58–9, 122–3.
3 Soldatenko, *Ukraina v revoliutsiinu dobu*, Vol. 1, pp. 989–90.

by the impact of the Bolsheviks' agitation on peace and land reform among the Ukrainian soldiers and peasants, with whose demands they increasingly agreed.

There was uproar at the Eighth session of the *mala rada* on 12 December when Martos said the Third Universal's abolition of private property in land had encouraged peasants and returning soldiers to steal land and inventory from all and sundry. Forests were being felled, the wood carted away, experimental seedlings uprooted from agricultural research stations. Martos was convinced by all this that the peasantry was not ready for collectivised agriculture or for socialism. The Ukrainian and Russian SR deputies attacked him and introduced a resolution calling for the comprehensive socialisation of land. The USDWP threatened to withdraw its members from the General Secretariat if the resolution was adopted. It was supported by the UPSF, the Mensheviks and the Bund, all of them insisting that only the Constituent Assembly once convened should deal with the land question. In the end the whole issue was taken off the table by an agreement to strike a commission proportionally representing all parties that would draft an alternative to Martos' bill based on the principle of full socialisation.[4]

The *mala rada* returned to the land question more than a month later on 18 January 1918. In the meantime the peasantry looked with ever deeper scepticism upon the Rada and with greater approval on the record of the Bolsheviks in Russia, who united with the left Russian SRs in the Soviet government in mid-November and adopted practically their entire programme on the land question.

2   The Outbreak of Anti-Jewish Pogroms

Soldiers deserted the front and headed for home, many of them still carrying weapons. Driven by hunger they begged and stole food from the civilian population, commandeering carts and horses along the way. Petty theft escalated into looting and violence; soldiers broke into stores of wine and vodka. Jewish shops and homes in the towns and villages of Kyiv, Volyn and Podillia closer to the front were the first to be attacked. These communities were made up mainly of women, children and the elderly, their able bodied men having been conscripted into the army. Pogroms broke out in September in Bakhmut, Zhytomyr, Ostrih, Kharkiv and Kyiv, and they grew in number and severity to the end

---

4   Doroshenko, *Istoriia Ukrainy*, Vol. 1, pp. 247–50.

of the year. A particularly savage pogrom in Pohrybyshche, Kyiv province, on 18 October spurred the General Secretariat into action. Condemning the violence, it ordered provincial commissars to deploy military units against any incidents of pogroms and to punish those responsible for the violence. They made arrests in several localities, but on the whole the Rada did not respond adequately, even after the fall of the Provisional Government when it assumed greater governmental responsibility. In December the Rada Secretariat of Jewish Affairs received 214 telegrams reporting pogroms in three provinces alone. The General Secretariat intervened again, with Petliura sending Ukrainian army units to suppress them and restore order. However, the dispatched units and the local police were overwhelmed by the sheer number of pogroms.[5]

In Odesa, a Jewish Fighters' Detachment was formed in August 1917. At its height it numbered some 600 well-armed members in 12 detachments, who protected the community from serious violence. There were three such detachments in Katerynoslav organised by Jewish socialist parties and one by the Union of Jewish Fighters (UJF). They also managed to prevent violent pogroms from taking place in Katerynoslav. There was another Jewish self-defence unit in Kharkiv. However, there were very few of them in the smaller towns and villages of the agrarian provinces closer to the military fronts and they were usually formed in the wake of pogroms in their localities, not before them.

The Union of Jewish Fighters grew out of a movement for self organisation among Jewish soldiers in the Russian army, taking place throughout 1917. Analogous movements were organised by the soldiers of other non-Russian nationalities. Initially they addressed the soldiers' cultural and educational needs, but over time they all politicised around the questions of national self-determination, council democracy and peace. In the case of Jewish soldiers the outbreak of pogroms made national self-determination first and foremost an issue of self-defence. Jewish soldiers of the 19th infantry division demanded that the Rada and the Provisional Government authorise special armed units made up of Jews and other nationalities and deploy them in the rear of the front to defend Jewish communities. Such units, they insisted, should be at the permanent disposition of the Rada and Jewish representative organisations. Soldiers' councils of the Third Siberian army corps and the Eleventh army committed themselves to the defence of Jewish communities. The Siberian Corps formed a unit from its own ranks to fulfil that obligation.

---

5   Vladyslav Hrynevych and Liudmyla Hrynevych, *Natsional'ne Viis'kove Pytannia v Diial'nosti Soiuzu Yevreiv Voiniv v KVO (lypen' 1917–sichen' 1918 rr.)* (Kyiv: Natsional'na Akademia Nauk Ukrainy, Instytut Istorii Ukrainy, Instytut politychnykh I etnonatsional'nykh doslidzhen', 2001), p. 15; Abramson, *Molytva za vladu*, pp. 136–9.

On 5 September soldiers in the Kyiv garrison formed a branch of the Union of Jewish Fighters of the Kyiv Military District, an inter-party military organisation united in the goal of 'the free development of the Jewish people in a free Russia'. The UJF was committed to consolidating the gains of the revolution, propagating democratic and republican principles, supporting the national and cultural development of Jewish soldiers in the Russian army and organising the defence of Jewish civilians against pogroms. It disavowed any involvement in domestic or international political conflicts unless they clearly threatened the safety of Jews. The UJF was formally apolitical but Zionism was undoubtedly the strongest ideological current in its ranks. Yoan Hohol, its first elected leader, was a Zionist.

The Kyiv organisation took the initiative to convene the first all-Russian conference of the UJF, held on 10–15 October. Delegates came from UJF branches in Odesa, Chernihiv, Syzran, Kyiv, Petrograd, Nizhni-Novgorod, Yelyzavethrad and from several armies. The all-Russian organisation they established was to be headquartered in Kyiv. Expressing no confidence in the Rada or in the Red Guards, the conference turned to the Provisional Government to approve a 'legalised, powerful Jewish self-defence, as mobile as the army itself … an organised self-defence such that it inspires serious respect'. In the first ten days of November, immediately after the Rada overthrew the Provisional Government, the UJF recruited soldiers to seven self-defence units. The one in Kyiv numbered two hundred fighters, in Odesa four hundred. Other UJF units were deployed in Tarashcha, Dymer, Bohuslav and Dashev. A unit of 120 was deployed in the town of Ovruch after a pogrom there on 15 and 16 December in which 62 shops owned by Jews were ransacked by soldiers and peasants from surrounding villages. The unit repelled further attacks in Ovruch and several surrounding villages.[6]

The UJF recognised the Ukrainian People's Republic and launched a campaign to convince the General Secretariat to permit Jewish soldiers to form special detachments for the defence of Jewish civilians. It tried to enlist the support of the Jewish National Council and the Rada Secretariat of Jewish affairs to convince the Rada's Secretariat for Military Affairs under Petliura that such units did not go against its plan to form a territorial Ukrainian army from the divisions of the Russian army. On 14 November, a week after agreement was reached with General Dukhonin, commander in chief of the Russian army, that plan was implemented in the Kyiv and Odesa military districts.[7]

---

6 Hrynevych and Hrynevych, *Natsional'ne Viis'kove Pytannia v Diial'nosti Soiuzu Yevreiv Voiniv*, pp. 6–7, 13–14, 19, 46–9, 121–2.

7 Dukhonin, who remained loyal to the Provisional Government after its overthrow in Petro-

Yoan Hohol appeared before three meetings of the Jewish National Council to seek its approval for the UJF's strategy. He asked the Council: if Muslims and Ukrainians could form their own units, then why not Jews? There were four hundred thousand of them in the Russian army, many of them on the fronts close to where pogroms were taking pace. The Council was dominated by the Bund, Poale Zion, Fareinigte and Folkspartei (the Zionist parties walked out at its first meeting in October), who disagreed with the UJF's course of action, saying it was harmful to the unity of the revolutionary democracy. Separate Jewish units, they argued, could provoke a hostile reaction from the Ukrainian army units and even more pogroms; they would further disorganise the military front and so contribute to the disintegration of the Russian state as a whole. Instead of the military detachments the UJF was proposing, the Jewish National Council advocated multinational civil defence units working under the direct command of the Free Cossacks. Rejecting the UJF's proposal, the Jewish socialist parties communicated their own proposal to the *mala rada*.

They also supported the Rada's plan for a Ukrainian army based on the territorial principle of recruitment, that all soldiers of the Russian army who were born in Ukraine, regardless of their nationality, should be transferred to the new regiments coming under the Rada's command. However, Jewish soldiers already had practical experience that such a plan was unworkable because they were being excluded from the new regiments. There were even cases when Jews, who insisted on serving in them, were threatened with death if they tried to stay. The UJF regarded Ukrainisation of the army as anti-democratic and discriminatory in practice, violating the Rada's own declared principles of national territorial and national personal autonomy. Nor were civil defence units under the Free Cossacks a realistic prospect. Jews were being refused membership in the Free Cossacks in localities where they applied to join.[8] Moreover, the Free Cossacks were ignoring attacks on Jews and their property, refusing to investigate and prosecute the perpetrators and in some places even taking part in such attacks themselves: in Bila Tserkva, Cherkasy, Zvenyhorod, Tarashcha, Kamenky and Novo-Pryluky.[9]

As an alternative the UJF proposed that soldiers who were unable or unwilling to join the new Ukrainised regiments be assigned by the Rada's general staff to the UJF as long as they agreed to serve under its command. The executive of

---

grad, was assassinated on 14 November by a bomb planted by Bolshevik agents at the railway station in Mohilev, near his headquarters.
8   Hrynevych and Hrynevych, *Natsional'ne Viis'kove Pytannia v Diial'nosti Soiuzu Yevreiv Voiniv*, p. 37.
9   Cherikover, *Istoriia progromnogo dvizhenia na Ukraine*, Vol. 1, pp. 95, 104–5.

the UJF took this proposal to the Jewish National Council meeting on 19 November for its approval. Hohol spoke about the urgency, the real possibility that the collapsing military front 'might flood all Ukraine under a bloody wave of pogroms'. Again the Council disagreed with the UJF, warning that Jewish self-defence units would be incapable of preventing pogroms on their own, that their presence may indeed provoke more of them, and that what was needed were civil defence units serving as part of the Free Cossacks.

On 28 November the Zionist representative Sheikhtman in the *mala rada* asked what measures were being taken to suppress anti-Jewish pogroms and whether the General Secretariat would permit Jewish soldiers to form their own detachments for the protection of their communities. Petliura answered that he saw no reason at all why such detachments should not be formed. That provoked an angry response from Rafes of the Bund, who accused the Zionists of 'making careers out of the pogroms'. He insisted that the defence of the Jewish population should not be built on the principle of self-defence.

> The Jewish population must be defended by the institutions of the government of Ukraine and responsibility for that should be placed on the General Secretariat. The army should be a common one if it is going to be built on the territorial principle. Building national military units will only inflame national enmity and lead to a strengthening of previous Jewish iniquity, the beginnings of which are already evident today when the Ukrainised officer schools won't accept Jews and they are excluded from the Ukrainised divisions ... Soon Jews will be refused work in the Ukrainised postal service, on the railways and in other institutions.[10]

Hrushevsky in the chair of the meeting nodded his head in approval while Rafes spoke. M. Shats-Anin (United Jewish Socialist Workers Party – Fareinigte) and M. Odin (Jewish People's Party – Folkspartei) supported Rafes from the floor, the latter confirming to the *mala rada* deputies that the Jewish National Council in its socialist majority opposed separate Jewish self-defence detachments.

The UJF tried for a while to work with the Secretariat of Jewish Affairs to overcome the alienation between Jewish and Ukrainian soldiers and officers. The Secretariat set about creating a special school to teach Jewish officers the Ukrainian language and to attach commissars for Jewish affairs to all units of the army. Avraam Lapidus, deputy head of the UJF, was appointed lead com-

---

10   Hrynevych and Hrynevych, *Natsional'ne Viis'kove Pytannia v Diial'nosti Soiuzu Yevreiv Voiniv*, pp. 24–5.

missar for this work in the general staff of the Kyiv Military District. Members of the UJF joined a commission to combat pogroms that was attached to the Secretariat. The Secretariat of Internal Affairs assigned to the UJF 50 out of 200 new political instructors for the Free Cossacks to eradicate antisemitism in their ranks. The UJF put forward its members to train as instructors, but then withdrew after a mere five of the 50 promised posts were given to them.

The General Secretariat was proving incapable of implementing its own policy or enforcing discipline in its army and the Free Cossack police force. Few Jewish soldiers and officers presented themselves at the recruiting centres. They were put in an impossible position: to stay in a Russian unit on Ukrainian soil was to demonstrate an unsupportive attitude towards the UPR, while at the same time they were being refused membership in the UPR's military and police forces.

On 22 December Moshe Zilberfarb gave up his longstanding opposition to Jewish self-defence detachments. He now believed it was too late to pursue the plan for mixed nationality civil defence units and unrealistic to expect that the Jewish communities would be defended by army units that refused to accept Jews in their ranks. 'Although the General Secretariat has adopted the territorial principle in building its armies, there is still antisemitism in their ranks, and as a result this principle is not being applied and Jews are not being accepted into the Ukrainised units. Therefore it is better to allow Jews to form separate units'.[11] On 4 January 1918 the Secretariat of Jewish Affairs formally backed Zilberfarb's change of position. Zilberfarb resigned a week later and on 15 January the newly appointed Secretary, Khurgin, sent an urgent telegram to the commander of the Kyiv Military District asking for permission to proceed with Jewish self-defence units as 'the only realistic way for the government to combat the wave of pogroms at this moment in time'.[12]

3   The Rada Trails the CPC in Seeking Peace

The Russian army had been disintegrating ever since the failure of its June offensive that cost it many thousands of lives. Soldiers would no longer follow orders; officers' authority now rested on persuasion and consent. In approximately a quarter of the regiments they had elected their own officers. The Council of People's Commissars' decree on peace and publication of the secret treat-

---

11   Ibid, p. 40.
12   I. Cherikover, *Istoriia pogromnogo dvizhenia na Ukraine*, pp. 102–3.

ies of the Tsarist state persuaded many more soldiers to stop fighting and start fraternising with the soldiers on the other side, or simply to desert and head for home. In a number of points along the front a de facto ceasefire was in place well before the CPC formally agreed one with the Central Powers on 3 December.

A struggle now ensued between the CPC, the Rada and the supporters of the ousted Provisional Government to impose their will on the Russian army along the Southwestern and Romanian fronts. General M. Dukhonin, appointed on 3 November as commander in chief of the army, whose headquarters (*Stavka*) were in Mohilev, Belarus, refused to submit to the CPC's order to prepare the army for ceasefire. He remained committed to holding the military front on the side of the Entente against German and Austro-Hungarian forces. Leaders of the centrist wings of the Russian SRs and Mensheviks, V. Chernov and M. Avkventsiev, evacuated to the *Stavka* after the CPC's supporters halted Krasnov's march on Petrograd. Here they planned to establish a united socialist government under Chernov's premiership. They had the support of the All-Russian Executive Committee of Railway Workers (*Vitkzhel'*), which could exert pressure on the Bolsheviks to accept the 'peaceful liquidation' of their government by isolating Petrograd and preventing the movement of pro-Bolshevik forces across the country.[13]

The more right-wing socialists and the Kadets had no faith in the peaceful restoration of the Provisional Government. They placed their hopes on Cossack leaders in the Don, Kuban and other settlements along Russia's southern borderlands. The Cossacks had served traditionally as a frontier guard and an internal security force of the Tsarist regime. The Don Cossacks' army under the command of General Oleksii Kaledin was now stationed along the Southwestern front. Kaledin was a supporter of the old regime; he had backed Kornilov's uprising against Kerensky's government and he prohibited soldiers' councils in his army. Rather, he was elected by the cossack ranks as their warlord (*otaman*) at their traditional assembly (*Okruh*). The relations in the cossack army remained caste-like even in the face of democratic aspirations that appeared among the younger rank and file. When the Bolsheviks came to power in Petrograd the *Okruh* declared its independence and formed a government, the South Eastern Union of Cossack Armies of the Don, Kuban', Tersk and Astrakhan, which sat in Novocherkassk, the capital of the Don region.[14] General Kaledin denounced the Bolsheviks' seizure in telegrams dispatched on 25 October to

---

13   Zdorov, *Ukrains'kii Zhovten'*, pp. 60–1.
14   Orlando Figes, *A People's Tragedy: The Russian Revolution 1891–1924* (London: Random House, 1996), pp. 556–60.

the Provisional Government, the Russian army headquarters, his own commanders in the field and a congress of rank and file cossacks then meeting in Kyiv. Addressing this same congress on 5 November after it reconvened in Novocherkassk, the civilian head of the South Eastern Union, M. Bohaievsky, announced that his government was supporting the restoration of the Provisional Government.[15]

The Tsentral'na Rada rejected the CPC as the central government of Russia and by the same token its claim to represent the UPR in peace talks. The Rada was holding out for an elected constituent assembly to form a government that represented the entire revolutionary democracy and the autonomous republics of non-Russian peoples. The General Secretariat sent its two representatives, Dmytro Doroshenko and Oleksandr Lototsky, to Mohilev on 8 November where they signed an accord with General Dukhonin to replace units of Russian soldiers with Ukrainian units along the Southwestern and Romanian fronts. Petliura, Rada Secretary of Military Affairs, dispatched a telegram on 11 November to units on the fronts, copied to the Mohilev army headquarters and the Don Cossacks, in which he told Ukrainian soldiers they were not obliged to obey the CPC as it did not represent them and had no right to conduct peace negotiations on their behalf. He called upon them 'to stand firm at this dangerous time, guard the front and maintain order. In your units put a stop to any attempts to fraternise or reach a truce'.[16]

Kaledin welcomed Petliura's call. The government of the South Eastern Union in a meeting on 14 November supported the General Secretariat's proposal for the construction of a federated Russian government on the conditions it would exclude the Bolsheviks and sue for a general, not a separate peace. The Rada and the South Eastern Union exchanged representatives, Yu. Cheremshansky, commissar of Cossack forces on the Southwestern front, coming to Kyiv and M. Halahan, an officer in the Bohdan Khmelnytsky regiment and member of the *mala rada*, going to Novocherkassk.[17]

The General Secretariat publicly supported the inclusion of the CPC in negotiations to form a united socialist all-Russia government, but it showed considerably more interest in co-operating with the opponents of the CPC. When the CPC ordered its forces to seize Russian army's headquarters in Mohilev, Dukhonin turned for help to the General Secretariat, which agreed on 18 November to the transfer of the headquarters onto the territory of the UPR. The transfer did not take place as M. Krylenko, Bolshevik commander-in-chief of the

---

15   Zdorov, *Ukrains'kii Zhovten'*, pp. 60–1.
16   Ibid, p. 64.
17   Ibid, pp. 64–5.

CPC's forces, seized the headquarters on 20 November. Dukhonin was killed by a bomb at the Mohilev railway station and only a few members of his general staff managed to escape. Two days later they and the military attaches of Britain, France, Italy, Japan, Romania and Belgium who were stationed at the *Stavka* evacuated to Kyiv by train. The Rada sent out a guard of 60 sailors to escort them the last few versts. It welcomed them into the capital with a military parade.[18]

The *mala rada* met on 21 November to consider its position on the War. General M. Shcherbakov, commander of Russian forces on the Romanian front, had informed the Rada he was entering negotiations for a ceasefire with his Romanian and Moldovan counterparts. He proposed the Rada send its representative to the talks. Addressing the *mala rada* on behalf of the left wing of the USDWP Yevhen Neronovych called upon it to seize the opportunity to assert Ukraine's independence:

> The Ukrainian People's Republic should take the issue of peace in its own hands as an independent state, inform the Council of Peoples Commissars as the Great Russian government, as well as the warring states and our 'allies'. Previously we kept emphasising the ties between Ukraine and Russia. But the changes which have occurred untie our hands so now Ukraine should consider itself a sovereign, independent state and fully realise its national self-determination.

The UPSR fraction of deputies supported Neronovych and put forward its own resolution that the Rada recognise the CPC as the central Russian government.

The USDWP leftists and the UPSR were challenged in the debate by the UPSF, Russian SRs, Poale Zion and the Mensheviks, all of whom opposed any attempt by the Ukrainian People's Republic to secure a separate peace or to recognise the CPC. However, Tiomkin from the Bund argued that the Rada should send its representatives to the front to secure a ceasefire, to inform the Entente and stick to its policy for a democratic peace which only a Russian central government, still to be formed, could negotiate on its behalf.

Characteristically, Vynnychenko wavered: he supported the Bund's position, but added that 'the Council of People's Commissars is widely regarded among the popular masses and the General Secretariat has to take that into account. At the same time we do not recognise the Council of People's Commissars as the government of the whole Russian republic'.

---

18   Bosh, *God bor'by*, p. 60.

The *mala rada* then adopted a compromise resolution tabled by the USDWP and UPSR to send its representatives to both fronts, for the Rada to turn to both sides in the War for peace talks, and to invite the CPC and the governments of other republics of Russia to join it in the talks. The resolution carried by 29 votes to eight, with all the votes opposed coming from the Russian and Jewish parties. However, the CPC had already begun negotiations the day before with the Central Powers in Brest Litovsk. The *mala rada* dispatched M. Liubynsky from the UPSR to Brest Litovsk, not to take part in the talks on behalf of the UPR, but 'to monitor and collect information'.[19]

Two days later the General Secretariat announced that in view of the disruption in communications between the military fronts caused by 'the events which took place at the headquarters of the commander-in-chief', that is Dukhonin's assassination and the flight of his general staff, it was unifying the Romanian and Southwestern fronts into a single Ukrainian front and placing it under the command of General Shcherbakov, who was then commanding the Romanian front. 'As it declares a truce on the Ukrainian front in the name of the UPR the General Secretariat considers it necessary to continue working to secure an immediate peace with the agreement of the states of the Entente'.

According to Khrystiuk, the General Secretariat's intention to seek prior agreement with the Entente was something entirely of its own making. 'The majority of the Ukrainian revolutionary democracy did not consider it at all necessary ... that much was clear from the *mala rada's* resolution'.[20]

On the same day, 23 November, the General Secretariat issued an invitation to the autonomous governments of the Don Cossacks, the mountain peoples of the Caucasus, Bashkiria, the Siberian Cossacks, Moldova, Crimea and 'likewise to the Council of People's Commissars in Petrograd' to join it in negotiations in Kyiv aimed at forming an all-socialist government on the basis of seeking a general, democratic peace and convening an All-Russian constituent assembly.[21]

This was a significant change in the Rada's position on the CPC: it recognised it as one government in Russia, while still rejecting it as *the* central Russian government. However, the formation of a central government made up of all the parties that received the General Secretariat's invitation of 23 November was already a lost cause. The CPC and the South Eastern Union were bitter class enemies. Minister Khyzniakov of the ousted Provisional Government made it

---

19 Khrystiuk, *Ukrains'ka Revoliutsiia*, Vol. 2, pp. 92–5; Doroshenko, *Istoriia Ukrainy*, Vol. 1, p. 226.
20 Khrystiuk, *Ukrains'ka Revoliutsiia*, Vol. 2, pp. 197–8.
21 Ibid, Vol. 2, pp. 54–5.

clear on a visit to Kyiv that the inclusion of Bolsheviks in any government was out of the question. The Rada could not possibly reconcile these differences between the invited parties.

The *mala rada* adopted its resolution on the War on 21 November in response to the CPC's initiative to start separate peace talks with the Central Powers and the growing public support for that initiative. Soldiers' councils were protesting the Rada's inaction.[22] The *mala rada* responded with a policy decision to join peace talks that involved all the extant governments in Russia, including the CPC, and that did not require the prior agreement, nor involvement for that matter, of the Entente. However, the General Secretariat could not implement that decision because it clashed with its own pursuit of an alliance with the South Eastern Union against the Bolsheviks. So it equivocated over recognising the CPC and seeking a unilateral peace settlement for the UPR. Instead, it sought the permission of the Entente, to whom it had no real obligation as an 'ally'. After all, the Rada did not exist when the War was declared in 1914. Such equivocation would soon become untenable and provoke a confrontation within the Secretariat between Vynnychenko and Petliura over the way forward for the army, the peace and the UPR's relations with the CPC.

The CPC desperately needed to sign a truce with the Central Powers so that it could deal with the opposition brewing at home. It was seriously concerned that Kyiv might become the organising centre for an anti-Bolshevik government involving the Rada, the ousted Provisional Government and the Don Cossacks. The main threat of counterrevolution was perceived to come from the Don Cossack troops demobilising from the Southwestern front, whom General Kaledin wanted to transport back into the Don region. On 24 November, Krylenko on behalf of the CPC entered into talks with Petliura, seeking the Rada's support to consolidate the ceasefire on the front and its agreement to permit Russian pro-Bolshevik units to cross UPR territory into the Don to confront Kaledin. Petliura turned down Krylenko, saying his government did not want to provoke a conflict with the Don Cossacks, that they had as much right as any soldiers to return to their Homeland. He refused to be drawn on the question of the ceasefire and simply asked him for more information. In fact, the Rada had established its own relations with the South Eastern Union. From 10 November Mykola Halahan, USDWP, took part in talks for a week in Krasnodar and Novocherkassk on behalf of the *mala rada* about the composition of a future federated Russian government. On 27 November military representatives from both sides held talks about joint operations against the

---

22   Vynnychenko, *Vidrodzhennia Natsii*, Vol. 2, pp. 138–44.

Bolsheviks, and on 4 December the Rada gave its formal agreement to allow Don Cossacks to cross its territory from the front to the Don.[23]

Kaledin was massing his forces to embark on a northwards march to seize the entire Donbas, from which he intended to advance on Moscow. On 26 November his forces smashed up the headquarters of the workers' council in Rostov-on-Don, killing two of its deputies. They captured the entire city on 2 December and two days later took Tahanrih. The Don Cossacks crossed into territory claimed by the UPR and attacked Bolshevik-led workers' councils in the coal mining communities of Makiivka, Rovenkivsk, Bokovo-Khrustalsk, Yanivsk, Mykytivka and Debaltseve. On 29 December they put down a poorly trained detachment of armed miners in Makiivka and went on to massacre 118 people, including 44 Austrian prisoners of war. The Cossack detachment responsible claimed to have authorisation from the Tsentral'na Rada to put down Bolsheviks in the area. The massacre led the CPC to break off relations with the Rada, holding it responsible for colluding with Kaledin or at the very least providing cover for his actions.[24]

The steady disintegration of the Russian army forced the Entente to seek alternatives to shore up its front against the Central Powers. In late September General Tabuis, France's ranking military representative on the Southwestern front, paid a visit to Petliura who briefed him on the Ukrainisation movement in the Russian army. Tabius asked for closer, but still informal, ties and invited the General Secretariat to publish more information about the Entente in its newsletter *Visnyk*. Tabius visited Petliura again on 13 November, this time with the British military attache in Kyiv. Petliura boasted to them that he could now call upon four hundred thousand Ukrainian soldiers on the front.[25] The Entente wanted to assemble several new corps from Ukrainised units of the Russian army, Czech prisoners of war captured from the Austrian army, Czech colonists and Poles settled in Ukraine. They would be stationed at the most vulnerable points along the Southwestern and Romanian fronts. In return for its co-operation the Entente was offering the Rada technical and financial assistance. The French government offered a loan from private banks to invest in the Ukrainian economy; the British said they could deliver provisions they were stockpiling in Vladivostok once they found a safe route across Russia.[26]

---

23   Zdorov, *Ukrains'kyi Zhovten'*, pp. 64–5.
24   Ibid, p. 97.
25   Doroshenko, *Istoriia Ukrainy*, Vol. 1, pp. 231–3; Viktor Savchenko, *12 viin za Ukrainu* (Kyiv: Nora-Druk, 2016), pp. 22–3.
26   Khrystiuk, *Ukrains'ka Revoliutsiia*, Vol. 2, p. 92.

The French and British governments formally accredited their diplomatic representatives to the Rada on 21 November. The Rada's leaders took this to mean that they recognised the UPR was an already independent state. Vynnychenko later acknowledged that was a dangerous illusion:

> We regarded our statehood, how 'real' it was, as more dependent on our allies' recognition of it than its recognition by our own masses. And we conducted ourselves in the matter of peace in the same way, so it suited our 'allies' rather than the masses.[27]

The relationship of military forces between the CPC, the Rada and the Don Cossack government now added its weight to the struggle for state power in Ukraine. While the CPC and the South Eastern Union immediately took a hostile stance towards each other, the relations between the CPC and the Rada initially were more open minded. The Ukrainised regiments that took part in the October seizure of power in Petrograd (those named after Taras Shevchenko, Pylyp Orlyk, Nalyvaiko and Chyhyryn) were sent back to Ukraine fully equipped with the approval of the CPC. As friendly as the Petrograd Bolsheviks were at first towards the Rada in the longer run their position was determined by the Rada's stance on the War, its relationship to the workers' and soldiers' councils in Ukraine and to the CPC itself. However, the CPC's capacity to influence the situation on the ground in Ukraine was still limited to telegraphic communications with the Rada and local Bolshevik forces.

By the end of November the Bolsheviks were turning public opinion against the Rada over its stance on the War, its relations with the Don Cossacks and its resistance to re-election by the councils. That emboldened them to challenge the Rada. Yet the balance of military force still remained in the Rada's favour. The 36,000 soldiers in the Kyiv garrison were divided in their loyalties: some 46 percent of them had voted for the UPSR and USDWP in the November Russian constituent assembly elections, 37 percent for the Bolsheviks and 7 percent for the Russian SRs.[28] The Bolsheviks were working within the Second Guards Corps, then demobilising and moving towards Kyiv from the Southwestern front. They thought they could take Kyiv by a combined assault of their forces from within and without, and then to legitimise their takeover at the All-Ukrainian Congress of Councils.[29]

---

27   Vynnychenko, *Vidrodzhennia Natsii*, Vol. 2, p. 201.
28   Zdorov, *Ukrains'kyi Zhovten'*, pp. 145–7.
29   Khrystiuk, *Ukrains'ka Revoliutsiia*, Vol. 2, pp. 77–8; Savchenko, *12 viin za Ukrainu*, pp. 11–

On 29 November at a meeting of the Kyiv Bolshevik party organisation Leonid Piatakov, head of the Revolutionary Military Committee of the Kyiv Council of Workers' Deputies, proposed an ultimatum be put to the Rada to withdraw troops from the capital that were hostile to the councils, to agree to hand local power to the Kyiv Councils of Workers' and Soldiers' Deputies, and to acknowledge that it remained the national government only temporarily, until the upcoming All-Ukrainian Congress of Councils. If it refused the Military Revolutionary Committee would make an armed assault on the Rada. His proposal was adopted only narrowly, by a majority of one or two, including Yevgeniia Bosh.[30]

The Kyivan Bolsheviks' challenge to the Rada was foolhardy because they were themselves divided and they had insufficient forces to carry through on their ultimatum. Crucially, the Kyiv organisation had rejected Bosh's earlier demand that they bring the Second Guards Corps right into the capital. The Rada, on the other hand, was prepared for the Bolsheviks in Kyiv and across the country. Overnight on 29–30 November Petliura deployed some 12,000 soldiers who disarmed 7,000 pro-Bolshevik troops and Red Guards in the capital. The Russians among them were deported on trains to the border with Russia while the Ukrainians were discharged immediately and sent home. The First Ukrainian Regiment under General Skoropadsky's command blocked the entry into Kyiv of the Second Guards Corps by tearing up railway lines and occupying stations along the route.[31] At the same time the Rada's forces disarmed Red Guard detachments in Katerynoslav, Luhansk, Mariupol, Mykolaiv and other centres. They dispersed the workers' councils in Poltava, Konotop and Ananiiv, arresting Bolshevik and Red Guard leaders whom they suspected of planning uprisings. In Odesa the Rada prevailed in a fire fight with Red Guards. They strengthened their contingent in the Kharkiv garrison and marched troops into Berdychiv, Vynnytsia, Zdolbuniv, Korosten and Koziatyn. On the Southwestern and Romanian fronts they arrested Bolshevik commanders and broke up soldiers' councils. The Bolsheviks suffered a comprehensive rout.[32]

Despite confirming its military superiority the General Secretariat still felt obliged to defend itself against the Bolsheviks' accusations of betrayal. It issued a statement on 30 November, insisting it was not plotting with the Don Cos-

---

12. Soldatenko claims the Bolsheviks did not plan to bring the 2nd Guards Corps into Kyiv for this purpose.
30 Soldatenko, *Ukraina v revoliutsiinu dobu*, Vol. 1, pp. 961–4.
31 Savchenko, *Symon Petliura*, p. 112.
32 Khrystiuk, *Ukrains'ka Revoliutsiia*, Vol. 2, p. 78n; Soldatenko, *Ukraina v revoliutsiinu dobu*, Vol. 1, pp. 961–4; Savchenko, *12 viin za Ukainy*, pp. 11–12; Savchenko, *Symon Petliura*, p. 112.

sacks against the CPC, that it would accept only socialists in an all-Russian coalition government, and that the first condition for talks with the government of the South Eastern Union was that it lift the state of martial law in the Donbas. Yet it also insisted 'that power locally should be in the hands of bodies chosen by universal, direct, equal and secret voting and not of groups of people who have been chosen incorrectly and episodically'. It would defend the revolutionary gains made by the peasantry, the most numerous and most oppressed class in Ukrainian society, and never permit 'its rebirth to be nullified by the agitation of anarchist elements coming in here from the Russian north'.[33]

4   The Bolsheviks Form a Ukrainian Organisation

The Bolsheviks of the Southwestern region convened a conference in Kyiv on 3 December to prepare for the All-Ukrainian congress of councils and to consider their own future as a party. Their comrades in the Donets-Kryvyi Rih region and the South were invited, but they ignored this conference and the All-Ukrainian congress of councils because they had scheduled their own regional congresses of councils to take place in Katerynoslav on 1–4 December and Kharkiv on 7 December.[34] Nevertheless, the Kyiv gathering made the first attempt in the history of the Bolsheviks to found their own Ukrainian national organisation. After months of the Kyiv Bolshevik party committee trying to substitute for a national leadership a wider circle of members finally recognised that they needed 'a different tactic in Kyiv and Poltava than in Tver and Kaluga'.[35]

There were 54 delegates, 47 with the right to vote and seven with consultative votes, from 29 population centres and two railway battalions. The Kyiv city and provincial organisation representing 5,800 members had 23 votes, accounting for practically half of the full voting delegates. They were followed by Chernihiv with seven, Poltava and Kremenchuk with six each and one each for Katerynoslav, Yelyzavethrad, Zhytomyr and the railway battalions. Kharkiv had nominated its leader Artem to attend, but he did not come. Not only were the provinces in the east and south practically absent, but those present were not

---

33   Khrystiuk, *Ukrains'ka Revoliutsiia*, Vol. 2, pp. 79–81.
34   *Robitnycha hazeta*, 6 December 1917, p. 3; Skrypnyk, 'Nacherk istorii proletars'koi revoliutsii', p. 81; Khrystiuk, *Ukrains'ka Revoliutsiia*, Vol. 2, p. 69; Soldatenko, *Ukraina v revoliutsiinu dobu*, Vol. 1, p. 996; Zdorov, *Ukrains'kyi Zhovten'*, pp. 143–4.
35   S. Shreiber, 'K protokolam pervogo vseuykrainskogo soveshchaniia bol'shevykov', *Litopys Revoliutsii*, 5–6 (1926), pp. 56–9.

proportionately represented: the four thousand strong Katerynoslav organisation, for example, was the second biggest but sent only one delegate. That was indicative of the lack of attention to the political maelstrom swirling around Kyiv by the Bolshevik organisations outside the northern provinces.

Four issues were on the agenda of this meeting: the national question, the Tsentral'na Rada, the Bolshevik party's organisation and its tasks in Ukraine, and its stand on an ultimatum to the Rada issued on 4 December by the Council of People's Commissars. Discussion on these issues took place over three evenings on the margins of the First All-Ukrainian Congress of Councils.

Two tendencies put forward opposing arguments and proposals. The first of these, articulated by Yevgeniia Bosh and supported by Alexandrov and Luxemburg, contended that the national question was a superfluous issue in the era of finance capitalism, an ideological tool wielded by the bourgeoisie against the workers' movement. To their mind, the Tsentral'na Rada was such a tool and it should be defeated by force of arms. All talk of national self-determination and the recognition of national autonomy for Ukraine had only incited nationalism, confused the workers and played into the hands of the petit-bourgeois intellectuals of the Rada.

The second tendency, articulated by Vasyl Shakhrai and supported by V. Zatonsky, H. Lapchynsky and A. Horwitz, took the position that the national question was a legitimate and important issue for the workers' movement. Once the Ukrainian nation affirmed its self-determination by establishing a republic, the Bolsheviks were obliged to recognise and defend it. Henceforth they should contest political power *within* the Ukrainian People's Republic and not *against* it. Engagement with the Rada was necessary through political, not armed, struggle in order to transform it into a genuine national council of workers', soldiers' and peasants' deputies. Shakhrai argued that the workers' movement was not strong enough in Ukraine to establish its own government. It needed time to win over the peasantry from their leaders in the Rada. Therefore the Bolsheviks needed to build a Ukrainian party organisation with its own elected leadership and centre in Kyiv. Its literature should be published in Ukrainian, understandable to the village proletariat and the peasantry.

Bosh's tendency, on the other hand, opposed any separate national organisation or any name other than the one the Bolsheviks already had. They needed no other political strategy than the one they had pursued to date, hardened against any opportunist concession to national demands.

In the resolution it adopted on the Tsentral'na Rada the conference took the view that the Rada's policies played into the hands of the growing counterrevolution and that it had become a focal point of attraction for Kaledin and other restorationist forces. 'By exposing the reactionary and chauvinistic policy of the Rada ... the party will use all means to fight against the current composition of the Rada and will strive in Ukraine, as it does in Russia, to establish the genuinely revolutionary rule of the Councils of Workers', Soldiers' and Peasants' Deputies'.

The conference then resolved to establish a Ukrainian organisation of Bolsheviks and name it 'RSDWP (Bolsheviks): Social Democracy of Ukraine'. It established a party centre in Kyiv called the 'Main Committee of the Social Democracy of Ukraine'. Nine members were elected to it: in descending order of the number of votes cast for each, they were Shakhrai, Aussem, Lapchynsky, Bosh, Zatonsky, Aleksandrov, Kulyk, Hrynevych and Horwitz.

It was a clear victory for Shakhrai's position. However, the significance of the resolution on party organisation lay more in its intent rather than in the number of Bolsheviks that supported it at the time. It was the first time the Bolsheviks took a decision to create a Ukraine-wide organisation, but the majority at this conference who supported the decision represented a minority of the total membership of the party in Ukraine, probably around one quarter. And this was why it was ignored by the central all-Russia party leadership. Lapchynsky, elected head of the new organisation, sent official notification to the Central Committee along with the conference resolutions, the list of members of the Main Committee, and a request for formal approval of the new organisation called Social Democracy of Ukraine. He never received a reply.

5   The Failure of Reconciliation

The First All-Ukrainian Congress of Councils opened in Kyiv on 5 December, two days later than scheduled and under the control of the Rada rather than the executive committee of the Councils of the Southwestern region which had originally called it. The previous day soldiers loyal to the Rada had taken over the mandate commission set up by the Kyiv Councils of Workers' and Soldiers' Deputies, seized its official seal, wrecked its premises and began to hand out voting mandates themselves. 'The Council of Soldiers' Deputies completely disappeared'. The Kyiv Workers' Council could not oppose the takeover because its Red Guards had been disarmed.[36]

The new mandate commission admitted to the congress some two thousand delegates, of whom 905 were from soldiers' councils and 607 from the peasant union *Selians'ka spilka*, both predominantly under UPSR leadership.

---

36   Bosh, *God bor'by*, p. 77.

DECEMBER: THE FAILURE OF RECONCILIATION 231

Another 150 delegates were admitted from 49 workers', soldiers' and peasants' councils. Among the last group there were some 60 Bolsheviks. The gathering was renamed as the All-Ukrainian Congress of Peasants', Workers' and Soldiers' Deputies. The Rada's representatives offered two seats on the congress presidium to the executive committee of the Kyiv Bolshevik organisation, but it refused to accept them on the grounds that the gathering was an improperly mandated congress.[37]

Most of the councils present were from the northern provinces of Chernihiv, Kyiv, Poltava, Podillia and Volyn. The councils in the industrialised southeast and the south were largely absent. Conditional support for the Rada that existed among the bigger urban councils was undoubtedly eroded by the Rada's use of force against those it accused of planning uprisings against it only days before. The Rada was convinced the Bolsheviks were implicated in a wider plan to destroy it. Krylenko, their supreme military commander, had disarmed and dispersed some six thousand Ukrainian soldiers who were trying to return home in formation. He ordered his own troops 'to come off the front, seize the railway stations and smash this counterrevolutionary den'.[38] In response the Ukrainian soldiers' councils of the Eighth, Tenth and Twelfth Armies sent telegrams to Krylenko accusing him not simply of refusing to recognise the Rada as their government, but actually trying to bring it down. The 8th Army council's words were plain and direct:

> Take your hands off our young republic. We know who we are putting into power and, if necessary, we ourselves will re-elect the Tsentral'na Rada. The Tsentral'na Rada and the entire working people of Ukraine will fight together with the Russian working people against the bourgeoisie, but not together with you because you have set one people against another. We do not want you to interfere in the internal affairs of Ukraine, we demand you move the Guards Corps which is wreaking destruction in Ukraine to the northern front and replace it with Ukrainian units. Your attempt to disperse the Tsentral'na Rada will be met by resistance from Ukrainians. We declare: enough persecution of Ukrainians, enough shedding blood of the toiling masses. We will throttle you in this blood.[39]

The congress began in a hostile atmosphere created by the threats coming from both sides. It became even more hostile when Petliura announced that

---

37   Soldatenko, *Ukraina v revoliutsiinu dobu*, Vol. 1, p. 996; Bosh, *God bor'by*, pp. 77–8.
38   Savchenko, *12 viin za Ukrainu*, p. 15.
39   Bosh, *God bor'by*, pp. 76–7.

the Council of People's Commissars had issued an ultimatum to the Rada on 4 December that threatened it with war. The Bolsheviks demanded from the floor that the telegram of the ultimatum that was dispatched to Kyiv be read out. Porsh, who was chairing the session, asked the delegates whether they wanted it read out; the overwhelming response from the floor was they did not.

The CPC's 'Manifesto to the Ukrainian people and ultimatum demands to the Ukrainian Rada' was composed of two parts. In the first part the CPC

> recognises the People's Ukrainian Republic and its right to secede from Russia or enter into a treaty with the Russian Republic on federal or similar relations between them ... recognises at once, unconditionally and without reservations, everything that pertains to the Ukrainian people's national rights and national independence.

To demonstrate that its recognition extended to all nations, regardless of the class character of their state, the CPC noted its position on Finland, formerly a Russian colonial possession:

> We have not taken a single step, in the sense of restricting the Finnish people's national rights or national independence, against the bourgeois Finnish Republic, which still remains bourgeois, nor shall we take any steps restricting the national independence of any nation which had been or desires to be a part of the Russian Republic.

In the second part of the Manifesto, the CPC charged the Rada with a 'two faced bourgeois policy' for refusing to recognise the rule of councils in Ukraine or to call immediately a national congress of councils.

> This ambiguous policy, which has made it impossible for us to recognise the Rada as a plenipotentiary representative of the working and exploited masses of the Ukrainian Republic, has lately led the Rada to steps which preclude all possibility of agreement.
>
> These, firstly, were steps to disorganise the front. The Rada has issued *unilateral* orders moving Ukrainian units and withdrawing them from the front, thereby breaking up the common united front *before* any demarcation, which can be carried out only through a formal agreement between the governments of the two republics.
>
> Secondly, the Rada has started to disarm Soviet troops stationed in Ukraine.

Thirdly, the Rada has been extending support to the Kadet-Kaledin plot and revolt against Soviet power. On the patently false plea of 'the Don and the Kuban' having autonomous rights, a plea that serves to cover up Kaledin's counterrevolutionary moves, which clash with the interests and demands of the vast majority of the working Cossacks, the Rada has allowed its territory to be crossed by troops on their way to Kaledin, but *has refused transit to any anti-Kaledin troops.*

Even if the Rada had received full formal recognition as the uncontested organ of supreme state power of an independent bourgeois Ukrainian republic, we would have been forced to declare war on it without any hesitation, because of its attitude of unprecedented betrayal of the revolution and support for the Kadets and Kaledinites, the most bitter enemies of the national independence of the peoples of Russia, the enemies of Soviet power and of the working and exploited masses.

At the present time, in view of the circumstances set forth above, the Council of People's Commissars, with the full cognisance of the peoples of the Ukrainian and Russian Republics, asks the Rada to answer the following questions:

1. Will the Rada undertake to give up its attempts to disorganise the common front?
2. Will the Rada undertake to refuse transit to any army units on their way to the Don, the Urals or elsewhere, unless it has the sanction of the Commander-in-Chief?
3. Will the Rada undertake to assist the revolutionary troops in their struggle against the counterrevolutionary Kadet-Kaledin revolt?
4. Will the Rada undertake to stop attempts to disarm the Soviet regiments and the workers' Red Guard in Ukraine and immediately return arms to those who had been deprived of them?

In the event no satisfactory answer is received to these questions within 48 hours, the Council of People's Commissars will deem the Rada to be in a state of open war with Soviet power in Russia and Ukraine.[40]

There was a clear contradiction in the Manifesto between the CPC's recognition of Finland's right to national independence but not Ukraine's. However, the Bolsheviks' leaders evidently did not consider it so, for either or both of the following reasons: they believed Ukrainians did not want to separate from Russia;

---

40 Lenin, *Collected Works*, Vol. 26, pp. 361–3. See also Zdorov, *Ukrains'kyi Zhovten'*, pp. 86–8.

or the proletariat asserting its class rule superseded the right of nations to their self-determination. The CPC now 'recognised' the Rada as merely a candidate, in its view unacceptable to the majority of people in Ukraine, to represent them in a Russian federated and soviet republic. The CPC was threatening the Rada with a war that it regarded as an internal class war between the Ukrainian 'bourgeois' and 'counterrevolutionary' Rada on the one hand and the Russian central Soviet authority on the other, which it claimed already represented the proletariat of Ukraine. It did not regard it as a war between nations and certainly not an interstate war: Ukraine was not Finland.

The CPC's Manifesto and ultimatum demands came as a complete surprise to the Ukrainian Bolsheviks at the Kyiv congress. They had not been consulted on it beforehand and they did not know its contents. Vasyl Shakhrai took the floor and attempted to explain their position and minimise the damage. Calling it all 'a misunderstanding' he pleaded with delegates not to allow their national passions to be inflamed by the ultimatum.[41] However, he went on to say that the source of the conflict lay in the contradiction between the Rada's words and its deeds: by allowing the Don Cossacks passage across Ukraine it sided with them against its own workers and peasants. The Rada would only continue the agony of the past months if it kept on trying to form a socialist coalition government and to make a 'socialist' out of Kaledin. This misunderstanding, said Shakhrai, should not drive a wedge between the Ukrainian and Russian masses; all the outstanding issues could be resolved peacefully through negotiations between Kyiv and Petrograd.[42]

The USDWP then went on the offensive. Volodymyr Vynnychenko threw the accusation of the Rada being 'bourgeois' back at the CPC, accusing it of repressing the Mensheviks in Russia, closing their newspapers and fomenting a national conflict in Ukraine.

> We have taken firmly in hand the task of building a reborn Ukrainian state. But that does not please the Bolsheviks, and it is the reason they are going on about the 'bourgeois nature' of the Tsentral'na Rada. They cannot admit openly and honestly they are fighting us as Great Russians. The Bolsheviks stand for the self-determination of nations, but they want to school us about the state ... We have had enough of these lessons. The Tsentral'na Rada will do only what is in the interests of the Ukrainian democracy ... The General Secretariat believes it necessary to use the

---

41 *Robitnycha hazeta*, 8 December 1917, p. 2.
42 Khrystiuk, *Ukrains'ka Revoliutsiia*, Vol. 2, pp. 70–1.

methods of political and class struggle and not the politics of blood and steel. As you can see there are no arrests, no violence in Ukraine.[43]

Petliura responded to the accusation that the Rada was disorganising the front by charging the Bolsheviks with withdrawing their own units and sending them into Ukraine to strengthen positions against troops loyal to the Rada. Hrushevksy emphasised the difference between calling for the re-election of the Rada, which he did not oppose for one moment, and this demand being made by a foreign power that was threatening it with war.[44]

The Bolsheviks returned to their party conference in the evening of 5 December where they had an opportunity for the first time to read the entire CPC Manifesto and ultimatum. There was broad agreement among them and they adopted a resolution that judged the ultimatum as the correct and logical response by the CPC: the General Secretariat was leading the Rada into a counterrevolutionary alliance with Kaledin. However, some delegates expressed reservations about its timing and the reaction the ultimatum had provoked among the Rada's supporters. Zatonsky felt that the CPC was badly informed about the situation in Ukraine. It had not foreseen that its threat to make war on the Rada would provoke a defensive nationalist reaction. The Ukrainian masses interpreted the CPC's ultimatum as a threat of international war by Russia against Ukraine, not a class war against their common enemy on the Don. They closed ranks even more tightly around the Rada rather than breaking with it over its policy toward Kaledin, the response the CPC had hoped its ultimatum would produce. Zatonsky went even further and warned that Soviet Russia could not make war simultaneously on the Don, in Siberia and in Ukraine. If there was no split, and he still did not foresee it, then Soviet Russia would be fighting a war against the Ukrainian people with only a small group of Bolsheviks on its side. It was necessary, therefore, for them to advise the CPC so that it could weigh its next step wisely. Zatonsky was supported in the debate by Aleksandrov who agreed that the ultimatum was badly timed. He believed it should have been issued much earlier. The conference minutes thus reported Aleksandrov's words:

> Now the Rada has sunk deep roots it will be necessary to wait until the Ukrainian people's faith in it dissipates. The split in the Ukrainian masses has begun but the ultimatum threatens to arrest it. We will be faced with waging war against the entire Ukrainian people, and not against the Rada.

---

43   Ibid, Vol. 2, pp. 71–2.
44   Ibid, Vol. 2, pp. 70–4.

The Bolsheviks returned to the congress of councils on 6 December where Shakhrai had an opportunity to speak again. Having seen the full text of the ultimatum and heard the leaders of the General Secretariat the previous day defending their policy towards Kaledin he ventured to correct himself and say that he did not, after all, consider the CPC's ultimatum to have been a misunderstanding.[45] It was Shakhrai's parting shot, for he knew there would be no real debate. Rumours had spread around the congress that the Rada was planning to arrest the Bolsheviks. Regardless of whether they had substance or not, the effect was to make the Bolsheviks and their supporters quit the congress. On the second day 124 delegates from forty-one councils out of the 49 in attendance walked out. They included the Bolsheviks, Russian left SRs and several members of the USDWP left wing. The UPSR lefts stayed behind with the other members of their party.

The remaining delegates declared themselves a constituent congress of peasants', workers' and soldiers' deputies of Ukraine, gave an overwhelming vote of confidence to the Rada, with only two opposed and 19 abstentions, and turned down the demand to re-elect it.[46] Not only had the congress failed to bring the Rada and the councils any closer together, but rather it galvanised them into opposing camps. The Bolsheviks were defeated, but it was a Pyrrhic victory for the Rada. As Khrystiuk later wrote:

> The Ukrainian democracy expressed its full confidence in the Tsentral'na Rada, withholding any criticism of its activities, although it did have the evidence for such criticism and was ready to make it. The spectre of a march on Ukraine by Muscovy was now throwing the Ukrainian democracy to the right, onto the preservation of a united national front and silencing the class struggle. That was one of the greatest misfortunes that Muscovy's war with Ukraine brought upon the Ukrainian revolution.[47]

The Rada's leaders had argued they had no right to prevent Don Cossacks or Russians from crossing Ukrainian territory on their way home. The Russian state had fallen apart into separate national state entities, the Don Cossacks had declared themselves such an entity that wished, like Ukraine, to become

---

45 A. Zdorov, 'Figura Molchaniia', Introduction to Vasyl' Shakhrai, *Revoliutsiia na Ukraine* (Odesa: T.Ye.S, 2017), p. 13.
46 *Robitnycha hazeta*, 5 December 1917; Skorovstiansky, *Revoliutsiia na Ukraine*, pp. 82–3; Vynnychenko, *Vidrodzhennia Natsii*, pp. 164–5.
47 Khrystiuk, *Ukrains'ka Revoliutsiia*, Vol. 2, p. 74.

an autonomous republic within a reconstituted Russian republic. Kyiv had no right to interfere and would therefore remain neutral in any conflict between the Russian Soviet republic and the Don Cossacks. However, it was not neutral to allow a counterrevolutionary force to be assembled on the Don that threatened not only the Soviet Russian government but also any Ukrainian government based on the councils, which the Rada itself claimed to be. Vynnychenko himself acknowledged

> the statehood we were creating was closer to the statehood of the Don Cossacks, closer to them. And that's why we weren't afraid to let them through ... we saw in the Don Cossacks our allies in the struggle for a federation. From that perspective the Don was closer to us than Petrograd, even though the latter had declared its recognition of the Ukrainian People's Republic.

Finally, Vynnychenko argued that the Rada did not have sufficient military forces to guard its own borders, nor to prevent a well armed Don Cossack force from crossing it even if it had wanted to.[48]

The General Secretariat replied to the CPC's ultimatum on 5 December, insisting the Rada was a government based on the councils of soldiers', workers' and peasants' deputies, but with a national composition at odds with the expectations of the Bolsheviks, as well as the Kadets and the Black Hundreds,

> who no doubt would like it to have a different national composition. But the General Secretariat gives these elements every opportunity to leave the territory of Ukraine for Great Russia where their national sentiments will be satisfied. Having just this in mind Ukrainian soldiers disarmed the anarchically pent up Russian soldiers who were conspiring against the government of the Ukrainian people and threatening to provoke a fratricidal war in Ukraine, to bring in all the anarchy and disorder which now pervades the territory of the People's Commissars.[49]

The General Secretariat reiterated the conditions on which it was prepared to work with the CPC: recognition of the right to self-determination of the Ukrainian people and the right to existence of the Ukrainian People's Republic; completion of the Ukrainisation of the armed forces, which required the

---

48   Vynnychenko, *Vidrodzhennia Natsii*, Vol. 2, pp. 139–42.
49   Soldatenko, *Ukraina v revoliutsiinu dobu*, Vol. 1, pp. 879–80.

free passage of Ukrainian soldiers from all fronts onto the Ukrainian front; non-interference by the CPC in the Ukrainian front and payment to the Rada from the state budget for the food supplies commandeered by the CPC's representatives in Ukraine and sent across the border into Russia. If the Council accepted these conditions, then war could be averted.[50]

The CPC immediately rejected the General Secretariat's reply and concluded that the Rada was in a state of undeclared war. It ordered Antonov-Ovsiienko to prepare a military expedition across Ukraine. He headed immediately for Kharkiv to establish a base for operations against Cossack forces under Kaledin in the south and the Rada in Kyiv to the west. Soviet Russia amassed troops along the borders of Ukraine at Briansk, Bilhorod, Bakhmach and Homel.[51]

6   One Republic, Two Governments

The delegates who walked out of the First All-Ukrainian Congress of Councils in Kyiv went on to Kharkiv by train to join up with the congress of councils of the Donets and Kryvyi Rih region. They arrived in Kharkiv on 8 December, at the same time as 1,600 Russian Red Guards, the lead detachment of Antov-Ovsiienko's expeditionary force under the command of Rudolf Sivers. On 8 and 9 December these forces supported some 3,000 local Red Guards to seize the main railway station, the telegraph and telephone exchanges and to disarm the Twenty-Ninth Division, take its armoured cars and arrest the Rada's military commander of Kharkiv. In the following days up to 16 December an additional 5,000 soldiers arrived in Kharkiv from Moscow, Petrograd and Tver under the command of Antonov-Ovsiienko and his chief of staff, the left SR Mikhail Muraviov. Control of the city would remain divided until the very end of December between regiments of the Rada, the CPC's expeditionary forces and the local Red Guards.

The CPC's instruction to Antonov-Ovsiienko was to deploy his forces against the Don Cossacks to the south and not to engage the Rada's forces unless necessary. The support Antonov-Ovsiienko's forces gave to local Red Guards against the Rada's soldiers was intended to secure them a temporary base in the city. All sides then upheld an uneasy truce. The CPC considered the Rada the lesser threat compared to the Don Cossacks; its relations with the Rada were not yet settled, they could possibly still be reconciled. Indeed, the forces loyal to the

---

50   Khrystiuk, *Ukrains'ka Revoliutsiia*, Vol. 2, p. 90.
51   Savchenko, *12 viin za Ukrainu*, p. 13.

Rada, who occupied the city garrison, still appeared to Antonov-Ovsiienko to retain military superiority.[52]

A complicated balance of local forces, both political and military, underlay the balance between the incoming forces of the CPC and the Rada. Local political authority rested with the Kharkiv Council of Workers' and Soldiers' Deputies, in which the Bolsheviks and left Russian SRs held a majority and which was chaired by the Bolshevik Artem, elected to the post on 24 October. The Council's Military Revolutionary Committee (MRC), created on 26 October, was composed of two representatives each from the Bolsheviks, left Russian SRS, USDWP and UPSR, plus one Menshevik Internationalist. Its head was Opanas Sivero-Odoievsky, from the UPSR's left wing, while his deputy was Artem. After the Provisional Government's fall, the MRC co-ordinated the forces of the Bolsheviks and Ukrainised army units in a combined and successful resistance against Kornilov's troops who had attacked Kharkiv from Bilgorod across the province's eastern border. 'The MRC recognised the liquidation of the Provisional Government, but not the authority of the Council of People's Commissars, recognising instead the authority of the Tsentral'na Rada'.[53]

Beginning with Artem himself, many Kharkiv Bolshevik leaders were hostile to the Rada and to the very idea their region belonged to an entity called Ukraine. They regarded it an integral part of Russia and saw no prospect for unity between its Russian working class and the Ukrainian peasantry, who were in fact a majority of the region's population. They intended to form their own Donets-Kryvyi Rih Republic and to ally themselves with the Russian Soviet republic under the CPC. It was for this very reason they were convening a congress of councils in Kharkiv. They resented their comrades coming from Kyiv to meddle in their affairs and they treated them as unwelcome guests. They refused at first to provide them with any accommodation, but when pressed in the early hours of the morning after they had arrived on the train from Kyiv the Kharkiv regional party committee offered them a cell in the city's prison. Bosh recalls:

> We headed through dark alleys to those familiar stone walls. An old and still unforgettable scene: sentries, identification on entry, a courtyard with a bag of stones, a warder and, finally, a prison cell. All this stirred up unhappy memories of bygone days and made me look with some alarm into the future …

---

52 Savchenko, *12 viin za Ukrainy*, pp. 17–18; Zdorov, *Ukrains'kyi Zhovten'*, p. 159.
53 Zdorov, *Ukrains'kyi Zhovten'*, p. 160.

> The accommodation was quite unhealthy. The cell had only just been refurbished and so it was very damp. Our bed linen became wet in the night and we all had to sleep fully dressed. With fresh plaster drying on the walls, rubbish strewn down the corridor and no water in the toilets, all this fouled the air so badly that by morning everyone was cursing and in a semi-conscious state. But such inconveniences were not important to us back then and for ten days the comrades lived voluntarily in such atypical accommodation. This was the hostel for members of the first Soviet government, given to them by their own comrades and the object of many malicious remarks on the part of those who were hostile towards us.[54]

They had arrived in Kharkiv in time to take part in a conciliation meeting called by the Mensheviks and the Bund between the Kharkiv Joint Council of Workers', Soldiers' and Peasants' Deputies, the city Duma and representatives of the Rada. Artem and Bosh were at this meeting, as was Petliura for the first part of it. They planned to consider the question of state power and several related issues: whether or not to allow the CPC's agents to ship grain, coal and steel out of the region into Russia; whether Russians demobilised from the tsarist army should be permitted to settle in Kharkiv; and whether to allow Russian Red Guard detachments to pass through the city on their way to the Don. Petliura said he did not object to any of these proposals, although he would not facilitate them. However, he insisted that Sivers withdraw his forces from the city and that he be informed of any further movements of Red Guards. The Bolsheviks would not agree to Peltiura's terms, insisting that Sivers' forces stay in the city until they could move on to the Don region.[55] The Bolsheviks feared the Rada-controlled garrison would move against their Red Guards before the incoming Russian forces decisively shifted the balance of military forces in their favour.

On the question of state power, three different positions were put to the meeting. The Mensheviks argued that the question should not be decided there, but at the upcoming congress of councils of the Donets and Kryvyi Rih region where a republic should be declared that answered to neither the Kyiv Rada nor the Petrograd CPC. The Kharkiv Bolsheviks supported the establishment of an autonomous republic for their region that recognised the Petrograd CPC. They resolutely opposed any kind of armed action against the Rada's forces and waited with some trepidation to learn of the latter's intentions. The Rada's supporters argued that, insofar as the first All-Ukrainian Congress of

---

54   Bosh, *God bor'by*, p. 101.
55   Zdorov, *Ukrains'kyi Zhovten'*, pp. 163–4.

Councils in Kyiv upheld the Rada as the government of Ukraine, so too should the parties and institutions present at the meeting. The Bolsheviks of the Southwestern region present at the meeting clearly disagreed that the Rada enjoyed the support of the workers' councils and said they would refuse to recognise it. But unlike their autonomist Kharkiv comrades, they were intent on reconvening an All-Ukrainian congress of councils in order to challenge the legitimacy and authority of the Rada as the government of Ukraine.

This last option risked provoking a pre-emptive attack by the Rada's forces, which the Bolsheviks and Mensheviks were desperate to avoid. The Bolsheviks then called for a break in the meeting in order to caucus separately to resolve their internal differences. After much debate they arrived at a joint position: to place the Red Guards on alert against a possible attack by the Rada's forces; to inform the conciliation meeting that only a few councils in fact supported the Rada at the Kyiv congress; and to call a meeting of the representatives of the entire regional Bolshevik party organisation for the following day, 9 December, to consider their way forward. The Rada's forces did not attack and the night passed peacefully. The next day the Bolshevik-led Kharkiv Council of Workers' and Soldiers' Deputies resolved to convene a new All-Ukrainian Congress of Councils on 11 December, which all the councils of the Donets-Kryvyi Rih region were invited to join instead of holding their own separate regional congress. They agreed to come, but as Bosh recalled they sent a delegation representing their region rather than simply appearing as representatives of individual councils.[56]

Two hundred delegates representing 82 councils took part in the congress held in Kharkiv on 11 and 12 December that declared itself the 'First All-Ukrainian Congress of Workers' and Soldiers' Deputies with the participation of Peasants' Deputies': 46 councils of the Donets-Kryvyi Rih region, 32 councils from the Southwestern region and four from the South. Representatives from seven soldiers' committees and military revolutionary committees also took part. There were also a few peasant representatives. The congress had just three items of discussion on its agenda: the principle of national self-determination, the practical question of state power in Ukraine, and the establishment of an autonomous Donets-Kryvyi Rih Republic.[57]

Three factions of the Boshevik party formed up and dominated the discussions. The Katerynoslav faction did not believe a Ukrainian state based on the councils was possible because of the military superiority of the Rada. Yakovlev,

---

[56] Bosh, *God bor'by*, pp. 86–8.
[57] Hamretsky, Tymchenko and Shchus, *Rady Ukrainy*, p. 299; Lapchynsky, 'Pershyi period Radians'koi Vlady', p. 161.

a leading Katerynoslavian, argued that without support from the peasantry any attempt to set up such a government would be purely adventurist. Rather, they should wait for the convocation of the All-Russian Constituent Assembly whose delegates had already been elected in mid-November.[58]

The Kharkiv, Donets and Kryvyi Rih Bolsheviks had their sights set on a republic of their own to be incorporated into Soviet Russia on terms of autonomy and federation. This faction's speakers argued that the industrialised provinces had stronger economic ties with Russia than with the agrarian Ukrainian provinces, that their workers belonged to a Russian working class and that the Tsentral'na Rada had no just claim to the region at all.[59]

The third Bolshevik faction was composed of the Southwestern group led by Yevgeniia Bosh from Kyiv, Vasyl Shakhrai from Poltava, Mykola Skrypnyk from Petrograd and Heorhii Lapchynsky, head of the Kremenchuk Council of Workers' and Soldiers' Deputies. This faction called for the immediate formation of a rival government for all Ukraine based on the councils that should ally itself with the Soviet Russian republic. To separate the region of Donets and Kryvyi Rih from the rest of Ukraine meant abandoning the peasantry to the Rada. Skrypnyk argued that the Ukrainian provinces, their working class and peasantry constituted a cohesive economic and social formation. Ukraine united politically under a government of all its local councils would serve to spread the revolutionary process westward into Central Europe. 'Skrypnyk ... characterised the social character of the Kharkovians' separatism as the ideology of Russian migrant workers who visit the Ukrainian industrial regions only temporarily in search of jobs'.[60]

Many workers' councils were choosing to recognise only their own authority, unencumbered by any regional or Ukrainian government, be it in Kharkiv or Kyiv. There are frequent references in memoirs to 'local patriotism' among the leaders of workers' councils who interpreted the slogan 'All power to the soviets' in the most literal and narrow sense. The Starobilsk Council organised its own regional government. In Odesa, Mykolaiv and Kherson, movements were afoot to proclaim them free cities. In December, the Odesa Council of Workers' Deputies sent a delegation to the Rada to negotiate such a status for its city. The Kremenchuk Council set up a state bank which printed its own legal tender.[61]

---

58 Lapchynsky, 'Pershyi period Radians'koi Vlady', pp. 161–2.
59 Ibid. See also Skrypnyk, *Statti i Promovy*, Vol. 2, p. 26; S. Sh., 'Iz istorii Sovvlasti na Ukraine', p. 172; Popov, *Narys Istorii*, p. 144.
60 Lapchynsky, 'Pershyi period Radians'koi Vlady', p. 162.
61 Maiorov, *Z Istorii Revoliutsiinoi Borot'by*, p. v; Lapchynsky, *Pershyi period Radians'koi Vlady*, p. 160; Popov, *Narys Istorii*, p. 135; H. Lapchynsky, 'Borot'ba za Kyiv. Sichen' 1918 r., *Litopys*

The position advocated by Skrypnyk gained support from a majority of delegates. The Congress adopted its main resolution 'On Power in Ukraine' on 12 December, with 110 delegates voting in favour and 13 Mensheviks and Right Russian SRs abstaining. The Congress resolved that

> power on the territory of the Ukrainian republic rests exclusively with the Councils of workers', soldiers' and peasants' deputies: locally in the hands of district, city, provincial and oblast councils and in the centre with the All-Ukrainian Congress of Councils of workers', soldiers' and peasants' deputies, its Central Executive Committee and the bodies it creates. Ukraine is declared a republic of councils.[62]

The Congress also proclaimed the Ukrainian republic a federated member of the Soviet Russian republic and instructed the new government it was about to elect to implement all the applicable decrees of the Soviet Russian government. It denounced the Tsentral'na Rada as 'bourgeois' and 'counterrevolutionary' and declared invalid all those laws and decrees it would henceforth adopt as well as those it had adopted previously that went against the interests of the working masses. It adopted decrees on land, workers' control of industry and democratisation of the army, and revoked the ban on the export of grain from Ukraine. In view of the inadequate representation of peasants the Congress resolved to convene an All-Ukrainian peasant conference no later than 20 January, which should elect representatives to take the twenty seats reserved for them in the Central Executive Committee of the Councils of Ukraine.[63]

The Congress also adopted a resolution entitled 'About the Donets-Kryvyi Rih Basin' that flatly contradicted the main resolution 'On Power in Ukraine'. Put forward by the Kharkiv Bolshevik party committee and supported by the Mensheviks and Russian SRs present, this resolution protested attempts both by the Tsentral'na Rada and the South Eastern Union to take the Donbas for themselves. Without mentioning at all the formation of the new Soviet Ukrainian government, it confirmed the intention of the same congress 'to seek the unity of the Donets basin within the borders of the Soviet [Russian] republic'. Shakhrai recalled that 'this resolution was ushered through on the motivation that the backward agrarian part of Ukraine should not be able to choke off in

---

Revoliutsii, 2 (March–April 1928), p. 209; Skorovstians'kyi, *Revoliutsiia na Ukraine*, p. 112; Skrypnyk, *Statti i Promovy*, Vol. 2, p. 27; Kuras, 'Borot'ba bil'shovykiv', p. 33; *Litopys Revoliutsii*, 3 (May–June 1931), p. 154.

62 Cited in Zdorov, *Ukrains'kyi Zhovten'*, pp. 169–70.
63 Bosh, *God bor'by*, p. 95; Zdorov, *Ukrains'kyi Zhovten'*, pp. 169–70.

a reactionary way the industrial working class of the region around Kharkiv. However, this resolution came to play an objectively national role, not a class one'.[64] Why such a resolution was allowed to pass can be explained perhaps by the Southwestern region Bolsheviks' desire not to drive their comrades from the eastern industrial region away from a joint congress they had only just persuaded them to take part in. It was, however, a sign of fundamental disagreement in their ranks.

The Congress elected a Central Executive Committee of the Councils of Ukraine (CEC) made up of thirty-three Bolsheviks, four Russian left SRs, one USDWP leftist and one Menshevik Internationalist.[65] This number gave representatives of the workers' and soldiers' councils double the number of seats on the CEC to those it reserved for the peasants' deputies.

The election of the People's Secretariat, functionally the same body as the Rada's General Secretariat, by the 39 initial members of the CEC proved a lot more difficult than the election of the CEC. This was because the overwhelming majority of the CEC were Bolsheviks who could not agree with each other. Once they became focussed on choosing the executive organ of their government the disagreements between them came again to the fore. The Bolsheviks then adjourned for a separate party caucus to decide their list of candidates to the People's Secretariat. It took them three meetings to come to an agreement.

At the first meeting Vasyl Shakhrai said that, despite all the previous decisions made in Kharkiv, it would be a mistake to create a Bolshevik government while the Bolsheviks still represented a minority throughout Ukraine. The People's Secretariat should not try to rule, but rather should engage in education and propaganda. 'We will not rule but enlighten'. Shakhrai had played a key role holding the left wing forces together at the Kyiv Congress and speaking on their behalf. He was a unifier whose words were taken seriously and they caused some consternation. While Bosh dismissed them and claimed that Shakhrai remained alone in his position on the CEC, his intervention did have a discernible impact. Some of those present now took the view that the People's Secretariat must be seen as representative of all Ukraine and that Ukrainian candidates should be nominated to it, and that its chairman at the very least must be 'a committed Ukrainian' so that the Rada could not claim it was a government of Russians.

A second group, while not disagreeing with the first, insisted that only candidates with political experience be elected to the People's Secretariat. A third

---

64   Shakhrai, *Revoliutsiia na Ukraine*, p. 104.
65   *Litopys Revoliutsii*, 1 (January–February 1928), p. 283.

group composed of Kharkiv comrades announced it would not take part in the election of the People's Secretariat on the grounds they were not sufficiently acquainted with all the candidates, that is with their comrades from other regions of the country.

In the second meeting of the Bolshevik fraction the second group that stressed political experience over considerations of nationality changed its position to support the election to the People's Secretariat of candidates 'with Ukrainian surnames wherever possible, but not to elect its chairman at this point in time'. The Kharkiv group was persuaded to nominate its own candidates. It then demanded four seats on a thirteen-person People's Secretariat, but the meeting agreed to give them only two. The third meeting finally agreed the list of Bolshevik candidates, which was then put to the six members of other political parties on the CEC. The meeting did not elect a chairperson of the People's Secretariat, but handed Bosh the responsibilities of the post in a temporary capacity.[66] She was the best choice on the basis of her experience and leadership qualities but she was a woman and of German descent. The fact she was a woman certainly carried more weight than her nationality in the party's decision not to make her the permanent chairperson.

The CEC elected the following of its members to the People's Secretariat:

Internal Affairs:	Yevgeniia Bosh
Military Affairs:	Vasyl Shakhrai
Education:	Volodymyr Zatonsky
Land:	Ye. Terletsky
Trade and Industry:	F. Serheev (Artem)
International Affairs:	S. Bakynsky (Ludwig Bergheim)
Labour:	Mykola Skrypnyk
Finances:	V. Aussem
Justice:	V. Luxemburg
Post and Telegraph:	Ya. V. Martianov,
Provisions and Supply:	E. Luhanovsky (Portugeiz)
Administrative Affairs:	Heorhii Lapchynsky
Transport:	V. Aussem, in a temporary capacity.[67]

All the members of the People's Secretariat were Bolsheviks, with the exception of Ye. Terletsky, a left Russian SR. By nationality, there were four Ukrainians, four Germans, two Russians, one Pole and one Jew.[68] Four of them knew the Ukrain-

---

66   Bosh, *God bor'by*, pp. 90–2.
67   It was left to a congress of railway workers to elect the permanent commissar. Bosh, *God bor'by*, p. 92.
68   Zdorov, *Ukrains'kyi Zhovten'*, p. 172.

ian language (Zatonsky, Skrypnyk, Shakhrai and Martianov).[69] 'The People's Secretariat considered it necessary to issue all laws and official publications in two languages, although often there was no-one in Kharkiv to translate them into Ukrainian, so a lot of material was published in an extremely laborious or simply ungrammatical Ukrainian language'.[70]

Two telegrammed messages to the new government were read out at the end of the CEC's deliberations. The first was from the CPC, which greeted its formation and promised henceforth to send it funds. A representative of the new government would be included in the Soviet Russian delegation at Brest Litovsk where the Central Powers had in principle accepted the CPC's peace terms and a ten-day pause in negotiations had begun.

The second telegram came from the headquarters of the CPC's supreme army command:

> The workers and peasants of Russia never doubted that the workers and peasants of Ukraine are brothers of the same toiling family, tightly bound together by the same interests, the same values and the same desire to cast off the oppression of capital ... We Russians never believed that the voice of the Tsentral'na Rada was that of the Ukrainian workers and peasants. By sending them the ultimatum we declared war on the Ukrainian bourgeoisie, which in concert with the world bourgeoisie wanted to exploit their aroused national feelings in order to drown in the blood of their brothers the gains won by the workers and peasants in the October revolution.[71]

The Central Executive Committee issued a manifesto on 14 December. Its first mention of the situation in Ukraine was in connection with the mounting counterrevolution.

> The capitalists, landlords and other parasites rose up in a desperate struggle against the worker-peasant revolution and chose for themselves as their bases of support first some sections of the military front, then the Don and then our Ukraine. The *Stavka* spoke out in the name of the front, Kaledin in the name of the Don and the General Secretariat of the Tsentral'na Rada in the name of Ukraine.

---

[69] Ibid, p. 165.
[70] Lapchynsky, 'Pershyi period radians'koi vlady na Ukraini', p. 168.
[71] Bosh, *God bor'by*, p. 97.

There was no mention of the mobilisations of the peasants, soldiers and workers from February to October. Rather, all attention was focused on the Rada:

> Under the guise of national self-determination the Tsentral'na Rada decided to turn Ukraine into a bourgeois republic that defends the interests of the capitalists and the officials, both Ukrainian and Russian ... it refused to obey the orders of the supreme command of the all-Russian army, it disorganised the front and so interfered with the conduct of peace negotiations, maliciously trying, as it now appears, to prolong the war until the spring in the interests of the Franco-British capitalists ... in support of Kaledin the Rada forbad the passage through Ukraine of revolutionary troops, treacherously disarmed soviet troops in Kyiv and tried to plunge the Ukrainian democracy into a fratricidal war with Russia.

The Manifesto charged the Rada had lost all legitimacy and right to rule. Therefore, the government of the Ukrainian People's Republic was henceforth the People's Secretariat appointed by the Central Executive Committee of the Councils of Ukraine. On its accession to power, the Manifesto went on, the spectre of a bloody war between Russia and Ukraine faded away, so that the Central Executive Committee considered its first responsibility was to reassure the Council of People's Commissars of Soviet Russia 'that there can be no war between Ukraine and Russia, that the Tsentral'na Rada wanted this war, not the working masses'.[72]

Work in the People's Secretariat preoccupied the entire Ukrainian Bolshevik leadership with the exception of Artem. The Secretariat's decisions were now taken to be decisions of the Ukrainian party committee, the Main Committee of the Social Democracy of Ukraine, established in Kyiv on 5 December. The party committee met only twice during the period from December 1917 to the Austro-German occupation in April 1918. The Kharkiv Bolsheviks continued to obstruct and sabotage the work of their comrades on the People's Secretariat. Their two members on the CEC did not attend its meetings but continued to demand four places on it. The CEC was given no premises of its own and so it had to hold its meetings at night in the building occupied by the Kharkiv Council of Workers' and Soldiers' Deputies and then later in the Kharkiv city Duma, which at the time was controlled by the Mensheviks. When it was allowed back into the workers' council's rooms it had to meet late at night after other party

---

[72] S. Sh., 'Iz istorii Sovvlasti na Ukraine', *Litopys Revoliutsii*, 4 (1924), pp. 176–9.

meetings were finished. Bosh recalls that it was here, on a window sill in the corridor, that the new government composed its first Manifesto to the Ukrainian people. Finally, on 17 January a unit of Red Guards secured the offices of the bourgeois newspaper *Yuzhnyi Krai* for the People's Secretariat and the CEC. They now had a place to meet as well as a printing press to issue their newsletter. The Kharkiv Bolshevik executive committee had refused them access to its own press. The printers agreed to work for the Secretariat even though the owners of *Yuzhnyi Krai* did not spare funds trying to persuade them to go on strike. The Kharkiv party committee was so outraged that the new government had acquired premises and a press without its permission that it called out CEC representatives to appear before it. The standoff was resolved only partially after the Russian Bolshevik Central Committee sent Sergo Ordzhonikidze to impose a settlement. The Kharkiv leaders now began a concealed boycott.[73]

Visiting Petrograd in January, Artem did not hide his determination to do away with this Ukrainian Bolshevik government altogether. Zatonsky recalled his appearance before the Central Committee, when he characterised the very idea of Ukraine as 'a reactionary undertaking'.

> The workers of the Donbas and the urban industrial areas on the whole are not Ukrainians. The peasants understand very little about these things. If on the Right Bank with Kyiv at its head there are some Ukrainians, then good for them. Let them do what they want. But here in the southern industrial region we simply have to organise a soviet power which is subordinated directly to Petrograd and not to dream up some kind of Ukraine.[74]

Undermined by their own comrades, the People's Secretariat and the CEC was a lame government, 'a centre without a periphery, a general staff without an army, having neither territory nor popular support nor military power'.[75] Lapchynsky recalled an angry Shakhrai:

> Shakhrai believed the People's Secretariat's bid to compete with the Rada's General Secretariat was the wrong strategy that would find little popular understanding or support. The Russian workers and urban middle classes saw no point in the Bolsheviks creating a government for Ukraine, while the Ukrainians who had welcomed the Rada's declaration

---

73   Bosh, *God bor'by*, p. 99.
74   Zdorov, *Ukrains'kyi Zhovten'*, p. 175.
75   S. Sh., 'Iz istorii Sovvlasti na Ukraine', p. 174.

of the Republic looked upon it with suspicion. The least organised Ukrainian workers continued to stay on the sidelines. The mounting hostilities between Kyiv and Kharkiv caused confusion and demotivation on both sides, leading people to withdraw altogether into their private lives.

Bosh and Shakhrai remained locked in dispute. Bosh insisted that opposition to the People's Secretariat came overwhelmingly from party leaders and functionaries and not from rank and file workers. She said the new government would gain understanding and support as long as it was given a chance to present its case, as its members did in the week immediately following the Kharkiv congress at meetings of railway workers, postal and telegraph employees and the Kharkiv Council of Workers' and Soldiers' Deputies. When Bosh tried to deliver a report about the decisions of the Kharkiv congress to a city-wide meeting of the Bolshevik organisation the chairman told her to limit herself to a statement lasting no more than five minutes. However, party members protested from the floor and demanded she be given enough time to make a full report. The meeting heard her out and voted unanimously to give full support to the new government. All members of the presidium abstained from the vote.[76]

The Rada's leaders questioned the very motives for the establishment of a competing Ukrainian government. Vynnychenko claimed 'the Kharkiv government got all its decrees from Petrograd and conducted its military operations using the forces of the Russian government'. It was a godsend to Petrograd, allowing it to claim the conflict in Ukraine was an internal matter, one in which it was not involved.[77] Ivan Maistrenko, a member of the UPSR, argued that the main reason for this government's formation was to legitimise a Russian military offensive against the Rada.[78]

There were deep disagreements among the Bolsheviks over the form that state power should assume, whether a nationally representative body of local councils was necessary or even desirable, or 'historically progressive' as they put it. Moreover, among those who did support the new government established at the Kharkiv congress there was a tension between those who supported it on the basis of the principle of national self-determination and those who saw it as an expedient way to win over the peasantry, to combat the Rada and take the power from it. Yet the fact that the Kharkiv Congress chose to fight the Rada in the name of the same Ukrainian People's Republic already signified

---

76   Bosh, *God bor'by*, p. 104.
77   Vynnychenko, *Vidrodzhennia nNatsii*, Vol. 2, p. 171.
78   Ivan Maistrenko, *Storinky z Istorii Komunistychnoi Partii Ukrainy. Chastyna persha* (New York: Prolog, 1967), pp. 41–2.

a considerable shift in the Bolsheviks' estimation of the national question in the revolutionary process. For as Mazlakh and Shakhrai wrote in 1919 in *Do Khvyli*, their polemic with Lenin, 'both the Tsentral'na Rada and the Central Executive Committee of the Councils, the two most authoritative institutions in Ukraine, were compelled by the facts, by events, the logic of the real revolutionary national liberation movement in Ukraine to come to the position of independence'.[79] By December 1917 a growing number of Bolsheviks were realising that a revolutionary government in Ukraine was not possible without an alliance between the workers and peasants or without confronting the national question as an integral part of their struggle for emancipation.

7 Civil War and the First Foreign Intervention

The General Secretariat publicly rejected the CPC's December 4 ultimatum, but it was deeply affected by its implicit threat of war. A dispute erupted between Vynnychenko and Petliura over the Rada's strategy which polarised the General Secretariat and the *mala rada*. Petliura opposed soldiers' councils and the election of officers by the ranks. He wanted to retain or restore the traditional hierarchical command structure and to employ experienced officers from the Russian army. There were many of them in Kyiv out of work. In November he started to recruit to a new Serdiuk regiment in which soldiers' committees were prohibited. Petliura also stood firm in support of an autonomous Ukrainian republic within a federated Russia and resisted the drift towards a separate peace with the Central Powers. In December he assured French representatives of his continued commitment to these goals, which were aligned with the Entente's efforts to keep Russia in the War. Moreover, he was counting on the Entente to help the Rada assemble and equip an army capable of fighting on two fronts, against German and Austrian forces on the Southwestern front and against Soviet Russian forces moving into Ukraine from the northeast. Petliura regarded Kaledin as an ally and conducted secret negotiations with him to bring Ukrainian regiments back from the Don region and the Southwestern front and to fight jointly with the cossacks against the Bolsheviks. In exchange he permitted the passage of cossack troop convoys from the Southwestern front through Poltava and Lozova down into the Don.[80]

---

[79] Mazlakh and Shakhrai, *On the Current Situation*, p. 54.
[80] Viktor Savchenko, *Symon Petliura*, pp. 121–5; Zdorov, *Ukrains'kyi Zhovten'*, p. 94.

Vynnychenko opposed Petliura on all these issues. He wanted to dismantle the Russian army altogether and replace it with a 'democratic worker-peasant army'. He conducted a campaign against Petliura's Serdiuk regiment and denounced his wider plan for a Ukrainian army under hierarchical command. He demanded that cossack troops stationed in Ukraine or trying to cross its territory be disarmed. He wanted to resolve the Rada's conflict with the CPC and to include it in a united socialist government on condition it withdrew its forces from Ukraine. Vynnychenko accused Petliura of inflaming the Rada's relations with the CPC and bringing them to the brink of war. Petliura had become a magnet for the UPSF, the Mensheviks, Bund and Russian SRs who refused to recognise the CPC as the government of Russia or to sue for a separate peace. Vynnychenko, on the other hand, drew closer to the left wings of the UPSR and USDWP. He saw Petliura as the main challenger to his authority in the Rada, a man who actively promoted a public image of himself as the decisive military leader in contrast to Vynnychenko, the vacillating playwright-turned-politician. Vynnychenko feared that, with a well-equipped and disciplined army under his command, Petliura could become Bonaparte and usurp the power of the Rada itself. Should he make an alliance with General Pavlo Skoropadsky, who commanded the First Ukrainian Division and was the elected leader of the paramilitary Free Cossacks, he could bring a force of seventy thousand bayonets into the capital. So Vynnychenko stepped up his campaign to oust Petliura and his closest supporters like Viktor Pavlenko, commander of the Kyiv military district.

The CPC viewed Petliura as the main culprit for its conflict with the Rada. It held him responsible for driving it over to Kaledin's side and trying to wreck the CPC's efforts to establish a ceasefire with the Central Powers. Petliura and Krylenko continued to spar with threatening telegrams to each other. When on 5 December the CPC accused the Rada of being in a state of war against it, it outlawed General Shcherbakov, the Rada appointed commander of the Ukrainian (Southwestern and Romanian) military front. General Dukhonin had been outlawed in November and he was killed soon afterwards. On 10 December Petliura received a copy of a telegram sent by Krylenko to the CPC delegation at Brest Litovsk that the Germans had intercepted and passed on to the Rada. It read: 'We will soon go after these gentlemen. The ceasefire has been signed to be in place for a whole month, so we can take an entire army and then we will see what such gentlemen as Petliura will do'.[81]

---

81 Viktor Savchenko, *Symon Petliura*, p. 119.

Having broken up Bolshevik-led councils and Military Revolutionary Committees on the Southwestern and Romanian fronts and prevented pro-Bolshevik forces marching from these fronts into Kyiv, Petliura now turned to face the Bolsheviks in Eastern Ukraine. The rival Soviet Ukrainian government was trying to implant itself in Kharkiv. Soviet Russian forces had crossed into territory claimed by the Ukrainian People's Republic. Petliura needed to take control of strategic railway lines and junctions in Eastern Ukraine along which the war would be fought. This was a war of movement rather than of position, involving the transport of relatively small numbers of troops along railway lines deep into enemy territory to seize strategic urban and industrial centres. It was a war without an established front line for population centres that were now full of competing local authorities and armed groups like the Red Guards, Free Cossacks and self-styled partisans acting in their own name.

The General Secretariat dispatched units of the Khmelnytsky and Polubotok regiments to suppress workers' and soldiers' councils that tried to take local government power into their hands. This was done in the name of suppressing the Bolsheviks among them who rejected the Tsentral'na Rada and recognised instead the authority of the CPC. The most violent suppressions took place on the Right Bank, notably in Korosten where seventeen workers were shot and in Uman where two members of the local workers' council, Piontkovsky, its head and a delegate to the Kharkiv Central Executive Committee of the Councils of Ukraine, as well as Baylis, a deputy, were shot dead.[82]

On 9 December the soldiers of the Poltava garrison, Ukrainians in their majority, adopted a vote of no confidence in the Tsentral'na Rada and arrested the garrison commander, Yu. P. Revutsky, a landowner appointed by the Rada. Revutsky in turn called upon Kyiv to send him a unit of the Khmelnytsky regiment. The unit arrived, surrounded and fired upon the Poltava Council of Workers' and Soldiers' Deputies. Its chairman, Drobnis, and several members of the executive committee were arrested and taken to the railway station to be shot. Some of them, including Drobnis, managed to escape but others were killed. Soldiers of the Khmelnytsky regiment looted Jewish businesses and robbed people on the streets. Strikes broke out across the city and the Poltava Council sent a representative to Kharkiv to ask for military assistance from the People's Secretariat.

On 12 December Petliura dispatched more forces to take control of the railway junctions south of Kharkiv at Lozova, Synelnykove, Yasynuvata and Oleksandrivsk (today Zaporizhzhia). The CPC forces under Antonov-Ovsiienko

---

82 Zdorov, *Ukrains'kyi Zhovten'*, p. 212; Bosh, *God bor'by*, pp. 117–18.

engaged Petliura's forces at Lozova, the key junction linking the railway lines of central Left Bank Ukraine with the Donbas and the Don. The battle for Lozova signalled the outbreak of open war between the forces of the CPC and the Rada. Antonov-Ovsiienko's units were at first repelled, but by 17 December they took Lozova and Antonov-Ovsiienko gave the order to his forces to move south towards Katerynoslav, Oleksandrivsk and the Donbas, to link up with the local Red Guards of those towns. Between 18 and 21 December they took Synelnykove, Pavlohrad and Kupiansk.

Petliura wanted to attack the CPC's forces in Kharkiv, believing he could take the city with some 10,000 men. The supply lines between Kyiv and Kharkiv were long and Petliura was having difficulty putting together a disciplined and sufficiently equipped army of this size. Moreover, the General Secretariat was divided over whether to make war on the CPC, to seek peace or to start isolating Ukraine from Russia by tearing up the railway lines. At its 15 December meeting it had to acknowledge that it was completely unprepared to fight a war with the CPC. Petliura, however, remained determined to attack its forces in Eastern Ukraine. He was hoping the Entente would help him by lending a Czechoslovak division standing outside Kyiv which at the time was obeying the French military command. The French command, however, would not permit the Czechoslovak division to support the Rada against the Bolsheviks inside Ukraine itself, but only to stand with it on the front against the Central Powers.

The straw that broke the camel's back was Petliura's attempt to introduce into the statute of the army of the Ukrainian People's Republic the requirement that all officers be appointed by its supreme command, in effect by Petliura. This requirement had been rejected explicitly by the All-Ukrainian Council of Soldiers' Deputies, a decision the General Secretariat was obliged to uphold. Vynnychenko seized on Petliura's defiance and persuaded his fellow secretaries to press for his dismissal. On 18 December Petliura was relieved of his duties, dismissed from the General Secretariat and replaced by Mykola Porsh, until then Secretary for Labour. The Serdiuk regiment was broken up into ordinary infantry detachments and soldiers' councils were re-instated. This deprived Petliura of a base of armed support should he attempt to challenge his dismissal.[83]

Vynnychenko's victory over Petliura gave him the upper hand in resetting the General Secretariat's strategy and reorganising its army, mending its relations with the CPC and ending Ukraine's involvement in the War. Yet while he was in a stronger position now with respect to the right-wing forces that

---

83   Savchenko, *Symon Petliura*, pp. 128–34.

coalesced around Petliura he faced ever growing pressure on his left flank from the Ukrainian Socialist Revolutionaries. They were demanding immediately a declaration of Ukraine's independence, peace with the CPC and the conclusion of peace with the Central Powers.

Porsh proved ineffective, if not incompetent, in his role as the new Secretary for Military Affairs. Reorganising the Ukrainised regiments of the old army into a worker-peasant militia would be difficult enough in times of peace. It would be suicidal in the midst of ongoing hostilities. It required abolishing the hierarchy of command and accepting only those former officers who were vetted by the socialist parties and elected by the ranks. On 21 December the Rada adopted a law establishing a popular militia. The following day Porsh gave the order to demobilise the Ukrainised units of the Russian army. On 24 December General Skoropadsky resigned his command of the First Ukrainian Division and handed it over to General Handziuk. However, Porsh took no other decisions about the defence of the Republic from the time of his appointment until early January. He did not have military training or experience or up-to-date information from the fronts. Russian forces were advancing across Right and Left Bank Ukraine to link up with rebellions by local Red Guards while Porsh anguished that the Rada's forces were falling apart as they came up against them.[84]

Even as the hostilities mounted between the Rada on the one side and the CPC, the rival Kharkiv government and the Red Guards on the other, efforts were still being made to resolve their differences peacefully. The first such effort came from the Ukrainian Military Revolutionary Committee (UMRC) of the Petrograd Soviet, which represented some twenty-two thousand sailors of the Baltic Fleet and soldiers stationed in the Russian capital. On 6 December the UMRC sent a letter to Lenin calling for a peaceful resolution of the CPC's conflict with the Rada and the transfer of all Ukrainian sailors to the Black Sea Fleet and Ukrainian soldiers in Petrograd to Ukraine. The CPC ordered the arrest of the members of the UMRC but then released them on 8 December.[85]

At the same time the Second All-Russian Congress of Peasants' Deputies that was meeting in Petrograd, acting on the request of its Ukrainian deputies, made its own intervention into the conflict. Emissaries from the Congress informed the General Secretariat that their main grievance with the Rada was its refusal to stop backing Kaledin's revolt. The Military Council of the Congress had decided to intervene on the fronts, to halt the Ukrainisation of the

---

[84] Savchenko, *Symon Petliura*, pp. 138–41; *12 viin za Ukrainu*, pp. 29–30.

[85] Stephen Velychenko, *Painting Imperialism and Nationalism Red: The Ukrainian Marxist Critique of Russian Communist Rule in Ukraine 1918–1925* (Toronto: University of Toronto Press, 2015), p. 57.

armed forces where it was taking place and to offer Ukrainian soldiers and sailors a choice: either they closed ranks with Russian soldiers and sailors against Kaledin or they laid down their arms. In other words, the All-Russian Congress of Peasants' Deputies went over the heads of the General Secretariat and appealed directly to its armed forces, to the only people who could actually implement the General Secretariat's military strategy with respect to Kaledin.[86]

The Congress also dispatched a delegation led by the Russian SR Prosha Proshian for mediation talks in Kyiv with Vynnychenko, Porsh and Hrushevsky. The delegation kept the CPC informed of these talks while the CPC agreed to hold Antonov-Ovsiienko back from marching on Kyiv, though his forces did engage the Rada's in Eastern Ukraine. The People's Secretariat of the rival Kharkiv government also held back from declaring war on the Rada, though not 'a merciless struggle' with it.

The mediation talks in Kyiv appeared to make a breakthrough after Petliura's dismissal as Secretary of Military Affairs. Proshian reported back to the CPC on 19 December and two days later the General Secretariat and the CPC both issued statements that preliminary agreement had been reached to start direct negotiations. The CPC issued its own resolution on the matter which defined the terms of the agreement as follows:

> Because the official representatives of the Tsentral'na Rada have expressed a desire to begin negotiations for the purpose of reaching agreement with the Council of People's Commissars, which from its side recognises the independence of the Ukrainian Republic;
>
> Further, that the Tsentral'na Rada acknowledges the counterrevolutionary character of Kaledin and his accomplices ... that the Council of People's Commissars everywhere and absolutely recognises the right of all nations, including the Ukrainian, to their state independence ... because it welcomes every effort to avert war with the Tsentral'na Rada if it did recognise the counterrevolutionary character of Kaledin's activity and did not prevent the prosecution of war against him ...
>
> The Council of People's Commissars considers it most desirable to enter into talks with the Tsentral'na Rada on these unresolved matters in order to remove all misunderstandings that flow from the politics of the Rada with respect to the general front and the anti-revolutionary uprising by Kaledin.

---

86   Zdorov, *Ukrains'kyi Zhovten'*, p. 92.

The Council of People's Commissars proposes to the Tsentral'na Rada talks towards an agreement which would meet the expressed conditions and considers the most suitable place for such talks to be Smolensk or Vitebsk.[87]

Three days later on 24 December Vynnychenko and Shulhyn, Secretary of Foreign Affairs, informed the CPC they were prepared to start talks on condition the Bolsheviks stopped their military advance through Ukraine, did not interfere in its internal affairs and recognised the Ukrainian People's Republic's sovereign right to decide its own relations with the government of the Don. They got no reply. The Kyiv Regional Council of Soldiers' Deputies stepped in to mediate but made no headway. Meanwhile, the Rada was rapidly losing control of towns and cities in the eastern provinces to local Red Guards and Antonov-Ovsiienko's forces. Porsh now backed away from the idea of negotiations with the CPC, claiming incredulously that they were unnecessary because by January 1918, 100,000 Ukrainian soldiers would return from the fronts and defeat the CPC's forces in Ukraine. The General Secretariat fell silent, without a political strategy or diplomatic avenue or the military force to control the territory it claimed for the Republic. The CPC sent another note to the Rada on 30 December; it went unanswered.[88]

Petliura was not deterred by his ouster from the General Secretariat. Within a few days he began organising an armed force of his own, called the Haidamak Camp of Slobidska Ukraine (*Haidamatskyi Kish Slobidskoyi Ukrainy*). Some officers of the UPR general staff resigned their posts and joined him. He received secret funding from the French mission in Kyiv. The Haidamak Camp was well equipped, but Petliura still lacked sufficient soldiers. The initial recruitment drive attracted some 180 volunteers; another 150 cadets from a Kyiv officer school joined in early January. Petliura's aim was still to take the fight to the Bolsheviks in Eastern Ukraine. Within a couple of weeks, however, his mission would change to defending Kyiv from their advance on it.

The Haidamak Camp was implicated in the abduction and murder of Leonid Piatakov, head of the MRC of the Kyiv Council of Workers' and Soldiers' Deputies. On 30 November Petiura ordered the arrest of Piatakov after he threatened military retaliation if the Rada did not remove soldiers from the capital that were hostile to the councils. But he was then quickly released along with other

---

87   Lenin, *Collected Works*, Vol. 26, pp. 398–9; Khrystiuk, *Ukrains'ka Revoliutsiia*, Vol. 2, p. 90; Zdorov, *Ukrains'kyi Zhovten'*, pp. 93–4.
88   Doroshenko, *Istoriia Ukrainy*, Vol. 1, p. 258; Savchenko, *12 viin za Ukrainu*, pp. 25, 29.

leading Kyiv Bolsheviks on the orders of the General Secretariat and they continued to agitate against the Rada. Piatakov was popular among the soldiers in Kyiv. He was elected to the All-Russian Constituent Assembly and to the Central Executive Committee of the Councils of Ukraine. He was still politically active in Kyiv when on 25 December a unit of Ukrainian soldiers wearing the distinctive head gear of the Haidamak Camp, a Caucasian fur cap with a red tail, burst into his home and arrested him together with his two brothers. His brothers were subsequently released, one of them, Mykola, having been severely beaten. But Leonid Piatakov disappeared without a trace. His abduction provoked widespread concern and aroused suspicion that Petliura was responsible. The General Secretariat denied all knowledge or involvement in the abduction and set up its own commission to investigate. It concluded that Haidamak soldiers or other soldiers wearing their uniform were responsible for Piatakov's abduction. Petliura's involvement was not established. On 16 January 2018 Piatakov's body, bearing signs of brutal torture, was found several versts outside Kyiv. If his murder had been meant to intimidate the Bolsheviks, it backfired and gave the Bolsheviks ammunition against the Rada, especially among the troops in the capital.[89]

From 17 December, when they defeated Rada forces at Lozova, Antonov-Ovsiienko's expeditionary force moved south. Its mission was to take control of the Left Bank provinces of Kharkiv, Katerynoslav and Kherson, to push Rada forces out of Poltava, sever its lines of communication with the Don and march against Kaledin's forces in the Donbas. Along the way Antonov-Ovsiienko armed the local Red Guards and joined them to fight for control of urban centres against the Rada's troops. Luhansk and Mariupol fell to them on 27 December, Kharkiv on 28 December, Katerynoslav on 29 December, Oleksandrivsk on 2 January and Poltava on 6 January.

Another Russian expeditionary force departed from Homel in Belarus heading south to Bakhmach, situated on the Chernihiv railway line to Kyiv. The south of Ukraine constituted still another theatre of erupting war, initially involving only local Red Guards and Rada forces. They fought twice over Odesa, first on 16 December and again on 15–17 January. The Bolsheviks took control of Mariupol on January 12, Mykolaiv on January 14 and Kherson on January 19. On the Crimean peninsula the dock workers and sailors of the Black Sea Fleet went over to the Bolsheviks, who took Sevastopol on 16 December, and by 2 January Feodosia, Kerch, Yalta, Yevpatoria and Simferopol.

---

89 Vynnychenko, *Vidrodzhennia Natsii*, Vol. 2, p. 155; Soldatenko, *Ukraina v revoliutsiynu dobu*, Vol. 1, pp. 1020–7; Savchenko, *12 viin za Ukrainu*, 30; *Symon Petliura*, pp. 141–2.

In Right Bank Ukraine, pro-Bolshevik units of the Second Guards Corps marched off the Southwestern front and tried to advance from Zhmerynka onto Kyiv. On 16 December the soldiers' councils of three armies on the Southwestern front rejected Petliura's authority and resolved to obey Krylenko, the CPC's commander. By mid-January 1918 the Bolsheviks controlled all of Kharkiv and Katerynoslav and parts of Poltava, Chernihiv, Kherson and Northern Tavria provinces. The Rada fully held onto Kyiv and Volyn and parts of adjacent provinces.

How did the Bolsheviks manage to take control of so many population centres? There were three contributing factors: the strength of local Bolshevik, anarchist and other left-wing forces; the added weight on their side of the incoming forces from Russia; and the collapse of morale among the Rada's forces.

Throughout December power in Kharkiv was shared uneasily between the Rada, Antonov-Ovsiienko and the MRC of the Kharkiv Council of Workers' and Soldiers' Deputies. The People's Secretariat had no military forces of its own until the night of 27 December when Shakhrai, by the power of his oratory, managed to win the third battalion of the Second Ukrainian Reserve Regiment over to the side of the People's Secretariat. Assisted by an armoured car provided by Antonov-Ovsiienko's forces, the third battalion then disarmed the whole regiment. The soldiers were given the choice to return home or join a new formation called the Red Cossacks. Three hundred out of the regiment's 2,700 soldiers joined. It became the first armed unit of the Kharkiv Soviet government, under the command of Vitali Prymakov. He was charged with turning the detachment into a fully fledged regiment, but this task proved impossible owing to the lack of time and weapons. On 29 December the Red Cossacks, Kharkiv's Red Guards and some Russian units, all of them acting under the command of Antonov-Ovsiienko's deputy Mikhail Muraviov, left for Poltava, some 150 kilometres to the southeast. The advance went smoothly and the original combined force of 600 grew considerably with the influx of new recruits along the way. Agitation by the Rada that Russian forces were advancing on Poltava backfired, alarming its own soldiers and leading them to retreat and disperse.[90] Muraviov took Poltava on 5 and 6 January.

The demobilisation of the Second Reserve Regiment in Kharkiv tipped the balance firmly in favour of the Bolsheviks, who then consolidated their control over the city. They suppressed the USDWP and UPSR as 'counterrevolutionary organisations'. The latter parties made four attempts in January and early Feb-

---

90   Bosh, *God bo'rby*, p. 127.

ruary to issue a joint newspaper, which the Bolsheviks confiscated each time, arresting their editors and distributors.

The dual power situation that prevailed in other cities shifted to the Bolsheviks' advantage when Antonov-Ovsiienko's forces advanced through the eastern provinces. Bosh received reports on 27 December of the hasty assembly of Red Guard units in Kryvyi Rih, Katerynoslav and other centres. A Bureau of the Revolutionary Military Committee was set up for the Donbas which gave factory and mine committees the responsibility to recruit ten workers from each enterprise to the Red Guards. The recruits were sent directly to assembly points to be outfitted, armed and despatched to their fighting positions. The time for these preparations was very short in localities where the Red Guards and Bolshevik-led workers' councils had been dispersed only weeks earlier either by Rada or Don Cossack forces.

The Briansk factory workers launched the uprising in Katerynoslav on 28 December. On one side there were 3,500 local Red Guards, on the other 1,500 Rada soldiers and a USDWP militia. Another 1,500 Red Guards from Moscow and Kharkiv arrived on the same day with an armoured train under Yegorov's command and joined the battle for the city centre and the main railway junction. The Rada's forces surrendered on the following day. Their defeat in Katerynoslav marked the beginning of their collapse across the south.

Antonov's intention was to hold Katerynoslav and prevent the further movement of Don Cossacks from the front. He planned to advance from here into the southern Donbas and destroy Kaledin's base of operations.[91] However, on 30 December the Petrograd CPC declared war on the Rada. The Kharkiv People's Secretariat followed suit on 4 January, calling for a general uprising across Ukraine. Two-thirds of the twenty thousand Russian Red Guards who had come into Ukraine continued south into the Donbas to attack Kaledin's forces. The remainder under Muraviov in Poltava, Yegorov in Katerynoslav as well as the new Russian expeditionary force which had crossed from Homel into Chernihiv province turned to advance on Kyiv.[92]

What contribution did the incoming Russian forces make to the defeats suffered by the Rada? The early Soviet Ukrainian historian M.M. Popov wrote that

> in the big proletarian centres of Eastern Ukraine such as Kharkiv and Katerynoslav the local Bolsheviks were neither strong enough nor de-

---

91 Savchenko, *12 viin za Ukrainu*, pp. 27–8; Bosh, *God bor'by*, p. 126.
92 Soldatenko, *Ukraina v revoliutsiiunu dobu*, Vol. 1, pp. 688–9.

termined enough ... to take power into their own hands. In Kharkiv and Katerynoslav they did that with the energetic participation and direct involvement of military units ... that came from the north, mainly units from the districts of Petrograd and Moscow ... It was precisely these units that enabled the rule of councils in Kharkiv.[93]

Estimates vary with respect to the numbers of fighters involved in these battles in December 1917 and the beginning of 1918. Valerii Soldatenko estimates approximately 150,000 on the Bolshevik side: 120,000 Red Guards, of whom 20,000 came from Russia; 32,000 soldiers from Russia, among whom there was a significant number of Ukrainians; and 6,000 to 7,000 local soldiers and workers who joined the Red Cossacks. Savchenko estimates the Bolsheviks could count on around 100,000 armed men in December 1917, including 40,000 Red Guards, half of them in Katerynoslav province, and 50–60,000 soldiers in the old army divisions garrisoned in the cities and coming off the fronts.[94]

There is little doubt that the collapse of morale in the Ukrainised regiments played a critical part in the outcome of the fighting across Eastern and Southern Ukraine in December and then in the fall of Kyiv itself in January 1918. The General Secretariat itself acknowledged on 15 December that it could rely on no more than 15,000 loyal troops. Vynnychenko and Porsh's attempt in the midst of the mounting hostilities to turn the Ukrainised regiments into popular militia was a major blunder that further undermined the Rada's defensive capacity. In the end, however, the war between the Rada and the Bolsheviks was decided not by the numbers of fighters alone nor by any technical advantages in arms, but by the willingness of men and women to fight and to die for their government. It was no longer a matter simply of raising their hands and voting for it. The Rada's erstwhile supporters were frustrated and demoralised by its failure to act decisively on land reform, to sue for peace or to break with Kaledin. They no longer knew whether they should be supporting the Bolsheviks or fighting them. A whole number of regiments voluntarily disarmed and declared their neutrality when they were confronted by the choice. Likewise, the peasantry by and large retreated to a neutral position. Dmytro Doroshenko, the conservative politician and historian, was impressed by the fervent support given by urban youth, especially Jewish youth, to the Bolsheviks when they approached their towns or cities. On the opposing side he witnessed dejection and depression,

---

93   M. Popov, *Narys Istorii Komunistychnoi partii (bil'shovykiv) Ukrainy*, 1928, p. 135.
94   Soldatenko, *Ukraina v revoliutsiinu dobu*, Vol. 1, pp. 1040–1; Savchenko, *Symon Petliura*, p. 134; Savchenko, *12 viin za Ukrainu*, p. 20.

an inability on the part of the Rada to mobilise practically any support from the working class. He was particularly bitter about its armed forces:

> The government had no armed forces. The Ukrainian army, all those numerous 'Ukrainised' regiments, divisions and corps, they melted like snow quicker than having been Ukrainised. The enthusiasm of the summer of 1917 disappeared without a trace until there was nothing left of those 'millions of bayonets' so proudly talked about. All those regiments ... that were born of the revolution, well, they no longer have a name nor even a number. They were simply some incidental gatherings of people who dissolved as soon as they reached Ukrainian territory because their slogan was 'Homeward bound!' That was how the Ukrainian regiment which came from Moscow broke up, the one which came 'to give glory to Ukraine's liberation' but managed to stay together for just one parade. That's how the Shevchenko regiment disappeared, the one which had been formed from the units of the Guards Reserve in Petersburg in the face of the Bolsheviks' opposition, which the Bolsheviks later armed and sent into Ukraine with the slogan: 'Bring the bourgeois Tsentral'na Rada to order' ... The old Russian army was falling apart and everything that issued from its body, all those Ukrainian units, turned out to be stillborn and useless for military action. They proved unable to organise a new Ukrainian army in time, dreaming as they did about some special democratic army, a 'popular militia'. It turned out that the Tsentral'na Rada didn't have anyone to turn to at the critical moment. In haste they started forming volunteer units, hiring an army of mercenaries ... Kharkiv, Poltava, Katerynoslav, Odesa and Chernihiv fell into Bolshevik hands, and now the Bolsheviks from the north and northeast were advancing on Kyiv.[95]

---

95 Doroshenko, *Istoriia Ukrainy*, Vol. 1, pp. 257–8.

CHAPTER 7

The First Treaty of Brest Litovsk

The Soviet Russian government agreed an armistice with the Central Powers on 3 December in the fortress outside Brest Litovsk, which at the time served as the headquarters of the Central Powers' military command on their Eastern front. Here, a week later, the two sides entered into peace negotiations. The principals involved in the first round included General Max Hoffmann, chief of staff of the Central Powers' forces on the Eastern Front; Richard von Kulhlman, the German foreign minister; Count Ottokar Chernin, foreign minister of Austria-Hungary; the grand vizier of the Ottoman Empire Talat Pasha and his foreign minister Nassimy Bey; from Bulgaria Prime Minister Vasyl Radoslavov and minister of justice Popoff. The Soviet Russian delegation was led by Adolph Joffe, who had negotiated the armistice on his government's behalf. It included his fellow Bolshevik Lev Kamenev, the Tsarist-era General Aleksandr Samoilo and the Marxist historian Mikhail Pokrovsky.

At the outset of negotiations Joffe set out Soviet Russia's conditions for concluding a peace: that there be no annexations, that is no seizure of foreign territory or the forcible annexation of foreign nationalities; the withdrawal of foreign troops from occupied territories; the restoration of the state independence of peoples who had lost it during the war; that nationalities living within existing states have the right to decide by referenda whether to remain in them, to join other states or to form new independent states of their own; the protection of the rights of national minorities; a peace without indemnities or war reparations; and that all of the conditions set out above apply to overseas colonies of the warring states as well as to their mainland territories.

In response, the German side declared itself in agreement with all of these conditions, much to the relief of the Russian side whose state was, after all, the one now threatened with foreign occupation and annexation. That relief, however, dissipated when General Hoffmann explained to Joffe that the Central Powers understood the principle of national self-determination to mean in practice

> allowing the voluntary secession of certain areas from Russia, to wit Poland, Lithuania and Courland [today Western Latvia] ... Livonia [today Northern Latvia and Southern Estonia] and Estonia. Hoffmann reported that Joffe was absolutely stunned by this revelation and burst into protests, while Kamenev raged and Pokrovsky asked in tears 'How can

one talk of a peace of understanding when you are tearing away nearly eighteen districts from Russia?'[1]

The Germans had no intention of permitting any popular referenda in these parts of the old Russian state it now occupied. Rather, they were relying on the German colonial minorities living there to demand separation from Russia and to establish client principalities of the German state guaranteed by Germany's continued military occupation. Germany's representatives utilised the language of national self-determination in the peace negotiations to keep pursuing its war aims against Russia. The Russian delegation at Brest Litovsk could not continue negotiating on such terms and requested an adjournment to consult with its government.

On 21 November the Tsentral'na Rada dispatched Mykola Liubynsky (UPSR) to Brest Litovsk to monitor them but not to take part in the actual negotiations for an armistice. There he was admitted to the Soviet Russian delegation, which allowed him to attend the talks as an observer. He remained into the first round of the peace negotiations and then he returned to Kyiv in mid-December to report what he had learned.

By this time the General Secretariat could see that its attempts to promote an alternative federated republic that could sue for peace with all the warring states on behalf of the UPR were getting nowhere. The impasse forced the Rada's hand. On 11 December the General Secretariat issued a declaration to all the warring parties protesting the conclusion of the armistice at Brest Litovsk without its participation, insisting that only the UPR, and not the CPC, could do so for the Ukrainian military front, and that until such time as a federated Russian republic was established only its prospective constituent parts held the right to conduct peace talks on behalf of their population and territory.

> The Ukrainian General Secretariat holds firmly to the principle of a general, common law peace and demands that its adoption be speeded up. Recognising the great efforts made by all sides to realise such a peace the General Secretariat considers it necessary for its representatives to take part in the negotiations at Brest Litovsk. At the same time it desires that the matter of peace be concluded at an international congress to which the Ukrainian government invites all the warring states.[2]

---

1 Fischer, *Germany's Aims in the First World War*, pp. 489–90.
2 Khrystiuk, *Ukrains'ka Revoliutsiia*, Vol. 2, p. 95.

The Central Powers responded to the General Secretariat's declaration on 13 December by inviting the UPR to the talks. The Entente continued to press on Vynnychenko and Petliura to stay in the War on its side and to refuse to take part in separate peace talks with the Central Powers. The French and the British upgraded the status of General Tabuis and Picton Bagge, their representatives in Kyiv, to the rank of diplomats. They dangled official recognition and material support from France, Britain and the USA before the Rada leaders. They were playing on Vynnychenko's frustration with the CPC and Petliura's preparedness to go to war against it.[3]

The Eighth session of the *mala rada* convened on 12 December to discuss the peace question. There was disquiet among its delegates that members of the General Secretariat, notably Vynnychenko, Shulhyn and Petliura, were involved in secret talks with the Entente even as they proposed entering the Brest Litovsk negotiations.[4] The disagreements that appeared at the previous discussion on this issue in the *mala rada* on 21 November resurfaced. The Russian SRs, Mensheviks and the Bund remained opposed to Ukraine, as well as Russia, taking part in separate talks. Zolotariov wrote in the 13 December issue of *Folkszeitung*, the Bund newspaper, that if the Rada signed a separate peace and exited unilaterally from the War that would end the co-operation between the Ukrainian and non-Ukrainian democracies. He argued that Ukraine was too weak economically and militarily to secure its independence against the Central Powers. It could only mean Ukraine would exit the Russian revolution and place itself under the protection of the Central Powers.[5] The UPSF also continued to oppose a separate peace, in the words of their foreign minister Shulhyn: 'we won't allow the Germans and Austrians to throw their regiments against the English, French and others. We stand for a general peace'.[6] But Shulhyn now argued that the Rada should send a delegation to Brest Litovsk to seek peace with Soviet Russia, not with Germany and Austro-Hungary. The UPSF and the USDWP believed that recognition of the Rada as a subject-participant of interstate relations would provide some protection to its sovereignty and territorial integrity. Vynnychenko continued to hedge his bets, saying that the General Secretariat was talking to states on both sides of the War, but not disclosing the substance of these talks even to the Central Committee of his own party.

It fell to the left wings of the USDWP and UPSR to inject some cold realism and urgency into the debate. They reminded the deputies how deserted the

---

3 Vynnychenko, *Vidrodzhennia Natsii*, Vol. 2, pp. 197–8.
4 Oleksander Sevriuk, *Beresteis'kyi Myr 9 II 1918* (Paris: Les Nouvelles Ukrainiennes, 1927), p. 4.
5 Rafes, *Dva goda*, p. 68.
6 Khrystiuk, *Ukrains'ka Revoliutsiia*, p. 97.

Ukrainian side of the military front had become and how far the talks at Brest Litovsk had progressed. Yevhen Neronovych said, 'The current Russian government – the People's Commissars – have already put the question of peace on an international footing in its full scope, and so to send a delegation to Brest is to engage with international peace'.[7] On 15 December the UPSR fraction put forward a resolution to the *mala rada* that the Rada take part in the talks at Brest Litovsk as an independent state. On the same day Mykola Liubynsky reported on his time as an observer at the talks and supported his party's resolution. The *mala rada* then adopted the resolution and appointed Vsevolod Holubovych, Secretary for Trade and Industry from the UPSR, to lead a delegation there that included Oleksandr Sevriuk, Mykola Liubynsky and Mykhailo Poloz from the UPSR and Mykola Levitsky from the USDWP.

The delegation received no formal instructions from the *mala rada* or the General Secretariat. It was left to Mykhailo Hrushevsky to hold a separate meeting with them. Doroshenko recalls what Hrushevsky told them:

> The delegation was to seek the inclusion in the Ukrainian Republic of all Eastern Galicia, Bukovyna, Transcarpathia, Kholm and Pidliassia [Podlachia], so that not a single scrap of Ukrainian land remained under foreign rule. Hrushevsky showed the delegates in great detail where the border lay across the northeast, taking care to include every little town, every village with a Ukrainian population. If Austro-Hungary did not agree to relinquish the Ukrainian territories it held (which was more than likely!) then Hrushevsky set down the *conditio sine qua non* for carrying on the negotiations: the creation from all the Ukrainian lands of the Austro-Hungarian monarchy of a separate crown land enjoying the widest possible autonomy.[8]

The Rada at that time had no contact with the Ukrainians on the Austro-Hungarian side, which naturally made its delegation's task more difficult. They would try and establish some contact with them on the way to the talks.

Poloz, Sevriuk, Liubynsky and Levitsky left Kyiv for Brest Litovsk on 17 December without Holubovych; he followed a short time later. Sevriuk recalls their arrival at Zbarazh in the Volyn Podillia uplands, where silence reigned across the snow-covered military front. They presented themselves to the Ukrainian soldiers in the trenches and asked for assistance to cross over to the German side.

---

7 Ibid.
8 Doroshenko, *Istoriia Ukrainy*, Vol. 1, p. 296.

> We ask them about troop numbers, the mood among them. Their answers are not encouraging. The army is like snow in the sun, they say. Who knows whether anyone will still be here on the front in a few days' time. As for the mood, well it is ugly. 'Conclude the peace quickly', we hear from all sides 'because otherwise there will be no-one left to do the fighting'.[9]

The soldiers escorted the delegation across the front line. It continued on via Ternopil and Lviv with a German military escort that assiduously shielded it from contact with the local population. From their automobiles 'ruined towns, burnt villages, misery and desolation pass before our eyes'. They arrived at Brest Litovsk on 19 December, the old town completely razed to the ground, its train station burned out, with only the fortress and several buildings left standing on the outskirts. The Rada delegation was quartered in one of these buildings alongside the other delegations.

The talks were still in adjournment when the Rada delegation arrived. Its first challenge, before they resumed, was to seek an understanding with the Russian delegation. Poloz, who represented the left wing of the UPSR, posed it thus: how could they present themselves as a separate delegation that nevertheless stood together with the Russians against the Central Powers? The Ukrainians and Russians held several joint meetings, chaired by Holubovych and Trotsky, the latter having replaced Joffe as head of his delegation. A basis for co-operation was found when the Russians agreed to recognise the Ukrainians as an independent party to the talks and the Tsentral'na Rada as the government of the UPR. Trotsky was to announce it at the start of the next plenary session of the peace talks. However, the Russian side unilaterally changed the agreed statement prior to the session, which gave rise to the first disagreement between the two parties.

The second disagreement concerned the prospect and desirability of concluding peace with the Central Powers at Brest Litovsk. Trotsky did not believe the Germans would resume their offensive because, as he saw it, the German revolution was about to erupt. The Russians would negotiate with the Germans, but only in order to preserve their revolutionary gains and to buy time until the revolution spread westwards. They were ready to sign a peace with the Central Powers, but not one that dictated the loss of so much territory that it threatened the survival of the CPC. That was the view of the majority of the Bolshevik Central Committee at that point in time and it allowed Trotsky to play the long game in the negotiations. The delegation from the CPC did not hide its con-

---

9 Sevriuk, *Beresteis'kyi Myr*, p. 5.

tempt for the governments of Germany and Austro-Hungary nor its readiness to help overthrow them at the first opportunity. Trotsky was appealing to the workers of Europe over the heads of their governments in order to put more pressure on them, hoping to accelerate their downfall. The Russian delegation was also calling for the talks to move to Stockholm where public pressure and exposure would be even greater. All that infuriated their German and Austrian counterparts.

The Ukrainians, on the other hand, believed the war was lost, that they were defeated, and to fail in these talks meant to invite a renewed German offensive. Their wider objectives in the talks differed from the Russians'. They approached Brest Litovsk as a positive opportunity to unite Ukrainian territories, to remove them from the War and to gain international recognition for the UPR as an independent state. For the Russian side the unification of Ukraine was not a pressing issue. They were more concerned about bringing the existing UPR into a federated Russia under the CPC. The prospect of finding common ground was proving difficult enough when Kyiv telegraphed a categorical instruction to its delegation that contact and co-operation with the Russian delegation could continue only on condition that Russia's armies halted their offensive inside Ukraine.[10]

Kuhlman, Hoffmann and Chernin returned from Berlin and Vienna. The Rada delegation met with them on 21 and 22 December and set out its main condition for taking part in the talks: the recognition both of the delegation and the Rada as the government of the Ukrainian People's Republic. Their aim at the talks was the unification of all Ukrainian territories in Russia and Austro-Hungary under the UPR. The territories in question on the Austro-Hungarian side held ethnically mixed populations and were claimed by other national movements or states as well, namely Eastern Galicia by the Polish, Northern Bukovyna by the Romanians and Transcarpathia by the Hungarians. The Rada delegation proposed plebiscites to resolve these claims. With respect to Kholm and Pidliassia, parts of the former Russian Empire settled by Ukrainian peasants and Polish nobility that were now militarily occupied by German and Austro-Hungarian armies, the Rada delegation proposed their direct transfer to the UPR.

The second round of peace talks which began on 27 December included for the first time the four representatives of the Tsentral'na Rada. Their average age was just under 30; for the CPC delegation's five leading members it was 40, for the Central Powers' five it was 50. The Ukrainian and Russian delegations sat

---

10 Sevriuk, *Beresteis'kyi Myr*, p. 6.

together on the inside of tables laid out in a horseshoe 'Π' formation, while the Central Powers faced them from the other side.

Holubovych made an opening statement on behalf of the General Secretariat. Trotsky responded to him, declaring that the CPC recognised the right of the UPR to take part in the peace talks on the basis of the right of nations to self-determination. The Rada delegation was not part of the Russian delegation, he said, nor did the CPC claim to speak on behalf of all the territory of the former Russian Empire.

Holubovych responded to Trotsky, thanking the CPC delegation for recognising the UPR. On 29 December the member states of the Central Powers also formally accepted the Tsentral'na Rada's delegation to the talks as an independent participant. But the Ukrainian delegation considered their main condition for taking part was still not met and it continued to insist that the Central Powers and the CPC recognise them as the representatives of the state of the independent Ukrainian People's Republic governed by the Rada and not merely an independent delegation to the talks. Their insistence yielded a result on 30 December when Chernin, with the agreement of the other states of the Central Powers, recognised the Rada's representatives 'as an independent delegation of plenipotentiaries representing the independent Ukrainian Republic. The formal recognition of the Ukrainian Republic as an independent State by the four Allied Powers is reserved for the peace treaty'.[11]

The Russian delegation, however, continued to limit itself to recognising the Rada delegation's right to take part in the talks, but not the state it represented. Trotsky delivered a lengthy exposition of the actual meaning of the CPC's stance. The CPC recognised that the national self-determination of Ukraine was genuinely taking place through the exercise of democratic freedoms by its workers, soldiers and peasants; they were forming their own representative councils and organs of local self government on the basis of general, equal and secret elections; political life in Ukraine was free, there were no occupation armies there to interfere in it. This endorsement was much appreciated by the Ukrainian delegation. However, Trotsky was still withholding recognition of the Tsentral'na Rada as the government of the Ukrainian People's Republic. Moreover, he was explaining the CPC's position on Ukraine in order to illustrate under what circumstances the CPC would recognise the political authorities of *any* territories of the former Russian Empire as genuinely representative, democratic and self-determining entities. He had in mind, of course, those ter-

---

11   *Proceedings of the Brest Litovsk Peace Conference 21 November 1917–3 March 1918* (Washington: Government Printing Office, 1918), p. 59.

ritories that were militarily occupied by Germany. Their populations did not enjoy democratic self government and they had not been given a chance to choose by plebiscite to which existing or new state they wished to belong. The CPC did not claim to represent them, but nor would it relinquish them into the hands of German occupation to further its war aims against Russia. It would not accept the cynical interpretation of the right to national self-determination that Hoffman had given Joffe in the first round of the peace talks.

Two immediate and related developments led the CPC delegation to backtrack on its acceptance of the Rada delegation to the talks. The first was the start of separate talks on 31 December between the Rada delegation and the Central Powers towards a bilateral peace treaty. The German delegation informed the Russian delegation of them, but they remained private and no transcripts of their proceedings were released. The ongoing multilateral peace negotiations were public and widely reported in the international press. Trotsky protested and called upon the Kharkiv Central Executive Committee of the Councils of Ukraine (CEC) 'to take steps to defend the interests of the Ukrainian People's Republic from the unprincipled, treacherous and covert games of the General Secretariat delegation'.[12] It was at this point that any remaining hope of reconciliation between the CPC and the Tsentral'na Rada was lost and war was declared on the Rada by both the CPC and the Kharkiv CEC.

The second development that caused the CPC delegation to backtrack was the adoption by the rival Kharkiv Ukrainian government of a resolution on 31 December rejecting any peace terms negotiated by the Rada delegation:

> Categorically we declare that any attempts by the Ukrainian Tsentral'na Rada to speak in the name of the Ukrainian people are acts of their own volition by bourgeois groups of the Ukrainian population directed against the will and interests of the labouring classes of Ukraine, and that any undertakings of the Ukrainian Tsentral'na Rada will not be recognised.[13]

The Kharkiv CEC recognised instead the CPC delegation as 'representatives of the federal government of Russia' whose jurisdiction extended to the territory of the UPR. The CEC decided to send as its own representatives to Brest Litovsk: its chairman Yukhym Medvėdev, Vasyl Shakhrai, People's Commissar for Military Affairs, and Volodymyr Zatonsky, People's Commissar for Education. They

---

12 Zdorov, *Ukrains'kyi Zhovten'*, p. 206.
13 I.B. Datskiv, 'Dypolomaty Ukrains'koi Tsentral'noi Rady u protystoianni z bil'shovyts'kymy delehatsiiamy Petrohrada i Kharkova na Berestes'kyi myrnyi konferentsii', *Gileia: zbirnyk naukovykh prats'*, edited by V.M. Vashkevych, no. 20 (Kyiv, 2009), p. 32.

all travelled via Petrograd where they met with Lenin. Zatonsky was persuaded to remain in Petrograd as representative of the Kharkiv government at the CPC. Medvedev and Shakhrai went on, arriving in Brest Litovsk on 8 January where they joined the CPC delegation.

Negotiations between the Austro-Hungarian and Rada delegations revolved around two issues: the UPR's claim on the Ukrainian territories held by Austro-Hungary and the latter's desperate need for Ukrainian grain and sugar. Chernin believed his side had the upper hand. His state was part of the winning coalition in the war and he regarded the Rada as part of the vanquished side. On 1 January Chernin clarified his government's position with regard to Ukrainian territories under Austro-Hungary, which amounted to a negation of the principle of national self-determination. He insisted there could be no discussion at the talks about the internal affairs of the Austro-Hungarian monarchy, no consideration of plebiscites or any other proposals concerning the administration of its territories and nations. He called upon the Ukrainians to recognise the 1914 border between Russia and Austro-Hungary as the UPR's border. Chernin was supported by Kuhlmann and Hoffman.

The Rada delegation, however, would not accept Chernin's position nor withdraw their own proposal. They knew how unstable his government was in Vienna with the growing unrest there, how much it needed to secure a peace treaty in order to restore order at home and to get food from abroad to feed its starving urban population. These facts weighed in their favour against Chernin's recourse to the fact of imperial possession and so they held out.

General Hoffman stepped in to propose a compromise. Insofar as the German and Austro-Hungarian armies were occupying Kholm and Pidliassia, Hoffman offered to secure these territories for the Ukrainian People's Republic against the Polish claims to them, which Chernin favoured, as long as the Rada delegation dropped its demand for plebiscites in Eastern Galicia, Northern Bukovyna and Transcarpathia.[14] Furthermore, the German side proposed that the Tsentral'na Rada in Kyiv formally declare its independence from Russia before proceeding to sign a peace treaty with the Central Powers. The Rada delegation felt it should consult its government on both these proposals and so asked for the talks to be adjourned. The talks had reached a point where all sides needed to return to their governments for further instructions. They were adjourned on 5 January, resuming again on 17 January.

During the pause the Rada in Kyiv faced a growing challenge from both its domestic and Russian opponents. Muraviov's army started its march on Kyiv

---

14   Sevriuk, *Beresteis'kyi Myr*, p. 9.

on 6 January. It was supported by local pro-Bolshevik urban councils and Red Guards. It advanced largely unopposed by the Rada's demoralised and disintegrating regiments. Simultaneously, the Bolsheviks organised an armed uprising inside Kyiv itself. The Ukrainian left SRs had become so implacably opposed to the General Secretariat under USDWP and UPSF leadership that they conspired to overthrow it, declare soviet power and make peace with the Bolsheviks. However, the coup conspirators were arrested at the last moment. Under the mounting pressure of these developments at home and with the expectation that international recognition as a state might somehow help protect it from its enemies, the *mala rada* adopted the Fourth Universal on 11 January which declared the Ukrainian People's Republic an independent state.[15] We shall examine these domestic developments in some detail in the next chapter. As we continue our examination of the peace talks at Brest Litovsk it is important to emphasise that the Rada wanted to sign an interstate treaty to extricate Ukraine from the World War and to help protect it from Soviet Russia, one of the states taking part in the same treaty talks. Indeed, the Fourth Universal was adopted as a declaration of independence from Soviet Russia, which the Rada now accused of delaying the peace talks at Brest Litovsk so that it could continue to make war against the UPR:

> The Petrograd Government of People's Commissars has declared war on Ukraine in order to return the free Ukrainian Republic under its authority ... We, the Ukrainian Tsentral'na Rada, have made every effort to stop this turning into a fratricidal war between two neighbouring peoples, but the Petrograd Government did not join us in this effort and carries on a bloody struggle with our people and our Republic.
>
> Apart from that, this same Petrograd Government of People's Commissars holds back from concluding a peace and calls for a new war, which it says is a 'holy' war. Again the blood will flow, again the unfortunate working people will have to sacrifice their own lives.
>
> We, the Ukrainian Tsentral'na Rada, elected by congresses of the peasants, workers and soldiers of Ukraine, can in no way agree to this. No war will we support because the Ukrainian people want peace and peace should come as quickly as possible.
>
> So that neither the Russian government nor any other prevents Ukraine from establishing the peace it desires, so that it can restore its

---

15   The Fourth Universal was backdated to 9 January.

> country to order, to creative work, to consolidate the revolution and our freedom, we, the Ukrainian Tsentral'na Rada declare to all the citizens of Ukraine:
>
> From this day the Ukrainian People's Republic becomes an independent, subject to no-one, free and sovereign state of the Ukrainian People.

The General Secretariat was so incapacitated by the mounting crisis that once again it held no proper consultations with its delegation returning from Brest Litovsk. 'Conclude a peace as quickly as possible – that was the only instruction'. So uncertain was its future that the General Secretariat authorised its delegation to ratify the anticipated peace treaty itself in the event the Tsentral'na Rada in Kyiv was unable for any reason to do so. Oleksandr Sevriuk now replaced Vsevolod Holubovych as head of the delegation. He demanded and got authorisation to negotiate separately with Medvedev and Shakhrai, the representatives of the Central Executive Committee of the Kharkiv government who had arrived in Brest Litovsk.[16]

On 16 January a train with an armed detachment pulled out of Kyiv carrying Sevriuk and Liubynsky to the military front. Levitsky had remained behind in Brest Litovsk. The rest of the delegation would soon follow. The train did not even make it to the front when it halted at the Shepetivka-Podilska station alongside an armoured train adorned with blue and gold flags and red flags.

> Red Army soldiers aimed their rifles at the windows of our carriages and surrounded the train from all sides. Commotion, cries and threats.
>
> Liubynsky immediately got up and was the first one out. They greeted him on the steps shouting threats. He turned to the crowd and asked for their representatives to come into the wagon. Three delegates entered the *coupé* and sat down. Each one is holding a revolver in his hand and has another weapon tucked under his belt.
>
> 'Who are you, where are you going and why?'
>
> Liubynsky started to answer in Russian. They interrupt and ask that he speak in Ukrainian as they are Ukrainians.
>
> 'We are a delegation of the Tsentral'na Rada going to Brest to conclude the peace'.
>
> The words 'Tsentral'na Rada' were quite enough. The Red Army soldiers stood up, told us we were arrested and they would take us immediately to Proskuriv where they would sort everything out.

---

16 Sevriuk, *Beresteis'kyi Myr*, p. 9.

Liubynsky made a futile effort to explain to them about the peace talks and our need to go right away to Brest.

'Things will be sorted out in Proskuriv' was their reply.

Outside the shouts and threats grew louder.

The Red Army soldiers were leaving when I stopped them and invited them to my *coupé*. They came in. It was no longer possible to deny we were representatives of the Tsentral'na Rada, but I turned their attention to the fact that we were authorised to negotiate not only with the Germans but also with the representatives of the Kharkiv Council of Workers' and Soldiers' Deputies (Sevriuk is referring to the Kharkiv CEC).

The argument was a good one, they started to listen to me more carefully, but still with mistrust. They asked for evidence. I took out the authorisation from the Tsentral'na Rada to negotiate with Medvedev. They read it carefully.

They rose, apologised for holding up the train, promised to order the immediate repair of the line ahead and wished us a good onward journey. Our train moved out.[17]

At the opening session of the third round of talks on 17 January, Trotsky announced he had just been informed by telegraph that a part of the Kyiv garrison had risen against the Tsentral'na Rada; it would not survive for much longer. Trotsky retracted the recognition he had previously accorded the Rada delegation. He now argued that recognition of the independence or dependence of a state should in no way be confused with recognition of one or another government of that state. Previously, when Trotsky had recognised the Rada's delegation and the UPR's right to be represented at the peace talks, the question of its government and its international legal position was far from settled. Even its territorial demarcation with the Russian republic was not agreed. The Kyiv Rada and the Kharkiv Central Executive Committee were still locked in a struggle to become the government of the UPR. According to Trotsky, Russia had no part in their struggle and it would be resolved by them alone. However, insofar as the Kharkiv CEC recognised the Petrograd CPC as the government of a federated Russia and the UPR as a constituent part of that federation, the Kharkiv delegation had a right to take part in the peace talks and was admitted to the Russian delegation. Therefore, Trotsky argued, any agreement reached between the Tsentral'na Rada and the Central Powers would have to be agreed also by Russia.

---

17   Ibid, p. 10.

Further discussion of this issue was postponed at Chernin's request until the Rada delegation returned, which it did in the morning of 19 January. In the meantime the telegraph line linking Brest Litovsk to both Kyiv and Petrograd broke down, preventing the latest news from reaching the site of the talks. This was to the advantage of the Rada delegation, as no-one could verify Trotsky's information concerning the uprising in Kyiv, which happened to be correct.

Oleksandr Sevriuk, at 24 years of age, rose to announce he had replaced his prime minister Vsevolod Holubovych as head of the Rada's delegation. Sevriuk's understanding was that Trotsky had twice recognised his delegation 'as the delegation of an independent state'. Indeed, all the delegations present had done so and proceeded on that basis right up to the adjournment of the second round of the talks. He dismissed Trotsky's argument concerning the unresolved internal struggle for power in Ukraine: by the same reasoning the Russian state should not be recognised either, as several nations inhabiting it, including the Crimean Tatars, the Moldavians, the Caucasian and Siberian peoples did not recognise the government of the CPC. Pointedly, he did not include the Ukrainians in this list, meaning the Rada delegation would not dispute the state credentials of the CPC. To Trotsky's news of the uprising in Kyiv, Sevriuk countered with his own news, that after fruitless efforts to constitute a genuine Russian federated republic the Rada had adopted its Fourth Universal, which declared the UPR an independent state and expressed its desire to live in friendship with all its neighbours. Therefore, in order to avoid further contradictory declarations by the Russian delegation 'the Ukrainian Delegation proposed a formal recognition of the Ukrainian Republic as an entirely independent State, dependent on no one, in order finally to establish both its international position as well as the Delegation's title'.[18]

Yukhym Medvedev then spoke on behalf of the Kharkiv CEC delegation. He pointed out the Ukrainian councils of workers', soldiers' and peasants' deputies were hitherto not represented at the talks; the Rada was not entitled to speak in the name of the Ukrainian people. Because it negotiated behind closed doors and away from the Russian delegation, it had further undermined their trust. The Kharkiv CEC agreed entirely with the Russian delegation's position and would refuse to recognise any agreements made by the Rada with the Central Powers unless they were approved also by Soviet Russia. However, Medvedev then went further:

---

18   *Proceedings of the Brest Litovsk Peace Conference*, p. 134.

The People's Secretariat is striving to create such conditions that the Ukrainian people as a whole, those living in Ukraine, Galicia, Bukovyna and Hungary, may exist independently of political frontiers as one entity. The political future of the whole of the Ukrainian people must also be settled by the free voting of the whole nation. We know the position taken up on this question by the Government of Austria-Hungary, which does not permit the discussion of the All-Ukrainian question at the peace negotiations. But we express our profound conviction that further democratic development will give to the Ukrainian people unity and freedom in fraternal harmony with all peoples.[19]

Medvedev's public support for the unity of the Ukrainian people across the frontiers of old Russia and Austro-Hungary was both an endorsement of the Rada delegation's objective in this regard and a criticism of their pursuit of this objective behind closed doors. It was a tacit recognition of some common purpose of the two Ukrainian delegations. During the third round of negotiations Medvedev and Liubynsky met several times in an attempt to work out their differences. The meetings took place without Trotsky's knowledge but with Kuhlmann's.

Liubynsky informed Kyiv about his contacts with Yu. Medvedev and reported to M. Porsh that Medvedev proposed Kyiv and Kharkiv authorise their respective diplomatic delegations at Brest Litovsk to start peace negotiations between themselves 'but mainly to stop this fratricidal war'.

Apart from that, Medvedev promised to 'chase all the Russian Bolsheviks out of Kharkiv' and to serve as a mediator in negotiations between M. Porsh and V. Lenin. It is interesting to note that when the UPR delegation was stopped on its way to Brest and declared that it was travelling to negotiations with Yu. Medvedev's delegation it was let through without any obstacle.[20]

'At that time', recalled Sevriuk, 'I was always struck by his deep interest, I would say even more by that sorrow and pain he felt for those subjugated Ukrainian lands. And I think that when he returned to the Russian delegation he must have raised the issue there and demanded that it be debated'.[21]

These talks on the side lines, however, had no perceptible impact on the further course of the negotiations at Brest Litovsk. The two Ukrainian delegations stayed apart, each becoming subordinated in its own way to the objectives pursued by the bigger powers present: for Kuhlman a peace treaty with the Rada

19   Ibid, p. 140.
20   Datskiv, 'Dypolomaty Ukrains'koi Tsentral'noi Rady', p. 36.
21   Sevriuk, *Beresteis'kyi Myr*, p. 13.

to wield against Russia; for Chernin a 'bread peace' to feed Austria's starving cities and one that would preserve its territorial integrity; for the CPC to hold out against the Central Powers and to prevent the Tsentral'na Rada securing a peace treaty with them.

The Central Powers' strategic objective was always to play the Tsentral'na Rada off against the CPC. It was now seeking two peace treaties, not one: first with the Tsentral'na Rada and then with the CPC, to use the first treaty to impose more onerous terms in the second. In the event the CPC refused their terms the Central Powers could go to war again. To clear the way for a peace treaty with the Tsentral'na Rada Chernin responded to Sevriuk's request and Trotsky's objections concerning the Rada's status. He declared on behalf of all the Central Powers that 'we have no reason to withdraw or restrict the recognition of the Ukrainian Delegation as an independent delegation and as a plenipotentiary representative of the Ukrainian People's Republic ... an independent, free and sovereign state which is in a position to make independent international agreements'.[22]

Chernin, Kuhlman and Hoffman told the Rada delegation they knew Trotsky's claim concerning their government's precarious position was not far from the truth. They urged them to make haste and agree a peace treaty. Chernin proposed a three-point agreement: that the war between the Central Powers and the Ukrainian People's Republic was over; they should establish diplomatic relations with each other; and the UPR should commit itself to supply the Central Powers with a million tons of grain and other foodstuffs. All other issues should be agreed later in bilateral relations between the states concerned.[23] The Rada delegation, however, declined Chernin's proposal and went away to prepare an alternative one. They understood their position was too weak to press for plebiscites in Eastern Galicia, Bukovyna and Transcarpathia. Count Chaki, Hungary's representative, refused even to discuss the status of Transcarpathia. The Turks, Bulgarians and Lithuanians present urged them to accept the terms offered by Chernin. Yet they were determined not to let go completely of the issue of Ukrainian territories under Austro-Hungary or those under German and Austrian military occupation that were formerly under Russia. On 20 January Sevriuk came back with their alternative proposal: the inclusion of Kholm and Pidliassia within the UPR; the creation of an autonomous crown land out of Eastern Galicia and Bukovyna; provision of one hundred thousand tons of grain and other foodstuffs to the Central Powers by the end of June 1918. Through two days of intensive discussion, they refused to waver

---

22   *Proceedings of the Brest Litovsk Peace Conference*, p. 134.
23   Doroshenko, *Istoriia Ukrainy*, Vol. 2, p. 314.

from their position. In the evening of 21 January Kuhlman and Chernin departed for Berlin and Vienna with the Rada delegation's proposal to consult with their own governments. As they were leaving both the CPC and Rada delegations fired off telegraphs to them that respectively claimed and denied that the Rada had already fallen in Kyiv. Neither was quite true: the Rada's forces in Kyiv had managed to suppress the Bolshevik uprising inside the capital, but Muraviov's forces were already at the gates. Berlin agreed with the Rada's terms on 23 January, but Vienna held out for more grain in exchange for a compromise on Ukrainian territories under its rule.

The leaders of the German and Austrian delegations returned to Brest Litovsk on 25 January. Trotsky made a last-minute attempt to prevent the treaty being signed by insisting that the only territory the Rada still controlled was under the rooms its delegation occupied in the fortress compound at Brest Litovsk; the Central Powers would be signing a treaty with a government that had lost control of practically all of Ukraine. However, the states that needed the treaty were not to be deterred by the facts on the ground and at 2am on the morning of 27 January the Tsentral'na Rada and the Central Powers signed the first peace treaty of Brest Litovsk.

The treaty ended the war between the Ukrainian People's Republic and the Central Powers. It established the frontier between the UPR and Austro-Hungary as that which stood between Russia and Austro-Hungary in 1914. Kholm and Pidliassia would be included in the UPR. The exact position of the frontier would be determined by a mixed commission on the basis of the ethnographic composition of the populations living alongside it and taking into account their wishes. A section of the treaty that was kept secret at the request of Austro-Hungary committed its government to join East Galicia and Bukovyna into a single crown land by July 1918.

There would be no reparations or indemnities for the costs of the war by any side. The treaty contained a detailed section (VII) pertaining to trade that was to be restarted by interstate commissions composed on the basis of parity. Tariffs would be maintained on the basis of the General Russian Customs Tariff of 1903, but Germany would gain freedom to transit its goods to Persia/Iran, something that Tsarist Russia had prohibited. With regard to the content of trade the treaty merely called for 'a reciprocal exchange of the surplus of their more important agricultural and industrial products, for the purpose of meeting current requirements'. However, the UPR agreed in a letter signed by Sevriuk and Liubynsky and kept secret to ship one million tons of grain and other food products by 1 July 1918.[24]

---

24 *Proceedings of the Brest Litovsk Peace Conference*, Section 3, pp. 9–23; Doroshenko, *Istoriia*

Kyiv had been taken by the Bolsheviks at the moment the treaty was signed and the ministers of the Tsentral'na Rada and the remnants of their army were fleeing westward. Why, then, did the Central Powers sign a treaty with a government no longer capable of implementing it? The Germans and the Austrians evidently had important economic and militarily strategic reasons of their own to conclude a peace treaty with Ukraine as quickly as possible. They could not do that with the Kharkiv Central Executive Committee because, like the CPC, it was bent on a social war with them, if not a military war.

> The result for the Germans was that the numerous advantages they had secured on paper could be realised only if they conquered the country and reinstated in Kyiv the government with which they had signed the treaty. The treaty was thus a sort of restraint order issued by the Germans for their own benefit and they did not hesitate to take immediate steps to secure their interests.[25]

25 *Ukrainy*, Vol. 2, pp. 316–17; Vynnychenko, *Vidrodzhennia Natsii*, Vol. 2, pp. 283–4; Stepan Vozniak, *Beresteis'kyi Dohovir 9 II 1918* (Cleveland: n.p., 1989), p. 53. Fischer, *Germany's Aims in the First World War*, p. 500.

CHAPTER 8

Battles for Kyiv

1   The March on Kyiv

The Soviet Army arrived on the outskirts of Kyiv on 22 January 1918. Four groups converged under the command of M. Muraviov. The first, which left Kharkiv on 29 December, was made up of the newly formed Red Cossacks led by V. Prymakov and Red Guards from Petrograd and Tver. As it passed through Poltava, Krovolets, Konotop and Kremenchuk between 5 and 11 January its ranks were swelled by the influx of local Red Guards. This group united with a second one coming northward from Katerynoslav and the Donbas via Konhrad (today's Krasnohrad) and Znamianka. It was composed of Red Guards from Katerynoslav, Makiivka and Yuzivka, a cavalry detachment led by Dmytro Zhloba and several anarchist and left SR brigades. The two groups now advanced together along the railways through Romodan and Hrebinka onto Kyiv.

From the north a third group of 1,000 Russian Red Guards from Briansk advanced through Vorozhba to Bakhmach. They were led by A. Znamensky (with the agreement of Kudynsky). There followed a fourth group composed of several detachments of between 200 and 300 men each, who left the military front and advanced into Homel and then to Bakhmach. Their leader was Eduard Berzin. Both groups left Bakhmach along the same Chernihiv railway line running southwest to Kyiv. Muraviov's entire army, numbering between 5,000 and 6,000 men, arrived on the eastern outskirts of the city aboard several trains.

On Right Bank Ukraine the Bolshevik-led Military Revolutionary Committee of the Seventh Army sent several units of the Second Corps for a third time against the Rada's forces in Vynnytsia. On 10 January they seized Vynnytsia and Vapniark. Then the Eleventh Army and the Separate Army (*Okrema*) left the Southwestern front and relocated in the region of Proskuriv. The road to Kyiv from the west was now open to the Bolsheviks.[1]

The Central Executive Committee of the Kharkiv government instructed Heorhii Lapchynsky and Yurii Kotsiubynsky, its Commissars for Administra-

---

1   Heorhii Lapchynsky, 'Borot'ba za Kyiv: sichen' 1918', *Litopys Revoliutsii*, 2 (1928), p. 212; Viktor Savchenko, *Symon Petliura* (Kyiv: Nora-Druk, 2016), pp. 143–5; Viktor Savchenko, *12 viin za Ukrainu* (Kyiv: Nora-Druk, 2016), pp. 30–1, 33.

tion and Military Affairs respectively,[2] to accompany Muraviov's army. Their mission was to ensure their government's decrees were implemented by civilian and military authorities in the areas liberated from the Rada. This was unlikely as the Kharkiv government was barely on its feet, little known outside its capital and the local councils did not want anyone superseding their authority. Lapchynsky and Kotsiubynsky presented themselves to Muraviov's staff at Liubotyn, a town outside Kharkiv where they were to board the train for Poltava.

> Examining our documents one of Muraviov's commanders read our mandate from the 'All-Ukrainian Council' and exclaimed: 'You are the kind of people we have been ordered to hunt down!' He pointed his revolver at our heads and led us away to his wagon, cursing and promising to 'guillotine' us at once. We barely managed to get him to phone Antonov's headquarters in Kharkiv. They ordered him to release us and give us a special train to Poltava because our train had left while we were being held under arrest.

Muraviov and his commanders treated the local councils they encountered with contempt:

> In Poltava itself ... right after the entry of Muraviov's army a fierce conflict erupted with the city's council in which the Ukrainian SRs, the 'left bankers' headed by Leonard Bochkovsky, Lev Kovaliov and Mykola Lytvynenko, were the most influential party. Infuriated by the tactless behaviour of the military commanders who regarded themselves masters of the city, the local council's executive committee adopted a resolution that asserted the only authority over Poltava province were the councils of workers' and peasants' deputies ... But their relations with the Central Executive Committee of Ukraine and its People's Secretariat were left vague in the resolution: the Poltavans were sceptical about the 'Kharkiv' government.
> ... Not understanding at all these nuances of local politics, Muraviov ordered the members of the executive committee into his wagon. He gave them a good shouting, ordered the arrest of their non-Bolshevik Ukrainian members and threatened to execute them ... Muraviov's chief of staff,

---

2 Kotsiubynsky replaced Vasyl Shakhrai in a temporary capacity when Shakhrai left for the Brest Litovsk peace talks.

comrade Liubynsky (Khlor), stepped up to arrest comrade Leonard Bochkovsky, leader of the Ukrainian SRs throughout Poltava province. Bochkovsky replied in Ukrainian to a question put to him by Khlor, who then shouted in Russian 'I order you to speak to me in an international way'! 'I can speak in English, German, French, Polish and Russian', Bochkovsky replied in Ukrainian, 'but I don't know which one of these you regard as international'. Only after that did Khlor understand he had done a stupid thing. Perhaps it was the same kind of 'naïve internationalist' who a few weeks later executed comrade Bochkovsky in Kyiv simply because he was carrying the red identity card of a member of the Tsentral'na Rada, which was written in the Ukrainian language. So Ukraine lost one of its most renowned revolutionaries ...

It was only the protests of Bolsheviks and Russian Left SRs present that prevented such an excess from taking place here. However, the leaders of the 'left bankers' felt compelled to step back from their work and leave Poltava. Governmental authority was now left exclusively in the hands of the Bolsheviks.[3]

Lapchynsky, head of Kremenchuk Council of Workers' and Soldiers' Deputies and commissar-emissary of the Kharkiv Ukrainian government, grew increasingly disillusioned with Muraviov during the two weeks he spent living with him in the same railway carriage on their way to Kyiv. He described him as

> an exceedingly ambitious person, narcissistic and petulant ... he left the impression of a disorganised, very nervous, almost hysterical person ... I don't think he was a good military specialist ... he had no relationship at all with the revolutionary movement. Politically and psychologically Muraviov was absolutely foreign to us. He could not imagine at all the tasks of the social revolution.[4]

In the light of what Lapchynsky and Kotsiubynsky witnessed on their way to Kyiv one is left wondering why they did not challenge Muraviov. After all, they represented the Ukrainian government which claimed the territory on which Muraviov's army was operating and which was recognised by the CPC. Was it their deference to Muraviov as the deputy of Antonov-Ovsiienko, himself appointed by the Petrograd CPC to lead military operations in Ukraine? Or the

---

3   Heorhii Lapchynsky, 'Borot'ba za Kyiv: sichen' 1918', *Litopys Revoliutsii*, 2 (1928), pp. 210–14.
4   Lapchynsky, 'Borot'ba za Kyiv', p. 215.

fact that neither Lapchynsky nor Kotsiubynsky exercised any direct authority over the army they were accompanying to Kyiv to install their own government-in-waiting in Kharkiv? They did get the opportunity a few days before the army reached Kyiv, when the Council of People's Commissars appointed Kotsiubynsky 'Commander-in-Chief of all military forces of the [Russian] Federation operating on the territory of the Ukrainian Republic'. Muraviov was deeply offended when he learned of the CPC's decision and he asked Antonov-Ovsiienko to allow him to return immediately to Kharkiv. Kotsiubynsky, however, believed it unwise to change leaders in the middle of the offensive and refused to take over Muraviov's command. This, despite Lapchynsky's and presumably even Kotsuibynsky's very low opinion of the military capability, political commitment and character of the lieutenant-colonel Muraviov.

2   Martial Law in Kyiv

News that the Bolsheviks had taken control of practically all Eastern Ukraine and were steadily converging on Kyiv exacerbated tensions in the capital. The city was overcrowded with demobilised soldiers and officers, Jews escaping the pogroms in the towns bordering the front, monarchists, bourgeois and landowners fleeing the civil war. According to a census taken in September 1917 there were 460,000 people registered as residents in Kyiv, making it the third most populous city of the former empire. Russians accounted for 50 percent of the population, followed by Jews at 19 percent and Ukrainians at 16 percent. But there were many people now living illegally in Kyiv without a residence permit, bringing the actual total closer to 650,000 and placing an enormous strain on housing, utilities and services.

In the three months since assuming power the Tsentral'na Rada had failed to organise an effective city administration. It faced resistance on the part of employees of the city Duma and the provincial administration who had worked previously under the Provisional Government and before that the Tsarist regime. The captains of industry and finance did not trust the Rada either, closing their businesses, locking people out of work and removing their liquid assets from Kyiv's banks. If the middle and upper classes regarded the Rada as a lesser evil than the Bolsheviks, they still mistrusted this upstart government. For them Kyiv was a Russian city, indeed 'the mother of All-Russian cities'. They were unhappy to see Ukrainian peasants in uniform marching around as though it were theirs and a government addressing them in the peasants' language. The Rada engendered more hostility when it tried but failed to expel everyone who had lived in Kyiv for less than one year, many of them Russians and Jews. Rafes noted that most urban dwellers were waiting for the Bolsheviks to arrive and rid them of this 'alien power which irritated them with its small but sensitive pin pricks'.[5]

The middle classes were an important factor in local politics, whereas the working class was relatively small. Kyiv initially was an administrative and trade centre, dealing in the transport, storage and processing of sugar and grain. There were railway workshops, factories producing agricultural and food processing equipment and, significantly, the Arsenal, which produced munitions for the army. However, the working class accounted for a considerably smaller proportion of Kyiv's total population than it did of Kharkiv's or Katerynoslav's, which had mushroomed in the wave of industrialisation before the War. Moreover, Kyiv had a less 'modern' working class in which craft and cottage industry workers still outnumbered its industrial workforce by around two to one.[6]

By the beginning of 1918 the Bolsheviks had taken control of most urban centres in Eastern Ukraine. On 4 January, the day the Kharkiv government declared war on the Rada, the General Secretariat declared Kyiv under siege and imposed martial law. Mykhailo Kovenko, appointed commander of the city, ordered a seven-day mobilisation of the Free Cossacks to police it. On the same day Mykola Porsh, Secretary of Military Affairs, ordered a full mobilisation of Ukrainian regiments and the immediate demobilisation of the rest of the Russian army. The Ukrainian regiments, however, could no longer be relied upon to hold together in the face of Bolshevik agitation, let alone in an armed confrontation. So Porsh took on two military formations with strongly anti-Bolshevik officers to try to stiffen the Rada's defences: Petliura's Slobidska Camp and the Galician Bukovynian Company. The latter was later renamed the First detachment of the Sich Riflemen and was made up of former soldiers in the Austrian army and led by Yevhen Konovalets and Andrii Melnyk.[7]

The Free Cossacks first appeared in the spring of 1917 in Kyiv province as an irregular paramilitary movement made up mainly of middle and wealthy peasants. Their aim was to protect their properties and localities from looting and disorder by army deserters. They quickly spread in the summer months across Katerynoslav, Chernihiv and Kherson provinces and into the Kuban.

---

5 Rafes, *Dva goda*, p. 78.
6 'Kyiv', *Encyclopedia of Ukraine* (Toronto: University of Toronto Press, 1988), pp. 502–12.
7 The Galician Bukovynian Company was later renamed the Sich Riflemen. Konovalets and Melnyk went on to become leaders of the Organisation of Ukrainian Nationalists in Polish-occupied Western Ukraine in the 1920s and '30s. Doroshenko, *Istoriia Ukrainy*, Vol. 1, pp. 279–81.

They then appeared in some towns, at first among railway workers. The USDWP was involved in organising them in Katerynoslav. Pavlo Khrystiuk described the social democrats' illusory hope that 'the worker Free Cossacks were the first shoots of a Ukrainian proletarian red army ... that could serve the local councils as their popular militia and defend the interests of the working people'.[8]

By the time their first national congress opened in Chyhyryn on 3 October, they had 60,000 members. Hopes of the kind Khrystiuk recounted were dispelled here when some 2,000 delegates to the congress elected Pavlo Skoropadsky, the wealthy landowner and commander of the Rada's First Ukrainian Division, as their leader, or *het'man*. They accorded the same title, but only in an honorary capacity, to Mykhailo Hrushevsky, president of the Rada. These bestowals of real and symbolic authority reflected a tension within the Free Cossacks. On the one hand there was the conservative nationalist entourage around Skoropadsky that belonged to the UPP and later the UPSI. They organised the congress and nominated him to become the het'man. On the other hand, there were the rank-and-file Free Cossacks who were awaiting from the Rada the resolution of land reform and an end to the War. The middle and wealthy peasants made up a majority of delegates at the congress. They gave their support to the conservative nationalist leadership who upheld private property in land, advocated Ukraine's immediate independence from Russia and opposed political or cultural autonomy for national minorities. These positions contradicted the principles set out by the Rada in its Third Universal a month later. Yet at the same time they sought official registration from the General Secretariat as a militia police force and their maintenance at public expense. After heated debate the General Secretariat registered and incorporated them under the Secretariat of Internal Affairs. When the Rada lost control of the eastern provinces and its army regiments started breaking up, the General Secretariat turned to the Free Cossacks for reinforcement. On 18 December they were transferred to the Secretariat for Military Affairs, which paraded 16 companies of Free Cossacks, around 1,000 fighters, in the capital on 30 December. Mykhailo Kovenko, their commanding officer and the general commander of Kyiv during the January state of siege, had recruited these companies from among the workers at the Arsenal, the Greter and Krivanek factory and the railway workshops.

Kovenko served in the War as an engineer on the Southwestern front. He was a member of the USDWP from 1916, elected in June 1917 to the Rada by the All-Ukrainian Council of Workers' Deputies. From September he worked for

---

8 Khrystiuk, *Ukrains'ka Revoliutsiia*, Vol. 2, p. 188.

the Elections Bureau of the Secretariat of Internal Affairs, training Free Cossack units to guard voting stations during the Constituent Assembly elections. It was presumably in this capacity that Kovenko began to pull together the Free Cossacks he eventually led against the Bolsheviks.

It was also during the autumn of 1917 that Kovenko resigned from the USDWP and joined the Ukrainian Party of Socialist Independentists (UPSI), launched by members the Ukrainian People's Party (UPP) and nationalist officers in the army.[9] His defection was symptomatic of the growing influence amongst the Rada's supporters of the once marginal Ukrainian People's Party. Formed in Kharkiv in March 1917 the UPP advocated as its long-term goal the independence of Ukraine, with ethnic Ukrainians taking all the positions within the government.

The party concentrated on building a Ukrainian army, first and foremost from divisions of the Russian army. It had some influence in the Polubotok and Khmelnytsky regiments and the 153rd Division. The party anticipated a new state leadership would come from the All-Ukrainian Soldiers' Congress, which should elect a *het'man*, declare independence and make peace with the Central Powers. It pursued this strategy over the summer months when UPP members also secured positions in the leadership of the Free Cossack movement. In December leaders of the newly launched UPSI made an unsuccessful attempt to persuade General Pavlo Skoropadsky, Symon Petliura and Mykola Porsh to seize power in a coup d'état, declare independence and replace all officers in the army with the UPSI's own people. More than anything they tried to include the UPSR in this plot. Skoropadsky, the lynchpin in their plans, broke off talks and the coup plot was abandoned. However, the UPSI nationalists' influence continued to grow in Ukrainian political and military milieus as tensions mounted between the Rada and the Petrograd CPC. The number of UPSI members in the Rada's general assembly of 822 deputies grew from 12 to 19. In December the party joined forces with a right-wing fraction in the UPSR to form a multi-party faction in the Rada, with S.A. Shekhulin (UPSR) as its head and Oleksandr Stepanenko (UPSI) its secretary. The Socialist Independentists would come to play a greater role in the looming military conflict between the Reds and the Rada 'when from their ranks sprang a considerable number of *otamany* [warlords]'.[10]

---

9 *Entsyklopedia Suchasnoi Ukrainy*: http://esu.com.ua/search_articles.php?id=34567http://sichovyk.com.ua/istorichna-slava/914-wiljne-kozactwo-unr [accessed 11 August 2018].
10 Goldelman, *Jewish National Autonomy in Ukraine 1917–1920*, p. 59; D. Mukha, 'Dialnis't Ukrains'koi Partii Samostiynykiv-Sotsialistiv, hruden' 1917–kviten' 1918', *Visnyk KHY imeni T. Shevchenka*, 2007; S. Herashchenko, 'Ukrains'ki Samostiinyky v natsional'no-vyzvol'nii

Over a period of seven days from 4 January the Free Cossacks carried out raids in 27 workplaces in Kyiv, including the Arsenal, the factories Greter and Kryvanek, the shipbuilding yards, the munitions factory at Demiivka, the railway mechanics' workshops and the railways administration. During the raids, many of which occurred at night, the Cossacks smashed up machinery and cut power lines. They interrogated workers and drew up lists of suspected militants whose houses were then searched. Two hundred were arrested and imprisoned in the Lukianivka and the Koso-Kaponir prisons, 40 of them beaten so badly they had to be treated in the hospital ward at Lukianivka. Some 1,500 rifles and tens of machine guns were seized in the raids. The premises of *Proletarskaia mysl'*, newspaper of the Kyiv Council of Workers' Deputies, were shut down. The editors launched a second paper, *Proletarskoe delo*, but its first edition was confiscated at the kiosks. The trade unions council and the factory committees council were ransacked. Four bakery workers were beaten when they called a one-day strike to protest against the repressions. A delegation of workers went to the Rada's headquarters where they were told it had nothing to do with the raids or the arrests. The workers demanded the Rada issue an order that the repressions stop, but none was forthcoming.[11]

3 The Fourth Universal

The Rada's delegation at Brest Litovsk returned to Kyiv on 5 January. It called on the government to declare the state independence of the Ukrainian People's Republic in order that it may sign a peace treaty with the Central Powers. The ninth plenary session of the *mala rada* convened on 7 January to deal with the matter, but first on its agenda was the long awaited Statute of National Personal Autonomy. The draft legislation was prepared by Moshe Zilberfarb, Secretary for Jewish Affairs, to replace the original statute of July 1917. The *mala rada* debated it for two full days and then adopted it unanimously.[12] Zilberfarb enthused that 'the law we have adopted is equal only to the acts of the great French Revolution. Then the rights of man were declared. Today we have proclaimed the rights of nations'. Rafes added: 'Not a single country in Europe has

---

borot'bi 1917–pochatku 1918 rr', https://vpered.wordpress.com/2010/02/18/українські-самостійники-в-національ/ [accessed 12 August 2018].
11   Bosh, *God bor'by*, pp. 116–17; Savchenko, *Symon Petliura*, p. 143; Zdorov, *Ukrains'kyi Zhovten'*, p. 214.
12   Abramson, *Molytva za vladu*, p. 112.

yet to know of a stronger act of such importance'. Representing the Zionists, N. Syrkin also spoke in its favour. Telegrams were sent of the news to the largest Jewish centres in Austro-Hungary, Russia and the USA.[13]

A draft of the Fourth Universal was hammered out from three competing resolutions submitted by Hrushevsky, Vynnychenko and Mykyta Shapoval. The Russian, Jewish and Polish parties were not consulted beforehand. According to Solomon Goldelman of Poale Zion, they were presented with the draft as a fait accompli in a closed session of the *mala rada* with all the other parties present.[14] The session went on continuously from 5pm on 10 January until close to midnight on 12 January. The debate focussed on the Rada concluding a separate peace, for which a declaration of the UPR's independence was deemed necessary. The three Ukrainian parties fell into line behind this argument, while the Mensheviks and the Bund remained opposed and the other parties undecided.

The Mensheviks and the Bund had agreed at the end of December 1917 that they would walk out of the Rada by 5 January, the day the All-Russian Constituent Assembly was scheduled to meet, if the Rada pushed ahead with a separate peace with the Central Powers. When it became clear that the General Secretariat was going for a separate peace, Alexandr Zolotariov, General Controller in the Secretariat, tended his resignation at the start of the *mala rada* debate on 10 January. The intention of the Bund was not to have its representative in the General Secretariat once independence was declared.

Rafes spoke for the Bund in the debate, taking aim at the Rada for its 'egotistic' attitude towards other nations and the CPC for its 'unprincipled, egotistic and devious' lip service to a general peace and the self-determination of nations. By agreeing to bilateral talks with the Central Powers, he argued, the Rada would make Ukraine the slave of German imperialism, and the aim of German imperialism was to dismember Russia. The Bund then issued a statement contending that a declaration of Ukraine's independence would hasten the disintegration of the Russian revolution and allow German imperialism to dictate its terms for a separate peace. It blamed 'the treacherous politics of the Bolshevik government' for creating the anarchy and provoking the civil war that stimulated separatist sentiments in Ukraine. These sentiments played into the plans of German imperialism to annex territory and to create a buffer of nominally independent states between Russia and Europe. The Germans

---

13 Cherikover, *Istoriia pogromnogo dvizhenia na Ukraine 1917–1921 gg*, Tom 1 (reprinted by Berlin Direct Media, 2015), p. 73.
14 S.I. Goldelman, *Zhydivs'ka Natsional'na Avtonomiia v Ukraini. 1917–1920* (Munich: n.p., 1967), p. 121.

would reverse land reform and strip Ukraine of its raw materials. Furthermore, the Bund contended that the declaration of independence was being made 'against the will of the Ukrainian democracy'. For its part, the Bund was taking part in the *mala rada*'s closed session only to press for amendments to the Fourth Universal that protected the rights of minorities, resisted Ukrainisation and other measures it believed would antagonise the population. But the Bund would vote against the Fourth Universal:

> We are going to fight for a stronger solidarity between the Ukrainian and Russian proletariat so that the bright day will come when the separation of Ukraine from Russia will be just a tragic episode in the life of both fraternal peoples.[15]

At 12.20am on 13 January the *mala rada* went into open session in the assembly hall of the Pedagogical Museum, which had been filling up with people, many of them members of the Rada's 800-strong general assembly. Hrushevsky gave a short introduction, explaining that disorder in the country had made it impossible to hold Ukrainian constituent assembly elections to resolve the country's international status but that the UPR needed to sign a peace treaty to end its involvement in the world war and to prevent it falling further into war with the Bolsheviks. Reading out the Fourth Universal, the declaration of independence, in its entirety Hrushevky was interrupted several times by ovations and shouts of approval. The Universal was then put to a vote by public roll call. Rada Secretary Mykhailo Yeremiiev read out the name of each member of the *mala rada* in turn. (The only other time such a voting procedure had been used was for the adoption of the Third Universal.) There were 49 members present: 39 of them, all members of the three Ukrainian parties and the Polish Socialist Party, voted in favour. Four voted against: the Mensheviks Mykhailo Balabanov, Dmytro Chyzhevsky and Kostiantyn Kononenko, and the Bundist Mykhailo Liber (Holdman). Six abstained: Yosyp Sklovsky and Kostiantyn Sukhovykh from the Russian SRs, Solomon Goldelman from Poale Zion, Max Shats-Anin from the United Jewish Workers Party Fareignikte, Pinkhus Dubynsky from the Jewish People's Party Folkspartei, and L. Pochentovsky from the Polish Centre.[16]

The result evoked disappointment and bitterness among some Rada deputies and members of the public gathered in the Pedagogical Museum. The

---

15 Rafes, *Dva goda*, pp. 71–5.
16 Doroshenko, *Istoriia Ukrainy*, Vol. 1, p. 268.

Ukrainian parties had joined in a unanimous vote a couple of days earlier to approve the statute on national personal autonomy for minorities; in return they were expecting solidarity with the declaration of independence. Hrushevsky now invited representatives of all the parties to address the meeting. On behalf of the USDWP and the Rada's Council of People's Ministers[17] Vynnychenko greeted the outcome of the vote and spoke optimistically about a future of peace, reconstruction and Ukraine's eventual membership in a worldwide federation. Sukhovykh from the Russian SRs regretted the outcome, saying the declaration of independence was premature. Then, 'the mere appearance of the well-known Liber who was to speak in the name of the Jewish Labour Bund ... called forth a storm of indignation'.[18] Hrushevksy was forced to clear the gallery and close the meeting.[19] When it was published, the Fourth Universal was backdated to 9 January, the day when the final debate on it had actually begun.

The USDWP and UPSR presented the declaration of independence to the public somewhat unenthusiastically, even apologetically. The socialist revolutionaries' newspaper *Narodna volia* explained:

> The declaration of independence was not the ultimate aim of Ukraine's rebirth. On the contrary, the bare slogan of independence doesn't have anything appealing about it for true socialists whose ideals are the greatest possible improvement in the wellbeing of every individual and the establishment throughout the world of brotherhood, equality and freedom. If at this time our socialist parties found it necessary to put this slogan on the order of the day they did it only because the circumstances demanded the declaration of independence ... in raising the slogan of independence the Ukrainian democracy will not retreat one single step from the idea of universal brotherhood, from the idea of a free union of all the countries of the world. On the contrary, all it did was to take an unavoidable step on the road to a worldwide federation of independent peoples because only those able to freely dispose of themselves can enter into a union with each other.[20]

---

17   The General Secretariat was renamed the Council of People's Ministers by the Fourth Universal.
18   Elias Heifetz, *The Slaughter of the Jews in the Ukraine in 1919* (New York: Thomas Seltzer, 1921), p. 15.
19   Abramson, *Molytva za vladu*, p. 112.
20   *Narodna volia*, no. 9, 1918.

Robitnycha hazeta, the USDWP newspaper was no less circumspect:

> The idea has taken hold among the Ukrainian democracy that it is necessary to proclaim the independence of the Ukrainian People's Republic as a way out of a situation created by circumstances beyond its control and as the only way to a genuine federation. Complete independence (without any state ties to other countries) arises from the fact that in these difficult times for us the Ukrainian democracy has understood like never before the great need of the working masses to live in a nationally independent state (not ruling out a federation with other states) because only in such a state can the class struggle unfold in all its scope, only in it can this struggle progress. Inasmuch as hope has been lost that the right of nations to their self-determination can develop through the general Russian revolution and in brotherly accord with all the labouring masses, at least for the immediate future, the Ukrainian democracy is compelled to take a different path, the path of complete independence. Freedom of national development is for it a question of life or death. Through independence to federation.[21]

4 The Socialist Revolutionaries Form a Government

The Ukrainian Party of Socialist Revolutionaries, the largest in the Rada but a minority in its government, now stepped forward to demand the USDWP-UPSF-led Council of People's Ministers resign. For while peace was at hand in Brest Litovsk, war with the Bolsheviks was well underway in Ukraine. The UPSR left wing was led by Mykhailo Poloz, Panas Liubchenko, Vasyl Ellan-Blakytny (Ellansky), Hnat Mykhailychenko, Opanas Sivero-Odoievsky, Serhii Bachynsky. It proposed to form a new government together with the USDWP left wing (led by Y. Neronovych) on a programme of immediate peace with the Bolsheviks and the establishment of council/soviet rule at the national level and locally throughout the country.[22] The centre-right of the UPSR (Mykola Saltan, Mykola Chechel, Mykola Shrah, Kuzma Korzh, Pavlo Khrystiuk) wanted to reconstitute the government on the basis of proportionality of party representation, to negotiate a new agreement with the workers' councils but to exclude the

---

21 *Robitnycha hazeta*, 22 January 1918.
22 The UPSR left wing was led by M. Poloz, P. Liubchenko, Mykhailychenko, Sivero-Odoievsky, S. Bachynsky and Vasyl Ellan-Blakytny; the USDWP left by Yevhen Neronovych and Yevhen Kasianenko.

Bolsheviks and to keep fighting them.[23] The two wings of the party could not find common ground. Their differences lay not only in policy but also in means.

The left wing no longer believed it could achieve its programme by reforming the government but would have to overthrow it. In December, while the Russian left SRs Mykola Alekseiev and Volodymyr Kachynsky were in Kyiv trying to mediate between the CPC and the Rada, they were consulting closely with their Ukrainian counterparts. The Ukrainian and Russian left SRs then made an agreement to co-operate in the All-Russian Constituent Assembly elections and to overthrow the Vynnychenko-led General Secretariat. They could not implement the first part of their agreement because the Constituent Assembly was forcibly dispersed by the CPC on 5 January. With regard to the second part, their main concern was that the Kharkiv CEC government might stand in the way of normal relations being established between Petrograd and a new council-based government in Kyiv. The CPC was made aware of these plans and concerns, which Stalin passed on by telegraph to Trotsky in Brest Litovsk. German intelligence intercepted this message and shared it with the Rada delegation, which then fed it back to Kyiv. Mykhailo Kovenko, the Rada's military commander of Kyiv, ordered the arrest of the coup plotters right inside the Pedagogical Museum while the ninth session of the *mala rada* was underway. The following UPSR leftists were arrested: M. Poloz, H. Mykhailychenko, O. Shumsky, O. Sivero-Odoievsky, H. Tkalia, A. Ovcharenko, O. Zarudnyi, A. Prykhodko, A. Polonsky and S. Bachynsky. Y. Ellan-Blakytny managed to escape. The Free Cossack detachment had orders also to arrest the left USDWP leaders Y. Neronovych and Y. Kasianenko, but they happened not to be there. M. Poloz and P. Liubchenko were arrested in Brest-Litovsk. The coup was foiled and the UPSR and USDWP left wings were cast out of the Rada.[24]

On 15 January a unit of the Zaporozhian Bohun regiment broke into the *mala rada* in session, protested the arrests and the deployment in the city of the Free Cossacks, who they said had criminal elements in their ranks. They threatened 'to disperse the bourgeois Rada', but then left without further ado.[25]

Desperate to find a way out of the impasse Vynnychenko proposed to the Council of Ministers the bizarre idea that it stage its own coup. This would have involved Mykola Porsh, Minister of Military Affairs and Mykhailo Tkachenko, Minister of Justice overthrowing Vynnychenko, the General Secretary, declaring the rule of councils and seeking peace with the CPC. However, ministers

---

23 The UPSR right wing was led by Saltan, Chechel, Shrah, Korzh and Khrystiuk.
24 Khrystiuk, *Ukrains'ka Revoliutsiia*, Vol. 2, p. 125; Doroshenko, *Istoriia Ukrainy*, Vol. 1, p. 260; Zdorov, *Ukrains'kyi Zhovten'*, pp. 215–16.
25 Savchenko, *12 viin za Ukrainu*, p. 41; Doroshenko, *Istoriia Ukrainy*, Vol. 1, p. 278.

were not prepared to go along with him and split 'the united national front'.[26] Vynnychenko was left with no option but to resign. On 16 January, the day before the handover of power to the UPSR centre-right, the USDWP Central Committee issued the following statement:

> We remain firmly convinced that an orientation towards the Bolsheviks, which manifests itself strikingly among the Ukrainian socialist revolutionaries, cannot save Ukraine from the danger it is now in; this orientation could sooner lose it altogether. Everyone knows that the Bolsheviks will heed no-one, they will not stop at anything but will scatter all before them, even the left SRs. Our party stands for a struggle against bolshevism, as against all utopianism that has nothing to do with socialism. And given this political submission of the SRs and the relationship of forces in the country which is now on the side of the peasant elements, in such a situation our party cannot remain in government. The revolution is now passing into a phase of anarchy, and after that it will move into reaction, and completely different elements, far removed from the proletariat, will come to the helm of the state. At this moment our party cannot take responsibility for such a political submission which is in evidence among the SRs.[27]

On 17 January a new Council of People's Ministers was formed under the premiership of Vsevolod Holubovych, composed of seven UPSR members and two from the USDWP, all of them from the centre-right of their parties.[28] The government immediately denounced the uprising and the general strike which had just begun in Kyiv: they were all, it alleged, vandals and looters. 'The city of Kyiv and all of Ukraine is overflowing with Bolshevik agitators and Red Guards sent in by the Petrograd authorities with big money'.[29]

As the uprising and general strike took hold and Muraviov's forces neared the outskirts of the city, the *mala rada* continued to sit in its ninth session

---

26 Vynnychenko, *Vidrodzhennia Natsii*, Vol. 2, pp. 220–2.
27 *Robitnycha hazeta*, no. 229, 16 January 1918.
28 Vsevolod Holubovych, Prime Minister and Minister of Foreign Affairs, L. Nenolovsky (Military Affairs), P. Khrystiuk (Internal Affairs), Stepan Perepylytsia (Finances, UPSR sympathiser), Ye. Sokovych (Roads), M. Kovalevsky (Provision), N. Hryhoriiv (Education), A Ternychenko (Agriculture), M Tkachenko (Justice, USDWP), D. Antonovych (Maritime Affairs, USDWP). See Doroshenko, *Istoriia Ukrainy*, Vol. 1, p. 291.
29 Cited in Andrii Zdorov, 'Arsenal i Kruty. 100 rokiv viiny. 100 rokiv pamiati'. http://www.historians.in.ua/index.php/en/dyskusiya/2389-andrij-zdorov-arsenal-i-kruti-100-rokiv-vijni-100-rokiv-pam-yati [accessed 8 May 2018].

and to adopt new laws. The most important of these for the UPSR majority was the land law of 18 January. Based on the resolutions of successive congresses of peasants' deputies in 1917, the draft of this law was hotly debated at the eighth session of the *mala rada* in December and then sent to a commission for inter-party conciliation. The new law abolished private property in land, water and underground resources, making them the common property of the citizens of Ukraine and assigning responsibility for apportioning them for use to peasant land committees and local organs of self-government. Land could no longer be bought or sold, only passed on as inheritance. Nor could labour on the land be bought or sold. Peasant families were to be apportioned as much land as their combined labour could put to productive use for their own needs. This law was adopted unanimously by the *mala rada*.[30]

The law on the eight-hour working day was also adopted by this session of the *mala rada*. There was no time left, however, before the Rada was forced to evacuate from Kyiv, to adopt a set of draft laws on workers' control of industry and banking, and co-decision-making of workers', peasants' and soldiers' councils with local governments.

5   The Uprising and General Strike

The Kyiv Bolshevik party committee prepared for the uprising from the beginning of January, and it persisted even as the Rada's forces detained its members and uncovered their weapons. On 12 January, the Kyiv Council of Workers' Deputies, in which the Bolsheviks now held a majority, declared its allegiance to the Kharkiv-based Central Executive Committee of the Councils of Ukraine. According to Yevgeniia Bosh, the Kyiv comrades were advised by the CEC not to launch the uprising without external support. Alexandr Horwitz, a 20-year-old member of the Kyiv committee who also served on the CEC, was the liaison between the two capitals. He received instructions from Kharkiv to hold back his comrades until M. Muraviov's forces reached the capital.[31] However, the uprising started a week sooner than planned, on 15 January, provoked by a number of developments: the Rada's declaration of independence, the active desertion or retreat into neutrality of at least half the soldiers of the Rada's regiments in the city, and the perception of the Bolsheviks in the factories that they were gaining support from workers who previously followed other parties.

---

30   For the full text of the law, see Khrystiuk, *Ukrains'ka Revoliutsiia*, Vol. 2, pp. 129–31.
31   Bosh, *God bor'by*, pp. 51–3.

The initiative came from below: rank-and-file militants in several workplaces launched the uprising in the night of 15 January before any decision was taken either by the Kyiv Council of Workers' Deputies or the Bolshevik city party committee. Rather, the latter bodies followed in the militants' wake. Crucially, it was when the soldiers who were supposed to guard the Arsenal came over to the side of its workers that they gained the confidence to launch the uprising immediately. Strategically the most important enterprise in Kyiv, the Arsenal, employed 3,000 workers and office staff in a complex of eighteenth-century buildings located in the upper city district of Pechersk. These were local Russians, Jews, Ukrainians and Poles, supplemented during the war years by metalworkers recruited from Russia and evacuated employees of the Warsaw Arsenal. It was the Bolsheviks' principal stronghold in Kyiv, but by no means their exclusive preserve. The workforce supported several parties, including Social Democracy of Poland and Lithuania, the USDWP, Russian and Ukrainian SRs as well as the UPSI who recruited a detachment of Free Cossacks at the Arsenal.

On 15 January the Rada ministries of labour and military affairs, both under Mykola Porsh, sent contradictory messages, possibly deliberately, to the workers at the Arsenal. First, a representative of the Labour Ministry promised them the machinery damaged by the Free Cossacks in earlier raids would be repaired and production restarted. Then the Ministry of Military Affairs sent an order by telegraph to remove all the coal from the Arsenal and put it at the disposal of the Rada's armoured trains. This second decision meant that production would be halted and the workers sent home. The Bolshevik-led factory committee met to consider their predicament. When a detachment of the B. Khmelnytsky regiment assigned to guard the factory declared its solidarity with the workers and was joined in this by representatives from the Shevchenko and Sahaidachnyi regiments stationed in the district of Pechersk, the factory committee decided to barricade the Arsenal and launch the uprising.

Syla Mishchenko, commander of the first company of the Sahaidachnyi regiment and a Bolshevik, led all his soldiers plus some volunteers from other companies, 450 in all, into the Arsenal. A full meeting of the insurgents elected a military revolutionary committee with Alexandr Horwitz as its head, Syla Mishchenko as military commander, Mykola Kostiuk, turner, and Ipolyt Fialyk, saddler, as members; that is, one Jew, two Ukrainians and one Pole respectively. Upon arriving at the Arsenal on 16 January at around 2am to remove its coal, the detachment of Free Cossacks met a hail of gunfire. The combined force of the Arsenal workers and the soldiers from Ukrainised detachments was somewhere between 700 and a thousand strong. They were well armed with rifles, machine guns and cannons. The fighting went on all night and into the morning. The insurgents held their ground. The Rada surrounded all of Pechersk with troops. Horwitz was wounded in the hand during the fighting. He tried to get to Podil to rally more support from workers but was captured and executed by Free Cossacks. Mykola Kostiuk then took over as head of the military revolutionary committee.

A ceasefire ensued in the morning of 16 January, followed by talks which went on until seven in the evening. When the talks proved fruitless the insurgents started firing their cannons in the direction of the Rada's seat of government at the Pedagogical Museum and into other parts of the city. Some of the Arsenal itself was set alight by the cannon fire.

In the evening of 16 January, the Kyiv Council of Workers' Deputies met with the trade unions and factory committees in the Commerce Institute. After a prolonged debate they agreed to launch a general political strike to back the uprising, overthrow the Rada and declare the rule of the Council. Menshevik and Bund leaders were opposed to the strike, but their rank and file tended to support it. The news delivered by Isaak Kreisberg, a Bolshevik, that the mutilated body of Leonid Piatakov, kidnapped on 25 December, had been found at Post Volynsk outside Kyiv swayed the meeting to a decisive vote in favour of calling the general strike by 266 votes to eleven. The meeting elected a combined strike and military revolutionary committee to co-ordinate different centres of the uprising.[32]

By midday on 17 January the general strike brought to a halt practically all production, distribution, retail trade, printing, education and transport in the city. Water and electricity were still available that day and into the night. Shooting could be heard coming from different points in the city. It was a sustained barrage in Pechersk around the Arsenal. The fighting continued all through the night. In the morning of 18 January a rumour spread through the city that a postal train had come off the rails and crashed into the main station. Water and electricity supplies were cut off. Despite the shooting that went on people ventured out of their houses with pails to buy water at privately owned wells. The queues grew, the price of water went up and looting of stores began.[33]

The uprising spread to other parts of the city, including the railway workshops by the freight yards and main station, the Jewish quarter of Podil by the Dnipro River and the outlying neighbourhoods of Shuliavka and Demiivka.

---

32 Andrii Zdorov, 'Khto pidniav zbroine povstannia v Kyevi v sichni 1918 roku?', *Liva Sprava*, 8 October 2010, http://www.istpravda.com.ua/digest/2010/10/18/639/ [accessed 15 August 2018].

33 *Nova Rada*, no. 13, 24 January 1918.

However, the combined strike and military revolutionary committee under Bolshevik leadership failed to co-ordinate these centres. Therefore, the Arsenal's military revolutionary committee served as the de-facto headquarters for the uprising across the whole city, though its ability to play that role diminished after the third day of fighting when the Rada's forces started cutting off the insurgent centres from one another. Then the Arsenal had to rely on intelligence gathered by youths, some as young as ten, who went out every day to spy on the movements and concentrations of Rada forces. When the ranks of the insurgents thinned out some of the youths, armed with rifles, replaced them on Volodymyr Mount, in Podil and Pechersk. The Arsenal workers' women prepared food and carried it to the men and boys. They went out into the streets of Pechersk to agitate against the Rada's forces.

On 18 January representatives of the Rada proposed new negotiations with the insurgents holed up in the Arsenal, to which they agreed. They met in the nearby Mariinsky palace, but the fighting went on as the talks got underway. The delegation from the Arsenal, led by Syla Mishchenko, set out its demands: to halt all military action against the workers, disarm the Free Cossacks, convene immediately a congress of workers' and peasants' deputies from Kyiv city and province, and call an all-Ukrainian congress of councils to elect a new national government. The Tsentral'na Rada's side had only one demand: that the insurgents lay down their arms in exchange for a general amnesty.

During a pause in the talks, a detachment of the Doroshenko regiment seized the Arsenal delegation and threw them in prison. Mishchenko later acknowledged that it was a mistake to include him in the delegation as he was the military leader at the centre of the uprising, and that his delegation should have first secured a general ceasefire across Kyiv before proceeding with any negotiations.[34]

The main railway workshops were a second focal point of the uprising. Throughout 1917 there were several political parties active among its workforce, including the Kadets, the Russian SRS, the USDWP and the Bolsheviks. In late December a meeting of 3,000 workers, having received an order to repair an armoured train for the Rada, resolved that 'in view of the fact that … the armoured train is intended to do away with workers who are conducting a struggle for a soviet government … not to carry on repairing the train but to disassemble what has already been repaired'. On the following day they took

---

[34] Andrii Zdorov, 'Arsenal i Kruty. 100 rokiv viiny. 100 rokiv pamiati', http://www.historians.in.ua/index.php/en/dyskusiya/2389-andrij-zdorov-arsenal-i-kruti-100-rokiv-vijni-100-rokiv-pam-yati [accessed 8 May 2018]; Savchenko, *12 viin za Ukrainu*, p. 41; *Nova Rada*, 17 January 1918.

the train apart. On 15 January, when the Arsenal workers barricaded themselves in against the Rada's Free Cossacks, a group of workers at the railway workshops followed suit. Not many workers there were ready to fight until Arkadii Dzedzievsky, a machinist, left SR militant (not known whether Russian or Ukrainian SR) and a brilliant orator, won over a railway workers' battalion of around two hundred men who until then supported the Rada. He did not try to persuade them to join the uprising but to insist on guarding the railway workshops themselves rather than allowing the Rada's troops into them. Guarding railway property was the reason why the battalion was originally formed, and now the question was posed, as had also been posed at the Arsenal: whose property was it and from whom should it be defended.[35]

The railway workers rebuilt the disassembled armoured train, which they put to good use. On 18 January they used it to secure weapons. Eighty insurgents disarmed another railway workers' battalion guarding wagons full of weapons and ammunition, brought their armoured train engine forward and shunted the wagons back into the workshops. They now had machine guns and cannons, and they quickly took instruction on how to use them. On the same day two hundred soldiers of the Polubotok regiment accompanied by an armoured car attacked the workshops, but they were repelled and suffered many casualties. After this defeat Rada commanders shot two of their scouts for wrongly informing them that the railway workers had no machine guns.

The railway workers were well armed and still confident when the Arsenal workers' delegation was seized at the Mariinsky palace. During the night of 19 January they tried to seize Kyiv-Tovarny railway freight station no. 1, where the Rada had its main military base. They attacked it with gunfire from the armoured train and cannon fire, forcing the Hrushevsky regiment out of the station. However, lacking infantry on their side, they could not hold the station. They were relying on the Serdiuk regiment nearby to help them, but its soldiers declared neutrality and so the railway workers were forced to retreat again. The following day they were engaged in street fighting and managed to advance into the city centre. However, they faced the same problem as before of insufficient forces to consolidate their gains and had to return to their original position that night.[36]

A third focal point of the uprising was Podil. On 16 January a large detachment of Red Guards advanced out of the Jewish quarter towards the city

---

35 Andrii Zdorov, 'Khto pidniav zbroine povstannia v Kyevi v sichni 1918 roku?'; N.S. Patlakh, 'V borot'bi za radians'ku vladu v Kyevi. Sichneve povstannia v zaliznychnomu raioni', *Litopys* Revoliutsii, 1–2 (1928), pp. 177–82.
36 N.S. Patlakh, 'V borot'bi za radians'ku vladu v Kyevi', pp. 177–82.

centre, seized the Starokyiv police precinct on St Sophia Square and the hotel Praha near the Golden Gates on Volodymyr Street. They attacked the Rada's headquarters at the Pedagogical Museum, raking the building with machine gun fire before being forced back. On the following day they came back, this time along Khreshchatyk, the main thoroughfare, which they held while trying to reach the Rada at the Pedagogical Museum again. They took heavy casualties as the Rada's units forced them back into Podil and cut them off from the other insurgent centres.

> The Red Guards' stunning operation could have given them control of the centre of the city and allowed them to seize the Tsentral'na Rada. Their predicament, however, was the further they ventured out the more exposed they became ... The Podil Red Guards contributed the brightest page to the history of the Bolsheviks' uprising in Kyiv but it was not their fault that the communists in the 1960s and '70s made heroes only out of the railway and Arsenal workers ... Practically all 250 of their fighters who came out on the first day of the uprising perished in it.[37]

Around 2,200 Red Guards in all took part in the uprising at the Arsenal, the railway workshops, in Podil, Shuliavka and Demiivka. They had two armoured cars and the armoured train. On the Rada's side there were around 2,000 fighters with three armoured cars. The general strike launched on 16 January to support the uprising involved far wider circles of workers. Many who traditionally followed the Bund, the Mensheviks and the right Russian SRs joined the strike, breaking with their leaders who continued to back the Rada or who retreated to a position of passive neutrality.[38] The number of people directly involved in the fighting was no more than one percent of the population, whereas in the general strike perhaps as much as 10 percent. Meanwhile, the rest of Kyiv's population waited without water, electricity or bread to see who would prevail. They included more than 20,000 recently demobilised soldiers and officers of the Russian army and over half the soldiers of the Ukrainised regiments the Rada had tried to mobilise, but who declared their neutrality. Many of them were not altogether neutral, for they were selling their weapons and ammunition to the insurgents.[39]

---

37 Andrii Manchuk, 'Sichneve povstannia. Rolia khlopchakiv', 29 January 2011. http://www.istpravda.com.ua/columns/4d4376f1674ac/ [accessed 20 August 2018].
38 Khrystiuk, *Ukrains'ka Revoliutsiia*, Vol. 2, p. 126.
39 Doroshenko, *Istoriia Ukrainy*, p. 1283.

The Rada convened a plenary session in the afternoon of 20 January in response to the news reaching the capital that a major pogrom that had broken out in Zviahel, Novhorod-Volynsk the previous day was still ongoing. Soldiers of the 27th regiment, peasants and even some government officials were targeting Jewish shops in the town, looting and setting them on fire. The police did not intervene. The pogrom was not preceded by any antisemitic agitation and there were no fatalities other than the accidental shooting of two soldiers by their own. Nevertheless, it was symptomatic of the incendiary climate building across the region from the front to Kyiv that was heavily populated by Jews.

I. Shekhtman from the Zionists opened the debate in the Rada plenary and drew attention to the ongoing antisemitic agitation in the capital: Jews were being accused *en masse* of supporting the Bolshevik uprising. Soldiers and Free Cossacks were attacking Jews on the streets as retribution for the casualties inflicted on them by the Red Guards. I. Shekhtman called on the Rada to condemn these attacks and appeal to the population to desist from pogroms. Ivan Martos, from the USDWP, spoke out against making an appeal, arguing that the Rada was not responsible for these attacks, but rather it was the Bund, the Russian SRs and the Mensheviks who had been agitating against the Rada in the Kyiv Council of Workers' Deputies and were now refusing to commit their own militias to its defence. Martos' ire was directed particularly at the Bund: 'Let the Bund itself issue a statement to the Kyiv population', he advised, 'and for that matter a statement that makes it clear it is the Bolsheviks alone and not the Bund who are opposing the Rada. If the Bund puts out such a statement in which it admits that all the gossip about the Tsentral'na Rada being "bourgeois" is a lie, then that statement will better protect the Jewish population from pogroms than any statement from the Tsentral'na Rada'.[40]

Martos did not make the same demand of the Russian nor indeed of the Ukrainian parties, although some of these nationalities' representatives were supporting the Bolshevik-led uprising, as were some Jews. In effect, Martos was demanding that Jews take collective responsibility for the actions of any one of their nationality.

The Southern Oblast Committee of the Bund had already issued a statement on 19 January in which it condemned the Bolshevik uprising and urged Jewish workers to defend the Rada. The problem for its leaders was that the rank-

---

40 *Narodna volia*, 23 January 1918, stenographic report of Rada plenary session reproduced as Appendix No. 23 in Vladyslav Hrynevych and Liudmyla Hrynevych, *Natsional'ne Viis'kove Pytannia v Diial'nosti Soiuzu Yevreiv Voiniv v KVO (lypen' 1917–sichen' 1918 rr.)* (Kyiv: Natsional'na Akademia Nauk Ukrainy, Instytut Istorii Ukrainy, Instytut politychnykh I etnonatsional'nykh doslidzhen', 2001), pp. 122–8.

and-file members of the Bund were refusing to distribute the statement and continuing to support the general strike, if not the uprising itself.[41] The Russian SRs had also issued an appeal to their supporters urging them to lay down their arms and return to work. The Menshevik deputy Chyzhevsky stood firm in the Rada plenary and insisted his party was not obliged to issue any statement at all. The UPSI deputy Lutsenko talked about the lack of trust in any of the minorities' representatives. Regardless of how they voted on the Fourth Universal he believed they were all opposed to the independence of Ukraine. The UPSR deputy Sknar asked rhetorically 'Why are these "minorities" now demanding a statement in their defence from that same Tsentral'na Rada whose authority they have been trying to destroy?'

Mykhailo Tkachenko, Minister of Justice, intervened near the end of the debate to ask the Bund and the Russian SRs why, if they supported the Rada, they had not sent their militia to fight with it against the Bolshevik uprising. 'You fight here with words alone, but in practice you don't fight'. The SRs protested that their militia had been disarmed by the Free Cossacks. Porsh countered that all they needed to do was to present themselves to the Rada's military command and they would have been given their weapons back. In the end the Rada plenary agreed to issue an appeal condemning the pogroms. Rafes doubted it would have much impact on a situation over which the Rada's civilian leaders were losing their grip.[42]

On the same day as this debate was taking place, a unit of the Free Cossacks arrested Yoan Hohol, leader of the Union of Jewish Fighters. Back in December the UJF (the Union of Jewish Fighters) had decided to convene its first All-Russian Congress in Kyiv on this very day, 20 January 1918. The organisation was pressing on with its plan to deploy self-defence units in Jewish communities at risk or under attack. It continued to define the act of self-defence as strictly humanitarian, disavowing involvement in any domestic or interstate political conflicts unless they threatened Jewish lives. However, the viability of an apolitical self-defence force was becoming untenable by the day. Even as it held to this position the UJF was arranging with Khurgin, the new Rada Secretary of Jewish Affairs, to receive weapons and uniforms from the demobilised Shevchenko regiment. However, the uprising in the capital put paid to all these efforts. The fighting made it impossible for all the delegates to the UJF congress to reach Kyiv. The 25 delegates who did decided to hold an informal private meeting. Having learned of its whereabouts, one of the Free Cossack units broke into

---

41   Rafes, *Dva goda*, p. 80.
42   *Narodna volia*, 23 January 1918; Hrynevych and Hrynevych, *Natsional'ne Viis'kove Pytannia v Diial'nosti Soiuzu Yevreiv Voiniv v KVO*, pp. 122–8; Abramson, *Molytva za vladu*, p. 147.

the meeting, arrested Hohol and several other participants, throwing the others out. Premier Holubovych was informed and he ordered their immediate release. Hohol was the only one who disappeared. His killers, who were never identified, were assumed to have been the Free Cossacks who took him away. His body was found only after Muraviov's army occupied the city. Ten thousand people, mainly from the Jewish community, came to his funeral.[43] After Hohol's murder the UJF ceased to act as a co-ordinating centre for Jewish self-defence detachments in Ukraine and Russia. Red Guards disarmed and demobilised them and other non-Bolshevik militias when they took Kyiv and other centres in January 1918. In Katerynoslav, the anarchists assisted the Red Guards, accusing the UJF of counterrevolutionary activity.

6   National Identity and Political Allegiance

An important issue raised by the January uprising concerns the place of national identity in the consciousness of the workers and peasants on both sides of the conflict. Their sense of common class interests was acute after ten months of revolutionary upheaval. Yet the perception of each other as enemies, to be precise as national enemies, overrode the sense of class solidarity for at least some of those involved. How did this happen?

As the conflict intensified people in leadership positions described the enemy on the other side increasingly in national terms or a combination of national and class terms. Their characterisations ranged from the simple identification of nationality to chauvinistic and racist depictions of Ukrainians, Russians and Jews. They could be crude caricatures or subtle insinuations. Any resort to language, ethnicity or nationality to identify someone's allegiance to one side inevitably appealed to prejudices on the other side. Or it drove people to identify positively with a particular nationality, for example by speaking its language, so as to align themselves publicly with one side in the conflict. Heorhii Lapchynsky described it thus ten years after the events in question:

> Insofar as the drive by the petit-bourgeois Rada against the worker-peasant revolution took place under Ukrainian chauvinist slogans a mood emerged among the revolutionary masses to identify everything Ukrainian with the counterrevolution. We know there were many real Ukrainians, workers and peasants, who didn't know or use any other language

---

43   Ibid, Vol. 1, p. 78.

than Ukrainian, but under the influence of this mood they renounced their nationality, naively believing an internationalist should not be a Ukrainian but ... a Russian. As for those comrades who were in Ukraine for the first time, here to fight for the interests of the Ukrainian workers and peasants against the local bourgeoisie, what else can I say: psychologically it was absolutely clear to them that a 'Ukrainian' was a supporter of the Tsentral'na Rada, whereas Ukrainian workers and peasants were 'simply workers and peasants'. That is why there was a complete mistrust of everyone who used the Ukrainian language, of every document written in Ukrainian (as it was with comrade Kotsiubynsky and myself in Liubotyn), of the members of revolutionary, pro-soviet but Ukrainian parties.[44]

Vynnychenko saw the Bolsheviks as coming into Ukraine to assert themselves both as Bolsheviks and as Russians over a people they regarded as of the same nationality as themselves, but of its 'Little Russian' branch, whose leaders were now spreading a petit bourgeois notion of a separate Ukrainian nation in order to divide the Russian proletariat. They believed that

> he who regards himself as Ukrainian is 'an enemy of the social revolution', an active and tenacious enemy. This made it easy for Russian nationalism to break out and fight against the Ukrainian national awakening under the pretext of fighting social enemies. It allowed the most ignorant Bolshevik elements to tear portraits of Shevchenko off the walls and stamp them underfoot, to hunt down Ukrainian schoolteachers in the villages, torment them and shoot them just because they were conscious Ukrainians.[45]

Members of the Ukrainian political parties succumbed to the same kind of identification of nationality with political allegiance as the Bolsheviks did. They blamed their own loss of popular support on the Bolsheviks, whom they regarded as a foreign Russian element that shared the same imperialist attitude towards Ukraine as the Tsarist autocracy. They cast the struggle as one between the Ukrainian peasantry and the Russian workers. Yet it was more complex than this: by January the peasants in the Ukrainian regiments were deserting the Rada in growing numbers, declaring neutrality or going over to the Bolsheviks.

---

44   Lapchynsky, 'Borot'ba za Kyiv. Sichen' 1918', pp. 213–14.
45   Vynnychenko, *Vidrodzhennia Natsii*, Vol. 2, pp. 271–2.

The UPSR historian and activist Pavlo Khrystiuk described the working class abandoning the Rada:

> A handful of brave patriotic revolutionaries was defending Kyiv ... Russian and Jewish workers who had been whipped up by the Bolsheviks' agitation launched an uprising right inside Kyiv which made it difficult to defend the capital. The more right-wing, anti-Bolshevik part of the Russian and Jewish workforce who followed the Russian social democratic Mensheviks, the right Socialist Revolutionaries and the Jewish Bund simply did not want to come out and defend Kyiv ... There took place before our very eyes a division of the workers and intelligentsia of Kyiv into two camps that was defined not so much by social class as by national belonging: on the one side there formed an anti-Ukrainian Russian-Jewish camp and on the other side the forces of the Ukrainian revolutionary democracy grew smaller and more isolated.[46]

Andriy Zdorov recounts an incident during the January uprising that illustrates the impact that conflating nationality with political allegiance had on the actual conflict. A company of Sich Riflemen composed of poor Galician and Bukovynian peasants, ex-prisoners of war from the Austro-Hungarian army, was fighting on the side of the Rada. Their commanding officers were staunchly anti-Bolshevik and the company was regarded as one of the Rada's most reliable. However, the rank-and-file soldiers sympathised with the uprising once they learned what its aims actually were. They formed a soldiers' committee to which they elected, among others, a certain Maksym Kopach. When the uprising began Kopach decided to go to the Bolshevik-led military revolutionary committee of Arsenal to see if he could somehow prevent his company from being deployed against the uprising.

> Maksym Kopach very quickly found common language with the workers there and they started discussing a concrete plan to neutralise the Sich Riflemen. Soon afterwards a leading member of the Kyiv Bolshevik committee came in, a 'headquarters' man' as Kopach called him. Upon seeing Kopach's uniform he went crazy: 'Petliurite bastard! Spy!' Kopach tried to explain that he was a representative of the Riflemen's committee, which was just like the soldiers' committees in the Russian army, and to prove it he showed him his letter of authorisation. In answer he got: 'What are you

---

46   Khrystiuk, *Ukrains'ka Revoliutsiia*, Vol. 2, pp. 126–7.

telling me?! It's written in that dog's language!' The 'headquarters' man' threw the letter in Kopach's face ... After that, of course, Kopach ended up in the basement and a full complement of the Sich Riflemen went in to put down the Arsenal insurgents.[47]

7 Uprising Suppressed, the Rada Cast Out

The Rada had its best military units outside Kyiv resisting the advancing Bolshevik-led columns: Petliura's Slobidska Camp, the Sich Riflemen (under Y. Konovalets), a company of the First Ukrainian Officers' School (under the command of Averki Honcharenko) and the Hordienko Cavalry Regiment (under Vsevolod Petriv), altogether around 2,400 fighters. They were ordered back into the city on 18 January to help the Free Cossacks and the soldiers still on the Rada's side to put down the uprising. At the railway station in Brovary, east of Kyiv, soldiers of the 1,300-strong Nalyvaiko regiment arrested their own officers, raised the red flag and vowed to prevent the 'reactionary' Petliura from re-entering the capital. Petliura's smaller force managed to disarm them but only 60 soldiers took up his offer to join them; the rest were dispersed. Their cannons and machine guns were made inoperable and left behind because Petliura did not have the capacity to take them back to Kyiv. The Nalyvaiko regiment soldiers returned to Kyiv on 19 January.[48]

Two small units of Georgian and Polish soldiers also took part in suppressing the uprising, while Romanian, Belgian and Czechoslovak troops standing in Kyiv under Entente command remained neutral, refusing even to take on guard duties on behalf of the Rada.[49]

The Arsenal was the first centre of the uprising to be put down. After four days of fighting the workers were exhausted and dispirited because Muraviov's army still had not reached Kyiv. Their electricity had been cut off, they were out of medical supplies, food and water and they were fast running out of ammunition. Many had died in the fighting. The soldiers who had deserted to their side at the beginning of the uprising surrendered on 19 January when Petliura brought fresh forces up to the walls of the Arsenal. On the morning of 20 January Petliura's soldiers broke into the Arsenal. Some of the workers managed to escape along underground passages while others retreated to the cellars. The

---

[47] Zdorov, 'Khto pidniav zbroine povstannia v Kyevi v sichni 1918 roku?'
[48] Savchenko, *12 viin za Ukrainu*, p. 37.
[49] Khrystiuk, *Ukrains'ka Revoliutsiia*, Vol. 2, p. 127.

remainder, somewhere between 200 and 360 (the historical accounts differ) were taken prisoner.[50]

What happened next is the subject of dispute among historians. V. Savchenko recounts that some tens of workers, those who continued to fight on in the underground passages and cellars, were shot inside the Arsenal. Those who surrendered were assembled in the courtyard in front of three machine guns. Petliura's soldiers demanded they all be shot, including the wounded. S. Petliura refused to allow it and they were led off to the Koso-Kaponir prison two kilometres away. Zdorov's account is different: after the workers and soldiers who surrendered were lined up one of Petliura's officers ordered ten machine gunners who had deserted to the insurgents from the Taras Shevchenko regiment to be shot on the spot. Another 25 workers and soldiers were killed on the road to prison.[51]

From 19 January the Rada's reinforcements isolated the centres of the uprising from each other and put them down. The workers at the main railway workshops held out the longest as they had their own fortress of sorts, ammunition to spare and an armoured train. However, they had failed to link up with the Podil Red Guards who had twice reached the city centre from the riverside. On 21 January after the Arsenal surrendered the city-wide military revolutionary committee decided to try to bring the uprising to an end. However, inasmuch as it had failed to co-ordinate the uprising in the first place, it had little authority among the insurgents. When three members of the committee, I. Kreisberg, D. Stohnyi and D. Itkind, came to the railway workshops to inform the workers of its decision, the workers took them for provocateurs and wanted to shoot them. They were saved only by the intervention of their own commander.[52] The railway workers decided to hold out. In the early hours of the morning of 22 January the Rada's forces mounted another attack, this time taking thirty prisoners. They were removed to the main railway station where seventeen of them were shot. In his memoir, N.S. Patlakh says that S. Petliura personally selected the group to be shot at the station and that the remainder of those captured were taken to the Bykivnia prison where they, too, were shot. The historian V. Savchenko says the executions at the main railway station were carried out without Petliura's knowledge.

The uprising came to an end. According to Patlakh the Rada's fighters stayed on the streets through the night of January 22, seizing workers and shooting

---

50   Zdorov, 'Arsenal i Kruty. 100 rokiv viiny. 100 rokiv pamiati'.
51   Ibid.
52   Patlakh, 'U borot'bi za radians'ku vladu u Kyevi'; Zdorov, 'Khto pidniav zbroine povstannia v Kyevi v sichni 1918 roku?'.

them on the spot. Ivan Klymenko, secretary of the Kyiv printing workers' union and a member of the Bolshevik MRC, recalled that Rada troops in the Podil district identified their enemies by their calloused hands. Four hundred insurgents died fighting, 50 were executed, and around 700 were wounded. On the Rada's side there were around 300 dead and 600 wounded. 'A mutual hatred flooded the streets and threatened to drown the great city. By the morning of 23 January Kyiv was quiet, weeping for its victims and preparing for new ordeals'.[53]

Muraviov's army reached Darnytsia on the edge of Kyiv on 22 January. There they met armed workers fleeing the city who told them how the uprising had been put down. The incoming army now consisted of around six thousand fighters with 25 cannons, three armoured cars and two armoured trains. Muraviov issued order no. 4: 'mercilessly to annihilate all officers, Kadets, *haidamaky*, monarchists and all enemies of the revolution'. He telegraphed Petrograd that he had already taken the city and liberated 500 workers from the Kyiv garrison, which was untrue. Rather, he was holding the bulk of his army on the Left Bank of the Dnipro River and sending small numbers of troops to probe the bridges. Encountering resistance from the other side, his units then used poison gas to take the bridges and flush out Rada troops dug into the cliffs on the Right Bank.

Muraviov did not have reliable information about the strength and disposition of the defending forces further inside Kyiv, so instead of mounting a full-scale attack he pounded Kyiv with artillery. At first intermittent, the shelling became practically continuous by 24 January.

> Heavy charges landed and exploded one after the other, sowing death and devastation and that unspeakable horror when people just went insane not knowing how to save themselves. All day and all night of 24 January until the morning of the 25th a veritable hurricane of fire raged. At night a malevolent red sky hung over a dead city with fires burning in every part of Kyiv. The populace completely lost their heads and hid themselves away in the lowest floors, the cellars and basements, listening in fright to the explosions above, ripping through their victims. No pen can write what was happening then in the city. People who had been in real warfare said they never experienced such a hell even on the front lines. Everyone was so unnerved that they just wanted it to end however it would, but to end.[54]

---

53   Savchenko, *12 viin za Ukrainu'*, p. 46.
54   *Nova Rada*, no. 14, 4(17) February 1918.

A delegation from the city Duma came out to Muraviov's headquarters on 25 January, offering to mediate, pleading with him to save their city from destruction. They told him that the Rada's forces were already leaving Kyiv, but Muraviov refused to stop the shelling. He sent the delegation back with an ultimatum to the Rada to surrender its ministers and commanders by midnight of the same day.

Meanwhile the *mala rada* had continued to sit, debating and adopting laws on land reform and the eight-hour working day. For its own protection it moved its last sessions out of the Pedagogical Museum to the Defence Ministry. Vsevolod Holubovych, Prime Minister, was determined to hold on in Kyiv until the Rada's delegation at Brest Litovsk signed the peace treaty with the Central Powers. Meanwhile, wrote Vynnychenko,

> shrapnel from cannons firing from the other side of the Dnipro showered the roof of the Tsentral'na Rada's building. Those cannons were our own, not ones brought from Moscow. They belonged to our Ukrainian military formations. Most of the Bolshevik army was made up of our own soldiers. Those very same Doroshenko and Sahaidachny regiments who had held their ground in Kyiv were now pulling our hair and kicking us in the spine.[55]

Around midnight of 25 January members of the *mala rada* and Cabinet of Ministers who belonged to the Ukrainian parties began to evacuate under armed escort. They left by the Sviatoshyn Road westward out of Kyiv in the direction of Zhytomyr. All told the retreating column numbered some 3,000 soldiers, irregular fighters and civilians. None of the Russian or Jewish party members went with them. Afterwards, there was some dispute as to whether they stayed in Kyiv because they did not want to leave or because they were not informed of the evacuation and were left behind. Dmytro Doroshenko acknowledged that the evacuation was organised privately at the Pedagogical Museum and not all members of the government were informed. Solomon Goldelman of Poale Zion was with Premier Holubovych the day before the evacuation took place and he was told nothing. Those who claimed the Russian and Jewish party members had elected to stay in Kyiv accused them of betraying their own government.

Vynnychenko went south instead of evacuating to Zhytomyr with other members of the Tsentral'na Rada. He spent eight days on trains talking with soldiers, peasants and workers, 'changing seats and neighbours at many stations':

---

55 Vynnychenko, *Vidrodzhennia Natsii*, Vol. 2, pp. 254–5.

At that time right after the Tsentral'na Rada's departure from Kyiv, whoever spent some time among the people and especially the soldiers could not but notice a particularly strong antipathy of the popular masses towards the Rada. By then I didn't believe any more in any particularly strong attachment of the people to the Tsentral'na Rada. But I never imagined there could be such hatred. Especially among the soldiers. And even more so among those who could not even speak in Russian, but only in Ukrainian ... With such contempt, fury and mockery they spoke of the Tsentral'na Rada, its General Secretaries, its politics. But what was so hard and awful to hear was how they all ridiculed everything Ukrainian: the language, songs, schools, newspapers and books ... It was like a son who was infuriated with his mother, whom he led out onto the square, tore off her clothes, beat her around the face, threw her in the mud and left her there naked, beaten, exposed to ridicule, humiliation and public shame. And he did this with such savagery, such smirking cynicism and fury as though in this way he was getting to feel his own pain for his mother's shame, he was reminding himself of that once great and passionate love which had now been insulted and subjected to mockery. And it was us, the Ukrainian democracy, the Ukrainian Tsentral'na Rada who had evoked and awakened this son's great love to his mother-nation. We, with our politics of the village girl wearing a gentlewoman's delicate gloves, we had caused him to lose faith in the national cause because we were the ones who defended this cause the most and provided it with leadership, and at the same time we ended up defending the social order of the generals.

The situation was like this not just in one or two instances, but the same everywhere from one end of Ukraine to the other.[56]

---

56   Ibid, Vol. 2, pp. 259–60.

CHAPTER 9

Kyiv under Bolshevik Rule

Muraviov entered Kyiv on 26 January after all of the Rada's forces were gone. On that day and the next his army executed more than 2,000 people.[1] Many of them were officers of the Russian army who had not taken part in the fighting, but who carried identity cards from the Tsentral'na Rada. They were executed where they were caught, many of them in the fashionable mansions of the districts of Lypky and Pechersk. The majority of deputies to the Rada evaded arrest because the Bolsheviks' intelligence was poor and they managed to hide in time. Some were caught and executed, including the former minister of land affairs, O. Zarudniy, the left UPSR member Leonard Bochkovsky and the editor of the UPSR newspaper *Narodna volia* Isaak Puhach.[2] Volodymyr Zatonsky, Commissar for Education in the People's Secretariat and its representative on the Petrograd CPC narrowly escaped being shot himself:

> I was facing execution and I saved myself by accident. There happened to be in my pocket a mandate with Lenin's signature on it. That's what saved me. Skrypnyk was spared only because someone else recognised who he was. It was just luck because when the patrol stopped me in the street I was carrying a Ukrainian language mandate of the All-Ukrainian Central Council of Workers', Peasants' and Soldiers' Deputies in Kharkiv ... We came into the city: corpses, corpses and blood ... that was when they were shooting everyone who had anything to do with the Tsentral'na Rada, right there in the streets. And I almost became one of them.[3]

The Bolsheviks were in control of Kyiv for three weeks, from 26 January by the Julian calendar to 28 February by the Gregorian. Thirteen calendar days were lost when the Gregorian calendar replaced the Julian, turning the first day of February into the fourteenth (there were no days of 1–13 February). For the first

---

1 Mykhailo Hrushevsky, *Na Porozi novoii Ukrainy. Statti I Dzherel'ni Materialy*, edited and with an introduction by Lubomyr Wynar (New York: Ukrainian Historical Association, 1992), p. 182. See also Doroshenko, *Istoriia Ukrainy*, Vol. I, p. 294, who cited the Austrian Diplomatic Mission's precise figure of 3,576 executed by the incoming army.
2 H. Lapchynsky, 'Borot'ba za Kyiv. Sichen' 1918 r.', *Litopys Revoliutsii*, 2 (March–April 1928), p. 218.
3 V. Zatonsky, Natsional'na problema na Ukraini (New York: Ukrains'ki Shchodenni Visti, n.d.), cited in M. Shapoval, Velyka Revoliutsiia in Ukrains'ka Vyzvol'na Prohrama (Prague: Vil'na Spilka i Ukrains'kyi Robitnychyi Universytet, 1927), p. 105.

two weeks the Bolsheviks felt themselves in the ascendancy, but from 20 February they were on the defensive and then in panic and retreat. The situation changed for them when the entire city learned, mainly by word of mouth, that the German army had crossed the western front line and was advancing on Kyiv. The Bolshevik government was not sufficiently embedded in the capital to defend itself. Moreover, the Soviet Russian delegation at Brest Litovsk had failed to conclude a peace with the Central Powers, as the Rada had done on 27 January, leaving the Kharkiv-based People's Secretariat exposed just as it was moving its headquarters to Kyiv.

Hryhorii Lapchynsky entered the city with Muraviov's army. He recalled that

> the soldiers killed every officer and *junker* (non-commissioned officer) they came across in the streets. This was the first truly mass terror during the revolution in Ukraine, and it had clear class criteria. Kyiv during the war was a centre for very many officers of all kinds, and so it was in the interests of the revolution, very useful to it, to kill as many of them as possible.

However, as Lapchynsky goes on,

> Persecution of the Tsentral'na Rada's supporters was a much worse matter because our soldiers did not always know how to distinguish in this regard. During the mass terror it was not just members of the Rada but people who were simply Ukrainian that suffered, including those who supported soviet rule, as opposed to those who supported the Rada.[4]

Khrystiuk, who witnessed the entry of Muraviov's army, claimed the attacks on Ukrainians were systematic:

> ... in Kyiv the Muscovite army was shooting everyone who spoke in Ukrainian and identified themselves as a Ukrainian. Of course it wasn't the communists who did this, but the ordinary 'brothers' and 'comrades' under the leadership of officers who had been schooled in the old times.[5]

The executions on 26 and 27 January were but the latest phase in a cycle of revenge killings that began a month earlier, a response to the Rada's brutal

---

4   Lapchynsky, 'Borot'ba za Kyiv', p. 218.
5   Khrystiuk, *Ukrains'ka Revoliutsiia*, Vol. 2, p. 136.

suppression of the January uprising which was itself preceded the week before by atrocities on both sides at Kruty station on the Chernihiv railway line and before that by the abduction, mutilation and murder of Leonid Piatakov.

After considerable debate, the People's Secretariat in Kharkiv adopted a decision on 28 January to move to Kyiv. Some of its members were worried they may become exposed to attack by the Rada's forces, but the view prevailed that Kyiv was after all the capital of Ukraine and that it would be easier to utilise the administration already established there by the Rada than to try to build one from scratch in Kharkiv. The Central Executive Committee of the Councils of Ukraine confirmed the decision of the People's Secretariat and on the following day the members of both government bodies boarded a train which brought them into Kyiv on 30 January.

Yevgeniia Bosh as commissar of internal affairs and the de facto leader of the government believed it would not have been necessary to move to Kyiv had it not been for the opposition in Kharkiv itself from the local Bolsheviks, Mensheviks and Russian SRs who had sabotaged her government's work over the entire previous month. Bosh believed the Bolsheviks could have made Kharkiv their impregnable fortress against the Rada and the Austro-German occupation that would follow in the wake of the Rada's collapse. Her vision was illusory, however, simply because the Bolsheviks were not united: they did not have an agreed strategy with respect to Ukraine and they were not all prepared to rally around a single national government. No sooner had the train carrying the People's Secretariat and the Central Executive Committee left Kharkiv than its local Bolsheviks led by Artem (Fedir Serheev) convened a second congress of councils of the Donetsk and Kryvyi Rih region. The congress established the Donetsk-Kryvyi Rih Republic that explicitly rejected any Ukrainian soviet government, recognising only the CPC in Petrograd. In February and March 1918 the Bolsheviks in Crimea and in Odesa were setting up their own regional governments on the same positions.

Meanwhile, the four members of the People's Secretariat who were already in Kyiv when it was captured (Lapchynsky, Kotsiubynsky, Aussem and Martianov) called a meeting on 28 January with the commanders of Muraviov's army, members of the Kyiv city Bolshevik organisation (Yan Hamarnyk, Andrii Ivanov, and Mykhailo Maiorov), and experienced revolutionary leaders whom they had released from Rada captivity (Hryhorii Chudnovsky, Yakiv Boiarsky, and Oleksandr Yegorov, the elected commander of the Separate Army of the Southwestern front). This meeting issued a declaration in the name of the People's Secretariat accusing the Rada of pursuing 'conciliation with the Ukrainian, Russian and foreign bourgeoisies' and 'concluding a shameful peace with the Austro-German imperialists'. They were not the 'northern barbarians and foreign invaders' that the Rada portrayed them to be, but 'representatives of the proletariat and poorest peasantry of Ukraine'.

> The armies of the Russian Federation came only as a loyal ally in the struggle against our bitter internal enemy – the Ukrainian nationalist intelligentsia and the groups of urban bourgeoisie and rural kulaks who backed them up ... Having seized power by force of arms, we the representatives of the workers and poorest peasants of Ukraine will hand it over only to the Congress of councils of workers, soldiers and peasants of Ukraine where the oppressed classes of the Ukrainian people will themselves express their will and decide how to build their lives.[6]

This meeting established a Military Revolutionary Committee with Chudnovsky at its head as commissar of Kyiv city. The MRC issued an order forbidding any further arrests, searches or requisitions without its authorisation. On the same day the Kyiv Council of Workers' and Soldiers' Deputies met and adopted a resolution demanding an end to summary justice, that all people accused of killing unarmed people or any other crime be brought before a revolutionary tribunal. The Council pointed out that the death penalty was abolished.

A full plenum of the Central Executive Committee of the Councils of Ukraine that took place in Kyiv five days later on 15 February (new style, Gregorian calendar) reaffirmed the Bolsheviks' intention to transfer all power in the hands of workers' and peasants' councils, to place all land in the hands of peasant land committees, all industry under workers' control, to establish a national bank and to call a Second All-Ukrainian Congress of Councils for 5 March.[7]

Chudnovsky ordered the city Duma to remove all corpses from the streets within 24 hours, making its chairman Yevhenii Riabtsov liable to a fine of 100,000 karbovantsi if he did not comply. The MRC also requisitioned glass and building materials to repair the buildings which had been damaged during the bombing. The owners of all retail and wholesale outlets, cinemas and theatres were ordered to re-open them.

On 17 February, 750 workers were buried in a mass grave in Oleksandr (Mariinsky) Park. It is not entirely clear who they included from among the following: the fatalities on one or both sides of the January uprising that ended on 26 January, the victims of the shelling of Kyiv, those who died fighting during the taking of Kyiv by Muraviov's army, or those who were executed by his troops.

---

6 Bosh, *God bor'by*, p. 134.
7 Ibid, p. 141.

The MRC was supposed to be a transitional authority transferring power from the military to the People's Secretariat as the national government and the Kyiv Council of Workers' and Soldiers' Deputies as the local government. There was agreement in principle on how to effect that transition, but in practice it did not take place without some conflict between the military and civilian authorities, with the MRC being pulled in both directions.

Muraviov had his own idea of how the transition should be carried out. His Order no. 14, attached to every telegraph pole in the city on 29 January, commenced with the warning: 'this power we carry from the far north on the tips of our bayonets and wherever we introduce it we uphold it by force of these bayonets'. The order confirmed that power had passed to the People's Secretariat and the Kyiv Council, but that arrests could be made only on the orders of Chudnovsky and the Kyiv MRC acting in conjunction with Mykhailo Remniev, commander of the Second Army and Muraviov's subordinate.

On arrival in the capital on 30 January Yevgeniia Bosh went immediately to the executive committee (*ispolkom*) of the Kyiv Council where she delivered a report on the general situation in the country. Members of the executive committee were angry about the arrests and executions carried out by Muraviov's soldiers and demanded they leave the city. But Muraviov would not submit to the civilian authorities and leave; on the contrary he decamped to the city centre and set up a parallel authority.

> The orders poured out of Muraviov's headquarters as from a horn of plenty. They were plastered over all the vacant spaces on buildings and telegraph poles. For the most part these orders ran counter to the resolutions of the local soviet authority. And along the city streets rolled Remniev in his car, a very dubious character who had wormed his way into Muraviov's general staff, with an armed group holding their rifles aloft, stopping cabs and cars, demanding in the name of soviet power their documents and to hand over any weapons. The townsfolk as well as responsible soviet workers were subjected to these raids. On the first day after our arrival in Kyiv, we were returning from a meeting of the Executive Committee when we were stopped by a car hurtling towards us with the men inside shouting 'Stop or we'll shoot!'. We were surrounded by a group of five or six men pointing their guns at us.
>
> To our question 'What's the matter?' we got the order 'Hands up' and Remniev *himself* walked up to us. After examining our documents, this self styled 'security' jumped back quickly into their car and raced off at full speed. All this caused panic among the population and gave rise to the

Mensheviks, the Bundists and Socialist Revolutionaries shouting about anarchy in the city caused by the rule of the Bolsheviks.[8]

Muraviov styled himself as the avenging sword of the Revolution. When he arrived in Kyiv, he proclaimed

> We come with fire and sword to establish soviet power. I took this city, striking at the palaces and churches ... I showed no mercy! On 28 January the Duma asked for a ceasefire. In response I ordered them to be gassed. Hundreds of generals, maybe thousands, we killed without mercy. That is how we took our revenge. We could have halted the anger of revenge but we didn't because our slogan is: show no mercy![9]

Muraviov appeared in many places to proclaim Russia united and indivisible once again and to denounce Ukrainians as traitors and Austrian spies. The inhabitants of Kyiv regarded him as a warlord. The Petrograd CPC tried to recall him after he refused the People's Secretariat's demand that he leave Kyiv and pursue the Rada's retreating army. Lenin then appointed him as commander of a 'Special revolutionary army to fight the Romanian oligarchy' and dispatched him to fight near Tiraspol on the Romanian front. The Kyiv newspaper *Nova Rada* reported on 21 February that he had arrived in Odesa two days earlier to take up his new post. Muraviov would fight in the south of Ukraine over the following two months against the advancing occupation forces of the Central Powers before retreating into Russia where in July 2018 he took part in the uprising of his party, the left Russian SRs, against the Russian soviet government and died.

The Bolsheviks could restore civilian government only with the co-operation of other political parties and institutions they did not control at the moment of their victory. They needed to engage with people who did not necessarily share their beliefs and to widen their social base of support. How this process unfolded can be observed in their efforts to restore essential services to Kyiv's population. They entrusted maintenance of law and order to the Red Guards of the Kyiv Council of Workers' and Soldiers' Deputies. The Council needed a minimum of 4,000 of them to cope with the armed criminal gangs that were still stealing from homes, shops and warehouses, the drunkenness and debauchery on the streets, and what the Bolsheviks believed was an ongoing campaign to

---

8 Bosh, *God bor'by*, p. 144.
9 Savchenko, *12 viin za Ukrainu*, p. 54.

sabotage their work by pro-Rada and Black Hundreds elements still lurking in the capital. However, the Council could not muster a sufficient number of Red Guards, who had been exhausted and seen their ranks decimated by the January uprising. Nor could it find ready recruits from among those who came into Kyiv as part of Muraviov's army. They considered their job was done and just wanted to return home. The Council even tried to recruit former members of the Free Cossacks who stayed behind after their defeat, but the recruitment of new workers to the force proved difficult and slow.[10]

Kyiv was critically short of food and the population stood on the edge of hunger. In general the cities in Ukraine were better supplied than in Russia, which depended on Ukrainian grain and other foodstuffs whose delivery was severely disrupted by the war between the Rada and the Petrograd CPC. The Bolsheviks in Russia had been pressing their comrades in Ukraine throughout January 1918 to collect and send food to Russia's starving cities. But the People's Secretariat found Kyiv itself so lacking in food that it ordered emergency supplies to be sent by train from Kharkiv.

The long-term solution was to restore trade between the capital and the surrounding rural areas. The countryside was beset by ongoing land seizures, burning of landlord estates and banditry, where no government was recognised or in control.[11] The People's Secretariat sent 70 agitators to the outlying villages and encouraged a letter writing campaign by Kyivans to their country relatives to stimulate the resumption of trade.[12] Peasants started to bring food into the city markets, but not in any appreciable quantity. They were discouraged by the price controls which the authorities imposed on essential goods so that Kyiv's workers could afford them. Second, currency itself was in very short supply and it was hoarded by the rich. And third, the soldiers in the capital intimidated the peasants. Red Guards and garrison soldiers got their provisions and fodder for their horses by using ration vouchers issued by the garrison commander Stohny. They could afford very little using these vouchers and so they resorted to detaining peasant traders and setting their own prices or simply seizing the food and fodder outright. The People's Secretariat tried to combat such practices with decrees threatening arrest and punishment. It also ordered all officers without a military or civilian posting who did not have relatives in the city who could support them to leave within three days.[13]

---

10   *Nova Rada*, no. 17, 21 February 1918; Bosh, *God bor'by*, p. 150.
11   *Nova Rada*, no. 20, 24 February 1918.
12   *Nova Rada*, no. 14, 17 February 1918.
13   *Nova Rada*, no. 18, 22 February 1918.

On 20 February the food supply divisions of the city Duma and the Council of Workers' and Soldiers' Deputies joined forces to start a trade in kind of manufactured goods for foodstuffs. The authorities decreed a monopoly on trade in foodstuffs, requisitioned manufactured goods from retail outlets and warehouses and took them to the outlying villages themselves. Private traders responded by hiding their goods, leaving the appointed government bodies with only the depleted stocks still held by the city's co-operatives.

The People's Secretariat took further, more drastic measures on 24 February. Placing the blame for the hunger on the capitalists, landlords and kulaks, it appealed to workers' and peasants' councils throughout Ukraine to seize all the food surpluses they could find, pay a fixed, non-speculative price for them, hold them in designated warehouses and distribute them in the first instance to peasants and workers who could not afford to feed themselves. Anyone concealing surpluses or selling at speculative prices was subject to prosecution before a revolutionary tribunal. Bosh recalled that this decree initially elicited some alarm, but the councils were able to supply people in need with a half a pound of bread a day and so averted the further onset of hunger.[14] In Kyiv the bread ration fell from three quarters to one half of a pound and in some places to one quarter. Rye and wheat were in such short supply that the nationalised city's bakeries resorted to adding ground peas and millet to the 'bolshevik' loaves they baked.[15]

As the prospect of a confrontation with the incoming German army grew closer, the Bolsheviks began to confiscate whatever they could take with them in retreat: cattle, sugar, carts and barrows, machinery and lathes from factories. 'The Ukrainian peasants, who in their great majority stayed neutral during the struggle of the Bolsheviks with the Ukrainian Tsentral'na Rada, and in certain places even sympathised with the Bolsheviks, began to take up batons and rifles to defend themselves from the plunderers'.[16]

The short supply of money in circulation was more of a problem of the Bolsheviks' own making. The People's Secretariat decreed the abolition of the *karbovanets*, the currency issued by the Rada, and replaced it with the Russian rouble. Working people could exchange *karbovantsi* for up to 100 roubles at a time to tide them over until they started to be paid in roubles. The People's Secretariat ordered the State Bank in Kharkiv to send a supply of rouble bank notes to Kyiv. But the incoming administration underestimated the amount of roubles it actually needed, not least because most of the city's workers and

---

14   Bosh, *God bor'by*, pp. 148–50; Doroshenko, *Istoriia Ukrainy*, Vol. 1, pp. 340–1.
15   *Nova Rada*, no. 22, 27 February 1918.
16   Khrystiuk, *Ukrains'ka Revoliutsiia*, Vol. 2, p. 151.

employees of government institutions had not been paid for January, and some not even for December. Long queues formed at the banks. The State Bank division of the Soviet Ukrainian government struggled to move its operations from Kharkiv and start supervising and servicing the operation of private banks in Kyiv. All the remaining gold reserves in the local banks had been removed by the Rada. The Rada's promissory notes that were originally underwritten by these reserves and were circulating as a *fiat* currency alongside the *karbovanets* were now practically worthless. The situation grew worse with each passing day. The People's Secretariat and the Kyiv Council did not have enough roubles to pay the salaries of the Rada and Duma employees they were co-opting as their own. Private sector employers faced the same shortages. By 25 February, the Kyiv Council had no money to pay the Red Guards for the most basic service of policing the city.

Upon hearing a report from Kreisburg, commissar for finances, on the shortage of roubles, the Kyiv Council called for the restoration of the *karbovanets* as legal tender and sent a delegation to the Central Executive Committee of the Councils of Ukraine to persuade it to act. The People's Secretariat then turned to the headquarters of the State Bank in Petrograd requesting an advance of one million roubles and the temporary restoration of the *karbovanets* until such time as there were sufficient roubles in circulation to satisfy demand. However, Yurii Piatakov as People's Commissar of the State Bank flatly refused to consider the proposal and instead issued an ultimatum refusing the Soviet Ukrainian government a single *kopek* if it restored the Rada's currency, even temporarily. Piatakov came to Kyiv to advise the Ukrainian division of the State Bank, whom he promised a fully adequate supply of roubles to cover the exchange of all *karbovantsi* still in circulation. He left Kyiv with raised expectations only to dash them when no banknotes at all arrived from Petrograd for the remainder of the Soviet Ukrainian government's stay in Kyiv. The shortage of bank notes affected the work and the reputation of the People's Secretariat across the country. Workers' and soldiers' councils in urban centres who turned to the Secretariat for funds were asked to wait, indefinitely as it turned out. So they turned away from it and appealed directly to the state bank in Petrograd.[17]

The Bolsheviks had barely declared their objectives with respect to governing the capital and the country when they were confronted by a mutual mistrust between themselves and the employees of public institutions. The Bolsheviks had shunned the Rada and the city Duma throughout the first year

---

17   Bosh, *God bor'by*, pp. 140, 143, 151; Rafes, *Dva goda revoliutsii*, pp. 81–2; *Nova Rada*, no. 14, 17 February 1918; no. 18, 22 February 1918; no. 21, 26 February 1918; Zdorov, *Ukrains'kyi zhovten'*, p. 199.

of the Revolution and so they had little experience of how they were run and little influence over their administrative personnel. If any, they could exert some influence through the relevant trade unions of teachers, postal and telegraph workers, and others who had a voice in the determination or implementation of government policy in their particular area. These Bolsheviks, however, had ceded leadership to other parties in these sections of the work force and concentrated instead on the industrial proletariat. And after the bloody January battles with the forces of the Rada the Bolsheviks were deeply mistrustful of everyone who had been associated with it. They were convinced that the Rada's leaders had left behind in Kyiv an underground network of agents to wreck the food supply and money supply and to undermine their authority among the population.[18] So they placed the state institutions they took over from the Rada (very few were to be replaced altogether) under the supervision of commissars, who approved all decisions taken and kept an eye on the employees at work. Not all Bolsheviks agreed with this system of intense scrutiny and close management, arguing that it was better to have ten reliable administration employees than 100 unreliable ones. The commissars in the ministries, moreover, were supervised by the Commissariat of Internal Affairs headed by Bosh. She became the ultimate decision-maker when commissars lower down the chain of command refused to take responsibility and pushed the issue at hand upstairs to her. So she was overwhelmed every day by delegations from all kinds of institutions demanding a decision to their petitions and appeals, such as hospitals and orphanages asking for food rations to feed people in their care. 'A sea of tears, hysteria and threats made it extremely difficult for us to undertake any kind of creative work'.[19] So difficult was the situation in the capital that the People's Secretariat and the Central Executive Committee had little time to devote to other parts of Ukraine.

The Bolsheviks also encountered political resistance among administration workers, especially in the commissariat of education. Commissar Zatonsky announced to the teachers' council of Kyiv that he was disbanding the All-Ukraine Teachers' Union, the largest in the country, because it was encouraging 'nationalism and chauvinism'. The Union supported Ukrainian as the language of instruction in the schools, which Zatonsky regarded as 'forced Ukrainisation'. In answer to a remark by a member of the Council that there also existed a Russian teachers' union, Zatonsky informed the meeting that he had no intention of disbanding it because the Russian teachers were 'internationalists'.[20] The

---

18   Bosh, *God bor'by*, p. 144.
19   Bosh, *God bor'by*, pp. 146–7.
20   *Nova Rada*, no. 16, 20 February 1918.

administrative workers in the commissariat of education then served notice they would work under Zatonsky only on condition that he did not question the pedagogical guidelines adopted by the All-Ukraine congress of teachers and that all teachers' unions were represented on the teachers' advisory council attached to the commissariat. Furthermore, they demanded that all employees of the commissariat (formerly of the secretariat) who were under arrest be released and that no employees could be arrested in the course of performing their duties.[21]

The Mensheviks and right Russian SRs sought a reconciliation with the Bolsheviks and the preservation of the Kyiv Duma in which they held a majority. Although they disagreed on many fundamental issues, these parties of the Russian democracy welcomed the restoration of unity between Russia and Ukraine which the Bolsheviks were trying to achieve. Vynnychenko wrote that

> the head of the Kyiv Duma, the right SR and despiser of the Bolsheviks (Riabtsov) greeted their entry as a moment of 'reunification of the single Russian proletariat' (read 'united and indivisible Russia'), while the Black Hundreds and counterrevolutionary press, inasmuch as it was allowed to publish, uttered those words plainly and praised the Bolsheviks and their entire national policy ...[22]

No deputies to the Duma from the main Russian, Jewish and Ukrainian parties suffered repression at the hands of the Bolshevik authorities. The Duma continued to meet in session, but the new authorities placed all its departments under the supervision of commissars who reported to the Duma's general supervisor, commissar Preobrazhensky. Meanwhile the Kyiv Council of Workers' and Soldiers' Deputies debated how to liquidate this institution altogether and absorb its functions and administrative personnel.[23]

On 27 January, the Military Revolutionary Committee closed down the monarchist Russian language newspaper *Kievlianin* and brought its editor Vasyl Shulhyn before a tribunal on charges of counterrevolutionary activity. Its presses were given over to the Kyiv Council of Workers' and Soldiers' Deputies to issue its own newspaper *Izvestiia*. The Council also took possession of

---

21   *Nova Rada*, no. 18, 22 February 1918.
22   Vynnychenko, *Vidrodzhennia natsii*, Vol. 2, pp. 271–2; see also Rafes, *Dva goda evoliutsii*, p. 83.
23   *Nova Rada*, no. 15, 19 February 1918.

the Rada's printing press. The liberal democratic Russian newspaper *Kiievskaia mysl* was also closed down, its premises handed over to the Secretariat of Internal Affairs and its presses began publishing the Russian and Ukrainian editions of *Viestnik/Visnyk*, the organ of the People's Secretariat. *Posliedni novosti*, a third Russian newspaper was permitted to continue publishing. All the capital's Jewish and Polish publications kept coming out. *Nova Rada*, organ of the UPSF resumed publication on 17 February, nine days after Muraviov's army entered Kyiv and after an interruption lasting two weeks that began during the January uprising. Ukrainian language bookshops remained open. The USDWP's *Robitnycha hazeta*, the UPSR's *Narodna volia*, the UPSR leftists' *Borot'ba* and the Mensheviks' *Rabochaia zhizn* stopped publication and did not resume until the end of February, once the Bolsheviks were losing control of Kyiv.[24] Volodymyr Vynnychenko, editor of *Robitnycha hazeta*, had fled Kyiv, and Isaak Puhach, editor of the *Narodna volia*, was executed by a unit of sailors of the incoming army. Presumably the newspapers' workers either left Kyiv with the Rada's leaders or went underground.

The newspapers that were published did not shy away from criticising the Bolsheviks nor reporting news that revealed their setbacks and vulnerabilities. Yevgeniia Bosh singled out the Bund's *Volkzeitung*, the UPSF's *Nova Rada* and *Neue Zeit*, organ of the United Jewish Socialist Party. This last paper exclaimed that 'Bolshevik terror has now destroyed all the gains of the revolution in Ukraine. True, it has restored the unity of the Russian front, but there is a bigger question: just which front has it restored: that of the all-Russian revolution or the all-Russian counterrevolution?'[25]

Serhii Yefremov and Andrii Nikovsky, who edited *Nova Rada*, became increasingly bold in their reporting and commentary. They provided a steady stream of news from Brest Litovsk about the CPC delegation's difficulty and the Rada's success in securing a peace treaty, about the Rada's forces holding out west of Kyiv, and then about the armies of the Central Powers crossing the southwestern front into Volyn. A blank space appeared in the news column of the 23 February issue, revealing the censoring hand of a commissar, but this was a faint-hearted attempt at restraint by the new authorities. Indeed, rank and file members of the USDWP called a meeting for 19 February and felt confident enough to discuss the restoration of the party organisation and the newspaper. A meeting of journalists and writers issued a protest on 21 February about restrictions on the press in Kyiv and other cities. The USDWP's *Robitnycha haz-*

---

24   *Nova Rada*, no. 14, 17 February 1918; no. 22, 27 February 1918; no. 25, 3 March 1918.
25   Bosh, *God bor'by*, p. 145.

eta started publishing again on 26 February, as did the Menshevik *Rabochaia zhizn*. Two issues of *Borot'ba*, organ of the newly regrouped UPSR left wing, also appeared at this time.[26]

The deep erosion of the Rada's social base and then its expulsion from Kyiv produced splits in the parties which were represented in it. The split in the UPSR appeared when the party's left wing tried and failed to overthrow the General Secretariat led by Vynnychenko. The rank and file of the Bund split when the Rada failed to halt the antisemitic violence. The USDWP left wing was also implicated in the attempted coup against the General Secretariat and some of its members like Yukhym Medvedev joined the rival Soviet Ukrainian government in Kharkiv. The split in USDWP ranks was consummated when the Kyiv branch met on 19 February without its longstanding leaders. One section of the branch led by Yevhen Neronovych and Yevhen Kasianenko, possibly a majority of those present, called for the recognition of the People's Secretariat as the government of Ukraine and the nomination of party members to the Kyiv Council and other soviet bodies. A 'significant part' of the branch, according to *Nova Rada*, continued to support the Rada and the election of a Ukrainian Constituent Assembly. Their differences proved too great to bridge, so the first group resigned from the party and established a new one, the Left USDWP.

The declaration of the organising committee of the Left USDWP acknowledged and indeed welcomed the 'brotherly aid' given to the councils in Ukraine by the working people of the Russian republic. It blamed the Rada under USDWP leadership for trying to build a bourgeois state on the basis of national objectives alone and in doing so becoming the class enemy of the workers of Ukraine. The Left USDWP charged it with discriminating against large sections of the working class, favouring only its 'own' workers, citing Vynnychenko at the eighth plenary session of the Rada where he called the supporters of soviet government 'traitors to their native land, lackeys and spies'. The Rada had incited the masses against bolshevism as an allegedly exclusive Russian phenomenon. By disarming the Red Guards and arming the Free Cossacks 'to the teeth' it had sown national hatred and splintered the unity of the proletariat; it attacked the workers' press; it was responsible for the execution of unarmed workers and in turn it had elicited a wave of national hostility towards Ukrainians by the incoming revolutionary army of Muraviov.

The Left USDWP denounced the Rada's separate peace with the Central Powers which, they argued, placed Ukraine at the mercy of German imperialism.

---

26   *Nova Rada*, no. 15, 19 February 1918; no. 22, 27 February 1918.

Therefore national self-determination was violated by the Tsentral'na Rada itself because it used it against the aims of the working class. For that reason we cannot remain a moment longer in the party from which there are only defections, and from which the workers of Ukraine have turned away in disgust.

The new party would stand by 'the positive gains of the revolution', including the delimitation of the UPR's territory according to the Third Universal and its federative ties with other republics of Russia; and the promotion of national forms in socialist culture, especially in the education system; thus using such gains to strengthen soviet government in the republic and the fraternal unity of the international proletariat.

That is why we are forming a separate Left USDWP and delegating our representatives to all the institutions of soviet power in Ukraine to undertake the most active work within them.[27]

Evacuating Kyiv on 26 January the Rada became a government on wheels. The 3,000 soldiers and irregulars who accompanied it diminished to around 2,000. Along the way Mykola Porsh was replaced as Minister of Defence by Oleksandr Zhukovsky at the insistence of General Oleksandr Osetsky, chief of staff of the Rada's forces. Symon Petliura refused to obey Zhukovsky; he poached fighters from other units to enlarge his own, planning to engage in partisan warfare against the Bolsheviks. Vynnychenko broke away from the fleeing government, disguised himself and headed south with his wife to Berdiansk. As the retreating column approached Zhytomyr, a delegation from the city Duma met it on the road and asked it not to enter. The Bolsheviks had learned of the Rada's presence in the area and dispatched forces from Koziatyn and Zhmerynka in the direction of Zhytomyr and Berdychiv. The Rada's column then retreated towards Sarny in northern Volyn gubernia. From there they cleared a railway line to link up with Kovel where German forces were stationed together with the 'bluecoats' (*syn'ozhupannyky*), a division formed out of Ukrainians from prisoner of war camps in Germany.[28]

Humiliated by their expulsion from Kyiv some of the Rada's forces in retreat exacted vengeance on the Jewish communities through which they passed. They attacked Jews on 17 February at the Sarny and Korosten' railway stations. On 23 February when Rada forces took the Borodianka railway station, they killed two Jews. In Klavdievo nearby, seven more were killed. Petliura and his

---

27 *Nova Rada*, no. 17, 21 February 1918.
28 Hrushevsky, *Na Porozi novoii Ukrainy*, p. 184.

deputy Oleksandr Zahrodsky were at the Borodianka station at the time. Petliura declined to meet a delegation from the town, while Zahrodsky told them he could do nothing to restrain his 'exasperated' soldiers.

Rada forces fired on a delegation from the Berdychiv Council of Workers' Deputies, the city Duma and *zemstvo*, all of them controlled by Jewish political parties; the delegation had come out to meet them as they approached the city. Twenty people were killed on the first day the troops occupied the town. USDWP members called for an inquiry into this pogrom on 3 March at a meeting of the *mala rada*, which was still sitting in Zhytomyr and was composed solely of Ukrainian party deputies. Bund member Davyd Lipiets (Petrovsky) came especially to Zhytomyr in a personal capacity to deliver evidence of the pogrom for the inquiry to consider. So polarised was the situation that Lipiets refused to stay and take part in it.[29]

The Bolshevik-led forces pursuing the Rada were neither numerous nor determined enough to fight them. Many soldiers wanted to return home, even more so once they learned that the Rada had signed a peace treaty with the Central Powers. Muraviov himself did not pursue the retreating Rada ministers, ignoring orders from Petrograd to do so. Much of his army spontaneously demobilised within a week of taking Kyiv, leaving him with some 2–2,500 soldiers. Similarly, the Bolshevik-led Second Corps what came off the Southwestern front had melted away by 15 February, its soldiers streaming through Fastiv into Kyiv or continuing on eastwards on their way home.

Two or three days into their retreat the Rada's Council of People's Ministers learned that its representatives in Brest Litovsk had signed the peace treaty with the Central Powers in the early hours of the morning of 27 January. They established communications with them by telegraph and began to consult about their next steps. On 30 January they decided at a depleted meeting of the Council by a vote of four in favour with one abstention to ask the Central Powers for military assistance to drive the Bolsheviks out of Ukraine.[30] The Germans had anticipated that they would need either to prop up or restore the Rada's government. General Hoffmann already had the text of such a request at the ready for Liubynsky, head of the Rada delegation, to sign. However, the Rada had an additional request: that Ukrainian prisoners of war in German camps be formed up into a division to take part in the intervention. This request was granted and the Rada formally asked the Central Powers to intervene on its side in the war with the Bolsheviks.

29　Cherikover, *Istoriia pogromnogo dvizhenie na Ukraine 1917–1921 gg*, Vol. 1, pp. 119–20.
30　A. Hrytsenko, *Politychni syly u borot'bi za vladu v Ukraini (kinets' 1917 r.–pochatok 1918 r.)* (Kyiv: Akademiia Nauk Ukrainy, Instytut Istorii Ukrainy, Istorychni Zoshyty, 1993), p. 14.

Twenty-nine infantry divisions and four cavalry regiments of the German army, some 230,000 soldiers, and a roughly equal number of Austro-Hungarian troops crossed the Southwestern front on 18 February (by the Gregorian calendar). German forces took Rivne and Lutsk on 19 February and Novhorod-Volynsk two days later. All the while the Rada's column continued to retreat from Zhytomyr via Korosten to Sarny, which it reached on 19 February and Rivne on 21 February. A delegation from the Rada composed of Porsh, Tkachenko and Zhukovsky went on ahead to meet the first incoming units of German and Ukrainian soldiers. The Council of People's Ministers issued a proclamation to the Ukrainian people on 23 February accusing the Soviet Russian government of invading and plundering Ukraine and trying to prevent it from making peace with the Central Powers, to whom it had been obliged to turn to for help:

> A division of Ukrainian prisoners of war, the Ukrainian Sich Riflemen from Galicia and the German army are coming into Ukraine to help the Ukrainian Cossacks who are fighting gangs of Russian Red Guards and soldiers. They are coming into Ukraine to eradicate disorder, to bring peace and good order to our country and allow the Council of People's Ministers to undertake the great task of building an independent Ukrainian People's Republic. These armies, our friends, are going to fight the enemies of the Ukrainian People's Republic under the direction of the Field Command of our state.[31]

The Rada ended its retreat and turned for Kyiv. Petliura rode at the head of his contingent in the pose of liberator, behind him the massive German army.[32] Oleksandr Sevriuk, the young UPSR member in the Rada's delegation at Brest Litovsk, remembers sitting in a railway carriage on the return journey somewhere between Sarny and Zhytomyr with fellow party member Mykhailo Hrushevsky.

> We two sat alone together and Professor Hrushevsky was crying. The Germans coming into Ukraine was the drama of his life. Those people, who in their hatred for everything Ukrainian had linked his name through lies and slander to Austrian or German intrigues, now had new ammunition in their hands. A bitter and unwarranted irony of fate![33]

---

31 Khrystiuk, *Ukrains'ka Revoliutsiia*, Vol. 2, pp. 141–2.
32 Vynnychenko, *Vidrodzhenia natsii*, Vol. 2, pp. 292–4.
33 Sevriuk, *Beresteis'kyi myr*, p. 12.

Bitter it was, but unwarranted? Hrushevky, the renowned historian of the Ukrainian people, knew better than any of his contemporaries how Ukrainian statehood had been lost before when the aspirations of the masses parted ways with the aspirations of their nation's elite. In the revolutionary war of 1648–49 Ukraine's cossack leaders agreed in negotiations with the Polish crown to return the peasants and the cossack ranks to feudal servitude as a condition for their recognition as an independent nobiliary estate, 'so that a cossack be a cossack and commoner a commoner obedient to his master'.[34] The masses abandoned their leaders, who then lost in battle to the Poles and so had to turn for support to the Swedish crown, the Turkish sultan, the Crimean khan and finally in 1654 to the Russian tsar. The fledgling Hetmanate, ripped away from the Polish Lithuanian Commonwealth, retained its national autonomy as a protectorate of Muscovy for but a short time.

Now, the Rada having lost mass support and control of practically all the Ukrainian gubernia appealed for help from the Central Powers. Three times its leaders sought to reassure the Ukrainian masses – in their February 23 proclamation and in separate appeals by Prime Minister Holubovych and Hrushevsky himself – that the German and Austrian armies were coming to their aid as friends, only to defend their national independence, not to interfere in their domestic affairs nor deny them the social gains of their Revolution. Yet it was abundantly clear that the Rada was putting the UPR and the Ukrainian masses at the mercy of German imperialism. It had no easy choice, caught as it was between the German hammer and the Bolshevik anvil. But its inability to stand its ground stemmed not from its international predicament alone, dire as it was after four years of bloody war, but from the fact that the Rada had lost the confidence and support of the peasants and workers on its home territory. Perhaps the bitter irony was that the man most expected to have learned this lesson of Ukrainian history did not foresee history repeating itself and the 1917 Revolution coming to such an end. Perhaps that was why Hrushevsky cried.

As the Central Powers' armies marched into Ukraine and pressed once again on Petrograd in the north, the Russian Bolshevik delegation returned to the negotiating table at Brest Litovsk. Having signed with the Rada, Germany set out more exacting and onerous terms in a new treaty, demanding an immediate cessation of hostilities between Russia and Ukraine, the removal of all Russian army units and Red Guards and the conclusion of a peace treaty between Rus-

---

34 Mykhailo Hrushevsky, *Istoriia Ukrainy-Rusy*, Vol. IX, Section V, p. 4. http://litopys.org.ua/hrushrus/iur90504.htm.

sia and the UPR under a Rada government. On 23 February Yukhym Medvedev and Vasyl Shakhrai returned from Brest Litovsk to Kyiv to seek the approval of the People's Secretariat about some of the points of the peace treaty being proposed inasmuch as the UPR, according to the 15 January resolution of the Third All-Russian Congress of Soviets, was now a federated republic of the Russian Socialist Soviet Republic. The People's Secretariat responded to Germany's terms by insisting there was no war between Russia and Ukraine. It would agree to the same general trade clause in the treaty that the Rada had signed, but not to the export of grain and other foodstuffs to Austria and Germany while Russian cities were starving. Crucially, the People's Secretariat could not agree to the Central Powers' demand that the Rada be returned to power in Kyiv. Should they insist, the UPR under the People's Secretariat and the Central Executive Committee of the Councils of Ukraine would continue to be at war with them.

A new delegation composed of Yevhen Neronovych, Volodymyr Zatonsky and Rudenko was elected to go back to Brest Litovsk to continue the negotiations. But the news came via telegraph from Stalin that Germany and Austro-Hungary declined to negotiate with a Soviet Ukrainian delegation. More ominously, its armies had crossed the Southwestern front into Ukraine. The news spread a sense of helplessness and despair through the institutions of the Soviet government.[35]

The People's Secretariat issued defiant calls to defend Kyiv from the occupying armies 'Over our dead bodies will they come into the capital of Ukraine!' It declared the city under siege, formed an Extraordinary Defence Committee, prohibited people gathering on the streets, imposed a night curfew and ordered all available weapons to be delivered to its headquarters in the Pedagogical Museum. It had run out of funds to pay its soldiers, so it ordered the confiscation of gold from the city's residents. As Bosh recalled, the Committee did not get the support of the local population or even of the Kyiv city Bolshevik party organisation, whose members believed it was hopeless to try to resist the German army.

> Depression grew in the ranks of the Kyiv proletariat, deepened even more by the panicky rumours ... the workers of Kyiv felt themselves really powerless and ... not seeing a way out of the situation they began, individually and in groups, to get out of Kyiv.[36]

---

35 Bosh, *God bor'by*, p. 156; *Nova Rada*, no. 18, 21 February 1918; no. 21, 26 February 1918.
36 Bosh, *God bor'by*, p. 159. See also Savchenko, *12 viin za Ukrainu*, p. 76.

The Kyiv Council of Workers' and Soldiers' Deputies started its meeting late in the evening of 23 February because there was an electricity blackout. The mood in the hall was tense. Not all members of the People's Secretariat were able to come. Skrypnyk and Zatonsky reported on the preparations for the state of siege. Zatonsky reported on the advance of German and Austrian armies, that Dvinsk (today Daugavpils is a city in southeastern Latvia) had been taken and that the CPC was ready to sign a peace treaty on German terms. There was panic in Petrograd in government circles as well as among the public. However, Zatonsky went on, Stalin had informed him that the Austro-Hungarian armies would not take part in the offensive so the predicament of the UPR was not that bad. The Germans were advancing along the line from Zhytomyr through Korosten to Kyiv. The forces of the People's Secretariat would engage them with an armoured train and, if that did not work, they would retreat and blow up the railway lines. He told the deputies not to worry, the Germans would not get into Kyiv. Skrypnyk added soberly that the government could fight for another ten to fifteen days.

The Council of Workers' and Soldiers' Deputies met again on the following day. Yevhen Neronovych, representing the Extraordinary Defence Committee, spoke with some optimism that they had attacked Petliura's detachment, they had aeroplanes ready to deploy if needed and that the situation was improving for them by the hour. 'Therefore, one more blow and the country will be cleared of these disorganised bands'.

Bosh then addressed the Council, offering an assessment of the broader political situation. The bourgeoisie in Ukraine was smashed, she said, but not quite dead. The Bolsheviks needed a revolutionary army, but as there was not enough time to mobilise it, they would have to rely on a temporary standing army of soldiers on monthly paid contracts. The councils were charged with protecting vodka stocks from looters, but they were discharging their responsibilities poorly across the gubernia of Kyiv, Podillia and Volyn. In Kyiv city itself they were faring far worse for lack of Red Guards. All kinds of delegations were demanding funds from Bosh, threatening to seize goods of value if they did not get any. She was working 18–20 hours a day and threatened to resign if she did not get more co-operation from the councils.

Some deputies criticised the Bolsheviks' policies and methods of governing, in particular the split they had created between the urban and rural population. They also accused the Bolsheviks of taking part in looting public property whereupon they were shouted down by the Bolshevik deputies. The Bundist Kheirets and Menshevik Dmytro Chyzhevsky were not allowed to finish their interventions. Chyzhevsky, once a deputy in the Rada, was threatened from the floor: 'It's strange that you are still alive'. The Council voted overwhelmingly, with only one opposed and 18 abstentions, to back the People's Secretariat. The left UPSR deputies introduced an amendment to the effect 'that the policies of the People's Secretariat should take account of national specificities'. It was rejected.[37]

In the early hours of 25 February several hundred people gathered outside the Kyiv Duma asking for more information about the peace treaty signed by the Rada and the Central Powers. A man climbed onto a nearby monument and began to read out aloud the text of the actual treaty (it was published in the newspaper *Nova Rada*, of quite limited circulation). An armed unit of Red Guards arrived on the scene, fired shots in the air and the panicked crowd fled in all directions.[38]

The Duma offered to mediate between the German and Ukrainian armies and the People's Secretariat. The Duma's intention was to prevent pogroms and other acts of vengeance against those who had supported or co-operated with the Bolshevik government. Revenge would fall in the first instance on the Bolsheviks who stayed behind, the trade unions and the Jews. It appointed a delegation of five deputies, one each from the UPSF, USDWP, the Russian SRs, Mensheviks and the Bund, to meet the incoming armies before they reached Kyiv. The Duma was ready to protect public order and government property using a neutral armed force, a Georgian unit stationed in Kyiv, while the Ukrainian soldiers supporting the Rada should remain outside of the city. The delegation wanted the Rada to agree to an amnesty of those taking part in the January uprising, a guarantee of freedom for trade unions and political parties, and a ban against summary justice or repression.[39]

Moshe Rafes, who served as the main point of contact between the Duma and the People's Secretariat, went to see Yevgeniia Bosh about the Duma's plan. She understood it to mean the 'painless liquidation' of the People's Secretariat and the Duma's assumption of power in Kyiv. On hearing Bosh's report of this exchange, the People's Secretariat decided to arrest the Duma deputies, but relented when the Central Bureau of Trade Unions threatened to withdraw all support for the Secretariat.[40]

On 26 February an explosion of munitions in two railway wagons spread alarm through the city. People thought the Germans had already started shelling. An emergency joint meeting of People's Secretariat, the Kyiv Council

---

37   *Nova Rada*, no. 21, 26 February 1918.
38   *Nova Rada*, no. 22, 27 February 1918.
39   Rafes, *Dva goda*, p. 84; *Nova Rada*, no. 25, 3 March 1918.
40   Bosh, *God Bor'by*, p. 159.

and the Bolshevik party leadership heard a report from Kotsiubynsky, commissar of war, that they would not be able to hold the city. The meeting resolved to remove all valuables from the State Bank and to evacuate the Soviet government to Poltava. Party members rushed to the Kyiv railway station to leave. Only three members of the People's Secretariat remained behind – Kotsiubynsky, Bosh and Aussem.

The Executive Committee of the Council of Workers' and Soldiers' Deputies also left Kyiv on 26 February without calling a plenary session of the Council or notifying anyone of their departure. They were in such a hurry that they left behind their rifles stored in the cellars of the Mariinsky palace. The members of the Executive Committee who worked at the State Bank closed it down properly and removed all the bank's valuables and papers. The amount of money taken from all the banks in Kyiv was rumoured to be in the order of 40 million *karbovantsi*.[41] The flight of the Council's executive committee left a deeply negative impression on the factory workers it had represented. The workers were left behind to close down production and organise a round-the-clock guard of their factories.

On 27 February the Bund and the Mensheviks called a meeting of the Kyiv Council of Workers' and Soldiers' Deputies in the Merchants Hall. The packed meeting called out the remaining members of the People's Secretariat, who arrived just as Rafes was proposing a new executive committee be elected. Bosh addressed this meeting and denounced Rafes for the Duma's plan to send a delegation to meet the German advance. The meeting supported her and resolved to prepare to defend the city. However, a joint meeting of the Presidium of the Central Executive Committee of the Councils and the People's Secretariat held immediately afterwards did not uphold this resolution, arguing it was too late as the incoming forces were but 30 versts (33 kilometres) from Kyiv. This meeting called on the members of the Bolshevik party's Kyiv Executive Committee who had fled to return to Kyiv. And the three remaining members of the People's Secretariat insisted on staying in Kyiv until they came back.

On 28 February the editors of the People's Secretariat bulletin *Viestnik/Visnyk* announced it would not be coming out as the print workers would no longer be able to travel the dangerous streets to work. That night Kyiv's main passenger station filled up with workers and their families carrying their household belongings, desperate to get out of the capital. From midnight train after train pulled out of the station. Bosh, Kotsiubynsky and Aussem were on one of these, heading for Poltava. As soon as they had gone the general staff and

---

41   *Nova Rada*, no. 28, 7 March 1918.

its remaining detachments of Red Guards and railway battalions left the city, crossing over to the Left Bank of the Dnipro in the morning hours of 1 March. By that time the Rada's *haidamaky* soldiers were entering from the other, western side of the city.[42]

42   Bosh, *God bor'by*, pp. 162–4, 188.

CHAPTER 10

The Pogroms in March and April 1918

The armies of the Central Powers swept through the Ukrainian gubernia to the Russian border in 70 days. They came over the Southwestern front on 18 February and marched in four groups along routes roughly parallel to one another before converging on the Donbas. The first group, made up of German divisions, departed from Brest Litovsk, passed through Homel, Chernihiv and Novhorod-Siversk before turning south for Kharkiv, which it captured in the first days of April. The second group, also German, left Kovel and met up with the Rada's forces on the way to Sarny, the furthest point to which the Rada had retreated from Kyiv. They then marched together to Kyiv, the advance units of Ukrainian soldiers entering the city on 1 March. From Kyiv they went on to capture Kremenchuk (25 March), Poltava (28 March) and Kharkiv (8 April). The Zaporozhian regiment, the UPR's largest military unit, marched ahead of this second army group on the way to Kharkiv, growing in strength to some 20,000 bayonets and swords, five armoured trains, 12 armoured cars, 64 cannons and four aeroplanes. The third was the Austro-Hungarian army group that set out from near Zhytomyr, passed through Vynnytsia and captured Katerynoslav on 2 April. A fourth army composed of Austro-Hungarian and German divisions marched out of Vynnytsia along a south easterly route between the Dnister and Buh Rivers towards the Black Sea. There it took Odesa (13 March) and Mykolaiv (17 March) before getting bogged down in a bitter fight to take Kherson (5 April). This army then proceeded across Northern Tavria towards Mariupol and Tahanrih in the far southeastern tip of territory above the Sea of Azov claimed by the UPR. A part of this army peeled off and went south to take Crimea, the port of Sevastopol falling to German forces on 29 April. And finally, a section of the UPR's Zaporozhian regiment and German forces left from Kharkiv for the south, captured Lozova and Kostiantynohrad (today Kropyvnytsky) and broke into the heart of the Donbas. They faced determined resistance there before the region fell to them in the last days of April.[1]

Along the way through the centre of the country, the second army group was supported by detachments of around 8,000 Free Cossacks. They controlled large swathes of southern Kyiv and northern Kherson gubernia. The Free Cossacks disarmed pro-Bolshevik remnants of the retreating Second Guards Corps

---

1 Bosh, *God bor'by*, Appendix, Map 2.

and blocked communications along the north-south railway lines. From the middle of March, they supported UPR forces operating in Poltava and Chernihiv gubernia. However, the German army command objected to their involvement in the campaign and ordered they be disarmed. The Rada complied at the end of March, banning their formations altogether.[2]

1   A New Wave of Pogroms

Between the time the Bolsheviks left Kyiv and the Rada's forces entered it, the Military Commissariat of Georgia sent out automobile patrols under its own national flag to keep order and calm. The city Duma sent a five-person delegation to Sviatoshyn to meet the Rada troops and try to negotiate their peaceful entry. In conversations with the soldiers there they learned how hostile they felt towards the residents of Kyiv, as though they were about to enter a foreign city.[3] They directed their hostility especially towards the Jewish population who they said had fired on them in their retreat, towards the Jews who served as commissars under the Bolsheviks' brief rule, and famous individual Bolsheviks like Trotsky and Joffe. 'Yid Trotsky is making war on Ukraine with support from the Jewish capitalists', they said. On hearing about this Yevhen Chykalenko, a prominent Ukrainian civic activist lamented: 'They will smother Ukrainian freedom in Jewish blood'.[4]

The Duma delegation met Petliura and Kostiantyn Prisovsky, who led the Separate Zaporozhian Detachment, the largest Rada unit returning to Kyiv. They told them the Bolsheviks had evacuated from Kyiv and expressed their fear that the incoming Rada forces could unleash a pogrom. Rafes recalled:

> We spoke with him as a member of a social democratic party. In reply Petliura said 'he cannot not give any guarantees; he knows about the feelings of the soldiers but he sees in them a thirst for vengeance, not antisemitism'. However, for safety's sake Petliura decided to lead the army into the city not through Jewish Podil but the suburb of Kurienivka.[5]

---

2 Savchenko, *12 viin za Ukrainu*, pp. 81, 100.
3 *Nova Rada*, no. 26, 5 March 1918.
4 Elias Cherikover, *Istoriia pogromnogo dvizhenia na Ukraine 1917–1921 gg*, Tom 1, Berlin 1923 (Berlin: Direct Media, 2015), p. 107.
5 Ibid; Rafes, *Dva goda revoliutsii na Ukraine*, pp. 83–4.

Rather than bringing all their troops into Kyiv the delegation proposed that the Duma itself retain responsibility for maintaining order in the city and protecting government buildings. It proposed a full amnesty be granted to those who took part in the January uprising against the Rada. The Duma wanted the Rada to reiterate its support for freedom of association of the trade unions and all political parties and not to permit acts of summary justice by its soldiers.[6]

The Rada's soldiers entered the city on 1 March ahead of the German divisions. Ministers of the government returned a few days later, and after them came the presidium and deputies of the *mala rada*.[7] Oleksandr Zhukovsky, acting minister of military affairs, and Prisovsky went to the city Duma, where they met its head Ye. Riabtsov on 1 March. They authorised the city police force to guard government buildings and to take control of the post, telegraph and telephone services. But Zhukovsky insisted that the police come under Prisovsky's direct command.

> I pointed out that the (Kyiv) police should be subordinated to the Gubernatorial Commandant for the sake of a greater concentration of authority, insofar as I don't have here enough forces of my own to defend the whole city. I have to increase my forces; that is what this moment requires. I declare the city in a state of siege, so let the population calmly take those orders that are given by the relevant individuals. The government does not mean to maintain order using force and the bayonet.

Prisovsky asked the Duma not to interfere in any of the workers' organisations. The Arsenal's workers approached the Duma for permission to gather for a meeting. Naturally, they were wary of the incoming authority, whose soldiers had suppressed the uprising in the Arsenal just six weeks earlier. According to the newspaper *Nova Rada*, the Duma responded by saying it had no concerns about the workers who were still in Kyiv and that they should hold their meeting.[8]

Prisovsky, given command over Kyiv gubernia, issued an order prohibiting arbitrary arrests, detentions or other acts of summary justice. Ensign Vlasenko of the Khmelnytsky Serdiuk Regiment, who presented himself as the 'Ukrainian commander of the city of Kyiv', provided further reassurance and advice: 'I promise you there will be no acts of summary justice whatsoever on the part of the Ukrainian army … I call on you to return to your good labours. Be assured

---

6 *Nova Rada*, no. 24, 2 March 1918.
7 Hrushevsky, *Na Porozi Novoii Ukrainy*, p. 184.
8 *Nova Rada*, no. 25, 3 March 1918.

that I stand by you and your work ... Rid yourself of bandit bolshevism which has given you nothing but trouble and unemployment'.[9]

Meeting Ukrainian officers on 1 March Zhukovsky gave them the order of the day: 'The Gubernatorial Commandant should immediately purge the city of Kyiv of its negative element. Establish a tight relationship with the Germans'.[10]

Kyiv came under martial law, a 'state of siege' as it was called then, enforced by the *haidamaky* and Free Cossacks, who were subordinated to Prisovsky and ultimately to Zhukovsky. They were joined two days later by the substantially larger German army, and soon after that by its high command. Being among the first to arrive, Petliura wanted to be seen as the liberator of Kyiv. He paraded his *haidamaky* on the square in front of St Sophia and had the Orthodox clergy hold a service to bless them. Hrushevsky, Holubovych and Zhukovsky saw in Petliura a posturing 'Ukrainian Napoleon' who might be preparing to usurp power in a coup. He was, after all, quite popular among the troops and the Kyiv conservative intelligentsia, both Ukrainian and Russian, for his anti-Bolshevism. The German high command was also suspicious of Petliura, knowing full well his contacts with the Entente. Such concerns led the Rada's Council of People's Ministers to relieve Petliura of his command on 12 March. His soldiers were reassigned to an infantry unit under lieutenant Sikevych and sent to the front to pursue the retreating Bolsheviks.[11]

Prisovsky on becoming Gubernatorial Commander handed the Zaporozhian Detachment over to Oleksandr Natiiev, when it was renamed a Brigade. Already while under Prisovsky and then under Natiiev the soldiers were subjected by nationalist officers to antisemitic agitation and calls for a Rada government without national minorities. Zhukovsky feared they were preparing to use the Brigade in a coup against the Rada and decided to send it out of Kyiv onto the front against the Bolsheviks. He met determined opposition to his decision from leading UPSI members I. Lutsenko, Oleksandr Stepanenko, and O. Ustymovych, and officers P. Bolbochan and Oleksandr Shapoval. It was not until mid-March that the Brigade left Kyiv.[12]

The pogrom began soon after the Rada's soldiers entered the centre of Kyiv. They began whipping people in the streets and making random arrests on the pretext of searching for 'Jewish commissars'. The arrested were taken to the Rada's army headquarters in the cellars of Mykhailivsky Monastery. Three

[9] *Nova Rada*, no. 24, 2 March 1918.
[10] Zhukovsky, *Vspomyny*, p. 145.
[11] Savchenko, *Symon Petliura*, pp. 185–8.
[12] Pavlo Hai-Nyzhnyk, *Kostiantyn Prisovs'kyi: biohrafichnyi narys*, http://www.hai-nyzhnyk.in.ua/doc/220doc.php; accessed 29 November 2018.

members of the Bund were among those murdered there – the shoemakers Khatkin and Lindheim and a deputy to the Rada, Sukhorovych-Lintam. Twenty-two bodies were dumped on Volodymyr's Mount, accessible from the back doors of the monastery. Other bodies were reported to have been thrown into the Dnipro River. Hardest hit by the violence were the Jewish neighbourhoods of Podil and Darnytsia.[13]

On 4 March head of the Duma Riabtsov made an impassioned appeal 'in the name of the future of the Ukrainian People's Republic' to *otaman* Donchenko of the Free Cossacks, reminding him that among Jews and Ukrainians there were both opponents and supporters of the Bolsheviks. 'I am asking you to stop this bloody vengeance and restore the rule of law'.[14] Ukrainian socialist deputies in the Duma visited the places where people were being held and demanded their release. They issued their own appeal to the soldiers: 'Don't besmirch Ukraine with summary justice and violence ... we believe you won't allow pillage and violence against innocent people no matter which nation they belong to'.[15] The Duma made further appeals to Zhukovsky and Prisovsky. Holubovych met representatives from the Jewish community who demanded he use the full force of his office as prime minister. He replied that the government was aware of the situation and there was no cause for alarm. A deputy minister for internal affairs, the acting commissar for Kyiv gubernia and the Kyiv city commissar Margulis toured the Podil district on 6 March. According to *Nova Rada* they concluded that the night before there had been no 'excesses or insurgencies'.[16] The Jewish community, however, felt the government remained indifferent to its fate because it regarded the claims of violence against its members as exaggerated.

A commission of the Duma collected evidence for the period of 1–8 March and found there had been 172 attacks on Jews, including 22 murders, 11 cases of torture, three rapes, 19 threats of execution, the arrest of 28 people on charges still unknown, and 16 people who remained missing. The commission's aim was to defend the Jewish community from the violence, but it was able only to gather evidence about it. When it made its findings public and Hrushevsky publicly read out the whole report, the Rada authorities started to issue orders to stop the violence. But that did not stop it as no attempt was made to apprehend or punish the perpetrators. The attacks on Jews in Kyiv lasted this time

---

13 Cherikover, *Istroiia pogromnogo dvizhenia na Ukraine*, p. 120; Rafes, *Dva Goda Revoliutsii*, p. 84; Abramson, *Molytva za Vladu*, pp. 148–9.
14 *Nova Rada*, no. 26, 5 March 1918.
15 Cherikover, *Istroiia pogromnogo dvizhenie na Ukraine*, p. 121.
16 *Nova Rada*, no. 28, 7 March 1918.

until 20 March. The Rada formed an investigating commission; the nominated representative from the Duma Ulianytsky walked out of it, protesting that it was not really investigating the pogroms but the activity of the Bolsheviks.[17]

Pogroms broke out in other parts of Kyiv gubernia: on 1 March in Korosten and in Radomyshl on the following day. In both places the commanders of Ukrainian army units demanded 'contributions' from the local community in the name of the central government of the Rada. There were further attacks in Buch, Hostomel, Khabno, Brovary and Hoholeve. In Hoholeve, they killed two Jews, looted households and publicly humiliated individuals.

The pogroms spread along the railway lines linking Kyiv to Poltava and Bakhmach as the Rada's forces advanced along them with the German armies. In March and April Jewish passengers at stations along these lines were beaten, robbed and killed. The worst violence took place in Hrebinka, where 18 people were killed, and in Romodan, where up to 40 were killed. Similar scenes were in evidence at the Bakhmach railway station. A German officer there claimed he could do nothing to prevent the attacks while neither the station master nor the local police took any preventative measures either.

Two reports on the pogroms were submitted by the Zionists (M. Grosman) and the United Jewish Socialist party (M. Shats-Anin) to the *mala rada* sitting on 16 April. Both were adopted on 20 April. However, some Ukrainian deputies, including Ukrainian Labour Party member Fedir Kryzhanivsky and the UPSR member Nikifor Hryhoriev, accused the Jewish deputies of exaggerating the gravity of the attacks. Hryhoriev called the authors of the reports 'a dishonest opposition'.

Pogroms continued to spread in the latter half of April to other towns in Kyiv and Poltava gubernia. One of these took place on 23 April in Tarashcha, Kyiv gubernia where a unit of soldiers looted and wrecked Jewish homes, wounding nine inhabitants, including four women. On 29 March Rada soldiers occupying Poltava started killing Jews on the streets, and then rounding them up and taking them to the local military college. There they were subjected to beatings, forced to beat one another, to shout slogans hailing a free Ukraine and denouncing 'zhydy' and 'katsapy', after which they were released. Officers of the incoming army denied any responsibility for these repressions, while the word on the streets of Poltava put the blame on colonel Oleksandr Shapoval, who belonged to the UPSI (not to be confused with Mykyta Shapoval of the UPSR).

Violence occurred in Konstantynohrad, Poltava gubernia, in which three Jews were killed, and at the beginning of April in Kremenchuk. The Kremen-

---

17   Cherikover, *Istroiia pogromnogo dvizhenia na Ukraine*, pp. 122–4.

chuk city Duma launched an investigation, but nothing came of it. Thus a wave of pogroms spread across Ukraine in February, March and April. According to Elias Cherikover, the historian and chronicler of the pogroms, 'this was the first encounter of the national army of Ukraine with the Jewish population'.[18]

Parallel to the pogroms carried out by the army were pogroms by peasants. These were of a more 'passive' kind: looting of Jewish homes and businesses, and non-Jewish residents resisting and boycotting investigations into them by the police. Appeals by Jewish community leaders to the gubernia police often resulted in accusations of wholesale collaboration with the Bolsheviks being hurled back at them and further threats of violence, which were sometimes actually carried out by army units sent into the settlement in question to restore 'order'. In some parts of Kyiv and Podillia gubernia the Ukrainian villagers drove out their longstanding Jewish neighbours. It became a more frequent occurrence that the Jewish residents of entire districts were compelled to give up their homes and flee to larger towns and cities.[19]

Just who bore responsibility for carrying out the pogroms in the population centres reclaimed by the Rada? Who condemned them and who tried to justify them? The Ukrainian press reported them, spoke out against them and called for their investigation by commissions under community control. However, they were not all prepared to identify those responsible, even at the general level of acknowledging the involvement of the Free Cossacks and units of the army. *Robitnycha hazeta* of the USDWP was forthright, the UPSR's *Narodna volia* less so. The UPSF's *Nova Rada* reported the pogroms, but distinguished itself by justifying them in the words of their perpetrators.

Nova Rada under the editorship of Serhii Yefremov and Anton Nikovsky, first reported repressions against Kyiv's Jews in its 5 March issue. It reported that army officers seeking revenge against the Bolsheviks for having executed so many of their fellow officers were pointing the Jews out to the soldiers; Black Hundreds elements were trying to start a pogrom against the wider Jewish community. The 6 March issue carried a denial by the Free Cossacks of any involvement in summary justice or executions that were being carried out by people in military uniform.

Nova Rada published an alleged eye-witness account on 7 March under the name A. Yarynovych, who turned out to be co-editor-in-chief Nikovsky writing under a pseudonym.[20] The author had gone to a Free Cossack encampment on

---

18   Cherikover, *Istroiia pogromnogo dvizhenia na Ukraine*, p. 130.
19   Ibid.
20   This according to Cherikover, *Istoriia pogromnogo dvizenia na Ukraine*, pp. 135–6.

Vasylkivsky Street to secure the release of Lazar Borysovych Furfurnyk (probably an invented name) who was rumoured to have been beaten nearly to death. Furfurnyk turned out to be unharmed and only 'mildly intimidated'. The Cossacks told the author that not a single Jew helped them when they were defending Kyiv in January and that Jews wearing Red Cross armbands took food and information as to their whereabouts to the Bolsheviks. When the Bolsheviks took power all the Jewish youth joined the Red Guards.

> We are not antisemites, says another. We know the Tsentral'na Rada gave national personal autonomy to Jews and we have nothing against that. But it is one thing to write laws, give speeches and publish newspapers, and another thing to fight. WE are soldiers and we respond to fire with fire, to a blow with blows, and to ambush and treason with caution and a show of strength.

'Hearing that sort of erudition, that people are acting out of conviction, that their logical construction is not a primitive one', Yarynovych/Nikovsky decided to plead for Furfurnyk's release into his own custody on the grounds that he did not believe he was a 'Bolshevik commissar' and he did not want the Cossacks to have an innocent man's death on their conscience. The Cossacks handed him over to this 'man of the word' and the entire incident ended happily. On returning from his visit the author reflected that the Jewish community should indeed disassociate itself from those of its members who worked with the Bolsheviks.

On the following day Nikovsky published another lengthy article entitled 'Jews and the Ukrainian army', this time under his own name.[21] He blamed the Jews of Kyiv for attacks on the Rada that led to its defeat and expulsion from the city.

> Finally they had to leave. 'Kyiv' was shooting them in the back all the way to the last small building before Sviatoshyn. Spotting their enemy individually and in groups they could see that it was all Jewish youths – university and high school students and workers ... Red Guardists, who were Jews in the main, were executing Ukrainians just because they were Ukrainian, while their fathers and brothers were informing, pointing out who among the Ukrainians was hiding and where, who was in favour of Ukrainian rule ... Kyiv accepted and recognised Bolshevik rule, that is, it accepts and recognises any rule as long as it is not Ukrainian.

---

21   *Nova Rada*, no. 28, 8 March 1918.

> The Cossacks have come again to Kyiv. To what have they come? To nothing other than a hostile city.

Nikovsky went on to accuse the city Duma, which had just released its report of the pogroms, of lumping together 'ordinary night murders and a few, careless acts by the cossacks'. He accused Jews of continuing to agitate against the Ukrainian government, of selling out to the Germans, seeking to work with them while waiting for the restoration of a Russian government, even a Bolshevik one. He exonerated the cossacks and Ukrainian army units on the grounds that they were still at war with their enemies, among whom there were many Jews. His thoughts returned to where he had rescued Furfurnyk just the day before:

> ... on Vasylkivsky Street such things are going on that one has to be on the lookout every step of the way lest some bullet of a national minority gets you ... Why have they not yet declared that the Kreisbergs, Reichsteins and Chudnovskys are criminals in the eyes of the Ukrainian state and of the Jewish people?

Cherikover observed on reading these lines: 'This was what the most moderate and solid Ukrainian periodical wrote in the heat of *haidamaky* violence, giving full moral and psychological justification for such violence'.[22]

Vynnychenko saw the pogroms as a consequence of *otamaniia*, that is warlordism, when military rule replaced civilian government and summary justice ruled. In his account of the 1919 pogroms, when Petliura was 'Chief Otaman' of the Directory of the Ukrainian People's Republic, he describes the social origins and ideological bent of the protagonists that we see already at work in the first months of 1918:

> ... there were two kinds of *otamaniia* which gave vent to the pogromist lode. One sort was the Black Hundreds, those openly counterrevolutionary and provocative Russian officers who made up a significant percentage of the commanders of the Ukrainian army. This *otamaniia* to a certain extent was the initiator and organiser of pogroms, which were useful and necessary for discrediting the Ukrainian government ...
>
> The second kind of *otamaniia* was of a fervent Ukrainian kind. The national moment was the main factor here. The sons of shop keepers,

---

22 Cherikover, *Istoriia pogromnogo dvizenia na Ukraine*, pp. 135–7.

middle landowners, priests and simple peasants, had been poisoned since their infancy by the spirit of antisemitism. Sharpening national conflicts and the alignment of Jewish workers with the Bolsheviks untied the hands of these dark souls, as though it gave them the right to pour out their angry emotions. And it is understandable that, given the opportunity, these types of people would rob and pillage and blackmail at will in such pogroms.[23]

When applied to the historical developments in the first months of 1918 Vynnychenko's second category of pogromists is synonymous with the Free Cossacks and the Ukrainian Party of Socialist Independentists. Goldelman says that 'from their ranks sprang a considerable number of *otamany*'.[24] Zhukovsky wrote: 'The majority of our Ukrainian Black Hundreds join this party. It presents itself as a democratic organisation, but that is just a label, a fig leaf with which it tries to conceal its nakedness'.[25]

2 Pogroms Carried Out by Red Forces

The Red Guards and army units led by Bolsheviks and Russian SRs carried out anti-Jewish pogroms in March and April 1918 in north eastern Chernihiv gubernia and Polissia in the regions of Hlukhiv, Novhorod-Siversk and Seredyna Buda. These pogroms took place during clashes with the German army advancing through this area towards the border between Russia and Ukraine. At the time the Soviet Russian government was encouraging local Red Guard units to resist the Austro-German occupation, but it was not providing coordination or leadership to them. Nor was there any active government policy to combat antisemitism among the fighters in these units.

Red forces retreating through Homel tried to carry out a pogrom in the town, but were repulsed by a Jewish self-defence group, in the process of which several pogromists were killed. The soldiers then spread word among peasants that they had been fired upon by Jews in their retreat. In Mhlyn the Jewish leader of the workers' council was killed while attending a meeting of the district council of peasant deputies. Incoming Red Army units then carried out a pogrom,

---

[23] Volodymyr Vynnychenko, *Vidrodzhennia natsii*, Section XII: Rozvytok reaktsiynostu rezhymu otamanshchyny.
[24] Goldelman, *Jewish National Autonomy in Ukraine*, p. 59.
[25] Zhukovsky, *Vspomyny*, p. 160.

wrecking Jewish homes, killing 15 people and injuring more. The First Lenin Regiment of the Red Army ransacked Jewish homes in the town of Surazh, this time without fatalities, in order 'to punish the counterrevolutionaries' who had greeted the incoming Germans with bread and salt, a ritual welcoming ceremony.

The Kharkiv newspaper *Sotsial-Demokrat* reported on 7 March a pogrom in the railway town of Hlukhiv that spilled over to the nearby village of Esman and went on for two and a half days. It occurred as control of the town was changing hands between the Baturyn regiment, which declared itself on the side of the Rada and drove the Bolsheviks out of Hlukhiv, and the Roslavlsky brigade of Red Guards from Kursk which was coming to the aid of the local Bolsheviks. The brigade, led by Oleksii Tsyhanko, decided 'to put all bourgeois and Jews to the sword'. Local workers and peasants joined the brigade in its violence, as did some of the soldiers of the Baturyn regiment itself, who insisted the town's Jews had employed them to fight the Bolsheviks. With great cruelty they killed over 100 Jews, men, women and children from proletarian and bourgeois families. They fired on the synagogue and tore up the scrolls of its Torah. The Rada-appointed commander in the town and all the officers of the Baturyn regiment were executed. The town council protested the killings on the second day, but to no avail. Over the graves of their partisans who died in battle with the Baturyn regiment the Red Guards placed memorial scripts bearing the words 'Long live the International'.

Pravda, central organ of the Russian Bolsheviks, reported on 8 March the events in Hlukhiv without disclosing that they included an anti-Jewish pogrom. The newspaper reported a military clash when 'the brave Roslavlsky regiment occupied Hlukhiv' and restored the rule of the town council. Soon after Easter the Hlukhiv council imposed a compulsory contribution on the Jewish community, threatening another pogrom if it did not comply.

On 19 March, a Red Army detachment killed 20 fleeing Jews in nearby Seredyna Buda. The entire district of Hlukhiv was gripped by fear, with many Jews hiding in the woods and fields. Some of them were apprehended by local peasants and turned over to the Red Army. The pogroms spread to villages in the adjacent Sosnyts district from which over 120 Jewish residents fled to the town of Korkhivka, then under German occupation.

On 6 April, just as the fighting between the Bolshevik-led forces and the German and Ukrainian armies was dying down, a pogrom broke out in Novhorod-Siversk, carried out this time by Red Army soldiers retreating from Sosnyts to Briansk. It began when the soldiers searched Jewish homes on the pretext of uncovering weapons, but in reality to steal from them. A second Red Army brigade entered the town under the command of the sailor Bereta; he called together the town's well-to-do Jews and demanded 750,000 roubles from them. The local Jewish self-defence detachment repulsed Bereta's brigade when it tried to start a pogrom and expelled it from the town. But the brigade returned and together with the town's policemen killed 88 Jews, seriously wounding another 11. Some of the town's Jews who fled were killed in the countryside, where the peasants refused to shelter them for fear of being executed themselves for doing so.

The Germans occupied Novhorod-Siversk on 7 April, but were pushed out again by Red Army detachments. The entire surviving Jewish population of the town followed them in their retreat. They returned to their homes again with the Germans on 8 April. The Bolshevik forces then retreated over the border to Pohar in Briansk gubernia, wreaking vengeance on the Jews living in villages along their path of retreat, killing eleven in Hrymiach. The violence spread further across the district and 24 Jews in all were left dead.[26]

Soon after the *Pravda* report about the 'brave Roslavlsky detachment', the official organ of the Russian Council of People's Commissars *Izvestiia* published its report on the Hlukhiv events, this time acknowledging that there was in fact an anti-Jewish pogrom. However, it stayed silent about who was responsible for it. The Bolsheviks then organised a public meeting and a special session of the Petrograd Soviet to protest the massacre of Jews in Ukraine and Armenians in the Caucasus. There was no mention at all of pogroms for which Red Army or Red Guard detachments were responsible, only those committed by Ukrainian, German or Romanian forces. The pogroms in Hlukhiv and Novhorod-Siversk were never investigated nor were any of the perpetrators brought to justice.

The north eastern Chernihiv gubernia was the only region where pro-Soviet/Red forces took part in pogroms of truly serious proportions. At that time there were antisemitic agitation and actions going on in many parts of Russia, but seldom of such gravity and violence. They attained serious proportions in Ukraine, Belarus (in Minsk, Vitebsk and Mohilev gubernia where Polish army units were also involved in them), and in Bukhara and Tashkent, Central Asia. In January 1918 pro-Bolshevik sailors carried out a pogrom against Simferopol's bourgeoisie and intelligentsia in which Jews were the principal victims. In the following month this same group in concert with forces under Muraviov's command tried, but failed to launch a pogrom in Odesa. Seventeen Jews accused of spying for the German and Ukrainian armies were tortured and shot in Haleshchyna near Kremenchuk.[27]

---

26   Cherikover, *Istoriia pogromnogo dvizenia na Ukraine*, pp. 143–9.
27   Cherikover, *Istoriia pogromnogo dvizenia na Ukraine*, pp. 149–51.

The vast bulk of pogroms were carried out during the civil war period by anti-Soviet forces. In his analysis of the pogroms in Ukraine the scholar Nahum Gergel found that armed forces of the Tsentral'na Rada and its successor, the Directory of the Ukrainian People's Republic, were responsible for 40% of all the recorded pogroms and 54% of those killed in them over the period 1918–21. Soviet army forces were found to have been responsible for just over 4% of the pogroms and 11% of the fatalities.[28] This contrast was in no small measure due to the education programme launched by the Jewish Commissariat under the Commissariat of National Affairs of the Soviet Russian government to combat antisemitism in the ranks of the Red Guards and the Red Army.

The scholar Brendan McGeever, who conducted research in the Kyiv and Moscow archives into the reports from Red Army units stationed in every gubernia of Ukraine in 1919, found antisemitism pervaded their ranks. Bolsheviks who wanted to fight antisemitism dared not approach some of the units for fear of being shot. Many peasants and workers in the Army equated antisemitism with soviet power: in the popular consciousness the Ukrainian ethnicity evoked an image of the worker and peasant as producer of surplus labour, while the Jewish ethnicity an image of the speculator, the extractor of this surplus labour. Thus the call of the pogromists in Hlukhiv 'to put all bourgeois and Jews to the sword'. Antisemitism was the ideological channel through which radicalised workers and peasants could move from revolution to reaction.[29]

The Bolsheviks opposed national oppressions in principle, but they did not know how to implement this position, how to act on it with regard to the oppression of Jews, as well as other nations. When the Jewish Commissariat set to work combating antisemitism there was not a single Bolshevik working in it. Left Zionists, Bundists and other Jewish socialists, who repeatedly pressed the Soviet government in the spring of 1918 to take action but got no response, took it upon themselves to write pamphlets and start discussion circles inside the Red Army to explain and fight antisemitism in its ranks. These were people 'at the margins of the Bolshevik project but at the heart of the Jewish renaissance'. They informed and equipped the Jewish Commissariat and other Soviet Russian institutions in their work combatting the more widespread and more lethal pogroms in 1919.[30]

---

28 N. Gergel, 'The Pogroms in the Ukraine in 1918–1921', *YIVO Annual of Jewish Social Science* (New York, 1951), pp. 237–52 (translation of the original published in 1928).

29 Brendan McGeever, 'Antisemitism and the Russian Revolution', a presentation recorded at Birkbeck, University of London, 24 November 2016, in the series Social Histories of the Russian Revolution, https://www.youtube.com/watch?v=fZXoJq6oDto [accessed 14 September 2018].

30 Ibid.

CHAPTER 11

Resistance to the Austro-German Occupation

The core of armed resistance to the Austro-German occupation was made up of around 30,000 fighters: 13,000 in the brigades of the Ukrainian and Russian left SRs and the anarchists, 12,000 in the Red Guards, and 4–5,000 in brigades brought in from Russia by Antonov-Ovsiienko.[1] The resistance was more widespread in the east and south than in the north and west, but uncoordinated and fragmented it was unable to withstand the vastly superior numbers and firepower of the German and Austro-Hungarian armies.

There were other factors contributing to the weakness of the resistance to the occupation. On 3 March, the Soviet Russian government signed a peace treaty with the Central Powers at Brest Litovsk that required it to recognise the Ukrainian People's Republic as an independent state under the rule of the Tsentral'na Rada, to make peace with it, to cease all agitation against its government and to remove all its military forces from its territory. While insisting publicly that the resistance was a purely local, Ukrainian affair, the Soviet Russian government continued clandestinely to provide the resistance with arms. However, once the resistance was pressed up against the border with Russia, the Bolsheviks instructed their comrades in Ukraine to destroy or take with them everything they could of economic or military value to the enemy and to withdraw into Russia. Soviet Russia could not back the resistance openly with conventional army units nor could it be seen to serve as its organising rear. News of the 3 March peace agreement sowed confusion in the ranks of the resistance. Why were they continuing to fight on alone if they were no match for the Austro-German armies? And if they must fight where was their rear guard, their source of reinforcement and safe haven?

> Everyone of us 'front line soldiers' could not help but ask ourselves the question: what was the rear doing where a huge number of our party and Soviet workers had assembled? And we came to the conclusion that in these conditions it was simply impossible to wage war against regular armies. But what exactly we should do no one really knew.[2]

---

1 Savchenko, *12 viin za Ukrainu*, p. 94.
2 Bosh, *God bor'by*, p. 216.

The news that Russia had agreed a peace with the Central Powers added to the recriminations and disagreements already circulating among the Bolsheviks in Ukraine. On 17 February, the day before the Central Powers advanced into Ukraine, Lenin ordered Muraviov to leave Kyiv for the Romanian front. Kotsiubynsky replaced him as commander-in-chief of the armed forces under the People's Secretariat. But Yegorov, Muraviov's associate and an experienced commander elected by the ranks, refused to obey Kotsiubynsky. Kotsiubynsky then had Yegorov's army committee arrested. Muraviov responded by arresting Kotsiubynsky's senior officers. After the Bolsheviks evacuated Kyiv and it fell to the Rada and the Germans, Muraviov blamed it all on Kotsiubynsky and other commissars in the People's Secretariat 'who acted from a narrow nationalist point of view'.[3]

The People's Secretariat mustered around 700 fighters in Kyiv to cover its retreat. The Red Cossacks' commander Chudnovsky positioned them in Darnytsia on the railway line between Kyiv and Hrebinka as a first line of resistance to the oncoming German and Rada forces.

On the way to Poltava a split occurred in the People's Secretariat between those who wanted to organise armed resistance and those who did not. Bosh, Kotsiubynsky, Aussem and Bakynsky belonged to the first group; they prepared to leave the Secretariat and join the front. They managed to recruit around 100 workers, the majority of them untrained, to send back to reinforce Chudnovsky's already retreating first line of resistance. Meanwhile, the second group led by Skrypnyk and Lapchynsky who held a majority in the People's Secretariat, began to revive the work of its commissariats. Skrypnyk now replaced Bosh as head of the Secretariat.

On 5 March, Kotsiubynsky tried unsuccessfully to bring under his command the Red Guard detachments in Kremenchuk, Kharkiv, Katerynoslav, and Chernihiv and to persuade them to come to the aid of Poltava, which was facing imminent assault. Two days later he gave up and resigned as commissar for war and commander-in-chief. The People's Secretariat replaced Kotsiubynsky with Antonov-Ovsiienko as commander-in-chief and Yevhen Neronovych as commissar for war. Antonov-Ovsiienko now attempted to get agreement from the three other soviet republics in the region, in Donetsk-Kryvyi Rih, Odesa and Tavria, to unite with the People's Secretariat in a Union of Soviet Republics of Southern Russia and to place their armed forces under his sole command. But the three republics refused and opted to fight on alone. Antonov-Ovsiienko then tried to induct peasants in Poltava and Kharkiv into brigades,

---

3 Savchenko, *12 viin za Ukrainu*, pp. 77–8.

but he had neither enough time nor resources to mobilise and prepare them to wage a partisan war.

Antonov-Ovsiienko got into serious disagreement with Skrypnyk because he insisted on taking orders directly from the CPC rather than from the People's Secretariat. On 18 March, he departed for Moscow to seek external military support. By this time the Red Guards had lost Bakhmach, Konotop, Hadiach, Zolotonosha, Kremenchuk, Cherkassy and the coastline of the Black Sea. They would not hold on for much more than another month. There was practically no hope the CPC would jeopardise the respite it had gained from the Central Powers by launching an offensive across the Russian-Ukrainian border.

The People's Secretariat managed to create new units totalling several hundred workers before it was forced to retreat once again from Poltava. Most of these workers had not been to a front before nor even knew how to handle a rifle. According to Bosh, some of these units were led by people without political commitment, drunkards and adventurists completely unknown to the Bolshevik party. They shied away from the fight, fled when fired upon, but knew how to take whatever they wanted by threatening violence against civilians whenever they passed through a settlement.[4]

Moreover, the workers simply were not willing to follow the Bolsheviks into resistance to the occupation forces. N.N. Popov, the noted Soviet historian of the 1920s, conceded that as early as January 1918 there was already 'some disenchantment with Soviet rule ... among workers and soldiers'.[5] Bosh wrote that by March the general mood in the working class was one of 'apathy, indecision, decomposition and reaction'.[6] In several places the Bolsheviks faced opposition and even uprisings against their own rule as the foreign occupation forces neared and they tried to mobilise workers into the Red Guards.

1 Poltava

On 10 March, the People's Secretariat quit Poltava and moved to Katerynoslav, where it set to work organising the Second All-Ukrainian Congress of Councils, originally scheduled to convene on 15 March. The resistance in Poltava continued to hold out, the German army having paused outside the city until heavy artillery and additional units were brought up from the rear. Meanwhile, the Bolsheviks were joined by 2,000 fighters from Moscow and two Czechoslovak

---

4 Bosh, *God bor'by*, pp. 168–215; Shakhrai, *Revoliutsiia na Ukraini*, p. 108.
5 N.N. Popov, 'Ocherki revoliutsionnykh sobittii v Kharkove', *Litopys Revoliutsii*, 1 (1922), p. 23.
6 Bosh, *Natsionalnoe Pravitelstvo*, p. 36.

divisions that had retreated there from Kyiv. The Czechoslovak divisions had an agreement with the Rada to leave for the French front; they now chose to stand their ground and fight the Central Powers in Ukraine.[7] But these reinforcements merely slowed the advance of the German and Rada forces, who broke into Poltava on 28 March. Around 600 Red Cossacks defending the city deserted to their side and turned their guns on their retreating comrades at the Poltava railway station. After the fighting was over these Red Cossacks were incorporated into the UPR's Zaporozhian regiment, but soon afterwards they were demobilised because they were considered too unreliable.

2 Katerynoslav

The Second All-Ukrainian Congress of Councils opened in Katerynoslav on 17 March after prolonged preparatory meetings of the separate party factions. The assembled delegates rose to sing Shevchenko's Testament, followed by the Internationale and the Funeral March in memory of fallen comrades.[8] In his speech Antonov-Ovsiienko declared that resistance to the occupation was the order of the day, 'to do what is needed to break the Germans and the *haidamaky* following on their tail'.[9]

The delegates came from towns and cities both occupied and still unoccupied by the incoming armies. There were many previously unaligned peasants and workers among them who signed up to the Bolshevik and left SR party delegations at the congress venue itself. They proved to be a politically fluid element, attending the meetings of more than one party fraction and changing sides in the voting on successive resolutions sponsored by the main parties.

The 964 registered delegates were split politically into two large camps of roughly equal size, and a small third one that came to hold a certain balance of power between them.[10] The left wings of the UPSR and Russian SRs joined forces to form the first camp; it was the first time these two parties were collaborating at a national level congress. The Ukrainian SRs held sway in the northern tier gubernia, the Russian SRs in the south. They both demanded all

---

7   Hrushevsky, *Na porozi novoi Ukrainy*, p. 187.
8   Mazepa, *Bol'shevyzm*, p. 51.
9   'Materialy pro Druhyi Vseukrains'kyi Ziizd Rad', *Litopys Revoliutsii*, 2 (29) (1928), p. 248.
10 According to V. Averin, there were 401 Bolsheviks, 414 combined UPSR and left Russian SRs, 27 Left USDWP, 27 Left Communists, 13 USDWP, six Social Democratic *obiedinisti*, two Bundists, three anarchists, four right and centre Russian and Ukrainian SRs, four Maximalists, 82 non-party independent delegates and eight unidentified (V. Averin, 'Do Druhoho Vseukrainskoho Ziizdu Rad', *Litopys Revoliutsii*, 2 (March–April 1928), p. 69).

out resistance to the Austro-German occupation. The Russian left SRS, buoyed by a considerable influx of their comrades from the Soviet Russian Republic, were guided principally by their complete opposition to both peace treaties signed at Brest Litovsk. The UPSR leftists were guided by their commitment to defend the independence of the Ukrainian People's Republic.

The Bolsheviks formed a second camp that was divided internally along three lines. The Katerynoslavians, led by Emanuiil Kviring, did not want to fight the occupation, but rather to make a pact with the Tsentral'na Rada and work towards a Ukrainian Constituent Assembly. A second group of Left Communists, who supported Nikolai Bukharin in the party, refused to recognise the Brest Litovsk treaty Soviet Russia had signed and wanted to resist the Austro-German occupation. A third group led by Skrypnyk argued that the congress should uphold the peace treaty signed by Soviet Russia at Brest Litovsk, declare the independence of the UPR as a Soviet Republic and continue to resist the occupation of Ukraine by the Central Powers. This group called on the congress to accept the treaty Soviet Russia had signed at Brest Litovsk as an international concession necessary to free its hand to deal with its domestic enemies. A narrow majority of the delegates supported this position. On the resolution concerning the nature of state power in Ukraine the Skrypnyk group refused to give any recognition to or to co-operate with the Tsentral'na Rada but denounced it as petit bourgeois, counterrevolutionary and the 'fig leaf' of German imperialism.

The USDWP leftists constituted the third camp. They did not want to write off the revolutionary gains of the Tsentral'na Rada or the institution itself. However, they regarded their own survival as inextricably tied to the struggle for a soviet government. They circulated the following resolution of their own, which in the end did not make it to the congress floor to be voted on:

> ... The further penetration of German armies into the interior of Ukraine will destroy not only the soviet government but also the government of the Tsentral'na Rada with all its Universals.
>
> ... The salvation at the very least of the Third and Fourth Universals issued by the Tsentral'na Rada, in which soviet organs of government are fixed, stands before the working masses of Ukraine. Otherwise the country will fall under the boot of a German military dictatorship.
>
> ... Without laying down its arms but having proposed an immediate truce the Congress is obliged to enter into peace negotiations with the Central Powers, which include also the Tsentral'na Rada, on the following terms: 1. Recognition of the peace treaty of the Tsentral'na Rada; 2. Withdrawal of German armies from Ukraine; 3. Immediate convocation

of an all-Ukrainian congress of workers' and peasants' deputies in Kyiv by a general commission established with equal representation from the Central Executive Committee (of the Councils of Ukraine) and the Tsentral'na Rada.[11]

In the first round of voting for the two main factions' resolutions, in which the USDWP leftists and the PPS delegate abstained, the left SRs got 414 votes and the Bolsheviks 400. The Bolsheviks then tabled an amended version of their resolution in which they softened the harsh terms in which they originally described the Rada and incorporated some of the USDWP leftists' resolution, but retained their essential position:[12]

> The working class and all the labouring masses of Ukraine consider the Ukrainian People's Republic a Soviet Republic that unites all workers living on the territory of Ukraine regardless of their nationality and that is closely connected through federal ties with the All-Russian Worker-Peasant Republic ... the working masses of Ukraine ... are ready to sign up to the same harsh conditions as those imposed on Ukraine by the peace treaty of the Tsentral'na Rada with Austro-Germany, but only on the binding condition of comprehensive non-interference of Austro-Germany in the internal life of Ukraine and the removal of Austro-German armies from all of the parts of Ukraine they have seized.[13]

This amended resolution gained the support of the USDWP leftists and was carried by a narrow margin of 427 to 400 votes.[14]

Thus the congress recognised the independence of a Soviet Ukrainian Republic, which meant different things to the different political factions present: Ukraine's independence from Soviet Russia, from the Central Powers or from the Tsentral'na Rada. This was the most the congress could achieve in uniting the various factions on the basis of the principle of national self-determination.

---

11 'Materialy pro Druhyi Vseukrains'kyi Ziizd Rad', *Litopys Revoliutsii*, 2 (29) (1928), p. 265. See also Maiorov, *Z Istorii Revoliutsiinoi Boro'tby*, p. iv; Yavorsky, *Revoliutsiia na Vkraini*, pp. 48–9; Mazepa, *Bol'shevyzm*, pp. 9, 48–50.

12 Averin, 'Do Druhoho Vseukrains'koho Ziizdu Rad', *Litopys Revoliutsii*, 2 (March–April 1928), pp. 69, 70–2.

13 Bosh, *God bor'by*, Appendix, pp. 55–6.

14 V. Averin, 'Do Druhoho Vseukrains'koho Ziizdu Rad', *Litopys Revoliutsii*, 2 (March–April 1928), p. 73. See also Skrypnyk, 'Nacherk istorii proletars'koi revoliutsii', p. 96; Popov, *Narys Istorii*, p. 146; Mazepa, *Bol'shevyzm*, p. 51.

It failed to elaborate a joint strategy to resist the advancing occupation forces or to restore Ukraine's independence in practice.

The congress elected a Central Executive Committee of the Councils of Ukraine composed of 49 Ukrainian and Russian left SRs, 47 Bolsheviks, five USDWP leftists and one member of the Polish Socialist Party. That seemed to prophesy continued rivalry between the evenly matched working class and peasant parties. There was, however, a new sensitivity to the need to present a government that was indeed Ukrainian. Volodymyr Zatonsky was made chair of the CEC and Mykola Skrypnyk head of the People's Secretariat, both of them Ukrainian speakers. From the USDWP leftists Yevhen Neronovych was confirmed as commissar for war and Mykola Vrublevsky was made commissar of education. Skrypnyk, Vrublevsky and Yuri Kotsiubynsky left for Moscow to establish formal ties with the Russian Soviet government on the basis of the congress resolutions.[15]

Yevhen Neronovych appeared dejected and exhausted at the congress. He did not head for Tahanrih where the bulk of his fellow government members were evacuating to, but returned to his native Poltava to visit his wife in the village of Velyki Sorochyntsi in the district of Myrhorod. According to Khrystiuk, Neronovych was bitterly disappointed that the congress rejected the Tsentral'na Rada altogether, and so he broke with the Bolsheviks and resigned his post in the government. He was detained in Velyki Sorochyntsi on 24 March, one day after his thirtieth birthday, by Rada soldiers of the Bohdan company, a remnant of the Bohdan Khmel'nytsky regiment. Commanding the company was Oleksandr Shapoval, member of the UPSI. Without a trial or even a tribunal Neronovych was shot on the following day for treason against the Tsentral'na Rada.[16]

After determined resistance Katerynoslav fell to Free Cossacks and German forces on 2 April. Red Guards and anarchists defending the city retreated to Yuzivka and then Mariupol and Sloviansk in the Donbas. Members of the new soviet government retreated all the way to Tahanrih, the easternmost city claimed by the UPR.[17] According to Panas Fedenko, a USDWP member in

---

15 A. Hrytsenko, *Politychni Syly u Borot'bi za Vladu v Ukraini (kinets' 1917 r.–pochatok 1919 r.)* (Kyiv: Instytut istorii Ukrainy, 1993), pp. 16–17.

16 Khrystiuk, *Ukrains'ka Revoliutsiia*, Vol. 2, p. 152. See also Artem Klymenko, 'Yevhen Neronovych: Zabuti heroi Ukrains'koi Revoliutsii', *Proletar Ukrainy*, https://proletar-ukr.blogspot.com/2018/03/blog-post_31.html.

17 In 1925, Tahanrih was annexed from the Ukrainian Soviet Socialist Republic by the Russian Federal Soviet Republic of the USSR.

Katerynoslav, the city population greeted the incoming forces, relieved at their liberation from the 'terror of the CEC'.

> The sentiments of the population in Katerynoslav, and of the workers in particular, who had endured the terror of the Red Guard spilled out at the first meeting of the Council of Workers' Deputies after the flight of the Bolshevik government. I was at that meeting together with (Isaak) Mazepa and we heard the speeches from members of the council – Russians, Jews and Ukrainians. None of them could find a good word to say about the regime of 'dictatorship over the proletariat' which had promised the workers fruit on the bough but instead brought to Ukraine the ruin of its economy and then carted off to Muscovy machinery, wagons, locomotives, all kinds of raw materials needed for industry and food products.[18]

3   Odesa

With 630,000 inhabitants Odesa was the largest city in Ukraine. The Bolsheviks had more than twice as much time there as their comrades did in Kyiv to entrench themselves before they faced the occupying armies of the Central Powers. The Rada's forces in Odesa were defeated on 17 January 1918 by the city's Military Revolutionary Committee and the Central Executive Committee of the Councils of Romanian Front, Black Sea Fleet, and Odessa Oblast (Rumcherod). The latter handed power to a Council of People's Commissars which declared the Odesa Soviet Republic as part of the federated (after 15 January) Soviet Russian Republic. The Odesa Soviet Republic claimed Bessarabia gubernia and parts of Kherson and Northern Tavria as its territories. The Council of People's Commissars held the full range of portfolios of any national government, including defence and foreign affairs. The Bolsheviks held eight commissariats, the two remaining ones were in the hands of Russian SRs. The Council did not recognise and did not co-operate with the People's Secretariat and the Central Executive Committee of the Councils of Ukraine that were elected in Kharkiv at the (rival) First All-Ukrainian Congress of Councils and that transferred to Kyiv in the wake of Muraviov's army at the end of January.

Party political influence was more diverse further down the institutional structure of the newly arising government in Odesa. The Mensheviks led the

---

18   Panas Fedenko, 'Isaak Mazepa v Zhytti i v Politytsi', *Nashe Slovo*, 3 (1973), p. 18.

trade unions of clerical, printing, tanning and food industry workers and the Trades Union Council itself. The anarchists had the strongest influence among the sailors of the Black Sea Fleet and the unemployed, the SRs among the railway workers, and the Ukrainian SRs and SDs were the dominant parties in the Council of Soldiers' Deputies. The city Duma was controlled by the Mensheviks, Bund and Russian SRs. With the exception of the Menshevik Internationalists and the Bolsheviks, all the socialist parties opposed building a government on the basis of the councils alone. However, they were prepared to work with the new government on condition it consulted with them and with all democratic organisations. Thus an interparty concord held for some time in Odesa.

Important social and democratic gains were secured with the introduction of the eight-hour day for all workers, including house servants, the institution of bargaining and the resolution of labour disputes, prohibition of night shifts by women, protection of minors, introduction of pensions, tax relief for artisans, and the confiscation by the commissariat of labour of all private sanatoria and nationalisation of health facilities for the benefit of the workers. The new authorities maintained good relations with the peasantry in the surrounding farming areas, unlike the situation that developed in Kyiv. However, the supply of food to the city was disrupted by the disturbances surrounding land redistribution. Just as in Kyiv the new Odesa authorities had difficulty ensuring an adequate money supply to private and public employers to pay wages and to service the retail trade.

Theft and burglaries grew to alarming proportions and the authorities seemed unable to stop them. The sailors on the ship *Sinop* entered into negotiations with the trade union of pickpockets to get their agreement not to rob the homes of persons or the persons themselves who were coming onto their ship for a fundraising benefit on 13 February. The pickpockets agreed and issued a statement: 'We, the representatives of thieves of Odesa give you our promise not to carry out any thefts on that day. We will patrol the city ourselves and forestall robberies. We ask you to permit three of our members to come to the benefit to maintain order'.

'And truly', recalls the Bolshevik A. Kirov, 'there were no reports filed that night in the commissariats of any burglaries or theft on the streets'.[19]

Military units of the Odesa Soviet Republic under Rumcherod's command were involved in a struggle with the Romanian army for control of Bessara-

---

19   A. Kirov, 'Rumcherod i Radnarkom Odes'koi Oblasti v Borot'bi za Zhovten'', *Litopys Revoliutsii*, 1 (January–February 1928), pp. 112–13.

bia gubernia.[20] Moldavian Romanians made up two thirds of the population of the gubernia, the remainder being mainly Ukrainians, Jews and Bulgarians. After the February Revolution, a powerful soldiers' movement grew among the 300,000 Moldavians in the Russian army and, in a process not unlike that which was occurring among Ukrainians in the Russian army, provided the impetus behind popular demands for national self-determination, land reform, democratic self government and the eventual unification of Moldavians with the Romanian nation in a single state. An autonomous Moldavian Democratic Republic was proclaimed by a National Council (*Sfatul Tarii*) on 15 December 1917. However, Moldavian soldiers who were initially supportive of the National Council came increasingly under Bolshevik influence after the Council failed to address their main demands, land reform in particular. It was into this situation that military units under Rumcherod's command intervened in Bessarabia and seized Kishinev on 14 January 1918. The Council of People's Commissars of the Odesa Soviet Republic claimed Bessarabia gubernia as part of its territory. The army of Romania, a member state of the Entente, then responded by taking Kishinev on 26 January and proceeding to occupy all of Bessarabia.[21]

Rumcherod retained leadership both of military operations and of the Supreme Collegia, a body endowed with extraordinary powers to oppose Romania's advance into Bessarabia. The Council of People's Commissars of the Odesa Soviet Republic maintained contact with representatives of the Entente, respected their diplomatic immunity and refrained from extending to resident French and British capitalists the same repressive measures it was applying against the local bourgeoisie (opening of their financial records and confiscating their wealth). The Entente was intent on strengthening the Romanian army so as to ensure the Romanian government was not forced to sign a separate peace with the Central Powers. Rumcherod, on the other hand, was trying to force the Romanian army out of Bessarabia and sought help from the French and British representatives to that end. An armistice was agreed between Romania and Rumcherod with the intercession of the Entente, but it was never honoured by the Romanian side, which continued to advance into Bessarabia.

Austro-Hungarian and German armies advanced south towards Odesa in the latter half of February, forcing Rumcherod to give up the fight with the

---

20 The eastern part of the principality of Moldavia was taken by Tsarist Russia in 1812 from the Ottoman Empire. It was Tsarist Russia's last imperial acquisition.
21 Bessarabia was incorporated formally into Romania after the Central Powers signed an armistice with Romania and the National Council of the Moldavian Democratic Republic proclaimed union with Romania on 9 April 1918.

Romanian army in Bessarabia. Thus Rumcherod recalled military units to the city of Odesa to prepare its defence. The CPC's expeditionary commander Muraviov also withdrew his 'Special revolutionary army to fight the Romanian oligarchy' from the region of Prydnistrovia, where it, too, had been opposing the Romanian army's advance to the Black Sea coast.

Most of the Russian army units stationed in the region were refusing to fight, so the Odesa Council of People's Commissars decided to form a new army out of Red Guards, sailors' units and those army units that took part in the January uprising on the side of the Bolsheviks. The army was to be filled out by a compulsory mobilisation of the city's workers, scheduled for 27 January: 'All workers in plants, factories, workshops and trade unions should not refuse to take up arms and join the ranks of the Red Guards in defence of the freedoms already won. Those who do not will be considered the assistants of the bourgeoisie and will be dismissed from work'.[22]

Similarly, soldiers who refused to join the new 'people's socialist army' were to be demobilised from their old units and deprived of food and lodging.

All told, the Council of People's Commissars mobilised 1,000 fighters. They were, in the main, members and supporters of the Bolshevik party, anarchists, left SRs and a battalion of Chinese fighters under the command of Yona Yakir, later to become a prominent Red Army commander. Muraviov gained 500 workers to his army, a poor showing in a city with 120,000 proletarians. The compulsory nature of the mobilisation came at a high political cost to the Bolsheviks, sparking demonstrations calling for an end to the war.

The opposition socialist parties in negotiation with the Bolsheviks maintained their readiness to defend the city from the advancing armies of the Central Powers, but on three conditions: they were included in military decision-making, they could deploy their militia under their own command, and that Rumcherod maintained a neutral position towards the forces of the Tsentral'na Rada coming with the Austro-Hungarian and German forces. These negotiations went nowhere and the opposition parties declared they would henceforth work only to defend the city's civilian population from military aggression, to prevent military operations rather than partake of them. The Menshevik party then adopted a resolution demanding power be transferred to a government chosen on the basis of the outcome of the November Constituent Assembly elections and issued a determined protest against the compulsory mobilisation 'which places the responsibility of blood letting upon the

---

22   A. Kirov, 'Rumcherod i Radnarkom Odes'koi Oblasti v Borot'bi za Zhovten'', *Litopys Revoliutsii*, 1 (January–February 1928), pp. 102–4.

workers'.[23] On 25 February the presidium of the Odesa republic's Council of People's Commissars ordered the closure of the Mensheviks' 'counterrevolutionary' newspaper *Yuzhnie rabochie* for inciting opposition to its authority and calling for its overthrow. Kirov, however, concedes in his memoir that 'the struggle against these actions was unsuccessful because the agitation of the conciliatory [i.e. moderate] parties more or less corresponded to the mood of wide sections of the working class at that time'.[24]

The Council of People's Ministers put all its military forces under the command of Muraviov when he arrived in the city and agreed to his personal dictatorship over the city. However, Muraviov antagonised the population and alienated it further from the Bolsheviks. He ordered all soldiers who did not belong to the garrison, the unemployed, all workers who did not belong to a trade union and anyone not registered as a resident to leave the city. A protest meeting of 4,000 soldiers sent a delegation to him, but he refused to receive it, threatening instead to turn his cannons onto the theatre where they were meeting and to send a Cossack unit against them. The soldiers were forced to end their protest. Muraviov told a meeting of representatives of the factory committees: 'I will not allow you workers to refuse to take up arms. And that's not all. I have a squadron here, and if I am forced to surrender Odesa I will burn it down, I will blow it up, I will leave the enemy nothing but ashes'.

Muraviov met with the city's bourgeoisie to demand money to finance his army:

> I will not surrender Odesa. The whole Black Sea Fleet is concentrated here and if it's necessary nothing will be left of your palaces and your lives. Within three days you must bring me ten million *karbovantsi* and woe to you if you don't. I will weigh you down with stones and drown you in the water, I will throw your families on the trash heap. Don't tell me there's no money left in the banks. You have the money in your strong boxes. Let's do this peacefully because it can be dangerous to argue with me.

Muraviov declared a state of siege and put the city under the control of sailors' brigades among whom there was a considerable number with criminal records. These brigades had a reputation of combatting 'counterrevolutionary elements' on their own initiative, disregarding all the rules of the civilian authorities. The level of crime and violence rose in the city and led to

---

23   Ibid, p. 108.
24   Ibid, p. 109.

clashes between Red Guards and sailors' brigades and demonstrations by workers against the state of siege. The Council of People's Commissars then lifted the siege and separated the command over standing forces of the Odesa military district from those of Muraviov.

Austro-Hungarian forces fought their way into the city with a loss of 500 soldiers' lives. The Council of People's Commissars and Rumcherod prepared to evacuate. The evacuation led to further clashes when the Odesa CPC tried to remove valuables from the State Bank and Treasury. It was blocked by a Jewish self-defence brigade, sailors of the merchant marine and workers from the Anatra factory who seized the commissar of labour Starostin and the deputy commissar of finances Kartsenko. They were released only after the valuables were returned.

Muraviov's forces retreated to the east of the city, while the soviet government ordered a full mobilisation to defend it, which the non-Bolshevik parties opposed by calling out a mass meeting of workers in protest. The mobilisation failed and a joint meeting of Rumcherod, the Council of People's Commissars and representatives of the Black Sea Fleet decided to send a delegation to meet the incoming Austro-Hungarian army to negotiate the terms of the city's surrender. But the delegation was ignored. Instead, on 12 March the city Duma successfully negotiated with the incoming forces a provision that all pro-Soviet armed units inside Odesa be allowed to leave with their weapons. The next day the Austro-Hungarian forces entered the city. The leaders of the Odesa Soviet Republic fled by ship or across land with the remnants of Muraviov's army. Most of the Black Sea Fleet sailed out of port bound for Sevastopol and Kerch on the Crimean peninsula.[25]

4 Mykolaiv and Kherson

One hundred and thirty kilometres northeast of Odesa, Mykolaiv fell on 17 March after one day of resistance by the city's Red Guards. The Duma greeted the occupiers, but soon afterwards the city's workers and soldiers rose up in rebellion. They seized a large part of the city and held it for four days. The same happened in Kherson, 70 kilometres southeast of Mykolaiv, after Austro-Hungarian troops entered the city on 19 March. Front line soldiers of the Russian army rose up, supported by the guns of a Bolshevik-led flotilla on the Dnipro River, an anarchist brigade led by Oleksii Mokrousov and a foreign unit

---

25 Ibid, pp. 112–14; Savchenko, *12 viin za Ukrainu*, pp. 82–4.

of internationalist fighters. It took the Austro-Hungarian forces 17 days to put down the uprising at a cost of more than 2,000 of their soldiers, greater than all the losses they incurred before reaching Kherson.[26]

5   Crimea

Five German divisions and one part of the UPR's Zaporozhian regiment marched on Crimea. Given its commanding position jutting out into the Black Sea, capturing Crimea was crucial both to the war aims of the Central Powers and Germany's long-term grand strategy in the east. The Rada had not claimed the peninsula as UPR territory in its Fourth Universal and it relinquished any claim to it in its peace treaty with the Central Powers.

The occupying forces were entering the terrain of a treble power struggle between the national movement of the Crimean Tatars, the left forces of Bolsheviks, left Russian SRs and anarchists, and the moderate socialist parties. In November 1917 more than 70% of the adult Crimean Tatar population took part in electing their national constituent assembly, the *Kurultai*. It elected a government, the Council of Directors, which then proclaimed the Crimean People's Republic. Yet inasmuch as the Crimean Tatars constituted 27% of the peninsula's population, it could only be a declaration of intent to build a democratic republic for all Crimeans, regardless of nationality, rather than to govern over the Crimean Tatars alone.

These elections took place simultaneously with elections to the All-Russian Constituent Assembly elections, in which the Mensheviks and the Russian SRs emerged the strongest parties. They formed a temporary government of their own for Crimea, the Council of People's Representatives, and waited for the All-Russian Constituent Assembly to convene.

In Crimea, the Bolsheviks received 5% of the votes in these elections, but their focus was on building a soviet government on the basis of the workers, soldiers' and sailors' councils in which they, the Russian left SRs and the anarchists were dominant. On 19 March 1918, a Bolshevik majority at the First Congress of councils, revolutionary committees and land committees of Tavria gubernia declared the Soviet Socialist Republic of Tavria, whose territory encompassed all of the Crimean peninsula and the adjacent mainland to the north from the Dnipro estuary down to the coast of the Sea of Azov.

---

26   Savchenko, *12 viin za Ukrainu*, p. 91.

The Tavria Soviet Republic's leaders prepared to defend their territory from the encroaching occupation forces while at the same time having to combat their domestic rivals. In April the Russian SRs and Mensheviks won majorities in elections to key workers' councils across this region, including Sevastopol. The trade unions went into opposition to the Tavria Soviet Republic. The *Kurultai* mobilised its own armed units. The Bolsheviks accused it of attempting to install a military dictatorship in league with the Tsentral'na Rada and suppressed it, driving its leaders underground or abroad to Turkey. On 21 April the Crimean Tatar movement rose in an armed rebellion along the south shore and in the mountains, which the Red forces of the Tavria Soviet Republic failed to put down. During the fighting the rebels captured and executed a majority of the members of the government of the Tavria Soviet Republic.[27]

The Red Army of Soviet Tavria numbering some 6,000 bayonets held a defensive line across its northern border. The German divisions broke through it, followed by the UPR's Zaporozhian unit under Petro Bolbochan. Now, the Rada's war minister Zhukovsky issued a secret order to Bolbochan on 11 April to lead his soldiers all the way to Sevastopol and seize the Black Sea Fleet. They reached Melitopol on 18 April and Simferopol on 24 April. The Germans learned of Zhukovsky's order and issued a determined protest. On 27 April Zhukovsky rescinded his order and apologised to the Germans for the 'misunderstanding' while Bolbochan withdrew to Melitopol.[28]

Zhukovsky regarded the Germans' refusal to allow Rada forces to take Sevastopol as a telling sign of their true intentions. Despite the UPR having relinquished any claim to Crimea at Brest Litovsk, the Rada government could not resist trying to steal a march on the Germans once they were both poised to invade the peninsula. Zhukovsky gave a sound reason for the attempt: it was strategically important for the defence of Ukraine to have its own fleet on the Black Sea. But it was a foolish and quixotic ploy against the Germans who had far greater forces on the same ground to pursue their own strategic interest.

> They were infuriated, like wild beasts. They surrounded our troops with machine guns and cannon and gave them three hours to think about it, either turn back or surrender their weapons and go no further. I say nothing about such arbitrariness on the part of the German command, but it goes a long way in showing with what good intentions the Germans came to help us build our state.[29]

---

27   Radio Svoboda series on the Crimean campaign of Petro Bolbochan: https://www.radiosvoboda.org/a/28446303.html.
28   Savchenko, *Symon Petliura*, p. 196.
29   Zhukovsky, *Vspomyny*, p. 173.

Meanwhile the Red forces managed until 29 April to hold back the Germans from entering Sevastopol. But once defence of the port city became untenable, sailors on some vessels of the Black Sea Fleet raised the Ukrainian flag in the hope that they would be recognised as belonging to the UPR and so not fall into the Germans' hands. Possibly they had learned of the Rada's intent to claim the fleet but still did not know it had backed down. On 30 April around 300 vessels with 3,500 sailors on board sailed out of Sevastopol, heading for Novorosiisk. Some 15 ships remained behind in port. On that day Sevastopol fell to the German armies.[30]

East of Crimea the occupation forces faced resistance as they advanced along the north shore of the Sea of Azov. Here fought the anarchist brigades of Makhno, Petrenko, Mokrousov, the sailors Polupanov and Stepanov, and the brigade of Marusia Nykoforova defending Berdiansk, Huliai-Pole and Polohy.[31]

6 Kharkiv and the Donbas

German forces and the Zaporoshian regiment reached Kharkiv at the beginning of April. The Bolsheviks mobilised resistance while preparing to evacuate. They sent trainloads of valuables across the border into Russia, including 100 wagons of grain, 50 locomotives and the uninstalled machinery of 17 factories, and then they retreated either east or south. The government and administration of the Donets-Kryvyi Rih Republic evacuated to Luhansk. German and Ukrainian forces entered and took control of Kharkiv on 17 April.

Seven thousand fighters belonging to the Red Guards and other insurgent detachments came together at the end of March into a Special Donetsk Proletarian Army. It merged with a second force of some 2,500 volunteers named the Fifth Army (beforehand known as Sivers' army) to make a last stand in the Donbas. On 4 April it engaged the expeditionary Donbas Group of UPR soldiers who seized Kostiantynohrad and then the strategic railway junction at Lozova on 8 April.[32]

The Bolsheviks were the governing party in the Donbas from the summer of 1917 when they won absolute majorities in the workers' councils and the councils became the local governments. After three years of degradation of industrial capital caused by relentless military production and the steady loss

---

30 Savchenko, *12 viin za Ukrainu*, p. 109.
31 Ibid, p. 101.
32 Savchenko, *12 viin za Ukrainu*, pp. 99–100.

of the youngest and most able workers to the fronts, any government whatsoever would have faced a formidable challenge to restore economic production to meet civilian needs and to raise the standard of living. By October all the industries in the region were nationalised under workers' control, which led to the flight of factory and mine directors and their skilled personnel. Production slowed down with the onset of winter and even halted in some enterprises. Workers failed to receive their wages and the supply of food to the Donbas region began to break down. The regional economy also suffered from the anarchist bands and criminal gangs that looted private and nationalised enterprises. Some of the smaller coal mines were reprivatised and returned to their former owners, from whom the workers now expected to start receiving wages again. However, as in Kyiv and Odesa after the Bolsheviks assumed power, the public authorities in the Donbas had great difficulty maintaining sufficient money in circulation once they were dependent on the Petrograd soviet government to supply it.

The Donbas was adjacent to the region to which Kaledin drew the Don Cossacks soldiers off the Southwestern Front. From here in December he sent them to put down the workers' councils that recognised the CPC as their government. The councils suffered from these repressions, losing some of their best leaders and activists.

The Bolshevik party lost members and the unity and discipline of its ranks declined. The experience of the party organisation in Horlivka-Shcherbynivtsi, a coal and mercury mining district, is illustrative of the general trend in the region. The Bolsheviks there numbered 7,000 on the eve of the seizure of power in October, 4,000 by December and 1,500 by mid-March, essentially reduced to their 'old guard' of February 1917. There were serious internal divisions and a growing alienation from their social base. The district workers' council in the process of combatting sabotage and looting 'resorted to excessive and dictatorial methods which were led by an executive committee called 'the council of seven''.

> This 'council of seven' conducted a ruthless struggle with all enemies and spoilers of the proletarian revolution ... without a doubt it was a mistake for this council to cut itself off from the working masses. It wasn't able to get their support for its harsh methods, and it was reproached quite rightly by the workers.[33]

---

33 M. Ostrohorsky, 'Z Istorii Bil'shovytskoi Orhanizatsii Horlivsko-Shcherbynivskoho Raionu Donbasa (1901–1918)', *Litopys Revoliutsii*, 5 (September–October 1930), p. 123.

A majority of the district party organisation opposed Soviet Russia signing its peace treaty with the Central Powers. Lacking support from Soviet Russia and facing insurmountable odds from the approaching armies more and more workers defected from the party. And finally, the district council administration faced 'protests and countermeasures from separate groups of backward and uninformed workers' when it started to evacuate with everything of value it could take, including food, raw materials and machinery. Even so, the incoming occupation army still faced determined resistance from the Horlivka miners in which 13 of them were killed.

The Central Powers completed their occupation of practically all the territory claimed by the UPR in the last days of April. An estimated 10,000 people had lost their lives resisting the occupation. The number of fatalities among the Rada, German and Austro-Hungarian troops is unknown. Hundreds of Jews died in the pogroms, thousands fled their ancestral homes. Many thousands of people of all nationalities were uprooted and displaced, orphaned, widowed, maimed and mentally disabled. And yet it was still not the end of the World War or civil war or further foreign interventions.

7   Tahanrih

The Second All-Ukrainian Congress of Councils ended its work in Katerynoslav on 21 March and the newly elected People's Secretariat and most of the CEC evacuated to Tahanrih. Yevgenia Bosh wrote that she went there 'in order to have a chance to work in peace'. She understood that the government elected in Katerynoslav had no future.

> By transferring to Tahanrih the Ukrainian soviet government isolated itself from the localities and departed the scene of political struggle. And not only from the masses: leading comrades who found themselves on the front and in the territory between the front lines saw no hope at all of getting support. The soviet government saw the transfer to Tahanrih as the beginning of its own liquidation.[34]

In Tahanrih the evenly matched rivals at the Second Congress turned to bitter feuding on the CEC: the 'revolutionary war' minded SRs denouncing the 'capitulationist' Bolsheviks, demanding from them the key portfolios of defence,

---

34   Bosh, *God bor'by*, p. 179.

finances and internal affairs in the People's Secretariat. The Bolsheviks held on to the Secretariat only with the support of the small left USDWP fraction. The SRS on the CEC threatened to walk out and form their own government. The two sides stood at the edge of open war and were already arresting each other's leaders. The Bolsheviks faced additional pressure from two other sources: the military commanders of the Russian left SRS (Kamkov, Karelin and Shteinberg) who had arrived in Tahanrih in March, determined to destroy the Brest Litovsk accords by drawing Russia into renewed war with the Central Powers; and the Military Revolutionary Committee of the Tahanrih Council of Workers' Deputies which at one point arrested their members on the People's Secretariat and seized its finances. Meanwhile the Russian CPC refused to lend their Ukrainian comrades support. Stalin expressed his position: 'You've played enough at Government and Republic, I think, now it's time to stop the game'.[35]

On 17 April the CEC dissolved the government and replaced it with a resistance organisation headed by the 'Insurgent Nine', made up of four Bolsheviks, four left Ukrainian and Russian SRS and one USDWP leftist. The CEC released its members to go back into the underground and mount a partisan war, while the members of the People's Secretariat left for Moscow.[36]

On 19–20 April, 69 representatives of these same parties held a conference in Tahanrih to consider merging into a single communist party of Ukraine. The Bolsheviks were the absolutely dominant party in terms of numbers. As in December in Kyiv when they decided to form Social Democracy of Ukraine, the Bolsheviks who took part in the April Tahanrih conference were mainly from the South Western region encompassing Kyiv, Poltava and Katerynoslav, not from Kharkiv, the Donbas or Odesa.

The 'right faction' of Katerynoslav Bolsheviks led by Emanuiil Kviring proposed an autonomous communist party whose Central Committee and congress decisions were to be subordinated to the Central Committee and congresses of the Russian Communist Party.[37] This faction viewed an armed struggle against the occupation forces as futile; it favoured recognition of the Tsentral'na Rada and a return to legal forms of struggle, in particular through the trade union movement. The 'left faction' of Kyiv Bolsheviks, led by Yurii Piatakov, remained opposed to the Rada and both Brest Litovsk treaties and wanted to continue the armed struggle for the renewal of a soviet Ukrainian

---

35   Savchenko, *12 viin za Ukrainu*, p. 102.
36   Bosh, *God bor'by*, pp. 179–84; Khrystiuk, *Ukrains'ka Revoliutsiia*, Vol. 2, p. 162; Shakhrai, *Revoliutsiia na Ukraini*, p. 108.
37   On 8 March 1918, the Seventh Congress of the RSDWP (Bolsheviks) changed the party's name to Russian Communist Party (Bolsheviks).

government. It placed its hopes more on the unabated revolutionary energy of the peasantry than on the working class, and it was relying on a close alliance with the left UPSR. Mykola Skrypnyk, supported by the group of federalist Bolsheviks around Hryhorii Lapchynsky, proposed a third way between these two factions: 'To establish an independent communist party with its *own* Central Committee and party congresses which is tied to the Russian Communist Party through the international commission for the Third International'. The right faction's proposal was rejected while Skrypnyk's was carried by a majority of 35 votes to 21. The new party was named the Communist Party (Bolsheviks) of Ukraine (CP(B)U).[38]

All three groups at the conference found their distinct objectives served by Skrypnyk's proposal: the Left Communists who wanted a platform from which to fight the Austro-German occupation without jeopardising Russia's peace with Central Powers; the Ukrainian Bolsheviks who had settled on the objective of an independent Ukrainian soviet republic and needed a party to realise it; and the left wings of the USDWP and UPSR who tried but failed to fashion the Tsentral'na Rada into a soviet government and then joined forces with the Bolsheviks and left Russian SRs to fight the Austro-German occupation. Skrypnyk, however, laid the cornerstone on which these three different groups came together. He was far sighted enough to see that the Third (Communist) International might offer the CP(B)U a new kind of relationship with the Russian party from which it had come, a relationship that institutionalised and better protected its right to national self-determination within the emerging international communist movement.

---

38 Soldatenko, *Ukraina v revoliutsiinu dobu. 1918 r*, pp. 165–70.

CHAPTER 12

Last Days of the Rada

> Those at the helm of Ukrainian politics shall not go in the footsteps of those *het'mans* whom our poet [Shevchenko] called the garbage of Warsaw and the scum of Moscow. This would be a repetition, word for word, of that unforgettable, shameful historical policy for which Ukraine paid with 250 years of slavery. You can't make the same mistake a second time. There is no justification for it.
> MYKHAILO HRUSHEVSKY[1]

∴

The armies of the Central Powers crossed Ukraine from west to east in seventy days, driving the Bolsheviks, left SRs and anarchists underground or out of the country altogether. Marching ahead of the Germans the Rada's forces entered Kyiv on 1 March, followed four days later by the Council of People's Ministers. The Rada began to take power again in the capital and sent authorised people into the bigger cities. Yet on 29 April, just as the German, Austrian and Rada armies completed their occupation of the country, the German high command overthrew the Rada government and replaced it with the puppet regime of *het'man* Pavlo Skoropadsky. How did the Rada come to such an end, to be felled by its international allies at the very moment of deliverance from its Bolshevik enemy?

At the heart of their relationship were the Brest Litovsk peace treaty, their agreement on economic co-operation and the Rada's request to the Central Powers to help them defeat the Bolsheviks. In exchange for military assistance the UPR would supply food and raw materials to Germany and Austro-Hungary. Its leaders publicly interpreted that bargain to mean the Central Powers would not interfere in their domestic affairs as they carried out the military intervention. However, this was patently impossible as the Bolsheviks, left SRs and anarchists were part of Ukraine's domestic affairs. And the Rada could not but realise that Ukrainian land and labour would have to feed and house the armies

---

1 Cited in Khrystiuk, *Ukrains'ka Revoliutsiia*, Vol. 2, p. 162.

of the intervening powers and provide wheat, sugar, coal and metals to their home countries. How could anyone separate UPR's domestic affairs from its international commitments? And did the Rada have sufficient popular support and institutional capacity in March 1918 to deliver its side of the bargain?

1   The Rada Returns to Kyiv

The Council of People's Ministers reconvened in Kyiv on 8 March in a state of disarray. Four ministers were missing, not seen since the end of January – Nykyfir Hryhoriev (education), Arystarkh Ternychenko (land affairs/agriculture), Stepan Perepelytsia (finance) and Mykola Kovalevsky (provisions supply). The other ministers were left holding more portfolios than they could handle – Mykhailo Tkachenko held justice and finance, Pavlo Khrystiuk internal affairs and education, Mykola Porsh labour and provisions supply, while Holubovych held the premiership, foreign affairs, trade and industry. Holubovych, moreover, was suffering from a lung disease.[2]

The Council issued a statement on Shevchenko's birthday, 9 March, assuring the population that the Third and Fourth Universals would be implemented, all land would be distributed to the peasantry, the eight-hour day and all other rights of labour enshrined in law would be upheld. The trade unions and workers' councils should function freely, but the councils were warned not to aspire to exercise state power. All nations of Ukraine were guaranteed full civil and national rights. The Rada intended to hand power over to the constituent assembly just as soon as the December election results were determined (if the records had not been destroyed) or fresh elections were held where necessary. And finally, the Council reiterated that the Germans were friends and allies of the UPR who would not interfere in its domestic affairs for the anticipated short duration of their stay.[3]

The centre-right wing of the UPSR, which held the majority in the Council since 17 January, knew it could not rule on its own. It wanted to form a new coalition government with the USDWP, the Jewish and Russian socialist parties. This, however, was unlikely given the enmity and divisions which had grown between and within these parties during the previous months. The USDWP and the UPSR had both split, their left wings agitating openly against the Rada government and calling for the inclusion in it of all the workers' and peasants'

---

[2] *Nova Rada*, no. 32, 13 March; no. 33, 14 March 1918.
[3] *Nova Rada*, no. 32, 13 March 1918.

councils. Their far left wings were preparing to join forces with the Bolsheviks and Russian Left SRs at the Second All-Ukrainian Congress of Councils in Katerynoslav, planned for 20 March.

USDWP members who stayed with the Rada disagreed among themselves whether to join a new coalition government. Their Central Committee had expressed the view in January 'that the revolution is now entering a stage of anarchy, after which it will pass into reaction, and completely different elements who are far from the proletariat will take the helm of the state'. Now, however, a majority of the Central Committee wanted the party to enter a coalition government, but the party's fraction in the *mala rada* did not. Instead, the fraction's deputies decided to recall Tkachenko and Porsh from Holubovych's cabinet. They believed the party would be of better use to the working class if it stayed in opposition to the government, furthering workers' rights with new legislation while at the same time rebuilding its own branches in working class communities.[4]

The Bund, Mensheviks and Russian SRs returned to the *mala rada* but refused to join a coalition government, choosing also to remain in opposition. They preferred the Rada to a Bolshevik-led government, but they were in fundamental disagreement with the Rada majority for having declared independence, signed a separate peace with the Central Powers and admitted their armies into Ukraine. They took these steps to mean the majority's complete rejection of membership in a Russian federated republic, to which they, of course, were still committed.

National antagonisms had been growing since the beginning of 1918, supplanting political differences as driving forces in the mounting civil war. Russian Bolshevik intervention from the northeast and Austro-German from the southwest hardened the perception that this was now a war between nations as opposed to social classes. Both, of course, were involved. The alienation felt between the parties of the national majority and the minorities continued to grow after the Rada returned to Kyiv, both in the field of 'high politics' and among the population at large. The centre of gravity of the party political system shifted to the right, with the Bolsheviks and the far left wings of the USDWP and UPSR cast out and the UPSI entering the *mala rada* for the first time as a fraction on the nationalist right. The UPSI thrived on antagonising the Russian and Jewish minorities.[5] The national minorities together constituted the

---

4   *Nova Rada*, no. 33, 14 March 1918.
5   Oleksandr Zhukovsky, *Vspomyny chasiv epokhy Velykoi Skhidn'oi Revoliutsii pochatka 1917–1919 rr. (Iz okopiv do tiurmy)*, Booklet 1919, edited by Pavlo Hai-Nyzhnyk (Kyiv, 2018), pp. 123, 160,

numerical majority of Kyiv's population by a considerable margin. They viewed with some foreboding the return of the Rada government with the Ukrainian and German armies. Each in their own way, these two armies looked upon Kyiv as foreign territory to be policed and subdued.

Several issues served to deepen the alienation between the nationalities in March and April. Foremost among them were the anti-Jewish pogroms and the Rada government's failure to punish the perpetrators in its own army and elsewhere. Second, the government decreed the compulsory use of Ukrainian language on the signage and notices of private businesses and public institutions, and in the provision of services by the courts, post and telegraph. All the Russian and Jewish parties protested these measures as 'immediate Ukrainisation'.[6] When the Ministry of Internal Affairs refused to deal with a request from the Kyiv Duma because it was written in Russian the editors of *Nova Rada* joined in the protest. They pointed out there was no law yet on the state language (though they wanted there to be one). No ministry could unilaterally decree Ukrainian as a state language; it was a constitutional matter. Therefore, the Ministry of Internal Affairs was violating citizens' rights by refusing to deal with the Duma's request.[7]

In public life the Russian, Jewish and indeed the Ukrainian city dweller were immersed in the Russian language and culture. Unless they were politicised into the new Ukrainian national consciousness – still a minority, though a growing one – people in the cities by and large remained suspicious of the Rada, poking fun at the Ukrainian language and passively resisting attempts to make Ukrainian the language of public discourse. Ukrainians were still stereotyped as illiterate rural commoners, and the urban dweller was not about to embrace their language on the strength of a decree, nor indeed on pain of punishment.[8] *Nova Rada* reported on 6 April that Ukrainian nationalists were ordering the arrest of people for speaking in Russian on the streets of Kyiv. The editors protested and demanded the authorities put a stop to it.

Third, there was considerable opposition to the law on citizenship adopted by the *mala rada* while it was still in Zhytomyr in late February. No deputies from the national minorities were present at its adoption. The law granted cit-

---

http://shron1.chtyvo.org.ua/Zhukovskyi_Oleksandr/Vspomyny_chasiv_epokhy_Velykoi_Skhidnoi_Revoliutsii_pochatka_191719_rr_Iz_okopiv_do_Tiurmy_Zapyska_k.pdf [accessed 1 October 2018].

6   *Nova Rada*, no. 41, 24 March; no. 43, 27 March 1918; Cherikover, *Istoriia pogromnogo dvizhenia*, pp. 117–18.
7   *Nova Rada*, no. 51, 6 April 1918.
8   Cherikover, *Istoriia pogromnogo dvizhenia*, pp. 114–15.

izenship to those who had lived in Ukraine for at least three years, who were gainfully employed and who had not committed any act directed against the Republic. Now, Kyiv and other cities of the south were filling up with Jews fleeing the pogroms in the surrounding countryside and refugees from the Russian north – expropriated landlords, nobility, military officers and soldiers, political opponents of the Bolshevik government. They occupied the remaining garrets and basements and slept on the floors of relatives and friends. The refugees had no residence permits nor ration cards and were reliant on the black market for food sold to them at exorbitant prices. Many of them had no right to citizenship according to the criteria of the new law.

In the first week of April, the Rada minister for Russian affairs Odynets expressed his concern in the *mala rada* about Russian officers, many of whom had served in the army of the UPR and who were now stranded and starving in Kyiv. A collection for them in the community had raised only 1,000 *karbovantsi*. The UPSI deputy Lutsenko attacked Odynets for asking the government to provide emergency support to these officers, claiming that many of them had not served in the UPR army at all but wanted to see the Rada overthrown. Lutsenko called for the officers to be interned in concentration camps. The UPSR deputy Saltan called for their deportation to Russia. A majority of the *mala rada*, however, called on the government to act humanely in the matter. This debate took place as the Kyiv press ran reports about the mistreatment of Ukrainian villagers living on the Russian side of the eastern border. The reports gave rise to calls from nationalist politicians for retaliation by the UPR government, including the deportation of Russians from Ukraine.[9]

The *mala rada* session of 17 March voted on a motion to ratify the Brest Litovsk treaty. The deputies of four Jewish parties joined with the majority to vote in favour of ratification. Three of the seven deputies who voted against ratification were Jewish – Rafes from the Bund, Sklovsky from the Russian SRs and Bisk from the Mensheviks. They bore the brunt of attacks from the floor and abuse from the gallery. So loud was the shouting that Hrushevsky in the speaker's chair cleared the gallery, the first time he had been forced to do so (in January he had threatened to clear the gallery when similar outbursts were made against deputies who voted against or abstained in the vote on the Fourth Universal). Rafes warned that a campaign had begun against the national minorities which would bury the revolution in Ukraine. Lytvakov of the United Jewish Socialist Party said he did not see any point in the national

---

9   *Nova Rada*, no. 53, 5 April; no. 54, 10 April 1918.

minorities participating in a state institution that had not consulted them properly in drawing up the Third and Fourth Universals and yet treated the voting on these acts as a test of the minorities' loyalty to the UPR.[10]

Two days later the leader of the UPSI, Oleksandr Stepanenko, called on the *mala rada* to close down the ministries of Jewish and Russian affairs and prohibit Russians and Jews from holding official posts in the UPR government as punishment for these minorities allegedly siding with Moscow against the the Ukrainian state.[11] Such threats coming from inside the legislative chamber of the Rada undoubtedly gave encouragement to the pogromists operating beyond its walls.

The labour movement was seriously weakened and its members divided by the January uprising, by the Bolsheviks' attempt to rule alone when they did come to power, and then by their flight eastwards ahead of the Austro-German occupation. Militants who stayed behind with their communities had little choice but to limit themselves to trade union issues and to channel their grievances through the parties present in the *mala rada*. The government, however, was fearful of any challenge to its fragile authority and determined to show its international allies that it could restore order. As internal affairs minister Tkachenko put it: 'the government's course right now is a firm rule ... so that we can fulfil our responsibilities before our allies, so that we stop the anarchy in the country'.[12]

Despite Zhukovsky's assurance at the beginning of March that 'the government has no intention to maintain order by force and bayonets', the state of martial law remained in place in Kyiv throughout March and April. Zhukovsky appointed Ukrainian commanders responsible for requisitioning what was needed for both German and Ukrainian units.[13] The units remained under their own separate commands, but they shared policing functions under an agreed division of labour. They had to co-operate as the Ukrainians held the political intelligence indispensable to policing the city while the Germans controlled all telephone and telegraph communications. However, there was ample evidence of friction between them, as well as between the military and civil authorities, not least because the Germans at practically every step demonstratively behaved to show they were in charge.[14]

---

10   Cherikover, *Istroiia pogromnogo dvizhenia*, p. 138.
11   Ibid, p. 119.
12   *Nova Rada*, no. 50, 5 April 1918.
13   *Nova Rada*, no. 61, 6 April 1918.
14   Zhukovsky, *Vspomyny*, pp. 146–7, 170–3.

On 9 April the *mala rada* unanimously adopted an interpellation directed to the ministries of justice and internal affairs concerning an estimated 200 to 300 people, including some who had fought against the Rada in January, who were imprisoned since the middle of March in unsanitary, cold and overcrowded conditions in the Starokyiv police precinct. No charges had been brought against them. The minister of justice S. Shelukhin confirmed that there were Bolshevik political prisoners among them and that they were being held in oppressive conditions, but in far fewer numbers than before. Hrushevsky protested to the German high command. The UPSR deputy Liubynsky expressed the hope that it was all merely a misunderstanding.[15]

Both the German and Ukrainian authorities took to muzzling the press. A unit of German soldiers confiscated the 7 March issue of the UPSR's newpaper *Borot'ba* and prohibited the following day's issue as well.[16] The German commandant of Kyiv summoned the editors of all the city's newspapers still coming out to induct them into a regime of censorship. His attempt met determined resistance, the *Nova Rada* rejecting any imposition of censorship on the front page of their next issue whilst inviting representatives of the German state to submit their news releases in the normal way.[17] In Odesa after the city was taken, UPR commissar Komorny closed down the Menshevik newspaper *Yuzhnie Rabochie*, the Bolsheviks' *Krasnoe Znamia* and Rumcherod's *Holos Revoliutsii*, all of them for agitating against the Rada. In Poltava *Svobodnaia mysl'* was closed, and in Katerynoslav the German commander shut down *Rabochie Bor'by*.[18]

The Rada prohibited the workers' councils from engaging in activity construed as aspiring to take over or share in government, limiting them to economic and social issues. This was, in effect, a ban on Bolsheviks, USDWP leftists and the left Ukrainian and Russian SRs. As a result the Mensheviks, the Bund and independent candidates took the majority of seats in elections to the workers' councils of big cities like Kharkiv, Katerynoslav, and Odesa. The Mensheviks reasserted their leadership of the trade unions.[19] In Kyiv, the Bolsheviks regrouped clandestinely a few weeks after the return of the Rada and elected a steering committee. They returned to public activity through the trade unions, issued leaflets in their own name and took part in preparing the first

---

15   *Nova Rada*, no. 55, 11 April; no. 58, 14 April 1918.
16   *Nova Rada*, no. 31, 10 March 1918.
17   *Nova Rada*, no. 46, 31 March 1918.
18   *Nova Rada*, no. 54, 10 April; no. 61, 18 April 1918.
19   Volyn, *Mensheviki*, p. 57; Fedenko, 'Isaak Mazepa', p. 18; *Pervii Siezd KP(b)U* (Kharkiv: Gosudarstvennoe Izdatel'stvo Ukrainy, 1923), p. 24; Popov, *Narys Istorii*, p. 143.

all-Ukrainian congress of trade unions which was held at the end of May, after the overthrow of the Rada.[20]

Trade union organisations were preoccupied with long arrears in the payment of wages and rising unemployment in both the private economy and public sector. On 18 March the ministry of transport called a halt to all road building and repair for military purposes. The halt had been decreed on 10 February under the Bolshevik government, but the work had gone on regardless. Six thousand people were thrown out of work without warning on 20 March, their wages in arrears.[21]

Union representatives started turning to the ministry of labour in mid-March with complaints that they were prohibited by 'administrators of the city' from meeting to conduct union work. They were assured their rights were guaranteed in law, but at the same time the ministry's officials did nothing to protect them from the military authorities. Similarly, the ministry appeared helpless to prevent punitive dismissals of workers, such as those elected to factory committees. The employers took advantage of martial law to ignore collective agreements, withhold wages, lock out their employees in response to threats of strike or close down their enterprises altogether.[22]

Mykhailo Tkachenko insisted that it was the state of martial law and not his own ministry of internal affairs that prohibited the celebration of the first anniversary of the February 1917 revolution. At the same time Tkachenko was at pains to point out that the government opposed, and would therefore prevent, any manifestation of opposition to the UPR and its army, which he believed was the real intention of the celebrations. With respect to May Day, a national holiday, the ministry of internal affairs said it would permit demonstrations even with martial law in force, but it was ready to put down any 'counterrevolutionary agitation'. The German command in Kyiv issued its own order on 28 April that required any group of workers who wanted to mark May Day or to hold any other public manifestation to get its permission first.[23]

Four USDWP deputies, M. Avdienko, L. Chykalenko, M. Kovalsky, and O. Hermaize resigned from the *mala rada* on 21 March in protest against the general course of the government. They cited:

---

20   *Bol'shevitskie organizatsii Ukrainy: opganizatsionno-partiinaia deiatel'nost'* (*fevral'* 1917–*iul'* 1918 *gg.*) (Politizdat Ukrainy, 1990), p. 644.
21   Hrushevsky, *Na Porozi Novoi Ukrainy*, p. 188; *Nova Rada*, no. 56, 12 April 1918.
22   *Nova Rada*, no. 31, 10 March 1918.
23   Khrystiuk, *Ukrains'ka Revoliutsiia*, Vol. 2, pp. 167–70; *Nova Rada*, no. 41, 24 March; no. 46, 31 March; no. 51, 6 April; no. 63, 20 April 1918.

The obligatory regulations of government agents prohibiting strikes, meetings and the like, the prevention of workers' organisations from carrying out their functions, central government institutions ignoring the trade unions when they hire workers, their refusal to recognise the collective agreement, the workers' demands for political pluralism (as opposed to their involvement with Bolshevism) ... these facts about the government's behaviour ... point not to the salvation but to the loss of all the gains of the revolution, including Ukrainian statehood.[24]

2   The Countryside

With winter coming to an end, the peasantry prepared for spring sowing of wheat and sugar beet. Food stores from the previous year were low, prices high, speculation rife and hunger stalked the towns and cities. Since the end of 1917 the peasants were seizing land, livestock and farming implements from the big landowners. Their elected land committees and district councils gave direction to the peasant upsurge, working on the basis of the same principles that lay at the heart of the Bolshevik and Rada laws alike: private ownership of land was abolished; sale and purchase of land and the hiring of labour on the land were prohibited; the land was to be divided equally and in accordance with the number of hands in a household that could work and subsist on it; they would hold the land in perpetuity and pass it on to their offspring; the landless, semi-proletarian members of the community were the first in line to receive parcels of land from the expropriated estates.

Dividing up the land caused disputes within villages and between them, but especially between the poorest peasants and the landlords who opposed any expropriation or redivision of land whatsoever. The poor were most radically inclined; they were called 'landless Bolsheviks'.[25] Some peasant committees refused to parcel out any land to returning Free Cossacks or soldiers who had served in the Rada's army, saying 'The Bolsheviks were going to give everything to us, they wanted only good for the people, while the Ukrainian army went with the landlords and the Germans'.[26]

The seizures evoked resistance not only from the big landowners but from middle and well-off peasants as well, those with holdings of between 12 and

---

24   *Nova Rada*, no. 38, 21 March 1918.
25   Zhukovsky, *Vspomyny*, pp. 67–8.
26   *Nova Rada*, no. 57, 13 April 1918.

100 *desiatyn*. In overpopulated areas with not enough arable land to distribute to the land hungry peasants and landless proletarians, the middle peasants stood to lose at least some of their holdings. They were uncertain whether they should sow their fields because some may well not be theirs in a few months' time.

The German and Austrian armies spread fear among the poor peasants that they would be forced to give back what they had taken and not be allowed to harvest what they were about to sow. Nevertheless, the peasants' determination to plant in the spring – one may even call it an instinct – was stronger than their fear of losing the harvest. It was only a question of whose fields the peasants would plough and sow. In 1918 sowing began around 1 April in Kyiv gubernia. In Radomyshl the peasants went out in an organised manner to plant the former landlords' fields. 'The landlords were left with a land parcel, each according to the labour norm. The kitchen gardens of the small holders remained with their owners as before'.[27] In some parts of sugar beet country the peasants were sowing their own plots but refusing to go out onto the fields of the plantations owned by the sugar refineries, either because their redistribution had not been agreed or because they did not have the draught animals for ploughing and the seed to sow. In still other parts the villagers now regarded the sugar beet plantations in which they had worked for wages as their common property; they did not divide them up but planted the fields together for a future collective harvest. 'They planted seeds all over the land. True, not like it is done in a proper economy, but all the same they planted them'.[28] By the end of April there were optimistic reports in the press that sowing of wheat and sugar beet were well underway in Podillia, Kyiv, Chernihiv and Poltava gubernia.[29]

The Central Powers had not made a specific provision in their economic agreement with the Rada as to how their armies would be fed. There was a general understanding that the Rada would supply at least one third of the armies' needs. In any case the Rada was quite incapable of doing that for the simple fact that it had little authority in the countryside. So the incoming army units forcibly requisitioned food, horses and buildings to accommodate troops. They issued paper receipts for these goods and services which they said would be honoured and reimbursed by the Rada government. The Rada was overwhelmed by the receipts, unable to pay their bearers.[30]

---

27 *Nova Rada*, no. 51, 6 April 1918.
28 Zhukovsky, *Vspomyny*, p. 167. See also *Nova Rada*, no. 65, 23 April; no. 67, 25 April; no. 68, 26 April 1918.
29 *Nova Rada*, no. 65, 23 April 1918.
30 *Nova Rada*, no. 24, 15 March 1918.

On the Right Bank in Podillia and Volyn the Polish landlords sent Polish legions armed by the Austrian army to take back land which had already been distributed by the peasant land committees in accordance with the Rada's law. The legions requisitioned bread and horses, meting out corporal punishment to those who refused to comply. The commander of one legion arrested all the members of the local government of Stara Syniava. Peasants retaliated with guns and home-made bombs. In the same region the Austrian army was demanding that local governments draw up inventories of livestock and food stores under pain of arrest and punishment for evasion, concealment or inaccurate records. An Austrian commander ordered the peasants of Rybnytsia to return a sugar refinery, its plantation and inventory to its former owner, threatening the death penalty for any delay in carrying out his order.[31] On the Left Bank the big Ukrainian landowners joined forces with middle peasants and Cossack farmers to put pressure on the Rada to repeal its land law.

On 20 March the German military command prohibited its units from imposing further requisitions of food on the population and entered into talks with the Rada Ministry of Provisions. This ministry already supplied the Ukrainian armed forces with food and was now expected to supply the German army as well.[32]

The German and Austrian army units supported large landowners who were still holding out against expropriation of their properties or trying to recover them. 'It is important for the Germans that the fields be sown, so they are forcing the peasants to return to the landlords what they have plundered so that they can start sowing'.[33] Some peasants were so afraid of punishment that they returned the cattle they had seized to the enclosures of the landlord at night and begged his forgiveness on their knees in the morning.[34] But in many other cases requisitions and military interventions provoked angry protests and armed resistance, leading to fatalities on both sides. Some of the fiercest battles took place in Uman, Nemyriv and Bratslav along the path of the Austrian army's advance southwest of Kyiv. Here Polish legions burned 140 homesteads and all their livestock in the village of Kachanivka.[35] The Rada government could do very little about these conflicts:

31   *Nova Rada*, no. 43, 26 March 1918.
32   *Nova Rada*, no. 39, 22 March 1918.
33   Yevhen Chykalenko, *Shchodennyk (1918–1919)* (Kyiv: Tempora, 2011), p. 46.
34   *Nova Rada*, no. 44, 28 March 1918.
35   Zhukovsky, *Vspomyny*, pp. 175–6.

> The villagers recognise no government; the Ukrainian government gives them nothing and hears nothing and looks on in fright as the German moves forward, taking away all the weapons and forcing them to return what they have plundered. Maybe he will even return them to serfdom ... The town proletariat and the peasants who have less than 10 *desiatyn* of land – all Bolsheviks, all hostile to the Tsentral'na Rada.[36]

The Germans were ruthless: 'for every German soldier killed or wounded they immediately shot ten insurgents or peaceful residents'.[37] They established their own courts martial. On 13 March, the *mala rada* first heard a report of one such court sentencing four Ukrainian citizens to minimum terms of five years' imprisonment. The deputies were indignant; they requested an explanation from the Council of People's Ministers, but got none.[38] On 18 March, one day after the Rada plenary ratified the Brest Litovsk peace treaty, the German high command issued an order requiring all its officers to establish courts martial. Many people convicted by these courts, among them members of the UPSR and USDWP, were sent into forced labour in coal mines and the reclamation of marsh land in Poland. The Rada minister of provisions resigned in protest on 19 March.[39] Mykhailo Tkachenko, the minister of justice, issued an instruction on 23 March asserting the supremacy of UPR law and prohibiting prosecutions of UPR citizens by the German military authorities. However, he resigned as justice minister on the same day (while retaining the internal affairs portfolio). His replacement, the UPSF member S. Shelukhin, apologised to the German high command for the 'bad impression' left behind by his predecessor.[40]

3 The Vice

The Rada was caught in a vice between the bourgeoisie and the landowners on the one side who wanted to revoke the social and democratic objectives set out in the Third and Fourth Universals, and the workers and peasants on the other side who feared the Rada would yield and revoke them under pressure. The latter listened carefully to all the rumours and insinuations that the Rada had

---

36 Chykalenko, *Shchodennyk*, p. 53.
37 *Vestnik Ukrains'koi Narodnoi Respubliki* (Tahanrih), 29 March 1918, cited in Soldatenko, *Ukraina v Revoliutsiinu Dobu. Rik 1918*.
38 *Nova Rada*, no. 33, 14 March 1918.
39 Savchenko, *Symon Petliura*, p. 193.
40 Khrystiuk, *Ukrains'ka Revoliutsiia*, Vol. 2, pp. 163–4; *Nova Rada*, no. 42, 26 March 1918.

already done that in a secret Fifth Universal and that it had invited the Central Powers into Ukraine to enforce the revocation.[41]

The big landowners, financiers and industrialists took the arrival of the Austro-German armies as an opportunity to press for the restoration of their property rights, the resignation of the UPSR government and the installation of a new one to serve their interests. They lobbied the German high command in Kyiv and its government in Berlin. The industrial bourgeoisie organised themselves quickly: an initiative committee was registered in Kyiv on 12 April that included the Congress of Industrialists of Southern Russia, Union of Coal Enterprises, Union of Anthracite Enterprises, Society of Factory and Plant Owners of Kharkiv, Katerynoslav, Odesa and Kyiv, the All-Russian Society of Sugar Refiners, the Kyiv and Kharkiv stock exchanges and the Kyiv Society of Agricultural Industries.[42]

The All-Ukrainian Union of Landowners,[43] which spoke for the Left Bank estates, and the Right Bank Polish landlords, had a more difficult task on their hands than the industrial and financial bourgeoisie. They had to wrest their property back from the peasants who were acting in conformity with the land law. They needed a wedge to divide the peasantry, which the Ukrainian Democratic Farmers' Party (UDFP) conveniently provided for them. Formed in March 1918 at a congress in Lubny by some 2,500 middle peasants and Cossack farmers from Poltava gubernia the UDFP campaigned for the abolition of the 18 January land law and the admission of the party's representatives to the government. They lobbied the Rada's ministries and the *mala rada* with mass delegations from Poltava, Kyiv and Volyn gubernia, and prepared for a national founding congress of the party, scheduled to take place in Kyiv on 29 April.[44] They came into bitter conflict with the peasant unions, whose members burned down the country estate of Serhii Shemet, organiser of the UDFP, in retaliation for its campaign against the land law.[45]

---

41   Hrushevsky, *Na Porozi Novoi Ukrainy*, p. 188.
42   *Nova Rada*, no. 65, 23 April 1918.
43   The renamed All-Russian Union of Landowners.
44   Khrystiuk, *Ukrains'ka Revoliutsiia*, Vol. 2, pp. 158–9; *Nova Rada*, no. 55, 11 April; no. 57, 13 April; no. 70, 28 April 1918.
45   *Nova Rada*, no. 62, 19 April 1918.

4   The Socialist Federalists' Campaign

The Ukrainian Socialist Revolutionaries knew they could not govern on their own. They tried unsuccessfully to persuade the other socialist parties to join the Council of People's Ministers. The Ukrainian Party of Socialist Federalists (UPSF), on the other hand, had no confidence in the UPSR government, regarding its policies as a Ukrainian version of Bolshevism. They launched a sustained attack to unseat the government, accusing it of incompetence and the pursuit of a utopian socialisation of land ownership that deepened the economic and political crisis. Serhii Yefremov, editor of *Nova Rada*, set the tone of their campaign:

> There is no government. Their portfolios are empty. Instead of influence over life they have just illusions, if anyone can still believe them; and then there is the fiction of work being done ... anarchy has taken hold of the cities and the villages, everywhere the government has disappeared without a trace.

Yefremov railed against the truly catastrophic situation, warning of 'the dangerous assistance from our present allies and the hostility of our former Russian partners'. And then he identified the principal culprit in his scenario as 'peasant anarchy' which he accused the UPSR of fomenting and which it could no longer control.[46]

The UPSF had served as an influential junior partner to the USDWP throughout the latter's leadership of the General Secretariat, until the USDWP was forced to cede to the UPSR in mid-January. It had far less influence over the UPSR: it enjoyed no popular mandate of its own, having gained only a few thousand votes in the November Constituent Assembly elections against the millions cast for the UPSR. Its only claim was to represent the majority of the Ukrainian intelligentsia. In fact it represented mainly the urban professionals and public servants who, like the middle classes in general, were exhausted by the War, desperate for stability and disillusioned with radical governments of all stripes. Now they felt liberated from their 'socialist captivity' of recent months by the Austro-German occupation and the UPSF came forward to articulate an alternative for them.

A 13 March editorial in *Nova Rada* proclaimed: 'We have to reject Bolshevik experiments to which our homegrown Lenins and Trotskys are returning once

---

46   *Nova Rada*, no. 37, 20 March 1918.

more. They have already declared Ukraine no more and no less than a "fortress of socialism" … we can't have any more of this'.[47] What the country needed, the editors went on, was a non-party government chosen on the basis of professional qualifications rather than ideology, with a strong and charismatic leader and a commitment to wage war on anarchy. Among the possible candidates mentioned for leadership were the social democrat Volodymyr Vynnychenko and the monarchist Dmytro Doroshenko. The newspaper also floated the banker and sugar magnate Abram Dobry for the finance ministry and the right-wing social democrat Valentyn Sadovsky for labour. Essentially, the UPSF was calling for a corporatist regime, allegedly non-ideological but in fact committed to rolling back the social and democratic gains of the lower classes. Makar Kushnir, member of the UPSF Central Committee, gave a speech on 20 March on the first anniversary of the Tsentral'na Rada (and the day the Second All-Ukrainian Congress of Councils opened in Katerynoslav) in which he told his audience that 'a new force is growing in Ukraine':

> It is the force of capitalism that brings progress and development. We need to recognise that no single country can develop without trade and industry, without a bourgeoisie. It's time for us to understand that it is impossible to shove the bourgeoisie aside from running the life of Ukraine. And the Ukrainian Tsentral'na Rada, our parliament, has to be reorganised so that all the cities, *zemstva*, the bourgeoisie, peasantry and workers, the socialist parties can work together to give direction to that life.[48]

The UPSF wanted a place in a new government of this kind. So did the nationalist UPSI, but in a government without any national minority ministers or ministries. *Nova Rada* mentioned several candidates recommended by the UPSI, including its own member Colonel Petro Bolbochan for military affairs and S. Shelukhin (UPSF) for the justice portfolio.[49]

The UPSF waged its campaign for the resignation of the UPSR government on two fronts: through the press and by intense lobbying behind the scenes with the representatives of big business, finance and trade. What the party lacked in terms of a popular mandate it made up for by its members' influential positions in government ministries. A most advantageous location for them in March 1918 was the newly created state commission for foreign trade, responsible for

---

47 *Nova Rada*, no. 32, 13 March 1918.
48 *Nova Rada*, no. 39, 22 March 1918.
49 *Nova Rada*, no. 34, 15 March 1918.

working out detailed export and import agreements with Germany and Austro-Hungary. Mykola Porsh headed up the commission. Kostiantyn Matsievych and Ivan Feshchenko-Chopivsky, both members of the UPSF, held key positions there. As deputy minister of trade and industry, Feshchenko-Chopivsky headed up the commission's division for export, import, finance and law. Delegations of businessmen from Germany and Austro-Hungary were arriving regularly in Kyiv to explore new opportunities for investment and trade, consulting with their Ukrainian counterparts, members of the commission and the German high command. Zhukovsky recalled the atmosphere: 'Everyone's appetite grew enormously when the prospect appeared of various railway concessions, trade ties with the Central [European] states, the export of all sorts of goods, provisions and raw materials. An entire stock exchange dealing in different interests and influences rose up alongside the state trade commission'.[50]

The Germans did not have confidence in the UPSR government's administrative capacity, finances, powers of coercion or, most important, its political will to deliver on their mutual agreements. Nor did the UPSF and the UPSI. With no other socialist party willing to join it and lend support, the government was forced to give way. Premier Holubovych shifted the balance in his Council of Ministers firmly to the right, leaving six ministries with the UPSR and giving four to the UPSF, three to the USDWP and one to the UPSI. None of the USDWP ministers were from the leadership of their party. Feshchenko-Chopivsky from the UPSF was elevated from deputy to full minister of trade and industry. There were no members of national minorities in the government nor functioning ministries for national minority affairs. It was not until April that M. Latsky from the Folkspartei accepted the post of Minister for Jewish Affairs with the agreement of the Bund, Poalei Zion and the United Jewish Socialist Party.[51]

The members of the new government were: from the UPSR – V. Holubovych (Premier), M. Kovalevksy (Land), M. Liubynsky (Foreign Affairs), Sokovych (Transport), and P. Khrystiuk (State Secretary); from the UPSF – S. Shelukhin (Justice), Prokopovych (Education), Feshchenko-Chopivsky (Trade and Industry), and O. Lototsky (State Controller); from the USDWP – M. Tkachenko (Internal Affairs), Koliukh (Food Provision) and Mykhailiv (Labour); from the UPSI – H. Sydorenko (Post and Telegraph); Independent: Klymovych (Finances).

The UPSR was forced to bend, but it did not buckle. Holubovych announced the new government's programme: land reform would be implemented in

---

50   Zhukovsky, *Vspomyny*, p. 179.
51   Hrushevsky, *Na Porozi Novoi Ukrainy*, p. 189; Goldelman, *Jewish National Autonomy in Ukraine*, p. 62; Khrystiuk, *Ukrains'ka Revoliutsiia*, Vol. 2, p. 162.

accordance with the Universals and laws of the Republic; the land committees would be strengthened by the addition of agronomists; the government's priority was to ensure spring sowing. With respect to labour, which faced an onslaught by the employers, the government promised to establish arbitration procedures and to enforce collective agreements. It would also launch new public works to reduce unemployment. Disabled people would receive training. The government would conduct foreign trade through a state monopoly, but permit private traders to operate under stringent state regulation. Local governments, co-operatives and private traders would all be permitted to engage in domestic trade.[52]

Despite taking four important portfolios in the new government, the UPSF was disappointed, complaining that it was essentially the same government with a few minor additions. But although they did not achieve a wholesale reorientation of the government's course, individual ministers could pursue their own agendas. Feshchenko-Chopivsky, for example, planned to restore private ownership to the Donbas mining and metallurgical industries and to stimulate recovery by trading its raw materials with the Central Powers. The trade unions would be involved, but there would be no more 'Bolshevik experiments' with industry.[53]

The UPSF stepped up its campaign to repeal the land law by promoting the upcoming inaugural congress of the Ukrainian Democratic Farmers' Party and publishing long interviews in *Nova Rada* with delegations of middle peasants coming to the capital that the government and *mala rada* steadfastly refused to receive. Those interviewed provided the newspaper's editors with the words to articulate what was already in their own minds:

> Socialisation has led to the complete ruin of agriculture. They called in the Germans. We asked: what for? To help of course. The Germans came and asked us: what is the biggest evil here? We told them. And they replied that they would help.[54]

Yevhen Chykalenko made the following entry in his diary on 7 April:

> I went to the anniversary celebrations of *Nova Rada*, sat in a tight circle with the editors. All the talk revolved around the Germans coming into Ukraine and the new cabinet of ministers. Everyone was saying it would

---

52   *Nova Rada*, no. 42, 26 March 1918.
53   *Nova Rada*, no. 65, 23 April 1918.
54   *Nova Rada*, no. 55, 11 April 1918.

be better if the Germans took everything in hand and appointed the ministers themselves because our own people can't manage, they won't bring peace to our young state. Our government headed by Hrushevsky thought it could rely on the village poor, on our Bolsheviks. They thought they are a force on which to build the state ... Our government ... supports these Bolsheviks and their committees and prohibits the return of what they have plundered from the landlords, saying in their Universals that it all belongs to the people. That's why everyone who desires peace and quiet wants the Germans to take control and provide order.[55]

5 The Germans Take Control

On 25 March, the Rada state commission on foreign trade headed by Mykola Porsh entered into negotiations for the new trade agreements with state representatives of Germany and Austro-Hungary, led respectively by baron Mumm von Schwarzenstein and earl Y. Fohach.[56] The formal objective of the negotiations was to fulfil the requirement set out in Clause VIII of the Brest Litovsk treaty: 'By 31 July it will be necessary to carry out the exchange of surpluses of the main agricultural and industrial goods for the purpose of covering ongoing needs'.

The German side had a formidable team in Kyiv: Field Marshall Hermann von Eichhorn's chief of staff, Lieutenant-General Wilhelm Groener, had previously organised Germany's Office of War Economy and ran its railways; ambassador Mumm von Schwarzenstein came from a prominent family of industrialists with interests in Eastern Europe. They were supported by 'a very active group of long-term planners from the Reich Economic Office ... This "economic office" was specially established to organise the economic penetration of the Ukraine'.[57] Their objectives in the talks were to tie the Ukrainian economy into service of Germany's and Austro-Hungary's needs for food and critical raw materials and to deny trade access to all other countries, in the first instance to Russia. They wanted a deregulated trade to ensure the unimpeded flow of grain, sugar, meat, timber, iron ore and manganese ore out of the country. The Ger-

---

55 Chykalenko, *Shchodennyk (1918–1919)*, p. 46.
56 Ihor Datskiv, 'Nimets'kyi chynnyk u zovnishnoekonomichnii politytsi UNR 1918 r', *Naukovi Zapysky: Seria Istorii*, pp. 20–5, http://shron1.chtyvo.org.ua/Datskiv_Ihor/Nimetskyi_chynnyk_u_zovnishnoekonomichnii_politytsi_UNR_1918_r.pdf [accessed 15 November 2018].
57 Fischer, *Germany's War Aims*, p. 237.

mans also wanted to alter the gauge of Ukrainian railway lines and to secure for themselves the Black Sea port of Mykolaiiv for the transport of mineral ores.[58]

The Ukrainian side's objective in the talks was to export Ukraine's surpluses under state control, with baseline prices for the main traded goods, and to use the earnings from exports to pay for the import of goods critical to the long-term development of the Ukrainian economy: increasing its productivity, efficiency and diversity. However, such objectives were beyond the powers of the Ukrainian side to secure in these negotiations. The best they could do was to resist the German positions and delay the agreement.

Conflicts arose over several key issues. The Germans and Austrians pressed for the export of 60 million poods[59] of bread grain by 31 July, which the Ukrainians insisted was too high as they expected a surplus of only 39 million poods after their domestic needs were met. Moreover, they were ill equipped to ship grain due to the damaged state of the railways and their own institutional incapacity. It was only on 5 April that the Council of People's Ministers issued a draft law for the *mala rada*'s ratification to create a state grain bureau responsible for trade with the Central Powers.[60]

The Germans and Austrians insisted that the UPR not trade with third parties without their agreement. The Council of People's Ministers countered by imposing export quotas on certain goods and insisting on a state monopoly for all exports. The Ukrainians also demanded their exports be matched in value terms by imports of ploughs, coal, oil and pharmaceuticals. The other side countered by raising the unit prices of these goods.[61]

On 11 April in the midst of the negotiations Eichhorn issued an order to the peasantry and the land committees. He was concerned that spring sowing was delayed despite the exhortations of the minister of land affairs and he doubted that the land committees had sufficient influence over the peasants to work in the landlords' estates. Therefore 'the Chief German Commander in Ukraine' ordered the peasants to comply with the following terms. First, whoever sowed the land owned the harvest from it and would receive a cash payment for it 'at the appropriate prices'. Second, peasants who took more land than they could work would be punished severely. Third, where the peasants could not sow all the land because the landlords still held on to it, the landlords must be allowed to sow it and the land committees must provide them with necessary seeds, horses and machinery. Though Eichhorn did not state it explicitly, he clearly

---

58   Ibid, p. 238.
59   Or 983,000 tonnes. One pood was equivalent to 16.38 kilograms.
60   *Nova Rada*, no. 42, 26 March; no. 50, 5 April 1918.
61   Datskiv, 'Nimets'kyi chynnyk', pp. 23–5; *Nova Rada*, no. 55, 11 April 1918.

meant that the peasants must provide their unpaid labour. He went on: 'The harvest in such cases will be the property equally of the peasants and those who have sown the land' – i.e. the landlords. Finally, Eichhorn instructed the land committees and the local governments, or the German military authorities should the former refuse his order, to issue peasants with certificates of the amount of land they had sown. In any event the military authorities required a full accounting by 15 May of all the land sown. They promised severe punishment for any theft or destruction of the harvest.[62]

The publication of Eichhorn's order, or 'law' as it became known, created an uproar in the *mala rada*, which denounced it as a violation of national sovereignty that threatened the agreements already made and those currently under negotiation between the UPR and the Central Powers. The *mala rada* called on the population to refuse to obey Eichhorn's order and for Prime Minister Holubovych to deliver its protest to the German and Austro-Hungarian governments, which he duly did. Land committees across the country issued their own protests.[63]

At first Kovalevsky claimed he had seen only a German copy of Eichhorn's order and that he was unable as minister of land affairs to intervene in the matter as it concerned foreign affairs. Nevertheless, he was sufficiently informed as to its contents to tender his resignation in protest. In an interview with *Nova Rada* two days later he charged Eichhorn with making a mockery of the land law and agitating against the socialist government.[64] All the while the editors of *Nova Rada* themselves continued to agitate against the government's land law, accusing it of destroying farmers' livelihoods and handing power in the villages to the worst elements. It was no wonder, they said, that the injured parties who could get no redress from their own government ended up appealing to the Germans for help. For *Nova Rada* the real issue needing attention was not the Germans interfering in Ukraine's domestic affairs but the 'utopian' and 'bankrupt' land law.[65]

Holubovych refused to accept Kovalevsky's resignation. He told a session of the *mala rada* on 18 April that Kovalevsky had been misinformed about Eichhorn's order and was unaware that his own ministry was issuing instructions that were quite similar in content. Eichhorn's order was simply a clumsy attempt to achieve the same objectives as those of the ministry of land affairs. Pavlo Khrystiuk, at the time State Secretary in the government, later wrote that

---

62 Khrystiuk, *Ukrains'ka Revoliutsiia*, Vol. 2, pp. 201–2, note 23.
63 *Nova Rada*, no. 58, 14 April; no. 59, 16 April; no. 62, 19 April; no. 66, 24 April 1918.
64 *Nova Rada*, no. 58, 14 April; no. 59, 16 April 1918.
65 *Nova Rada*, no. 59, 16 April 1918.

'the German military authorities indicated ... that the order was drawn up with the agreement and understanding of the minister of land affairs M. Kovalevsky. Nobody believed their statement, however it proved impossible to verify it, all the more so because M. Kovalevsky did not speak out against it anywhere afterwards'.[66]

The Germans were baffled. The Rada minister's inconsistency could be explained by his objection not so much to the content of Eichhorn's order but to the fact that it was issued by the German command, thereby further undermining the already shaky authority of the Rada. Eichhorn's reason for issuing the order was that neither the minister of land affairs nor the land committees could persuade the peasants to sow the fields still held by the big landlords. He was moved to act in the midst of the trade negotiations by a sense of urgency, not to miss the time window available for spring sowing. At that very moment the German negotiators were trying to persuade the Ukrainian side to agree to export grain that would be needed to feed its own population, given the anticipated size of the summer harvest. Thus, it is reasonable to believe that Kovalevsky's ministry was pressured to agree to the intervention by the German army in order to maximise the coming harvest, even if it violated the land law and the UPR's sovereignty. However, the government did not want to disclose any of its humiliating subordination to its own citizens.

The two sides signed a new trade treaty on 23 April that was to remain in force until 31 July. The treaty provided for the collection and export of 60 million poods of grain by a Ukrainian state monopoly assisted by a German purchasing company. Iron ore, manganese and timber would be traded on the market, but within quantitative limits and from a baseline of agreed minimum prices. Ukraine's trade with other states required prior permission of the Central Powers.[67] The treaty not only met all of Germany and Austro-Hungary's expressed needs, but also set prices for coal and grain, the two main items to be traded, that were substantially to their advantage.[68]

The Germans were by now exasperated with the Rada, the 'kiddies in their ministerial baby carriages' as Groener had taken to calling them.[69] They had no confidence the Rada would implement its side of the agreement. Their Foreign Ministry in Berlin wanted to keep working with the Rada, while the German delegation in Ukraine favoured replacing it with a government based

---

66 Khrystiuk, *Ukrains'ka Revoliutsiia*, Vol. 2, p. 202, note 23. See also Vynnychenko, *Vidrodzhennia natsii*, Vol. 2, p. 319.
67 Datskiv, 'Nimets'kyi chynnyk', pp. 23–5.
68 Soldatenko, *Ukraina v Revoliutsiinu Dobu. Rik 1918*.
69 Fischer, *Germany's War Aims*, p. 539.

on landlords, middle peasants, financiers and industrialists, all of whom had been lobbying the delegation assiduously for that very purpose.

General Erich Ludendorff identified General Pavlo Skoropadsky as a candidate to head up such an alternative government. On 24 April the German command in Kyiv set its plan in motion to overthrow the Rada by putting to its representatives and separately to Skoropadsky an identical set of conditions for a government that Germany could accept: the introduction across the entire country of Austrian and German courts martial; the formation of a Ukrainian army only with the agreement and under the direct supervision of the German command; the removal of 'undesirable elements' from government institutions; the restoration of private property in land, financial compensation for redistributed land and the retention of large agricultural estates; the removal of all restrictions on free trade and export of foodstuffs and raw materials to Germany and Austro-Hungary; and new elections to a national government only when order had been completely restored.[70]

The Tsentral'na Rada rejected the conditions out of hand and issued a protest to Eichhorn and Schwarzenstein. Groener met with Skoropadsky, who accepted the conditions with a few reservations. The Germans assured Skoropadsky they would prevent any popular protests or challenges to his assumption of power, while at the same time officially maintaining their neutrality. Already on 24 April their army units occupied the strategic points in the capital. The events of the following days showed the Germans were indeed the masters of the overthrow and Skoropadsky their puppet.

The one serious challenge to the overthrow of the Rada could have come from the railway workers, who were critical to military operations, communications, domestic and foreign trade. Zhukovsky addressed the All-Ukrainian Congress of Railway Workers on 23 April in Kyiv, and *Nova Rada* reported obliquely that he warned them of an imminent danger from enemies of the Ukrainian Republic.[71] However, there is nothing in Zhukovsky's memoirs to suggest he did any more than that at the congress. The problem was that the railway workers were split politically. Two competing unions were meeting in Kyiv at the same time in April, the Fourth Delegated Congress of South Western Railway Workers and the All-Ukrainian Union of Railway Workers. The Mensheviks and Russian SRs led the first union, the USDWP and UPSR the second. There were several exchanges of delegations between the congresses to try to reconcile them, but they failed. So there was little prospect, if any, that an attack on the Rada might

---

70   Soldatenko, *Ukraina v Revoliutsiinu Dobu. Rik 1918*; Fischer, *German War Aims*, p. 540.
71   *Nova Rada*, no. 66, 24 April 1918.

unite the railway workers in resistance to it. In any event the German command was ready for them: in the event of a strike their armed forces were poised to occupy all important stations, workshops and freight yards, to escort strike breakers to work and to detain the leaders and agitators of the strike.[72]

The Rada was finished. However, a clandestine group organised around internal affairs minister Mykhailo Tkachenko launched a desperate, last minute attempt on 24 April to stop the Germans from carrying out their plan. The self-styled Committee for the Salvation of Ukraine, a conspiracy that also involved ministers Kovalevsky and Liubynsky, kidnapped Abram Dobry, the Kyiv banker and sugar magnate. They took him to Kharkiv in a sealed railway carriage and held him under guard in the city's Grand Hotel. Rumours flew around Kyiv as to the motive and identity of the kidnappers. The Germans turned immediately to the Rada and demanded Dobry be found within 24 hours and his kidnappers brought to justice. Tkachenko pretended he didn't know anything and publicly ordered the Kyiv chief of police Bahatsky to track the kidnappers down.[73]

Dobry was head of the Kyiv branch of the Russian Bank of Foreign Trade, a member of the Bank's board, a board member of the All-Russian Society of Sugar Refiners and board director of five separate refineries in Ukraine. He built up the sugar industry, which boomed in the decade before the First World War and became a prime target for German capital investment. Dobry served as an important conduit between German and Russian banks. Intimately involved in sugar production, its financing and trade, he traded very successfully on his own account and for his German counterparts.

In March 1918, Dobry was recruited on the recommendation of the UPSF to the Rada's state trade commission and the tripartite commission for the settlement of payments for trade between Ukraine, Germany and Austro-Hungary. Thus, he was instrumental in drawing up the new trade treaty signed on 23 April. During this period the Germans engaged Dobry separately to buy up food supplies for them that the Rada government could not secure. He was possibly also the private shipper by rail of these supplies to Austro-Hungary and Germany, which the Rada government repeatedly tried to stop. He kept close contact with the German military and diplomatic missions in Kyiv and he lobbied them for the removal of the Rada in favour of a government of landowners and big business. Premier Holubovych lamented from the rostrum of the *mala rada* that 'Dobry sold himself to the Germans'.[74]

---

72 Soldatenko, *Ukraina v Revoliutsiinu Dobu. Rik 1918*.
73 *Nova Rada*, no. 70, 28 April 1918.
74 Savchenko, *Symon Petliura*, p. 201.

On 25 April, Field Marshall Eichhorn responded to Dobry's kidnapping by ordering German military field courts be set up across the whole country to deal with criminal violations of law and order. The Ukrainian courts would deal henceforth only with civil matters. All street gatherings were banned. Newspapers that agitated against the existing order would be closed down. Eichhorn's spokesman told the press: 'We see his arrest as a provocation that is aimed actually at us ... People who are working with us are being arrested. That shows the present government is unable to ensure their safety'.

Note that Eichhorn's spokesman referred to Dobry's abduction as an arrest, rather than a kidnapping, by which he signalled that the Germans already knew Ukrainian officials were involved. He added that the German military command held precise information about further arrests being planned by the still unknown 'salvation groups' and that was why it was obliged to interfere into the internal affairs of Ukraine in order to maintain law and order.[75]

The *Nova Rada* editorial on 27 April took the same position as it had in response to Eichhorn's first decree, that the Ukrainian government led by the UPSR and not the German military command bore primary responsibility for the introduction of martial law: 'we have neither a leadership nor any accountability in our political circles'. On the same day the UPSF recalled its members from the Council of People's Ministers citing its disagreement with critical policy decisions.

The Germans knew from their own intelligence service that the kidnappers came from the Rada's leadership. Within a few days they discovered where Dobry was being held and freed him. The Committee for the Salvation of Ukraine had intended to kidnap 27 prominent citizens who were working closely with the Germans and thereby to disrupt the plan to overthrow the Rada. However, they managed to kidnap only Dobry and they failed even to hold him. The Germans then arrested Tkachenko, his right-hand man Haievsky in the internal affairs ministry (who organised Dobry's kidnapping), and M. Liubynsky, the foreign minister. Kovalevsky fled Ukraine.[76] It was a poorly planned and indecisive assault on German power, conducted in the manner of a counter-coup rather than an uprising. Carried out clandestinely by ostensibly private individuals and not openly in the name of the Rada, they had targeted close collaborators of the German occupation, not the occupation authorities as such.

---

75   *Nova Rada*, no. 69, 27 April 1918.
76   P.P. Hai-Nyzhnyk, *Vykradennia bankira A. Dobroho v kvitni 1918 roku (rekonstruktsiia ta analiz podii)* (Kyiv: M.P. Drahomanov University Publishers, 2014), pp. 221–3.

German army units reinforced their positions across Kyiv on 24 April. They were assisted by the UPR's Sich Riflemen on the following day in disarming other Ukrainian army units. In one night, from 26 to 27 April, German units surrounded, disarmed and disbanded the First Ukrainian (Blue Coats) Division, the UPR's most loyal and disciplined soldiers who had just returned to Kyiv from the front. In the morning the German command ordered Skoropadsky's supporters to be armed.[77]

The *mala rada* went into session three times on 27 April, twice behind closed doors. Some deputies denounced Eichhorn's second order, threatened armed rebellion and abrogation of the Brest Litovsk treaty. Others criticised the policies of their own government and demanded it be thoroughly reshuffled. No-one mentioned the disappearance of Dobry. Nothing was decided.

On Sunday, 28 April, Volodymyr Vynychenko, sun-tanned and refreshed from his sojourn in the south, delivered a speech to the reassembled *mala rada*. He reviewed only the setbacks of the Ukrainian national movement before he himself had gone south, accusing the 'non-Ukrainian democracy' of abandoning their Ukrainian comrades. He did not appear to have anything to say about the preceding three months or the critical situation at hand. Rafes rose to respond to Vynnychenko's accusation and made an appeal for unity of the multinational proletariat against German imperialist designs on Ukraine. It was around 4pm when Rafes' speech was interrupted by a unit of 50 German soldiers marching into the meeting. According to Vynnychenko, the soldiers ordered the detachment of Sich Riflemen guarding the *mala rada* to stand down or face 'severe punishment and dispersal'.[78] According to Zhukovsky, the detachment offered no resistance but 'on the contrary, it clearly carried out the order to fall into line, which meant there were nests of treason hiding inside it'.[79] The officer in charge of the German unit held warrants for the arrest of those the German high command believed were the ringleaders of the Committee for the Salvation of Ukraine. Hrushevsky, who was chairing the meeting, protested the intrusion and was duly silenced. Holubovych was made to stand in a corner facing the wall. Haievsky, Zhukovsky and Liubynsky were led away under escort. Someone warned Tkachenko, who was sitting in his office at the time, but he refused to go into hiding. He was arrested later on his way home. Kovalevsky was not present either; he managed to escape and went into hiding in Henichesk on the coast of the Sea of Azov. After four hours of detention the German unit allowed all the remaining *mala rada* deputies and members of the government to leave

---

77   Soldatenko, *Ukraina v Revoliutsiinu Dobu. Rik 1918*.
78   Vynnychenko, *Vidrodzhennia natsii*, Vol. 2, p. 326.
79   Zhukovsky, *Vspomyny*, pp. 191–2.

the building and then left themselves. The Sich Riflemen resumed guarding the building. Fractions of the political parties held their meetings in the same building that night.[80]

The *mala rada* met one final time on 29 April, adopted the Constitution of the Ukrainian People's Republic. It was reminiscent of the meeting at the end of January when the *mala rada* adopted its landmark laws on socialisation of land and the eight-hour working day even as shrapnel fired from cannons across the Dnipro River was showering onto its roof. This time, however, the impending oblivion hung silently over the Rada. The deputies held their fraction meetings in the evening and went home, never to return. The Sich Riflemen left their posts and took Hrushevsky and his wife with them for safekeeping in their barracks. On their way they were attacked by an assailant wearing a Sich uniform. Vynnychenko identified him as a Russian officer. Accounts vary: according to Savchenko, Hrushevsky was unharmed but his wife suffered a serious stab wound from the assailant's bayonet. Khrystiuk wrote that Hrushevsky was shot in the chest, his wife in the hand.[81]

That night Hrushevsky, Petliura, Porsh and Konovalets of the Sich Riflemen held a secret meeting in the barracks. They were helpless to prevent the overthrow of the Rada: General Oleksandr Hrekiv, who had replaced the arrested Zhukovsky as minister of military affairs the day before, had disappeared. Lieutenant Colonel Oleksandr Slivinsky, in charge of the UPR military general staff, had already gone over to Skoropadsky, as had some from the ranks of the Sich Riflemen. Overnight the UPR's cavalry chief of staff Lieutenant Colonel Arkas also defected.[82]

Nova Rada's 29 April editorial, written but not published because the paper did not come out that day, again exonerated the German command. It called for the resignation of Holubovych's government 'which had allowed it to come to this, to the point where the authorities of a neighbouring government had to arrest its members'. That evening unidentified army officers wearing red and white armbands broke into the newspaper's press building with an order in Russian from the ministry of internal affairs to close down the newspapers *Nova Rada*, *Borot'ba* and *Vidrodzhennia* (organ of the ministry of military affairs). They placed the building under guard. The original order was replaced

---

80   Vynnychenko, *Vidrodzhennia natsii*, Vol. 2, p. 326; Khrystiuk, *Ukrains'ka Revoliutsiia*, Vol. 2, pp. 167–74; Hai-Nyzhnyk, *Vykradennia Bankira A. Dobroho*, pp. 24–5; Savchenko, *Symon Petliura*, p. 200; *Nova Rada*, no. 71, 9 May 1918.
81   Khrystiuk, *Ukrains'ka Revoliutsiia*, Vol. 2, p. 174; Vynnychenko, *Vidrodzhennia natsii*, Vol. 2, p. 326; Savchenko, *Symon Petliura*, p. 201.
82   Savchenko, *Symon Petliura*, pp. 202–3; Zhukovsky, *Vspomyny*, pp. 91–2.

on the following day with one from the German command. It offered the editors permission to restart publishing on condition the newspaper submitted to censorship, which the editors rejected. *Nova Rada* reported these developments of 29 April in its 9 May issue, when it started to publish again under conditions of censorship.[83]

The Ukrainian Democratic Farmers' Party chose 29 April as the day to convene its founding national congress. Thousands of members streamed into Kyiv in the preceding days. Field Marshall Eichhorn had kindly agreed to assist the party in finding a venue and accommodation for the delegates.[84] However, at some point the UPSF party leadership lost control of its members and the proceedings did not go according to their plans or the expectations of the party leaders who had so assiduously promoted the congress over the previous weeks. Yevhen Chykalenko made the following entry in his diary:

> … Germans have shaken down the members of the Tsentral'na Rada and taken away the minutes of their meeting. Meanwhile this is what happened with (Serhii) Shemet's Ukrainian democratic farmers' congress. The Kyiv organisation of the All-Russian Union of Landowners, having learned from the newspapers about the congress on 29 April in the Merchants Hall, decided to hold their own congress in the circus on the same day. They made every effort to bring out as many big landowners as possible and they saw to it by fair means and foul to lure over to themselves the people who had come for the Ukrainian national congress. They managed to do that very effectively owing to the ignorance of our peasants, and as a result up to eight thousand people, according to some reports, gathered at the congress of the All-Russian organisation or, as they called it, the 'All-Ukrainian' organisation.[85]

The congress in the circus took place under German armed guard. Speaker after speaker denounced the Rada, its ministers and the peasant land committees, calling for a strong hand to restore law and order. At 2pm around 500 Russian officers arrived to reinforce the German guard and at 3pm Skoropadsky arrived with his entourage. He met applause and calls from the floor for a dictator, a *het'man*. Skoropadsky embraced all the members of the presidium and walked out onto the stage:

---

83   *Nova Rada*, no. 71, 9 May 1918.
84   *Nova Rada*, no. 70, 28 April 1918.
85   Chykalenko, *Shchodennyk*, pp. 59–60.

Gentlemen! I thank you for entrusting me with power. I do not take on the burden of this momentary power for my own benefit. You know yourselves that anarchy has spread everywhere and only a strong hand can restore order. On you, farmers and right thinking circles of the population, will I rely. I pray to God to give us strength to save Ukraine.

The farmers lifted Skoropadsky aloft and carried him out of the circus. He proceeded to the ancient church of St Sophia, where he swore an oath of loyalty to Ukraine. The Orthodox clergy held a *moleben* prayer service outside on the square as archbishop Nykodym performed the ritual of cropping Skoropadsky's hair and anointing him with holy oil.[86]

Skoropadsky issued 'a Charter to the whole Ukrainian nation' which appeared on the walls of Kyiv the following morning. In it he declared himself 'het'man' of all Ukraine', abolished the Tsentral'na Rada, its *mala rada*, ministries and the peasant land committees. Until elections to a Parliament could be held, he would personally appoint and instruct a Council of Ministers to govern. 'All the orders (laws) of the previous Ukrainian government as well as the Provisional Russian government are withdrawn and repealed'. Private property was fully restored. The peasants would receive plots through a land reform for which the landowners would be compensated. Rights of the working class would be upheld, living conditions improved, especially those of the railway workers who did not leave their posts (i.e. did not strike) during the recent troubles. Attached to Skoropadsky's Charter was an initial set of laws, countersigned by his first appointed '*Otaman* of Ministers' Mykola Ustymovych, a rich Poltava landowner and descendant of Ukrainian Cossack nobility. The laws gave the *het'man* absolute authority over all institutions of the state, including the government, the administration of justice and the armed forces. They declared Orthodox Christianity the religion of the Ukrainian State, as it was now to be called. In effect, Skoropadsky's Charter, his Laws and his repeal of all laws adopted since the February 1917 revolution aimed to return Ukraine to the *ancient regime* of the Tsars.[87]

Internationally the German government presented the regime change as an entirely domestic affair while its representatives in Kyiv instructed Skoropadsky to bring the Ukrainian political parties of the Rada into his government so as to lend it a democratic and even left-leaning facade. These parties made a counter offer which the Germans refused even to consider: to dilute the

---

86 Khrystiuk, *Ukrains'ka Revoliutsiia*, Vol. 3, p. 4.
87 Khrystiuk, *Ukrains'ka Revoliutsiia*, Vol. 3, pp. 4–8.

Rada's land law and admit the bourgeoisie and landowners into government in exchange for the Germans dismissing Skoropadsky and restoring the democratic republic. Ambassador Schwarzenstein simply told them 'zu spät' – 'it's too late'. The following day Skoropadsky ditched Mykola Ustymovych as his 'otaman of ministers' and replaced him with Mykola Vasylenko, a Kyiv university professor and member of the Russian Kadets who was on good terms with the UPSF. Vasylenko assembled a cabinet of Kadets, Octobrists and monarchists representing the agrarian, industrial and financial bourgeoisie, with a sprinkling of like-minded Ukrainians. Vynnychenko called 29 April 'the day that power passed from the hands of the national Ukrainian petit bourgeois democracy to the non-Ukrainian big bourgeoisie'.[88]

88   Vynnychenko, *Vidrodzhennia natsii*, Vol. 2, p. 326.

Epilogue

The first year of the Revolution ended with the dissolution of the Soviet Ukrainian government in Tahanrih, the overthrow of the Tsentral'na Rada in Kyiv and Pavlo Skoropadsky's installation by the German General Staff. Within days peasants' and workers' organisations showed they would not be intimidated. On 10 May, 12,000 peasants came to Kyiv for the Second All-Ukrainian Congress of Peasant Deputies only to be dispersed by troops, their leaders thrown into jail. They reconvened three days later in the Holosivsky forest outside the city and resolved to fight the Austro-German occupation and its client regime. In the same week 500 delegates from more than 100 towns and cities gathered clandestinely in Kyiv for the First All-Ukrainian Trades Union Congress. They founded a national-territorial trade union central, the first in the country's history, and resolved to rebuild the labour movement, support the peasant movement, reclaim their democratic and social rights and restore the Ukrainian People's Republic. Their struggles would go on through two further long cycles, the second against *het'manshchyna* which lasted until November 1918 when the Austrian and German armies withdrew and Skoropadsky's regime fled with them, and a third cycle marked by civil war, anti-Jewish pogroms and foreign interventions known as the *otamanshchyna* (rule of warlords) that ended in February 1920 with the victory of the Red Army over all contenders for state power in Ukraine. These two cycles of the Revolution are the subject of a further work.

References

Newspapers

Borot'ba (Geneva): February–November 1915.
Borot'ba (Vienna): 1 January–26 June 1920.
Nasha Pravda (Vienna): 9 April 1921–15 July 1922.
Nova Doba (Vienna): 6 March–17 July 1920.
Nova Rada (Kyiv): 14 January–9 May 1918; 12 January 1919.
Robitnycha Hazeta (Kyiv): April–December 1917.
Robitnycha Pravda (New York): 1922.
Robitnychyi Holos (Akron, Ohio): 1922–26.
Robitnychyi Prapor (Sofia, Bulgaria): 1915.
Robitnychyi Vistnyk (New York): 1919.
Robitnyk (Cleveland, Ohio): 1916, 1917, 1919.
Soborna Ukraina (Vienna): 12 October 1921–18 May 1922.
Vil'ne Zhyttia (Odesa): 31 March–3 July 1918.
Vistnyk Tovarystva Prosvity (Katerynoslav): 18 March–30 July 1917.

Periodicals

Chervonyi Shliakh (Kharkiv): 1923–31.
Dzvin (Kyiv): 1913–14.
Krytyka (Kyiv): 1928–30.
Literaturno-Naukovyi Vistnyk (Lviv): 1902–13.
Litopys Revoliutsii (Kharkiv): 1922–28; 1930–33.
Nova Hromada (Vienna): 1923–24.
Nova Ukraina (Prague): 1922–28.
Ukrains'kyi Istorychnyi Zhurnal (Kyiv): 1957–81.
Zhyttia i Revoliutsiia (Kyiv): 1925.
Visty Ukrains'koi Tsentral'noi Rady (Kyiv): 1917.

Primary Sources in Books and Pamphlets

Bachynsky, Yuliian 1924, *Ukraina irredenta*, 3rd edn, Berlin: Vydavnytstvo Ukrains'koi Molodi.
Bahalii, D.I. 1925, *Taras Shevchenko i Kyrylo-metodiivtsi*, Kyiv: Derzhavne Vydavnytstvo Ukrainy.

Borba za Oktiabr na Artemovshchyne 1929, Kharkiv: Proletaryi.

Bosh, Yevgeniia 1918. *Natsional'noe Pravitel'stvo*, n.p.: n.p.

Bosh, Yevgeniia 1925, *God bor'by. Bor'ba za vlast' na Ukraine s aprelia 1917g. do nemekts'koi okupatsii*. Mosow: Gosizdat.

Chykalenko, Yevhen 2011, *Shchodennyk (1918–1919)*, Kyiv: Tempora.

Doroshenko, Dmytro 1969, *Moi Spomyny pro Nedavnie Mynule, 1914–20*, Munich: Ukrains'ke Vydavnytstvo.

Doroshenko, Dmytro 1947, *Istoriia Ukrainy*, 2nd edn, Augsburg: P. Pohasyi.

Drahomanov, Mykhailo 1937, *Vybrani Tvory*, edited by P. Bohatsky, Prague/New York: Ukrains'ki Postupovi Tovarystva v Amerytsi.

Dubnow, S.M. 1975, *History of the Jews in Russia and Poland*, translated by I. Friedlaender, New York: Ktav Publishing House.

Eideman, R. and Kakurin, N. *1928, Hromadians'ka Viina na Ukraini*, Kyiv: Derzhavne Vydavnytstvo Ukrainy.

Fedenko, Panas 1968, *Vlada Het'mana Skoropadskoho*, London–Munich: Vydavnytstvo Nashe Slovo.

Fedenko, Panas 1968, *Marksysts'ki i bol'shevytski teorii natsional'noho pytannia*, Munich: Institute for the study of the USSR.

Fedenko, Panas 1973, 'Isaak Mazepa v zhytti i v politytsi', in *Nashe Slovo* (Munich), no. 3.

Goldelman, Solomon 1968, *Jewish National Autonomy in Ukraine 1917–1920*, translated by Michael Luchkovich, Chicago: Ukrainian Research and Information Institute.

Grinevich, V. 1923, *Professional'noe dvizhenie rabochikh v Rossii*, Moscow: Izdatel'stvo Krasnaia Nov.

Grinevich, V. 1928, *Istoriia Ukrainy v styslomu narysi*, Kharkiv: Derzhavne Vydavnytstvo Ukrainy.

Halahan, Mykola 1930, *Z moikh spomyniv*, Lviv: Chervona Kalyna.

Hermaize, O. 1926, *Narysy z Istorii Revoliutsiinoho Rukhu na Ukraini*, vol. 1: RUP, Kyiv: Knyhospilka.

Hrushevsky, Mykhailo 1917, *Yakoi Avtonomii i Federatsii Khoche Ukraina*, Vienna: SVU.

Hrushevsky, Mykhailo 1944, *A History of Ukraine*, New Haven: n.p.

Hrushevsky, Mykhailo 1954–58, *Istoriia Ukrainy-Rusy*, 10 vols. 2nd edn, New York: Knyhospilka.

Hryhoryiv, N. 1934, *Ukrains'ka Borot'ba za Derzhavu v Rokakh 1917–20: Chomu Ukraintsi ne Vderzhaly Svoiei Derzhavy*, Scranton: Narodnaia Volia.

Kautsky, Karl 1910, *The Class Struggle (Erfurt Program)*, translated by William E. Bohn, Chicago: Charles H. Kerr and Co.

Khrystiuk, Pavlo 1921, *Ukrains'ka Revoliutsiia. Zamitky i Materiialy do istorii ukrains'koi revoliutsii 1917–20 rr*, 4 vols, Vienna: Ukrains'kyi Sotsiolohichnyi Instytut.

Kolesnikov, B. 1923, *Professional'noe dvizhenie i Kontrrevoliutsiia. Ocherki iz istorii professional'nogo dvizheniia na Ukraine*, n.p.: Gosudarstvennoe Izdatel'stvo Ukraine.

REFERENCES

Kuchyn-Oransky, H. 1924, *Dobrovol'cheskaia Zubatovshchina*, Moscow: Trud.

Lenin, V.I. 1942, *Collected Works*, Vol. XIX, New York: International Publishers.

Lenin, V.I. 1956, *The Development of Capitalism in Russia: The Process of the Formation of a Home Market for Large Scale Industry*, Moscow: Foreign Languages Publishing House.

Lenin, V.I. n.d. *Selected Works: The Years of Reaction and the New Revival*, New York: International Publishers.

Lenin, V.I. 1974, *Lenin on the Jewish Question*, edited by Hyman Lumer, New York: International Publishers.

Levynsky, V. 1913, 'Narid i Sotsiializm', in *Kalendar Rus'koho Narodnoho Soiuzu na 1914 rik*, Scranton: Narodnaia Volia.

Levynsky, V. 1920, *Yedyna nedilyma sovits'ka Rosiia*, Kyiv-Vienna: Nova Doba.

Levynsky, V. 1920, *Sotsiialistychna Revoliutsiia i Ukraina*, Kyiv-Vienna: Nova Doba.

Luxemburg, Rosa 1976, *The National Question: Selected Works by Rosa Luxemburg*, edited and with an introduction by Horace B. Davis, New York: Monthly Review Press.

Maiorov, M. 1922, *Iz Istorii Revoliutsionnoi Bor'by na Ukraine: 1914–1919*, Kyiv: Derzhavne Vydavnytstvo Ukrainy.

Maiorov, M. 1928, *Z Istorii Revoliutsiinoi Borot'by na Ukraini: 1914–1919*, Kyiv: Derzhavne Vydavnytstvo Ukrainy.

Maistrenko, Ivan 2019, *Borot'bism. A Chapter in the History of the Ukrainian Revolution*, translated by George S.N. Luckyj, edited and with an introduction by Christopher Ford, Stuttgart: Ibidem.

Maistrenko, Ivan 1954, *Borot'bism. A Chapter in the History of Ukrainian Communism*, translated by George S.N. Luckyj, New York: Research Program on the USSR.

Marx, Karl, and Friedrich Engels 1948, *The Communist Manifesto*, New York: International Publishers.

Marx, Karl 1947, *The German Ideology*, New York: International Publishers.

Marx, Karl 1959, *On the Jewish Question*, New York: Philosophical Library.

Mazepa, Isaak 1922, *Bol'shevyzm i Okupatsiia Ukrainy. Sotsiial'no-ekonomichni prychyny nedozrilosty syl Ukrains'koi revoliutsii*, Lviv-Kyiv: Vydavnytstvo Znattia to Syla.

Mazepa, Isaak 1946, *Pidstavy Nashoho Vidrodzhennia*, Chastyna Persha, n.p.: Prometei.

Mazepa, Isaak 1950, *Ukraina v Ohni i Buri Revoliutsii 1917–1921*, 3 vols, 2nd edn, n.p.: Prometei.

Mazlakh, Serhii, and Vasyl Shakhrai 2019 [1919], *Do khvyli: Shcho diietsia na Vkraini i z Ukrainoiu*, reprint of the 1919 original edition, edited by Andrii Zdorov and with introductions by Andrii Zdorov and Artem Klymenko, Odesa: Astroprint.

Mazlakh, Serhii, and Vasyl Shakhrai 1970, *On the Current Situation in Ukraine*, edited by P.J. Potichnyj, Ann Arbor, MI: University of Michigan Press.

Milonov, Yu. (ed.) 1924, *Putevoditel' po Rezoliutsiiam Vserossiiskikh S'ezdov i Konferentsii Professional'nikh Soiuzov*, Moscow: V.Ts.S.P.S.

Pervi S'ezd KP(b)U 1923, Kharkiv: Gosudarstvennoe Izdatel'stvo Ukraine.

Petrovsky, D. 1920, *Revoliutsiia i Kontrrevoliutsiia na Ukraine*, Moscow: Gosudarstvennoe Izdatel'stvo.

Polak, Thalia (ed.) 2012, *The Autobiography of Esther Polianovsky Salaman*, n.p.: n.p.

Popov, N.N. 1930, *Narys Istorii Komunistychnoi Partii (bil'shovykiv) Ukrainy*, Kharkiv: Proletaryi.

Porsh, Mykola 1907, *Pro Avtonomiiu*, Kyiv: Prosvita.

Porsh, Mykola 1908, *Pro Avtonomiiu Ukrainy*, Kyiv: Prosvita.

Porsh, Mykola 1912, 'Vidnosyny Ukrainy do ynshykh raioniv Rosii na robitnychomu rynku na osnovi materiialiv pershoho vseliudnoho perepysu', in *Literaturno-Naukovyi Vistnyk* (Lviv), Books II and III.

Porsh, Mykola 1913, 'Robitnytstvo Ukrainy. Vysnovky z pratsi pro ukrains'ku ekonomiiu i robitnytstvo', in *Zapysky N.T. Sh.*, Book XII.

Porsh, Mykola 1918, *Ukraina v derzhavnomu biudzheti Rosii*, Katerynoslav: Kameniar.

Rafes, M. 1920, *Dva goda revoliutsii na Ukraine. Raskol Bunda*, Moscow: Gosudarstvennoe Izdatel'stvo.

Sadovsky, V. 1932, *Pratsia v USSR*, Warsaw: Ukrains'kyi Naukovyi Instytut.

Sevriuk, Oleksandr 1927, *Beresteis'kyi Myr*, Paris: Les Nouvelles Ukrainiennes.

Skorovstansky, V. (Shakhrai, V.) 2017, *Revoliutsiia na Ukraine*, reprint of the originial 1919 Saratov edition, edited and with an introduction by Andrii Zdorov, Odesa: T. Ye. S.

Shapoval, Mykyta 1927, *Velyka Revoliutsiia i Ukrains'ka Vyzvol'na Prohrama*, Prague: Vil'na Spilka i Ukrains'kyi Robitnychyi Instytut.

Shapoval, Mykyta 1936, *Sotsiolohiia Ukrains'koho Vidrodzhennia*, Prague: Ukrains'kyi Sotsiolohichnyi Instytut v Prazi.

Shapoval, Mykyta 1958, *Het'manshchyna i Dyrektoriia. Spohady*, New York: Ukrains'ka Hromada im. M. Shapovala.

Siry, Yurii 1915, 'Vidrodzhenie Rosiis'koi Ukrainy', in *Kalendar Ukrains'koho Narodnoho Soiuzu*.

Skrypnyk, M. 1929, *Statti i Promovy*, Vol. II, Kharkiv: Derzhavne Vydavnytstvo Ukrainy.

Slabchenko, Mykhailo Ye. 1925, *Materiialy do ekonomichno-sotsiial'noi istorii Ukrainy XIX stolittia*, Kyiv: Derzhavne Vydavnytstvo Ukrainy.

Trotsky, Leon 1967, *History of the Russian Revolution*, 3 vols, London: Sphere Books.

Volobuiev, Mykhailo 1962, 'Do problemy ukrains'koi ekonomiky', in *Dokumenty Ukrains'koho Komunizmu*, edited by Ivan Maistrenko, New York: Prolog.

Vynnychenko, Volodymyr 1920, *Vidrodzhennia Natsii*, 3 vols, Kyiv-Vienna: Dzvin.

Vyshnivsky, Oleksandr 1978, *Povstans'kyi Rukh i Otamaniia*, Detroit: Universal Slavic Printers.

Yavorsky, Matvii 1923, *Revoliutsiia na Vkraini v ii holovnishykh etapakh*, Kharkiv: Derzhavne Vydavnytstvo Ukrainy.

Yurkevych, Lev 1913, *Klasy i Suspil'stvo*, Kyiv: Vydavnytstvo Dzvin.

Yurkevych, Lev (Rybalka, L.) 1969, *Rosiis'ki Sotsiial-demokraty i natsional'ne pytannia*, New York: Suchasnist.

Zahorsky, Symon 1909, 'Robitnyche pytannia v sil'skim hospodarstvi Poludnevoi Rosii', in *Literaturno-naukovyi Vistnyk (Lviv)*, Vol. XLV, Book III.

Secondary Sources

Abramson, Henry 2017, *Molytva za vladu. Ukraintsi ta Yevrei v revoliutsiinu dobu (1917–1920)*, translation from the English by Anton Kotenko and Oleksandr Nadtoka of *A Prayer for the Government: Ukrainians and Jews in Revolutionary Times, 1917–1920*. Kyiv: Dukh i Litera.

Adams, Arthur E. 1963, *Bolsheviks in the Ukraine: The Second Campaign. 1918–1919*, New Haven: Yale University Press.

Anderson, Perry 1974, *Lineages of the Absolutist State*, London: New Left Books.

Antonovych, M. 1966, *Istoriia Ukrainy*, 2nd edn, 3 vols, Winnipeg: UVAN.

Apter, David 1968, *Some Conceptual Approaches to the Study of Modernisation*, New Jersey: Prentice Hall.

Bahro, Rudolf 1981, *The Alternative in Eastern Europe*, translated by David Fernbach, London: Verso.

Baron, Salo 1964, *The Russian Jew under Tsars and Soviets*, New York: Macmillan.

Bloom, Solomon F. 1967, *The World of Nations: A Study of the National Implications in the Work of Karl Marx*, New York: AMS Press.

Borys, Yurij 1960, *The Russian Communist Party and the Sovietisation of Ukraine: A Study in the Communist Doctrine of the Self-Determination of Nations*, Stockholm: n.p.

Boshyk, George Y. 1981, 'The Rise of Ukrainian Political Parties in Russia 1900–1907: With Special Reference to Social Democracy', PhD dissertation, Oxford University.

Braichevsky, Mykhailo Yu. 1972, 'Pryiednannia chy Vozziednannia?', in *Shyroke More Ukrainy: Dokumenty Samvydavu z Ukrainy*, Paris-Baltimore: P.I.U.F.-Smoloskyp.

Brovkin, Vladimir 1987, *The Mensheviks after October: Socialist Opposition and the Rise of the Bolshevik Dictatorship*, Ithaca: Cornell University Press.

Carter Elwood, Ralph 1974, *Russian Social Democracy in the Underground: A Study of the RSDRP in the Ukraine 1907–1914*, Assen: Van Gorcun and Company.

Cherikover, Elias 2015, *Istoriia pogromnogo dvizhenia na Ukraine 1917–1921gg*, Tom 1, Berlin: Direct Media.

Davis, Horace B. 1967, *Marxist and Labour Theories of Nationalism to 1917*, New York: Monthly Review Press.

Deutsch, Karl 1966, *Nationalism and Social Communication*, 2nd edn, Cambridge, MA: MIT Press.

Dmytryshyn, Basil 1956, *Moscow and the Ukraine, 1918–1953: A Study of Russian Bolshevik Nationality Policy*, New York: Bookman Associates.

Dubyna, K.K. (ed.) 1967, *Istoriia Ukrains'koi RSR*, 2 vols, Kyiv: Naukova Dumka.

Fanon, Frantz 1968, *The Wretched of the Earth*, New York: Grove Press.

Frankel, Jonathan 1981, *Prophesy and Politics: Socialism, Nationalism and Russian Jews, 1862–1917*, Cambridge: Cambridge University Press.

Gajecky, George 1978, *The Cossack Administration of the Hetmanate*, Volume 1, Cambridge, MA: Harvard Ukrainian Research Institute.

Gellner, Ernest 1964, *Thought and Change*, London: Weidenfeld and Nicolson.

Gitelman, Zvi Y. 1972, *Jewish Nationality and Soviet Politics: The Jewish Sections of the CPSU, 1917–1930*, Princeton: Princeton University Press.

Gramsci, Antonio 1959, *The Modern Prince and Other Writings*, New York: International Publishers.

Gramsci, Antonio 1971, *Selections from the Prison Notebooks*, edited and translated by Quintin Hoare and Geoffrey Nowell Smith, New York: International Publishers.

Guthier, Steven L. 1971, 'The Popular Base of Ukrainian Nationalism in 1917', *Slavic Review*, March.

Guthier, Steven L. n.d., 'Ukrainian Cities during the Revolution and the Interwar Era', University of Michigan, mimeographed.

Haienko, Fedir 1958, *Profesiini spilky S. Soiuzu. Ukrains'kyi Zbirnyk*, Book 13, Munich: Institute for the Study of the USSR.

Hamretsky, Yu. M., Zh.P. Tymchenko, and O.I. Shchus 1974, *Rady Ukrainy v 1917 r*, Kyiv: Naukova Dumka.

Hechter, Michael 1975, *Internal Colonialism: The Celtic Fringe in British National Development 1539–1966*, Berkeley: University of California Press.

Heifetz, Elias 1921, *The Slaughter of the Jews in the Ukraine in 1919*, New York: Thomas Seltzer.

Herlihy, Patricia 1981, 'Ukrainian Cities in the 19th Century', in *Rethinking Ukrainian History*, edited by Ivan L. Rudnycky and J.P. Himka, Edmonton: C.I.U.S, University of Alberta.

Hobsbawn, Eric 1973, *The Age of Revolution: Europe 1789–1848*, London: Cardinal.

Holubnychy, Vsevolod 1961, 'Sotsiialistychni teorii natsional'noi problemy', *Suchasnist*, 8.

Holubnychy, Vsevolod 1969, *Try lektsii pro ekonomiku Ukrainy*, Munich-New York: Vydavnytstvo Ukraina i Diiaspora.

Holubnychy, Vsevolod 1982, *Selected Works of Vsevolod Holubnychy: Soviet Regional Economics*, edited by Iwan S. Koropeckyj, Edmonton: C.I.U.S., University of Alberta.

REFERENCES

Horlach, M. 1966, *Virna Opora Partii Komunistiv*, Kyiv: Vydavnytstvo Kyivs'koho Universytetu.

Hroch, Miroslav 1970, 'The Social Composition of the Czech Patriots in Bohemia, 1827–1848', in *The Czech Renaissance of the 19th Century*, edited by Peter Brock and H. Gordon Skilling, Toronto: University of Toronto Press.

Hrynevych, Vladyslav, and Liudmyla Hrynevych 2001, *Natsional'ne Viis'kove Pytannia v Diial'nosti Soiuzu Yevreiv Voiniv v KVO (lypen' 1917–sichen' 1918 rr.)*, Kyiv: Instytut Istorii Ukrainy, Instytut politychnykh i etnonatsional'nykh doslidzhen', Natsional'na Akademia Nauk Ukrainy.

Hrytsenko, A.P. 1965, *Robitnychi Fortetsi Sotsialistychnoi Revoliutsii*, Kyiv: Naukova Dumka.

Hrytsenko, A.P. 1973, 'Struktura i Sklad Promyslovoho Proletariatu Ukrainy v 1917 r', in *Velykyi Zhovten' i Hromadians'ka Viina na Ukraini*, Kyiv: Naukova Dumka.

Hrytsenko, A.P. 1992, *Ukrains'ki Robitnyky na shliakhu tvorennia natsional'noi derzhavy: pershii vseukrains'kii robitnychii z'izd 11–14/24–27 lypnia 1917r*, Kyiv: Instytut Istorii Ukrainy, National'na Akademiia Nauk Ukrainy.

Hrytsenko, A.P. 1993, *Politychni Syly u Borot'bi za Vladu v Ukraini (kinets' 1917r–pochatok 1919r)*, Kyiv: Instytut istorii Ukrainy, Akademia Nauk Ukrainy.

Hrytsenko, A.P. 1997, *Politychni Syly v Borot'bi za Vladu Rad 1920 rik*, Kyiv: Instytut Istorii Ukrainy, National'na Akademia Nauk Ukrainy.

Hudzenko, P.P. 1965, *Sotsialistychna Natsionalizatsiia Promyslovosti v Ukrains'koi RSR*, Kyiv: Naukova Dumka.

Hunczak, Taras 1969, 'A Reappraisal of Symon Petliura and Ukrainian Jewish Relations 1917–1921', *Jewish Social Studies*, 31, no. 3.

Hunczak, Taras (ed.) 1977, *The Ukraine 1917–21: A Study in Revolution*, Cambridge, MA: Harvard Ukrainian Research Institute.

Hurzhii, I.O. 1958, *Zarodzhennia Robitnychoho Klasu Ukrainy (kinets XVIII – persha polovyna XIX st.)*, Kyiv: Derzhavne Vydavnytstvo Politychnoi Literatury URSR.

Keep, John L.H. 1976, *The Russian Revolution: A Study in Mass Mobilisation*, London: Weidenfeld and Nicolson.

Kirianov, Yu. Y. 1971, *Rabochie Iuga Rossii 1914–fevral 1917 g.*, Moscow: Izdatel'stvo Nauka.

Kobersky, Karlo 1933, *Ukraina v Svitovomu Hospodarstvi*, Prague: Ukrains'ka Strilets'ka Hromada v S.Sh.A.

Kohn, Hans 1944, *The Idea of Nationalism: A Study in its Origins and Background*, New York: Macmillan and Co.

Kononenko, Konstantyn 1958, *Ukraine and Russia: A History of the Economic Relations between Ukraine and Russia (1654–1917)*, Milwaukee: Marquette University Press.

Kostiuk, Hryhory 1960, *Stalinist Rule in the Ukraine: A Study of the Decade of Mass Terror*, New York: Praeger.

Kostiuk, Hryhory 1971, *Teoriia i Diisnist'*, Munich: Suchasnist.

Krawchenko, Bohdan 1985, *Social Change and National Consciousness in Twentieth Century Ukraine*, Basingstoke: Macmillan.

Kuras, Ivan Fedorovych, and Petro Lohvynovych Varhatiuk (eds) 1990, *Bol'shevitskie organizatsii Ukraine: organizatsionno-partiinaia deiatel'nost', fevral' 1917–iul' 1918 gg.: sbornik materialov I dokumentov*, Kyiv: Politizdat Ukraine.

Lawrynenko, Yuri 1953, *Ukrainian Communism and Soviet Russian Policy Toward the Ukraine, An Annotated Bibliography. 1917–1953*, edited by D.I. Goldstein, n.p.: Research Program on the USSR.

Los, F. Ye. (ed.) 1967, *Istoriia Robitnychoho Klasu URSR*, 2 vols, Kyiv: Naukova Dumka.

Mace, James E. 1983, *Communism and the Dilemmas of National Liberation: National Communism in Soviet Ukraine 1918–1933*, Cambridge, MA: Harvard Ukrainian Research Institute.

Maistrenko, Ivan 1967, *Storinky z Istorii Komunistychnoi Partii Ukrainy. Chastyna Persha*, New York: Prolog.

Manning, Clarence A. 1951, *Twentieth Century Ukraine*, New York: Bookman Associates.

Manning, Clarence A. 1953, *Ukraine under the Soviets*, New York: Bookman Associates.

Melnyk, M. 1926, 'Vos'ma rokovyna zahal'noho straiku na zaliznykh shliakhakh Ukrainy', *Vestnik Profdvizhennie Ukraine*, 15–16, August.

Myhul, Ivan 1984, 'Ukrains'ka Radians'ka Istoriohrafiia pro Ukrains'ku Revoliutsiiu ta 1920 roky', *Suchasnist*, September.

Nairn, Tom 1975, 'The Modern Janus', New Left Review, 94, November–December.

Nesterenko, O.O. 1962, *Rozvytok promyslovosti na Ukraini. Chastyna II*, Kyiv: Vydavnytstvo Akademii Nauk URSR.

Palij, Michael 1976, The *Anarchism of Nestor Makhno 1918–21: An Aspect of the Ukrainian Revolution*, Seattle: University of Washington Press.

Petrivsky, D. 1951, 'Chy buv zahal'nyi zaliznodorozhnyi straik v Ukraini 1918 roku?', *Vil'na Ukraina*, 10.

Pidhainy, A.S. 1977, 'The Formation of the Communist Party (Bolsheviks) of Ukraine', PhD dissertation, McGill University.

Ponomarov, O.M. 1971, *Rozvytok Kapitalistychnykh Vidnosyn u Promyslovosti Ukrainy XVIII st.*, Lviv: Vydavnytstvo L'vivs'koho Universytetu.

Potichnyj, Peter J. 1972, *Soviet Agricultural Trade Unions 1917–70*, Toronto: University of Toronto Press.

Radkey, Oliver H. 1950, *The Election to the Russian Constituent Assembly of 1917*, Cambridge, MA: Harvard University Press.

Reient, Oleksandr Petrovych 1993, *Robitnytstvo Ukrainy i Tsentral'na Rada*, Kyiv: Akademiia Nauk, Instytut Istorii Ukrainy.

Reient, Oleksandr Petrovych 1994, *Bil'shovyzm I Ukrains'ka Revoliutsiia 1917–1920rr. Sproba vyznachennia kharakteru i dynamika sotsial'nykh protsesiv*, Kyiv: Instytut Istorii Ukrainy.

Sadovsky, Valentyn 1937, *Natsional'na Polityka Sovitiv na Ukraini*, Warsaw: Pratsi Ukrains'koho Naukovoho Instytutu.

Schechtman, Joseph 1969, 'Jewish Community Life in the Ukraine (1917–1919)', in *Russian Jewry 1917–1967*, edited by Gregor Aronson, Jacob Frumkin, Alexis Goldenweiser and Joseph Lewitan, translated by Joel Carmichael, New York: Thomas Yoseloff.

Skliarenko, Ye. M. 1966, *Robitnychyi Klas Ukrainy v Roky Hromadians'koi Viiny*, Kyiv: Naukova Dumka.

Skliarenko, Ye. M. 1974, *Narysy Istorii Profspilkovoho Rukhu na Ukraini 1917–20*, Kyiv: Naukova Dumka.

Soldatenko, V.F. 2004, 'Novitni vydannia i doslidzhennia z istorii Ukrains'koi revoliutsii (1917–1920 rr)', in *Aktual'ni problemy vitchyznianoi istorii XX st. Zbirnyk naukovykh prats' prysviachenykh pamiati akademika NAN Ukrainy Yuria Yuriovycha Kondufora*, Kyiv: n.p.

Soldatenko, V.F. 2010, *Ukraina v revoliutsiinu dobu: Istorychne ese-khroniky*, 4 vols, Kyiv: Svitohliad.

Soldatenko, V.F. 2011, *Revoliutsiina doba v Ukraini (1917–1920 roky): lohika piznannia, istorychni epizody, kliuchovi postati*, Kyiv: Parlaments'ke vydavnytstvo.

Soldatenko, V.F. 'Novi pidkhody do osmyslenniu istorychnoho dosvidu i yrokiv revoliutsiinoi doby 1917–20rr. v Ukraini', in *Revoliutsiia i Reformy Novitnoi Istorii*, http://istznu .org/dc/file.php?host_id=1&path=/page/issues/24/24/soldatenko.pdf [accessed 6 October 2017].

Suprunenko, M.I. (ed.) 1977, *Istoriia Ukrains'koi RSR*, Vol. 5, Kyiv: Naukova Dumka.

Szajkowski, Zosa 1969, 'A Reappraisal of Symon Petliura and Ukrainian Jewish Relations 1917–21. A Rebuttal', *Jewish Social Studies*, 31, no. 3.

Tcherikower, Elias 1965, *The Pogroms in the Ukraine in 1919: Di ukrainer pogromen in yor 1919*, New York: YIVO Institute for Jewish Research.

Tobias, Henry J. 1972, *The Jewish Bund in Russia from its Origins to 1905*, Stanford: Stanford University Press.

Velychenko, Stephen 2015, *Painting Imperialism and Nationalism Red: The Ukrainian Marxist Critique of Russian Communist Rule in Ukraine 1918–1925*, Toronto: University of Toronto Press.

Verstiuk, V.F. (ed.) 2011, *Studii z Istorii Ukrains'koi Revoliutsii 1917–21 rokiv: na poshanu Ruslana Yakovycha Pyroha: zbirnyk naukovykh prats'*, Kyiv: Instytut istorii NAN Ukrainy.

Volin, S. 1962, *Mensheviki na Ukraine 1917–21*, Inter-University Project on the History of the Menshevik Movement, Paper No. 11, New York, September.

Wallerstein, Immanuel 1976, *The Modern World-System*, New York: Academic Press.

Wallerstein, Immanuel (ed.) 1975, *World Inequality: Origins and Perspectives on the World System*, Montreal: Black Rose Books.

Zdorov, Andrii 2007, *Ukrains'kyi Zhovten': Pobitnycho-selians'ka revoliutsiia v Ukraini (lystopad 1917–liutyi 1918rr.)*, Odesa: Astroprint.

Index

Locators in italic refer to table or maps. Thus, 26t1 refers to table 1 on page 26.

agricultural production
  of *horodovi* Cossacks 12–13
  in Hetmanate 21
  Ukrainian imports and exports 29, *30t2*
  wage earners in Ukraine *45t5, 51t7*
  distribution of Ukrainian workers *54t9*
  See also land reforms; land rights; sugar industry
agricultural proletariat
  estimated numbers of 45–46, *51t7*, 53–54
  seasonal workers 23, 38, 45–48, 152
Alexander I, (Tsar), limits on Ukrainian language imposed by 59
Alexander II (Tsar)
  Temporary Rules promulgated by 42, 79
  EMS *ukaz* 59, 91
All-Russian Congress of Soviets, Second Congress 158
All-Russian Constituent Assembly 138, 166, 242, 257, 287, 291, 357
All-Russian Council of Peasants' Deputies, national autonomy and federalism supported by 134
All-Ukrainian Congress of Councils – First Congress, Kyiv
  resistance by USDWP's leaders to Rada's re-election at 191, 206–7
  support of workers' and soldiers' organisations for its convocation 201–8, 210
  CPC's Manifesto and ultimatum delivered to 232–35
  first meeting in Kyiv 230–38, 351
All-Ukrainian Congress of Councils – First Congress, Kharkiv 242–49
  All-Ukrainian Congress of Councils – Second Congress, Katerynoslav 347–51, 361, 366, 378
All-Ukrainian Council of Peasants' Deputies
  elected by All-Ukrainian Peasants' Congress 122–23
  seated in Rada plenary assembly 129, 142
  Second Plenum called for end to war 154
  Third Plenum addressed War and land reform 209–10
All-Ukrainian Council of Soldiers' Deputies
  seated in Rada plenary assembly 129, 142
  affirmed popular election of officers and soldiers' committees 253
  See also All-Ukrainian Soldiers' Congresses first and second
All-Ukrainian Council of Workers' Deputies 284
  seated in Rada plenary assembly 129, 142
All-Ukrainian Soldiers' Congress, First
  called for end to War and reorganisation of Russian army 122
  called for for Provisional Government's recognition of Ukrainian national autonomy 122–23
All-Ukrainian Soldiers' Congress, Second
  First Universal adopted by soldiers' deputies 125–26
  Provisional Government's attempts to ban 135, 137, 192
All-Ukrainian Workers' Congress – First Congress
  participants of 130
  resolutions of 129–33, 148–49
All-Ukrainian Peasants' Congress 122–23, 154
Antonov-Ovsiienko, Volodymyr 169, 238–39, 253, 255–58, 345–46
Arsenal, Kyiv 186, 283–6, 333
  support for Petrograd Soviet adopted by workers of 128, 186, 294
  Kyiv branch of the USDWP in 181
  uprising at 294–98, 303–5
Artem (F. Serheev) 239, 244, 245, 248
Aussem, V. 230, 245, 311, 329, 345
Austro-Marxism
  Brunn Congress of 1899, 68–69
  on national political autonomy for minorities 68–70, 74, 84, 99
  influence on USDWP 87

INDEX

Bakynsky, Serhii   205, 245, 345
Baranovsky, Khrystian   140–41
Bauer, Otto   78
Black Hundreds   *See* Union of Russian Peoples (Black Hundreds)
Bochkovsky, Leonard   129, 201, 280, 281, 309
Bolbochan, Petro   334, 358, 378
Bolsheviks
    conception of democratic centralism   71–76
    delegates on workers' councils in Ukraine   157–58
    on People's Secretariat of Kharkiv CEC   244–45
    See also Bosh, Yevgeniia; Kyiv Bolsheviks Piatakov, Hryhorii; Piatakov, Leonid; Zatonsky, V.
    establishment of the MRC of   312
Bolshevik uprising in Kyiv
    preparation for   293
    general strike in support of   295, 298
    at Arsenal   294–98, 303–5
Bolshevik rule of Kyiv   309–3, 345–6
Borochov, Ber   83–84
Bosh, Yevgeniia   229–30, 245, 248–49, 311, 318, 327, 329
Brest Litovsk
    First Treaty of   262–78, 326, 348, 364, 368–9, 375
    See Also Entente, Central Powers
Brotherhood of Saints Cyril and Methodius   87–88
Bund   *See* Jewish General Workers' Union

Capitalist development in Ukraine   21–23
Central Executive Committee of the Councils of Ukraine (CEC)
    election of in Kharkiv   170
Central Powers   173, 177–8, 210, 212, 220, 223–5, 246, 250–51, 253–4, 262
Cherikover, Elias   217–219, 297, 323, 335–337, 339, 342, 367, 369
Chudnovsky, Hryhorii   311, 312–13, 345
Committee in Defence of the Revolution
    in Kharkiv   159
    in Kyiv   156, 159–61

Communist Party (Bolsheviks) of Ukraine (CP(B)U)
    establishment of   363
    Ukrainian influx into   6–7, 190, 363
Cossacks   11–19
    See also Don Cossacks; Free Cossacks; Hetmanate; Khmelnytsky, Bohdan
Council of People's Commissars (CPC)
    election   114
    Manifesto and ultimatum to Rada   232–38, 250
    peace terms proposed at Brest Litovsk, by   246
Crimea   9–11, 15, 64, 179, 257, 311, 331, 357–9
Crimean Tatars   274, 9–11, 15, 274, 357

Dobry, Abram   378, 386–88
Donbas   22, 25, 39, 41, 50, 57, 85, 96, 103–4, 115, 145–7, 155–6, 158, 167, 175, 178, 186, 191–2, 225, 243, 248, 253, 257, 259, 279, 331, 341, 350, 359–362, 380
Don Cossacks   164, 220–21, 224–25, 229–30, 233, 237, 246–47, 255, 259
Donets-Kryvyi Rih region   54, 146, 154, 158, 181
    Donets-Kryvyi Rih Republic   191, 239, 241, 359
Drahomanov, Mykhailo   88–93
Dubynsky, Pinkhus   288

Economy of Ukraine
    after Russian annexation   21–2
    Russian investment in   22–23
    foreign trade in   24–29
    expatriation of capital from   29–33
    integration with all-Russian market   28–9
    underdevelopment of   33–35
Eichhorn, Hermann von   381–387, 390
EMS *Ukaz*
    banning of Ukrainian language   59, 91
Engels, Friedrich   63–71, 76, 87
Entente   118, 177–8, 210, 220–25, 250, 253, 264, 304, 334, 353

Fareinigte   *See* United Jewish Workers' Party
Federalism   68–70, 74, 84, 99, 133–4, 163, 164n153, 188–9

Feshchenko-Chopivsky, Ivan   123, 130, 379–80
First Universal   *See* Tsentralna Rada universals
Folkspartei   *See* Jewish People's Party
Fourth Universal   *See* Tsentralna Rada universals
Free Cossacks
   emergence of   283–84
   antisemitism   217–19, 299
   Skoropadsky (Pavlo) elected as leader of   251
   raids on Kyiv workplaces   286
   targetting of left USDWP leaders   291
   suppressed Kyiv uprising   294–97
   involvement in pogroms   335, 337, 340
   peasant committees refuse land to   372

Galicia   20map 2
   panshchyna in   10, 11
   influence of Drahomanov in   90–92
   Russia's claims on   109, 110–11, 186
   Austro-Hungary's interests in Eastern Galicia   265, 267, 270, 276–77
General Secretariat   *See* Tsentral'na Rada – General Secretariat
Gergel, Nahum   343
Goldelman, Solomon   45, 159, 196, 285, 287–8, 307, 340
Grosman, M.   336

Hetmanate
   establishment of   14–15
   serfdom in   18–19
   as protectorate of Muscovy   15, 18
   trade and industry of   21
   literacy among Ukrainian men   58–9
   See also Khmelnytsky, Bohdan; Skoropadsky, Pavlo
Hilferding, Rudolf   67–68
Hohol, Yoan   216–8, 300–301
Holubnychy, Vsevolod   27–8, 79
Holubovych, Vsevolod   265–66, 268, 272, 274, 292, 301, 307, 325, 334–35, 365–66, 379, 383, 386
Hopner, C.I.   190
Horwitz, Alexandr   229, 230, 293, 294

Hrushevsky, Mykhailo   117–20, 163, 255, 265, 268, 284, 335, 287, 288, 289, 324–25, 334, 335, 364

industrialisation
   mobilisation of rural population to urban centres   2
   impact of Russian annexation on   21, 24
   construction of railways   25
   branches of production in Ukraine (1904)   26–27, 26t1
   foreign investors in   24–29, 33–34, 46–47
   migrant labour   47
   seasonal labour   38, 47, 51–52, 92, 152, 181

Jewish General Workers' Union (Bund)
   silence of Stalinist Ukrainian historians on   7
   auto-emancipation of Jews advocated by   80
   self-defence committees to fight pogroms organised by   81
   advocated defence of Jews by UPR armed forces in   1917–18, 218
   Sixth Bund Congress in Ukraine   81
   readmission to RSDWP 1906   82–83
   as mediator and conciliator in social democratic camp   138
   opposition to Zionism   83
   affinity to Mensheviks   82–83, 195
   branches and membership of   194
   in Jewish National Council   199, 217
   representation in Rada   194–200
   opposed Fourth Universal   288
Jewish National Council   199, 216–18
Jewish People's Party (Folkspartei)   142, 196, 199, 217, 288, 379
Jewish Social Democratic Party (Workers of Zion) (Poale Zion)   83–84, 130, 142, 159, 174, 179, 194, 296–97, 199, 217, 222, 287–88, 307
   See also Goldelman, Solomon
Joffe, Adolf   262–63, 266, 269, 332

Kadets   *See* Russian Constitutional Democratic Party
Kasianenko, Yevhen   160n142, 291, 321
Kautsky, Karl   34, 66–7, 69–71, 79, 81, 99

Kharkiv 145–57
   Committee in Defence of Revolution in 156
   Bolshevik delegates on workers' councils in 158
   Russian SRs in 175
   Kharkiv Council of Workers and Soldiers Deputies splits over Rada 191
   Kharkiv Council of Workers' and Soldiers' Deputies first big city council to recognize Rada 201–2
   dual power in Kharkiv between Rada and Bolsheviks 239–43
   rival First all-Ukrainian Congress of Councils held in Kharkiv 241
   CEC elections in Kharkiv 245
   Manifesto by CEC to workers and peasants in Ukraine 246–248
   Bolsheviks needed support from Russia to take control of 260
   Austro-German and Rada occupation of 331, 359
   See also Donets-Kryvyi Rih region; Zatonsky, Volodymyr
Khmelnytsky, Bohdan 14–16, 18, 21, 126
Khmelnytsky Regiment 121–22, 140, 221, 252, 285, 333
Khrystiuk, Pavlo 120, 284, 290–91, 303, 310, 365, 379, 383
Kotsiubynsky, Yurii 279–82, 302, 311, 329, 345, 350
Kovenko, Mykhailo 283–85, 291
Kreisberg, Isaak 159–60n142, 192, 295, 305
Kremenchuk Council of Workers' and Soldiers' Deputies 203, 242, 281
   See also Lapchynsky, Hryhorii
Kryvyi Rih   *See* Donets-Kryvyi Rih region
Kulyk, Yu. 230
Kviring, Emanuiil 348, 362
Kyiv Council of Workers' Deputies
   opposition to soldiers' movement 121
   on Ukrainisation of schools 128
   in Kyiv Committee in Defence of the Revolution 156
   involvement in seizure of power 160–63
Kyiv Councils of Workers' and Soldiers' Deputies
   vote on soviet government and state power in Ukraine 204–205

   demand to Rada to face reelection 227
   premises wrecked by Rada soldiers 230
   closure of newspaper 286
   general strike in support of Kyiv uprising 295, 298
Kyiv Council of Workers' and Soldiers' Deputies
   demand to end summary justice by Muraviov's soldiers 312–13
   failed to restore order in Kyiv 314–16
   flight of its executive committee from Kyiv 329
Kyiv gubernia 20map 2
Kyiv Union of Struggle for the Emancipation of the Working Class 85, 92

Labour Zionism 83–84
land reform
   Stolypin land reform (November 1906) 47
   confiscation of landed estates demanded 123, 130, 209–10, 213–14
   land seizures and redistributions 122–23, 130, 153–54, 164, 212–13, 352, 372–74
   land law of Rada 18 January 212–14, 293, 372–74, 376, 380, 383, 391–92
   repeal of Rada land reforms in Skoropadsky's Charter 391–92
language and literacy
   EMS *ukaz* of Tsar Alexander II 59, 91
   Russian as language of social mobility 60
   See also Ukrainian language; Yiddish language
Lapchynsky, Hryhorii 188–9, 229–230, 242, 245, 279–82, 310–11, 345, 363
Lenin, Vladimir I. 67, 71–74, 77, 81–83, 85, 100–102, 134–5, 157–9, 169, 170–73, 314, 345
Lesia Ukrainka, (pen name of Liarysa Kosach) 92
Levitsky, Mykola 365
Liubynsky, Mykola 265–66
Lutsenko, I. 300, 334, 368
Luxemburg, Rosa 75–79, 81, 87–88, 229

mala rada   *See* Tsentral'na Rada – *mala rada*
Martianov, Ya. V. 245, 246, 311

Martos, Ivan   214, 299
Martov, Julius   80
Marx, Karl   3, 62, 63–69, 81
Mazepa, Isaak   6, 53, 180–81, 351
Medvedev, Yukhym   208, 275, 269–70, 272–76, 321, 326
Mensheviks
  presence in Ukraine   185–90
  allied with Bund   82–83, 195
  position on national question   186–9
  strength in trade unions   104, 370, 385
  in Provisional Government   103–4
  In Kyiv Duma   319, 328
  In Odesa   351–2
  In Kharkiv   242–3, 247
  in workers' councils   147–8, 157, 186, 339
  orientation to Tsentral'na Rada   134, 137, 142, 156, 179, 365, 159, 165, 365
  opposition to Rada seizure of power   159, 162, 164–5, 169
  opposed Rada's separate peace with Central Powers   222, 264, 287–8
Muraviov, Mikhail   238, 258–59, 270, 277, 279–82, 292–93, 301, 304, 306–7, 309–15, 320–21, 323, 342, 344, 345, 351, 354–56
  persecution of Ukrainians by   306–7, 310–11, 313–15, 321
  in Odesa   351, 354–56
Mykhailo, Maiorov   192, 311

Nalyvaiko regiment   122, 226, 304
national autonomy
  Austro-Marxist conception of   68–71, 74, 84, 99
  as defined in Temporary Instruction of Provisional Government   141–42, 155, 157, 202
national liberation struggle
  social democrats' interpretations of   5–6, 87
  Stalinist estimation of   6–7
  Marx on national liberation of Ireland   65–66
national question and national movement
  and capitalist development   64–67, 76
  Yurkevych on   99–102
  Luxemburg on   76–79
  Marx and Engels on   63
  Austro-Marxists on   63–68
  Kautsky on   69–71
  Lenin on   71–75
  Holubnychy on Marxist treatments of   79
Neronovych, Yevhen   183, 208, 222, 265, 290–91, 321, 326–27, 345, 350
Nikovsky, Andrii   159, 320–321, 337–39

Odesa
  literacy in   58
  population by national groups in 1897   55, 56, 351, 353
  support for First Universal in   129
  workers' councils formed in   115, 145, 158
  councils' support for Third Universal   203–4
  Menshevik-Bolshevik co-operation in   185, 193
  Rada prevailed over Red Guards in   227, 257
  Jewish self-defence in   215–216
  Bolshevik-led government of   351–57
Odesa Soviet Republic
  Bessarabia gubernia claimed by   353
  Council of People's Commissars of   351, 353–56, 370

Pale of Settlement   42, 79
paramedics and midwives, All-Ukrainian Union of Paramedics and Midwives   148, 151
Patlakh, N.S.   305–6
People's Secretariat
  in Kharkiv   244–45
  in Kyiv   315, 327
  split over response to Austro-German occupation   345
  in Poltava   345–46
  dissolved in Tahanrih   361–2
Petliura, Symon   110, 122, 160, 207, 213, 215–6, 218, 221, 224–5, 227, 231, 235, 240, 250–58, 260, 264, 279, 283, 285–86, 304–5, 322–24, 327, 332, 334, 339, 389
Petrograd
  massacre at Winter Palace in 1905   103
  protests in force abdication of Tsar   112
  emergence of dual power in   113
  Bolshevik-led seizure of power in   159–67

Petrograd Soviet of Workers' and Soldiers' Deputies
  USDWP resolution to unite workers' and soldiers' deputies into   112
  political composition of   113
  Ukrainian Military Revolutionary Committee of   158, 254
  Ukrainian Soldiers' Congress in support of   123
  Rada delegation seeking national autonomy rebuffed by   125, 131
  response to pogroms in Chernihiv   342
Piatakov, Hryhorii   135, 162–63
Piatakov, Leonid   192, 227, 256–57, 295, 311
Piatakov, Yurii   160–62, 317, 362
Poale Zion   See Jewish Social Democratic Party (Workers of Zion) (Poale Zion)
Pogroms   42, 79, 105, 109, 214–16, 299–300, 331–340, 343, 367
Polish Democratic Centre   142, 165, 179
Poloz, Mykhailo   265, 290–91
Polubotok regiment   122, 139–40, 252, 285, 297
Porsh, Mykola   31–33, 53–4, 58–9, 95–100, 106, 131, 159, 183–4, 205, 208, 232, 253–56, 260, 275, 283, 285, 291, 294, 300, 322, 324, 365–66, 379, 381, 389
Postal and telegraph workers' union   150
Provisional Government
  formation of   112–14
  on Tsentral'na Rada's declaration of Ukrainian national autonomy   123–25
  Temporary Instruction to Rada from   141, 155, 157
  overthrow of   155, 158–59, 161–63, 166

Rada   See Tsentral'na Rada
Rafes, Moshe   138, 140–41, 165–66, 196, 218, 283, 286, 300, 328, 332
railway workers
  as key section of working class   49
  in RUP   94
  All-Ukrainian Railway Workers' Union   149–50
  All-Russian Union of Railway Workers   170–220
  efforts to unify unions on an industry wide basis   104
  debates over national autonomy among   128–129
  recruited to Free Cossacks   284
  in Kyiv uprising   297, 305
  failure to unite against overthrow of Rada   385–6, 391
Revolution of 1648
  roots of   14–15
  extension of serfdom to cossack society   14, 18–19
  failure to establish independent nation state   33
Revolutionary Ukrainian Party (RUP)
  founding of   93
  rural workers as a priority of   93–94
  urban workers' concerns   94–95
  turn to Social Democracy   95–97
RSDWP   See Russian Social Democratic Workers' Party (RSDWP), Bolsheviks
Rubach, M.A.   45, 49, 51
RUP   See Revolutionary Ukrainian Party (RUP)
Russians in Ukraine
  as national minority   53–8
  Russian as language of social mobility   60
  as minority with status of social and political majority   124–5, 200, 234, 301
  national autonomy for   114
  perception of threatened status of   134–5
  as part of Kyiv population 1917   282
  treatment of Ukrainians as "little Russians"   302
  Ukrainian nationalist sentiment against   369
Russian Social Democratic Workers' Party (RSDWP)
  founding of   82–7
  resolution on national question adopted by Second Congress   74, 85
  in 1905 Revolution   105–7
  See also Lenin, Vladimir I.; Bolsheviks; Mensheviks
Russian Socialist Revolutionaries (SRs)
  and First Universal   134
  and Third Universal   165
  and All-Russian Constituent Assembly   166, 357
  and General Secretariat   179

Sadovsky, Valentyn 183, 378
Schwarzenstein, Ambassador Mumm von 381, 385, 392
Second All-Ukrainian Congress of Councils *See under* All-Ukrainian Congress of Councils
Second RSDWP Congress *See under* Russian Social Democratic Workers' Party (RSDWP)
Second Universal *See* Tsentral'na Rada universals – Second Universal
Secretariat of Jewish Affairs *See* Tsentral'na Rada – Secretariat of Jewish Affairs
Serheev, F. (Artem) 245
Sevriuk, Oleksandr 265–66, 272, 274
Shakhrai, Vasyl 229–30, 234, 242–50, 258, 269–70, 272, 280, 326
Shapoval, Mykyta 159, 287
Shapoval, Oleksandr 334, 336, 350
Shats-Anin, Max 218, 288, 334, 336
Shelukhin, S. 370, 375, 378–9
Shevchenko regiment 122, 226, 261, 265, 300
Shevchenko, Taras 78, 87–8, 90–91, 122, 128, 302
Sich Riflemen 283, 303–4, 324, 388–89
Skoropadsky, Pavlo 251, 254, 284–5, 364, 370, 385, 389–92, 393
Skrypnyk, Mykola 86–7, 190, 201, 245–46, 309, 327, 345–46, 348, 350, 363
Socialist Ukrainian Party (SUP) 92–93
Society of Ukrainian Progressives (TUP) 116–17
soldiers' movement
 formation of 121–22
 link between workers and peasants provided by 120, 151
 opposition to Provisional Government 127, 164
 Mensheviks' opposition to 189
Soviet Socialist Republic of Tavria 357–58
Spilka *See* Ukrainian Social Democratic Union (Spilka)
Stepanenko, Oleksandr 285, 334, 369
Steshenko, Ivan 92
sugar industry
 sugar refiners' syndicate organised in Ukraine (1887) 27
 Ukrainian exports 29
 industry workers in Ukraine 48t6

All-Russian Congress of Sugar Industry Workers 152–53
All-Russian Society of Sugar Refiners 376, 386
sugar magnate Abram Dobry 386–388
SUP *See* Socialist Ukrainian Party (SUP)

Teachers, All-Ukrainian Teachers' Union 151
Terletsky, Ye. 245
Third Universal *See* Tsentral'na Rada universals – Third Universal
Tkachenko, Mykhailo 155, 159, 183, 291–2, 300, 324, 365–66, 369, 371, 375, 379, 387–88
trade
 Kyivan Rus trade with Scandinavia and Byzantium 9
 impact of Russian annexation on 21
 terms of trade negotiated by UPR with Central Powers 381–82
 Serheev, F., as People's Commissar for Trade and Industry 245
 Holubovych (Vsevolod) as Secretary for Trade and Industry 265–66, 365
 Feshchenko-Chopivsky as Minister of Trade and Industry 379–80
 See also industrialization
Trade unions, in Ukraine 147–53
Treaty of Pereiaslav (1654) 16
Trotsky, Leon 136, 169, 171, 175–78, 266–69, 273–76, 277, 291, 332
Tsentral'na Rada
 elected leadership of 120
 national autonomy as its goal 116–17, 119–26, 133–38
 national autonomy negotiated with Provisional Government 139–41
 parties seated in 141–42, 179
 Temporary Instruction issued by Provisional Government to 141–42, 155, 157, 202
 Provisional Government overthrown by 114, 168, 393
 national personal autonomy for minorities adopted by 195–99, 217, 289, 338

INDEX

Donbas Bolsheviks' attitude to 186, 192, 243
CPC's Manifesto and ultimatum to 232–38, 250
abolition of private property in land by 212–14, 293, 372–74, 376, 380, 383, 391–92
evacuation from Kyiv by 293, 307–8, 328–30
pogroms by armed forces of 343
dissolution of Rada by Skoropadsky 391
Tsentral'na Rada – General Secretariat
apportioning of seats in 139, 165
USDWP control over 143
In Kyiv Committee in Defence of the Revolution 156, 159–60
declaration as the government of Ukraine 164
renaming as Council of People's Ministers 197
rejection of CPC's Manifesto and ultimatum by 250
suppression of workers' councils by 252
See also Vynnychenko, Volodymyr
Tsentral'na Rada – *mala rada*
debates and adoption of land law 213–14, 293
Fourth Universal (declaration of independence) adopted by 271, 286–88
Statute of National Personal Autonomy adopted by 286
pogroms discussed in 323, 336
Constitution of the Ukrainian People's Republic adopted by 389
Tsentral'na Rada – Secretariat of Jewish Affairs
staffing and priorities of 196
addressed pogroms 218–9
Statute on National Personal Autonomy drafted by 196–200, 286–87
Tsentral'na Rada universals – First Universal
declaration of autonomy 126
support from workers 129
rejections by Russian left and right parties 134
Tsentral'na Rada universals – Second Universal 138, 195–96

Tsentral'na Rada universals – Third Universal
declaration of Ukrainian People's Republic 164–67
support from workers' and soldiers' councils 202–8
declared abolition of private property in land 212–14, 284
Tsentral'na Rada universals – Fourth Universal
declaration of independence of Ukrainian People's Republic 288–90
TUP *See* Society of Ukrainian Progressives

UDFP *See* Ukrainian Democratic Farmers' Party (UDFP)
UJF *See* Union of Jewish Fighters (UJF)
Ukrainian Democratic Farmers' Party (UDFP)
Opposed Rada land law 376, 380
founding national congress 390–91
Ukrainian language
and division of labour 5, 67–68, 167
literacy 58–60
Alexander I's restrictions 59
Alexander II's Ems *ukaz* 59–60
first socialist publications in 90–91
as language of government 114
as language of instruction in schools 118, 128, 189, 318
championed by All-Ukrainian Teachers' Union 151–52, 318–19
newspapers and books for soldiers in 129
Ukrainian speaking sections of Bolshevik party created 192
plan to train Jewish officers in 218
identification of language with counterrevolution 301–2
Ukrainian Party of Socialist Federalists (UPSF)
TUP renamed as 117
shared Rada leadership with USDWP 117
supported soldiers' movement 140
resisted land redistribution 212–24
opposed separate peace of Rada with Central Powers 222, 264
UPSF newspaper *Nova Rada* on pogroms 337–39
sought to involve Germany in bringing down Council of People's Ministers 375–78
quit Council of People's Ministers 387

Ukrainian Party of Socialist Independents (UPSI)
　associated with Free Cossacks　284
　launch of　285
　Stepanenko (Oleksandr) as secretary of　285, 334, 369
　recruited workers at Kyiv Arsenal　294
　See also Bolbochan, Petro
Ukrainian Party of Socialist Revolutionaries (UPSR)
　contested Rada's leadership　142–43
　adopted soviet platform at Third Congress　210–11
　drafted Rada land law of 18 January　213–14, 293
　suppressed in Kharkiv by Bolsheviks as "counter-revolutionary"　258–59
　led Rada Council of People's Ministers　292–93, 377–81
　See also Liubynsky, Mykola; Poloz, Mykhailo; Shapoval, Mykyta
Ukrainian People's Republic (UPR)
　declaration by Tsentral'na Rada　164–65, 167
　rival Bolshevik government of UPR declared in Kharkiv　249
　declaration of UPR state independence　288–90
　Holubovych (Vsevolod) as premier of　379–80, 383, 386
　UPR Constitution adopted by *mala rada*　389
　dissolution of UPR by Skoropadsky　391
　First All-Ukrainian Trades Union Congress resolved to restore UPR　393
Ukrainian Social Democratic Union (Spilka)　96–97, 105–7
Ukrainian Social Democratic Workers' Party (USDWP)
　populist and anarcho-socialist forerunners of　87–90
　emergence of Ukrainian social democracy　90–97
　evolution of programme and strategy　97–102
　split by 1905 Revolution　105–7
　as leading party of Rada　142–3
　working class exercise of power debated at Fourth Congress　183–85

split of Left USDWP　321
party relinquishes responsibility to govern　291–92, 366
Left USDWP enters Soviet Ukrainian government of CEC　350
Union of Jewish Fighters (UJF)
　all-Russian conference of　216
　defence of Jewish civilians　215–19
　All-Russian Congress attempted in Kyiv　300–301
　accusations of counterrevolutionary activity directed towards　301
　See also Hohol, Yoan
Union of Landowners
　elected to All-Russian Constituent Assembly　175
　attempt to restore property rights addressed during Austro-German occupation　376
　congress in Kyiv Circus　390
Union of Russian Peoples (Black Hundreds)　237, 115, 137, 315, 319, 339–40
United Jewish Workers' Party (Fareinigte)
　in Jewish National Council　199, 217
　in Rada　142, 196
　See also Shats-Anin, Max; Zilberfarb, Moshe
UPP　See Ukrainian People's Party
UPR　See Ukrainian People's Republic (UPR)
UPSF　See Ukrainian Party of Socialist Federalists
UPSI　See Ukrainian Party of Socialist Independents
UPSR　See Ukrainian Party of Socialist Revolutionaries

Vasylenko, Mykola　392
Volobuiev, Mykhailo　22, 28
Volyn　20map 2
Vynnychenko, Volodymyr　5–6, 120, 123, 126, 131, 133, 140–41, 154, 183, 207, 213, 224, 234, 249, 251, 253–54, 255–7, 260, 264, 287, 289, 291–92, 302, 307–8, 319, 322, 339–40, 388, 392

women workers　50–51
workers' councils
　formation after fall of autocracy　115

comparative support to Provisional Government in Russia and Ukraine 136
orientation to Tsentral'na Rada 168
spread across Ukrainian gubernia 145–47
regional organisations of 146
comparative influence of Mensheviks, Bolsheviks in 146–47, 157, 167, 185
petit bourgeoisie involvement in 135, 147
divided over Bolshevik seizure of power 178
influence of USDWP in 182, 187
recognition of Rada as national government 201–7
opposed to recognition of Rada 242–43
in Crimea 258
suppressed by Rada 365, 370
Working class
peasant sources of 37–40
Russian migrant sources of 40
Jewish artisans in 41–43
numerical growth 43–51
national composition of 152–57
literacy of 158–60

Yefremov, Serhii 120, 320, 337, 377
Yiddish language
clandestine literature published by Bund in 81
as official language of Rada 198
Zionist movement's preference for Hebrew 198
Yurkevych, Lev 99–102, 106, 110

Zapovit (Taras Shevchenko's *Testament*) 126, 347
Zatonsky, Volodymyr 159–61, 189, 193–94, 229–30, 235, 245–46, 248, 269–70, 309, 318–19, 326–27, 350
Zhukovsky, Oleksandr 322, 324, 333–35, 340, 358, 366–67, 369, 372, 379, 385, 388–89
Zilberfarb, Moshe 159, 196–97, 219, 286
Zolotariov, Oleksandr 196, 264, 287